Free Press/Free People

Free Press/Free People
The Best Cause

by

John Hohenberg

 The Free Press, New York
Collier-Macmillan Publishers, London

John Hohenberg, with a background of twenty-five years of newspaper experience in New York, Washington, at the United Nations, and abroad, is Professor of Journalism at Columbia University's Graduate School of Journalism and Administrator of the Pulitzer Prizes. He is the editor and commentator for *The Pulitzer Prize Story* and *The New Front Page* and is the author of *The Professional Journalist, The News Media, Foreign Correspondence: The Great Reporters and Their Times*, and *Between Two Worlds.*

Copyright © 1971, 1973 by John Hohenberg

Printed in the United States of America

The Free Press
A Division of the Macmillan Company.
866 Third Avenue, New York, New York 10022

Collier-Macmillan Canada Ltd., Toronto, Ontario
First Free Press Paperback Edition 1973

This edition is reprinted by arrangement with The Columbia University Press

Library of Congress Catalog Card Number: 70-133912

printing number
1 2 3 4 5 6 7 8 9 10

For my colleagues
on the newsfronts of the world,
with whom I spent so many happy
and challenging years.
*

Foreword

John Hohenberg's latest book well serves both the press and the people in explaining the essential interrelationship between those journalists to whom freedom of expression is indeed "the best cause" and the people whose precious freedoms rest upon it.

This volume is no mere glorification of the press, but a lucid, analytical exposition of its role and especially its impact upon mankind through the years.

It is a timely work—rich in documentation of the endless struggle for human liberty and penetratingly aware of the dangers to the press and the people when government attempts to shackle the press by destroying public confidence in what people read and hear.

We of the Knight Newspapers thank John Hohenberg for providing sorely needed clarification of how the press protects the public interest even as others seek to weaken its capability to stand as guardian of our constitutional rights.

Further, we rejoice in being privileged to have played some small part in making *Free Press/Free People: The Best Cause* a notable and lasting contribution to public knowledge.

> JOHN S. KNIGHT
> President, Knight Foundation
> Editorial Chairman, Knight Newspapers

Preface and Acknowledgments

In the lovely green uplands of the Japanese home island of Honshu, there is a thickly populated central area that shivers almost daily under the impact of swarms of small earth shocks. Now and then, an earthquake strikes. Villages are wiped out. Some people die. But for the rest, life goes on in the ceremonious Japanese way.

Not long ago, when the Japan Meteorological Agency proposed to build a seismological observatory in the vicinity as a possible source of warning against disaster, the uncomplaining public mood changed. People became excited. A terrible spasm of fear and protest swept over a large part of the area. Irrationally and unreasonably, the less educated among the citizenry felt that the observatory, far from being a protection against earthquakes, might actually cause them.

At the height of the clamor, a Japanese scientist in the area quite by chance recognized a telltale fissure at the edge of a settled community — a sign of the initial stages of a landslide. He sounded the alarm. Through his efforts, all residents were evacuated and no lives were lost when the disastrous slide actually occurred. The opposition to the observatory collapsed. It stands today in the city of Matsushiro, in the heart of the earth tremor belt, a monument to the triumph of the spirit of free inquiry over blind suppression, of the rule of reason over ignorance.

The struggle for freedom of expression has not always ended so happily. In the five hundred years since Johann Gutenberg first used movable type to print a Bible on his renovated wine press, the iron heel of control more often than not has ground out the right of free publication. There is a tragic similarity of purpose between the torture, imprisonment, and burning at the stake that became the lot of the medieval heretics who used the printing press, and the harsh Soviet-led invasion of our own time that crushed free publication in Czechoslovakia. An authoritarian system's first line of attack on any people's liberties has always been the independent press. And so it remains today.

But even in the most libertarian societies, the press is never completely secure because it cannot lift itself out of the morass of troubles that inevitably surround it. "How beautiful upon the mountains are the feet of him that bringeth good tidings, that publisheth peace," cried Isaiah. But, as the journalists of every era must learn anew, the public reaction is seldom anything approaching beautiful to those who bring bad tidings. Let the press reveal the idiocies of government (as, for example, the hollowness of the predictions that victory was in hand in the Vietnam War) and the super-patriots are certain to rise up with screams of "Treason!" Let television bring on the home screen the Chicago police clubbings of demonstrators before the 1968 Democratic National Convention and many are sure to say that such things should not be displayed to the nation because they may lead to more rioting.

There is a sensitive and little understood relationship between free people and a free press, the subject of this book. One may not necessarily guarantee the other, but it is nevertheless true that one cannot exist without the other for very long in any country and in any age. That is the verdict of history. Every informed person in an open society subscribes to the principle proclaimed by John Milton: "Give me the liberty to know, to utter, and to argue freely according to conscience, above all liberties." But in a time when man is busily perfecting and stockpiling the means for his own ultimate destruction, even some of the supposedly enlightened among the mass of human beings apply Milton's impassioned words only to their own beliefs and not to those of their opponents.

Clearly, the very turbulence of our era calls for a serious examination of the interaction between a free press and a free society. It is not sufficient, however, to consider the matter in terms of the noble guarantees of freedom of assembly and freedom of the press that are written into the Constitution of the United States and others (including a high-sounding pronouncement in the Soviet constitution). Nor can it be thought of in the simplistic terms of a Fourth of July tribute by a Chamber of Commerce speaker to the freedom of the press — a tiresome view that has done more to alienate public sympathy than attract it. All the drum-beating of editors' and publishers' societies for public support of free press campaigns has yielded pitifully small results.

In working out the details of this study during the past two years, the temptation has been great to concentrate on the cases of the martyrs and other distinguished losers who have sacrificed their fortunes and sometimes their lives as well in the cause of a strong and independent press. Had this course been followed, the undoubted result would have been an obituary of the free press, which would be somewhat premature at this date. Similarly, it would scarcely have been edifying to limit this work to either the heroes of the press, of whom there are too few, or the villains, of whom there have always been too many.

What has determined the style, concept, subject matter, and organization of this book more than anything else is the audience to which it is addressed. All too often, works on the free press are intended almost exclusively for those who are its practitioners and the exercise, therefore, closely resembles that of a man who talks to himself in front of a mirror. This one seeks a wider, nonprofessional audience — an audience that has its doubts about what the press has accomplished in the past and is likely to achieve in the future. That in itself should insure that the discussion will not be theoretical and it certainly will not be conducted in a drab if scholarly monotone. If the free press has any leading characteristic, it is controversy; if it has a principal weakness, it is a tendency to make an interminable fuss about small matters if it can find no great issues worthy of its attention. Very likely, some of these and other journalistic faults may be found in these pages; if so, it will scarcely be accidental, considering the closeness of the author to his subject.

This book, in summation, is about people. It concentrates on those who fought for freedom of the press and, through it, the freedom of the individual, on those who supported them and opposed them, and on those others who benefited from or were penalized by their efforts. In this sense, what is attempted here is a biography of a cause—the "best cause," in the words used in defense of John Peter Zenger at his trial for criminal libel in colonial New York. While much of it necessarily deals with the United States, Great Britain, and Western Europe, where the battle for a free press primarily has been and still is being waged, those who have struggled against even greater odds elsewhere in the world have an honored place in this narrative. The interplay of free publication and free people has changed the course of history in the past; without doubt, it will happen again.

While there are no novel historical materials here, beyond the reporting that took me to the principal cities of the United States and Western Europe in one summer and to Czechoslovakia and the Soviet Union in another, this work brings together in one volume all that has impressed me and fascinated me for many years about the relationship of the journalist to the cause of personal liberty. My six previous books on journalistic subjects and a quarter-century as a working newspaperman have served to prepare me for this one, in many ways the most important of all, and my travels in both Europe and Asia during the past decade have given me access to many differing points of view. There has been sufficient research—the text itself is the best measurement of that—but the footnoting so characteristic of scholarly work has been dropped. With Samuel Eliot Morison, I devoutly hope that a certain amount of erudition, based on past performance, may be taken for granted.

To Columbia University and Grayson Kirk, who was president at the time this project was undertaken, I express my thanks for the university's sponsorship. A particular expression of gratitude is also due the Knight Foundation and John S. Knight, its president, who is also editorial chairman of the Knight newspapers, for making available a grant to the university for the project in the summer of 1968. It made possible a number of visits to archives, libraries, newspapers, and other news organizations in the United States, Great Britain, and Western Europe, as well as Czechoslovakia and the Soviet Union. Included were many interviews here and abroad with editors and publishers of newspapers,

eminent members of their staffs, executives in broadcast journalism and leading practitioners, government authorities directly
and indirectly concerned with problems of the free press, and
several valued academic critics of press performance who contributed a great deal. There are, in addition, two to whom I am
deeply indebted — J. Montgomery Curtis, who first suggested the
study to Columbia, and my dearest and most constant companion and adviser, Dorothy Lannuier Hohenberg, without whom
this long effort could not have been undertaken. They and all
others are absolved of responsibility for what is written here — a
burden that is mine alone.

I well recall asking Dr. Kirk, at our first conversation about
the matter, whether it might not be wiser for the university to
select a historian or a sociologist to conduct the work because a
journalist could scarcely be expected to suppress his prejudices
in favor of his own profession. The response was that, for both
the university and for me, this was a risk that could conscien-
tiously be undertaken. The public will have to judge the result
for itself. To my fellow journalists, I bequeath these lessons of
the past and the present in the hope that they will help to point
the way toward a brighter future.

John Hohenberg, Columbia University, June, 1970

For this paperback edition of *Free Press/Free People* I have
written a commentary in the form of an epilogue which follows the
former concluding chapter. In the main, it deals with the events of
the two years after the publication of the original work—and especially with the deepening controversy over the role and powers of
the free press in the United States and elsewhere. I am indebted to
Charles Smith, Editor-in-Chief of The Free Press, for suggesting
this vital addition to the book, and to Robert J. Tilley, Editor-in-
Chief of The Columbia University Press, publishers of the hard-
cover edition, for agreeing to let me do it.

John Hohenberg, Columbia University, August, 1972

Contents

Foreword   vi
Preface and Acknowledgments   vii

Prologue
  1. At the Dawn of History   1
  2. The Greek Example   2
  3. The Dissenters of Israel   8
  4. From a Chinese Blacksmith   10
  5. The Printer of Mainz   11
  6. A World Without Freedom   13

  I. The Winds of Doctrine
  1. News for the King   16
  2. "The Times Are Daungerous"   20
  3. The Press in the Americas   27
  4. Truth Goes to Trial   38
  5. The Press after Three Hundred Years   43

 II. The Violent Journalists
  1. Sundown in London   46
  2. The Newspaper War   48
  3. "Congress Shall Make No Law . . ."   59
  4. At the Barricades   70
  5. The Merchant of News   80
  6. "The Thunderer"   82
  7. The Swiss Doctor's Prescription   88
  8. The Press after Four Hundred Years   96

III. New Vistas, New Goals
  1. The Reformers   100
  2. Member of the Establishment   107
  3. A New Birth of Freedom   114
  4. On Liberty   126

IV. The Imperial Age
    1. Swaraj   129
    2. "Dangerous Thoughts"   135
    3. The Warmakers   141
    4. The Persecuted   149
    5. The Wisdom of Liang Chi-chao   156
    6. New Channels for News   159

V. A World in Turmoil
    1. Catastrophe   162
    2. The Battle for America   171
    3. War and the Press   178
    4. The Battle for Russia   184
    5. The Peace that Failed   193
    6. The Press and the Peace   198

VI. The Old Order Changes
    1. The Lion at Bay   205
    2. The Conscience of Europe   213
    3. The Jackal   216
    4. Der Fuehrer   220
    5. The Might of Asia   228
    6. The American Ordeal   233

VII. Total War
    1. The Fall of Europe   240
    2. The Power of the Soviet Union   248
    3. The Misfortunes of War   253
    4. Tragic Victory   261
    5. The Press after Five Hundred Years   272

VIII. Under the Super-Powers
    1. Cold War   281
    2. The Lamps Go Out in Prague   289
    3. Nehru's India   294
    4. On the Red Tide   301
    5. The "Forgotten War"   306

IX. The Balance of Terror
    1. McCarthy 313
    2. The Thaw 318
    3. The "Hundred Flowers" 323
    4. Good Neighbors—and Bad 326
    5. Eyeball to Eyeball 332
    6. The Great Red Schism 341
    7. An American Tragedy 343
    8. The Uses of the Press 347

X. The Lonely Struggle
    1. The Czech Spring—and the Fall 351
    2. Dissent in the Soviet Union 362
    3. Mao's Way 373
    4. In China's Orbit 378
    5. The Fate of India 389
    6. Japan: Forge of Asia 392

XI. Into a Revolutionary Age
    1. The Third World 397
    2. The Divided House of Europe 406
    3. The Decline of Fleet Street 422
    4. The American Giant 439

XII. Free Press/Free People
    1. The Press Today 462
    2. New Roles for the Press 466
    3. The Explosion of Techniques 473
    4. Television vs. the Press 482
    5. The Free Press on Trial 489

Epilogue 499

Index 513

Prologue

1. At the Dawn of History

More than two thousand years before the birth of Christ, a Sumerian king used the word "freedom" for the first time in recorded literature. He was Urukagina, king of Lagash, and he restored the rights of his people in a manner that most modern politicians would approve. First, he drove out the tax collectors. Next, he knocked down the special privileges of the high priest who used church property and church personnel for his own benefit. And finally, he pledged to protect the widows and orphans of Lagash from being victimized.

It would be pleasant to record that Urukagina's reforms were widely recognized and admired, and as wisely copied in the ancient world, but unfortunately freedom is not so easily won or even retained. Within ten years a more authoritative king, a well-disciplined tyrant from a neighboring city, overthrew the benevolent dictator of Lagash. He vanished from history, with the exception of a few deep scratches of cuneiform script on the ancient sun-baked bricks of Mesopotamia.

In Babylon seven hundred years later, there arose another ruler who laid down the first great code of law with the words that the gods had dispatched "me, Hammurabi, the obedient, god-fearing prince, to make manifest justice in the land, to destroy the wicked and evil-doer, that the strong harm not the weak." These were eloquent words for a time when the awesome trinity of miracle, mystery, and authority had overwhelmed the feeble gropings toward freedom of person and freedom of thought.

Hammurabi's justice, however, was scarcely based on the principle of freedom and equality. For all his admirable declarations, he approved of selling debtors into slavery unless they could pay up, and he fixed maximum wages for his remaining labor. What people thought of the innovations and limitations of this enlightened despot are lost to history because there was no way of recording public opinion. The power of written language was used primarily by the rulers of men to glorify themselves as super-beings, not to communicate wisdom. No one had yet thought of giving a voice to people in the mass.

2. The Greek Example

It remained for the Greeks to bring civilization to a dazzling peak in the ancient world. In that brief and glorious time when Athens was a beacon of wisdom and tolerance, her great ones used all their arts to disseminate thought and knowledge to those about them. No man was suffered to dictate to an Athenian citizen. He was free, for the first time in the world's history, to think and speak as he pleased. For at the height of its prestige, Athens regarded freedom of expression for its citizens as fundamental. The learned Greek thus made the finest of all contributions to the enlightenment of peoples — the spirit of free inquiry and the tireless pursuit of truth.

During the era when their city-state was small and their voting citizenry limited to a few thousand, the Athenians enjoyed the most effective of all systems of communication — person to person. Their most important news came to them at first hand. Frequently, it could be discussed, analyzed, and weighed as to probability with those who were in the best position to make decisions. Any Athenian who cared to be his own correspondent could become one and he could also inform his distant friends by letter if he chose to do so.

Nearly everything important about the public's business was in the open because that was the key to Athenian democracy. Often, the public insisted on being consulted about the touchy relations with other city-states and the threats of encroachment by larger foreign powers. Even in the necessarily secret councils of defense, the news sometimes got out and it was just as well that it did; otherwise, on the eve of Salamis, Aristides might never have heard of a dispute among Greek captains and come to the aid of his bitter enemy, Themistocles, in time to persuade the divided naval staff to accept Themistocles' plan of battle.

There is no record of anything approximating a Greek newspaper or newssheet primarily because it was not necessary to their way of life. Anything their scribes could have written and distributed concerning the news of the day would have been old by the time it was circulated in the agora, the market place. Therefore, the Greek writer who thought something of himself reserved his ability for works far more durable than the bits and pieces of daily intelligence that could be obtained by any citizen at the source.

The only modern approximation of this system of news dissemination and analysis would be a continuous national television program of the proceedings of the Congress of the United States or the British House of Commons, with all the chief figures of government subject at all times to questioning by individuals or committee. The very idea no doubt would draw anguished cries of protest from the honorable members in the two leading democracies of the world today.

And yet, in ancient Athens, such an accounting was expected. In the market place and in the council, in the shaded grove of the great philosophers, and sometimes even in the glittering theater, the Athenians learned from those best qualified to tell them whatever was of interest to themselves and their community. Pericles, the first statesman of his age, never walked in any street, after assuming power, except those that led to the market place and the council hall. And while he let his representatives dispatch the routine business of the day, he never failed to address the electorate himself on matters of the highest importance.

Whatever came to the Athenians at second hand was usually reported to them by ambassadors or heralds, sent by friendly city-states or others, and sometimes by enemies demanding concessions. In times of political contests, the issues were discussed before the public by those most concerned and the orators who adhered to each faction. As for gossip, no less an authority than St. Paul observed in a later age when he appeared before the Areopagus (Upper Council), "All the Athenians and strangers which were there spent their time in nothing else but to tell or hear some new thing."

The height of Athenian prestige and power as the world's first democracy came during the Periclean era in the fifth century, B.C., and it was Pericles himself who proclaimed its virtues. There were those like the historian, Thucydides, who contended that the democratic manner was a mere mask for one-man aristocratic rule. But few could doubt Pericles' intentions after he set forth his creed in his celebrated funeral oration in 431 B.C. for those who had died defending Athens in the first year of the Peloponnesian War.

"Our government is called a democracy because its administration is in the hands, not of the few, but of the many," he said. "Yet, while as regards the law all men are on an equality for the settlement of their private disputes, as regards the value set on them, it is as each man is in any way distinguished that he is preferred to public honors, not because he belongs to a particular class, but because of personal merits. . . . And not only in our public life are we liberal, but also as regards our freedom from suspicion of one another in the pursuits of everyday life; for we do not feel resentment at our neighbor if he does as he likes, nor yet do we put on sour looks which, though harmless, are painful to behold. But while we thus avoid giving offense in our private intercourse, in our public life we are restrained from lawlessness chiefly through reverent fear, for we render obedience to those in authority and to the laws, especially to those laws which are ordained for the succor of the oppressed and those which, though unwritten, bring upon the transgressor a disgrace which all men recognize."

In this encouraging atmosphere of freedom, man's creative genius burst into a brilliant display of literature and art that has been a source of inspiration and instruction ever since for all the civilized world. For at the time of Pericles, Socrates walked the streets of Athens and gave his wisdom to the youth, Euripides and Sophocles wrote their most imposing dramatic works, and Aeschylus concluded his career as a tragic poet. If it is true, as

Xenophanes wrote, that "all men's thoughts have been shaped by Homer from the beginning," then certainly these children of Homer preserved and enlarged immeasurably his precious heritage to mankind.

It is no accident that, with the flowering of Greek literature, there was an almost magical burst of creativity in the other arts. Sculpture and painting flourished as never before and seldom since. The Parthenon was built. And education was so highly esteemed that most Athenian youths eagerly sought it. Once, Socrates observed mildly to a promising youth that he must have done a great deal of thinking. The boy doubted it, but remarked that he had often wondered about many things. The delighted Socrates exclaimed, "That shows the lover of wisdom, for wisdom begins in wonder!"

Such idealism even penetrated the most practical of the arts, politics, for Pericles broadened the participation of Athenians of all classes except the slaves in the operation of the Athenian government. He preserved and strengthened the century-old reforms of Solon, who eliminated slavery for debt, canceled mortgages on Athenian farms, and limited the amount of land a citizen could hold. As for the institution of slavery itself, the Athenians were no worse than the other people of their times and probably a good deal more humane. And yet, such was the stimulus of the Periclean age that Euripides became the first to condemn slavery in these burning words:

> That thing of evil, by its nature evil,
> Forcing submission from a man to what
> No man should yield to.

The most that Plato would say a generation later was that "a slave is an embarrassing possession," but Aristotle, while upholding slavery, conceded: "There are people who consider owning slaves as violating natural law because the distinction between a slave and a free person is wholly conventional and has no place in nature, so that it rests on mere force and is devoid of justice." Had Athens been able to maintain her position in the ancient world, it is evident that there would have been no limit to the extension of the principles of individual freedom and free expression.

Wherein, then, did Athens fail? Clearly, the long and desperate circumstances of the Peloponnesian War which raged for twenty-seven years until the surrender of Athens in 404 B.C., drained off much of the vitality of the Athenian people and lessened their enthusiasm for all that Pericles had wrought. Even worse, in their vengeful search for victims, the Athenians fastened on the noble spirit of Socrates, accusing him falsely of corrupting the city's youth and introducing the worship of strange and alien gods. Such was the disgraceful depth to which even the Athenians tumbled in their mistaken belief that new ideas, and not their own internal weakness, had undone them.

Yet, although Socrates forfeited his life to assuage public clamor and the light of freedom eventually was snuffed out in his land, the practices of Athenian democracy did not die. His martyrdom in the search for truth remained to ennoble those who sought to learn from him and the great ones who lived in his era and followed him. This was the gift of Athens to the world.

It was never possible again to duplicate the person-to-person relationship between the Athenian public and its chosen servants, even though statesmen and commoner politicians have tried in every age to recreate it. The world grew too large for the practice of such an intimate democratic tie between the governors and the governed.

But had it not been for the Greek example, it is doubtful that Julius Caesar, in his service as First Consul of Rome, would have felt so deep a need for public accountability that he established the first daily newssheet, the *Acta Diurna*, which was written by his scribes and posted in his capital. In it were reported a summary of the Senate's transactions and other official current material, as well as the more notable births, deaths, and similar news of public interest. True, this was not a newspaper and it did not cause journalists to arise in Rome as independent public figures to watch, examine, and dispute the course of government. But Caesar's publication was the beginning of the dissemination of official written government news in the Western world.

There is nothing to show that the *Acta Diurna* made any particular impression on the people of Rome. The men of quality and the citizenry had their own methods of keeping themselves posted. The first of these, of course, was gossip in public places. But superior people, who would not deign to gather such morsels themselves, employed scriveners to note down the day's events for them, and some of these were widely circulated among the upper classes. It was the birth of the penny-a-line journalist.

Outside Rome, people had many ways of gathering information. Caesar observed that it was a curious practice of the Gauls to halt travelers on the road and traders in town to oblige them to "give a clear and full account both of the district they have come from and of the news they found current in it." In seaports, the arrivals of ships invariably brought fresh intelligence that was passed along by word of mouth. Heralds of kings and emperors and their nobility appeared from time to time in public places to announce what it was deemed the public should know. Consequently, during the long midnight of barbarism that descended over the Western world, the average man knew little of what his rulers did and was discouraged from making inquiries. It was a case of the rulers demanding and receiving loyalty from the bottom up, and seldom feeling any need for a similar show of loyalty from the top down. After all, with the exception of an occasional revolutionary or heretic, who was there to question them? It is no wonder that the cause of public enlightenment languished.

Eventually, the ancient Greek ways were spread anew before the nations of the earth and eagerly studied, but the spirit of free inquiry was slow to rise again. The nobility, the military, and the church, having possession of the sources of the news, were reluctant to share their knowledge with the common herd. The Athenian reliance on an informed public as the basis of representative government was regarded as an intolerable weakness, not a source of strength. And the Athenian spirit, while it was widely praised, was even more widely mistrusted.

3. The Dissenters of Israel

For the ancient Israelites, that "stiff-necked people," liberty was precious because it was so rare. As the inhabitants of a tiny and well-nigh powerless land at the crossroads of the ancient world, they lay at the mercy of their enemies after their brief period of splendor under David and Solomon. Yet, no less than the Greeks, they contributed magnificently to the triumph of the free spirit, for that was the very soul of their gift to the world, the Bible.

Through the prophets of Israel, those angry and inspired men, the right of dissent against kings was enshrined. Such voices, determined and unafraid, cultivated a matchless sense of moral indignation that spread throughout the land. In consequence, there arose among the people of Israel a respect for learning that has withstood the battering of centuries of ignorance and a reverence for social justice that still has the power to move and to inspire.

It is remarkable that so few men and so weak a people could have exerted such an influence on mankind's quest for freedom because freedom, for much of the history of ancient Israel, was little more than a vision. With Solomon's death and the division of his kingdom into northern Samaria and southern Judea, its fate was foreordained. In 722 B.C., the Assyrians bore the ten northern tribes into slavery, and the Babylonians, in 587 B.C., made captives of the Judeans, wrecked Jerusalem, and destroyed Solomon's temple. Had it not been for the prophets, who rallied the spiritual forces of their people at a time of unexampled trial, Israel might have faded into the shadows of history with its ancient oppressors.

With the Assyrian conquest, Amos denounced the high living of the wealthy and powerful of Samaria for bringing a blight upon the land. "Hear this word, ye kine of Bashan that are in the mountains of Samaria, which oppress the poor, which crush the needy, which say to their masters, Bring and let us drink," cried the indignant prophet. "The Lord God hath sworn by His holiness that, lo, the days shall come upon you, that he will take you away with hooks, and your posterity with fish-hooks."

Such was the voice of doom in Israel. But there was hope, too; for, in the midst of his lamentations, Amos predicted that Israel would one day be reborn in its ancient home. And Isaiah, sickened by the ravages of the invaders, held up a sublime vision of the world in which people "shall beat their swords into plowshares and their spears into pruning hooks, nation shall not lift up sword against nation nor shall they learn war any more." To those who mourned and suffered, he said gently: "Awake and sing, ye that dwell in the dust: for thy dew is as the dew of herbs, and the earth shall cast out the dead."

It remained for Jeremiah to set an example of stubbornness, courage, and faith for his beleaguered people—the forthright defiance of a king who did not want to hear his harsh truths. The Babylonians were at the gates of Jerusalem and Zedekiah, the king, was angered because Jeremiah was predicting the fall of the city. For this dismal but truthful forecast, the great dissenter was cast into prison.

"Where are now your prophets," Jeremiah taunted, "which prophesied unto you, saying, The King of Babylon shall not come against you, nor against this land?"

When Jeremiah's terrible prophecy was realized, and Zedekiah was blinded in his fallen city and led off to captivity, it could not have failed to impress the survivors of the battle that the prophet was spared. For he had called for widespread moral reforms, threatening doom if his warnings were not heeded, and he had warned against the false optimism of the Judean leaders who tried to stand up to the might of Babylon.

There was good reason for the Israelites to revere such prophets as Isaiah, Amos, and Jeremiah and keep alive their words and their hopes in the years of captivity. Out of the later blossoming of a Judeo-Christian civilization that they helped to create came an overwhelming urge toward individual freedom that has profoundly influenced all peoples. With the invention of the printing press, that influence was so magnified that the doctrine of freedom became an ideal in lands where it had never before existed.

4. From a Chinese Blacksmith

Long before the warring Western world learned the useful art of public news dissemination, the ancient Chinese had their living newspaper. The newsman gathered his own intelligence compounded of rumor, gossip, and a few grains of truth, wrote it in bulletins on a thin sheet of bamboo, fastened the sheet sail-fashion to a bamboo pole, and hoisted the pole over his head by thrusting it between the back of his neck and his shirt. Then, lustily beating a gong, he gathered a crowd, elaborated orally on his news, and collected his small fees. Thus were the Chinese, that most inquisitive of peoples, given the substance for their teahouse small talk.

Just when the Chinese first turned to printing from wooden blocks is not entirely certain, but they were several centuries ahead of the West. They had known the arts of paper making and the use of ink for more than a thousand years when Europe plunged into the Dark Ages. Several identical copies exist of a book attributed to a scholar, Wang Chieh, and published in A.D. 868. However, the invention of block printing is generally ascribed by Chinese historians to another scholar, Feng Tao, who died in A.D. 954. By the time of the Sung dynasty (960-1279) book printing from blocks was fairly common in China, causing the works of Confucius, Mencius, Lao-tze, and others to be broadly distributed among the elite class and learned people generally.

It was no scholar but an humble Chinese blacksmith, Pi Sheng, who is credited with the invention of movable porcelain type about A.D. 1000. It occurred to him to cut Chinese characters on the soft surface of plastic clay, then harden it in a hot fire. There is a sound reason for the failure of Pi Sheng's invention to revolutionize the art of printing in China. The Chinese language contains so many thousand characters that there seemed to be little future for movable type in China; it did not, in fact, displace wood-block printing for many years.

Movable metal type, made of copper, was invented in Korea shortly after A.D. 1400, and independently discovered in Germany a bare two generations later. China did not have its own metal type until the reign of Emperor K'ang Hsi (1662-1722) when, at the suggestion of Jesuit priests, he had 250,000 beautiful examples of copper type cast for the exclusive use of the government printing office. By that time, the Western world had long since caught up with and passed China in the use of the printed page.

The living newspaper of the Chinese countryside continued to serve the people as their own form of news dissemination throughout this era, and for a long time thereafter. For the rulers of China found many uses for printing other than news dissemination, including the making of playing cards and money in addition to books. Historically, the first continuous publication in newspaper format is ascribed to China, the Peking *Gazette*, but this was only a record of royal edicts in its original form and intended for the use of officers of the realm. It dates from the eighth century and went out of existence with the coming of the Chinese Republic of 1912. In the Han dynasty, some eight hundred years before, there was a monthly written record called *Miscellanies*, which also was a form of government record, but it was no more a newspaper than the Peking *Gazette*. For news, the ever-inquisitive citizen of China still had to wait for the gong of the ancient news vendor and the gossip of the teahouse.

The Chinese emperors, like the contemporary absolute rulers, were disinclined to let their people know too much of what was going on.

5. *The Printer of Mainz*

When Marco Polo returned to Italy at the end of the thirteenth century after his long sojourn in China, he related many wonders he had observed at the court of the Great Khan. Although he told of Chinese printing methods, it was scarcely a matter of high priority with him or anybody else. In any event, communications between his native Venice and the rest of Europe were so poor that more than a century passed before the first printing press began to operate in the Western world. Even then, for fear of outraging the mighty ones of church and state who controlled the copying of great books by hand, the earliest printers deliberately concealed the invention of movable type for fear that they might be punished for multiplying in unreasonable amounts the important volumes that were then available. In all probability an equally compelling motive was the highly developed commercial instinct, not uncommon among printers, which may have led them to hope that they could pass off a well-printed version of a book as a valuable handwritten copy and thus keep the price high.

Whatever their reasons, the first printers were so zealous about retaining their secrets that relatively little is known even today of the manner in which they operated. By general agreement among historians and journalists, the honor of being the first to use movable type in the operation of a printing press has long been accorded to Johann Gutenberg of Mainz, Germany, in about 1440. Statues have been raised to him, although no record has been found to show what he looked like. Even the beautiful printed works that have been ascribed to him bear no signature.

This much is reasonably certain about the first printer in the Western world:

He was born in Mainz and chose to use his mother's name, Gutenberg, rather than his father's name, Gensfleisch. For a time he lived in Strasbourg and later returned to Mainz, where he opened a printing shop and produced his first works around 1440 on a converted wine press. He engraved his own metal type faces and cast the shank of each one to a suitable size to fit his press. When he had completed a page of type, inserting each piece by hand, he securely fastened it, placed it on the flat-bed of his press, inked it with a leathern ball, and placed a sheet of paper over the type. Then, lowering a flat wooden surface over the paper by applying a lever to a large wooden screw device, he was able to obtain a good imprint. With luck, and the unceasing labors of two husky young men, fifty to sixty pages an hour could be printed through this method. However, it is doubtful that Gutenberg chose to work so fast. He was too much the artist and too little the business man.

To complete his great work, the 42-line Gutenberg Bible, begun about 1450 and completed before 1456, he had to borrow money from a Mainz goldsmith, Johann Fust. He finished the Bible, but was unable to repay Fust and lost the shop. Another printer, Peter Schoeffer, Fust's son-in-law, took over and made a go of what had been a losing venture from the outset. Schoeffer was the first to print in color and the first (1457) to print a dated book. Very quickly, other printers began emulating him and Mainz became the center of a thriving new industry.

Had it not been for a military accident, one of those strange quirks of war that bring unintended results, the art of printing might not have spread as quickly as it did. But just as the printers of Mainz were establishing themselves firmly on the banks of the Rhine, the invading armies of Nassau sacked the city. Saving whatever they could of their equipment, the printers fled and set up in business elsewhere — in Nuremberg, Cologne, Augsburg, and Strasbourg, and later in every ancient center of influence in Europe.

Nobody in the German states even bothered to experiment with a newssheet until 1505 when an Augsburg printer, Erhard Oeglin, put out a broadside announcing the discovery of Brazil. It was much safer, and far more profitable, to stick to books rather than displease the authorities with news disclosures that unnecessarily excited the public. By 1500, the best sellers included 291 editions of Cicero, 91 of the Latin Bible, 95 of Virgil, and 57 of Horace.

In pain and in tragedy, Europe began to emerge from the Dark Ages. But Johann Gutenberg, who had made possible the attack on superstition and ignorance by creating the instrument for a free press, died in obscurity in 1468 — a glorious failure.

6. *A World Without Freedom*

The world of Gutenberg was a world of serfdom and slavery, of justice by torture, of voracious armies that spread death and devastation throughout the fairest lands. It was a world without pity and a world of little hope, a world in which labor was driven to its tasks with the whip and the branding iron, and deference to religious authority was enforced by the horrible cruelties of the Inquisition. Feudal anarchy ruled the Western world and the terror of Oriental despots dominated the East. The heart of Europe had been torn apart by the Hundred Years' War, the Turkish hordes had laid waste to the Middle East and captured Constantinople, and the Mongols had imposed their will on the rest of Asia by fire and sword. Half the working class of England had been wiped out by the Black Death, and nothing had been done there or anywhere else to halt the recurrence of the pestilence. Even in the most civilized lands there was hunger and fear and outright terror.

No one then alive who knew the ways of that oppressed world could have failed to take warning from the fate of the fiery English "hedge priest," John Ball, and the Lollards, the "poor priests," who tried at the risk of their lives to attack the dominant evils of their times. One hundred and sixty-six years after King John granted the Magna Charta, that great charter which was regarded as the cornerstone of English liberties, Ball cried out for freedom in 1381 in these challenging words: "Good people, things will never go well in England as long as goods be not in common, and so long as there be villeins and gentlemen." The peasant revolt that followed was put down in a torrent of blood and Ball himself, convicted of high treason, was drawn, hanged, and quartered. The Lollards and their leader, John Wyclif, were as savagely persecuted.

In Bohemia, the saintly Jan Hus, who followed Wyclif's campaigns for reform within and without the established church, was convicted as a heretic and burned at the stake. All the glitter of the Medicis in Florence at the outset of the Renaissance and all the stubborn bravery of Martin Luther in stimulating the Reformation could not conceal the essential ugliness of life in the fifteenth and sixteenth centuries and the hopelessness of a world enmeshed by arbitrary rule.

It is not surprising, therefore, that the printers in the German states were so secretive, docile, and respectful as they worked at their new trade. Seeing what was going on all about them, they could not be blamed for their caution. And yet, on the eve of the discovery of America, fifty years after Gutenberg, every necessary ingredient of a free press except one was in existence. The missing quality was courage. But where individual freedom and liberty of thought were so rare, so precious, and so feared by those in authority, it took time for printers to develop a belief in the untrammeled right of publication. Against the awesome power of church and state, they had only their cumbersome presses, a little ink, and a few sheets of paper. And yet from these humble instruments were to flow the ideas and matchless words that would change forever the face of Gutenberg's world.

I. The Winds of Doctrine

1. News for the King

An unruly horde of professional newsmongers infested the public places of Paris in the sixteenth century. They pressed their services on everybody they could for a fee and used whatever sources that were available for a strange output of military information, political gossip, ballads, jokes, and scandals. Because their roots were deep in the era before the coming of the printing press, they gaily disregarded the competition of the first printed broadsides, such as Christopher Columbus' widely copied Letter on the First Voyage. The oral tradition of news circulation was still stronger than this complicated and confusing new medium of print.

Surveying the disorderly Parisian scene, Prince de Condé exclaimed in despair, "The evil is without a remedy!"

Convinced of the undoubted supremacy of the spoken word as the quickest and surest way of cashing in on perishable intelligence, the newsmongers expanded their services. They set up lists of private subscribers for their tart and amusing satires on contemporary figures, always in demand in Paris. A few of the more enterprising of these *nouvellistes* employed people to freshen the flow of gossip. And with the formation of these primitive editorial bureaus, they set about killing off the threat of printed competition by circulating the much faster handwritten letters.

But printed news couldn't be so easily dismissed. What happened was that both newsmongers and printers opened themselves up to punishment whenever they transgressed on affairs of state and aroused the displeasure of the government. Whippings, brandings, and imprisonment in the Bastille were common enough for those who trafficked in both the oral and the printed methods of news circulation.

It was inevitable that the government would move into this confused and unregulated traffic in news, pseudo news, and unadulterated gossip, particularly with the spread of printing and the willingness of printers to assume editorial risks. As early as 1566, the Magistracy of Venice had challenged both printers and gossips by posting official accounts of the Dalmatian War in public places and collecting a small coin, called a *gazetta*, from those who stopped to read.* Sheets of the same type had been posted even earlier in Switzerland. At the beginning of the seventeenth century, these broadsides developed into the first newspapers that were regularly circulated in a few large cities of the German states — the *Avisa Relation oder Zeitung* (1609), the *Frankfurter Journal* (1615), and the *Frankfurter Postamtzeitung* (1616).

Why not a French newspaper?

If independent printers had become bold enough in Germany to publish such newssheets, it was obvious that French printers sooner or later would emulate them. Such publications could be highly profitable to those who were willing to take the gamble. People wanted news. They trusted the sanctity of print. Consequently, a newspaper was almost certain of acceptance by a far wider public than the narrow and privileged circle that could be reached by the weak and untrustworthy voices of the *nouvellistes*.

Under these circumstances, the great Cardinal Richelieu decided to establish the first official French newspaper — the *Gazette de France* — and commissioned a learned physician-journalist, Dr. Theophraste Renaudot, to be the editor, He began bravely enough in 1631 with the declaration: "In one thing only will I yield to nobody — I mean in my endeavor to get at the truth. At the same time I do not always guarantee it, being convinced that among 500 dispatches written in haste from all countries, it is impossible to escape passing something from one correspondent to another that will require correction from Father Time." In a sad admission of the imperfections of his age, he added: "History is the record of things accomplished. A *Gazette*

* The source of the name, *Gazette*, used by many newspapers.

is the reflection of feelings and rumors of the time which may or may not be true."

A skeptical Paris accepted the fledgling eight-page newspaper with reserve. Was Dr. Renaudot publishing his news for the people or for the king? And was the government quite as interested in getting at the truth as the editor said he was? Such questions required hard answers that weren't immediately forthcoming. Regardless of the public regard for Dr. Renaudot, which was considerable, the same trust and affection did not extend to his powerful patron, Cardinal Richelieu, a stern and autocratic figure. Soon, it was also noised about that the melancholy Louis XIII, apparently having little else to do, was a frequent contributor to his *Gazette*. The royal correspondent was accustomed to write his own paragraphs, take them around to Dr. Renaudot's office, and see that they were properly put into type. It made the doubters nod sagely, their worst suspicions confirmed. What else could be expected, after all? If the paper existed to print news for the king, why should not the king contribute news to the paper?

Dr. Renaudot must have done much to please his masters. It was not long before he obtained letters patent conferring on himself and his heirs the exclusive right of printing and selling, in any way they wished, "the gazettes, news, and narratives of all that has passed or may pass within and without the kingdom." Such a sweeping news monopoly was scarcely an auspicious beginning for the press in France. Within a little more than two centuries, it was to be followed by an even more imposing monopoly under the direction of the Agence Havas.

The *Gazette de France*, which was to become the *Journal Officiel* at a later date, began each issue with news from abroad and followed with such domestic news as its royal sponsors permitted it to print. It did not, by itself, end the traffic of the oral newsmongers. They continued to operate during the wars of Louis XIV because of public demand for news of the progress of the Grand Monarch by whatever means possible. But with the appearance of better newspapers that successfully challenged the monopoly of the *Gazette,* notably the *Mercure Galant* in 1672, the oral news vending tradition slowly disappeared.

The policy of government control and influence of the press, inaugurated in France by Louis the Just and his great cardinal, set an ominous precedent for the rest of Europe. In Russia, Peter the Great took a commanding interest in whatever news he authorized for publication in his new capital beside the Neva and even read proof on some of the more sensitive contributions to his press. In Prussia, Frederick II paid 100 ducats to have an unfortunate Cologne gazette printer beaten up for publishing a paragraph that displeased him. In Austria, the *Allgemeine Zeitung* of Augsburg had to change its name and move from place to place because it offended the government.

It was in England, however, that the hounding and persecution of nonconformist printers and venders reached a depth that was not exceeded by even the cruelties of the Spanish Inquisition. Under Henry VIII, no printer was safe except those who adhered without question to the royal will. For at the outset of his struggle with the Church of Rome, the king sought to placate the pope by drawing up a list of heretical books influenced by the Reformation. These could not be printed nor imported on pain of the severest punishment. For selling a copy of a book by William Tyndale, a Protestant author, a bookseller named Thomas Hittin was executed in 1530. Such printers and booksellers as Richard Bayfield and John Teukesbury were burned at the stake for heretical publications in 1531, and James Bainham followed them to the stake in 1532. Following Henry's break with Rome in 1534, he turned just as vengefully on the Catholics, beginning with Sir Thomas More's execution. Even the publication of a street ballad with political overtones became ground for arrest and severe punishment.

Nor were the royal Tudor ladies, Mary and Elizabeth, any more merciful. Mary established the Stationers Company in 1557, a printing monopoly confined to the most docile members of the black art. Elizabeth used the Star Chamber Court to cast rebellious Puritan printers into prison. As for William Carter, who had the daring to publish pro-Catholic pamphlets in this anti-Catholic land, he was summarily hanged.

With good reason, therefore, the upper strata of English society continued to rely on the work of their own newsmongers, the intelligencers, whose private sources of information were not always under the ruthless control of the crown. Both in their oral and written reports to their patrons, these informants continued to fulfill a public need. In consequence, they flourished for at least two centuries after William Caxton set up his first press at Westminster in 1476 under the Sign of the Red Pale.

Viewing the crushing restrictions on news publication both in England and elsewhere in Europe from his vantage point in Paris, the ebullient Dr. Renaudot could scarcely be blamed for observing somewhat smugly in his *Gazette* after his first year's work:

"The publication of Gazettes is indeed new; but in France only can this novelty find favor which it can always easily retain. ... If the fear of displeasing the age in which they live has prevented many good authors from touching the history of their time, what ought to be the difficulty of writing that of the week, indeed of the day, even, in which it is published?"

The difficulty, as Dr. Renaudot must have been the first to realize despite his mask of professional optimism, lay neither with the press nor its struggling people. The hand of royal power, despite feeble challenges, remained in firm control of communications in Europe.

2. *"The Times Are Daungerous"*

In a warning letter to his noble patron in the British diplomatic service overseas, John Chamberlain, one of the most trusted intelligencers in London, wrote toward the close of the reign of James I: "The times are daungerous and the world grows tender and jealous of free speech."*

It was an unsettled era. The king was having increasing trouble with Parliament. His wavering policies had outraged Catho-

---

* To Sir Dudley Carleton in Ostend, February 16, 1622.

lic and Protestant alike. And to compound his difficulties, the printers were finding new ways to evade the strict controls that had been imposed by the Tudors, persuasion and bribery among them. As the unhappy James informed the Venetian ambassador: "If I were to imitate the conduct of your republic and begin to punish those who take bribes, I should not have a single subject left."

Public corruption was so widespread that the stern lawgiver, Edward Coke, warned the House of Commons: "Make what law you will, inflict what punishment you will; little good will come of it if offices be bought and sold. He that buys must sell." Scandal, however, continued to reach into the highest places, for on May 3, 1621, the lord chancellor of the realm, Sir Francis Bacon, was barred forever from public office upon his admission that he had been guilty of such a crime.

This was the moral and political climate in which the first prototypes of newspapers began appearing in England. At first, wary printers pirated their *Mercuries, Corantos*, and *Courants*, as they called them, from Dutch newssheets and news books, regulations being less stringent in Holland. But in 1621, Nicholas Bourne, Nathaniel Butter, and Thomas Archer produced English products. Archer, in the words of a contemporary intelligencer, was promptly sent to jail "for making, or adding to, his publications without authority."

Despite King James's angry proclamation condemning "the great liberty of discourse" in the land, Butter and Bourne kept their press busy in London. On September 24, 1621, they issued their *"Corante, or Newes from Italy, Germany, Hungarie, Spaine, and France,"* but tried to appease the censor by noting that it was taken from "Dutch Coppy printed at Franckford." Once Archer had regained his liberty, he and Bourne on May 23, 1622, issued their first *Weekly Newes*, again a compendium of items from Europe that had been lifted from the Dutch. Butter added a news book on August 2. Then, on August 23, the partners printed an issue in which they advertised continuity of publication and proposed "to continue weekly, by God's assistance, from the best and most certain intelligence." They kept it up for twenty-three consecutive issues without restraint, a record for the time, before they had to give up.

For a decade, the leather-lunged *"Mercurie* girls" cried their wares as the publication of news books became more popular, even though they changed title and seldom were able to maintain continuity between issues. Butter and Bourne printed a number of these products, including a *Swedish Intelligencer* that described the battles of King Gustavus Adolphus. Archer tried to make a go of something he called *Mercurius Britannicus*, but the public would have none of it. The traffic in foreign news might have gone on indefinitely in this manner if the Spanish ambassador had not complained in 1632 to the new monarch, Charles I, that the scurrilous news books had offended the court of Austria. Under a Star Chamber edict, Charles promptly forbade the publication of news from abroad in England.

Having learned by this time that the profit in printing newssheets was usually worth risks, the printers turned their attention from foreign scandals to the ills at home. People suddenly found that they could get along nicely without worrying about what the king of France was doing, or what new deviltry was being concocted in Rome. It was almost a revelation when Parliament, the center of a storm that was shaking the entire realm, became the subject of a blizzard of freshly printed news books, termed *diurnals* or journals.

With the abolition of the king's Star Chamber in 1641, John Thomas put out the first regular parliamentary reports, his *"Diurnall Occurrences."* Scriveners skilled in a kind of primitive shorthand began taking down speeches. The most prominent and industrious, Samuel Pecke, a "bald-headed buzzard" with "long runnagate legs," set himself up in a stall in Westminster and became, in effect, the father of all parliamentary reporting. But Parliament, in its epic struggle with the king, was just as suspicious of the press as royalty. Pecke was tossed into prison twice for his interpretations of various speeches, a harsh method of inducing objectivity in the press. From his punishment, as well as others freely meted out to printers and reporters for the same crime, it became evident that Parliament, too, had little use for a free press.

The control of the news thus became one of the issues between King Charles and Parliament. It is probable that the authors of the handwritten intelligencers had a part in this, for the rival printed medium was wrecking their business. The intelligencers were distributed on Tuesdays, which was post day, but the wily printers were beating them by getting out their parliamentary reports on Mondays. Still, whatever damage the intelligencers were able to do, they scarcely wanted to endanger themselves in the process. But that was precisely what happened when Parliament, on June 14, 1643, substituted its own press control organism for the king's Star Chamber. A single licenser, Henry Walley, clerk to the Company of Stationers and himself a one-time publisher of Ben Jonson's work, took control thereafter.

It was the eve of the decisive conflict between king and Parliament. Consequently, the lone Royalist publication, *Mercurius Aulicus*, had to be put out in Oxford and secretly smuggled to its subscribers in London. Women found selling Royalist pamphlets were dragged off to Bridewell Prison and whipped. Some news books were issued in French to escape the severe penalties of books printed in English that displeased the parliamentary licenser. Finally, the licenser himself went into the news book business in competition with those whose work had to go before him for approval.

In this tense atmosphere, John Milton made the famous speech before Parliament in 1644 (later published as his "Areopagitica,") in which he uttered the familiar lines: "Though all the winds of doctrine were let loose to play upon the earth, so truth be in the field, we do injuriously by licensing and prohibiting, to misdoubt her strength. Let her and falsehood grapple; who ever knew truth put to the worse, in a free and open encounter?"

There was a limit, however, to the poet's concept of free publication. He made no plea for the circulation of Royalist tracts,

but taunted the licenser on his ineffectiveness in failing to suppress the secret circulation of the royal journal. He did not call
for a sweeping withdrawal of all acts of repression against printing. Instead, he argued that laws previous to those of June 14,
1643, were sufficient to control the press. Finally, he termed
"fire and the executioner" the best remedy against books that
had a bad effect.

Milton's concluding words, rather than his poetic faith in the
ultimate triumph of truth, attacked the very heart of censorship
as a governmental weapon: "This I know, that errors in a good
government and in a bad are equally almost incident; for what
Magistrate may not be misinformed, and much the sooner, if liberty of printing be reduced to the power of the few; but to redress willingly and speedily what hath been erred, and in highest authority to esteem a plain advertisement more than others
have done a sumptuous bribe, is a virtue, honored Lords and
Commons, answerable to your highest actions, and whereof
none can participate but the greatest and wisest men."

The poet's passion was understandable, for he had been attacked before Parliament for writing pamphlets upholding the
right of divorce for incompatibility, his first wife having left him
after a year of marriage. However, it was not in his original defense, but somewhat later, that he declared: "I wrote my 'Areopagitica' in order to deliver the press from restraints with which
it was encumbered."

Unhappily, he failed. His magnificent speech attracted scant
attention in its own time, although it was widely published, and
it has since been mentioned often but seldom read in its en-
tirety. He himself moved in precisely the opposite direction from
the press freedom he came to advocate. For after the execution
of Charles I in 1649, Oliver Cromwell chose Milton to preside
over the spreading of the winds of Cromwellian doctrine across
all England and the poet readily agreed.

In 1651, Milton became both the editor and chief censor of the
official Cromwell publication, *Mercurius Politicus*, which replaced nearly two hundred publications that had been circulating more or less freely in England. While he did not remain long

at his post, he was Cromwell's faithful servant for years. Nor was the Lord Protector's tight control of the press relaxed either with Milton's departure or the addition of a new publication, the *Publick Intelligencer*, in 1655. If truth happened to be in the field, it was in the handwritten newssheets that were smuggled in and about England beginning in 1652. Like Woodrow Wilson's celebrated demand for "open covenants openly arrived at" some three centuries later, Milton's noble phrasing exceeded both his human powers and his intentions.

The struggle went on.

With the Restoration and the accession of Charles II, Henry Muddiman began to direct the winds of doctrine as the exclusive publisher of news books from 1660 to 1663, a right conferred on him through the revival of the royal system of licensing. Muddiman had had plenty of practice. He had been the trusted publicist and news book writer for General George Monck, Cromwell's lieutenant in Scotland, who played such a key role in the restoration of the Stuarts to the English throne.

Under the printing regulation act of 1662, a veteran Cavalier, Roger L'Estrange, became licenser of the press and took over from Muddiman the two government-controlled news books, the *Intelligencer* and the *Newes*. Promptly, in the *Intelligencer* of August 1, 1663, L'Estrange laid down a policy of restrictive publication that was in keeping with the spirit of the times:

"A Publick *Mercury* should never have My Vote; because I think it makes the Multitude too Familiar with the Actions, and Counsels of their Superiors; too Pragmaticall and Censorious, and gives them, not only an Itch, but a kind of Colourable Right and License, to be Meddling with Government."

If there was to be no "Publick *Mercury*," obviously there would have to be a government newspaper on the French model, put out by official sanction. Thus was founded the first English newspaper, the London *Gazette*, in 1665. Begun while the royal court was at Oxford on November 16, 1665, in the period of the Black Plague, the semiweekly official organ was known as the Oxford *Gazette* for its first twenty-three issues before assuming its regular nameplate.

Its reception was about what might have been expected of a government publication. Muddiman, its first editor, broke precious little news in the *Gazette* because he still maintained his own highly profitable and independent newsletters to his subscribers. Then, too, the *Gazette*, as the voice of the court, proved to be both stuffy and difficult to read. Between the busy printers and intelligencers and the lively gossip that circulated in the London coffeehouses, the *Gazette* had little chance of attracting much public attention or earning public respect for its credibility.

In 1679, Parliament refused to renew the 17-year-old printing regulation act, giving rise to the publication of a score or more of independent newspapers. But it was not until the Revolution of 1688 and the rise of the two-party system of a free England in the reign of William and Mary that the archaic licensing system was repealed. Even so, when the first English daily newspaper appeared on March 11, 1702, in London, it turned out to be a single small sheet titled *The Daily Courant*, which was printed on one side only with material lifted from foreign newspapers. Clearly, the first publisher, Elizabeth Mallett, considered it safer to rely on foreign intelligence than to risk publishing some domestic item that would displease the government. After two weeks, she gave up.

A more determined publisher, Samuel Buckley, successfully revived the *Courant* a month later with a rousing appeal to his readers in his issue of April 30, 1702, to trust him to conduct the "proper and only business of a news writer" as follows:

"First, giving the freshest advices from all quarters, which he (the publisher) will certainly be able to do—let the post arrive when it will—by coming out daily. And next, delivering facts as they come related without inclining to either one side or the other. And this, too, he will be found to do by representing the same actions, according to the different accounts which both sides give of them, for which the papers he cites will be his vouchers. And thus having fairly related what is done, when, where, by which side reported, and by what hands transmitted hither, he thinks himself obliged not to launch out of his province, to amuse people with any comments and reflections of his own; but leave every reader to make such remarks for himself as he is capable of."

One may wonder if Buckley's objectivity was the result of journalistic virtue or prudent respect for the latent powers of government repression. But whatever his motivation, the editor of that first *Courant* inaugurated the most vital tradition in English language journalism. For with the rise of the independent newspaper in years to come, the responsible majority would adhere to the principle of separating editorial comment from the news columns. It would, however, take a corps of trained, professional journalists to deliver Buckley's "facts as they come related."

Until then, the contest between truth and the winds of doctrine would continue to be an unequal affair in every land on earth.

3. *The Press in the Americas*

When Sir William Berkeley became the royal governor of Virginia in 1642, he noted his feelings about a free press and free education in a report to the Lords Commissioners of Foreign Plantations in London in these well-remembered words: "I thank God, we have not free schools nor printing; and I hope we shall not have these hundred years. For learning has brought disobedience, and heresy and sects into the world; and printing has divulged them and libels against the government. God keep us from both!"

The Lords Commissioners obliged him as far as the press was concerned. For seventy-five years after Jamestown was established in 1609 as the first permanent English colony in the Americas, there was no press in Virginia; in fact, it was not until 1730 that a permanent press of any kind was established there. Governor Berkeley thus nearly achieved his pious hope.

The Spaniards were much quicker to export printers and their equipment to the New World, but they made certain that both were kept under the strictest control. An Italian from Brescia,

Giovanni Paoli,* set up a printing shop in Mexico City by grace of the Spanish government and the Catholic Church in 1539, printed a newssheet about a Guatemalan earthquake in 1541, and brought out his first religious book in 1543. Antonio Ricardo, who had worked in his shop, became the first printer in Peru in 1580. In Ecuador, controlled printing began in 1626, and other Spanish dominions in Latin America followed. But there is no known instance of free publication in the region until the eighteenth century. Printing in Spanish territory was a privilege, granted by the rulers and carefully supervised, not a basic right to be freely exercised.

Elsewhere, the European colonizers of the New World essentially agreed with the English governor of Virginia and the rulers of New Spain that printing was a potential danger to authority. The Portuguese in Brazil didn't have a press in their entire territory until 1747, the French in Quebec waited until 1759, and the Dutch in Guiana until 1793. However, in none of these colonies was there any marked urge toward freedom of thought nor any distinctive movement toward individual freedom of any kind.

The first document to be signed by free men in the name of human liberty anywhere in the New World was the Mayflower Compact, drawn up by the Pilgrims before landing at Plymouth in 1620, which called for self-government under a rule of law. Its forty-one signers pledged to "combine ourselves together into a civil Body Politick" and promised to "enact, constitute and frame such just and equal laws ... as shall be thought most meet and convenient for the general Good of the Colony."

If this noble motive was so soon to be twisted into an intolerance as fierce as any they themselves had faced in England, and if a new order conceived in freedom was so quickly to degenerate into a grim and formidable theocracy, that was a testimonial to human perversity from which not even the Puritans were exempt. It is shameful that they drove out one of their noblest minds, Roger Williams, rather than hear out his protests against

---

* Paoli worked for the Spaniards under the name of Juan Pablos. There is a Mexican memorial to an even earlier printer, Esteban Martin, in 1533, but little else is known of him and none of his works has survived.

religious intolerance. But it is also a tribute to the opportunities for freedom in New England that he was able to found the colony of Rhode Island as a "shelter for persons distressed of conscience."

This strange duality of freedom as an ideal and intolerance as a way of life, so characteristic of the people of Massachusetts Bay Colony, seemed also to govern their attitude toward the dissemination of knowledge. Two of the Pilgrims' leaders, William Brewster and Edward Winslow, had little use for the printing press even though they had themselves been printers in Holland. There was too much else to do.

It took a well-to-do nonconformist clergyman, the Rev. Jose Glover, to seek funds for both a college and a printing press in the colony after a brief visit in 1634. When he returned home, he quit his Surrey parsonage, obtained sufficient money to buy a press and type, and recruited a locksmith, Stephen Daye, with two husky sons, Stephen Jr. and Matthew, to open a printing shop. The Rev. Glover never lived to see his press in operation. On his second voyage across the Atlantic, this time with his wife and the Dayes, the clergyman died at sea but his widow went ahead with the printing shop in Cambridge in 1638. That same year a tiny college began holding classes in the same town, having been founded in 1636 under a grant of the colony; in 1639, it took the name of a clergyman, John Harvard, who had bequeathed to it half his estate of nearly £800 and 320 books.

Proudly the Rev. Edmund Browne wrote from Cambridge on September 7, 1638: "Wee have a [t] Cambridge heere, a College erecting a library, and I suppose there will be a presse this winter." No other place in the New World could point to such signs of progress in the human condition at the time.

The Dayes began cautiously, publishing the *Freeman's Oath*, a small almanac, and their first book, the historic *Bay Psalm Book*, dated 1640. In the following year, the Daye press's uncertain future was assured for Elizabeth Glover, the clergyman's widow, was married to President Henry Dunster of Harvard College. Through this altogether happy circumstance, Harvard acquired a press and the press a sponsor. The youthful Matthew Daye,

succeeding his father as the college printer, also served as a
steward of Harvard until his death in 1649. Harvard then turned
from the Dayes to the founder of the most imposing printing
family in colonial America, Samuel Green, then thirty-four years
old. It is noteworthy that Green operated the college press for
forty-three years, but even more important that he had nineteen
children, three of whom spread the printing art through the land.

Despite the high literacy of the colony and the loud professions of adherence to learning and freedom of conscience, the
printers continued to be wary of publishing anything that would
offend. They had reason for their caution. In 1662, the Massachusetts legislature clamped censorship on the press through a
licensing law at a time when Harvard still had the only working
printer in the province. It is scarcely an accident that one of the
earliest licensers was Increase Mather, the leader of the Puritan
theocracy, who later became president of Harvard. To print
without a license was to be accounted an enemy to the government "and to be proceeded against as such with the utmost
severity." Whatever freedom there may have been in Massachusetts, the printers enjoyed none of it. The saving of their souls
was more important than the unrestricted right to print what
they wished.

It was no different elsewhere in British America. Governor
Thomas Dongan of New York received these instructions from
James II soon after the province had been wrested from the
Dutch: "And for as much as great inconvenience may arise by
the liberty of printing within our Province of New York, you are
to provide by all necessary Orders that noe person keep any
press for printing, nor that any book, pamphlet or other matters
whatsoever bee printed without your special leave and license."

Against such prohibitions, it took an exiled printer of demon-
strably poor judgment, Benjamin Harris, formerly a London
bookseller, to attempt the unlicensed publication of what has
been accepted since as the first newspaper in the Americas,
Publick Occurrences, Both Forreign and Domestick, dated September 25, 1690. In a previous publication in London, he had

"exposed" what came to be known as the Popish Plot, an imaginary conspiracy that Catholics planned to slaughter Protestants and burn the city. Arrested later for printing a seditious pamphlet, he was tried before a rascal even more notorious than he, the infamous Justice William Scroggs, who sentenced him to nine months in prison. Upon his release, the luckless bookseller-journalist fled to Boston, where he opened a coffeehouse.

Publick Occurrences, issued by the shop of R. Pierce of Boston, was printed on three sides with a fourth page blank, and was only 6 x 10-1/4 inches in size. In addition to licensing violations, Harris displeased the authorities by running two items that were likely to cause trouble for the provincial government. One dealt with the atrocities of Indians against their captives and the other imputed the grossest immorality to the king of France. In a licensed publication, such things were generally held to be published with the approval of the government unless it showed its displeasure quickly. Within four days, an official statement was issued disowning *Publick Occurrences* and expressing the government's "high resentment" of the newspaper. It was ordered suppressed, and all published copies destroyed. Thenceforth, the governor and council warned that they were "strickly forbidding any person or persons for the future to Set forth anything in Print without License first obtained."

The first American newspaper, in consequence, perished after a single issue. Its publisher, however, continued to run his coffee shop, sold books, and seemed not too displeased with himself; eventually, he returned to London, put out another newspaper, the London *Post*, but never established a reputation for himself except as a kind of scatterbrained opportunist with poor judgment and worse luck.

It is worth asking whether his ill-starred American venture was really a newspaper. Certainly, it was his intention to publish news; moreover, his sheet looked like a newspaper and his items, whether or not they were true, purported to be news. Yet, under the circumstances, nobody but a character like Harris would have attempted to publish and he had no mourners when he failed. *Publick Occurrences*, therefore, remains a curiosity and it has little significance in the long and difficult struggle for the right of free publication.

With the close of the seventeenth century, it was obvious that the English colonies could not exist much longer without some kind of communications system. Boston, the largest city, had 7,000 population and there were nearly 50,000 people in Massachusetts as a whole. In all the colonies, nearly a quarter of a million people were sharing in a way of life that pointed increasingly toward a closer community of interest along the Atlantic seaboard and a greater separation from both the dominion and customs of the Old World. At length, in 1692, the British government authorized a minimal step—the creation of an intercolonial postal system and the appointment of a series of postmasters. At last, a distinctively American form of journalism became possible.

The earliest days were slow and uninspired, quiet and devoid of the kind of conflict that is inevitably stirred up by controversialists of the Ben Harris stripe. The first to attempt to disseminate news in a systematic manner was the Royal Postmaster of Boston, John Campbell, a shrewd and careful Scot, quite the opposite of the publisher of the unlamented first American newspaper. With his appointment in 1700, Campbell industriously circulated a handwritten news letter in the European manner to a growing list of clients. After all, as the postmaster of Boston, he had access to the news and his character as well as his office was a guarantee of its reliability.

Within four years, Campbell discovered that he could not handle his news business by longhand, even with help. Consequently, through a business arrangement with the print shop run by Bartholomew Green on Newbury Street, Boston, the postmaster issued the first American newspaper of continuous publication, beginning April 24, 1704. It was called the Boston *News-Letter*, which announced in large type that it was "published by authority" and committed itself to a policy "for the Publick Good, to give a true Account of all Foreign & Domestick Occurrences, and to prevent a great many false reports of the same."

If Campbell expected to clean up with his small single sheet, printed on both sides in two-column format, he was soon disappointed. Proclamations and other official news, news clipped from foreign newspapers, and a scattering of innocuous news items of varying origin did not send his circulation soaring. He charged his subscribers twopence a copy, or twelve shillings a year, but after seven years confessed that he couldn't sell 250 copies of an edition. He went from weekly to bimonthly publication without much better results and fell many months behind the news he lifted from his foreign contemporaries. When he finally gave up his newspaper in 1723, his printer, Bartholomew Green, continued it in the same pattern without electrifying the subscribers.

The unexciting nature of the Boston *News-Letter* meant that there was room for competition but it was slow to arise because of repressive laws and high costs, the most powerful enemies of free journalism. However, when Campbell retired as postmaster in 1718 and refused to turn his publication over to his successor, a new paper began that touched off, quite by accident, a revolution in colonial journalism. It was the Boston *Gazette*, published by authority as was its rival, with the new postmaster, William Brooker, as editor and an ambitious young printer, James Franklin, as its hired publisher. Within a year Brooker lost his job and his successor, Philip Musgrave, took the paper away from Franklin's printing shop. The outraged Franklin, encouraged by friends of an equally independent turn of mind, revenged himself by starting a new newspaper, the *New-England Courant*, on August 7, 1721. It was the beginning of the free press in America, for it was published without license and dared to oppose constituted authority in what it believed to be the public interest.

Necessarily, James Franklin did not undertake so important a venture by himself. His most important resource was his younger brother, Benjamin, who even then showed wisdom and journalistic skill far beyond his lowly status as an apprentice. Together, the Franklins counted among their supporters people who were dissatisfied with and even in a rebellious mood against the strict authoritarianism of the Puritan masters of Boston. It is not surprising, therefore, that the *Courant* struck hard at established authority in its very first issue.

The blow, however, was not very well aimed. What James Franklin tried to do was to discredit an attempt by Cotton Mather to use the then experimental practice of inoculation to fight a developing smallpox epidemic in Boston. The tests, conducted by a privately educated physician, Zabdiel Boylston, preceded by seventy-five years the development of smallpox vaccine by Edward Jenner in London. When the *Courant* announced it would oppose this "doubtful and dangerous practice," Cotton Mather invented the "Hell-Fire Club," to which he immediately consigned the first newspaper. He also denounced "the practice of supporting and publishing every week a libel on purpose to lessen and blacken and burlesque the virtuous and principal ministers of religion in a country."

James Franklin lost his crusade. The Boylston experiments, in retrospect, did more good than harm. The pioneering physician inoculated 240 persons, beginning with his own son, and only six of his patients died. The power of the theocracy tightened about the lone journalistic rebel. In less than a year, James Franklin was in jail for contempt of government, the result of a slur on the province's campaign against piracy. While he was released in a month, he wasted no time in resuming his attack on his theocratic enemies; in turn, they awaited a favorable moment to silence him for good.

The Mathers' opportunity came on January 14, 1723, when the *Courant* observed: "There are many persons who seem to be more than ordinary religious, but yet are on several accounts worse, by far, than those who pretend to no religion at all." This was *lese majesté*. The government invoked its censorship powers against James Franklin, forbidding him to publish his newspaper "or any other pamphlet or paper of the like nature, except it first be supervised by the Secretary of this Province." It was a blow from which the first crusader in American journalism never recovered.

Now, Benjamin Franklin came from the back shop at the age

of seventeen to take charge of the *Courant*. He had been born on Milk Street in Boston on January 17, 1706 as a member of the large and perpetually hungry family of a thrifty soap maker and, after the most rudimentary education, had been apprenticed at the age of twelve to his older brother, James. Nevertheless, the Mathers must have discerned at once that they were dealing with a cooler, wiser, and far more subtle journalist. For, having witnessed the inevitable result of a continual policy of confrontation with the government and the church in the province, Ben announced in the *Courant* of February 11, 1723, that "the present undertaking . . . is designed purely for the diversion and merriment of the reader." So that there could be no misunderstanding, he added: "The main design of this weekly paper will be to entertain the town with the most comical and diverting incidents of human life.... Nor shall we be wanting to fill up these papers with a grateful interspersion of more serious morals, which may be drawn from the most ludicrous and odd parts of life."

It must have discomfited the grim and angry James to note that the *Courant*, under the lighthearted direction of his self-educated apprentice brother, was able to put on circulation and increase its price. There was still another surprise when a wise old lady, who had been contributing engaging pieces to the paper under the name of Silence Dogood, turned out to be the impish Ben himself. But worse was yet to come. Ben finally sickened of pretending to be a responsible editor when James, having publicly released him from his indenture as an apprentice, still was holding him to a secret agreement to the contrary. And so, after seven months of running the *Courant*, Ben walked out, knowing that James could do nothing to him without disclosing a fraud against the laws of the province.

James advertised for a new apprentice for the *Courant*, but there was not another, in the New World or the Old, to equal Benjamin Franklin. Three years later, after insupportable losses, the *Courant* died. James Franklin was heard from now and then after that as the government printer for Rhode Island and the founder of the *Rhode Island Mercury*, but he never achieved eminence again. But his brother, after reaching Philadelphia, showed such strength and will and keen intelligence that he made himself a leading citizen within five years, obtained sufficient backing to put out his own newspaper, and became a commanding figure in British America.

In issuing the *Pennsylvania Gazette* for the first time from his thriving printing shop in Philadelphia on October 2, 1729, Ben Franklin sagely announced: "To publish a good newspaper is not so easy an undertaking as many people imagine it to be." Although he now was an experienced professional printer, a shrewd businessman, a first-rate writer and respected philosopher, he found the *Pennsylvania Gazette* a much more difficult undertaking than the *New-England Courant*. He had to gather and write most of his own news, watch his editorial policy to insure a proper respect for free inquiry without arousing the hostility of the authorities, set much of his own type, and hustle for advertising and circulation whenever he could. Then, too, his printing rival, Andrew Bradford, was the postmaster and blocked his mail deliveries. But Ben bribed the carriers to make sure that the *Gazette* reached its proper destination. He succeeded to such an extent that he was soon able to buy out his less-talented partner, Hugh Meredith. It was no wonder that the erstwhile Boston runaway was both famous and well-to-do in Philadelphia before he was twenty-five years old, widely respected and regarded as a man who would make his mark in the world.

Franklin was a journalist of principle, for he took positions in the *Gazette* on the issues of the day and he saw to it that various shades of opinion were represented in its columns. "If all printers were determined not to print anything until they were sure it would offend nobody," he once wrote, "there would be very little printed." Yet, his early experience in Boston made him more prudent than bold, for he well understood that a rising young printer could more easily get into trouble with the authorities than a man of property and substance.

In every way he could imagine, he turned his energies to the achievement of an unassailable position as a man of independent means. He published books and sold them in his shop, imported others, helped establish the first foreign language newspaper in the colonies at Germantown, financed his likeliest apprentices in establishing newspapers elsewhere in the colonies, formed the first subscription library, and produced his first bestseller, *Poor Richard's Almanac.*

Franklin wanted money, to be sure, but it was not the be all and end all of his efforts. He was ever alert to the public interest, but his was a practical form of crusading that achieved results. In the *Gazette* on February 4, 1735, he posed as an elderly citizen and wrote a letter to himself as editor warning that Philadelphia needed better fire protection. He called for the licensing of chimney sweeps as a means of fire prevention and he pointed to a system of volunteer firemen in Boston that had reduced fire hazards to a large extent. "An ounce of prevention," he cautioned his fellow-Philadephians in the style of "Poor Richard," his homespun philosopher, "is worth a pound of cure." One of the prime results of this kind of discreet campaigning was the formation of the Union Fire Company by Franklin in 1736, the first of the volunteer groups that for many years made Philadelphia an outstanding example of safety from fire in early America.

The enterprising publisher also tried to reform the city's system of police protection, but in this he was less successful and his efforts had to be spread out over a much longer period. Not every crusade succeeds overnight, as he sadly discovered. What he wanted was a broad and equitable tax on businesses and private householders to enable the city to select career watchmen and pay them for regular services. He proposed that such a system should replace the old method under which each ward constable drafted householders to serve with him by night but let them off for a year upon payment to him of six shillings. It wasn't easy to break up an established police racket, Franklin learned, even in colonial Philadelphia.

Through such concern for the welfare of his fellow citizens, Franklin's fame spread throughout the colonies. By the time he was forty years old, he had the fortune that gave him the independence he desired. Because he had been diligent in making friends of powerful and important men, he had influence. And through his manifold activities in helping spread newspapers throughout the colonies as the underwriter or partner in many such printing enterprises, his views as a public man were assured of a respectful hearing. He was, in effect, the founder of the system of group publication that is so prevalent and important a factor in American newspapering today.

4. Truth Goes to Trial

In one of his earliest "Silence Dogood" pieces in the *New-England Courant*, Benjamin Franklin selected a passage from an essay, published in a London newspaper, that became a fundamental principle of the printer-publishers of colonial America:

"Without freedom of thought, there can be no such thing as wisdom; and no such thing as public property, without freedom of speech: Which is the right of every man, as far as by it he does not hurt and control the right of another; and this is the only check which it ought to suffer, the only bounds which it ought to know. . . . Whoever would overthrow the liberty of a nation must begin by subduing the freedom of speech; a thing terrible to public Traytors."

The quotation was from the work of two London newspapermen, John Trenchard and William Gordon, who collaborated under the pen name of "Cato" beginning in 1720 to formulate a theory of free speech and free press that had the widest influence at home and in the American colonies. It was "Cato" who first argued in favor of a policy that truth must be admitted as a defense against a charge of criminal or seditious libel, a crime against the state. Up to that time, there had been agreement in the courts on the enforcement of the old English common law that held, on ground of public safety: "The greater the truth, the greater the libel." Yet, "Cato" insisted that a defendant who was able to prove the truth of a charge of seditious libel should be acquitted on the basis that the public had a right to know the truth about its government.

This notion of public policy was so novel at the time that not even John Locke, a veritable apostle of liberty in England, found himself able to sustain it. In his brilliant defense of personal liberty, the eloquent philosopher backed away from criticism of the common law of seditious libel. In framing the "Fundamental Constitutions of Carolina," he wrote this provision: "No person whatsoever shall speak anything in their religious assembly irreverently or seditiously of the government or governors, or of state matters."

The colonial governors, councils, and even the assemblies in America were even less impressed with "Cato's" arguments. Rather, they appeared far more inclined to agree with Machiavelli that the fatal weakness of popular government was the freedom of people to "speak ill" of it and that it was a wise Prince who insisted on being "talked of with Reserve and Respect." Yet, through the enthusiasm of the colonial press, the doctrines of "Cato" spread through the land. They became, in effect, a popular cause second only in importance to the fair administration of Parliament's Habeas Corpus Act of 1679, a safeguard against illegal imprisonment.

While there were scores and possibly hundreds of cases in which either the colonial governors or popular assemblies initiated punishment for verbal or written attacks that were classified as "seditious words," it was not often in colonial history that the power of the courts was invoked. The judges, after all, were the people of the king and juries were likely to be respectful of their instructions. When the case of a poor New York printer came before the court, therefore, it did not unduly disturb the profligate royal governor of New York, William Cosby.

The defendant was John Peter Zenger, the 36-year-old printer-publisher of the New York *Weekly Journal*, a struggling new newspaper that had first appeared on November 5, 1733, in opposition to the government organ, the New York *Weekly Gazette*. Zenger, an emigrant from the German Palatinate, was semiliterate in English; up to the time he had been selected to run the *Journal*, he had had a difficult time supporting a large family. Under his name, prominent New Yorkers who opposed

Governor Cosby and his regime proceeded to the attack by every means at their command.

The methods that were used by such leading citizens as James Alexander and Lewis Morris, despite their professions of anonymity, made the small, poorly printed *Journal* required reading in the city. Before long, Zenger was the talk of the town. In his columns, the high sheriff was burlesqued as a monkey who "fancied himself a general," an adviser to Governor Cosby was depicted as a "large spaniel ... with his mouth full of fulsome panegericks," and the governor himself was accused of using arbitrary power, suppressing trial by jury and undermining "the choicest of our fundamental laws."

The new chief justice of the province, James Delancey, charged the grand jury at the beginning of 1734 to inquire into the "seditious libels" that "with the utmost virulency have endeavored to asperse his Excellency and vilify his Administration." But such was the popular feeling against the governor that the grand jurors refused to indict. In October, the chief justice again demanded action without avail. The frustrated governor in the following month caused his own council to issue a warrant for Zenger's arrest on a charge of "raising sedition." On November 17, 1734, he was seized and thrust into jail but he did not come to trial until August 4, 1735. To his subscribers he wrote: "I hope ... by the Liberty of Speaking to my servants thro' the Hole of the Door of the Prison, to entertain you with my weekly Journall as formerly."

During Zenger's long imprisonment, the *Journal* continued to come out mainly through the efforts of his wife. But the editorial brain behind the campaign was that of James Alexander, an admirer of "Cato" and a legal reformer who had at one time been attorney general of New Jersey. It was Alexander who kept the case alive and, very possibly with the help of Benjamin Franklin, persuaded the distinguished Philadelphia lawyer, Andrew Hamilton, then almost eighty years old, to represent Zenger. But his engagement was kept quiet until the day of the trial.

Long before the opening of the court, the small room in New York's old City Hall at the corner of Nassau and Wall streets

was crowded with citizens of all stations in life. It was a hot
August day and the room was breathless. Zenger, ashen-faced
after his long imprisonment and almost devoid of hope, was led
in. Chief Justice Delancey and his associate, Justice Frederick
Philipse, took their places on the bench in black gowns and long
grey wigs and gravely surveyed the troubled scene before them.

With little delay, a jury of twelve citizens headed by Thomas
Hunt as foreman was selected — a jury that would have much to
do with the future of a free press in America. The crowd waited,
quietly and attentively, for the government to present its case,
fully realizing that this was a fateful day in the history of the
land. The attorney general, Richard Bradley, formally read the
charges to which the defendant had pleaded innocent. These
were a part of the information he had been obliged to file against
Zenger because the grand jury had resolutely refused to indict.
They included accusations that the editor had committed seditious libel by alleging in his newspaper that the governor had
arbitrarily displaced judges, deprived defendants of trial by jury,
denied the vote to eligible citizens, and created new courts without the consent of the legislature.

The great advocate, Hamilton, took up the burden of defense.
Stern, white-haired, and imposing in the dignity of his advanced
age, the Philadelphian courteously addressed his opening remarks to the court: "I do (for my Client) confess that he both
printed and published the two Newspapers set forth in the Information, and I hope in so doing he has committed no crime."

Up jumped Attorney General Bradley, thinking he had quickly
won the day, and demanded that the jury find a verdict for the
crown. But Hamilton reproached his excited opponent with
these stern words: "You will have something more to do before
you make my Client a Libeler; for the Words themselves must
be Libelous, that is, *false, scadalous and seditious*, or we are not
guilty!"

The crowd, which had been aghast at first when the old lawyer seemed to be throwing his case away, now took new heart,
for this was a line of defense that had never before been undertaken in New York. And yet it was, as every literate citizen in

the courtroom knew, the argument of "Cato" that truth was, and of necessity had to be, a defense against seditious libel if any popular government was to exist in fact as well as in name.

Justice Delancey could have disposed of the matter summarily by directing the jury to find for the crown, but he was only thirty and inexperienced and he hesitated. When the more mature attorney general fell into argument with the distinguished counsel for the defense, the court let the two lawyers proceed. At length, the chief justice intervened to make his ruling: "You cannot be admitted, Mr. Hamilton, to give the Truth of a Libel in evidence. A Libel is not to be justified; for it is nevertheless a Libel that it is true."

It was the break in the case. After respectfully disputing the right of the court to make such a ruling, Hamilton turned unexpectedly to face the twelve men in the jury box and said: "Then, Gentlemen of the Jury, it is to you we must now appeal, for Witness to the Truth of the Facts we have offered and are denied the Liberty to prove; and let it not seem strange that I apply myself to you in this Manner. I am warranted to do so, both by Law and Reason. . . . You are Citizens of New York; you are really what the Law supposes you to be, honest and lawful Men; and, according to my Brief, the Facts which we offer to prove were not committed in a Corner; they are notoriously known to be true; and therefore in your Justice lies our Safety."

The attorney general broke into furious argument. The chief justice sat on the bench, bemused. The crowd in the hot courtroom sat as if transfixed. And the jurymen watched and listened, their faces immobile, while the pale-faced defendant seemed almost to have been forgotten.

Again and again, Hamilton returned to the theme that free men, by which he broadly meant the jury, had both the right and the duty to contain the arbitrary authority of the government. "Power," he said, "may justly be compared to a great River, while kept within its due Bounds, that is both Beautiful and Useful; but when it overflows its Banks, it is then too impetuous to be stemmed, it bears down all before it, and brings Destruction and Desolation wherever it comes. If then this is the nature of Power, let us at least do our Duty, and like wise Men who value

Freedom use our utmost care to support Liberty, the only Bulwark against lawless Power, which in all Ages has sacrificed to its wild Lust and boundless Ambition the Blood of the Best Men that ever lived."

The old lawyer rested his case, then, with his emotional final appeal — words that will live in a disordered and embattled world for as long as the free press exists:

"The Question before the Court and you, Gentlemen of the Jury, is not of small nor private Concern, it is not the Cause of a poor Printer, nor of New York alone, which you are now trying: No! It may in its Consequence affect every Freeman that lives under a British Government on the Main of America. It is the best Cause. It is the Cause of Liberty; and I make no Doubt but your Upright Conduct this Day will not only entitle you to the Love and Esteem of your Fellow-Citizens; but every Man who prefers Freedom to a Life of Slavery will bless and honor You, as Men who have baffled the Attempt of Tyranny; and by an impartial and uncorrupt Verdict, have laid a noble Foundation for securing to ourselves, our Posterity and our Neighbors, That, to which Nature and the Laws of our Country have given us a Right — the Liberty — both of exposing and opposing arbitrary Power (in these parts of the World, at least) by speaking and writing Truth."

The jurors deliberated only a short time before returning to the courtroom with an agreed verdict. When the clerk of the court solemnly asked them whether John Peter Zenger was in fact guilty of printing and publishing seditious libel, Foreman Thomas Hunt cried out defiantly: "Not Guilty!" Cheers rolled over the jubilant courtroom. Chief Justice Delancey's efforts to rebuke the crowd and halt the celebration were all but ignored. For this was a day on which to savor a victory in the name of the free press — a day that would not soon come again.

5. The Press after Three Hundred Years

In the three centuries from Johann Gutenberg to John Peter Zenger, the press found only small, isolated islands of freedom in a vast sea of authoritarian control. If these few islands existed mainly in England and the American colonies, it was almost entirely due to the preoccupation of the English-speaking peoples with the long struggle for individual freedom and their support of the valiant printer-publishers who challenged their governments.

This was not an uprising of the governed against their governors. Far from it. Certainly, the thirteen small weeklies that existed in the American colonies by the middle of the eighteenth century could not by themselves have made the crown tremble. The best that most editors could hope for was 500 or 600 circulation at that period, although Benjamin Franklin did better with his newsy and well-edited paper in Philadelphia. Nor did the larger and more important newspapers of England enjoy a much stronger position.

The editorial content of the English language press did not send the subscribers into rhapsodies very often. Geniuses like Franklin were lamentably few either in the home country or America. And unhappily, the government quietly moved to subsidize those writers of talent whom it could not intimidate by threat of prosecution or tax out of existence. Daniel Defoe received many favors from Robert Harley, one of Queen Anne's most influential ministers, and apparently gained control of the Edinburgh *Courant* and *Scots Postman* with such funds; in return, he wrote in favor of some of the government's policies. Jonathan Swift, too, was in Harley's stable of writers for a time. During the administration of Robert Walpole, when secret subsidies to the press reached a peak, the government paid between £5,000 and £10,000 a year to various newspapers and journalists. This kind of hanky-panky was sufficiently known by informed persons on both sides of the Atlantic to affect the credibility of the press in England.

Had it not been for the reformers from the time of John Lilburne, English journalism in its early years might have been looked on less as a trade than as a disgrace. As the chief pamphleteer for the Levellers, a sect of extremists during the Puritan Revolution, he spent much of his life in prison or exile because of his insistent crusading for freedom of the press. "All things being duly weighed," he wrote, "to refer all Books and Pamphlets to the judgment, discretion or affection of Licensers, or to put the least restraint upon the Press, seems altogether inconsistent with the good of the Commonwealth, and expressly opposite and dangerous to the liberties of the people, and to be carefully avoided, as any other exorbitancy or prejudice in Government." The papers of "Cato"—which so mightily influenced the outcome of the Zenger trial—were in this fearless liberal tradition.

Thus, the Zenger case became a landmark in the history of the free press in both the New World and the Old. Although it was many years before the principles on which the Zenger jury acted were incorporated into law, the precedent had been set in a tiny courtroom in New York's City Hall. A principle of law had been established, however long the courts hesitated before accepting it. Truth, henceforth, could not be ignored as a defense against libel in any jurisdiction that pretended to act in behalf of a free and open society. There would be more martyrs in the cause of a free press, but each case would only intensify the struggle until a jury's right to determine law as well as fact became firmly established.

This was the real significance of the Zenger case and the principal reason for the enormous interest in its outcome. Zenger himself never again attained such prominence. Upon his release, the day after the verdict, he went back to his newspaper and, as one of his first acts, arranged for the publication of an account of his trial. He was named public printer in New York in 1737 and in New Jersey a year later. When he died in 1746, his wife published the *Journal* for two years, then turned the paper over to a son, John. In 1751, having long since fallen from its once great popularity and usefulness, it suspended publication.

Such was the manner in which a free press gained a foothold in the New World that Columbus had discovered and began publishing the news independently for the first time of government control. It was the true measure of progress that had been achieved from the time that Columbus' Letter on his First Voyage had been printed and circulated to an unbelieving public.

II. The Violent Journalists

1. Sundown in London

The journalists of eighteenth-century London inhabited a little universe that was peculiarly their own. In the tumble-down offices of their thin little sheets, they held their conferences with all the gravity of cabinet ministers and decided on policies with the sweeping grandeur of kings. Sometimes, to their own surprise, and always to their gratification, they found that they exercised a unique and compelling power over the affairs of government.

From the time of the "Glorious Revolution" of 1688 and the lapse of the government's licensing power, both ministries and monarchs pondered the problem without arriving at any agreeable solution. In 1712, with Queen Anne's assent, a stamp tax was levied on the press — the first of the odious "taxes on knowledge" — as a means of exercising some semblance of control and at the same time adding to the revenues of the crown. It didn't work. Almost as soon as it was passed, it was evaded with a flourish for it contained enough loopholes for the least enterprising of journalists to crawl through. Nor did bribery accomplish very much. A journalist in an era of light morality could be bought, but he didn't necessarily remain bought. Of course, the old recourse to punishment for seditious libel still remained in England; however, prison sentences had little effect on the outburst of critical warfare both for and against the government.

Thus the free press, in an early phase of its evolution, conducted itself with the utmost extravagance. For all his failings, Daniel Defoe proved the essence of his power as a journalist by helping bring down a Tory government with his ceaseless attacks in his *Review*. Nor were writers like Joseph Addison and Richard Steele less effective as political journalists, although their work was more sedate and polished. On the Tory side, the brilliant Jonathan Swift—the "terrible dean"—was able to defeat a foeman as illustrious as the duke of Marlborough. And such novelists as Henry Fielding in the *Champion* and Tobias Smollett in the *Critical Review* showed full command of every weapon of journalistic invective when they chose to use them. Even the awesome Dr. Samuel Johnson lent his talents on occasion to political journalism, particularly during his attack on Parliament—the "Senate of Lilliput," he called it—in Cave's *Gentlemen's Magazine*.

None of these created the sensation of John Wilkes's issue No. 45 of the *North Briton* of April 23, 1763, in which he attacked the "blind favor and partiality" of King George III, a ready target despite his scant three years on the throne. Wilkes, a nonconformist journalist with a boundless capacity for indignation, wrote that the crown had "sunk even to prostitution" and roared on in a fine fury: "Every friend of his country must lament that a prince . . . can be brought to give the sanction of his sacred name to the most odious measures, and to the most unjustifiable public declarations from a throne ever renowned for truth, honor and unsullied virtue."

The king clapped Wilkes inside the Tower of London but couldn't keep him there. His immunity as a member of Parliament saved him. Efforts to suppress the *North Briton* failed. It didn't matter that Wilkes lost his seat in Parliament in the following year and had to flee the country. He had become famous. The number 45 for years thereafter was a symbol as popular and as revered as the Churchillian V for Victory.

Wilkes's diatribe had an even greater effect in the American colonies. Because of the repressive policies of his government, King George already had become an odious figure to the fledgling American press. Once the *North Briton*'s issue No. 45 reached Boston and New York, it became the signal for outbursts of public disapproval stimulated by an angry press. Governor Francis Bernard of Massachusetts wrote home: "To send you all the incendiary papers which are published on this Occasion would be endless."

The king and his ministers chose to ignore the danger signals.

Following the end of the seven-year war against France, the British treasury was almost bare and the king determined to replenish it by whatever means he could. The result was the Stamp Act, which brought Benjamin Franklin to London at the head of a colonial delegation soon after it was laid before Parliament in 1765. The protest failed, as Franklin had known it would. To his neighbor, Charles Thomson, he wrote in a reflective mood on July 11 after the new tax on the colonies had been approved by Parliament and signed by the king:

"We might as well have hindered the sun's setting. That we could not do. But since 'tis down, my friend, and it may be long before it rises again, let us make as good a night of it as we can. We may still light candles."

The night would be long and hard before the sun rose on an independent United States of America.

2. *The Newspaper War*

The twenty-three small newspapers in colonial America scarcely seemed to be a formidable enemy for the British empire ten years before the first volley at Concord bridge. Nevertheless, these few printing shops became the forge of American liberty. They were scattered from Boston and New York to Savannah; in two colonies, New Jersey and Delaware, there were none at all. Nor were the newspapers printed in large numbers, the greatest circulation being only about 2,000 copies a week. Few could get along on their subscriptions because the delinquency rate was so high; consequently they had to depend on a certain number of advertising notices. As Benjamin Franklin was the first to point out, the taxes under the Stamp Act hit them harder than anything else. This may have explained a part of the motivation of the colonial press, but it scarcely accounted for the massive public response. The spirit of revolt already was in existence. The "Sons of Liberty," taking their name from the well-publicized protest of Isaac Barré's against the Stamp Act in Parliament, sprang up overnight to spread the movement.

Boston, that "hotbed of sedition," led the attack on the Stamp Act. Its strongest voice was the Boston *Gazette*, which the indignant Governor Bernard denounced as "an infamous weekly paper which has swarmed with Libells of the most atrocious kind." The publishers, two independent-minded young printers, Benjamin Edes and John Gill, were, in the governor's view, "Trumpeters of Sedition," but he did not dare to proceed against them. The Sons of Liberty, of which Edes was a leader, were a power in the land, leading street mobs against their foes; in some cities, there was virtual anarchy. Moreover, the best people in the provinces supported them.

As John Adams wrote to the *Gazette*: "The stale, impudent insinuations of slander and sedition, with which the gormandizers of power have endeavored to discredit your paper, are so much the more to your honor. Be not intimidated." With his cousin, Sam, and other Bostonians like John Hancock, James Otis, and Josiah Quincy, John Adams did his journalistic stint for the *Gazette* by "cooking up paragraphs" and working "the political engine" to keep the protest at full blast. Sam Adams boasted: "Where there is a spark of patriotick fire, we will enkindle it." And they did.

In New York, under the patronage of "King" Isaac Sears of the local Sons of Liberty, John Holt turned his New York *Gazette* into a full-throated propaganda organ. The usually mild-tempered Cadwallader Colden, the lieutenant governor of the province, raged that Holt and his fellow editors "used every falsehood that malice could invent to serve their purpose of exciting the People to disobedience of the Laws & to Sedition." In Pennsylvania, William Bradford, the third of the Bradford printing dynasty, published his *Pennsylvania Journal* with the black rules of mourning when the Stamp Act took effect. Nor was Franklin's *Pennsylvania Gazette* any less inflammatory. It revived the famous political cartoon that its publisher had drawn first in 1754 at the time of the French and Indian War—a rough sketch of a snake divided into pieces representing the various colonies and labeled, "Join or Die." Across the land, the press carried the motto: "The United Voice of all His Majesty's *free* and *loyal* subjects in America — LIBERTY, PROPERTY and NO STAMPS."

Between the printer-publishers and the lawyers, America was in a state of insurrection during the brief life of the levy. It could not be collected. Newspapers published their editions without stamps. From New England to Georgia, they carried Patrick Henry's "If this be treason..." speech and published the Virginia Resolves that he had fashioned. The Sons of Liberty terrorized the government's stamp collectors and forced a number of them to resign. Finally, on March 8, 1766, Parliament was obliged to repeal the hated law.

In retrospect, it was undoubtedly an effective colonial boycott of British products that forced the repeal more than the newspaper agitation, but the pattern of resistance was now set. The press and its supporters knew what panic it could cause in the offices of the British governors and in London. Consequently, with the imposition of new taxes under the Townshend Acts of 1767, the press war burst out again with renewed virulence.

While the cannonading against the Townshend taxes increased in Philadelphia, New York, and less populous centers, it was Boston once more that bore the brunt of British displeasure. The Massachusetts Assembly was dissolved in 1768 and British troops were sent to keep the peace. Yet, in spite of the uproar, Edes and Gill and their journalistic associates in Boston were able to pull off a coup that resulted in the recall of their old enemy, Governor Bernard. In triumph, they obtained and published copies of the governor's secret correspondence on conditions in the colony in both their own Boston *Gazette* and the rival Boston *Evening Post* on April 3, 1769. Hastily, the British ministry acceded to the Provincial Council's demand for the governor's recall. When he sailed for home on August 1, the *Gazette* in its farewell called him a "Scourge to this Province, a Curse to North America, and a Plague to the Whole Empire."

The New York and Boston newspapers now turned their fire on the British military occupation. And the virtual impossibility of keeping order in the largest cities in the land plus the damage that was being done to British trade by the colonial boycott caused the British government to reconsider. As 1770 began, there were almost nightly clashes between the colonials and the British "bloody-backs." In New York, on January 18, the so-called Battle of Golden Hill was fought and several soldiers and civilians were injured. In Boston, on March 5, British troops fired into a rioting crowd and killed five persons—the Boston Massacre, as it immediately became known in the patriot press.

The British ministry had had enough. On April 12, 1770, Parliament removed all the Townshend taxes except one, the tax on tea, and this was the greatest mistake of all. However, the rioting in American cities died away. The trials growing out of the Boston Massacre were postponed to let tensions relax. In the comparative calm that followed, even so confident a revolutionary as Sam Adams began to worry. In the first place, his cousin, John Adams, had given in to his libertarian conscience and defended the accused British soldiery in the cases growing out of the Massacre. In the second, the British government appeared to present no new issue to exploit, for the tea tax in itself seemed fairly innocuous at the moment. "If the People are at present hushed into Silence, is it not a sort of sullen silence?" Adams asked. But in his response, he betrayed his own uneasiness: "Too many are afraid to appear for the publick Liberty, and would fain flatter themselves that their Pusilanimity is true Providence."

During the next three years, the patriot extremists and the colonial press had a difficult time keeping the spirit of resistance alive. But in one way and another, they did so. Out of sheer necessity, Sam Adams formed what amounted to the first press association—his committees of correspondence which soon linked the colonies in a network of eighty "bureaus," or correspondence centers. In 1772, the communication between all points from Boston to Savannah was being managed with such efficiency that concerted planning could be undertaken by the leaders of colonial resistance.

By this time, a new newspaper had come to Boston—the *Massachusetts Spy*, founded by Isaiah Thomas, then only twenty-one years old but expert in every art of the controversial journalism

of his day. With the *Gazette* and the *Evening Post*, he had contrived from 1770 to maintain an incessant agitation. In the patriot offensive against Governor Thomas Hutchinson, Bernard's
successor, Thomas took the lead in another of those journalistic
exploits that had made life for British authority so uncertain in
America. Through Benjamin Franklin's mission in London, the
Boston patriots obtained copies of Hutchinson's private correspondence and published it serially in the *Spy* and other papers.
The only really damaging statement by the governor was his
argument that "there must be an abridgment of what are called
English liberties." Despite that, he managed to hang on in office
for another year and meanwhile struck back at Franklin by causing his dismissal as deputy postmaster of the colonies.

The excitement over the Hutchinson disclosures had barely
died down when the newspapers of Boston, Philadelphia, and
New York disclosed that the East India Company was about to
unload a half a million pounds of tea in America. The almost
forgotten threepenny tax on tea now became a major issue. The
Massachusetts Spy cried out that taxes were being "extorted
from us without our consent." The New York *Journal* warned
that a monopoly on tea would lead to other British monopolies,
to the disadvantage of the colonial shippers. The *Pennsylvania
Journal* went so far as to warn that tea contained a slow poison
that produced a horrible, lingering death.

When the first tea ship, *Dartmouth*, entered Boston harbor on
November 28, 1773, the Boston *Gazette*'s office became the
headquarters for the leaders of the resistance. And it was from
this strategic point that the determined Edes sent his compan-
ions in the Sons of Liberty, disguised as Mohawk Indians, to
the historic "tea party" on December 16 in which 18,000 pounds
of tea were dumped into Boston harbor. The *Massachusetts Spy*,
in its issue of December 23, crowed: "How will you settle this
account, Mr. Hutchinson?"

The British closed the port of Boston on June 1, 1774, until the
East India Company was repaid for its losses. Salem became the
temporary seat of government. In the next few months, other
"Intolerable Acts" followed and America turned sharply toward

an armed resistance. The Boston *Gazette* warned: "Our sister colonies behold in this metropolis a specimen of what they may expect after we are subdued." Many a patriot newspaper flaunted Franklin's "Join or Die" cartoon from its masthead. The able and ingenious Paul Revere, who had cartooned the British as a wicked dragon at the time of the stamp tax agitation of 1765 and as murderers in his 1770 sketch, "The Boston Massacre," now drew a rousing "America in Distress" cartoon — a helpless woman victim surrounded by villainous British physicians.

The inevitable consequence, for which the press clamored, was the meeting of the First Continental Congress in Philadelphia from September 5 to October 26, 1774. Although it respectfully petitioned the crown for a redress of grievances, it also went ahead on a more practical plane with a Continental Association to boycott British trade. It charged the press with the duty of exposing all violators of the boycott as "enemies of American liberty," unleashing a vigilante spirit that created panic among the Tories.

The freedom of speech and of the press, for which the colonial patriots were fighting, as it turned out, was limited to the "right" expression of sentiment. As for the Tories, they were so far in the wrong that this privilege was not for them. In an appeal to the people of Quebec for sympathy, the Continental Congress declared that the importance of press freedom "consists, besides the advancement of truth, science, morality, and arts in general, in its diffusion of liberal sentiments on the administration of government, its ready communication of thoughts between subjects, and its consequential promotion of union among them."

It was quite an interpretation of what constituted "liberal sentiments" that could be properly diffused; as for the illiberal sentiments, the patriots punished those who harbored them by boycotting the foremost Tory organ in America, Jemmy Rivington's New York *Gazetteer*. The Committee of Inspection for Newport, R. I., argued against the printing of "wrong sentiments" in the recovery of American liberties. In Boston, John Adams attacked the "scandalous license of the Tory presses." And in Philadelphia, Francis Hopkinson cried, "When the press becomes an engine for sowing the most dangerous dissensions, for spreading false alarms, and undermining the very foundations of government, ought not that government . . . silence by its own authority such a daring violator of the peace, and tear from its bosom the serpent that would sting it to death?"

The crusade for freedom had come full circle; the patriots, having won the right to print what they believed in defiance of the power of the British government, now were quick to deny the same right to their opponents on the eve of war. The invasion of Tory printing shops, the destruction of presses, the confiscation of newspapers that attacked the patriot cause would come later. But with the approaching conflict, it was clear that a free people, fighting for its existence, could not tolerate a free press for any except those who agreed with them.

The new governor of Massachusetts, General Thomas Gage, saw that events were heading toward a climax. Soon after relieving the distraught Hutchinson, Gage had written to his superiors that the Americans were set on civil war. Parliament rejected the petition for the redress of colonial grievances. Little more was needed to show that the British government had embarked on a policy of force. The Boston Tories already had appealed to the British to act against the patriot leaders. In one letter, this postscript was added: "Don't forget those trumpeters of sedition, Edes and Gill."

But Edes and Gill did not take warning. The wiser Isaiah Thomas smuggled his press, type, and paper out of his Boston office on the night of April 16, 1775, put them on the ferry to Charlestown, and from there transported them by cart to Worcester. There, he set up the *Massachusetts Spy* again but didn't print at once; instead, he hurried back to Boston for the crisis. On the night of April 18, when the warning signal flashed from the Old South Church that the long-awaited British military expedition had begun to move, he helped Paul Revere spread the warning. He was at Concord and Lexington for the opening battles of the Revolutionary War next day and on May 3

issued the first eyewitness account in the *Spy* under the headline:

AMERICANS! LIBERTY OR DEATH! JOIN OR DIE!

He began with this appeal:

"Americans! Forever bear in mind the BATTLE OF LEXINGTON
—where British troops, unmolested and unprovoked, wantonly
and in a most inhuman manner, fired upon and killed a number
of our countrymen, then robbed, ransacked and burned their
houses! Nor could the tears of defenseless women, some of
whom were in the pains of childbirth, the cries of helpless
babes, nor the prayers of old age, confined to beds of sickness,
appease their thirst for blood! or divert them from their DESIGN
OF MURDER AND ROBBERY!"

The report of the engagement that followed, with 60 casualties
among the Minute Men and 260 for the British, was even more
highly partisan. It was intended, not as an objective account of a
battle, but as a propaganda tract to inflame the colonies into
united resistance. As such, it brilliantly succeeded. For on the
basis of the reporting in the *Spy* and other journals, which were
widely disseminated, the colonies closed ranks.

The patriot press suffered casualties through the appeal to
arms. Ben Edes managed to get out of Boston with his press and
type and began printing the *Gazette* at Watertown on June 5, but
his partner, Gill, was imprisoned by the British. The *Essex Gazette*
had to move from Salem to Cambridge. The Boston *Evening
Post* suspended publication. The Tories suffered, too. In New
York, Jemmy Rivington's *Gazetteer* was sacked by a patriot mob
and he himself was forced to flee to a British warship in the harbor. But despite that, a total of thirty-eight newspapers still operated in the colonies as the Second Continental Congress gathered in Philadelphia on May 10.

Benjamin Franklin, his long mission to Britain a failure, had
been on the Atlantic on the way home at the time of the fighting
and learned of the opening battles only when he arrived at Philadelphia. Then in his seventieth year, he had few hopes left and
no illusions as he took his place among the delegates in Carpen-
ter's Hall. To a friend in Kent, John Sargent, he wrote: "It now

requires great wisdom on your side the water to prevent a total separation." There was no wisdom. On August 23, the king proclaimed the Americans to be rebels. The last chance for a reconciliation was gone. But curiously, with the exception of such stalwarts as Sam Adams, the American leadership could not bring itself to face up to Franklin's "total separation." Instead of a great debate over independence, the colonies sank into a maze of legalisms.

There occurred then a towering event in the history of human freedom — the publication of a pamphlet called *Common Sense* in January, 1776. In it, at one bold stroke, Tom Paine set the course of British America toward independence by arguing in the language that the dominant middle class best understood — self-interest. Within three months, the pamphlet sold 120,000 copies; soon afterward, a half million. It was also reprinted by enthusiastic newspapers everywhere so that every literate patriot in America must have read it within a relatively short time and felt its influence.

Paine's masterwork burst upon an America torn by doubt, fear, and frustration with the dazzling clarity of a bright summer morning. It argued the case for American independence by pointing to Britain's systematic exploitation of the colonies and calling for an end to it. Independence, in Paine's words, would lead to a better economic arrangement. As for government, he called it no more than a utility and expressed his preference for policies that were the most likely to provide security and freedom "with the least expense and the greatest benefit."

While *Common Sense* attacked the monarchical principle and what its author called the errors of the English form of government, it was self-interest that remained the key until the shattering conclusion: "The sun never shone on a cause of greater worth. . . . The blood of the slain, the weeping voice of nature, cries, 'TIS TIME TO PART." As George Washington said, it was a "flaming argument" and it swept through the land with ever-mounting effect. There no longer was any doubt that America would declare for independence. The only remaining questions were when and how.

On July 3, 1776, in an announcement jointly published in the *Pennsylvania Journal* and the *Pennsylvania Gazette*, the news was broken to the people and to the world: "Yesterday, the CONTINENTAL CONGRESS declared the UNITED COLONIES FREE AND INDEPENDENT STATES." After the adoption of the Declaration of Independence on July 4, the Congress distributed copies across the land and asked all papers to publish it. From July 6, when the *Pennsylvania Evening Post* printed the first mass copies in Philadelphia, until August 2, when it was run in the *South Carolina* and *American General Gazette* in Charleston, thirty of the thirty-two newspapers then operating in the new nation devoted their issues to the famous lines of Thomas Jefferson that asserted freedom for the 3 million people of America.

In beleaguered New York City, where British warships already crowded the lower bay, a jubilant populace heard the Declaration read on July 9, and celebrated by pulling down the gilded leaden equestrian statue of George III in Bowling Green. The leaden figures, appropriately enough, soon were melted into bullets at Litchfield, Conn. Truly, as Sam Adams had said, the people regarded the Declaration of Independence "as though it were a Decree promulgated from heaven." Such attitudes could not have been shaped without the patriot press and the great journalist of the Revolution, Tom Paine.

Soon, he was writing: "These are the times that try men's souls. The Summer soldier and the sunshine Patriot will, in this crisis, shrink from the service of their country; but he that stands it now, deserves the love and thanks of man and woman. Tyranny, like Hell, is not easily conquered."

This new work, the first of the "Crisis Papers," appeared on December 19, 1776, in the *Pennsylvania Journal* after the British had taken New York City and pursued Washington's defeated army southward that first dismal winter of the war. Never were words more calculated to restore the resolution of a beaten army and never did a soldier-journalist render greater service to his commander. When the first copy of Paine's work reached Washington on a dreary Christmas along the Delaware River, he ordered it read to every squad of his command. Then, he led the surprise attack on Trenton at dawn next morning to wrest both the city and state from British command.

In the darkest hours of a new nation, one Tom Paine was worth an army and the press that published him gained in stature and prestige. As Ambrose Serle, the British official in charge of the Tory press of New York observed of his patriot rivals: "One is astonished to see with what avidity they [the newspapers] are sought after, and how implicitly they are believed by the great Bulk of the People ... Government may find it expedient, in the Sum of things, to employ this popular Engine."

But a press that was illuminated by Paine's work and stimulated by a noble cause could not so easily be subverted. Despite British efforts to undermine the patriot newspapers and encourage those who published the Tory press in British-occupied cities, the case for a British-dominated America steadily lost friends. The controlled British press, even with the expert guidance of Jemmy Rivington, could make little headway. The patriot editors were more of the mind of Isaiah Thomas in the *Spy*: "Should the liberty of the press be once destroyed, farewell the remainder of our invaluable rights and privileges! We may expect padlocks on our lips, fetters on our legs and only our hands at liberty to slave for our worse than EGYPTIAN TASKMASTERS, OR—FIGHT OUR WAY TO CONSTITUTIONAL FREEDOM."

Fight they did. Throughout the war, the patriot press served primarily to maintain communications in whatever manner possible and to stimulate public morale for long periods when ultimate defeat seemed more likely than victory. Neither in the United States nor in England was there any systematic war correspondence; indeed, the information that was published on military developments was not always reliable.

Washington was alert, however, to the use of the press in his own interest. He saw to it that Tory newspapers were carried through his lines and he subscribed to patriot newspapers that were delivered to him in the field. He also made certain that the press publicized punishments imposed by courts martial, and in other ways tried to maintain and broaden this method of communicating with his troops. In the winter of 1777, for example, he helped establish the *New Jersey Gazette* to keep his troops informed and contributed some useless tenting for the paper mill stock.

Another measure of the usefulness of the press during the war was the volume in which newspapers were published. At the time of the British surrender at Yorktown, thirty-five papers were still being published in the United States and their total circulation was probably around 40,000. This must have been considerably magnified by the number of hands through which each copy passed. Of the total, perhaps a score of the papers survived the entire war and even these either had to shift their bases for the most part or suspend publication temporarily because of the course of battle. Others gave up, new ones began, and some changed ownership but kept going; in sum, about seventy papers in all appeared at one time or another during the war. Of these, only fifteen were Tory for part or all of their histories. At the end, nearly all the Tories had to suspend publication and go into exile.

For all its difficulties and its journalistic faults, this was a vigorous and a vital press. As Vernon Louis Parrington wisely observed, on the whole it was not a liberal press but its final effect was profoundly liberalizing.

3. *"Congress Shall Make No Law . . ."*

"What signifies a declaration that 'the Liberty of the Press shall be inviolably preserved?' " demanded Alexander Hamilton in one of his *Federalist* papers. "What is the liberty of the Press? Who can give it any definition which does not leave the utmost latitude for evasion? I hold it to be impracticable; and from this I infer, that its security, whatever fine declarations may be inserted in any Constitution respecting it, must altogether depend on public opinion, and on the general spirit of the people and of the Government."

Had the choice remained to the future founder of the New York *Evening Post*, there would have been no specific Constitutional protection for freedom of the press or, indeed, any of the other provisions of the Bill of Rights. Due in large part to his leadership, with the somewhat hesitant concurrence of the "Father of the Constitution," James Madison, the Bill of Rights was omitted entirely from the work of the Federal Constitutional Convention that met in the old State House in Philadelphia from May 25 to September 17, 1787. As Hamilton argued, "Civil liberty is only natural liberty, modified and secured by the sanctions of civil society."

It was widely recognized, despite the omission, that a number of states would refuse to ratify the Constitution without the inclusion in some manner of a Bill of Rights with guarantees for the rights of free speech, free press, freedom of religion and free assembly. Jefferson, leader of the anti-Federalist cause, pleaded for a Bill of Rights in letters to both Washington and Madison. "The inconveniences of the want of a Declaration (of rights)," he wrote, "are permanent, afflicting and irreparable."

Why had the delegates refused to act, knowing that Jefferson would lead an anti-Federalist clamor for a Bill of Rights? There is no clear explanation. Some delegates evidently assumed that the separate states either had given or could give these rights sufficient protection if necessary. Others, principally legal scholars, had a deep-seated aversion to the intrusion of the federal government into areas in which its powers could not be clearly and specifically defined. Still others were tired after the long hot summer and simply wanted to go home.

To men of such demonstrated devotion, talent, and determination as Madison and Hamilton, the strategy of obtaining the necessary ratification of the Constitution by nine states was based in the main on expediency rather than principle. The end, in this case, wholly justified the means, and the objective as always was the creation of a strong central authority in the American government. Therefore, even though they had passed over the Bill of Rights in framing the Constitution, they had to reconsider to still the clamor of the anti-Federalists.

Actually, as it turned out, Madison was far from reluctant to proceed. His record on the key issue was good. At the outset of the war, he had helped draft the Virginia Declaration of Rights in 1776 and its Article XIV: "That the freedom of the press is one of the great bulwarks of liberty and can never be restrained by despotic government." Other states had gone farther. Pennsylvania's Constitution of 1776 made free speech and free press a constitutional right: "That the people have a right to freedom of speech, and of writing, and publishing their sentiments; therefore, the freedom of the press ought not to be restrained." Moreover, it was a matter of extreme interest to both Madison and Hamilton that the moderate John Adams, in 1780, had led in the adoption of Article XVI of the Declaration of Rights of the Massachusetts Constitution: "The liberty of the press is essential to the security of freedom in a state; it ought not, therefore, to be restricted in this commonwealth."

As the ratification process began, the dictates of expediency grew stronger. Several states, in fact, ratified only because Washington himself, no doubt with Hamilton's approval, suggested that a Bill of Rights could be inserted in the Constitution by amendment. There was no contest in Delaware, the first to ratify, on December 7. In Pennsylvania, the Federalists beat down a strong move for the adoption of amendment and delay, ratifying on December 12 by 46 to 23. There was no significant argument in the next three states to approve — New Jersey, Georgia, and Connecticut.

But in Massachusetts, shortly after the convention met on January 9, 1788, a straw vote showed the delegates stood 192 to 144 against ratification. This was the showdown for the party of Hamilton and Madison on the Bill of Rights and the Federalists, in a move that spread confusion among their opponents, agreed to support nine Constitutional amendments in the form of a Bill of Rights. It won over the leading anti-Federalists, old Sam Adams, and the convention voted Massachusetts' ratification, 187 to 168, on February 7. Then came easy victories in Maryland and South Carolina, after which New Hampshire, overcoming an early majority against the Constitution, voted its approval on June 21 mainly because of an agreement to submit a dozen amendments. That was the ninth state, providing the necessary majority for the adoption of the Constitution, but the victory was no cause for Federalist jubilation. They could scarcely go ahead without Virginia and New York, the most populous and powerful of the states.

In the Virginia convention, meeting on June 2, Madison himself took the floor to lead the fight against the anti-Federalists under Patrick Henry. Characteristically, Jefferson took so equivocal a position that both sides claimed his support, but Madison quickly let it be known that he would accept a Bill of Rights. The proposals piled up in such volume that the Federalists, in order to carry the day, agreed to a Bill of Rights with twenty articles and also endorsed some twenty other changes. In the preamble to the Virginia proposal was the statement that "among other essential rights the liberty of Conscience and of the Press cannot be cancelled, abridged, restrained or modified by any authority of the United States." It was just as well Madison capitulated; the final vote was a narrow 89 to 79 for approval.

In New York, Hamilton had an even closer call and also had to accept a Bill of Rights in order to defeat the rampant anti-Federalists led by Governor George Clinton. Swallowing his words that a Constitutional free press guarantee was unnecessary in the state that had inherited the tradition of John Peter Zenger, Hamilton's Federalists agreed to a proposed amendment "that the Freedom of the Press ought not to be violated or restrained." It wasn't even in the state constitution at the time and would not be, curiously enough, until Hamilton put it there. But that was still some years off.

Even the agreement on a Bill of Rights did not give Hamilton and John Jay sufficient leeway to go ahead with a vote. Instead, working with great skill, the wily Hamilton stalled until favorable news came in from New Hampshire and Virginia. Then, he proceeded to a vote on ratification on July 26 and won by only 30 to 27. Had he maintained his obdurate position against a Federal guarantee on press freedom, there is little doubt that the whole ratification process would have been in the deepest trouble. The approval of North Carolina and Rhode Island completed the long and difficult compaign.

With the inauguration of Washington as president and John Adams as vice-president on April 30, 1789, and the convening of the first session of Congress in New York City, Madison himself moved to make good the Federalist pledges. He introduced a series of Constitutional amendments on June 8, of which the House accepted seventeen and the Senate fifteen. Out of a conference, there emerged twelve which were submitted to the states. In a little more than two weeks, ten states ratified. The eleventh, Virginia, finally approved after a long wrangle on December 15, 1791, bringing the first ten amendments into law as the Bill of Rights.* In a world that was deeply stirred by the French Revolution, the American action was a heartening reaffirmation of the dedication of the new nation to the principles of freedom.

At long last the government of the United States was committed under the First Amendment's forty-four words to protect free speech and a free press in these familiar terms: "Congress shall make no law respecting an establishment of religion, or prohibiting the free exercise thereof; or abridging the freedom of speech, or of the press; or the right of people peaceably to assemble, and to petition the government for a redress of grievances." The intentions of the framers would be debated, interpreted, and fought over in countless courts until the forty-four words grew into a turgid legal torrent that would one day threaten to overwhelm those they were intended to benefit.

By 1800, Philadelphia had six dailies; New York, five; Baltimore, three; and Charleston, two; while Boston inhospitably refused to support two upstart dailies. The first of the dailies, the *Pennsylvania Evening Post*, a one-time weekly, had appeared in 1783 but succumbed in eighteen months to the competition of a better newspaper, the *Pennsylvania Packet and Daily Advertiser*, which began in 1784. Few, however, found the public to be enthusiastic about their wares.

The dark era of political journalism was just beginning in the

---

* The two rejected amendments would have fixed the size of the House of Representatives and forbidden members of Congress from raising their own salaries.

United States and partisanship was poisonous on all sides. Hamilton, always attracted to the notion of using the press as a political weapon, inspired and funded the first administration daily, the *Gazette of the United States*. It was soon ridiculed as the "court *Gazette*" in New York and its first editor, John Fenno, a Boston schoolteacher and reliable Federalist, was in deep trouble. He had shown unusual journalistic candor in his first issue, April 15, 1789, by pronouncing its purpose as the illumination of "the people's government in a favorable light." There wasn't much interest in that kind of a newspaper, as Fenno quickly found out. He was able to obtain only about 1,000 subscribers in his first year; in 1793, he had to obtain a $2,000 loan from Hamilton. Somehow, the paper staggered along until 1818.

The "court *Gazette*'s" principal anti-Federalist rival, Philip Freneau's *National Gazette*, had a much shorter but wilder history, appearing for the first time as a semiweekly in Philadelphia on October 31, 1791. Jefferson, as secretary of state, saw to it that Freneau, the "poet of the Revolution," received $250 a year from a sinecure office in the department as a translator and lent his support in other ways. Before long, tongues were wagging in the capital over the warfare between the rival organs of the secretaries of the treasury and state. So the Hamilton–Jefferson feud broke into the open.

No effort was spared in the *National Gazette* to disparage and undermine the Federalists through the most vicious abuse. While Freneau protected Jefferson by swearing that his patron had never written for the paper, Hamilton angrily told President Washington: "I cannot doubt from the evidence I possess that the *National Gazette* was instituted for political purposes and that one leading object of it has been to render me, and all the measures connected with my department, as odious as possible." For all its noble guarantees, the free press in the United States did not present a very pretty spectacle.

Jefferson, thrown on the defensive, responded with a 4,000-word letter in which he argued: "No government ought to be without censors & where the press is free, no one ever will. If virtuous it need not fear the fair operation of attack & defense.

Nature has given to man no other means of sifting out the truth either in religion, law or politics. I think it is as honorable to the government neither to know, nor notice, its sycophants or censors, as it would be undignified & criminal to pamper the former & persecute the latter."

But Jefferson's disclaimers of responsibility did not appease the wrathful Washington. In 1793, the first secretary of state resigned. Having lost his sponsor, Freneau suspended the *National Gazette* after two years with less than 1,500 circulation. Like its rival, the "court *Gazette*," it was an ignoble failure.

There was much worse to come. A scurrilous sheet flaunting the name *Aurora* (formally, it was the *General Advertiser of Philadelphia*) took up the anti-Federalist cause when the *National Gazette* faltered. Its editor, the 21-year-old grandson of Benjamin Franklin, Benjamin Franklin Bache, soon made himself an anathema to President Washington by calling him a "despot" and an "anemic imitation of the English kings." The *Aurora* broke the text of John Jay's treaty with Britain in 1795 despite Washington's efforts to keep it secret. And when the *Pennsylvania Packet* carried Washington's Farewell Address exclusively, Bache wrote in the *Aurora* of the great national hero: "If ever a nation was debauched by a man, the American nation has been debauched by Washington. If ever a nation has suffered from the improper influence of a man, the American nation has suffered from the influence of Washington."

Such violence could only beget violence. An infuriated mob invaded the *Aurora*'s office and shop, beat Bache, and wrecked the premises. Both he and Fenno died soon afterward in the yellow fever epidemic that swept Philadelphia. In eight years, Bache had lost $14,700 on the *Aurora*. Another violent but more talented editor, William Duane, succeeded him, married his widow, and conducted himself in such a contentious manner that an effort was made to deport him (he proved he was American-born). Later, when he agitated against the Alien and Sedition Acts, he was arrested.

William Cobbett, the English satirist who established a partisan Federalist daily called *Porcupine's Gazette* on March 4, 1797, made just as miserable an impression and also lost money during his relatively brief career in Philadelphia. A $5,000 libel verdict returned against him for attacking the eminent Dr. Benjamin Rush's treatment of yellow fever victims put *Porcupine's Gazette* out of business. It was typical of Cobbett that he left Philadelphia before the jury returned its verdict and sailed for England, where he continued to justify his reputation as the "contentious man."

Major Benjamin Russell's *Columbian Centinel* of Boston and Noah Webster's *American Minerva* of New York were somewhat less devoted to political brawling, although both were strong Federalist organs. Major Russell, a veteran of the Revolutionary War, had founded the *Centinel* in 1784 as a semiweekly and had 4,000 circulation by 1800, the result of enterprise and sound news policies. As for the more distinguished Webster, whose spelling book eventually sold 60 million copies, his *Minerva* was the first to run an editorial page in 1796, three years after its initial appearance. But Webster soon grew tired of the constant uproar of political journalism and sold out.

Had all papers been as useful and as moderate as the *Minerva*, American journalism might have been spared one of its most disgraceful episodes and the government of the United States might have averted a relapse into the dark era of politically inspired prosecutions of the press. But as the excesses of the pro-French anti-Federalist press increased, and the danger of war with France mounted, the Federalist-dominated Congress of 1798 hastily passed the Alien and Sedition Acts. While the alien laws had little effect, most French citizens choosing to leave the country voluntarily, the Sedition Act stirred up such a tumult that it eventually wrecked the Federalist Party and destroyed President John Adams' administration.

The sedition law's provisions were sickeningly familiar to the printers who had been struggling against them since the time of Wilkes. Imprisonment for not more than two years and a fine of not more than $2,000 was the punishment decreed for any person who was convicted of uttering, writing, or printing any "false, scandalous and malicious" statement "against the Government of the United States; or either House of the Congress of the United States, with intent to defame . . . or to bring them . . . into contempt or disrepute." During the two-year period of the Sedition Act, it led to twenty-five arrests, fifteen indictments, eleven trials and ten convictions. At the same time, common law proceedings brought about five other convictions. In all, eight newspapers were involved in guilty verdicts in one way or another.

Dr. Thomas Cooper, editor of the Reading (Pa.) *Weekly Advertiser*, was jailed for six months because he called President Adams incompetent. For criticizing the army, Charles Holt, editor of the New London *Bee*, went to prison for three months. For reprinting another paper's criticism of President Adams, William Durrell of the Mount Pleasant (N.Y.) *Register*, also received a three-month term but the president pardoned him. However, there was no presidential mercy for David Brown, a New England workman who erected a liberty pole in Dedham to protest taxes and post a placard seeking "Downfall to Tyrants in America." He drew the harshest sentence of all, eighteen months in prison.

A strange combination of Madison, Jefferson, and William Duane's *Aurora* finally opened fire on the Alien and Sedition Acts and, in the process, brought down the Adams administration. In the Virginia Resolutions, written by Madison, and the companion Kentucky Resolutions, written by Jefferson, the repressive laws were declared unconstitutional. Duane, having founded the *Indian World* in Calcutta and suffered deportation back to England, was an old hand at jousting with authority; having been arrested under the Sedition Act, he struck back in his paper by exposing a Federalist plot to steal the approaching presidential election. Such actions brought about the "Revolution of 1800" and Jefferson's election as president. With the expiration of the Alien and Sedition Acts, the new president halted further prosecutions, remitted fines and caused indictments to be dismissed. By reason of Jefferson's action, the fighting Duane did not have to spend a day in jail.

One of the Sedition Act cases, however, remained to plague the new administration for several years. The defendant, James

Thomson Callender, had been jailed for nine months in Richmond and fined $200 for attacking President Adams in a pamphlet. Later, he vainly demanded the postmastership of Richmond when Jefferson became president and later circulated vile tales about the eminent Virginian's private life in revenge. To appease Callender, Jefferson finally offered him $50 but withdrew it when the renegade called it "hush money." At this juncture, the New York *Evening Post*, which Hamilton had founded in 1801, published an article based on the supposed Jefferson–Callender relationship. A Federalist editor, Harry Croswell, reprinted the *Post's* article in his paper, the *Wasp*, published at Hudson (N.Y.), and was indicted on a charge of seditious libel.

Hamilton, feeling morally responsible, entered the case after Croswell had been found guilty in the lower court and carried the editor's appeal to the state's highest court in Albany. There, finally, he answered his own challenging question as to the meaning of liberty of the press. It was, he said, "the right to publish, with impunity, truth, with good motives, for justifiable ends though reflecting on the government, magistracy or individuals." The language he used was reminiscent of the defense of that other great Hamilton in the Zenger case, for he pleaded that the jury must be given the power to decide both the fact and the law in any case of seditious libel.

The state's attorney general, Ambrose Spencer, clung to the old English common law concept that a libel was punishable, whether true or false, "because of its evil tendency, its tendency to a breach of the peace." And this was pure Tory doctrine, emanating from a Democratic prosecutor and meeting firm opposition from the leading Conservative spokesman in the land. Truly, where freedom of the press was concerned, American political values were being thoroughly scrambled.

The appeals court was equally divided, 3 to 3, in returning its opinion in the Croswell case in 1804; however, the support of Hamilton's argument by Judge James Kent, founder of the Columbia Law School and a leading legal commentator, had a powerful effect. While Hamilton could not upset the Croswell verdict, he did succeed in influencing his home state to change its constitution. In 1805 the legislature approved a law that at last gave the jury the right to decide whether an alleged libel was a criminal offense in law and to consider truth as a defense if published "with good motives and for justifiable ends." In this manner, Hamilton, the first opponent of a guarantee of the rights of the free press in the federal Constitution, in effect wrote one of the most liberal interpretations of its function into the New York constitution.

Yet, as was the case in England, the relaxation of the laws affecting the press by no means ended the prosecutions for seditious libel. Not even the end of the Sedition Act and the accession of Jefferson's anti-Federalists, now called Democrats, saved the more aggressive editors. Nor did the spreading practice of permitting truth to be entered as a defense reduce substantially the number of convictions.

There was one other untoward result of the Croswell trial. The Albany *Register* published some disparaging remarks on the career of Aaron Burr, who had narrowly lost the presidency in 1800 to Jefferson, which were attributed to Hamilton while he was in Albany for the appeal. This became the basis for Burr's challenge to the duel at Weehawken Heights on July 11, 1804, in which Hamilton was killed.

Jefferson, whose apostrophes to the liberty of the press are so often reprinted and whose criticism is as often forgotten, emerged from this dark period as the patron saint of the free press in America. His feelings about the press, in all truth, were mixed. At a low point in his fortunes, when he was beset by unfair press criticism, he wrote: "Nothing can now be believed which is seen in a newspaper." More typical of the greater portion of his career was this familiar affirmation of faith: "The basis of our governments being the opinion of the people, the very first object should be to keep that right; and were it left to me to decide whether we should have a government without newspapers or newspapers without government, I should not hesitate a moment to prefer the latter. But I should mean that every man should receive these papers and be capable of reading them."

Hamilton's philosophy was never as grandly stated, but he,

too, helped give greater liberty and a sense of direction to the American press, despite its attacks upon him.

For Madison, the "Father of the Constitution" and probably of the Bill of Rights as well, the lash of an opposition press fell the hardest when he was least able to bear up under it. For when he led the nation into the War of 1812 after it had been virtually forced on him by the jubilant Western War Hawks under the leadership of Henry Clay, the press was the first to attack him. In the *Columbian Centinel* in Boston, Major Benjamin Russell editorially denounced what he called this "useless and unnecessary war." Nor were the thunders of dissent heard only in New England. In Baltimore, the *Federal Republican* was wrecked by a mob that was infuriated by its antiwar position. When the proprietors and staff continued to print after repairing their presses, the mob returned with a cannon, bombarded the building, and later shot two of the staff, Generals James M. Lingan and "Light Horse Harry" Lee, both Revolutionary War heroes.

It was only with the accession of President James Monroe in 1816 that the nation buried its differences and turned inward to begin the hard task of rebuilding both its spirit and its capital after the British invasion. Major Russell in the *Centinel*, ever ready with a good journalistic phrase, called it "The Era of Good Feelings."

4. At the Barricades

In the hot and oppressive summer of 1789, Paris plunged into a crisis that was to change France beyond recall and shatter the peace of Europe. King Louis XVI, taking advantage of a brief recess of the newly summoned National Assembly on July 11, had dismissed the minister on whom his despairing subjects had rested their hopes for reform, Jacques Necker. Next afternoon, before the Palais Royal, the symbol of absolute authority in the French kingdom, anxious citizens gathered to discuss the dismaying news.

To Camille Desmoulins, a 29-year-old journalist who had come to the Palais Royal with the notion that he might find there the beginning of an insurrection against royal power, the orderliness of the people was disappointing. To sustain his own courage, he had two pistols in his pockets; he reflected dismally that he might as well have left them at home. All at once, on impulse, he decided that this was his moment to address the people and sprang to a bench nearby. The crowd reacted as if a signal had been given. A few words, and it would become a mob. A few cries, and it would set all Paris aflame.

"Citizens!" Desmoulins began.

"There is not a moment to lose. I have just come from Versailles. Necker is dismissed. His dismissal is the tocsin of a St. Bartholomew's for patriots! This evening all the Swiss and German battalions will sally forth from the Champs de Mars to cut our throats. We have only one recourse — to rush to arms and wear our cockades as a means of recognizing each other."

The crowd stormed with applause. Desmoulins saw that the people, as if by a miracle, were with him and tears came to his eyes. "Friends!" he concluded. "The signal is given. Watching me are spies and saboteurs of the police. At least, I will not fall into their hands alive." He brandished his two pistols aloft. "Let all citizens follow my example!"

Now the Parisian mob was set loose and Desmoulins was carried along with it. Two days later, on July 14, he was at the Bastille when an unarmed people attacked the gray bastion of empire, killed the governor, the Marquis de Launay, and freed the prisoners. The French Revolution had begun, but there was no mention of it next day or for days to come in the *Gazette de France*, the government newspaper. To report such things, in the king's view, was to condone them. With all Paris in turmoil, and unrest sweeping the provinces, the news had to be spread by the clandestine press and foreign newspapers that were smuggled across the border.

To Frenchmen, the timidity and cowardice of the relatively few newspapers that operated under heavy censorship in the land had long been a source of bitter jest. In his witty satire on the French nobility, *The Marriage of Figaro*, Pierre Augustin

Caron de Beaumarchais riddled the French press with this speech of his hero: "They all tell me that if in my writings I mention neither the government, nor public worship, nor politics, nor morals, nor people in office, nor influential corporations, nor the opera, nor the other theatres, nor any one who has aught to do with anything, I may print everything freely, subject to the approval of two or three censors."

It was, of course, the truth. For all Dr. Renaudot's aspirations to tell the truth in the *Gazette de France*, he had been rendered helpless by his royal master and the same fate had befallen his successors for more than a century and a half. As might have been expected under the circumstances, a French underground press had flourished for more than a century. The example of the seventeenth-century *Les Nouvelles Ecclesiastiques*, which circulated privately to keep alive the efforts of Cornelis Jansen to reform the Roman Catholic Church from within, was heartening to secular journalists as well. In the flysheets that were printed clandestinely and furtively passed from hand to hand throughout France were recorded the scandals of the court, the oppression of the people, the complaints against the regime, and the news of foreign lands.

This underground press had survived Louis XIV's campaign to suppress disloyal printers, some of whom were sent to the galleys for life and others either strangled to death or burned at the stake. When French refugees had begun printing their attacks on their government in Holland and sending their products across the border, the Grand Monarch—like a number of dictators who were to follow him—used this primitive version of a free press as an excuse to launch his invasion of the Netherlands in 1672. The Dutch, fearful thereafter of French displeasure, taxed and fined the nonconformist printers to try to keep them under control.

The competition from the underground press, however, forced the French regime to loosen its information policies ever so slightly. The *Gazette* in 1772 became a daily paper, but—in the opinion of a disgruntled citizenry—it was "good only for toilet paper." Another daily, *Le Journal de Paris*, began publishing in

1777 without adding significantly to the flow of news. Taking courage from the examples of Voltaire and Rousseau, the proprietors of the underground press redoubled their attacks on the weakening regime of Louis XVI. When he finally agreed to Necker's proposal to summon the Estates General on May 8, 1789, to liberalize his government, one of its first demands was to establish freedom of speech and of the press, the prime requisite of a free people.

Comte de Mirabeau, whose purpose was to create a constitutional monarchy on the British model, at once began publishing his newspaper, *Les États Généreaux.* He was followed by Jacques Brissot de Warville, who had been trying for two months to force the police to let him circulate his new publication, *Le Patriote Français.* It was the start of a mammoth cycle of newspaper publication in France that has never been equaled, either in intensity or numbers, in any country for a relatively brief time. The underground press surfaced. Politicians who wanted a voice founded new newspapers. Printers, alert to public desires and conscious of financial rewards, tried to circulate as many newssheets, both genuine and spurious, as they could.

When the third estate, the commoners, broke away from the clergy and nobles in the Estates General on June 17, 1789, and formed the National Assembly on the motion of the Abbé Siéyès, the free press received still another boost. On August 26, 1789, after the storming of the Bastille, the Assembly adopted its Declaration of the Rights of Man with this provision in Article 11:

"The free communication of thoughts and opinions is one of the most precious rights of man. Every citizen may accordingly speak, write and print with freedom, but shall be responsible for such abuses of this freedom as shall be defined by law."

In a nation that had never before known a free press, it was only natural that both amateur and professional journalists, in their rush to print, would overlook the implied warning in the free press clause. Despite the noble tone of the words, they might just as easily have been written for Tory England as by the National Assembly for revolutionary France. There was no prior restraint on publication, but those who abused their rights in various ways that remained to be defined could be punished — and the punishment could be severe.

Nevertheless, the jaunty Camille Desmoulins, the hero of the Bastille, was prompt to establish his *Revolutions de France et de Brabant*, in which he could be as bold and bloodthirsty as any journalist of the era. Jean Paul Marat, the revolutionary physician, brought his paper, *L'Ami du Peuple*, up from underground and made it the leading journal of the extreme radicals. His leftist rival, Jacques Rene Hébert, spewed out hate and threat with every issue of his paper, *Le Père Duchesne*, a hint of what he was to do during the Reign of Terror. Beside these formidable revolutionary newspapers, the mildness of the *Mercure de France*, with its advocacy of a limited monarchy, went almost unnoticed. It was almost as if every politician in France had a compulsive fascination for journalism and either had written for the newspapers or aspired to do so.

Within four years of the passage of the Declaration of the Rights of Man, 435 newspapers were founded in France, about 150 in Paris alone, but many of them did not last very long. The largest, *Les Revolutions de Paris*, was reputed at one time to have reached 200,000 circulation.

The new order was short-lived. When the king hesitated to ratify the Declaration of the Rights of Man, rumors swept a hungry Paris that foreign intervention threatened the Revolution. It required the prestige of the marquis de Lafayette to rescue the royal family from the Versailles mob and lead them, as virtual prisoners, to Paris on October 6, 1789. With the death of Mirabeau at the beginning of 1791, Louis XVI lost his strongest supporter among the revolutionaries and the only genuine newspaper voice. He was obliged to approve the Constitution of 1791, with its free press guarantees based on the rights declaration, but by that time the liberty to speak and to publish freely had long since vanished. As was the case in the American Revolution, a newspaper in France had the choice of publishing what was agreeable to the revolutionary leadership or going out of business.

By 1793, with France at war against Britain, Spain, and the Netherlands and the king executed, all pretense of press freedom vanished. The new National Convention, in a decree, called for the death penalty for all persons who were convicted of writing for the monarchy and against the republic. Almost immediately, two journalists were executed. During the period of the Directory that followed, forty-five publishers and editors were exiled, forty-two journals were suspended, and the editors and publishers of eleven newspapers adjudged to be hostile were arrested and their presses smashed.

The revolution, meanwhile, had already begun to devour its children and the revolutionary journalists were among the first to go. Marat was assassinated by Charlotte Corday on July 13, 1793. That December, seeing that Robespierre and his Jacobins were in the ascendancy, Camille Desmoulins began a newspaper, *Le Vieux Cordelier* (The Old Friar), to try to save himself and his idol, George Jacques Danton, the leader of the Cordelier faction, from almost certain execution. In desperation, the young journalist assailed the terror that he had helped to unleash and thereby sealed his own fate. He was condemned to death with Danton as an enemy of the revolution and spent his last moments writing his defense before he went to the guillotine. Danton, a lion of courage to the last, called to his executioner as he stood on the scaffold: "Don't forget to show my head to the people. It's worth the trouble." Hébert, the journalist who had campaigned for pitiless execution of all traitors to the revolution in his newspaper, did not long survive them. He, too, died on the guillotine. So, too, at last, did Robespierre.

If the revolutionaries crushed freedom of the press even while they proclaimed their love of liberty to the world, Napoleon Bonaparte made the surviving French newspapers his tools. "They say only what I wish," said with infinite contempt. And he was, of course, eminently correct. When he replaced the Directory, he clamped a punitive censorship on all forms of publication in France that lasted for fourteen years and was pitiless to all who violated his decrees. When his government branded the newspapers of the Department of the Seine as "instruments in the hands of the enemies of the republic," he approved a decree of January 17, 1800, which in effect put his real and fancied press foes out of business. He allowed no more than thirteen newspapers to publish in Paris under government inspection; in the provinces, he permitted no new newspapers to appear and took measures to reduce those then in existence.

If the dictator was quick to toss French journalists into prison, he was even more severe with his enemies in the foreign press when he was able to lay his hands on them. During his campaign against Austria in 1809, his forces captured an Augsburg printer, Johann Palm, who had been circulating a clandestine newspaper attacking both the French and the German princes who were cooperating with them. On Napoleon's orders, Palm was executed by a French firing squad. However, that did not still the resistance of the German press. Long after Palm's martyrdom, the *Rheinische Merkur*, edited and published by Joseph Goerres, attacked Napoleon with such resolution and effectiveness that he called the newspaper the "fifth great power."

Under Napoleon as emperor, the press had still greater troubles. In 1811, he confiscated all newspapers and made them the property of the state without bothering to consider payment to the proprietors. He cut down the number of publications still more drastically, permitting only four (*Le Moniteur, Gazette de France, Journal de L'Empire* and *Le Quotidien*) to publish in Paris and only one in each department of France under the control of the prefect.

Napoleon tried in every way possible to seal off France from foreign newspapers, as well. Such important publications as the *Gazette de Leyde* of the Netherlands was ordered seized at the frontier. The Minister of Police had standing orders to intercept all English newspapers that were sent into France in the guise of mail. Napoleon even instituted a law suit in the English courts at one point against a refugee Frenchman, M. Peltier, for making fun of him in a satiric journal, *L'Ambigu*. When the *Argus*, a German newspaper, failed to comply to the letter with Napoleon's orders, he instructed his police: "The paper must be better managed or it will be suppressed."

In the cynical manner of all military dictatorships, Napoleon set up an information machine, complete with censors and personal newspapers, that were responsive to his every mood. To this apparatus he added what he called a Bureau of Public Opinion, whose business it was to create favorable public attitudes — one of the earliest attempts to manipulate public opinion. While he marched across Europe and swept the Russian armies before him on the road to Moscow, this system worked to his advantage. But once his fortunes broke, the restless French public found out soon enough that his information system was a poor cover for his lying communiques. He was not the first war lord, nor the last, to learn too late that he had destroyed himself by trying to conceal his defeats by calling them glorious victories.

The habits of mind that are imposed by a dictatorial regime are not immediately exorcised, however, with its collapse. The French press, ruined by years of Napoleonic corruption, was not purified and liberated by his fall and his exile to Elba. Before Waterloo, it was as ready as ever to believe in his professions of good will for his people. To Benjamin Constant, he put on a new face and a new front in which all things were possible among reasonable men:

"Tell me your ideas. Freedom of speech, free elections, responsible ministers, freedom of the press? . . . I am agreeable to all this. Especially freedom of the press. To try and crush this any longer would be absurd. . . . I am the man of the people. If the people really want freedom, I must give it."

Constant, agreeable to the dictator's new mood, produced sixty-seven articles of an "Additional Act to the Constitution" that provided France with at least the outward trappings of a democratic state. But it meant little. Only about 1.5 million votes were cast for it because most of France abstained in instinctive mistrust of this sudden and unbelievable convert to democratic ways. At Waterloo, when final defeat came to Napoleon and he was banished to St. Helena, his brief vision of democracy vanished. To the end of his days in exile, when his spirits were low, he could be seen reading the text of his old dispatches from a bound volume of *Le Moniteur* which he rested lovingly on his knees. He was the only one who believed them.

When Louis XVIII was propped up on the French throne by

the victorious allies after the Congress of Vienna, he granted a new charter to his people. In it was this guarantee: "Frenchmen have the right of publishing and causing to be printed their opinions provided they conform themselves to law." This so-called right was curiously observed. The British, having noted the ease with which Napoleon corrupted the French press, began buying favorable opinions as well among the journalists of post-Napoleonic France. It was a despicable game at which any number could play and the French government entered into it soon with subsidies for compliant journalists both at home and abroad. Nor were all of them mean, unprincipled scoundrels of little importance. Among the most eminent of all the French government's pensioners was the Paris correspondent of the *Allgemeine Zeitung* of Augsburg, Heinrich Heine.

It was not a system that could long endure. By 1830, eager hands were reaching up again to tear apart the sullied white flag of the Bourbons and journalists once again were leading the insurrection. Among them, the most daring and the most determined was the swarthy, courageous Alexandre Dumas, a journalist by profession at twenty-eight but a soldier of fortune at heart. He was his d'Artagnan come to life—that gallant character he was to immortalize years later.

That spring, the imperious but foolish Charles X had tried to assert his will by dissolving the rebellious French Assembly. But an even more hostile group had been returned to power, causing jubilation among the Parisian newspapers. The king responded on July 26 by signing decrees abrogating the rights of the press, again dissolving the Assembly, disfranchising at least 75 per cent of the electors of France, and setting new elections for September. The forty-four most important journalists of Paris, led by the 33-year-old editor of the *National*, Adolphe Thiers, one day to be president of France, served a manifesto on the king:

"The government has this day lost the character of legality which commands obedience . . . As for ourselves, we resist. It is for France to judge how far her resistance should extend."

The newspapers came out in defiance of the royal ban on publication. At *Le Temps*, the leader of the Paris press, mounted gendarmes closed in to make arrests but the editor, M. Baude, locked the doors of his plant and drew up his editorial staff and printers in a double line at the gates. The commander of the gendarmes sent for locksmiths but two of them fled at the sight of the menacing crowd and the police. Before the police could act, the streets of Paris boiled over with enraged humanity.

Once again, the citizens were at the barricades. Soon the Royal Guards were under attack at the Tuileries. Dumas was there, surging in with the invaders as the Guards retreated. The 79-year-old marquis de Lafayette, who had assumed command, assigned the young journalist to go to Soissons and bring back 6,000 pounds of powder. With only two men to help him, Dumas seized the Royal Magazine at Soissons — an incredible feat — and bore the powder back to Paris in triumph. Behind him he left a dazed and terrified commander who had surrendered when the journalist threatened to blow out his brains.

Within three days, his forces hurled back at every point, Charles X was in flight and the nation belonged to the revolutionaries. They called to the throne Louis Philippe, the duke of Orleans, who had taken part in the Revolution of 1789 and fought at Valmy and in the Netherlands. With the fall of the Hotel de Ville, the last stronghold of monarchical absolutism in France, Louis Philippe entered the building and joined the marquis de Lafayette, who had preceded him. In the presence of the duke and Lafayette, the Chamber then convened and listened to a declaration of new principles of government. Until the recital came to the press, the newest master of France said nothing. Then he heard these words: "A jury for offenses of the press."

"This is a useless clause, my dear general," said the duke to Lafayette, "for, as I hope, there will be no more offenses of the press."

At the conclusion of the reading, the duke placed his hand on his heart and said: "As a Frenchman, I grieve for the evil done to the country and for the blood that has been spilled. As a prince, I am happy to contribute to the happiness of the nation."

Lafayette put a tricolor flag in Louis Philippe's hand, escorted him to a window, and showed him to the cheering populace. The white flag of the Bourbons came down and the tricolor replaced it. To all save the skeptical Dumas, who watched the scene, the day was glorious. As a journalist, he had heard such pretensions of loyalty to the people's will on other occasions and had just as often seen them disregarded. And yet, on this day, the journalists of Paris had a right to celebrate. They had proved, at least once in their lifetime, that the pen could triumph over the sword.

5. The Merchant of News

By a quirk of history, the French journalist who did the least to overthrow the absolute rule of the Bourbons in 1830 was the one who profited the most by it. His name was Charles Havas and, soon after those brave July days, he became the proprietor of a struggling new correspondence bureau for journalists in the Rue Plâtrière. There had never been a journalist quite like Havas in the history of France; certainly, there has never been one since. For if Dumas was the incarnation of d'Artagnan, then surely Havas was a figure out of Balzac's *Human Comedy*—that same Balzac who criticized him with such fury in later years as *le maître-jacques* of the French press. For Havas managed to serve, satisfy, and prosper under diverse masters for many years; a shadowy figure, disinclined to strut before the applauding populace like Dumas, he knew how to acquire and wield power.

Little is known of Havas' early life beyond his birth and baptism in Rouen in 1783; however, by 1806, at the age of twenty-three, he had made enough of himself to attract the favorable attention of Gabriel-Julien Ouvrard, who fancied himself as one of Napoleon's bankers. The youth profited from the commercial licenses that Ouvrard, among others, was empowered to grant to businessmen to trade under Napoleon's continental system, and eventually set up in business for himself in Nantes as a supplier to the imperial armies.

These entirely pleasing prospects changed suddenly, however, for in 1808 Havas turned up in Lisbon as a banker and man of affairs, married a young lady of French parentage, and became the father of a daughter. If there had been a temporary breach between Havas and the Napoleonic regime, the damage evidently was repaired for by 1811 he and his wife were back in Paris where their first son was born. Under circumstances that have never been entirely clear, he became one of the proprietors of the *Gazette de France*, a mark of his favor with the regime. As long as Napoleon's star was rising, all went well with Havas. In 1814, he was a rich man; the following year, after Waterloo, he was near ruin.

Havas' taste of newspapering with the *Gazette de France* led him to continue in journalism with the *Phare de la Loire*, and perhaps others. He became immersed enough in the business of newsgathering to learn how to intercept government messages on the semaphore telegraph system that Claude Chappé had spread across France—a fruitful source of intelligence. However, under a new regime, he could not easily recoup his losses, even with the tiny correspondence bureau he established in 1826. When the July revolution burst over Paris four years later, he was at the *Constitutionnel* office but he was no Adolphe Thiers or Alexandre Dumas. He remained modestly in the background, leaving the heroics to others. But once Louis Napoleon came to the throne, and the press again enjoyed a brief period of relative freedom, the businesslike journalist saw a great opportunity and grasped it.

The Havas correspondence bureau became a financial service, complete with carrier pigeons to beat the competition with the latest market prices. Next, he merged with a small rival bureau and in 1835 announced the formation of the first news agency, the Havas Agency of Paris. With the founding of the first two cheap French mass circulation newspapers a year later— Emile de Girardin's *La Presse* and Armand Dutacq's *Le Siècle*, the Havas Agency came into its own. Within a decade, through the invention of the telegraph, Havas dominated France as a merchandiser of news and reached out for new power and new authority on the European continent.

His chief rivals, as it turned out, were in his own office — Paul Julius Reuter and Bernhard Wolff, both Germans by birth and journalists by accident. In 1849, Wolff returned to Berlin and founded the telegraph bureau bearing his name that developed into a powerful instrument of a resurgent Germany. Two years later in London, Reuter began the news agency that is still as symbolic of Britain as the Union Jack. Even though they did not adopt Havas' methods, Reuter and Wolff eventually entered into a tripartite compact with him under which they exploited news as a worldwide monopoly. For seventy-five years, they allowed only a small voice to others in the gathering and distribution of global news — notably the angry but politically impotent Americans.

It was inevitable that Havas' power to control and channel the news as well as his close contact with his government would stir resentment, suspicion, and even hatred. When Balzac launched his famous attack in *La Revue Parisienne*, he embellished in print all the charges that were being whispered in Paris about the Havas Agency and its founder. The worst of these was that Havas was collecting from the government, by vending his service to government departments, and then collecting from the newspapers by selling them news that did not displease the government. In later years, when the Havas Agency began a prosperous advertising service, which went only to papers that cooperated, such accusations were to gain in both fury and credibility.

In the end, despite all the controversy, it was not the gallant musketeer, Alexandre Dumas, who influenced the course of the independent newspaper in France by fighting for freedom at the barricades of Paris. What he did has been very largely forgotten by a world far too preoccupied with other things, although his "Three Musketeers" live on as amiable musical comedy caricatures. It was instead Havas, the shadowy merchant of news, whose news agency system came to dominate the world's communications to the public.

6. *"The Thunderer"*

A new London newspaper struggled for survival under the least favorable of circumstances toward the close of the eighteenth century. It was the *Times* and its 50-year-old publisher, John Walter, had to direct its uncertain destinies from a Newgate prison cell where he was serving a sixteen-month sentence for libeling the duke of York.

Walter had begun his newspaper adventure with a broadsheet called the *Daily Universal Register* in 1785, which three years later became the *Times*. His libel trial and sentence occurred the following year, when the paper was trying to establish itself against the stiff competition of the London *Morning Post, Chronicle, Oracle, Sun,* and others. Under less-determined ownership, the *Times* might have gone under but the first John Walter was a brave, stubborn, and resourceful man. Besides, the French Revolution had created a demand for a *news*paper of the type he envisioned. Once the unchastened publisher finished his sentence and returned to his office, a modest establishment in Printing House Square which was also his home, he did everything he could to make up for lost time. As a sop to compensate for his imprisonment, the government gave him the Customs printing and other small gratuities, but they didn't last long. From the outset, the *Times* was too hard to handle.

However much the public may have demonstrated its willingness to support an independent press in Britain, the theory of the free newspaper still had only a grudging acceptance in the law of the land toward the close of the eighteenth century, as the *Times*'s experience indicated. The dominant view, as enunciated by Lord Chief Justice Mansfield, still rested on the commentaries of Sir William Blackstone, the first Vinerian professor of English law at Oxford. In Blackstone's high Tory interpretation, freedom of the press consisted primarily of freedom from prior restraint upon publication; however, he argued that the printer must suffer punishment for disseminating "bad sentiments," which were evidently to be defined at the discretion of the judge. Neither the Lord Chief Justice nor Blackstone had admitted the right of a jury to define the truth of a libel charge, the test set up in the Zenger case. British juries had declined in a few instances to penalize the publication of so-called "bad sentiments," notably in the case of the "Junius" letters that were printed in Henry

Sampson Woodfall's London *Public Advertiser*, but the Lord Chief Justice remained adamant.

It was only when he submitted the issues in the Woodfall case to Parliament after the Revolutionary War that a change in the legal atmosphere became evident. Then, with Edmund Burke leading the fight, the efforts of English liberals from the days of "Cato" scored an encouraging advance. In Charles James Fox's Libel Law of 1792, the verdict in the Zenger case was recognized in English law in these words: "On every such (criminal libel) trial the jury sworn to try the issue may give a general verdict of guilty or not guilty upon the whole matter put in issue . . . and shall not be required or directed by the Court or judge . . . to find the defendant . . . guilty merely on the proof of publication by such defendant . . . of the paper charged to be a libel, and of the sense ascribed to the same in such indictment or information."

The enthusiasm of editors, publishers, and book printers was scarcely unrestrained over the Fox law, for they had long since come to realize that, even among people who professed to cherish freedom, the spirit of the times had much to do with the right to print and the right to speak freely. The nobility of the law was one thing; the matter of its enforcement quite another. And with the disturbing ideas of the French Revolution spreading unrest in Britain and the United States, both governments were on guard. As a result, despite the new liberalism of the Fox Act, two hundred informations were on file in England for seditious libel within a year after its adoption. In the spreading record of convictions was recorded the grim truth that juries of free men could be as frightened as governments in times of tension, and sometimes were even more likely to convict when entrusted with the right to decide whether publications or utterances were in truth seditious.

British juries voted seditious libel convictions against a lawyer for saying he wanted a better constitution and no king and against a clergyman for preaching against oppressive taxation. Nor were the punishments light. It was lucky for Tom Paine, who was prosecuted for seditious libel in London in 1792 for disrespectful sentiments in *The Rights of Man*, that he could escape to France before a jury's guilty verdict was returned. The great liberal, Lord Erskine, argued in vain in Paine's behalf that "his opinions indeed were adverse to our system, but I maintain that opinion is free, and that conduct alone is amenable to the law." The jury didn't believe him.

It was a tribute to the courage and vitality of the English press that neither the odious stamp taxes—the "taxes on knowledge"—nor restrictive prosecutions halted its growth or its determination to maintain an independent position. The fight to report the proceedings of Parliament, which had been waged surreptitiously, also burst into the open during this trying period. Defied by both reporters and newspapers, the House of Commons halted enforcement of its ancient rule of secrecy in 1771 and the Lords followed four years later. By 1789, therefore, James Perry of the London *Morning Chronicle* was sending reporters into Commons in relays to give his readers a running story of the previous night's session in his paper. It was an engaging newspaper custom that his rivals emulated whenever they could.

Crusading against malpractice in government also began to pay off. Under John Walter II, younger son of the founder, the *Times* boldly embarked on a policy of complete independence of government and in 1804 attacked Lord Melville, the treasurer of the navy, for incompetence. With Melville's subsequent impeachment, the *Times* was vindicated and established as a new kind of authority in the land. One of the *Times*'s editorial writers, Edward Sterling, subsequently began a leader on social and political matters with these words: "We thundered out the other day an article on social and political reform." The phrase may have amused Fleet Street, but it stuck. From then on, the *Times* became "the Thunderer."

There was need in Britain at the time for a thunderous, rebellious press. English goods could not be sold easily in post-Napoleonic Europe. The bottom had fallen out of English industry, for war plants were closed. With 400,000 troops discharged from military duty, unemployment became critical. But the government, instead of easing the crisis, adopted measures that had exactly the opposite effect. The Corn Law of 1815, enacted to protect the interests of farm landlords, brought about higher prices for bread by excluding foreign grain until home-grown grain reached what amounted to a "famine price." The Bank of England resumed specie payments, which had the effect of deflating the currency. And while a 10 percent income tax was dropped, so many new duties were enacted that prices generally soared.

The demand for Parliamentary reforms became overwhelming under the leadership of William Cobbett, the "contentious man" who had been obliged to flee from the United States. In his *Political Register*, he delivered such slashing attacks on the government that he became a marked man.

In 1817, Parliament passed the Coercion Acts that temporarily suspended the right of habeas corpus for the first time in British history, raised the newspaper stamp taxes, and obliged all newspaper publishers to post security in advance for fines that might be incurred for seditious or blasphemous publications. Cobbett had to give up. Despite the large circulation of his *Political Register*, he was ruined by the government's action. He also sold his thriving *Parliamentary Debates* to Luke Hansard and his sons. Then, barely beating prosecution, he fled once again back to the United States and for several years supported himself as a Long Island farmer and writer.

Leigh Hunt and his brother, John, the editors of the liberal weekly *Examiner*, whose agitation was considered as dangerous as Cobbett's, went to jail from 1813 to 1815 on conviction of libeling the Prince Regent, later George IV, but they continued to edit their paper from jail. Lord Byron was among the many who visited the poet and his brother to encourage them. When they emerged, they continued to campaign in the *Examiner;* in addition, Leigh Hunt contributed to other publications. If his name did not lead all the rest like that of his hero, Abou Ben Adhem, it was always high on the list of the fighters for reform.

The most obdurate and the most persecuted of all the journalists during the Reformist agitation was Richard Carlile, a mild-mannered bookseller and the proprietor of the weekly *Republi-*

can. In all, he spent nine years in jail for his beliefs at various times in his career, but edited his paper from behind the bars. He also brought out suppressed books by Robert Southey, William Hone, and Tom Paine.

It was inevitable that such prosecutions also would extend the attack on press freedom in England. A group calling itself the "Constitutional Association for opposing the Progress of Disloyal and Seditious Principles" began seeking indictments against both newspapers and individuals it disliked. In defending a rival paper, the *Times* itself was indicted but the Constitutional Association had no luck with its campaign. The tide of public sentiment finally was beginning to swing against seditious libel prosecutions in England and juries simply refused to convict. It was a positive advance toward a wider freedom of the press, but at first it changed no laws and halted no taxes.

While the *Times* was not a Reformist power on the same level as Cobbett, the Hunts, and Carlile, it did not shrink from an attack on the highest and most powerful elements in the government when it was deemed necessary in Printing House Square. Thus, when the unfortunate Carlile was being prosecuted for libeling the royal household in the reign of William IV, it was pointed out in his defense that the *Times* had done much worse. In *Times* editorials, the household had been called "a nest of voracious vermin," "a set of lords by way of menial servants," and "domestics of a limited monarch at so many thousands each per annum for wearing out their lives in irksome yawning attendance on a King who feels oppressed by their contiguity of person." On another occasion, a *Times* editorial called members of the House of Commons "hired lackeys of public delinquents."

With this kind of resistance to constituted authority, and with editors of principle going to prison instead of meekly submitting, the cause of reform gained strength over a decade or more of effort. The protectionist movement was breached, reducing taxes on some imports. Relief legislation was passed to ease the hardships of workers. And while a new law permitted workers to combine to improve their wages and hours of employment, they were forbidden to strike. An antiquated criminal code was revised, sharply reducing the number of crimes that had been made punishable by death. But perhaps the major reform, in which the press played a key role, was the Reform Act of 1832 that made Parliament more truly representative of the people.

"The Thunderer" was neither the first daily in England nor the richest nor the largest. But it became the most important early in the nineteenth century because it was the most authoritative and spoke for the leading segment of opinion in the land. If that opinion increasingly became also the opinion of the government as well, it was a tribute to the newspaper's power. A year after the passage of the Reform Act, for example, the government of Lord Grey was urging the passage of an important bill that had been introduced in Parliament. The *Times*, however, disapproved and editorially denounced the measure, an audacious step for the conservative middle-to-upper class press of the era. In the language of the age, it "made a great sensation" and shook the government. All of which caused the admiring Charles Greville, the busy English diarist and clerk of the government's Council in Ordinary, to write of the affair: "It is no small homage to the power of the press that an article like this makes as much noise as the declaration of a powerful Minister or leader of the Opposition could do in either House of Parliament."

The independent newspaper had come of age as a trusted leader of public opinion. Even the independent editor was now respectable. For upon his return from his second exile in America, William Cobbett, no lofty *Times* man but for thirty years the boastful editor of "tupenny trash," was elected to Parliament.

7. *The Swiss Doctor's Prescription*

The *Zürcher Zeitung* was a sick newspaper. It had survived some of its contemporaries, but not by much. From 1,000 copies an issue during the Napoleonic wars, its most prosperous time since its first appearance on January 12, 1780, it had sunk to a mere 419 copies in 1820. The proprietors, Orell, Gessner, Füssli, & Company, were prosperous printers but they could not sustain losses from their newspaper indefinitely. Their first recourse, as usual with publishers who are in trouble, was to look for a new editor.

Johann Heinrich Füssli, who had been running the paper, was much impressed with a public-spirited botanist and physician, Dr. Paulus Usteri, who had also been a correspondent for the *Allgemeine Zeitung* of Augsburg and the president of the short-lived Helvetic Republic's Senate. He had everything a successful editor required — talent, integrity, toughness, vitality and, most important of all, a competitive independent spirit. Furthermore, he wanted the job.

Usteri's prescription for the ills of his country, his people, and his newspaper was awesomely simple: a free people, free speech, and a free press. But all these, of course, had been proscribed by the great powers at the Congress of Vienna, which had made Switzerland a loose confederation of twenty-two self-governing cantons after Napoleon's downfall. In addition, there was a tough censorship that obliged all Swiss newspapers, including the *Zürcher Zeitung*, to stick to watered-down foreign news dispatches.

Nevertheless, the new editor applied his prescription to his newspaper without hesitation. On June 22, 1821, he changed its name to the *Neue Zürcher Zeitung*, made it a triweekly instead of a biweekly, and decided to print Swiss news in his paper instead of a starvation diet of foreign news. It was little short of revolutionary for that era and Usteri, in consequence, found himself famous overnight.

The great powers didn't take kindly to the *Neue Zürcher Zeitung* even if a grateful populace did. Anything that stimulated public support for a Switzerland free of great power control was not compatible with their interests. Therefore, they regarded criticism directed at them in the Swiss press as a breach of the pledge of neutrality under which the confederation had been set up. As German, Italian, and French political refugees began streaming across the Swiss border, the position of the champion of freedom, the *NZZ*, became even more difficult.

It was to be expected that the Holy Alliance would take drastic action. All too soon, the wily Count Clemens von Metternich of Austria, the moving spirit of the Alliance, forced upon the reluctant Swiss his own version of the Alien and Sedition Laws, quite literally the *Press- und Fremdenkonklusum*, on July 14, 1823. Under this statute Switzerland was obliged to give up power to grant political asylum to refugees and it also bowed to the enforcement of the strictest censorship on all news and comment.

Despite all their difficulties, Usteri and his collaborator, Füssli, made headway in their long and dogged campaign to arouse greater public support for a free country, free speech, and a free press, for the spread of education and tolerance, for continued resistance to foreign influence. Both were elected to the greater council — the Grosser Rat — of the canton of Zurich. From that austere platform, as well as in the columns of the *NZZ*, they fought for their cause with such success that Zurich became the first of the Swiss cantons to remove press censorship.

Füssli retired from the *NZZ* in 1830, his lifetime's ambition fulfilled, and died two years later at the age of eighty-seven. Usteri, whose prescription had worked such miracles, was elected mayor of Zurich but died unexpectedly a month later. There were others, no less able and determined, to carry on. With the acceptance of a new constitution by an overwhelming vote in the cantons, the *NZZ* on September 13, 1848 published the news that Switzerland had become a federal state — a free union, no less independent than the United States, with its own foreign policy and army, a single revenue system, a customs union and currency. Had he lived, Usteri would have been proud, indeed, of his country and his newspaper that brilliant September day.

The success of the Swiss doctor's prescription gave fresh courage and renewed hope to many a journalist and political refugee who watched the *NZZ*'s long campaign. Foremost among these impoverished exiles, whose presence in Switzerland had always been defended by the *NZZ*, was a hot-tempered young Genovese lawyer, Giuseppe Mazzini, who had devoted his life to the cause of Italian independence. Both his underground newspaper, *Giovine Italia* (Young Italy), and his revolutionary activities had often embarrassed the Swiss but, out of principle, they provided a haven for him as long as they could, despite repressive laws that were forced upon them. Mazzini's clandestine sheet, smuggled over the Italian border and read with longing and enthusiasm by the youth of Italy, became the inspiration for a violent upsurge of sentiment for freedom in his native land. He already had spent a year in prison for planning an Italian revolt that did not come off in 1832. He also tried to stir up an invasion of Savoy from his Swiss base in 1834; when that failed, he was obliged to move his base to London.

Despite his mistakes, Mazzini retained a hold on Italian youth. However, his place at the head of the Risorgimento was taken gradually by a cooler and more effective patriot of moderate bent, Count Camillo Benso di Cavour. *Giovine Italia*, like its editor, also was soon surpassed by a less sensational newspaper that had a broader appeal to Italians of all ages and classes, Cavour's *Il Risorgimento*. But between them, with the help of the determined soldier-exile, Giuseppe Garibaldi, these two inspired the Italian people into long years of resistance that eventually made possible a united Italy.

Elsewhere in Western Europe, the islands of freedom were pitifully few in the years immediately after the downfall of Bonaparte. The censorship exercised by the French, in effect, was taken over by the censorship of the Holy Alliance as exercised by Metternich from Vienna. As a result, there were lamentably few editors who dared to attempt to emulate Paulus Usteri and the *Neue Zürcher Zeitung* in a campaign for freedom.

In the German states, the home of the first newspapers, the triple-headed monster of censorship, licensing, and taxes combined to keep venturesome spirits in line. In Prussia, as early as 1727, advertising was restricted to official publications known as *Intelligenz Blätter*, and independently owned newspapers were warned that they would lose their licenses if they accepted advertising. The censors were strict, eliminating virtually all criticism that might displease their particular regime. And, of course, the taxes on the press inevitably tended to grow heavier rather than lighter as the controls were applied.

It is a journalistic miracle, in such an atmosphere, that any independent newspapers managed to survive. And yet, such was the vitality of German journalism of the era that it brought into being one of the most famous journals, Christian Voss's *Vossische Zeitung*, the old Tante Voss (Aunt Voss) that survived until the Nazis came to power. The *Kölnische Zeitung*, the *Hamburgische Correspondent* and the *Allgemeine Zeitung* all struggled to maintain at least a semblance of news coverage although the difficulties were enormous. Baron Johann Cotta, the engaging bookseller who published the *Allgemeine Zeitung*, had to move his operations successively to Tübingen, Stuttgart, Ulm, and finally Augsburg during the Napoleonic wars and the era that followed.

In Austria, Metternich's police and his censors attacked the few struggling Viennese newspapers with such venom that only two of substance finally remained, the official *Wiener Zeitung* and the government-approved *Beobachter* (Observer). The Hungarians and the Slav peoples under the rule of the Hapsburgs were not even permitted the use of newspapers published in their own languages, but were obliged to turn to poorly printed and inadequate papers in German.

The dismal pattern of repression was broken in the United Netherlands, in which the Congress of Vienna had attempted to unify the Netherlands, Belgium, and Luxembourg in 1815. A determined Belgian editor, Louis de Potter, and his *Courrier des Pays Bas*, refused to submit to stringent press controls that had been set up by William of Nassau, who had assumed the Dutch throne as William I. Although he was jailed for his defiance, other Belgian newspapers took up his cause and printed appeals which he managed to slip out from his prison. The agitation became so great that the Belgians rebelled, declared their independence on October 4, 1830, and, in one of their first legislative acts, gave this guarantee of a free press:

"The press is free. Censorship may never be reestablished and no surety bond may be exacted from writers, editors or printers. In matters concerning the press, closed hearings may be held only with unanimous consent. Jury trial is required in all criminal cases and in all hearings of political and press offenses."

In the burst of vitality that came with freedom, a new and independent Belgian press was born and shaped in the spirit of the first Dutch newspapers that had shown Europe what a free press could do. What happened in Belgium eventually led the Dutch to reassert their own liberties and establish an independent press once again. But as the Dutch learned to their cost, the tyrannical rule of William I and his successor, William II, could not be overthrown at once. It was not until 1843 that Jan Thorbecke, a liberal-minded professor at the University of Leyden, was able to establish a Dutch voice of reform, the *Nieuwe Rotterdamse Courant*.

In Greece, too, the revolutionary struggle was long and hard and here also the press played a major role. As early as 1790, *Ephemeris* (Journal) was edited in Vienna by the Greek patriot poet, Rigas Fereos, and smuggled across the Balkans into Turkish-held Greece. After a revolutionary uprising began in Greece on August 1, 1821, presses had to be brought in from neighboring countries because the Turks had permitted none to operate inside the captive nation; from London alone, four printing plants were shipped. Lord Byron gave up his beloved England and sacrificed his career as a poet to edit one revolutionary paper, the *Ellenika Chronika*, and just before his untimely death was also helping edit the *Greek Telegraph*. In all, more than sixty papers were in operation in Greece during the seven-year revolution, but independence did not help their professional cause. It was many years before the Greek press achieved even a precarious freedom.

The press in the Scandinavian countries suffered similar disappointment in the latter part of the eighteenth and early nineteenth centuries.

In Denmark, there were two brief years of press freedom because Johann Frederick Strünsee, the German physician to the demented Christian VII, insisted on it. With the abolition of censorship, the physician-dictator's enemies used the fledgling Danish press to publish charges that he had become the lover of the young queen, Caroline Mathilde, causing his downfall and execution. For many years thereafter, the press was published only by royal decree, the most notable example being Ernst Heinrich Berling's weekly government paper in Copenhagen which, after a century and a half, became the independent *Berlingske Tidende*.

In Sweden, there was a six-year period beginning in 1766 when censorship was lifted for the small and impoverished newspapers of the land; however, it was only during the long reign of Charles XIV, Napoleon's Marshal Jean Baptiste Jules Bernadotte, beginning in 1818, that a free press finally became possible for a united Sweden and Norway. As for Finland, these were the most heroic years of the press's fight for existence, for the few Finnish newspapers were controlled under Swedish rule. The Russians, who succeeded the Swedes as Finland's overlords, repressed all hope of freedom for more than a century.

In Spain, where no fewer than sixty-five decrees enabled the government to regulate the press and impose death sentences on rebellious editors by the end of the eighteenth century, the Napoleonic invasion brought a temporary change of policy. Spain had not lacked for talented journalists from the sixteenth century on. Francisco Fabro Bremundan, founder of Spain's most enduring periodical, the *Gazeta Nueva*, and Francisco Nipho y Cagigal, founder of at least twenty newspapers and periodicals, led in the establishment of a thriving if closely regulated press. When the French took it over at the beginning of the nineteenth century and bent it to their own purposes, however, the defiant Cortes, meeting in Cadiz, approved a free press law on October 19, 1810.

The decree was without precedent in Spanish history; yet, even under the stimulus of foreign invasion and national necessity, the law was adopted by only a vote of 68 to 32. It declared in sweeping terms that "all groups or particular persons, regardless of condition or state, [shall] have the freedom to write, print and publish their political ideas without the need for licensing, review, or any approval prior to publication." Its purpose was to serve "not only as a brake on the arbitrariness of those who govern, but also as a means of arriving at knowledge of true public opinion." This was quite a declaration for Spain; as a result, in the three years that the Cortes met in Cadiz, more than fifty newspapers began.

But as soon as the emergency was over, unhappily, the traditional urge to keep the press in check returned with greater virulence than ever. In less than a year after Madrid was liberated from the French in 1813, Ferdinand VII issued a royal decree nullifying all the laws of the Cortes and added a special manifesto for the press which ruthlessly crushed all liberty of expression. Editors of liberal mind either fled or were thrown into jail. And the score of newspapers that were being published in Madrid quickly were reduced to two miserable, government-approved sheets.

Under the stresses of the Napoleonic era, there was even a spark of press freedom in Russia but it also was put out as soon as the danger had passed. Peter the Great, early in the eighteenth century, had established the first Russian newspaper, *Vedomosti* (Gazette), to help modernize the country. Although it was an official journal on which the czar himself sometimes read copy in 1703, and although only 1,000 four-page copies were circulated, it was a decided innovation in an illiterate and backward land. However, under Catherine the Great, the hesitant trend toward freer expression was abruptly halted; at the borders, foreign literature was seized and at home the private printing shops were closed.

Jean Francois de la Harpe, a distinguished Swiss teacher and contemporary of Dr. Paulus Usteri, brought the principles of freedom to Russia with him when he became the tutor of Alexander I at the beginning of the nineteenth century. De la Harpe had lectured at the Lycée in Paris; consequently, he was imbued with the heady notions of the French Revolution. To the Russian intellectuals, he must have seemed heaven-sent; soon, in the new *Magazine of Russian Letters*, they were arguing for a free press, free speech, and the abolition of serfdom. However, the cautious Alexander, preoccupied with the imminent danger of attack, never let the press get out of hand even though he relaxed censorship for a time.

Once Napoleon was driven from Moscow and forced into his disastrous retreat, the czar returned to his familiar absolutist principles just as the Spanish monarchy did. In Alexander's later days, he was, like Metternich, an implacable autocrat of the Holy Alliance. Instead of liberalism, he caused the frenzy of a brutish repression to march across Europe from the east. As for the Russian press, it vanished into the darkness of royal control. The influence of de la Harpe and Swiss humanism was brushed aside. With the abortive revolution of 1825, the reactionary years of Nicholas I began and Russia's course was set toward absolutism.

Although the Holy Alliance dominated much of post-Napoleonic Europe, the image of personal liberty remained a cherished if unattainable dream for millions of repressed peoples. Among those of wisdom and discernment, it was not forgotten that even the haughtiest autocrats in moments of sheer desperation had granted a short spell of freedom to the press in order to rally popular support against military danger. It was also an observable phenomenon that the press had served as a guarantor of personal liberty in those few lands that were fortunate enough to win and maintain their own freedom.

Thus, the prescription of the Swiss physician-editor, Usteri, became precious to many who had never seen his newspaper nor heard of his own struggles. To all who yearned for a better world in the discouraging era of which he was a part, the ideal represented by free peoples, free speech, and a free press became the compelling force of their lives.

8. The Press after Four Hundred Years

In the middle of the nineteenth century, the newspapers of the United States and Britain were the most representative examples of a free press in a world that had its doubts about the principle and the practicality of such an institution. In Canada, Australia, and a few European centers of popular sovereignty — Switzerland, the Scandinavian countries, and the Low countries — the principle of independent publication was accepted and free newspapers were showing encouraging growth. But in France, the press swung violently between periods of great liberty and the cruelest repression. And in Germany and Italy, a vigorous group of underground newspapers cried incessantly for national independence. In much of the rest of Europe, as well as the rest of the world, the real struggle for freedom of the press had scarcely begun. The ruthless hands of autocratic government, in consequence, still held the balance of power over most of the globe.

There is no doubt that the American press was the strongest group of independent newspapers in any nation in the middle of the nineteenth century. From 1,200 newspapers in 1833, the press in the United States had grown to 3,000 by 1860, of which more than 300 were dailies; as for periodicals, there were more than 1,000 by mid-century. The vitality of the press was best illustrated in New York City, where thirty-four new dailies were published in four years beginning in 1833, of which nearly half survived. There were numerous papers as well in Western and Southern cities — ten in St. Louis, nine in New Orleans, ten in Cincinnati, twelve in San Francisco and more than 400 in the state of Illinois.

Beginning with the publication of the New York *Sun* in 1833 by a 23-year-old job printer, Benjamin H. Day, the penny papers had captured a faithful and ever-widening public. It was followed, with even greater success, by the New York *Herald*, which James Gordon Bennett founded in 1835 and which was to dominate the American press for fifty years; Horace Greeley's serious and high-minded New York *Tribune* in 1841, and Henry J. Raymond's New York *Times* ten years later. Two of the penny papers outside New York, the Philadelphia *Public Ledger* and the Baltimore *Sun*, helped finance and promote Samuel Finley Breese Morse's invention of the magnetic telegraph in 1844. The New York papers, for their part, took a leading role in 1848 in forming the first wire service, the New York Associated Press, the forerunner of the modern global agency of the same name.

It had taken all the genius and inventiveness of the industrial revolution to make possible such cheap, mass-produced newspapers. With the invention of the steam engine by James Watt in 1770, both paper-making and printing operations became practical on a larger scale. Nicolas Louis Robert invented a machine for making the first continuous cylinder roll of paper in 1798 in France. Within a few years, his invention was perfected in England by the brothers Henry and Sealy Fourdrinier who, by 1803, were able to modernize the paper-making industry. Then came the pioneering Koenig-Bauer steam cylinder press, developed for the *Times* of London in 1814 and improved upon by an Englishman, David Napier, in 1830. But the penny press needed much faster equipment, which was supplied in 1846 with the invention of the first rotary press by the American firm of R. Hoe & Co., with a capacity of 16,000 papers an hour. A year later, Hoe offered his "Lightning" presses with six to ten cylinders bearing curved and locked type forms, which could turn out 20,000 sheets an hour.

Among the American dailies, the *New York Herald*'s 77,000 circulation was the largest by 1860. It was also believed to be the largest in the world, exceeding the 70,000 of the *Times* of London and the lesser circulations of the cheap English and French press. However, nothing could touch the 200,000 circulation of Greeley's weekly *Tribune* throughout the United States; in influence and prestige, it far exceeded the 45,000 copies of the daily *Tribune* and made a famous and powerful figure out of its editor.

Yet, although there were three times as many newspapers in the United States as there were in England and France in 1833 and an even greater proportion by 1860, no single American paper had the worldwide acceptance of the *Times* of London. It was the most extravagantly admired for its authority and influence, its independence, and the excellence of its news coverage. The New York *Herald*, the New York *Tribune* and the *National Intelligencer* each had virtues, but none was on the rarified journalistic level of the "Thunderer."

It was a proud moment for American journalism when Greeley, author of the phrase, "Go West, young man," turned instead to London and in 1851 testified before Lord Milner's Parliamentary Commission against the remaining British "taxes on knowledge." Four years later, the last British stamp taxes on newspapers and advertising were removed, causing an expansion of the British press that was proportionately comparable to the American experience.

If there were many who worried about the excesses of the free press in the United States and Britain, they had good reason for their concern. Warmongering, sensationalism, irresponsible campaigning, and cheap appeals to the worst in humankind were scarcely calculated to sit well with a thoughtful public. There could be grave doubts about the wisdom of John L. O'Sullivan's rallying cry for support of America's "Manifest Destiny" in the New York *Morning News* of December 27, 1845 — a faith that invoked Divine right to justify possession of a continent. And there could be both shock and horror over the cheers with which much of the penny press greeted the expansionist Mexican-American War of 1846-1848. But for all the undoubted failings of popular sovereignty and the free press, the alternatives to both were so repugnant to free peoples that they put up with the defects of their press to guarantee their own liberties.

III. New Vistas, New Goals

1. The Reformers

All France seemed to have turned itself into a huge banquet hall toward the end of 1847. Night after night, the news from Paris concerned what had been said and done by influential people, gathered around a sumptuous dinner table. In a somber mood, all the rest of Europe watched and waited, for this strange spree of high living presaged trouble.

The French banquets were extraordinary affairs. Even the French workmen, so accustomed to the sour wine of discontent and the black bread of despair, were inordinately interested. For the real menu was social reform, based on the most violent and vitriolic after-dinner speeches that had been heard in France since the storming of the Bastille.

It was now Louis Philippe's turn to tremble.

The corruption of the Assembly, capital punishment for political offenses, the continuing censorship of the press, and the hard lot of the workers were the issues upon which the banqueters seized. And the silk weavers of Lyons, who had to work sixteen hours for a pitiable 11 sous a day, responded with the cry: "Live working or die fighting." It was evident enough that another day of reckoning was approaching in France.

The doctrine of the brotherhood of man as it was developed by Claude Henri Saint Simon, the idealistic French philosopher, had a deep appeal to the seething Paris of mid-century. The communal schemes of Charles Fourier and the anarchism of a young French printer, Pierre Joseph Proudhon, both had a following. And in an obscure corner of the City of Light, the exiled editor of the *Rheinische Zeitung*, Karl Marx, already was discussing with his friend, Friedrich Engels, the principles they would incorporate in the *Communist Manifesto*.

But next to Adolphe Thiers, the 50-year-old founder of *Le National* and twice premier of France, the dominant journalist in the

Paris of the banquets was Louis Blanc, the Socialist editor of the newspaper, *Reform*. "To the able-bodied citizen, the state owes work!" he exclaimed. "To the aged and infirm it owes aid and protection. This result cannot be obtained unless by the action of a democratic power."

As Louis Philippe well understood, these were not empty words. A two-year depression in both agriculture and industry had robbed him of whatever prospect he may have had for popular support. When Blanc called for a series of social workshops under government control to provide work relief for the unemployed, the then novel proposition had a decided appeal. And when the editor proclaimed the doctrine, "From each according to his abilities, to each according to his needs," he was trying to express popular desires rather than a Communist slogan.

A particularly large and therefore dangerous political banquet had been scheduled in Paris for February 22, 1848, but the fearful Louis Philippe prohibited it. Instead, he called upon the liberal-minded Thiers that day to supplant the arch-conservative premier, the historian Francois Guizot, but the journalist refused. The king had waited too long. That day, the barricades went up in Paris and the fighting began.

Guizot resigned next day, February 23, and the tumult might have subsided but for a senseless military attack. Trigger-happy soldiers, on guard before Guizot's residence, fired wildly into a crowd and killed twenty-three people. Within a matter of minutes, Paris plunged into insurrection. By next morning, the mobs were streaming through the streets crying: "Long live the Republic!" Louis Philippe abdicated in favor of his grandson, the comte de Paris, and took off with his queen as plain "Mr. Smith" in a horse and carriage for the Channel and England. By sheer good luck, he made it.

For the second time in French history, a republic was proclaimed. The comte de Paris was quickly brushed aside in favor of a fusion provisional government, with Louis Blanc as the leader of the left wing and the poet, Alphonse de Lamartine, at the head of the right. Within twenty-four hours, Blanc had his national workshops in operation although, as it turned out, they gave little work and even less relief. He also proclaimed his revolutionary ten-hour day for Paris (eleven in the provinces) but he couldn't enforce it. He was a better journalist than a ruler.

When the National Assembly was elected in April, the true temper of the nation was seen; the conservatives won 500 seats, the Royalists about 200, and Blanc's radical reformers less than 100. At once, the conservative Assembly named General Louis Cavaignac to be a kind of bourgeois dictator to repel a threatened working-class revolt against the outcome of the election. It also dissolved Blanc's workshops. The Parisians rioted. From June 24 to 26, 1848, General Cavaignac threw the might of the French army against the mob. In the bitter and bloody street fighting of those terrifying June days, the revolt was crushed. Once again, reaction was victorious in France.

That July and August, the Assembly cracked down with one of the severest press censorship laws in French history, making it impossible for Blanc to continue his paper. Other laws clamped control on political clubs and suppressed the secret societies that had caused so much social ferment. The banqueting stopped. And on December 10, in the national elections, France turned to the adventurous nephew of Napoleon I, Prince Louis Napoleon Bonaparte, as its president under a new constitution.

Before long, the leaders of the Left saw that their weak republic was fading. A new dictator was in power, a new empire was in the making. In the Assembly, Victor Hugo thundered at the monarchists: "You are all dead! You do not belong in our century, in our world!" Over the cries of the deputies he shouted: "Because we have had a Napoleon the Great, must we have a Napoleon the Little?" But regardless of what they did, neither Hugo nor Alexandre Dumas nor Louis Blanc could stop this new Napoleon. The people were against them, and two years later the people paid for their folly. On the night of December 2, 1851, the opposition politicians and the opposition journalists were snatched from their beds and jailed, the Assembly was dissolved, and troops stormed into Paris. Two days later, the dictator's troops repelled a weak insurgent rising and fired on the unarmed civilians of Paris in what became known as the "Massacre of the Boulevards."

The news bulletins raced across the Channel to England by way of the new "submarine telegraph" — the cable that had been laid between Dover and Calais. Out of the thousands of French citizens who were arrested nearly 20,000 received prison sentences and half were exiled to Algeria. By decree on December 2, 1852, the second empire came into being under his majesty, Napoleon III. That barometer of repression, the press, sank to a low ebb, for all newspapers were put under police control and editors could be appointed and discharged by the minister of the interior on nomination by the proprietors. Any paper could be suspended at any time without reason. If a paper was established, it had to be with government authority; moreover, the proprietor had to deposit 50,000 francs with the government in Paris to insure his good behavior toward the regime. And there was a stamp tax on each paper that was sold.

Hugo, Dumas, Blanc, and others of their illustrious company fled to England. There, the underground press took up the attack against the new Napoleon, led by Hugo's own paper, *Chatiment*. It was a desperate time for the French press, but the best papers survived and a few new ones were born. To Girardin's *La Presse* was added in 1854 a little boulevard sheet called *Le Figaro*, the property of Hippolyte Villemessent. Still later, in 1863, Moise Millaud produced the French equivalent of the American penny paper, *La Petite Presse*, for which he charged one sou. It was an immediate success.

There was one family of French journalists that profited even more — the ever-accommodating Charles Havas and his sons, the proprietors of the now imposing Havas News Agency. With its wires spread across Europe and under the English Channel, it had made Paris one of the world's greatest news centers. Through it, the government of France could — and did — impress its views on what people read in their newspapers. Mainly, this had been Charles Havas' doing, for he made himself indispensable under Louis Philippe as a dispenser of news and a friend of the regime. With the accession of Napoleon the Little, the founder of the Havas Agency quietly retired in his seventieth year and left his prosperous business to his faithful and diligent sons, Auguste and Charles-Guillaume. Their father had made all France his province. They extended Havas to the world, reaching agreement with Reuters and Wolff in 1859 on a news cartel that eventually embraced the New York Associated Press. At Havas, whatever the state of France, it was business as usual.

The shock waves of revolution that emanated from France in March and April of 1848 rocked all Europe, unseating old rulers and bringing temporary reforms from frightened governments. But with few exceptions, the forces of conservatism were able to rally by midsummer. The risings were put down with military force. Upstart leaders had to flee. And old regimes, sometimes with new faces, took up where they had left off, but with greater watchfulness. Yet, while it lasted, the upsurge of 1848 produced heady results that made a formidable impression on suffering peoples.

Nowhere was the effect more remarkable than in old Vienna, the lovely gray capital of the Austro-Hungarian empire. Here, the first statesman of Europe, the 75-year-old Prince Metternich, toppled from power before the onslaught of a 36-year-old Hungarian journalist, Louis Kossuth. As a member of the Hungarian Diet in Budapest, he had helped achieve the adoption of Magyar as the country's official language. He also had defied strict Hapsburg censorship to publish his *Diet Bulletin* so that his constituents would know what was going on. For this, he spent three years in prison from 1837 to 1840. When he emerged, he founded the Hungarian newspaper *Pesti Hirlap* (Pest News) in Budapest in 1841 and published it for four years until it was suppressed. With the proclamation of the Second French Republic, Kossuth on March 3, 1848, eloquently demanded independence for Hungary before the Hungarian Diet. That was the beginning.

Within ten days, the Viennese broke into rioting and a deputation demanded the resignation of Metternich. Eluding the mob after his palace had been set aflame, the aged prince, in blue swallow-tailed coat, faced King Ferdinand in the Hofburg and remarked, with conscious irony, that his presence no longer seemed to be required. With the frightened monarch's assent, Metternich and his wife mounted an ordinary laundry wagon on March 13, drove from a riotous Vienna, and went into exile in England.

Two days later, in an imperial manifesto issued in Vienna, a constitutional assembly was summoned and press censorship was abolished. In Hungary, without asking Vienna's leave, Kossuth pushed through a democratic constitution that guaranteed free expression. When the emperor gave the Austrians something less, the barricades went up before the Hofburg and he had to flee to Innsbruck.

Kossuth was the man of the hour. Newspapers, so long suppressed in both Austria and Hungary, fairly poured from the presses. There were more than two hundred in Austria, ninety of them dailies, including the imposing new journal, *Die Presse*, founded by August Zang. In Hungary, more than eighty papers and magazines flourished, among them Kossuth's revived *Pesti Hirlap*. Italy, Bohemia, Moravia, Galicia, Dalmatia, and Transylvania all rose against Austrian rule, encouraged by Kossuth's example. But wild demonstrations were no substitute for government.

It didn't take long before the Austrian military went into action to recover lost ground. Count Alfred von Windischgraetz, the military governor of Bohemia, captured Prague and Field Marshal Joseph Radetzky, military governor of Upper Italy, conquered a Sardinian-Piedmontese army at Custozza. The military governor of Croatia, Count Joseph Jellachich de Buzim, invaded Hungary, then joined the other commanders in capturing Vienna. Through the maneuvering of Prince Felix zu Schwarzenberg, King Ferdinand abdicated on December 2 in favor of his 18-year-old nephew, Francis Joseph.

That was the end for Kossuth. All the revolutionary reforms he had made possible in Austria-Hungary meanwhile were undone by Francis Joseph. Censorship once again was imposed on the press. In Austria, fewer than twenty papers remained; in rebellious Hungary, only three. As an honored elder statesman,

Metternich quietly returned to Vienna to live out his days while Kossuth retired in chagrin to Italy. Reaction had triumphed in the domain of the Hapsburgs as well as in France.

It was inevitable, under these circumstances, that the hopes that had been aroused in 1848 for a union of the weak German Confederation would be dashed. True, in the excitement over the proclamation of the Second French Republic, King Louis of Bavaria had abdicated in favor of his son, Maximilian II, and liberal reforms had been promised in a half-dozen other German states. But in Berlin, Frederick William IV ordered his troops to fire on a riotous mob, killing two hundred people, and shattering the prospect of a peaceful change to a new order. Frightened after four days of fighting, the king agreed to summon the Prussian Diet to draft a constitution for all Germany but he made no further concessions. When the National Assembly met at Frankfurt-am-Main and asked all members of the German Confederation to end censorship at once, the *Vossische Zeitung* issued an extra with the headline: "THE PRESS IS FREE!" The news was premature. As Frederick William and his fellow rulers recovered their nerve, they forgot their promises, reestablished the Confederation in its original form, and left everything in Germany as it had been.

Almost overlooked in the military and political uproar was the issuance of Karl Marx's *Communist Manifesto* in Brussels early in 1848. In laying down the principles of Socialism for the workingmen's clubs he had helped establish, the 30-year-old German exile concluded: "The proletarians have nothing to lose but their chains. They have a world to win. Workingmen of all countries, unite!" If the little pamphlet won few readers at the outset, Marx's own importance as a radical leader was nevertheless enhanced. The Belgian government, under pressure from Prussia, ordered him out. He fled to Paris in time to witness the February revolution of 1848 in which his friend Louis Blanc played so historic a part. But he did not tarry. With the news of the first German risings, he returned to his homeland and reissued his old radical paper in Cologne as the *Neue Rheinische Zeitung.* But it was to no avail. In the end, he was arrested for inciting to armed resistance in Germany, and exiled once more. From 1849 until his death in 1883, the founder of the doctrine of world Communism lived in London, supporting himself at various times as a correspondent for the New York *Tribune* and the *Presse of Vienna*. In this fashion, his work for the free press helped provide him with the time he needed to write his masterpiece, *Das Kapital*, which led his follower, V. I. Lenin, to victory in Russia in less than seventy years.

Although the British government was typically generous to Marx and other political exiles, it was quick to suppress a threatened rising in 1848 of a workingmen's reform movement called the Chartists. Only Switzerland, the Netherlands, Denmark, and Sardinia really benefited in the end. As for the violent journalists of 1848, some of the best fled to the United States. And in France, the banquets of hope ended in squalor and despair.

2. *Member of the Establishment*

A 23-year-old junior parliamentary reporter for the *Times* burst into his modest flat in London's St. James Square on a lovely spring morning in 1841 and exclaimed to his startled roommate: "By Jove, John, what do you think has happened? I'm the editor of the *Times*."

John Thadeus Delane had reason for excitment. He had been chosen to lead a great newspaper although he was the youngest member of its staff and had just received his degree from Oxford. His roommate, John Blackwood, might have been forgiven if he had reflected, as he could have, that journalism is a topsyturvy business.

Delane had been born into the Establishment that had so much to do with running the country. He was the second of the four sons of the *Times*'s financial manager, William Frederick Augustus Delane, a lawyer, and a neighbor of the *Times*'s proprietor, John Walter II, in Berkshire. Having known John Delane from childhood on, Walter was well aware that the young man was not much of a student. Nor had he been a sensation as a writer or thinker at Oxford. Outwardly, he seemed to be just another handsome and well-mannered young Berkshire squire who had been taken on by the *Times* as a junior in the House of Commons press gallery. His observable enthusiasm, however, was horses, not newspapers.

Yet, in the inscrutable ways of journalism, Walter had suddenly put this untried youngster in charge of a newspaper that even then was the acknowledged leader in the land. The *Times*, with 40,000 circulation and unmatched prestige, dwarfed the *Morning Advertiser*, with 7,000, and the *Daily News*, *Morning Herald*, *Post*, and *Chronicle* with 3,000 or less each. It had become a vital part of the British Establishment under the regime of its late editor. Thomas Barnes, and now exercised more influence on government policies than many a cabinet minister.

As Barnes's youthful successor, Delane tossed aside whatever inhibitions he may have had about following a great man and made a bold beginning. Under his direction, the *Times* took a loss in railway advertising in order to press a campaign against worthless railway shares that were then flooding the market. And while the cabinet in 1845 was debating whether to repeal the Corn Laws, which would stimulate the flow of foreign grain into Britain and cut the price of bread, the young editor himself wrote the story that the decision to repeal had been made. As it turned out, the news was premature — but it was right. His source had been the incoming prime minister, Lord Aberdeen.

On these and other occasions in his first decade at the *Times*, Delane showed he had the indispensable gift of the great editor — to be ahead of the news. In the conviction that Russia meant to destroy Turkish power and that Britain might be drawn into an Eastern war, he visited the Crimea in 1852. When he returned, he wrote some pieces about his travels, read a number of books about Russia, and was impressed in particular with the work of another traveling English journalist, Laurence Oliphant, who had written a volume entitled, *Russian Shores of the Black Sea*. The editor made the writer a special correspondent. All preparations were undertaken to cover a war that had not yet been declared.

Russia, determined to curb Turkish power, occupied the Danubian principalities in the summer of 1853. After their protests had been rejected, the Turks declared war on October 4 and called for help. When the British and French fleets entered the Black Sea to protect the Turkish coast line early in 1854, Russia severed diplomatic relations with both Western powers. So far, everything moved ahead in the stately but fatal diplomatic quadrille that European nations had used for centuries to go to war. But on February 28, 1854, the *Times* interrupted the movement with an exclusive disclosure that the British and French governments had served a secret ultimatum on Russia. This was most inconvenient, for it raised the possibility that the British public now might decide it didn't really think the protection of Turkey was worth a war. In the House of Lords, Lord Derby cried out: "How is it possible that any honorable man, editing a public paper of such circulation as the *Times*, can reconcile to his conscience the act of having made public that which he must have known was intended to be a cabinet secret?"

Delane, who had been present at the proceedings, responded in next day's *Times:* "We hold ourselves responsible not to Lord Derby or the House of Lords, but to the people of England for the accuracy and fitness of that which we think proper to publish. Whatever we conceive to be injurious to the public interests, it is our duty to withhold; but we ourselves and the public at large are quite as good judges on that point as the leader of the Opposition."

On March 11, 1854, after Russia had ignored the ultimatum, Delane revealed another closely held Foreign Office secret. It was a proposal that the czar had made to the British government for the partition of Turkey—a suggestion that had been indignantly rejected. Its disclosure at so sensitive a moment, when the issue of war or peace still was so delicately balanced, again drew Lord Derby's condemnation of the *Times*. Once again Delane answered in print the following day:

"This journal never was, and we trust never will be, the journal of any Minister, and we place our independence far above the highest marks of confidence that could be given us by any servant of the Crown. . . . As long as we use the information we obtain and the influence we possess for the honor and welfare of the country, the people of England will do us justice."

The British and French declared war on Russia March 28, 1854. At the insistence of Count Cavour, the prime minister of Sardinia, that little kingdom in the following year entered the war on the side of the Western powers; eventually, Cavour's foresight would provide Sardinia with French military help against the Austrians. But neither he nor anybody else was really prepared for war, and the British were the least prepared of all. Lord Hardinge, the British commander-in-chief, admitted as much to the inquisitive Delane before the beginning of hostilities and the *Times* promptly opened a campaign to equip the troops. It was the first danger signal.

Up to this point, the *Times*'s record in the Crimean adventure indicated willingness, even eagerness, to prepare public opinion for the decisions that had led to war. While governments had used newspapers before in an effort to shape public opinion, this was one of the earliest instances—perhaps the earliest—in which a great independent newspaper had lent itself willingly to underwrite governmental news management. There could have been no other explanation for the series of exclusive news and policy revelations in the *Times* that brought shrieks of anguish from the Loyal Opposition and no real complaint from the government. Lord Aberdeen's friendship for Delane, in this respect, paid off.

Had this been the whole object of the *Times*'s coverage of the Crimean War, the newspaper would soon have been discredited with the large and influential public it served. But fortunately for Delane, he had sent William Howard Russell, a moon-faced 34-year-old correspondent, at the head of a large crew to cover the war with the brusque and effective directive: "Tell the truth." Here, the *Times* and the government parted company, and Delane found that he could no longer support his friend, Lord Aberdeen. For the story that his newspaper told was one of utter incompetence of military leadership.

As Russell revealed the incredible suffering of the ill-clothed, half-starved British troops in the Crimea during the winter of

1854-55, pressure mounted on the *Times* to keep its complaints to itself. Lord Raglan, the Crimean commander, accused Russell of giving aid and comfort to the enemy, which discomfited the correspondent not at all. Lord Clarendon, the foreign minister, wrote in despair: "Three pitched battles gained would not repair the mischief done by Mr. Russell and the articles upon his letters." Queen Victoria herself demanded to know what justification the editor of the *Times* could give for trying her officers. The Prince Consort, branded Russell "a miserable scribbler."

Delane stood fast. To Russell and his colleagues, he continued to insist: "Tell the truth." To his government and the nation, he replied: "Publicity is my trade. Details the public wants and details it shall have." But like any good editor, caught up in such a crisis, he went to see for himself in the fall of 1854 and found ample confirmation of everything that Russell had written.

Necessarily, the editor of the *Times* received preferred treatment. And yet, on board the H.M.S. *Britannia* off the Crimean coast, he found the crew desolated by cholera. After the landing of the troops from the fleet, he wrote, "It is painful to see how weak they are." As for the despised Turks, he found to his surprise that they were "infinitely better supplied and better appointed than either the French or English."

With Delane's return, he began pounding at the government for winter's supplies for the troops, but received no encouragement. He turned to the public for assistance and within a few weeks raised £25,000 for relief and hospital supplies. It was the *Times*'s campaign, too, that brought the "Lady of the Lamp," Florence Nightingale, and her thirty-eight nurses to the military hospitals of the Crimea to lessen the suffering of the sick and the dying.

All this, of course, would not have been possible without the steadfast front-line reporting of Russell under conditions that would send many a war correspondent today to headquarters howls of protest. In the Crimea, nobody at headquarters would listen. And although Russell at one point made an injudicious offer to submit his letters to the command to be read before they were sent, Lord Raglan refused to deal with him. In this war there was no censorship; evidently it was considered unmilitary and even unpatriotic to deal with those merchants of treason, the correspondents.

Russell let nothing stop him. He seemed to be everywhere — in the line of battle, behind the lines, in the hospitals, and always with the troops. He was at the Alma River, before Sebastopol, at Balaclava for the tragic charge of the Light Brigade, at Inkermann, but he could not write of the glory of war. Instead, he warned the public at home early in 1855 that the British army was "used up and ruined . . . misery in every form and shape except defeat."

Delane pressed home this complaint with such vigor that the House of Commons set up a Select Committee of inquiry into the *Times*'s charges. The Aberdeen government fell under the savage assault of its one-time friend, Delane. Lord Palmerston came in as the new prime minister and the sardonic Lord John Russell observed: "The *Times* aspires not to be the organ but the organizer of government."

Under Palmerston, reinforcements and supplies flowed to the British forces in the Crimea but it was not until September 11, 1855, after a siege of 316 days, that Sebastopol fell. Three days later, Russell reported in a dispatch dated "Inside Sebastopol" that the Union Jack had been hoisted over the ruins of the Crimean fortress and the bodies of its Russian defenders. It was the first instance in which a newspaper could rightfully claim to have influenced the course of a war through its fearless and well-justified attacks on the conduct of its own government and the sagacity of its military command.

The *Times*'s circulation in this period had gone as high as 70,000 on the strength of its Crimean War performance, giving its enemies in the government an opportunity for revenge. The repeal of the "taxes on knowledge" was being discussed, but one governmental proposal was to substitute postal for revenue stamps for newspapers. However, under the contemplated standard of four ounces for postal charges, the *Times* would have been put to heavier cost than its rivals because it was generally a bigger paper. Consequently, Delane let it be known that he would organize his own press delivery system independent of the government if the discriminatory postal revenue proposal was adopted. The *Times* accused the government of a plot to raise up "an inferior and piratical press, and sacrificing a revenue of £200,000 a year."

While the *Times* won its battle, with the "taxes on knowledge" being abolished, new rivalry developed but it was scarcely "inferior and piratical." The *Daily Telegraph*, after a shaky start, had been taken over in 1855 by its printer, J. M. Levy, who made it a penny paper and put on 27,000 circulation within a few months. An even more formidable rival was the *Daily News*, founded by Charles Dickens in 1846, which took on a brilliance that was attractive to liberal Britain with its championship of the American crusade against slavery. As a penny paper, the old *Morning Post*, too, showed more life under its proprietors, Algernon Borthwick and his correspondent son.

The *Times*, therefore, did not lack for competition in the critical years following the Crimean War, although no editor showed the capacity of Delane. His policy of keeping a balance between the government and the opposition and mixing high society with his politics paid large dividends. It gave him powerful friends in both parties. It also provided him with access to the most exalted news sources. He was the repository of an imposing amount of valuable and accurate information, which he used judiciously and often to good effect. There never had been a better political reporter in all Britain than this quiet, well-mannered, hard-working Squire of Printing House Square.

By that period, Delane was immersed in an even more sanguinary struggle — the American Civil War. To prepare himself, he had made a brief American visit in 1856 and returned with a large-sized prejudice against the Northern cause that was to betray him into many an injudicious act. Washington, to him, had been an "odious village," and New York City a colossal bore. Of Boston, he had written that "nobody seems to have anything to do but lounge in and out of the hotels and gossip and drink." As for the American press, he had judged it to be "too corrupt"; and yet, he had added, "it would be dangerous as well as unavailing to bribe it in our interests."

Such an attitude earned the *Times* the hatred of the North during the Civil War and did not notably contribute to the advancement of British interests, which in this instance had corrupted Delane's judgment of news. Moreover, the *Times* steadily lost the support of the liberal section of British opinion to the *Daily News,* which championed the antislavery cause and the leadership of Abraham Lincoln. As the fortunes of the South steadily declined, it became clear that British policy had been mistaken from the outset.

Under such pressures, Delane lost patience. He allowed his natural anti-Americanism, never very well disguised, to get the better of him. On October 14, 1862, he permitted the *Times* to demand editorially: "Is the name of Lincoln ultimately to be classed in the catalogue of monsters, wholesale assassins and butchers of their kind?" It was the lowest point in his 36-year career as editor of the *Times.*

When Delane was the disinterested champion of truth, he established new standards of performance and responsibility for the free press. As a member of the Establishment, he brought new respect to his ink-stained trade and almost succeeded singlehandedly in making a profession of it. But as a partisan, he was only human. In all these guises, he presided over the *Times* until his death in 1879. "I have not stirred from this place since I last saw you," he wrote to a staff member in his latter days, "and I believe not a column has been published in the *Times* which has not had some of my handwriting in the margin."

It was the farewell of an editor.

3. A New Birth of Freedom

William Lloyd Garrison, a stern, 26-year-old Yankee printer, celebrated New Year's Day in Boston in 1831 by running off the first copies of his four-page newspaper, *The Liberator,* for fewer than fifty subscribers. He was uninterested in fame, wealth, or

power, the goals of so many journalists of his day. With his feeble weapon, he began a furious attack on the powerful and ever-
spreading institution of Negro slavery in the United States in
these terms:

"I will be as harsh as truth, and as uncompromising as justice.
On this subject, I do not wish to think, or speak, or write, with
moderation. ... Urge me not to use moderation in a cause like
the present. I am in earnest—I will not equivocate—I will not
excuse—I will not retreat a single inch—*and I will be heard.*"

Garrison was a man of iron and his soul was flint. The sparks
he struck during the thirty-five years he ran his little paper
helped set the conscience of America aflame. Let the Bennetts
and the rest make their fortunes in the development of the
commercial press with every device to trick the masses into buying. Garrison conceived of a free press with an entirely different
mission. To carry it out, he defied mob violence, jail, and death
itself. He preached sedition, even treason. He encouraged
revolt, turning aside the warnings of more reasonable men.

Garrison had been born to poverty and drifted into a print shop
by chance. In Newburyport, Mass., his birthplace, little formal
education was available but he learned the printing trade beginning at the age of thirteen in a seven-year apprenticeship to the
owner of the Newburyport *Herald*. After an unfortunate experience with an Abolitionist paper in Baltimore, he set up his own
in Boston. "I WILL BE HEARD," he insisted in his boldest type.
And he was.

When Nat Turner led his abortive slave revolt in the Virginia
tidewater country in 1831 and killed fifty-five whites before
being caught and hanged, Garrison among others was blamed
for incitement to riot. On another occasion, in 1835, a Boston
mob dragged him from his print shop through the cobbled
streets with a rope around his waist, screaming that he was a
"damned Abolitionist." When he helped sponsor an Abolitionist meeting in New York, Bennett's *Herald* complained: "That a
half-dozen madmen should manufacture opinion for the whole
country is not to be tolerated."

But Garrison was contemptuous of *Herald* editorials. His *Lib-*

erator never had more than 3,000 circulation; to make ends meet, he lived on bread and water when his funds ran low. He was eternally coining slogans such as: "No Union With Slaveholders." In every issue of his paper, he sought to stimulate his friends, outrage his foes; in his anxiety to attain his goal quickly, he sometimes could not distinguish between them. He even quarreled with John Greenleaf Whittier over Whittier's advocacy of political action to achieve the emancipation of the slaves.

To Garrison, there was no substitute for total militancy, massive confrontation. Invariably, he adopted shock tactics when he wanted to make an impression. At a meeting in Boston on July 4, 1854, he held up a copy of the Constitution of the United States, shouted that it was a "covenant with death and agreement with hell," and publicly burned it. Such outrageous tactics made him more of an embarrassment than an ornament to the Abolitionist cause and cost him whatever chance he may have had to be its leader. But it didn't bother him. While the blacks were enslaved in the United States, nothing would do for him save all-out struggle.

In a nation that sought a new birth of freedom, many another like Garrison served with utter selflessness in the Abolitionist campaign, forfeiting their property, their well-being, and sometimes their lives as well. His friend, Whittier, aroused such resentment in Philadelphia with the *Pennsylvania Freeman* that a mob wrecked and burned the paper's shop. Another Abolitionist sheet, the Utica (N.Y.) *Standard and Democrat*, was sacked. Cassius M. Clay's *True American*, in Lexington, Ky., was seized and he was banished from the state. In nearby Newport, Ky., William Bailey's *Free South* plant was destroyed.

Still another Kentuckian, James Gillespie Birney, was driven out of the state in 1836 when he began publishing the *Philanthropist*, an Abolitionist weekly. And when Birney moved to Cincinnati to begin all over again, his printing shop was wrecked. As Garrison and others had learned, the North could be no more hospitable to Abolitionists than the South. Subsequently, the *Philanthropist* reappeared under the editorship of Dr. Gamaliel Bailey, the founder of the more famous *National Era* in Washington, D.C.

The *Era* was the paper that first published serially Harriet Beecher Stowe's *Uncle Tom's Cabin*.

The greatest sacrifice to the Abolitionist cause by the journalists of the 1830s and 1840s was that of Elijah Parish Lovejoy, who began his crusade in St. Louis. When some of the best citizens in town attended a mass meeting in October, 1835, to try to persuade him to tone down his St. Louis *Observer*, he stood up before them and said: "The path of duty lies plain before me, and I must walk therein, even though it lead to the whipping post, the tar barrel or even the stake."

Like Garrison, Lovejoy was a New Englander, as unyielding in principle as the rocky coast of his native Maine. He had been born in the town of Albion in 1802, graduated in 1826 from what is now Colby College, and studied theology at Princeton. As the editor of the *Observer*, a Presbyterian weekly, he carried on his Abolitionist campaign for three years before he was obliged to move to another river town, Alton, Ill., on June 21, 1836. But he had even less success in Alton, where a mob destroyed his newly purchased press after he had been at work there for less than a year. He bought another but that, too, was wrecked; had it not been for his wife, who clung to him and shrieked for help, he might have been trampled by the angry citizenry.

Instead of giving up, Lovejoy ordered still another press with funds that his friends had provided. On the night of November 7, 1837, while he and a handful of loyal associates were guarding that press in an Alton warehouse, a mob came for him and this time he was shot and killed. The building was spared, but the press was destroyed. It was the bloody end of the *Observer*. The martyr's brother, Owen Lovejoy, carried on his work as the pastor of the Congregational Church at Princeton, Ill., and, as a congressman, helped form the Republican Party and elect Abraham Lincoln.

Of the forty or more Abolitionist newspapers that were founded, edited, and published by Negroes before the coming of the Civil War, few survived for very long. The first, *Freedom's Journal*, appeared between 1827 and 1830 in New York City, the work of the Rev. Samuel Cornish and the first black college graduate in the United States, John B. Russwurm, Bowdoin, Class of 1826. Like such others as the *Colored American* and the *Elevator*, *Freedom's Journal* died for lack of public support. But when a truly influential paper such as the *North Star* began appearing in 1847 under the leadership of Frederick Douglass in Rochester, N. Y., mobs soon began to form to wipe out the black press. Douglass' home was burned and a dozen volumes of his paper were destroyed. He managed to keep it going under a different name until 1860.

As the clouds of civil conflict settled over the land, the largest and most responsible newspapers in the North assumed the leadership of the cause that Garrison and Lovejoy and Douglass had done so much to sustain. Horace Greeley in the New York *Tribune*, Henry J. Raymond in the New York *Times*, Joseph Medill in the *Chicago Tribune*, and Samuel Bowles III in the Springfield (Mass.) *Republican* welded the antislavery press into a formidable engine at the time of John Brown's raid on Harper's Ferry in 1859. When old Brown went to the gallows for his mad attempt to ignite an antislavery insurrection, the Springfield *Republican* proclaimed: "John Brown still lives!" And many another paper prominently published Ralph Waldo Emerson's inspired comment that old Brown had "made the gallows glorious like a cross."

But the South was not without journalistic defenders. Bennett's New York *Herald* went so far as to try to pin the blame for Brown's deed on Senator William H. Seward of New York because he had warned at Rochester of the coming of an "irrepressible conflict." It didn't matter to Bennett that Seward had spoken *before* the Brown raid. The publisher accused the senator of plotting "national disruption." But in the end, it was Bennett and not Seward who had to change course. For with the attack on Fort Sumter that marked the beginning of the Civil War on April 12, 1861, a mob obliged Bennett to display the American flag in front of his building — a wholly unaccustomed act of patriotism for the pro-Southern publisher.

As for the New York *Tribune*, which had been temporizing with the secessionists, it shifted policy drastically after Sumter and clamored: "On to Richmond!" Although the Union forces were in poor shape, the *Tribune* insisted on calling for a decisive test of arms. When the government gave in to this ill-informed editorial pressure and sent the luckless Army of the Potomac southward, it met disaster at Bull Run. In his latter days, a contrite Greeley contended that his managing editor, Charles A. Dana, had made the decision in his absence to press for a quick victory. But regardless of who was responsible, it was an appalling instance of the influence of the journalist on history.

If the *Tribune* became undependable and the *Herald* a potential enemy, Lincoln nevertheless was able to count on the New York *Times* and its editor, Henry J. Raymond, as his steadiest supporters. Raymond was a comparatively late-comer among Lincoln's stalwarts. The *Times*'s editor, an associate of Boss Thurlow Weed of New York State and his leading vote-getter, Senator Seward, had opposed Lincoln's nomination for president by the Republicans at Chicago during the 1860 convention. His choice had been Seward. But like good party men, once Lincoln's nomination had been assured, Seward, Weed, and Raymond all had swung over to Lincoln and Seward had been named secretary of state. It was only with the coming of war that Raymond had put his doubts of Lincoln aside. Then he unfurled a huge American flag outside his building and wrote in the *Times:* "The great body of our people have but one heart and one purpose in this crisis in our history."

That was the *Times*'s policy throughout the war and Raymond dedicated himself to it. Energetic, quick-witted, graceful and still in his middle years, he was well qualified to serve as one of Lincoln's foremost counselors and confidants — "my political lieutenant general," as the president called him. He had been born in 1820 on an upstate New York farm near the village of Lima, graduated from the University of Vermont, trained by Horace Greeley as his assistant on the New York *Tribune*, and elevated through Thurlow Weed's friendship to be Speaker of the State Assembly at the age of thirty-one. Then, in a break with what appeared to be a promising political career, he had joined two partners, George Jones and Edward B. Wesley, in starting the New York *Times* in 1851 with $40,000 in borrowed capital. Ten years later, housed in a fine new five-story building on Park Row, the *Times* had 40,000 circulation, and enough advertising to show a decent profit.

In the fall of 1861, Raymond consented to stand for the State Assembly again to bolster his party and, upon his election, was chosen once more as the Speaker. From that politically powerful eminence, he was able to exert influence in Albany and there was additional reason for the Lincoln administration to be respectful to him in Washington. He found himself drawn into the president's inner circle as the war dragged on and was often in Washington, conferring with Seward or the secretary of war, Edwin M. Stanton, or Lincoln himself. Their policies, if not their thoughts, often appeared to guide the editorial pages of the *Times* in consequence.

Raymond let nothing diminish his loyalty to Lincoln. The *Times* was one of the few newspapers that ran the president's Gettysburg address in full and gave it the attention it deserved. When the Republican National Convention assembled in Baltimore a few months later, the editor drafted the platform, sponsored the vice-presidential candidacy of Andrew Johnson of Tennessee, and insured Lincoln's renomination in guiding the traditional roll-call of the states. As the leader of the New York delegation, largest on the convention floor, he was elevated thereafter to the chairmanship of the National Union Executive Committee and took charge of the president's reelection campaign.

The gloomy summer of 1864, when Northern armies made so little progress, gave way to better times. Atlanta fell on September 2 and the Confederacy was about to be split by General William Tecumseh Sherman's march to the sea. Raymond, hardpressed for party funds, used every device to obtain money for Lincoln's reelection drive, even including ill-concealed demands on federal employees for contributions. He rallied campaign organizations by pulling hard on all the influence the *Times* could generate. To insure full strength for his party in ever-critical New York State, he even ran for the House from the Sixth Congressional District. On election day, his efforts were rewarded. The president was reelected overwhelmingly. His "political lieutenant general" was elected to Congress, but by only 464 votes.

Now, despite the pressure of his official duties, Raymond tried to resume his responsibilities at his long-neglected *Times*. During his preoccupation with politics, many things had happened to change the character of American journalism. The military, political, and journalistic wars all had been hard-fought, and for essentially the same broad objective — a nation of free people, bound together by indissoluble ties.

As Raymond most of all had reason to know, the focal point of every effort to sway public opinion during the war had been the press in New York City, then as now the communications capital of the country. Of the seventeen dailies in the metropolis at the outset of the war, five had been Copperhead sheets, four others anti-administration but somewhat less in sympathy with the South, and five remained pro-Administration. The rest had been political ciphers.

Despite the turbulence of the New York press, it had remained relatively free from censorship. The *World* and the *Journal of Commerce* had been suspended for two days each by the military for publishing a false presidential proclamation calling for the draft of 400,000 men in 1864, and the author of the hoax had been jailed for three months. The *Journal of Commerce* and four other papers, in a separate action, had lost their postal privileges after a federal grand jury had named them as rebel sympathizers. The record had not been a bad one, considering how hard pressed the Lincoln administration had been in wartime.

Outside New York, there had been even less censorship despite the existence of at least 150 papers characterized by the *Journal of Commerce* in 1861 as "opposed to the present unholy war." The Union's mainstays, in addition to the New York *Times*, had included such papers as the Chicago *Tribune*, Washington *Chronicle*, Philadelphia *Press*, Philadelphia *Inquirer*, Springfield *Republican*, and Albany *Evening Journal*. One of the major anti-Administration organs, Wilbur F. Storey's Chicago *Times*, was closed down for three days in 1864 by military order but reopened through the intercession of President Lincoln himself. The Copperhead Philadelphia *Evening Journal* was suspended by military command in 1863 and its editor imprisoned for a few days until he promised to reform, but the paper died before he could change his mind and his policies. There were a few other censorship cases, none as important as these two.

Mob action, as it developed late in the war, was infinitely more dangerous to the newspapers that consistently took an anti-Administration tack. Even some of Lincoln's stalwarts among the press, for that matter, had to take extreme measures to defend themselves. During the 1863 draft riots in New York, Raymond and a friend and fellow stockholder, Leonard Jerome,* each manned a Gatling gun while armed *Times* employees mobilized to defend the building against a mob. When the neighboring *Tribune*'s windows were smashed by rioters who sought to burn down the building, Raymond sent a detachment of *Times* men who helped the police repel the attack. Cannons had to be trained on Park Row by federal troops before the uproar ended.

The virulence of patriot mobs against the Copperhead papers could not be so readily contained. Toward the end of the war, when the editors with Confederate sympathies were setting up a steady clamor for peace at any price, literally scores of Copperhead organs were attacked by outraged citizens and some were destroyed. In San Francisco, after Lincoln's assassination, mobs wrecked five anti-Administration newspaper offices.

In the South, plagued by shortages of paper, ink, and labor, the censorship was more severe and the mortality among newspapers was catastrophic. Those that managed to print had to be wary of using sensitive military information because of an efficient and watchful Confederate censorship. If they survived the scrutiny of their friends, they were well-nigh certain to be put out of business by their enemies as the advancing federal forces soon demonstrated. Papers in New Orleans, Vicksburg, and Memphis that did not submit to federal control were suspended.

---

*Father of Jenny Jerome and Winston Churchill's grandfather.

One, the Memphis *Appeal*, became a portable newspaper and was published in ten towns in four states before the war ended.

The relative freedom with which the war was reported in the North stimulated a prodigious flow of information from the battle-fronts, much of it reliable. The 150 or more special correspondents who took to the field used the telegraph in such imaginative ways that they changed the historic methods of presenting the news. Instead of the long, wandering essay so suitable to the mails and mounted couriers, crisp, telegraphic bulletins and compact news summaries became the order of the day for all except exclusive battle accounts. Competition rose to heights never before experienced in journalism. The correspondent who failed to "run for the wire" with his news soon learned that he could expect to be hopelessly beaten.

Of all the papers that covered the war, the New York *Herald* spent the most money, $500,000, and employed the largest number of correspondents, no less than sixty-three in active service at various times. The *Times* and *Tribune* in New York each had a score of correspondents in the field. In the west, the Chicago *Tribune* had twenty-nine correspondents with the Union armies. There wasn't a major newspaper in the North that didn't have its own dependable men in the field. For the rest, they used the first wire service of the era, the Associated Press.

In addition to the obvious risks of being killed or wounded in action, there were other drawbacks to being a correspondent in the most thoroughly covered war in history up to that time. Commanders on both sides raised the age-old complaint that the correspondents were revealing too much military information and, of course, it was true. These were risks that had to be taken if a free press was to be maintained in wartime to insure widespread public support. At one point in the spring of 1862, General Henry W. Halleck expelled all correspondents from the Union forces in the East. To this the *Times* responded:

"More harm would be done to the Union by the expulsion of correspondents than those correspondents now do by occasional exposures of military blunders, imbecilities, peccadilloes, cor-

ruption, drunkenness, and knavery, or by their occasional failures to puff every functionary as much as he thinks he deserves."

Despite everything that General Ulysses Simpson Grant tried
to do to protect him, the military storm center in the North was
General Sherman, who had no patience either for the press or its
correspondents. The general hustled correspondents out of his
ranks as fast as he discovered them lurking within his lines. It
was his fixed conviction that General Robert E. Lee and the
Confederate high command learned much more from the Northern papers than they did from their own spies. Once, when Sherman was told that three correspondents had been killed by a
shell burst, he exclaimed: "Good! Now we shall have news of
hell before breakfast." At another time, when a correspondent
pleaded against summary expulsion on the ground that he
sought only the truth, the irate general snapped: "We don't want
the truth told about things here—that's what we *don't* want!"
Later in the war he had the satisfaction of convicting Tom Knox
of the New York *Herald* at a court martial for publishing information of value to the enemy. It required intervention by President Lincoln to set aside the sentence, but the stubborn Sherman
refused to readmit Knox to his command.

Throughout the war, battle scenes were sketched by combat
artists under fire and reproduced on wooden blocks, engraved
by hand, for newspaper use. Maps, too, were widely used to
acquaint readers with the progress of the war. Because of the
pressure for large daily press runs, anywhere from 75,000 to
125,000 for the leaders when there was big news, the time was
ripe for other experiments. One of the most valuable, the stereo-
typing process (the molding of solid curved plates of type to fit
on rotary presses in half-cylinder shapes) was introduced by the
New York *Tribune* to increase the speed of its presses. And in
Philadelphia, the *Inquirer* in 1863 used for the first time a web
perfecting press that enabled both sides of a roll of paper to be
printed from one feeding.

The most novel contribution to journalism, Mathew B. Brady's
magnificent collection of Civil War photographs, unfortunately

could not be generally reproduced in the newspapers of the time. It was not until 1877 that Frederic Eugene Ives, of Litchfield, Conn., pioneered in photoengraving by inventing a halftone process to reproduce photographic shadings of black and white. The marvel was not that Brady could take photographs; after all, others had done it before him. But he did his work in such superb fashion and captured such monumental battle scenes and lifelike figures on his cumbersome cameras that he became outstanding among the journalists of his era. In his own way he, too, was devoted to the principle of "all the news of the day."

At Appomattox, Brady arrived too late to photograph Grant and Lee together in the McLean farmhouse where the surrender was arranged. But he went to Ford's Theater in Washington after Lincoln's assassination on April 14, 1865, and recorded the melancholy scene for posterity. It was the end of a chapter in American history. Few of those who were so intimately associated with Lincoln during the ordeal of the republic ever attained again the high sense of purpose and mission that animated them during his lifetime. It was as if their greatest roles had been played with the glow of national attention upon them. After that, all else was shadowed.

For Henry J. Raymond, the tragedy was survival. At forty-nine years of age, he had outlived his time. His health had been broken by his wartime exertions, his hand trembled, and his movements were uncertain. Not even the prestige and the success of the *Times* seemed to make much difference to him. He lingered on for four years after the assassination of Lincoln and died of a stroke on the night of June 19, 1869. His last major work had been an 800-page biography of Lincoln. His monument was a great independent newspaper, his bequest to his city and his country.

For Horace Greeley, broken in mind and body, the end came on November 29, 1872, in a sanitarium at Pleasantville, N.Y., a little more than three years after the death of his "little villain." His hope for high office had been broken by his futile campaign for the presidency.

Not even Mathew Brady survived the ill fortune that dogged

so many of Lincoln's associates. He could interest no one in government after the war in the purchase of his photographic collection, to which he had devoted his best years. He was down on his luck and needed money. Yet, far from realizing the $100,000 the war pictures had cost him, he could not collect a penny for years. In 1875, when Congress finally voted him $25,000 for his picture collection, it was too late to help him. His activity diminished. When he died in 1896, he was almost destitute.

These were the journalists who helped bring about a new birth of freedom in their land. Whatever their shortcomings, theirs were the ideals of Lincoln. If they had been able to put into words their feelings for the future of their people and their country, they would have been at one with the sometime editor of the Brooklyn *Eagle* and occasional war correspondent, Walt Whitman,

For you these from me, O Democracy, to serve you ma femme!
For you, for you I am trilling these songs.

4. On Liberty

The middle of the nineteenth century was a rare and precious time in the history of the Western world. It was an era when the philosophy of a libertarian government, particularly in the United States and Britain, coincided with the dominant mood of public opinion. Consequently, the usual tensions between a popular government and a free press tended to come into balance. Thus encouraged, journalists took whatever advantage they could of the opportunities that the times provided.

In Europe, the hesitation of autocratic rulers enabled the press to burst its bonds. But when it became clear that the course of free expression was likely to lead to a revolutionary seizure of power, as it did in some places, the old order rallied and reasserted its authority. Just the opposite occurred in Britain, where the development of the *Times* and its rivals gave the public a new and valuable checkrein on government. And in the

United States, where the free press gained an authority and independence it had never known before, a hard-pressed federal government accepted it as a necessary outpouring of public opinion and criticism even in time of war.

There were excesses. There always are in such times. In accepting the principle of an independent press, an open society assumes risks as well as benefits on the theory that the public good eventually will be served by a policy of full disclosure, limited only by the requirements of national security. In the middle of the nineteenth century, the risks were greater and the benefits fewer. The martyrdom of an Elijah Lovejoy could scarcely be set off against the benefits of a system that also produced a William Lloyd Garrison, a Horace Greeley, or a Henry Jarvis Raymond. But the public accepted the system for what it was, with few exceptions, and the government limited its interference to the minimum. It was far from a perfect system, but it suited the needs of the United States better than any other that could have been devised.

It was no journalist but a retired official of the East India Company, John Stuart Mill, who best stated the philosophy behind such a system of freedom of thought, discussion, and publication. In his essay, "On Liberty," he wrote in 1859:

"The time, it is to be hoped, is gone by when any defense would be necessary of the 'liberty of the press' as one of the securities against corrupt or tyrannical government. No argument, we may suppose, can now be needed against permitting a legislature or an executive, not identified in interest with the people, to prescribe opinions to them and determine what doctrines or what arguments they shall be allowed to hear. . . .

"Were an opinion a personal possession of no value except to the owner, if to be obstructed in the enjoyment of it were simply a private injury, it would make some difference whether the injury was inflicted only on a few persons or on many. But the peculiar evil of silencing the expression of an opinion is that it is robbing the human race, posterity as well as the existing generation—those who dissent from the opinion still more than those who hold it. If the opinion is right, they are deprived of the opportunity of exchanging error for truth; if wrong, they lose what is almost as great a benefit, the clearer perception and livelier impression of truth produced by its collision with error."

Mill did more than reaffirm the judgment of John Milton. The precise declaration of the basis for free expression and free publication became the foundation on which an independent press erected its defenses for the remainder of the nineteenth century and the most despairing hours of the century that was to follow.

IV. The Imperial Age

1. Swaraj

India was torn by revolt in the spring of 1857. In May, the Bengalese soldiers of the East India Company, the sepoys, struck at the city of Meerut. Soon, they took Delhi and Cawnpore and besieged Lucknow. To the British, it was mutiny. To the Indians, smarting under a century of oppressive foreign rule, it was a blow for *swaraj*, independence.

Charles John Canning, the governor general, wasted no time in snapping the shackles of censorship on the hapless Indian press with his "Gagging Act" of June 13, 1857. True, Indian journalists had been campaigning in a restricted way for social reforms and often had been suppressed before to punish them. But in no instance had it been found this time that they had been guilty of stimulating the sepoy uprising.

As for the British press, which lusted for revenge on the unspeakable Indians, Lord Canning told his Legislative Council quite candidly that his law was not aimed at such loyal newspapers. He did think, of course, that British journalists should be careful of publishing passages that could be "turned to mischievous purposes in the hands of people capable of dressing them up for the native ear." But that was about all. A less prejudiced observer, the historian George Trevelyan was to write later of these same loyal newspapers: "The tone of the press was horrible. Never did the cry for blood swell so loud among the Christians and Englishmen in the middle of the nineteenth century."

But it wasn't cricket to rebuke a British journalist in India.

No one except the Indian journalists dared make even a mild protest, and what they wrote was quickly expunged by vigilant censors, licensers, and self-appointed agents of a panicky regime. Above the uproar, however, the voice of Imperialism could be heard in defiance of every liberal principle that animated

British opinion at home. As the governor of Bombay, Mount Stuart Elphinstone, put the position in his defense of the "Gagging Act": "If ... a despotic form of government is, indeed, the only one suitable to the state of the country as well as the only one possible for us, it follows that if the unrestricted liberty of the press is incompatible with this form of government, and with the continuance of our rule in the country, that it must be curtailed."

The rebellion raged on into the next year until the British drove the sepoys from their strongholds and raised the siege of Lucknow. Because the Indians were unable to tell their own story, the world heard only that ignorant and superstitious mutineers had indulged in a senseless orgy of sadism and killing because they resented the coating of cartridges with beef and pork grease, a desecration of religious beliefs to Hindu and Muslim alike. Little was heard of the ruthless British absorption of Oudh and Sind and other complaints or of the savagery with which the British ripped into the rebel ranks. Instead, such correspondents as William Howard Russell celebrated the valor of Sir John Lawrence, the British commander, and the heroism of General Henry Havelock, his colored neckerchief floating in combat like the white plume of Henry of Navarre.

The Indian press, having struggled for years against British authority, did not give up easily. Dr. George Buist, the British editor of the Indian-owned Bombay *Times*, launched an attack on the "freedom tigers, treacherous barbarians, and cruel savages" that almost exclusively populated India and demanded: 'Blood for blood!" The Indian shareholders met and fired him. An Indian language newspaper, the Bengali journal *Som Prakash*, was suppressed and at once resumed publication under another name. The prestigious *Amrita Bazar Patrika* of Calcutta, which had been printed in Bengali, changed overnight into an English-language newspaper to evade the "Gagging Act" and thereby began its growth into one of the great newspapers of India.

The First War for Independence, as the Indians called this

English-designated mutiny, resulted in the abolition of the East India Company and the assumption of the rule of India directly by the crown. Lord Canning, as the first viceroy, decreed mild and generally ineffective reforms that brought Indians for the first time into minor roles in the government of their own country. But for the Indian press, he kept his guard up and generally acted as if the emergency were over.

The queen's viceroy was wrong. Far from being ended, the struggle for *swaraj* had just begun. Even in defeat, the Indians saw that the British were far from invulnerable. The sensitivity of the rulers to the opinion of their subject peoples was nowhere more marked than in the treatment of the press. And it was the press, in consequence, that became the spearhead of an attack on authority that would last for nearly a century.

The importance of the newspaper in the campaign for independence had grown steadily from the era of the first governor general of India, Warren Hastings. Never one to suffer criticism, Hastings expelled William Bolts, a Calcutta merchant of Dutch extraction, when he signified his intention of starting a newspaper in 1766. The governor general showed little more mercy to James Augustus Hickey, founder of the Bengal *Gazette*, first weekly in India, when he began publication on January 29, 1780. In less than two years, the unfortunate Hickey was sued for libel, found guilty, fined, imprisoned, and deprived of his newspaper for having had the bad taste to criticize the government.

As other papers appeared in Calcutta, Madras, and Bombay, the British raj permitted pro-government organs to operate under close scrutiny and put the others out of business as soon as possible. Imprisonment, expropriation of printing plants, and deportation were the lot of editors who tried to function as an independent force. One of the victims, the Irish-American William Duane, was forced out as editor of the Bengal *Journal* and, soon after he had started the *India World* in 1795, was escorted by British soldiers to the first available outbound ship. By the time he reached Philadelphia, the future editor of the *Aurora* had learned at first hand the disadvantages of maintaining a free press. But it didn't stop him, any more than it discouraged his fellow journalists in India. They were tough—and they had to be.

When the marquess of Wellesley became governor general, he announced that he considered printing presses in India to be an "evil of the first magnitude, useless to literature and to the public." Thereupon, he appointed a press censor, set up strict regulations for all publications, and decreed immediate deportation for all non-Indian violators of his rules. The few existing newspapers managed to struggle along despite his displeasure.

With the easing of press regulations in 1818, two new editors brought out impressive publications in India. The first was an ex-sea captain, James Silk Buckingham, who produced the bi-weekly Calcutta *Journal*. The other was his friend and close associate, Raja Ram Mohan Roy, the father of Indian journalism, a social reformer of strength, vigor, and originality. Aided by Buckingham, Mohan Roy took over the new Hindu weekly, *Sambad Kaumudi* (Moon of Intelligence), which had been founded in 1821, and made it widely respected. He also founded a Persian-language newspaper in which he attacked social problems, much to the discomfiture of the British authorities. They didn't quite know what to do about the vernacular press and were dismayed by the prospect of a large number of newspapers published in languages they could neither read nor understand.

The Buckingham–Roy alliance was smashed within two years. Despite British professions of tolerance for the press, Buckingham's criticism of government officials resulted in the cancellation of his license to publish and his deportation in 1823. In the same year, a new Vernacular Press Act forced Roy and his fellow publishers of Indian language newspapers to obtain licenses and to face heavy penalties if they printed anything that aroused hatred or contempt of the government.

Just when the Indian journalists were suffering the most inconvenient forms of government repression, relief came to them in an unexpected manner. Lord William Bentinck, the governor general in 1835, had to resign and return home because of ill health at a time when press reforms were under consideration. Sir Charles Metcalfe, senior member of the Council, acted as his successor and asked the Council's legislative member, Thomas Babington Macaulay, to draft a new press act.

It was difficult to say whether the British or the Indians were more surprised at the outcome. For what Macaulay did, in effect, was to repeal all previous press legislation and substitute the principle of free and responsible publication. In place of licenses, newspapers merely had to register with the government; instead of pre-publication censorship, editors were given freedom to print but were held responsible for libel, sedition, or calumny. It was a Blackstonian version of press freedom but, to India, it had the effect of Holy Writ.

The brave Metcalfe, who knew exactly what he was doing, accepted Macaulay's draft and made it Act XI of 1835. To his detractors, he replied that a denial of freedom of expression was to contend that "the essence of good government is to cover the land with darkness." He went on: "Whatever may be the consequence, it is our duty to communicate the benefits of knowledge. If India could be preserved as a part of the British Empire only by keeping its inhabitants in a state of ignorance, our domination would be a curse to the country, and ought to cease."

Metcalfe paid dearly for his enlightened policy. He was passed over for permanent appointment as governor general, sent out to the Northeast Provinces in a minor post and soon called home. But the liberal course he pursued lasted for more than twenty years in India and stimulated the growth of the Indian language press as a force for progress in that beautiful and unhappy land. Until repression returned in the wake of the 1857 uprising, the Indian journalists learned the meaning of a free press and never again slackened their campaign to achieve it.

During the remaining years of the nineteenth century, the pendulum of press control swung to the extremes of censorship and strict regulation from time to time, but it never again was as harshly administered as it was under the East India Company. For one thing, the viceroys learned by experience that suppression was not a practical way of dealing with a vigorous and combative press; for another, the Indians never hesitated to defy the law and go to jail if necessary in pursuit of freedom.

Some of the outstanding newspapers of India were founded in the quarter-century after the tragic uprising—the *Hindu* of Madras, the *Times of India* in Bombay, the *Pioneer* of Allahabad, the *Statesman* of Calcutta, and the *Civil and Military Gazette* of Lahore. But of equal importance were the scores of sickly-looking little Indian language papers that sprang up all over the subcontinent. Together, they contended for a primacy over Indian public opinion and sought to make themselves heard in the outside world.

It was an unequal struggle. The world wanted to believe in the charm of a picturesque and romantic India, basking under the kindly authority of British rule, as it was portrayed by a one-time reporter for the *Civil and Military Gazette*, Rudyard Kipling. And that was the way Kipling wrote of the land. He had learned his craft well, beginning in Lahore at the age of seventeen in 1882, and going on in 1887 to the *Pioneer* in Allahabad. Subsequently, the outside world by the millions learned to love the India of Kim and Tommy Atkins and to appreciate the nobility of the British in shouldering the "white man's burden." In this effort, Kipling had the undoubted assistance of many a traveling foreign correspondent who was conditioned to see India only through his eyes.

There was, however, another India—the India of a half-million villages and desolate habitations in the teeming cities where Kipling's tales meant nothing because they were in a foreign language that 99 percent of the people of India did not understand. Here, the magic of the master story-teller could not penetrate; instead, each miserable little Indian language newspaper that could be obtained was read aloud to crowds of illiterates and passed from hand to hand until it was in tatters. It was another India—another world.

This was the country of the resolute successor to Raja Ram Mohan Roy. His name was Bal Gangadhur Tilak and his paper, published in the Marathi language, was called *Kesari*. Let British soldiers come into a native quarter, searching houses, and the redoubtable Tilak shouted for justice. If Kipling conjured up the vision of the Widow of Windsor as the supreme authority, Tilak appealed to the great Maratha hero, Shivaji, to sustain his people in their desolation. While Kipling wrote his jingles and his Barrack Room Ballads in celebration of the British raj, Tilak was tried for sedition in agitating against the British military and went to prison for eighteen months.

"*Swaraj* is my birthright," Tilak roared, "and I will have it!"

Kipling, without doubt, prevailed on the world for almost a century to accept his glamorous vision of India. But in the longer view, India itself was won by Tilak and his successor, Mahatma Gandhi. In the end, they were revered as national heroes by hundreds of millions of people who had never heard of Kipling.

2. "Dangerous Thoughts"

With the benign encouragement of their rulers, Japanese artists poked fun at a group of big-nosed, round-eyed barbarians who had just arrived from a mysterious and far-distant land in the summer of 1853. The leader of the peaceful invasion, one Beriri, and his smoke-belching black ships were caricatured in primitive newssheets called *kawaraban*, which were circulated to all parts of the empire.

Often, the pot-bellied Beriri, in naval uniform, was shown brandishing his sword before brave and defiant Japanese; on other occasions, he and his men were depicted groveling ignobly before their heroic Japanese hosts, or viewing with dazed appreciation the charms of surpassingly beautiful Japanese ladies. Occasionally, he was paid the high compliment of being sketched with such other illustrious foreigners as Napoleon or the sultan of Turkey.

Certainly, the visit was a sensation. It suited the interest of the shogun or military governor and his henchmen at Edo (later Tokyo) to create the impression that they didn't take the affair seriously. In the annals of the Tokugawa shogunate, no foreigner had ever made much headway in Japan. Except for a trickle of Dutch trade, the country had been closed to the rest of the world for over two hundred years, and had gotten along very nicely in isolation. The shogun intended the people to know that he would deal with the barbarians in his own good time; accordingly, he relaxed his strict control of the circulation of news and encouraged the purveyors of the *kawaraban*.

It didn't help him. Under the frowning guns of the black ships, Japan's isolation suddenly ended. At Kanagawa on March 31, 1854, Commodore Matthew Calbraith Perry of the United States Navy—the despised Beriri of the *kawaraban*—obliged the Japanese commissioners to sign a treaty opening two of their ports to American ships. Regardless of the ridicule in the newssheets, that change couldn't be kept a secret for very long from the Japanese people. As for the American public, the progress of the Perry expedition was related to them first with poetic flourishes by Bayard Taylor, a correspondent for the New York *Tribune*.

When Townsend Harris arrived in Japan two years later as the first American consul general, the *kawaraban* took particular delight in caricaturing him and his beautiful Japanese girl friend, Okichi. Nevertheless, the first Japanese-American commercial treaty was signed in 1858 and others followed. Before long, an isolated people began learning of many new things, among them the independently owned and circulated newspaper that dared to criticize the government.

Although Japan was the last of the world's major nations to develop a press system, the history of government regulation and journalistic defiance was repeated here with some typically Japanese embellishments. For one thing, the shogunate was being torn apart by the pressure of foreign powers from the outside and the inner rising of adherents of the imperial court in the ancient capital of Kyoto. For another, there was no such thing in a recently awakened Japan as movable type.

From the sixteenth century on, there had been a handful of officially approved newssheets carrying translated material from the Dutch that had been circulated to selected officials. The people hadn't minded this news filter system; they had had their street ballads, their legends, their skimpy newssheets of local scandal printed on tiles or woodblocks and hawked by *yomiuri* (town criers). But up to the time of Perry and Harris, no one had had the temerity to put out anything resembling a privately owned newspaper with an independent spirit.

When the press did come to life in Japan, therefore, it was under the most disagreeable circumstances. Very soon, the public was caught up in an unequal struggle between the weak but determined challenge of a handful of primitive newspapers and the power of a gravely weakened but still formidable feudal government. With the overturn of the shogunate in 1867 and the accession of the boy-emperor Meiji in the following year, there was temporary hope of a greater degree of freedom of publication. New newspapers began circulating in the big cities, but most of them died. The Meiji press regulations were even more stringent than those of the shogunate.

It is difficult to characterize many of the early Japanese journalists as men who waged a great struggle for principle. Some of them had been adherents of the shogunate and were thrown into prison for their disloyalty to the emperor. Others were adventurers. Still others published for purposes that could be only dimly discerned. But once the Meiji restoration was firmly established and the opposition had been put down, a different breed of journalist began to emerge — men who were fiercely devoted to the principle of free publication. Although their efforts seemed hopeless at the time, they resisted the Meiji publication laws that forbade newspapers to circulate without government approval and laid down the strictest injunction against irresponsible criticism of public officials.

The issue, as it developed, was over the promulgation of a liberal constitution and the formation of a national assembly and a multiparty political system. It might have been expected that the atmosphere would be friendlier to liberalism and the commitment to a democratic society, but the early Meiji government was critical of "dangerous thoughts" — a label for subversive activity that had been handed down from shogunate days. In the single year of 1876, eight years after the restoration, no fewer than fifty-eight editors were thrust into prison for utterances that were deemed to be violations of the law.

Foreign journalists in Japan, too, were treated harshly. To make certain that all publications could be controlled, the government specified that it was illegal to issue newspapers that were not printed in Japanese — a law that was enforced for years. J. R. Black, a pioneer British journalist in Japan, wrote that almost every editor of the era, Japanese or not, spent time in jail and paid fines under such stringent regulations. Yet, he noted that persecution actually strengthened the growth and importance of the press in Japan. It gave the early newspapermen a sense of commitment and dedication to the public interest.

The example of Genichiro Fukuchi, one of the earliest leaders of the Japanese press, is an illustration of how difficult it was for a fearful government to suppress opposing opinion. Having attacked the youthful Emperor Meiji's advisers, the editor was tried, convicted, and imprisoned for inciting to revolution. But when he was released, he was unrepentant. With vigor, he threw himself into the campaign for a National Assembly as the editor of a new and powerful Tokyo *Nichi Nichi* (Tokyo Daily Press, the forerunner of today's *Mainichi Shimbun*) beginning in 1872. He set new patterns for Japanese journalism by writing signed editorials on the issues of the day, became a strong liberal voice with a potent influence on government, and lived to see some of his proposed reforms put into effect. Another eminent editor, Yukichi Fukuzawa, Japan's "Great Enlightener," founded Keio University and also the *Jiji Shimpo*, one of the best of the early newspapers, after surviving the displeasure of the regime.

Not many editors were as fortunate. One of the bravest, Ryuhoku Narushima, wrote an allegory that held up the restrictive press and libel laws to ridicule. When he was arrested, he was dragged through snowy streets by the police before being brought to court and forced to confess a long catalogue of faults. Although he was let off with only a four-month prison term, mild for the era, he eventually lost his newspaper because the government forced so many temporary suspensions upon it. Another editor who had to give up his newspaper under government pressure, Shunsan Yanagawa, died soon afterward at the age of thirty-eight.

It was only because of the idealism and stubbornness of the Japanese journalists that newspapers were able to make progress under such difficult circumstances. Yet, had it not been for the proclamation of the Japanese Universal Education Law of 1872, the rapid development of the press would not have been possible. The first Japanese daily, a *Mainichi Shimbun* (Daily Newspaper) of Yokohama, was founded in that year. It was also in this era that the greatest of Japanese newspapers began — *Yomiuri Shimbun* in 1874, *Asahi Shimbun* (Rising Sun) in 1879, and *Mainichi Shimbun*, as it now exists, in 1883. If there had not been sufficient public understanding of the role of the independent newspaper and popular support of its operations, none of the "Big Three" could have survived.

Despite such repressive measures as an 1875 libel law and the decision of the home ministry in the following year to put out of business by administrative order any offending newspaper, "dangerous thoughts" continued to be published and editors continued to go to prison. Yet, by 1877, there were 225 newspapers in Japan. A decade later, the total had increased to 470. Movable type long since had been introduced and steam presses had been imported to do away with the hand crank cylinders, operated by husky young men with the benefit of liberal applications of *sake*. The press was now a power in the land.

When the National Assembly came into being and held its first session in 1890, it was scarcely a surprise to the public that a number of journalists had been elected to the House of Representatives. That amounted to public recognition of their value. After all, if it had not been for the incessant press campaign, the Assembly might never have been created. As might have been expected, the speeches of many of the leading journalists in the House coincided neatly with the editorial positions of their newspapers in opposition to the government. Criticism of the regime became so violent that the House was dissolved in two successive years to try to get rid of the malcontents and in each year new elections were held. Not many of the critics were defeated, however.

As the opposition press was quick to reveal, the general election of February 15, 1892, reeked of fraud. Charges were published that the government had tried to give orders to count out the opposition in numerous local districts in order to increase its own strength in the House. The bitterness was so general that violence spread throughout the land. At least twenty-five persons were killed and nearly four hundred others injured. The government had to proclaim martial law to restore order. In this manner, many opposition newspapers were suppressed and their printing presses seized.

Journalists without papers used the rostrum of the House to shout their defiance of the government. The papers that still managed to appear spread the charges of the government's interference with the electoral process. But when the votes were tabulated, victory rested with the antigovernment parties. It scarcely was the occasion for great satisfaction to a bemused and wondering public; it could not be said that the spectacle of democracy at work in the Orient was either inspiring or edifying.

During the first five years of the National Assembly, the legislators regularly tore apart budgets and submitted bills of impeachment. But the government just as regularly suspended the Assembly, then was obliged to dissolve the House and seek new elections. Each time, the opposition won a majority. Nor was there any peace between the House of Representatives and the less active House of Peers. The lower House would pass a bill revoking the government's anti-press laws, a testimonial to the strength of the journalists who were members, but the upper House would reject it. Despite the activity of the free press, it was clear that representative government in Japan was in deep trouble.

When the Japanese military defeated a corrupt and incompetent China in the war of 1894-95, a violent nationalist spirit swept the island nation. The press, with few exceptions, led the cheering. Warlike newspapers of the character of *Kokumin*, which had campaigned for the conflict, registered huge circulations. To many a journalist, the free press seemed to be at the peak of its power in Japan. Actually, it was the beginning of the end. In the public glorification of the military, the reactionary forces in the government had found a weapon to batter the newspapers into submission. It was to be used with deadly effect in the twentieth century, a time when "dangerous thoughts" would become a crime against the nation.

3. The Warmakers

At the outset of a career of ruthless conquest that made Germany the most feared and hated power in Europe, Prince Otto von Bismarck compared himself to Caliph Omar, the barbaric Muslim conqueror who created an empire by destroying all in his path with fire and the sword. "I cannot deny," Bismarck wrote, "that there is a sort of Caliph Omar instinct in me, prompting me not only to the destruction of books (all but the Christian Koran) but to the annihilation of the means of producing new ones. The art of printing is the chosen instrument of anti-Christ."

When the letter was written on June 30, 1850, the young Prussian militartist could only dream of the power that he hoped would be his one day. When he achieved it in 1862 as the premier of Prussia under Wilhelm I, he chose not to try to destroy the always feeble independent German press; instead, he bent it to his will. There was nothing particularly original about this. Napoleon, Francis Joseph of Austria Hungary, and the Russian czars had been his instructors. His unique contribution to the ancient and dishonorable art of press manipulation was the almost diabolical efficiency with which he practiced it and the incredible lengths to which he was willing to go to manage even a small item of the news.

From the outset of his long reign as Germany's "Iron Chancellor," the instrument Bismarck used in his dealings with the newspapers was his government's Press Bureau. Under the Imperial Constitution, he had virtual life-or-death power against any newspaper. But the Press Bureau gave him a choice of methods. Through it he maintained a huge slush fund to distribute bribes to journalists at home and abroad, placed desirable articles, issued covert threats and warnings to those he mistrusted, floated rumors and denied them when necessary, and made the most vile and unprincipled attacks against his choice victims.

Upon those who were willing to work with him and his government, he bestowed only contempt, never gratitude. The compliant newspapers were eternally damned as the "reptile press" that crawled on its belly before its master. Its editors and writers were his "ink sparrows," "press cattle," and "inky scamps." He once exclaimed in fervent denunciation: "Decent people do not write for me!" No government propagandist before or since has ever been quite as devastatingly candid.

From Berlin, as a result, there emanated a stream of thinly disguised propaganda that eventually became a torrent and polluted the press of almost every neighboring country except Britain. And even here, Bismarck's agents had standing instructions to try to get their material in the British press. They seldom succeeded, but of course Bismarck scarcely expected that Germany would ever be trusted in Whitehall. To counter what he deemed to be the dangerous influence of Reuters and Havas, he made the Wolff Agency a semiofficial German news bureau and thereby destroyed its credibility. It became more mistrusted throughout the world than even his own client press.

The frequency with which even mild press comment was punished in Germany led the few papers of consequence to create an institution known as the "sitting editor," adapted from an old Russian custom. What this amounted to was that there would be a real editor, with a disguised title, and several "sitting editors" whose duty it was to serve whatever prison term Bismarck decreed. At one time, for example, the *Frankfurter Zeitung* had five editors in prison at the same period. In 1878, 127 periodicals and 278 other publications were suppressed for suspected socialistic leanings. And in 1890, a critic estimated that Bismarck had inflicted jail terms totaling more than a hundred years on obstreperous German editors.

If Bismarck was a strict master in time of peace, he demanded absolute loyalty from his press in time of war. Consequently, when he picked a fight with Austria over Schleswig-Holstein in

1866 and humbled the Austrian army at Königgrätz, the German press with one voice roared its approval. And when he sent his tricky Ems telegram to Napoleon III, provoking him into the disastrous war of 1870 through a deliberate insult to French honor, not a single German newspaper dared to protest. With the creation of a united Germany as the first military power of Europe, the end sublime of all Bismarck's machinations, the isolated remaining press critics simply were condemned as traitors and treated as such. "Deutschland Über Alles," needless to say, included the German press.

The absence of realistic press criticism of government became a dominant factor of German life in Bismarck's time, and in the end it hurt him. For when Kaiser Wilhelm II succeeded to the throne in 1888, arrogant in his belief that he ruled by divine right, not a voice within his realm could be raised against him. Within two years, the new kaiser amassed such authority that he was able to dismiss Bismarck with ease. A thoughtful German censor even eliminated the famous Punch cartoon, "Dropping the Pilot," from the magazine before it was circulated in Germany. The Reich, under its new kaiser, headed off on a new course that was to bring it into collision with mightier forces in less than a quarter of a century — and its press was helpless to protest.

In Great Britain, where the independent press could not be so easily disregarded, the always touchy business of preparing public opinion for war and for the support of sometimes unpopular conflicts had to be handled quite differently, although the end result could be just as unpalatable. As the dominant military force in the world at the beginning of the twentieth century, the British had more experience than the Germans in dealing with newspapers and realized quite well what penalties had to be paid in the loss of public confidence when the credibility of the press was deliberately undermined. Consequently, when risks had to be undertaken that involved war or the possibility of war, leading newspapers often were welcomed as unofficial partners of government if they chose to accept such status. If not, the more sophisticated masters of Victorian policy were content to have the press follow a parallel course in what amounted to a common interest. As for those newspapers that chose to dissent, their criticism had to be borne — up to a point.

Both the advantages and the disadvantages of so shaky a government–press alliance were graphically illustrated during the Boer War at the high tide of British imperialism. The *Times*, a loyal supporter of the government on this issue, had been involved in South African affairs for nearly a decade before fighting actually began as an ally of Cecil Rhodes, the diamond king, who was the prime minister and virtual dictator of the Cape Colony. Through a self-styled South African expert, Flora Shaw, a mild-looking British spinster, the *Times* also had mounted a stiff campaign against Rhodes's foe, Paul Kruger, the president of the neighboring (and gold-rich) Transvaal. It was Miss Shaw's duty as roving correspondent to record in detail the misdeeds of the Boer republic in its persecution, whether fancied or real, of the British within its borders. She did her job with such commitment that, as a Select Committee of the House of Commons later determined, she shared complicity with Rhodes in the ill-fated raid of Leander Starr Jameson on the Transvaal on December 30, 1895. The *Times* itself was exonerated, and Rhodes lost his political leadership while Jameson and his associates served moderate jail sentences.

In the ensuing years, the British conveniently forgot what they didn't want to remember of the sorry affair. But in the Boer republic, the recollection of the Jameson raid served to strengthen the resolution of the Boers. They could not forget, particularly when they saw British troops massing on their borders in an undisguised effort to make them more amenable to British penetration of their country. When the time came for armed resistance, they fought from 1899 to 1902 against the might of the British empire and won the sympathy of the world at large.

The compliant conservative sector of the British press, led by the *Times*, successfully swung public opinion for a time behind the government's war policy, but it was hard put to justify Britain's proposed annexation of Boer lands. At that point, embarrassing questions began to rise among people who had never seen any reason at the outset for an imperial war against a small, struggling nation. From the field, a young champion of empire, the soldier-correspondent Winston Churchill, wrote in a dispatch: "The difficulty of rallying public opinion ... has caused the most dangerous delay in the dispatch of reinforcements."

The government, after rallying its forces, was able to produce the needed reinforcements despite mounting opposition; in the end, 350,000 British troops eventually wore down 60,000 Boers. But in Britain as elsewhere, liberal opinion was outraged by the senseless brutality of the British occupation, the burning of Boer farms, the herding of thousands of Boers and their families into concentration camps. The war was worse than unpopular. It became a criminal activity in the eyes of such champions of the Boers as the American war correspondent, Richard Harding Davis.

Charles Prestwich Scott, the editor of the Manchester *Guardian*, led the liberal press of Britain in an all-out campaign against British "methods of barbarism," Sir Henry Campbell-Bannerman's phrase. Scott did more than oppose the *Times* and the other conservative proponents of the war. In the *Guardian*'s editorial columns, he demanded self-government for the oppressed Boers, denounced the hunting down of rebel chieftains and the demands for their unconditional surrender. To his standard he drew the London *Daily News*, which came under new ownership and deserted the pro-war camp; the *Westminster Gazette*, the *Morning Leader*, and the *Star*, and a notable group of journalists that included Henry W. Nevinson, G. K. Chesterton, and Hilaire Belloc.

Both Scott and the *Guardian* were penalized for their attack on their government in time of war, even though the war had become unpopular with the liberal part of the British public by that time. So many threats were made against the editor and his paper that the police often had to mount guard over both. Scott, who also was a member of Parliament, was publicly reviled. In one cartoon in an opposition newspaper, he was depicted as the recipient of a bribe from Kruger, the Boer leader. Some subscribers canceled his paper. In the pro-government press, he was held up to scorn as little more than a traitor. But the ceaseless agitation that he led at length forced an angry and divided Britain to come to terms with an outnumbered foe and insured self-government for South Africa.

What the Union of South Africa did with its hard-won liberty is another and even more tragic story. Its achievement, however, was due in no small measure to the efforts of C. P. Scott and the *Guardian* and their devoted supporters. That, of course, could not excuse the role of an independent press in creating a climate of opinion in which such a war could be planned and prosecuted by a less-than-benevolent government. What it did do was to demonstrate the essential rightness of a theory of government that permitted an opposition press to express its critical views even under the stresses of war.

If there were such demonstrable excesses in the practice of independent journalism in Victorian Britain, the extravagance with which a few powerful newspaper proprietors abused their privileges in the United States amounted to a public scandal. Bismarck, in his own way, could not have been more cynical than the leaders of the yellow press in New York at the outset of the Spanish-American War. Following the explosion of the battleship *Maine* in Havana harbor on February 15, 1898, Joseph Pulitzer's New York *World* proclaimed: "WAR SPIRIT RISES FROM WORLD'S EVIDENCE." And once the conflict began, William Randolph Hearst's New York *Journal* trumpeted: "HOW DO YOU LIKE THE JOURNAL'S WAR?" The moderately liberal Edwin Lawrence Godkin, editor of the New York *Evening Post*, observed with devastating effect: "No one—absolutely no one— supposes a yellow journal cares five cents about the Cubans, the *Maine* victims, or anyone else. A yellow journal is probably the nearest approach to hell existing in any Christian state."

Pulitzer, a Hungarian immigrant and an ex-Union soldier of the Civil War, had made the journalistic practice of public service an article of faith when he founded the St. Louis *Post-Dispatch* in 1878. After invading New York in 1883 as the new proprietor of the *World*, he pledged himself to "expose all fraud and sham, fight all public evils and abuses . . . and battle for the people with earnest sincerity." He won national recognition with a successful campaign to bring Frederic Auguste Bartholdi's Statue of Liberty to New York and place it on a pedestal in the harbor. Thereafter, Pulitzer began crusading in earnest. He disclosed the bribing of aldermen for a streetcar franchise, attacked bad tenement construction, fought the white slave traffic, and soon made himself a political force to be courted and feared. His *World* became a resounding success, envied and even hated by some of his rivals.

If Hearst had not come to New York in 1895 and transformed his newly purchased *Journal* into the *World*'s principal rival, Pulitzer's subsequent history might have been quite different. Hearst staked everything on sensation and unashamed self-promotion, the qualities that had enabled him to make a success of his San Francisco *Examiner*. To the youthful and arrogant Californian, backed by his inherited gold-mining millions, the irascible Pulitzer was an obstacle to be swept aside. Although he was now blind and forced into the perils of absentee ownership, Pulitzer let himself be goaded into a circulation battle by his younger rival. The result was appalling.

Once the *Maine* went down, the *World* rivaled the *Journal* in beating the war drums. The wrathful Godkin assailed their "gross misrepresentation of facts, deliberate invention of tales calculated to excite the public, and wanton recklessness in the construction of headlines." The new owner of the New York *Times*, a Chattanooga printer named Adolph S. Ochs, who had bought the paper out of bankruptcy for $75,000 in 1896, called for a law to forbid "freak journalism." But nothing could dissuade the Hearst and Pulitzer staffs once the circulation war had been joined. Both *Journal* and *World* sales soared to new heights.

It should not be imagined, however, that Hearst and Pulitzer were able to bring on war with Spain solely by their own efforts. A powerful war faction in the United States had been anxious to fight over Cuba for a number of reasons, which were best explained by Theodore Roosevelt with a frankness that he himself thought "our timid friends would call brutal." While he was assistant secretary of the navy in 1897, he wrote: "I would regard a war with Spain from two viewpoints: First, the advisability on the ground both of humanity and self-interest of interfering on behalf of the Cubans, and of taking one more step toward the complete freeing of America from European domination; second, the benefit done to our people by giving them something to think of which isn't material gain, and especially the benefit done our military forces by trying both the Army and Navy in actual practice." There was one other consideration, which was not precisely noble, either: the decline of the $100 million annual American trade with Cuba to next to nothing.

If either Hearst or Pulitzer gave such things a thought, it was purely coincidental. Hearst wanted circulation and Pulitzer didn't want to let Hearst get ahead of him. In the resultant agitation the purposes of the American war party and the New York rivals coincided. It is possible that the national war fever might not have risen to the height required for a declaration of war if the press had not done so much to stimulate it. Even so, McKinley hesitated for two months after the sinking of the *Maine* before sending his war message to Congress. The Senate approved on April 19, 1898, by only 42 to 35, although the House whooped it up by 310 to 6. Hearst, accepting the vote as a personal tribute, announced to his staff that it was "Our War." He couldn't have done much worse.

For both Pulitzer and the *World*, the war was a disastrous experience. The temporary 1 million circulation won by the newspaper shrank quickly with the coming of peace after three months' fighting. The excessive costs of war coverage could not be made up and constituted a rather large loss. While Hearst went on from one sensation to another, Pulitzer disgustedly withdrew from the excesses of yellow journalism. He had had enough. In the twilight of his career, he defied the then President Theodore Roosevelt who had brought a criminal libel suit to silence the *World* for criticizing his seizure of Panama. It was the blind publisher's final act to uphold the freedom of the press and served to atone, in a way, for the excesses of 1898.

However, the damage had been done. Wherever independent

newspapers were published, they learned from the American example that war news meant big circulation figures. To those with responsible managements, the temptation to wallow in gore was resisted. The lesson of the *World* had shown that sensationalism did not insure profits — and, as Pulitzer would have been the first to agree, profits were not the ultimate end of free journalism in any case.

Unhappily, such sober conclusions did not always make an impression. In the Russo-Japanese War of 1904, it was the example of Hearst instead of the far more responsible Pulitzer that dazzled the Japanese press. Inspired by the victories of the Japanese war machine on land and sea, Japanese correspondents emulated the Americans in sensational feats to get the battle news home first. If the Japanese military encouraged them, and thoughtfully used the first effective military censorship in history to restrain their foreign journalistic rivals, it was only to be expected. They had learned the arts of manipulating public opinion from the highly moralistic West.

And so, the warmakers — whatever their political beliefs — approached the height of their power as the twentieth century began. With few exceptions, the free press did little to restrain them or even criticize their acts. For such negligence, the world was to pay a terrible price in the lengthening years that stretched ahead.

4. The Persecuted

Harold Frederic toured Russia in 1891 for the New York *Times* to learn whatever he could of the apparently systematic persecution of the Jews with czarist approval. From time to time, the Western world had received skimpy reports of pogroms, a Russian word meaning riot but almost universally applied to attacks on the empire's 5 million Jews. Yet, there had been no protest to the Russian government. And inside Russia itself, a weak and heavily censored press dared not raise its voice.

Frederic, then the London correspondent of the *Times*, reported at first hand on a number of murderous mob assaults on

Jews, often with the complicity of the Russian authorities. Such challenges to the authority of the czarist empire were not taken lightly at a time when Pan-Slavist expansion was the order of the day. The Russian government barred Frederic from the country, which didn't matter to him, since he had no intention of returning. His articles in the *Times* were published later under the title: *The New Exodus: A Study of Israel in Russia.* More than 300,000 Jews thereafter emigrated from their Russian pales in a single year, providing additional evidence — if any was needed — of the truth of his reports.

Yet, inside Russia nothing changed. The government, sure of its ability to choke off any uprising, tightened its hold. To the harshness of anti-Semitism as an official policy was added a closer surveillance of all other minorities. The censorship that Frederic had momentarily penetrated became even more effective, the press even more subservient.

From the time of the founding of the Russian press in the era of Peter the Great, it had been tied closely to the regime. The czar himself made it so. The care with which he supervised the first Russian newspaper, *Vedomosti* (Gazette), established in 1703, was proof of his determination to keep so powerful an instrument under his control. Even though it was an official journal, which published only news and foreign press excerpts of which he approved, he permitted just 1,000 copies of each four-page issue to be printed and sometimes read proof himself.

The great czar and his successors developed the tightest of all censorships. The few newspapers that existed were forbidden to criticize anybody in authority, to use such terms as "bureaucracy" which might seem disrespectful, or even to use exclamation marks or dots that might indicate displeasure with the system. In the time of Catherine the Great, a magazine called *Vsiakaia-Vsiachina* (Every Little Thing) was circulated and printers were permitted to reproduce the works of Voltaire and Rousseau. But when such heady ideas of personal freedom were circulated at the same time as a peasant uprising that had to be hastily crushed, Catherine soon enough decided censorship was a better policy. Her successor, Paul I, closed all printing houses and forbade the importation of foreign literature.

Alexander I, emboldened by the liberal notions of his Swiss mentor, Frederic La Harpe, relaxed the traditional surveillance in 1805 to permit a group of progressives (by Russian definition) to found the *Magazine of Russian Letters*. In it, they campaigned cautiously for a free press and greater personal liberties until the Napoleonic invasion ended their hopes. In the reign of Nicholas I, who followed, the remaining liberals were scattered from Siberia to England by the severity with which the Decembrist uprising of 1825 was suppressed.

A clandestine press sprang up outside Russia then and was regularly smuggled across the border. The most famous was *Kolokol* (The Bell), published in London by the exiled revolutionary, Alexander Herzen. In it he sought to make the dormant Russian social conscience peal like a bell "with a tone which shall not cease to reverberate until ... a joyful, orderly and quietly heroic bell begins to ring in every man."

Alexander II aroused the expectations of the Russian intelligentsia by freeing the serfs, initiating mild judicial reforms, and creating district councils (*zemstvos*) as a form of local self-government. Two reform journals, *Russkoe Slovo* (Russian Word) and *Savremennik* (Contemporary), campaigned for a few years for greater freedom in Russia but an attempt on the czar's life caused them to be suppressed. A liberal paper, *Novoye Vremya* (New Times), survived by turning itself into an unofficial government organ. But a newspaper that was timidly critical of the regime, *Golos* (Voice), was put out of business after running up 30,000 circulation. A number of others were suspended for weeks, even months, while their editors were in prison.

When Alexander was killed by a bomb hurled by terrorists on March 13, 1881, at a time when he was considering reforms, one of the bloodiest purges in Russian history followed. Spurred by the son of the victim, Alexander III, the state security police wiped out the rich young rebels and revenged themselves as well on all whom they suspected of Nihilist, Socialist, or other radical sympathies. In the holocaust, as might have been expected, there were more Jewish victims than at any time since the Jewish massacre of 1648 in Russia.

It served the purpose of the new czar to call for the "Russification" of the empire. "Out with the hated foreigners!" was the official policy. It became easy, under such a program, to sacrifice the Jews to the ideal of Pan-Slavism, to herd them into pales in the cities of Western Russia and forbid them to own land or otherwise improve their lot. Nor did the accession of Nicholas II in 1894 halt the persecution. He carried on as his father would have wished him to do. The severity of the punitive censorship exercised by his regime from its earliest days was sufficient insurance that the Russian press would go on printing what it was told to print and omitting what it was told to omit. In such an autocratic society, a free press had no chance to make itself heard, or even to exist.

What there was of the newspaper and periodical press practiced sentimentality and sensation, for the most part, to try to capture the attention of younger people. Except for a few illustrated weeklies, the largely illiterate masses remained outside the scope of public communication. The best a serious newspaper could do was 25,000 readers, *Novoye Vremya*'s total; even so, it had little credibility because of its known dependence on the government. The other Moscow daily was the official *Vedomosti* (Gazette), which few people read and no one believed. Of the illustrated weeklies, *Niva* reached a record high of 200,000 on a thin gruel of fake sentiment and romantic nonsense. For foreigners, the *Journal* of St. Petersburg was published in French but it took care to reveal nothing unpleasant that was going on inside Russia. In the provinces, the only surviving sheets were those that willingly used the official line.

The Dreyfus case, which came so close to destroying France at the turn of the century, should have conveyed its warning to the czarist government. For Georges Clemenceau's attacks in *La Justice* did more than unmask the anti-Semitic plotters who had wrongfully convicted Captain Alfred Dreyfus of treason at his 1894 court martial. They were aimed at every reigning autocrat in

Europe. And when Emile Zola's "J'Accuse!" first appeared in *L'Aurore*, it reverberated across Europe and made itself felt in the Winter Palace and the Kremlin. Yet, official Russia learned nothing from the twelve-year campaign in the press and on the public platform that established the innocence of the central figure of France's *cause célèbre*.

The 1903 pogrom in Kishinev, in which several thousand Jews were killed, was sufficient evidence that the czarist regime still believed it could do whatever it pleased. It expelled D. D. Braham, the correspondent of the *Times* of London, for his report on Kishinev. Theodore Herzl, the Zionist leader, made a personal appeal for mercy to the Russian authorities after the sixth Zionist Congress, but it had no effect. Yet, the Russian Jews fiercely opposed Herzl's proposal to investigate a British offer of Uganda, in Africa, as a Jewish national home. The weary Herzl said of the Zionist delegation from Russia: "These people have a rope around their necks and still they refuse!" Palestine was his last hope.

Such outbreaks as Kishinev lent strength to the exiled radicals who were trying to organize a revolt against the czars. In Geneva, Vladimir Ilyich Ulianov, known as N. Lenin, and Georgi Plekhanov, his ally, had founded a newspaper, *Iskra* (Spark), in 1900 as the organ of the "Russian Social Democratic Labor Party." Lenin, as editor, printed the paper wherever and whenever he could, but always had it smuggled into Russia. He resigned after the 1903 London Congress of the party even though he and Plekhanov had headed a faction that won more *(bolshe)* votes than the opposition, led by Julius Martov and Leon Trotsky, which had fewer *(menshe)* votes. It was the genesis of the Bolshevik and Menshevik factions of what later became the Communist Party of the Soviet Union.

Lenin founded a weekly, *Vperyod* (Forward), in 1904 and soon began to have an impact on the parties inside Russia, from the mild liberals who had formed the Constitutional Democratic (Cadet) Party to the Social Revolutionaries (SR), descendants of the conspirators against Alexander II. Events played into his hands, for the czarist government stumbled into a war with the

Japanese over Manchuria and Korea in 1904 for which it was poorly prepared. Within fifteen months, the Japanese military had crushed Russian arms on land and sea and forced the czar to sue for peace.

Out of the national humiliation, there arose demands for change in the corrupt and pitiless system of government. The revolutionary spirit, so long suppressed, began to rise. Toward the end of 1904, the local zemstvos demanded the creation of a national assembly and a broad grant of individual liberty. The czar's troops gave the regime's answer on "Bloody Sunday" — January 22, 1905. Without warning, they fired on a peaceful procession of 200,000 people who were on their way to petition the czar in St. Petersburg and left more than 250 dead and wounded sprawled on the ground. At his retreat, Yasnaya Polyana, Leo Tolstoy mourned the dead and proclaimed the end of an era in Russia.

But the 1905 revolution, with its strikes, street fighting, and assassinations, was short-lived. The frightened Nicholas II found it expedient to make temporary concessions. He removed his most reactionary ministers. To placate the Cadets and other liberals, he decreed the establishment of a popularly elected lower house (Duma) of a bicameral national assembly. The liberal Count Sergei Yulyevich Witte was called to the premiership amid great expectations that a new constitution would be drafted.

The underground and exiled press sprang to life and new papers joined them daily. Both Lenin and Trotsky were among the new editors. Toward the end of 1905, nearly 1,700 newspapers and periodicals were being published in Russia, about twenty-five in Moscow and double that number in St. Petersburg. To Tolstoy, Russia was heading for a form of government that was "entirely different." But to the czar, regaining his courage as he saw his beaten troops returning home from the Far East, the country had to be brought back under his control. He let loose reactionary gangs, known as "Black Hundreds," to terrorize the cities and the countryside. Although he let the Duma meet, he withdrew all real power from it. By spring, 1906, he had summoned sufficient resolution to dismiss Witte from office. The tide of revolt ebbed swiftly. Autocratic power was restored.

Nowhere was the effect of the change seen more clearly than in the drastically curtailed activity of the press. Before the end of 1906, the sorry record of Russian newspaper suppression and editorial punishment had been resumed. Censorship was restored. Many of the journalists who had come home to Mother Russia had to flee again. Others returned to their underground activity. For Lenin, back in his Swiss exile, it was a disaster; for Leon Trotsky, who had taken a leading part in the street fighting, it meant imprisonment in Siberia until he was able to escape. The regime felt so confident of its strength in 1907 that it saluted the New Year by welcoming a correspondent of the *Times* of London back to St. Petersburg.

While the czar made gracious gestures toward world peace by taking a leading part in two international meetings at The Hague, the press was a more accurate barometer of his real intentions. Between 1906 and 1911, there were nearly a thousand instances of newspaper suppression in Russia, with fines totaling more than $200,000. The jailing of editors became commonplace. No liberal politician could ever feel safe in his home. As for the Jews, they continued to leave Russia by the hundreds of thousands whenever they could.

It was typically Russian that the celebration of the two hundredth anniversary of the first Russian newspaper was canceled by the police when it became known that a mild resolution advocating freedom of the press was to be a feature of the proceedings. Under such dismal conditions, it is remarkable that any kind of a press could maintain itself. On the eve of World War I, out of 2,167 newspapers and periodicals published in Russia in 1912, 317 were suppressed and even more suffered the same fate the following year. The labor press had a particularly hard time of it, one paper losing thirteen editors in five months through imprisonment and finally being confiscated. During the coverage of the notorious Kiev trial of a Jew, Mendel Beiliss, on false charges of ritual murder, the government prosecuted 102 newspapers, fined 43, suppressed 3 and jailed six editors. But, according to a New York *Evening Post* correspondent of the era, "rabid utterances of the anti-Jewish journals, which screamed for the blood of Mendel Beiliss, enjoyed an absolute immunity from censorial interference."

The few thoughtful remaining journalists in Russia appealed for reason. One of the most respected, Eugene Markov, editor of the journal, *Russian Speech*, wrote with plaintive earnestness: "Let us recognize honorably and clearly the existing world ... cease the despotic system of proscriptions and intolerance. . . . Let us be, in a word, enlightened citizens of Russia."

His plea, like those of so many others, went unheeded. His journal was suppressed. With the coming of World War I, the incredible misrule of the Romanovs carried Russia into the abyss of revolution.

5. *The Wisdom of Liang Chi-chao*

With the end of the disastrous Chinese-Japanese War in 1895, a small but active reform party, Ch'ian Hsio Hui, founded a newspaper, *Wai Kung-pao*, in Shanghai and bestowed the principal editorial responsibilities on an inexperienced, 22-year-old journalist, Liang Chi-chao. With enthusiasm, but little appreciation of the consequences, Liang began attacking the Manchu regime. Neither the party nor the paper lasted very long under the government's displeasure.

Not at all deterred, Liang found fresh financial support in Shanghai and began publishing another paper, *Shih Wu Pao*. In his initial announcement to the public in 1896, he wrote: "The strength of a nation depends on whether the channels of communication are open or not. In the case of a man, if his arteries are obstructed, he sickens. In the case of a country, if knowledge is not disseminated, the people remain dull and ignorant. ... To remove obstacles and achieve mutual understanding, means are many, but the first step is the creation of a public press. ... To remedy the incapacities of the people and the rulers, to enable both to see, to hear and to articulate — this is the function of the press."

Liang's second newspaper also collapsed under the weight of the government's disapproval. This time, he fled to Japan where he edited several revolutionary journals and was honored with a $140,000 Manchu price that was put on his head. The regime, belatedly noticing the attraction of newspapers for a limited but influential public, established what it called a newspaper by imperial decree on September 12, 1898. But the Empress T'zu Hsi, having larger plans than mere press warfare, abruptly put the new publication out of business in twelve days.

It soon became evident that the empress was behind the increasing anti-foreign agitation of the Righteous Harmonious Fists, the fanatical I Ho Ch'uan, or Boxers. When they began their hopeless armed rebellion against the foreign centers in China in 1900, the world once again received the news almost entirely from non-Chinese sources. Not an independent voice of consequence existed in the Manchu domain. Consequently, with the defeat of the Boxers, the foreign press published in the treaty ports became the most important source of news about the declining years of the empire.

From afar, Liang Chi-chao wrote: "What led to the European renaissance? Nothing other than freedom of thought, freedom of speech, and freedom of publication. These three freedoms are truly the mother of our civilization." But inside China, few heard him; even for those who did, there was no hope of freedom in the desolate land.

Dih Ch'u-ch'ing made an effort to establish another independent newspaper in Shanghai in 1904 with predictable results. In the first issue of his *Shih Pao*, he carried an editorial that began: "At the present time most Chinese officials and politicians, ignorant of the situation of the world and going on easily with their corrupt habits and conservative ideas, are so behind the times that they seem as if they were living in the dark ages. . . . China needs a guide of the right kind at her critical moment. In view of this, we start the *Shi Pao*."

Like Liang, Dih escaped imprisonment by fleeing to Japan.

The few hundred newspapers that continued to publish in China during the concluding years of the Manchu regime were either foreign-owned or mere copies of newspapers that were being put out in the treaty ports in English. The important ones were smuggled in. At the Tungshan Higher Primary School, an eager student received a volume of Liang's most important newspaper, *Hsin-min Ts'ung Pao*, and devoured its ideas. His name was Mao Tse-tung. In his own first article, written soon afterward and pasted on the school wall for all to see, he proposed Liang for foreign minister of a new regime. Even as a lad, Mao had large ideas.

When Sun Yat-sen's revolution began on October 10, 1911, at Wuhan, the end of the Manchu dynasty unfortunately did not lead to the adoption of Liang's liberal ideas. Some 800 newspapers, including Sun's own journal, gained a respectable readership for a short time. But four months after his election as the first president of the Chinese Republic on December 28, 1911, Sun bowed out in favor of another old reformer, Yuan Shih-kai. Yuan, founder of the tiny reform party that had sponsored Liang's first little newspaper in Shanghai, might have been expected to favor the growth of the press; however, the intervening years had changed him. Now he promulgated a press censorship law that provided for police surveillance of all newspapers and was the equal in severity of anything the Manchus had decreed.

In *Hsin-Min Ts'ung Pao*, Liang wrote of his despair. And at the First Normal School in Changsha, his youthful admirer, Mao, continued to read him and absorb his ideas. But when Mao tried to put some of these ideas on paper, an unfeeling schoolmaster rebuked him. That, the teacher said, was not the way to get ahead in China. If Mao had any observations on this display of wisdom, it is not recorded in either his works or those of his biographers. But it is clear enough that Liang's wisdom and his longing for a free press in China were almost entirely brushed aside in his native land. To the despairing journalists of China, the independent newspaper was a lost cause. As for Mao Tse-tung, he quickly lost whatever faith he might have had at the beginning in the power of a free press. He was to write: "Power grows out of the barrel of a gun."

6. New Channels for News

In the early years of the twentieth century, world news was generally what Reuters said it was. After more than fifty years of effort, the British agency's supremacy as a global news agency was unchallenged, envied by its allies and its rivals alike. Havas, having become a major dispenser of advertising as well as news to the French press, and Wolff, the semiofficial German news agency, were content to continue as Reuters' partners in the grand cartel. Each had its own satellite agencies and each had its own carefully designated areas of operations, which remained satisfactory. As a result, the old news alliance continued despite mounting German suspicions of Reuters and Havas.

There had been a change in the representation of the grand cartel in the United States, but it hadn't made much difference to the European partners. With the formation of the Associated Press of New York as a national corporation, replacing the regional organization of the same name, the Americans claimed Canada as a part of their news sphere. During the next decade, the AP also set up a few foreign bureaus although these did not by any means make them independent of the cartel. Such moves did not disturb Reuters. As always, the first law of the flow of news was that it follows the lines of dominant world power. And Britain, despite all challenges, remained No. 1.

However, the world was changing, as the crusted and decaying Russian and Chinese empires were learning. Even the well-entrenched members of the grand cartel, if they had been alert, would have realized that imperial domination of the world's news channels no longer was possible. But they failed to grasp the significance of such novel channels of communication as the telephone and radio. Nor were they geared to compete for the use of these unfamiliar media. For years after the first typewriter and teletype came into use in 1872, and Thomas Alva Edison produced the first incandescent lamp in 1879, Reuters clung to the stylus carbon copier and gaslight. For speed, the horse-drawn cab was still the old reliable, while the new automobiles of Karl Benz, Gottlieb Daimler, and Henry Ford could be regarded only as innovations. And even though Alexander Graham Bell had perfected the telephone in 1876, Melville E. Stone, general manager of the AP, was still insisting in 1910 that the distribution of news by long distance telephone wires was impractical.

Guglielmo Marconi's wireless (the United States Navy popularized the term "radio") had a more immediate acceptance but was unable to establish a firm financial base for a decade or more. It proved its effectiveness by flashing the result of the Kingstown Regatta in 1898 to the Dublin *Daily Express* and duplicated its success the following year at the America's Cup races for the New York *Herald* and the Associated Press. After Marconi received the first trans-Atlantic wireless signal in 1901, the *Times* of London was convinced of its usefulness and covered the naval actions of the Russo-Japanese War with a wireless-equipped steamer. But the device was expensive and, aside from infrequent though dramatic uses at sea, it could not compete at first with the cables.

Then, on the night of April 14, 1912, the 21-year-old David Sarnoff, as a radio operator atop Wanamaker's Department Store in New York, picked up the first distress signal from the S. S. *Olympic*, nearly 1,500 miles at sea: "S.S. *Titanic* ran into iceberg. Sinking fast." President William Howard Taft himself ordered all other stations off the air so that Sarnoff could do his work unimpeded. For three days and nights, the youthful operator stayed at his instruments, relaying the story of the sinking of the pride of the White Star Line to the world. From the *Olympic* and the *Carpathia*, he received the names of the 700 survivors of the great ship that had carried more than 1,500 passengers to their deaths.

After that, radio no longer could be ignored as a channel for news, although many a newspaper continued to pretend for two decades or more that it didn't exist. The wiser editors knew better. They could envision it as a news medium that would one day take away from the press the sharp and potent quality of being first with events.

Within the sensitive inner circle of the American government, the demonstration of radio's power drew a more positive and far-reaching response. Under the Radio Act of 1912, as approved by Congress, all stations within the jurisdiction of the United States became subject to government authority and licensing in peacetime and seizure in wartime. Five years later, in World War I, American radio consequently passed into government control. By the time David Sarnoff became the president of the new Radio Corporation of America, the government's right to license the most potent of the new media of news communication had been established beyond doubt in the United States; elsewhere, most governments reserved the exclusive rights for radio operation to themselves.

The press had acquired a rival.

V. A World in Turmoil

1. Catastrophe

Theodor Wolff, editor of the *Berliner Tageblatt*, had just returned to Berlin from the annual Kiel Week regatta. He was still in a pleasant glow over the festivities he had witnessed as the guest of Albert Ballin, chairman of the Hamburg-American Line, aboard the liner *Viktoria Luise* on the lower Elbe. Kaiser Wilhelm II had been a member of the party just six days before — a most gracious and merry kaiser who had slapped his knee and roared with laughter when Felix von Eckhardt told of falling overboard from the yacht of Herr Krupp von Bohlen. "Wilhelm II was never freer from haunting cares," Wolff wrote that gay evening. "No comet of dire portent passed across the night sky, the Elbe lapped peacefully at the ship's side, the guests aboard the *Viktoria Luise,* animated by many good drinks, felt that life was pleasant, and Germany too was a ship of good fortune."

All that changed abruptly for the editor of the *Tageblatt* when a telegram dated June 28, 1914, was thrust roughly in his hand, bearing news from a town in Bosnia, Sarajevo. Archduke Francis Ferdinand, the heir to the Austro-Hungarian throne, and his morganatic wife, Sophie, duchess of Hohenberg, had been killed there only a short time before by a Serbian student, Gavrilo Princip. From his associates, Wolff learned that the Kiel Week celebration had been canceled, that a visiting British squadron had suddenly sailed away, that London, Paris, Vienna, St. Petersburg, and Belgrade were in a state of tension. All waited anxiously to see what would happen in Berlin. Wolff thought that a shudder had passed over all Europe as if, at that horrible moment, "men had seen the Medusa's head."

Almost the first thing Wolff was told at the German Foreign Office, with which he maintained a respectful and regular contact, was that there was no cause for alarm. All foreign correspondents at the Wilhelmstrasse were being informed that Germany stood for peace and that, even if war did develop between Austria and Serbia, it could be localized. Wolff waited a few days; then, in common with thousands of other Germans, decided to take advantage of the beautiful weather and departed with his family for a vacation in the Netherlands. It did seem to him that everything would blow over. The Foreign Office was so very reassuring.

Beneath the artificial calm in Berlin and Vienna, however, there was anxiety, agitation, and anger that were pushing unprincipled men into desperately unwise decisions. The Austrian war hawks who wanted to punish Serbia, and perhaps absorb her into the empire, pressed the aged Francis Joseph to grasp the opportunity of the moment. The German ambassador to Austria, the militant Heinrich von Tschirschky, backed them up with the warning, "Now or never!" But the Austrian emperor wanted to hear from the All-Highest in Berlin just how far Austria could go in proceeding against Serbia, and on July 4 sent him a secret letter. Next day, the German kaiser sent word to Vienna that Austria-Hungary was to make its own judgment of what to do against Serbia, that Germany was prepared for a hostile attitude from Russia and that, in any case, Germany would stand at Austria's side "with her usual loyalty as an ally." It was the notorious "Blank Check." Having sent it, the All-Highest serenely took off on his yacht, the *Hohenzollern*, for a cruise in Norwegian waters on July 6 while in Berlin his faithful servants pointed to his public show of disinterest as a sign of his peaceful intentions.

Wolff, sunning himself at Scheveningen in Holland, was completely unaware of what was going on. The first indication he received that war was in the air came from a rival newspaper, the official *Norddeutsche Allgemeine Zeitung*, which on July 19 stated that the European press was recognizing Austria-Hungary's right to reckon with Serbia. This was the language of inspired reportage; as an old hand at that game, Wolff recognized quickly enough that the government was preparing public opinion for something dreadful. If he needed further proof, he got it from the banking reports of a "political depression" and the steadily falling stock markets.

The editor of the *Tageblatt* did not receive a summons from the Wilhelmstrasse until the morning of July 23 when he was told to be in Berlin next day without fail. But he didn't relish being ordered around like an office boy and balked. Next day, he saw a. crowd collecting around a bulletin board, wandered over, and learned for the first time that an Austro-Hungarian ultimatum to Serbia had been delivered in Belgrade at 6 P.M. on July 23. It was now painfully clear to him why he had been ordered home. As soon as he was able to, he picked up a *Frankfurter Zeitung* and realized that it would be impossible for Serbia to accede to all ten demands from Vienna within the time limit, forty-eight hours.

But even more severe shocks were in store for the unfortunate editor. When he reached Berlin on July 25, he saw that the *Tageblatt*, in its report of the ultimatum, had backed Austria and warned the world that Germany would act against any power that interfered to aid Serbia. It was not what he would have said, and it went contrary to his instructions to reserve comment on all critical matters in his absence; however, the deed was done now and the Foreign Office without doubt was highly pleased. The *Tageblatt* was being as faithful to the government line as Bismarck's old *Kreuz Zeitung*. The *Vossische Zeitung* and the *Frankfurter Zeitung* were warning, as Wolff would have wanted to do, that the demands from Vienna had gone very far. Only the *Vorwärts* and the rest of the Socialist press were shouting in alarm that Austria was pushing all Europe into war.

That day, Wolff decided he must have it out with the Foreign Office. He confronted the foreign minister, Gottlieb von Jagow himself, at the Wilhelmstrasse and was astonished to learn that the Austrian ultimatum had been served on Belgrade with Germany's support but without Germany's prior knowledge of the terms. "But suppose Russia does not draw back, what then?" Wolff demanded. "We should surely be involved in a world war without wanting it."

Jagow was soothing. "I do not regard the situation as critical," he said softly.

Just before the expiration of the ultimatum, Serbia sent an astonishingly meek reply to Vienna in which all but two of Austria's ten demands were granted. To any responsible government, that would have been sufficient ground for negotiation. But the Austrians had put reason behind them and Berlin did nothing to dissuade them. Two hours after the expiration of the ultimatum, the government's mouthpiece, the *Lokal Anzeiger*, thrust a black bulletin into its windows saying that Serbia had rejected Austria's demands. It wasn't true, but truth had long since become the first casualty of the rising war spirit in central Europe

The kaiser decided next day to break off his cruise and head for home but Wolff saw little evidence that the All-Highest intended to make a final effort for peace. The editor of the *Tageblatt*, however, did want to make a gesture against war in some fashion; after some hesitation, he protested to the Foreign Office against mob demonstrations that had been going on outside the Russian embassy. In response, the Wilhelmstrasse issued a polite semiofficial statement saying the affair had been "regrettable." When Sir Edward Grey, the British foreign secretary, proposed a mediation conference on July 27, Wolff expressed hope that Austria and Germany would accept. But they declined, despite affirmative reactions from France and Russia. That same day, the wires carried the news that the official Italian Socialist Party paper, *Avanti*, had demanded a policy of neutrality for Italy and its editorial director had written, "Let a single cry arise from the vast multitudes of the proletariat and let it be repeated in the squares and streets of Italy: 'Down with the war!'" The peace-loving editorialist was a 31-year-old journalist, Benito Mussolini.

Wolff learned next day, July 28, of the Austrian declaration of war against Serbia and the shelling of Belgrade. Two days later he brooded over a bulletin that Russia had called for a general mobilization against Austria, which Vienna quickly matched. And at noon on the following day, he picked up an extra by the official *Norddeutsche Allgemeine Zeitung* with the announcement that

Germany had sent an ultimatum to St. Petersburg demanding that Russia suspend its mobilization within twelve hours. In the evening Kaiser Wilhelm shouted from a window of his palace to an excited throng of 200,000: "The sword is being pressed into our hand!"

Wolff knew that everything now depended on what the British government would decide to do, for he realized that the kaiser was counting heavily on British neutrality. It wasn't at all certain. Wolff, as a faithful reader of the *Times*, could have quoted its significant editorial in response to Germany's declaration of an "imminent state of war" — a prelude to mobilization — on July 31: "We can no more afford to see France crushed by Germany, or the balance of power upset against France, than Germany can afford to see Austria-Hungary crushed by Russia and that balance upset against Austrian and Hungarian interests." But nobody at the Wilhelmstrasse wanted to listen to the *Times*. The Foreign Office specialists were impressed by the antiwar cries of the Manchester *Guardian*, London *Daily News*, and even *Punch*. Wolff could have told them that the *Times* was a better barometer.

But the kaiser pushed ahead recklessly. He authorized a virtual ultimatum to France, demanding to know by 1 P.M. on August 1 what the French proposed to do if Germany went to war with France's ally, Russia. And he refused to make a response to a British demand as to whether Germany was prepared to respect Belgian neutrality in the event of war. A German declaration of war on Russia was prepared, to be handed to the czar's government at the expiration of the ultimatum to St. Petersburg at 5 P.M. on August 1.

Early that afternoon, the worried Wolff waited upon the under-secretary of state, Alfred Zimmerman, to learn if there had been any response to the belligerent notes that had been flying from Berlin in all directions. Zimmerman had something from the French. As expected, Paris had replied that France would act in her best interests; that, of course, meant mobilization for war, which was already under way. But from Russia, there was only ominous silence. The telephone rang and Wolff, sitting beside Zimmerman's desk, gathered from the conversation that the caller was General Count Helmuth von Moltke, the Army chief of staff. "Moltke wants to know whether things can start," Zimmerman said casually.

Wolff decided to hang around. Toward 5 P.M., he saw the austere Theobald von Bethmann-Hollweg, who had been chancellor since 1909, leave the Foreign Office with Jagow, who had a piece of paper in his hand and seemed quite pleased. The editor rushed to intercept his best source — Zimmerman. "Have Bethmann and Jagow gone to the palace?" he asked. Zimmerman responded: "Maybe. It seems the British are not coming in." The crowds on Unter den Linden already were shouting "Mobilization!" and officers, in open cars, were waving their swords and handkerchiefs. It must have occurred to Wolff, as it did to the foreign correspondents at the Wilhelmstrasse, that some kind of a message had come through from the German ambassador to London, the erratic Karl Max, Prince Lichnowsky.

That, as he later discovered, was exactly what had happened. The prince had talked that day by telephone to Sir Edward Grey at the British Foreign Office to determine under what circumstances Britain might be neutral in a German-Russian war. The foreign secretary thought he had made it clear to the German ambassador that Germany would have to stay out of war with anybody for Britain to make such a commitment. But Lichnowsy had a different understanding and, as soon as he had hung up, wired Berlin in jubilation that the British might stay out of the war after all.

What happened then at the kaiser's palace was strange, almost incredible. As Wolff soon found out, the All-Highest summoned his chancellor, foreign minister, and Army chief of staff and told them that the British were prepared to discuss French neutrality under a British guarantee, even though Germany was going to war with Russia. It was what the kaiser desperately wanted to believe; all evidence to the contrary was swept aside.

"So," the kaiser said, "we simply march to the East with the whole army."

Moltke objected: "Your Majesty, it cannot be done." He explained that he had a million men poised to strike at France through Belgium, the old Schlieffen Plan brought up to date.

"Your uncle," the kaiser cried, referring to the Moltke of 1870, "would have given me another answer."

Moltke pointed out that it was only a short time before 7 P.M., when the first German units were to occupy Luxembourg, the opening gambit in the Schlieffen movement. Since July 29, the German embassy in Brussels had had an ultimatum which was to be presented to the Belgian government at 7 P.M. August 2, demanding that the Belgian army stand aside within twelve hours and let the German forces through. The war machine already was in motion, but the kaiser ordered it stopped. He then telegraphed King George V an offer of a twenty-four delay in action against France if Britain would consider being neutral.

Wolff and his fellow editors were stunned at the dramatic turn of events. But within four hours, when Moltke was summoned to the palace and told to proceed with his plans, the dismal news circulated that Lichnowsky had made a mistake—that another telegram had come from London that the British were unlikely to make a "positive proposal." Actually, the German war machine wasn't at all delayed. Luxembourg had been invaded on schedule, and within twenty-four hours was occupied. The Belgian ultimatum was presented, as planned, and as quickly rejected. The German army rolled on—a seemingly irresistible gray-green mass.

For Wolff and the *Tageblatt,* as for the rest of the German press, nothing now remained but to print whatever was handed out by official sources in Berlin, Military censorship already had closed all telegraph offices in Germany and cut off all information except the carefully screened semiofficial Wolff Agency bulletins. Taking advantage of its news control and its docile press, the German government put out a stream of deliberately false reports as soon as the French mobilization took effect. French bombers had attacked the Nuremberg area, French troops had opened fire on German frontier posts without a war declaration, French aircraft had been seen over Baden and the Rhineland—these were among the false stories given currency by Berlin and placed before German press people. An official report said: "France has thus opened the attack on us and produced a state of war. The safety of the empire compels us to resist." It was not the first time, nor the last, that German warmakers would resort to the big lie. The German war declaration against France followed on August 3.

With the invasion of Belgium, Britain mobilized but German censorship tried to soften the blow. There was no detailed reporting of the speech of Sir Edward Grey before the House of Commons on August 3 in which he presented the issue and the choice: "If, in a crisis like this, we run away from these obligations of honor and interest as regards the Belgian treaty. . . . I do not believe for a moment that, at the end of this war, even if we stood aside, we should be able to prevent the whole of the West of Europe opposite us from falling under the domination of a single power. . . . and we should, I believe, sacrifice our respect and good name and reputation before the world and should not escape the most serious and grave economic consequences."

The House stormed with applause. Britain then dispatched an ultimatum to Berlin to stop the invasion of Belgium within twenty-four hours, acting under the British treaty's pledge to protect Belgian neutrality. Once again, the German censors let through only the bare detail. It was not until next day, August 4, that Bethmann-Hollweg at last let the German people and their press know the seriousness of their position.

That night, the *Tageblatt's* editor chanced to meet the head of the Foreign Office political section, Wilhelm von Stumm, who volunteered the news: "Now it is done — England has just declared war on us."

Wolff asked timidly if he might not put out an extra edition to let the nation know about it. Stumm agreed, saying it would have to be revealed sooner or later anyway. It didn't make much difference. The editor hustled off to get the *Tageblatt* on the street.

While he was thus occupied, Sir Edward Goschen, the British ambassador, was given the German government's rejection of the British ultimatum. When he asked for his passport, the indignant Hollweg exclaimed: "Really, it is like striking a man from behind while he is fighting for his life against two assailants!"

Goschen replied that Britain had pledged her honor to maintain the neutrality of Belgium and was going to war in defense of her treaty obligations.

Bethmann was furious. "But at what a price! Just for a word — neutrality — a word which in war time has so often been disregarded — just for a scrap of paper, Great Britain is going to make war on a kindred nation who desires nothing better than to be friends with her. My whole policy has tumbled down like a pack of cards!"

Goschen walked out in tears. The Germans would never understand the meaning of a "scrap of paper," and the civilized world would never forgive them for their part in making war inevitable.

As soon as the *Tageblatt's* extra hit the street, a mob bore down on the British embassy and smashed every window it could reach. A howl arose to the fire-flecked skies: "Gott strafe England!" For even then it was realized that the failure to read British intentions correctly had been the most damaging of all Germany's colossal miscalculations. When the British protested the violence just before their departure, Jagow said that it had been the *Tageblatt's* fault. Its extra had caused the German peoples' passions against Britian to boil over. The faithful Wolff accepted his rebuke in silence. Instead of thanks, he received nothing but abuse for his pains — a symbol of the role into which the press had been relegated in this ruthless military state.

With Sir Edward Grey, the editor of the *Tageblatt* could have said that night: "The lamps are going out all over Europe. We shall not see them lit again in our lifetime."

The calculated propaganda and outright lying that marked the beginning of World War I established a noxious pattern for a whole succession of wars that followed. If the German government set a precedent in its cynical treatment of its press and public, it was not alone. Over the years, others followed the same perfidious path. For the sake of swaying public opinion, no trick was too low, no act too extreme. Censorship besmirched the truth and buried it under a foul swath of deceit. In due course, the solemn word of governments ceased to be believed by the large segments of their peoples and national honor was thought, even by the youngest and least experienced, to be a pitiful myth of distorted history. That, in a sense, was the greatest tragedy of all.

2. The Battle for America

A new official German Information Office opened in New York City in August, 1914. It became the principal German propaganda agency under the direction of Dr. Bernhard Dernburg, a former colonial minister, who had come to the United States in the guise of a Red Cross official. He had experienced help from the German ambassador in Washington, Count Johann von Bernstorff; Professor Hugo Munsterberg of Harvard, and a youthful German-American editor, George Sylvester Viereck, who put out a subsidized weekly, the *Fatherland*.

Bernstorff's expenditures in the United States ran into the millions in his campaign to influence American opinion. Although the British had thoughtfully severed the German cables at the outset of the war, the ambassador's communications with his own country were good. He had two German-built radio stations in the United States that were in regular contact, under United States Navy supervision, with Germany's powerful station at Nauen. A few correspondents chose to use this German channel for their dispatches, but most of those who covered the war shied away from it; the news emanating from it might just as well have born the stamp, "Made in Germany."

Before long, the German Information Office secretly bought control of the New York *Evening Mail;* a magazine, the New York *International Monthly,* and founded a news agency, the International Press Exchange. Through these and other sources, German news and views were distributed to a very large audience. If one of the top German operatives had not been negligent in leaving a portfolio of such secret propaganda activities on a New York elevated train in 1915, the campaign might have achieved greater results.

Such disclosures, however, did not stop the German effort in the United States even though they were decidedly inconvenient. The theme of Germany's appeal was best illustrated in a much-quoted manifesto of ninety-three German intellectuals, issued in October, 1914, calling on the West to defend the "pure cause" of the Fatherland. Against the embattled white race, of which the Germans even then had appointed themselves as the chief defenders, the manifesto complained that the Allies were summoning the black and yellow races and the treacherous Slavs to tear down the white homeland of Goethe and Beethoven. Racism had always been a dependable weapon in Berlin, but it was difficult to export.

The British maintained an even more effective Allied propaganda effort in the United States with distinguished French assistance. From Wellington House in London, seat of the official British wartime propaganda agency, an American office was established with outlets in Washington and New York. Gilbert Parker, a Canadian-born member of Parliament, took charge of the American operation with a staff that included a 25-year-old Oxford don, Arnold J. Toynbee. Like the German propagandists, Parker worked with his ambassador, Sir Cecil Spring-Rice, who had far more entrée to the elite in Washington than Bernstorff.

As for the French ambassador, Jean Jules Jusserand, his intimate relationships with the White House and with presidential advisers were of such nature that he was a one-man propaganda agency. His prestige was so great that he was given the first Pulitzer Prize in History in 1917 for his wartime memoir, "With Americans of Past and Present Days," although the award had been intended by Joseph Pulitzer to be reserved solely for Americans.

The British ran a businesslike propaganda operation — press services to newspapers, newsreels, propaganda movies, magazine articles, domestic and imported lecturers, distribution of documents and tracts, services to libraries and the like. The theme was the war guilt and imperialistic aims of Germany's war machine, and the essentially aggressive character of those who shaped the destinies of Germany, from Bismarck to Nietzsche. The glorification of the superman, in Nietzsche's teachings, the worship of German Kultur, as defined by Hegel, and Treitschke's tribute to power as the first attribute of the state — all were belabored in the British propaganda effort.

But the key piece in the Allied case for American support was the report of an official British commission, headed by Viscount James Bryce, on "alleged German outrages." The groundwork had been prepared by the foreign correspondence from Belgium and France detailing the destruction of cities, the shooting of unarmed civilians, and the brutal repression of normal living in occupied areas. To this, the Bryce Report added the benediction of scholarship. Its principal theme was that the German military, deliberately and brutally, had used terror as a weapon of intimidation. As evidence, it detailed the execution of several thousand civilians and the widespread destruction that had been practiced by German military commanders in their invasion of Western Europe. To be sure, official denials were made in profusion by the German government and perfectly well-intentioned correspondents in Berlin cabled their own rebuttals to charges of bestiality. But the Bryce Report struck home in the United States because there was a predisposition to believe the worst of the Germans among the legions of Allied sympathizers.

Yet, Washington maintained a cautious neutrality and there was little doubt that American public sentiment, by and large, supported that policy. The reports of German crimes in Belgium piled up. The British nurse Edith Cavell was executed by a German firing squad on unconvincing charges of being a spy. German submarine commanders began sinking Allied shipping with a loss of American life at sea, notably in the case of the British liner *Falaba*. But the Wilson administration did not bestir itself although there was every reason to believe that German U-boat commanders had orders to sink all enemy shipping on sight.

At this critical moment in German–American relations, the German embassy took matters in its own hand on May 1, 1915, by advertising a warning in the American press to travelers against sailing in the war zone on British or other Allied ships. That day the Cunard liner *Lusitania* left New York for Liverpool with 1,257 passengers and a crew of 702, and a cargo of food, cartridges, and empty steel shrapnel shells. On the afternoon of May 7, some fifteen miles off Old Kinsale Head on the southwest Irish coast, the German U20 torpedoed the great ship and sank her in eighteen minutes. The British Admiralty was the first to issue news of the tragedy to correspondents in London and advised them that survivors were being landed at Queenstown (Cobh). For once, all censorship was lifted and the story of the tragedy went out with a rush. Within a short time, it became known that 1,153 persons, including 114 Americans, had been killed — among them Elbert Hubbard, Charles Frohman, and Alfred Gwynne Vanderbilt.

In the sharp exchange of notes between Washington and Berlin that followed, President Wilson's tone became increasingly tough, Secretary of State William Jennings Bryan resigned in protest, and Bernstorff notified his government privately: "We might as well admit openly that our propaganda here has collapsed completely under the impact of the *Lusitania* incident. . . . Our propaganda cannot begin again until this storm has abated." The chief propagandist, Dr. Dernburg, was hustled home before the State Department forced him to leave.

Bernstorff, in retrospect, had an impossible job to begin with. An examination of the relevant materials of the era demonstrates beyond doubt that the basic sympathy of the American people was with the Western Allies (but not Russia) from the beginning of the war. This, however, was very largely due to heritage — a national outlook derived from British and French culture — rather than any sudden storm of emotion. The internationalist section of the American press, in its exertions to cover the war and comment on it, served in this sense to confirm and strengthen an existing public mood rather than lead it in new directions. There was never a chance of a public movement on a nationwide scale to put America in the war on the German side; rather, the issue lay between neutrality and intervention to aid the Allies.

The best evidence of the limits of the influence of the press at that particular juncture in American history was the disastrous experience of William Randolph Hearst in trying to swing the national mood in an exactly opposite direction. Hearst had no particular love for Germany, but he was rabidly anti-British (and later was to become even more violently anti-French). If he could have been said to have followed any particular line in conducting the policies of his newspapers, it was the pro-Irish sentiment that motivated such a large section of his readership in New York and Boston. More than any other factor, that accounted for his anti-British line.

This led him into a good many tortuous editorial turns and twists, but it was characteristic of the way he operated. His New York *American*, for example, condemned the sinking of the *Lusitania* on May 8, 1915, but on June 6 the same paper called it "justified" under the rules of "civilized warfare." When the *American* concluded on November 23, 1916, that the "Teutonic powers are winning the war," the delighted Germans distributed millions of copies of the paper. The Chief enjoyed the pro-German dispatches of William Bayard Hale who, as it later became known, also was receiving $15,000 a year from the German government. But the worst of all Hearst's mistakes was to meet three times with a mysterious Levantine from Paris known as Paul Bolo Pasha, who later was arrested by the French, court-martialed, and shot as a spy. The Chief shrugged it off: "I did not know that Bolo Pasha would turn out to be a spy."

The upshot of such adventures was the British decision on October 11, 1916, to bar the Hearst press from its cables, followed by similar French action eighteen days later. In response, Hearst ordered little American flags to be printed in his papers and proposed the publication of patriotic editorials. Even for so tough and arrogant a character as this one, it proved impossible to go against the tide of prevailing public opinion.

In the psychological war abroad, everybody from the outset tried to bottle up bad news. The French put wandering correspondents in prison while the first Marne battle was in progress. As for the British, it took a censorship slip-up to permit Arthur

Moore, correspondent of the *Times* of London, to expose the desperate situation of the tiny British Expeditionary Force—the "Old Contemptibles"—at Mons. In Germany, Theodor Wolff's *Berliner Tageblatt* was suspended three times for criticizing the government. Maximilian Harden's *Zukunst*, which attacked the conduct of the war in 1917, was suspended and he was reduced to the role of a military clerk. When Georg Bernhard's *Vossische Zeitung* told the Germans to "tighten their belts" because the war would last longer than expected, his evening edition was confiscated. The *Breslauer Volkswacht*, which protested the killing of women and children in the Zeppelin raids on London, was put out of business. As for the Socialist *Vorwärts*, which continually campaigned for peace, it was suspended so often that its adherents didn't know when to expect to read it.

On the Allied side, the press had more of an impact on the conduct of the war. Lord Northcliffe, the Napoleonic proprietor of the *Times* and the *Daily Mail*, wrathfully attacked the War Ministry when the *Times* disclosed on May 15, 1915, that a shortage of high explosive shells had caused a British attack to fail in France. He was warned the circulation of both his papers would fall, and he himself might be imprisoned. "Better to lose circulation than lose the war," he said. His papers were burned on the floor of the London Stock Exchange.

Northcliffe persisted in his fight to overthrow the Asquith government, despite all obstacles, and succeeded. At the end of 1916, David Lloyd George became prime minister in a coalition cabinet. The press lord's brother, Cecil Harmsworth, wrote: "The London liberal daily papers are full of denunciations of Northcliffe, whom they regard as the arch-wrecker of the Asquith government. There is truth in this, of course, but it is not the whole truth."

In France, much the same function was performed with even greater effectiveness by the ferocious Tiger, Georges Clemenceau, who made his newspaper, *L'Homme Libre* (The Free Man), the scourge of the French government from the day the war began. Although he was seventy-three years old in 1914, neither age nor infirmity nor the tight French censorship deterred him.

As a former premier of France, he had been appointed president of the Senate Commission of Military Affairs and knew in detail of the manifold blunders of both the government and the general staff. He began printing what he had learned.

At first *L'Homme Libre* appeared with blank spaces on its pages — the work of the censors. Clemenceau snarled and struck even harder. He revealed the gross negligence of the French Medical Corps, the obsolescence of French military hospitals, and the inadequacy of French transport (the railroad cars marked "Quarante Hommes Huit Chevaux.") The French government blanked out more of *L'Homme Libre* and finally suppressed the little sheet altogether. With the joy of battle, Clemenceau at once brought out *L'Homme Enchainé* (Man in Chains); within a few weeks, it attained 100,000 circulation because it was the most widely read of all French newspapers at the front.

With the opening of the German assault on the French fortifications at Verdun on February 21, 1916, there was a moratorium on criticism in *L'Homme Enchainé*. Once more, as at the Marne in 1914, France was in mortal danger. In the ten months of the combat at Verdun, a million soldiers were killed — the worst carnage of any battle in history. ' It was," Clemenceau said, "a sustained nightmare out of hell. I gave up scrapping with the government for awhile to do everything I could to cheer our boys. How we managed to hold the Boche at Verdun was indeed a miracle."

Following Wilson's narrow victory for reelection on November 7 over Charles Evans Hughes, the long American balancing act between German submarine warfare and British retaliation on the high seas came to an end. On January 31, 1917, Germany notified Washington of the renewal of unrestricted submarine warfare on the following day. The United States severed relations with Germany on February 3; on April 6, in response to Wilson's idealistic war message, Congress declared war. The Allied campaign of persuasion had been successful in the end, not because of any propaganda tricks, although they were used in volume, but because the necessities of war had forced the Germans into desperation policies. Once again, it was the force of events—and the manner of the telling of the news—that carried maximum impact on public opinion. This was the major factor in the winning of the battle for America.

3. War and the Press

"It is the wisdom of successful government," wrote David Lloyd George, "that it should harness the powerful but unruly natural elements to some beneficent task." In that spirit, he cast about in 1917 for a method other than the repressive Defense of the Realm Act to handle his greatest press problem—his sometime enemy and wartime ally of necessity, Lord Northcliffe.

Did the press lord desire to be ambassador to the United States? Lloyd George was willing, but Northcliffe said no. He did warn the prime minister that the job of informing Americans about the British war effort was not being done very well. That gave Lloyd George a hint of how to proceed. He proposed the establishment of a permanent British War Mission in Washington, once the United States entered the war, and sounded out President Wilson on the acceptability of Northcliffe to head it. Wilson didn't mind the War Mission; as for Northcliffe, he was unenthusiastic. He had enough trouble with his home-grown press lords without importing another.

When Lloyd George pressed Northcliffe to take the job, despite Wilson's coolness, the mercurial publisher accepted. The prime minister was pleased. At one stroke, he had taken care of two problems—the need for better British propaganda in the United States and the easing of violent press criticism at home. Or so he thought. But once Northcliffe reached Washington, Lloyd George discovered that not even 3,000 miles of Atlantic Ocean could insulate him from journalistic barbs. The publisher received a flow of inside information from his staff, notably Wickham Steed, then the foreign editor, and sent back continual instructions to pepper away at the government.

To a kindred spirit, Josephus Daniels, the American secretary of the navy, who also was the publisher of the Raleigh (N.C.) *News and Observer*, the ever-critical Northcliffe remarked on the failures of British censorship: "My country has been stupid. Every day we are told, 'Don't print this, don't print that.'" It was Northcliffe's conviction, which Daniels shared, that people were "entitled to the news, good and bad, and that knowledge would stimulate both patriotism and sacrifice."

This was the theory to which Northcliffe adhered later in the war when he became chief of British propaganda directed at enemy countries. While he maintained his newspapers' independence, he never again was the unrestrained critic of government that he had been earlier in the war. To that extent, Lloyd George did ease his press burden. It was a typically British way of solving an always touchy relationship between a democratic government and a free press in wartime.

The French did it differently. With Georges Clemenceau, such an accommodation simply was not possible. As a former premier of France and a French senator, he had been drawn into the war effort both as an official and agent of the government but he saw neither a conflict of interest nor personal inconvenience in continuing his devastating criticism in *L'Homme Enchainé*. In this respect, French journalistic tradition was far different from the narrower professionalism in the United States and Britain. It went back to Camille Desmoulins and Alexandre Dumas, who conceived of the mission of the journalist as constant criticism and continual attack on government in the public interest.

Determined to repress a defeatist campaign that was draining the strength of France in the wake of the failure of the great offensive of early 1917, Clemenceau denounced the regime for its softness in a full-page editorial. The censor blanked out the page. When the same thing happened next day, the old Tiger warned that, if the offense was repeated a third time, he would speak from the rostrum of the French Senate. The censor's third assault on *L'Homme Enchainé* was his last. As a result of Clemenceau's attack on defeatists on July 22, 1917, before the Senate, the government of Alexandre Ribot fell. When President Raymond Poincaré put in Paul Painlevé as a stopgap premier, the Tiger growled: "Poincaré is a man who knows everything and understands nothing."

From then on, Clemenceau was unrestrained in his attacks. "I ask no quarter, I give no quarter!" he wrote. Poincaré, no friend of the savage old journalist, had to ask him to the Elysée Palace on November 13, 1917, to form a government but they wasted no courtesies on each other, not even a handshake.

"You have made it impossible for anyone else to form a government," the president said. "Suppose you take on the job. Let's see what you can do."

"Good!" snapped Clemenceau. He returned to his lair at *L'-Homme Enchaîné*, called in the men he already had decided on for his victory cabinet, and took office. As his chief censor, he designated one of his closest associates, Georges Mandel, with instructions to be tough in the application of the law. It took a journalist to know how to do such things to other journalists. As for himself, he permitted articles critical of the government to continue to be published in *L'Homme Enchaîné* and other newspapers. To the foe, he showed no quarter; to the weak and irresolute and the defeatists in his own land, he was merciless. He brought about the downfall of Joseph Caillaux and his imprisonment, the exile of another cabinet minister, Louis Malvy; the exposure of two defeatist newspapers, *Bonnet Rouge* and *Le Journal*, and the trial and execution of Bolo Pasha and Mata Hari as traitors to France.

It was Clemenceau who insisted on a commander-in-chief for all Allied forces following the arrival of General John J. Pershing and the vanguard of the American Expeditionary Force. It was Clemenceau, too, who won the appointment for Ferdinand Foch, ultimately the architect of victory. But always, the Tiger was conscious of the importance of getting out the news at the right time. At the second Battle of the Marne in 1918, when the Germans were within reach of Paris once more, the censorship was so tight that there was little reason for correspondents to be at the front. They could send nothing. But once Foch's lines held, and the tide turned, Clemenceau let the news pour out. As a journalist, he best understood how to work with journalists. Troublesome though the French solution may have been, it produced results.

Behind the German lines, the last year of the war was the most severe on the press. The censors, never amenable to anything of a critical nature, disciplined editors with jail sentences and shut down their papers if they deviated very far from the publication of official bulletins. Yet, the military was not satisfied. On January 2, 1918, just before Field Marshal Paul von Hindenburg opened his last campaign in the West, he forwarded a telegram from the crown prince to his father, the kaiser: "I beg you to forbid the circulation of the three newspapers — *Frankfurter Zeitung, Berliner Tageblatt,* and *Vorwärts* — on the Western front. The damage which these three newspapers have done during recent months to sentiment among our men is lamentable. It is not a matter of indifference to us leaders how the officers and men view things in the great decisive struggle. To my great joy, I see that they are taking stern measures in Berlin."

In Austria-Hungary, the reaction was even more panicky in the face of the deteriorating military situation. The *Neue Freie Presse, Neues Wiener Tageblatt,* and other papers all received punishment for publishing news that was either inconvenient or embarrassing to the regime. At one point, merely because they published reports on food conditions, fifty-five provincial papers in Austria were forbidden to appear. The Socialist organ, the *Arbeiter Zeitung,* was disciplined as frequently as *Vorwärt's* in Berlin.

Nothing that happened to the press and public of any of the European belligerents was in any way comparable to the star-spangled campaign of censorship, patriotic advertising, and propaganda that was mounted in the United States. The organization primarily responsible for the publicizing of the American cause, as espoused by Wilson, was one that he had created himself by executive order on April 13, 1917, just a week after the declaration of war. It was the Committee on Public Information, headed by George Creel, an energetic and bombastic former editor of the *Rocky Mountain News* of Denver and a political associate of the president's. Creel defined his task, as so many propagandists have since his day, as a "fight for the minds of men."

He surrounded himself with hardheaded professional propagandists such as Carl Byoir, Edgar Sisson, Harvey O'Higgins, Guy Stanton Ford, and Edward L. Bernays.

Creel's imaginative use of advertising, in which both private advertisers and the media purchased space and turned it over to his committee, did much to help promote the successful war loan drives in the United States. His Four Minute speakers, backed by films and posters, were active before organizations of all kinds. But it was in the publication and circulation of Wilson's speeches abroad that the Creel committee attained its highest degree of usefulness. Nothing quite like this had ever been done before; certainly, in penetrating enemy lands with the text of Wilson's "Fourteen Points" for peace, Creel made a magnificent contribution to the art of psychological warfare. That he was able to recruit so effective an organization and perform with such efficiency on a little less than $5 million for eighteen months demonstrates the essential sparseness and economy of the entire operation.

It was not Creel's function to censor or punish. He formulated the principle of voluntary censorship by the American press at home. In a relatively brief statement of that principle he defined ship sailings, troop movements, and similar events of a basically military nature as material the press should not publish. All else, he insisted, could be used. He stood for a policy of "unparalleled openness" and had little trouble with it because the United States had a basically good story to tell and was coming out on the winning side. Had the American fortunes suffered serious reverses, Creel's methods might have been put to a much more severe test. As it turned out, he had the support of a comparatively complacent press during wartime; even to the most critical liberals, the chief villains of censorship were the Post Office and the Attorney General's office.

Such punishment as was meted out to the American press emanated in the main from the Espionage Act of 1917, which contained some of the broadest and most restrictive sanctions against publication in American history. A maximum penalty of twenty years in prison and a $10,000 fine was ordained for the circulation of false reports in wartime that interfered with the

American armed forces or aided the enemy, and for willful attempts to obstruct recruiting or enlistment in the armed forces or to cause insubordination, disloyalty, mutiny, or refusal of duty in wartime. There were other sanctions in the Sedition Act of 1918, but they were repealed in 1921, and the Trading With the Enemy Act was not generally applied to the press.

Under a provision of the Espionage Act that barred the mails to material advocating treason, insurrection, or forcible resistance to any law of the United States during wartime, the Post Office refused to handle more than seventy-five publications. Most of them were either Socialist or German-American, sometimes both; if they agreed to refrain from further discussion of the war, they resumed their Post Office privileges. The most prominent case was that of Victor Berger's Milwaukee *Leader*, which was banned; Berger, a Socialist member of Congess, was convicted of sedition and expelled from the House of Representatives. Another Socialist daily, the New York *Call*, was refused mailing privileges. The *Masses*, a radical magazine edited by Max Eastman, had its August, 1917, issue placed under the ban because of four antiwar cartoons. It took a presidential pardon in 1921 to free Eugene V. Debs, four times Socialist candidate for president, following his imprisonment for sedition because he had attacked the Allies.

In a number of wartime cases, appeals to the Supreme Court were not possible until the end of the conflict. But out of one of these, the judicial review of *Schenk vs. United States*, in which the defendants had mailed circulars to draft-eligible men to resist conscription, came one of the historic principles of civil liberties in the United States. In upholding the conviction and the constitutionality of the Espionage Act, Justice Oliver Wendell Holmes established the "clear and present danger" test for the First Amendment:

"We admit that in many places and in ordinary times the defendants in saying all that was said in the circular would have been within their constitutional rights. But the character of every act depends on the circumstances in which it is done. ... The question in every case is whether the words used are used in such circumstances and are of such a nature as to create a clear and present danger that they will bring about the substantive evils that Congress has a right to prevent. It is a question of proximity and degree. When a nation is at war many things that might be said in time of peace are such a hindrance to its effort that their utterance will not be endured so long as men fight and that no Court could regard them as protected by any Constitutional right."

There was a creaking and jerry-built military censorship abroad during the war but it broke down as the American Expeditionary Forces swelled its ranks with the addition of a million fresh troops in 1918. General Pershing had entrusted the job to a veteran correspondent, Frederick Palmer of the New York *Herald*. But as a public relations major, Palmer was in almost constant trouble with his former colleagues and a resentful military command. He let out too little to please the journalists and too much to please the generals. He had too much responsibility and too little authority. It was predictable that he wouldn't last a year.

Under a combination of regular Army officers and a scattering of journalists acting as military public relations people, the system didn't work too well for the remainder of the war. But with only about sixty American correspondents at the front, the daily crises could be handled. Only five lost their accreditation, the most prominent being Heywood Broun of the New York *Tribune* and Wythe Williams of the New York *Times.* Roy Howard's unfortunate United Press dispatch of the "false armistice," causing premature jubilation four days before the war ended on November 11, 1918, was a symbol of the uncertainty and confusion of a considerable part of American wartime reporting. No press system could barter away its critical heritage in the interests of greater national security, even in the emergency of a world war, and maintain its effectiveness. And that was as true in the United States as it was in other belligerent nations.

4. The Battle for Russia

The danger signals were flying over Russia for all who wished to see them at the beginning of 1917. The Russian army was dis-

integrating under remorseless German attacks. Out of a force of
14 million men, no less than 1.7 million had been killed in action
or died of other causes, many more had been wounded, and at
least a million soldiers were wandering aimlessly behind the
lines.

Yet, to an Allied military mission that came to Petrograd in
January of that year, the grandees of the czar's government pre-
tended all was well. In vain did the French ambassador, Maurice
Paléologue, warn his delegation that Russia was near disaster.
Despite the ambassador's efforts, Minister of Colonies Gaston
Doumergue said on returning to Paris, "I have brought back an
excellent impression from my journey. It is clear that Russia is
filled with a unanimous will to pursue the war."

The British delegation received similar warnings while in Petrograd from Sir George Buchanan, the British ambassador, and
a British political agent, R. H. Bruce Lockhart, but also disregarded them. Lord Milner, the British chief of mission, reported
on his return that there was a "great deal of exaggeration in the
talk about revolution" in Russia. At that stage the British believed only what they wanted to hear. The Foreign Office had
gone so far as to advise the *Times* to play down the assassination
of the disreputable monk, Gregory Rasputin, a favorite of the
czarina, on December 29, 1916. Yet, the *Times*'s correspondent,
Robert Wilson, kept warning his editors of "grave disorders"
ahead. Such messages, too, were disregarded.

In the United States, the Russian embassy in Washington and
the Russian Information Bureau in the Woolworth Building in
New York contrived to feed the American press the same soothing syrup. They led the American banking community and the
ineffectual liberals to discount brief newspaper reports about
a possible uprising against the czar. Even the volatile Leon Trotsky, who was publishing the revolutionary journal, *Novy Mir*
(New World), in New York, could not believe that a crisis was
near.

What went wrong? To the Western world, everything seemed
to hinge on the combat along the Western front from the Swiss
border to the North Sea. Nothing except the military issue received primary attention either from the press or the public, and

leading statesmen were just as blind. What a few obscure revolutionaries were or were not doing in Russia didn't seem to
matter.

In Petrograd, however, the atmosphere was tense. As the
Duma gathered on February 27, the czar brought in troops and
the regime tightened censorship in anticipation of disorders. On
March 5, just before leaving for the front, the czar even signed
an undated decree for the dissolution of the assembly. That day,
munitions workers struck, and those in other war plants followed. On the Nevski Prospekt, roving bands of people heard
street agitators call for "Bread and Freedom." Still, it scarcely
seemed revolution was at hand.

By March 10, the Petrograd military garrison was patrolling
the streets with armored cars, but the demonstrations mounted.
Shots were fired. Yet, the people stood their ground. Two days
later, on the eve of the dissolution of the Duma, the Pavlovsky
regiment mutinied. Other units joined the leaders. Within a matter of hours, all Petrograd was in the hands of the mob. A Duma
committee, meeting in the Tauride Palace, tried to reestablish
order. But it was overpowered by the first meeting of the Petrograd Soviet of Workers' and Soldiers' Deputies, which called for
the creation of a "peoples' power."

The frightened czar, who had left his field headquarters by
train, was diverted to Pskov and abdicated there on March 15.
In Petrograd and Moscow, the rioters celebrated. In only a
week, with less than 200 dead, they had toppled the three-cen-
tury-old regime of the Romanovs. With the monarchy in ruins,
and its weak successor government struggling to restore public
order in the midst of war and riot, the press burst its bonds for
the first time in Russian history. New papers appeared. Old ones
came up from underground. But in the Russian manner, each
became the organ of a political group. Of independence in the
Western sense, there was none. What freedom meant for this
new Russian press was the priceless opportunity to contend for
the mastery of their torn and bleeding nation. And this they did
with the ruthlessness of politically motivated journalists. They
brandished the club of propaganda and shoved aside the healing
art of understanding. Their objective was power, not truth.

The Petrograd Soviet, which had founded the newspaper *Izvestia* (News) on February 28, used it to announce the famous Revolutionary Order No. 1 on March 14, the eve of the czar's abdication. Addressed to the armed forces of the nation, the order called on the lower ranks to choose committees that would be responsible to the Soviet. Officers' privileges were abolished and they were told they could no longer be harsh toward their men. "This is the death of the army," said a monarchist, V. V. Shulgin. It was more than that. It was the beginning of a drive that would place all power in the hands of the Soviets.

Under the control of the Menshevik faction, *Izvestia* temporarily joined the Social Revolutionary Party in supporting the Duma's provisional government headed by the liberal Prince Georgi Yevgenyevich Lvov as premier and Pavel N. Miliukov as foreign minister. The Petrograd Soviet at first refused to cooperate, but the emotional Alexander Kerensky, in a passionate speech, persuaded its members to reverse themselves. Thereupon, he took his place in the government as minister of justice and embarked on a fatal policy of continuing the war in support of Russia's Western allies.

The Bolsheviks, through their newspaper *Pravda* (Truth), hit the streets of Petrograd a short time afterward with an appeal to complete the revolution. The young editor, Vyacheslav M. Molotov, featured a Lenin slogan, adapted from Marx: "Proletarians of all countries, unite!" But Lenin himself, taken as completely by surprise as Trotsky, was still in Zurich trying desperately to find a way to smuggle himself into Russia. In his absence, *Pravda* wavered. Founded in 1912, it already had suffered a two-year suspension and its editors wanted to keep it alive. Soon, the paper was supporting the Lvov government's decision to continue the war. As one of the paper's younger editors said upon returning from Siberian exile, it was "absolutely impractical" to end the war at that moment. His name: Joseph V. Stalin. Nor was he alone. His fellow-exile, Lev B. Kamenev, wrote on March 28 in Pravda: "It [the Russian army] shall remain staunchly at its post, answering bullet with bullet and shell with shell."

Lenin, in Switzerland, was almost in despair over the Lvov regime's March 19 manifesto "to bring the war to a successful conclusion." To his friend, Inessa Armand, he wrote late in March: "It seems we will not get to Russia. . . . Transit via Germany cannot be arranged." And then, suddenly, everything changed. General Erich von Ludendorff, the German Army chief of staff, gave the order to send Lenin and his associates across Germany in a sealed train on the assumption that the revolutionaries would take Russia out of the war if they gained power. On April 16, Lenin arrived at the Finland Station in Petrograd—his rendezvous with destiny. To his supporters there, he cried at the end of a brief address: "Long live the Socialist Revolution!" He had come home to rule Russia.

The world press, preoccupied with the drama of the czar's fall and the collapse of the Russian army, paid little attention to the arrival of the 47-year-old agitator and the strange manner in which his travel across Germany had been arranged. Who, after all, was N. Lenin? A disreputable character who styled himself a journalist and was actually a Bolshevik (then popularly depicted as a wild bearded character, bomb in hand). He had a few ragged supporters; some said a thousand or so, others only a few hundred. The notion that this man would become the dictator of Russia, with power mightier than the czar, was not seriously entertained by anybody in the West. In Russia itself, there were few enough who would have believed it possible.

Lenin didn't have it in him to wait and wonder. He struck hard. On April 20, he published his "April theses" in *Pravda*, calling for a policy of opposition to "imperial war" and withdrawing support at once from the provisional government. He demanded the formation of a Soviet republic, the nationalization of land, banks, and production, and the transformation of the Social Democratic Party into the Communist Party. His battle cry was: "All power to the Soviets!" To support his program, he rallied his tiny Bolshevik faction. But when the second Soviet Congress was held in Petrograd on June 3, nothing happened.

Kerensky, by this time, had become minister of war. The British and French sent the elite of their diplomatic service to see him and plead for continued Russian commitment to war. President Wilson sent a mission headed by Elihu Root, former secretary of state, for the same purpose. The dazzled Kerensky, seeing a mirage of power, ordered a Russian attack in Galicia July 1, but whole regiments refused to go into action. The attack was broken. Kerensky and the allies had done the one thing that made Lenin's eventual victory possible.

Under Bolshevik influence, a rising began in Petrograd on July 16 but Kerensky had just enough troop strength left to disperse the mob. He ordered the seizure of *Pravda*, the hotbed of insurrection. Leon Trotsky, who had arrived May 17 from New York City, was put in prison. Lenin fled to Finland. The first Bolshevik surge for power, spontaneous and poorly planned, had been a failure, but Lenin had learned something from it — the importance of planning and central direction.

The agile Kerensky now vaulted into authority as premier with a coalition government that proved to be even weaker than its predecessor. For when General Lavr G. Kornilov marched on the capital with his troops, the Kerensky regime was so powerless that it liberated Trotsky so that he could take command of the Petrograd Soviet's military resources and marshal resistance. He wasn't needed. Most of Kornilov's troops deserted before he reached Petrograd. From then on, it was just a matter of time until Kerensky was overthrown. When Lenin secretly returned from Finland on October 22 and took command of a new Bolshevik bid for power, everything was in readiness for a coup. This time, there would be no resistance that counted. The Russian structure of government lay in ruin.

Although there were knowledgeable correspondents in Moscow, not much of this seeped into the world press. Between the censorship inside Russia and the indifference of editors in the West, little news was published. It was no secret to the diplomatic community, of course, that Kerensky was a mere shadow premier. Sir George Buchanan warned him on August 31 at he must find some way to maintain order or he would not last out the year. Yet, both the French and British watched with indifference and the United States couldn't understand what was going on. The German military, always alert, sent agents swarming across the border to help bring about the rise of a government that would sue for peace; to the high command, it didn't matter one whit if the Bolsheviks came to power as long as they backed out of the war.

One of the first correspondents to sense that he was on the threshold of great events was John Reed, who arrived from New York at the beginning of September with his beautiful and impetuous wife, Louise Bryant. "We are in the middle of things," he wrote home, "and believe me it's thrilling." He was then thirty years old and was writing for the Socialist daily, the New York *Call*, and Max Eastman's *Masses* magazine. He was a seasoned and sensitive correspondent although a fellow member of the Harvard class of 1909, Walter Lippmann, had belittled him in the *New Republic*. Having been in Russia earlier in the war, the new arrival was able to find out soon enough what the Bolsheviks were planning.

On October 26, the leadership of the new Military Executive Committee of the Petrograd Soviet was given to Leon Trotsky and the Bolshevik Central Committee formulated plans for the uprising. Kerensky had been foolish enough to give them arms. Now, they were to be turned against him. After some debate the plans were affirmed on October 29. That same day, Reed cabled the *Call:* "It is possible the proletariat will finally lose its temper and rise." Two days later, Maxim Gorki's paper *Novaia Zhizn* (New Life), disclosed that the revolt was to coincide with the opening of the Second All-Russian Congress of Soviets. Lenin, annoyed at the premature disclosure of his plans, flared that Gorki and his associate Grigori Zinoviev, were "traitors." To try to save the situation, Trotsky denied the report. Both Lenin and Trotsky might have saved themselves the trouble. They could have announced the revolution at the head of a brass band, marching down the Nevski Prospekt, and neither Kerensky nor his Western allies would have been in any position to stop them. However, the Gorki leak caused the postponement of the opening of the Congress from November 2 to 7; yet, all Kerensky could do was wait helplessly for events to engulf him.

In the great hall of the Smolny Institute in Petrograd on the evening of November 6, Trotsky addressed a preliminary meeting of the delegates. Having deserted the Mensheviks, the leader carried the meeting for the Bolshevik cause with his magnetic oratory and cried out: "Insurrection is the right of all revolutionists! When the downtrodden masses revolt, it is their right!"

Reed learned that troops loyal to the Bolsheviks had seized all communications centers, bridges, and railway stations. At 3:30 A.M., the cruiser *Aurora*, anchored in the Neva River off the Nikolayevsky Bridge, trained its guns on strategic points, and fired blanks—the signal for the attack.

By 10 A.M. on November 7, Trotsky was able to issue a proclamation that the government had fallen. All that remained was to take the great Winter Palace, from which Kerensky already had fled into exile. With a rag-tag crew of Red Guards, Reed and his Louise were in the first wave inside the palace while the cannon boomed outside. Soon it, too, was in Soviet hands. Reed wrote: "There was all great Russia to win—and then the world!" An enormous change in the history of the entire century had been accomplished in twenty-four hours at a cost of a score of dead among all factions. No wonder the Congress of Soviets cheered Lenin as their leader that night when he proclaimed: "We shall now proceed to construct the Socialist order."

As head of the Council of People's Commissars, with Trotsky as commissar for foreign affairs, Lenin moved to consolidate the Bolshevik victory. He called for peace with Germany, seized all private property, and abolished hired labor, with the enthusiastic approval of his Congress. And on November 10, emulating every successful dictator in history, he prohibited the publication of all opposition newspapers. *Izvestia* became the organ of the government, *Pravda* the mouthpiece of the Communist Party, and *Glavlit*, a holdover from the czarist regime, resumed its function as the Soviet censorship organization. The two government news agencies, the Petrograd Telegraph Agency and the Soviets' own Press Bureau, were merged into the Russian Telegraph Agency, or Rosta, the forerunner of Tass. Old newspapers and old journalists were swept ruthlessly aside and some of those who celebrated the coming of new times perished with them. Sick and weakened from his exertions as a Soviet propagandist, John Reed died in Russia in 1920 and was interred in a grave beside the Kremlin wall. Thus, the infant Soviet press was born in servitude to the Soviet state. It was the beginning of a powerful and far-reaching new press system under absolute state control that was soon to rival the 250-year-old independent press of the West.

Behind this screen of newsprint, Lenin's government concluded peace with Germany at Brest-Litovsk on March 3, 1918, and falsified the news of the assassination of the czar's family at Ekaterinburg (Sverdlovsk) on July 16, 1918, saying that only the czar had been executed. It was a long time before the world learned the truth; even then, within Russia, few knew or cared. The first concern of the Soviet government was for the security of the state; beside it, little else mattered.

With British, French, and American forces occupying Murmansk and Archangel in North Russia and Japanese troops in possession of Vladivostok in the Far East, the new Red Army under Trotsky had all it could do to hold off the counterattacking White detachments and the roving Czech Legion. The Germans at the earliest moment took advantage of the turmoil in Russia by moving a million troops to the Western front and hurling them toward the Marne and Paris in the spring of 1918. Had not American troops and materiel arrived in sufficient strength to bolster the sagging Allied defenses and help the counterattack, Lenin might well have seen the West staggered by the German juggernaut he had unleashed. But in this first devastating global struggle, the power of the United States maintained for a time the fundamental structure of Western Europe despite the Russian withdrawal from the war. It was enough to insure an armistice on Allied terms on November 11, 1918, the overthrow of the kaiser, the creation of the pathetically insecure German republic, and the decimation of the Austro-Hungarian empire.

Out of that initial clash of American and Soviet interests emerged a very substantial proportion of the public attitudes each would adopt toward the other. In the sixth of his Fourteen Points, President Wilson had said: "The treatment accorded to Russia by her sister nations in the months to come will be the acid test of their good will, their comprehension of her needs as distinguished from their own interests, and of their intelligent and unselfish sympathy." Unhappily, there was no good will on either side, little comprehension, and an utter lack of sympathy between the two nations that were to become the world's super-powers. Such demonstrable hostility could not help but lead to a formidable and enduring campaign of opposition in which the free press of the United States and the controlled press of the Soviet Union remained in a perpetual confrontation.

5. *The Peace that Failed*

Woodrow Wilson had inspired such a mirage of faith in his ideals and his nobility of purpose after the armistice of November 11, 1918, that the world press made a glittering pageant of his movements from the moment he arrived in Paris on December 14. Herbert Bayard Swope cabled the New York *World:* "Never in the many comings of emperors and kings, of dignitaries great and little, has there ever been the like in the city's history to compare with this coming of Wilson."

So much for hearts-and-flowers sentiment in the *World*, the "President's paper." On the same day, the basic hostility between the president and the press was disclosed when Swope, acting as the chairman of the American correspondents' group, signed a letter with Lawrence Hills of the New York *Sun* that complained to the president's confidant, Colonel Edward M. House, about the arrangements for conference coverage. The correspondents wanted daily briefings by a major American official, such as the British and French already had provided for their correspondents, and access to meetings. The response was icy. The conference sessions were to be closed. The president would not meet the press. He intended to respect the confidences of the other members of the Big Three, Georges Clemenceau of France and David Lloyd George of Britain. As William Allen White observed, "He (Wilson) believed in the white light of publicity chiefly for the other fellow, and that was his mistake."

Like most of his fellow academics, Wilson had never been able to overcome a thoroughly snobbish dislike of newspaper correspondents and a perpetual suspicion of both editors and publishers. He once told David Lawrence with lofty disdain, "I am thoroughly useless for publicity purposes." It was not an attitude that was calculated to endear him to the correspondents. Nor did he intend to favor them when he called for "open covenants . . . openly arrived at." He referred here to the processes of diplomacy and not to the prospect, which horrified him, that the press would be present at all negotiations. This was something that he had not intended at all.

It would be a grievous error, however, to blame the press entirely for Wilson's loss of stature at Versailles and for the disastrous turn in American foreign policy that followed. His visionary attitudes did not help him, either. He had lost the 1918 elections to the Republicans, who now controlled Congress, but had not thought of including a Republican in the peace delegation as a gesture of faith in the Senate, where approval of treaties had to be won. He also had not taken into account the possibility that a war-weary people might repudiate his leadership, as well as his party's. Thus, with the aloof reserve of his aristocratic nature, he stood apart from his friends and enemies alike; annoyed by his attitude, disturbed by his secrecy, and outraged by his refusal to tell them what was going on, the American correspondents simply turned elsewhere for their information. He lost them, almost to the last man.

George Creel, who had brought a task force of his press agents to Paris, received the same treatment from the president whom he had served so diligently. Nevertheless, Creel did not give up as quickly as the correspondents did; through Colonel House, he arranged to provide the historian, Ray Stannard Baker, as a daily briefing officer for the American delegation. He also set up a press department at 4 Place de la Concorde, near the delegation's headquarters in the Hotel Crillon. But Baker turned out to be little more than a dummy because Wilson seldom told him anything he could announce. He could not function in the manner of Lord Robert Cecil, Norman Angell, and Sir George

Riddle for the British, or Andre Tardieu and Louis Aubert for the French. Just about the only pipeline for American opinion that was available to the correspondents was Colonel House, who almost immediately fell into a wrangle with the ever-suspicious Secretary of State Robert Lansing for meddling with affairs of state. If the three-score American correspondents therefore mirrored British and French opinion more than that of their own government, and reported that the American delegation was split from top to bottom, they only reflected the realities of Versailles.

The disunity and disaffection among the Americans spread as far as Washington, where the president's press secretary, Joseph Tumulty, was keeping watch at the White House. Once, Tumulty tried to warn his chief that he was needlessly antagonizing the press and received a truly Wilsonian reply that this was "a matter which I admit I do not know how to handle." The despairing Creel reported: "No American newspaperman could win a word from him with reference to any controversial matter until decisions were reached and duly announced." The more his dream of a peaceful world safeguarded by a League of Nations was misunderstood, the farther he retreated from the correspondents whom he regarded as his tormentors. Eleven days after the opening of the peace conference on January 19, 1919, Creel disbanded his publicity operation and sent his people home. He had never been given a chance.

In addition to Wilson's senseless hostility and secrecy, there was a particularly mischievous censorship in both France and Britain that cast even more of a pall over Versailles. At one time, Premier Clemenceau was given a copy of a message by an American correspondent and discussed it with President Wilson before permitting it to be transmitted to the United States. While French censors thus scrutinized American dispatches, they did nothing to halt the continual abuse of Wilson by an influential segment of the French press that was responsive to Clemenceau. If the American president failed abysmally in his press relations, Clemenceau turned out to be a brilliant success. As a journalist, he well understood the art of news management and turned it to his advantage, as did Lloyd George, no mean hand at journalism himself.

London proved to be just as formidable a barrier to news that displeased the British as Paris was for material that offended the French. It soon became known that a punitive censorship was being applied against those who published dispatches that annoyed Lloyd George. In one instance, the London *Morning Post* and its Versailles correspondent drew fines for publishing an article on military affairs over the objections of censorship. In another, a New York *World* exclusive on reparations was held up forty-eight hours by a British censor because the author, Herbert Bayard Swope, had filed through London; however, when after suitable delay he gave the story to Hills of the New York *Sun*, his grateful competitor filed directly through Paris and beat him on his own story. It is not unknown for correspondents to confirm their own exclusives by thoughtfully planting the story among the opposition, but this is the only known instance in which the confirmation was published ahead of the original article.

The stiff competition of the journalistic war, and the pressure it generated among the correspondents, eventually became a major cause of the president's estrangement from Colonel House. Already under suspicion as a source of some of the poisonous material that correspondents were sending from Paris, House had his troubles with both Secretary Lansing and Mrs. Wilson. Both accused him of leaking material without presidential authority, although he denied it. Nevertheless, when Wilson himself made the charge, accusing his friend of "giving away everything" that he had won in Paris, the break became complete.

The result of the strife in Paris was a flow of mostly unfavorable reports on Versailles to the United States. One of the leading correspondents, Frank H. Simonds of the New York *Tribune*, cabled: "The League of Nations is dead. The treaty of peace is impossible." The Hearst newspapers attacked the League Covenant, centering their fire on Article X as a provision that would force the United States into war at the League's behest. It wasn't so, as the League's melancholy history subsequently proved, for nobody was ever willing to fight to save the world organization. Yet, the misrepresentation was so persistent and the bad publicity so overwhelming that the League's defenders in the United States were swamped. The gentle William Allen White, leaving his Emporia *Gazette*, went out to speak against his fellow-Republicans, Senators Henry Cabot Lodge and William E. Borah, to persuade Americans to enter the League. There was little he could do, however, to reverse the tide that was running so heavily against Wilson. Even the New York *World* virtually gave up toward the end.

And so, at Versailles, an unrepentant and angry Germany signed a peace treaty on June 28, 1919, that could not insure peace or even the continued existence of the victors, the vanquished, or the new nations that were born in the Hall of Mirrors. Yet, Czechoslovakia and Yugoslavia came into being, bright with hope, and resolute Poland was reassembled in a kind of historical jigsaw puzzle with a narrow corridor through a seething Germany to the port of Danzig. As for the Germans themselves, the levying of reparations, a $15 billion indemnity in a disarmed nation and the loss of Alsace-Lorraine as well as a colonial empire were not as galling as the forced admission of war guilt. For here was planted the seed of a newer and more terrible war a generation hence, and one that a cardboard League of Nations could not stop.

Stubborn, obdurate, inflamed by both the press and the opposition of the Republican-controlled Senate, Woodrow Wilson rejected all compromise and took his case for the League to the American people. It was too late. Public opinion against the League had become frozen, and the League and the peace were so interwoven that the defeat of one meant the defeat of the other. To the correspondents who joined the president on his campaign train on September 3, 1919, he was gallantry itself in what most of them recognized as a futile effort. After traversing seventeen states in twenty-one days over an 8,000-mile route, the end came suddenly. At Pueblo, Colorado, the president was stricken and obliged to return to the White House for treatment. On October 2, he suffered a paralytic stroke of which Mrs. Wilson and his physician, Rear Admiral Cary T. Grayson, kept the nation in ignorance.

For more than a year, Mrs. Wilson listened to cabinet officers and delegations from Congress, consulted her husband if she was able to do so, and then reported back with what were said to be his decisions. Grayson wrote of that surpassingly strange era in American history: "Some thought it flattery to tell her that she was governing the country and doing it extraordinarily well. 'Do you call that a compliment?' was her scornful retort."

On March 19, 1920, the Senate rejected the Versailles Treaty by 49 to 35. It was the beginning of the return of the United States to isolation. With the election later that year of the small-town Ohio newspaper publisher, Warren Gamaliel Harding, the nation began a new era under a new president. The Republican press called it "normalcy."

6. The Press and the Peace

The American journalists who had played their part in the undoing of Woodrow Wilson and his dream turned to other things with the coming of peace. The 57-year-old William Randolph Hearst began promoting the 20-year-old Marion Cecilia Davies into movie stardom. The Chicago *Tribune* spawned the era of tabloid journalism with the birth of its offshoot, the New York *Daily News*. The New York *Sun*, which had lapsed into journalistic senility, fell into the hands of the newspaper butcher, Frank Munsey, who slaughtered it for a profit. The pacifist Oswald Garrison Villard saw his weekly, the *Nation*, decline into a pale liberal journal, unsure of the isolationism it had done so little to halt.

For the first time in the country's history, a newspaperman presided over the White House and tried, with flaccid mind and unsure grasp, to govern a people with an almost reckless bent for independence. Let it be said, in defense of the craft from which he emerged, that Harding was not a very good publisher and a minor figure in the journalism of his time when he became a United States senator from Ohio. Despite that, he emerged as a symbol of all that could go wrong with the presidency—a name conjured up in a smoke-filled room, an easy-going man who would let his friends disgrace his cabinet and besmirch the White House itself with scandal before his death in 1923. In his time, he watched the growth of a wildly speculative spirit among money-mad people and called it prosperity. He permitted his government to go into the Washington Naval Conference of 1922 with such incredible faith in a peaceful future that it agreed to sink the main strength of the American Navy. Even as a journalists' president, he was a failure; for one thing, he became the first president to insist that all questions put to him would have to be submitted in writing, and for another, he was less than candid about his operations and those of his friends.

For the internationalist press in the United States, it was a confusing time. Concentrated in the main along the Eastern seaboard, a few powerful newspapers faced up to the reality that they were out of tune with the dominant sentiment of the country. The leaders, the New York *Times* and the New York *World*, adopted widely divergent policies in what amounted to a struggle for survival. Under the wise guidance of Adolph S. Ochs, the *Times* became the complete newspaper—the journal of record—and succeeded in making itself indispensable as a massive and impartial news source. The *World*, with the dynamic Herbert Bayard Swope as executive editor and Walter Lippmann in charge of its editorial page, turned into the greatest crusading newspaper in the land—the fierce opponent of the Ku Klux Klan, the scourge of a peonage system in Southern prisons, and the righteous foe of Tammany Hall. Within a decade, the *Times* was the first newspaper in the United States and the *World* was dead, its virtues buried in the dust of the market place.

In only one sense did American journalism break out of the isolationist mold of thought that had settled over public opinion. That was in the increasing interest of the wire services and a handful of newspapers in a better rounded foreign report, a feeling that grew out of their wartime experience. If the Associated Press remained a willing although increasingly restless partner of the grand cartel with Reuters and Havas, the more exuberant

United Press insisted on a free hand in all its contacts abroad. Beginning in South America and later in Asia, the two American agencies began competing actively for foreign clients in utter disregard of the outcries from London and Paris. For although Reuters and Havas had split up the business that came to them through the demise of Wolff as a competitor, they also saw that the Russians, with their Tass agency, were a new and powerful threat. The old European services did not relish the American competition, but there was very little they could do about it.

Although the grand cartel arrangements for dividing the world into zones of influence lingered on until 1934, they had little practical value. The old British dominance of the news died with the end of World War I. In Canada, Australia, New Zealand, and South Africa, a vigorous and independent press was flourishing and had little reverence for the traditional ties of empire or the wishes of a little publishing coterie in London. Such newspapers as the Melbourne *Age*, the Sydney *Morning Herald*, the Toronto *Star* and *Globe* and *Mail*, the Montreal *Star*, the *Rand Daily Mail* and Johannesburg *Star* did not need lessons from Fleet Street.

As the shadows cast by an uncertain peace began to lengthen, new burdens were cast on the system of independent newsgathering throughout the world. As a counterweight to the Soviet system of press control, an authoritarian press began to emerge in postwar Europe; in Italy and Germany, its presence was felt very soon. And in France, where Havas controlled both the advertising and news for a large section of the press, it was inevitable that there would be both government influence and widespread corruption. Such things had been a part of French journalism for too long a time and were not easily overcome. Except for Switzerland and the Scandinavian countries, the independent press in Europe was weak and it scarcely existed in much of Asia, Africa, and Latin America. Nor did its general performance in its traditional American, British, and European strongholds generate much confidence in its future; with a few brilliant exceptions, it was merely doing business as usual. To the infant gabble of radio, a new-born competitor, it turned a deaf ear. Few had any idea that an electronic medium that was distinguished chiefly by static and a paucity of talent would seriously challenge the sanctity of print as a major source of news within a generation.

Underneath the stagnant surface of the old journalism, the people and the forces of renewal and creativity already were at work. Some were destined to build new journalistic empires, others to pioneer with fresh ideas in new lands. And there were the inevitable tragedies — the gallant ones who sealed their own doom by challenging forces with powers greater than they could command.

The press barons of New York knew nothing at the end of World War I of a 24-year-old night-school law graduate, Samuel Irving Newhouse, the son of Russian immigrant parents, who was trying to make a winner out of the tiny *Times* of Bayonne, N.J. But beginning in 1919, when he put the paper on a profitable basis for his law firm, which had inherited it as a debt, he decided to invest his own slender funds in other small newspapers. It was the beginning of the Newhouse chain, which would become one of the largest in the land in the next quarter-century.

In Akron, Ohio, John Shively Knight came back from France and service with the American Expeditionary Forces to join his father, Charles L. Knight, at the *Beacon Journal*. The elder Knight was a hard-fighting, progressive editor and publisher. First as reporter, and later as editor and publisher following his father's death, the younger Knight patiently acquired the knowledge and the resources that would enable him to become the directing editorial force behind another dominant and powerful newspaper chain.

But for Knight's fellow Ohioan, Don R. Mellett, editor of the Canton *News*, the struggle to build better and more responsible newspapers brought tragedy. With the support of the *News*'s owner, former Governor James M. Cox, Harding's unsuccessful rival in the 1920 election, Mellett had crusaded against an evil combination of corrupt police and underworld influences in Canton's business life. On July 16, 1926, when it appeared that he was on the verge of an exposure of the culprits, he was shot and killed outside his own home by gangland gunners. It was one of the reasons that Cox, another successful group proprietor, sold the *News* and expanded his interests in other parts of the land.

For Frank E. Gannett, who had been obliged to work his way through Cornell University, an early interest in journalism led to the acquisition of a group of small-city daily newspapers in the Northeast. And from these beginnings, his heirs spread his group across the country in later years. The three sons of Herman Ridder, the publisher of the old German-language *New Yorker Staats-Zeitung*, used their heritage to build themselves another influential chain. Yet, few in New York would have given Bernard, Victor, and Joseph Ridder much chance for national power when they purchased the old *Journal of Commerce* in 1926 and the St. Paul *Pioneer Press* in the following year. The odds were even more against Roy Thomson, the ambitious son of a Toronto barber, who was peddling Crosley radios in Canada at about that time. However, he was to become the owner of more newspapers than anybody else in the world — and in the United States, as well; a British peer, and the proprietor of the *Times* of London.

To two young newspapermen in Baltimore who threw up their jobs because they wanted to found a news magazine, the postwar world was the least inviting of all for they had little money, scanty prospects, and no regular work to sustain them. But Henry Robinson Luce, the China-born son of a Presbyterian missionary, and Briton Hadden, a native of Brooklyn Heights, had a dream of greatness that stimulated them. They had been at Yale together and had served together in the army, as well. In 1922, when both left the Baltimore *News*, they set out to raise money to bring out their news magazine and after nearly a year had $86,000.* Their product was *Time*, the Weekly News-Magazine, and Vol. 1, No. 1, was dated March 3, 1923. It was the foundation of the greatest magazine empire in the world. But that first thin though lively publication was puny, indeed, compared with such established institutions as the *Literary Digest*, the *Saturday Evening Post*, or *Collier's*, the giants of their day. All were to die and *Time–Life–*

---

* An original investment of $50 in Time, Inc., would have amounted to $74,461 in 1968.

Fortune were to pyramid the Luce interests into a fat skyscraper in Rockefeller Center.

To others among the adventurous young American newspapermen of the postwar period, the prospect of facing up to new times in foreign lands was more inviting than the pursuit of fame and fortune at home. Gershon Agronsky, who had left the Jewish Correspondence Bureau in New York at the age of twenty-three to enlist in the Jewish Legion in 1917, was such a journalist. Although he had been brought to America as a child by his Russian immigrant parents and obtained both his education and his professional beginnings in Philadelphia, he was thrilled by the dream of a Jewish National Home in Palestine. And so he went back to Jerusalem with his family after World War I, sustained himself by serving as a one-man correspondence bureau for the American and British press, helped found the first Hebrew daily, *Ha 'aretz*, and threw himself into the work of the Jewish Agency for Palestine. He was to establish the first English-language daily in the Holy Land, the *Palestine Post*, and as Gershon Agron was to become the first journalist of the State of Israel.

For Edgar Parks Snow, a youthful reporter on the Kansas City *Star*, the future meant China—a land hopelessly torn by internecine strife in the postwar world. When he reached Shanghai in 1928 at the age of twenty-two, he headed for J. B. Powell's old *China Weekly Review* and produced a letter of introduction from Dean Walter Williams of the University of Missouri School of Journalism. It was Snow's passport to journalism in Asia. He remained, first as a correspondent for the Chicago *Tribune*, and later for the *Saturday Evening Post*. He was to become the first English chronicler of the celebrated "Long March" of the Chinese Communist armies to Yenan and the biographer of that strange and powerful Chinese idol, Mao Tse-tung.

For Ernest Hemingway, who also had begun on the Kansas City *Star* as a reporter and driven an ambulance on the Italian front in World War I, the future meant Paris. He corresponded for the Toronto *Star*, hung about on the fringes of Gertrude Stein's expatriate Left Bank set, and all the while worked on a novel, *The Sun Also Rises*. He was to win the Nobel Prize for Literature.

For the Harvard-educated Dr. William Edward Burgardt Du-Bois, editor of *The Crisis*, the future meant Africa. At a series of Pan African Congresses during the 1920s, the teacher and journalist put forward an action program for Negro freedom, voting rights, and abolition of the color bar. It was his misfortune that the Communists infiltrated his movement and even won his own loyalty for a time. But even worse, his efforts were overshadowed by the rival program of Marcus Garvey, who started the *Negro World* in order to support his claim to be the Provisional President of Africa. Even though Garvey's grandiose scheme collapsed with his trial and imprisonment on mail fraud charges and his deportation to his native Jamaica, his influence on African nationalism was more lasting than that of the idealistic Harvard intellectual, DuBois.

For Lincoln Steffens, the old journalistic muckraker, the future was the Soviet Union. After accompanying William C. Bullitt to Moscow on a postwar fact-finding mission, the enthusiastic Steffens burst in upon Herbert Bayard Swope at the Versailles peace conference and exclaimed, "I have seen the future and, by God, it works!" The less than admiring Swope may not have been convinced but younger and more idealistic Americans were.

It was scarcely sufficient, therefore, to picture the American journalism of the 1920s as a debilitating mixture of Hearstian isolation, jazz journalism, anti-British nonsense by Colonel Robert R. McCormick of the Chicago *Tribune*, and Jovian detachment by the New York *Times*. The twenty-five newspapers that Edward Wyllis Scripps left to his heirs on his death in 1926, and the manner in which they were developed by his partner, Roy Howard, set new patterns of responsibility in group ownership in the United States. The other young proprietors who were rising to power, and the young journalists who scattered from the United States to far places, also showed no hesitation in breaking with old notions about the press. All were to have an impact on their society and the history of their times.

VI. The Old Order Changes

1. The Lion at Bay

Lord Northcliffe, in a cheerful mood despite a recent spell of illness, dashed off a letter of congratulations on June 15, 1919, and in it signaled for a change in national policy. The congratulations were for Captain John Alcock and Lieutenant Arthur Whitton Brown, who had that day won Northcliffe's £10,000 prize for making the first nonstop trans-Atlantic flight in 16 hours and 12 minutes. The policy change he sought was more generous treatment for Ireland, for he wrote: "I rejoice at the good augury that you departed from and arrived at those two portions of the British Commonwealth, the happy and prosperous Dominion of Ireland."

It was the first suggestion that Northcliffe's *Times* would be for dominion status for Ireland, which at that time was anything but happy and prosperous. Up and down Fleet Street, the rumor spread that it was part of a campaign to embarrass the prime minister, David Lloyd George, and that the *Times* was being "used." There was probably some truth to the story, for Northcliffe was a good hater. Despite the rectitude of the policy, that in itself could not account entirely for the *Times*'s dramatic change of front and the heavy circulation and advertising losses that followed.

There was more than enough evidence of bad feeling between the Napoleon of Fleet Street and the prime minister. After their wartime cooperation, Northcliffe had tried to turn Lloyd George out of office at the "khaki election" and lost. He also had attempted to determine who would be on the British delegation at Versailles and the prime minister had told him to "go to hell." Lloyd George had crowed over his enemy: "Northcliffe thought he could run the country. I couldn't allow that." Out of pique, Northcliffe had removed Geoffrey Dawson as editor of the *Times* early in 1919 and replaced him with the foreign editor, Wickham Steed, who was less inclined to be friendly with the government.

Whatever doubts there may have been of the press lord's sincerity in his pro-Ireland campaign, there could be none about his courage. He told Steed to go ahead with the *Times*'s pressure on the government even though the paper's advertising had declined 9 percent in twelve months. Its losses were now £1,000 a week and its circulation was down to a puny 110,000 daily. Of course, the rest of the Northcliffe empire still prospered and the *Daily Mail*'s circulation stood at 1.73 million, which even its proprietor termed "stupendous" for that period.

Despite the risks, Steed kept demanding an Irish peace in both the editorial and news columns of the *Times*. He proposed a form of Irish federation with separate legislatures for Ulster and the rest of Ireland. Although the British government reluctantly accepted the general principles, which would have reduced Northern Ireland to the six Protestant countries of Ulster, the Sinn Fein would have none of it. At that juncture, it appeared that the *Times*'s dangerous and costly gamble with public opinion on Ireland had failed. "The *Times*," Steed wrote, "can rarely have been more unpopular in England than during this period."

Steed would have been first to concede that the Irish policy lacked public support because there was a general unwillingness to admit that Britain's status in the world had changed. Yet, with the strengthening of the United States as a world leader and the emergence of the Soviet Union, it was painfully apparent to even the most patriotic British people that theirs was no longer the all-dominant empire of yore. The Irish were not alone in clamoring for freedom. Eyed by hostile Arabs, the Jews were trying to build a homeland in Palestine in fulfillment of a British pledge. And in India, a little brown man in a loincloth, Mohandas K. Gandhi, was preaching nonviolent noncooperation with the British raj. After the sacrifices of World War I, Britain no longer had the vitality to face down all these challenges to her authority; indeed, some papers already were calling for a withdrawal from the Middle East on grounds of economy. Clearly, the lion was at bay.

To the *Times*, Ireland was the test of British policy in the post-war world. It was the era of the Black and Tans, so named after the color of their uniforms, the ferocious auxiliaries of the Royal Irish Constabulary who were recruited from the worst elements in England. The murders, burnings, kidnapings, and hangings on both sides amounted to nothing less than open warfare between the Sinn Fein and Britain. Even after the Government of Ireland Bill was passed and given the king's approval on September 23, 1920, the warfare continued. For the Sinn Fein still balked at accepting the separation of the six counties of Northern Ireland, the key to the whole arrangement.

Steed conceived it to be his duty as the editor of a great independent newspaper to try to restore peace. To that end, he dealt with an envoy of Arthur Griffith, that man of stone, the printer-turned-journalist who for a generation had led the Irish Republic Brotherhood and now was the provisional head of the Irish Republic. But these efforts, too, came to nothing for on Sunday, November 21, 1920, gunmen mowed down fourteen British officers in Dublin. In retaliation, the city of Cork was nearly ruined by fire, and six Sinn Feiners were executed at Mountjoy Gaol, Dublin.

It was almost enough for Northcliffe, who had been weakening on the *Times*'s Irish campaign. In the spring of 1921, the Chief suddenly turned on Steed, complaining that the *Times* was a burden—"financial, personal and social . . . the last straw which makes the load unbearable." Northcliffe's health had been failing for some time and he had been growing irrational, but Steed had not expected to be set upon so abruptly. He pleaded for a month's grace from the Chief to consider what the paper should do about Ireland. Before the month was out, King George went to Belfast on June 22, 1921, and called for a truce in a speech opening the Northern Ireland Parliament. The result was the opening of negotiations between Eamon de Valera, the president of what was then known as the Irish Republic, and Lloyd George in London.

For the *Times*'s editor, these negotiations became all-important. When at length the Anglo-Irish Treaty was signed on December 6 and the Irish Free State was formally recognized, not even de Valera's repudiation of his own negotiators could mar the *Times*'s celebration. With its continued advocacy of peace and reconciliation, the paper had made a recognizable contribution to the outcome.

For Northcliffe, however, that was not good enough. The *Times*'s financial situation had grown worse. In the spring of 1922, Steed was demoted to a mere personal adviser. From then on until Northcliffe died on August 14, 1922, in London, the paper had no editor although Steed did what he could to keep things in order. A little more than two months later, the *Times* was sold to Major John Jacob Astor and John Walter IV, the board chairman, on October 23. It was the end of Steed, whose stubbornness had helped bring peace to Ireland; when the more pliant Geoffrey Dawson returned to the job, it was a signal that the *Times* would stand for a gracious kind of conservatism. For Dawson associated only with the best people, some of whom were to become known shortly as the "Cliveden set."

The influence of the press was far from beneficent in another dangerous area for a weakened Britain—the Middle East. Here, the Northcliffe papers played an uncertain obbligato to the trumpet call of the Beaverbrook press for a "bag-and-baggage" withdrawal of British arms and influence for a wide range of overseas commitments. This was the policy primarily of the Canadian-born Max Aitken, who had become the multi-millionaire Lord Beaverbrook, the proprietor of the powerful *Daily Express* and the *Evening Standard* in London. As the wartime minister of information of Lloyd George's cabinet, Beaverbrook had been one of the strongest supporters of the government. But once the armistice came, he turned violently toward isolation.

To Beaverbrook, the Middle East was an unnecessary drain on Britain. With more than a touch of malice toward the 500,000 Jews who were struggling to maintain a precarious foothold in Palestine, his papers suggested that British support for their cause had been an unwarranted burden on the taxpayers and an abandonment of the Arabs. The Jewish settlers in Palestine were wholly supported by their own agencies at the time and drew nothing from the British treasury, but that scarcely mattered to Beaverbrook. To him, and to other mistrustful publishers, Zionism was a questionable cause. They compounded their own lack of understanding by spreading doubt and confusion about the Palestine issue among their readers.

Zionism—the movement for the restoration of a Jewish homeland in Palestine—was hardly a new idea. It had been infused with vitality and supported at a dramatic moment in World War I by precisely the British government that was now being asked to abandon it. After considerable negotiation with Zionist leaders, the Lloyd George cabinet had authorized the issuance of the Balfour Declaration, as drafted by Foreign Minister Arthur James Balfour, on November 2, 1917:

"His Majesty's Government view with favor the establishment in Palestine of a National Home for the Jewish people, and will use their best endeavors to facilitate the achievement of this object, it being clearly understood that nothing shall be done which may prejudice the civil and religious rights of the existing non-Jewish communities in Palestine or the rights and political status enjoyed by Jews in any other country."

Such was the rather enigmatic pledge of support for the return to Jerusalem—the ancient Jewish dream that dated from the destruction of the last Jewish state in A.D. 70 and the dispersion of most of its inhabitants. The ever-generous C. P. Scott of the Manchester *Guardian* did much to bridge the chasm between dream and reality. Soon after World War I began, he sought out the Zionist leader, Chaim Weizmann, a Russian-born, German-educated chemist who had invented synthetic acetone for use in making explosives. The journalist, persuaded of the rightness of the Zionist cause, brought Weizmann to Lloyd George's attention without delay, both for his importance as a scientist and his devotion to the restoration of a Jewish homeland. Out of gratitude for Weizmann's war services, and perhaps somewhat conscious as well of Scott's importance as a liberal spokesman, Lloyd George endorsed in general the aims of Zionism. But in the detailed negotiations with Balfour, the outcome was not really what the Zionists had envisioned.

When the Council of the League of Nations ratified Britain's mandate over Palestine on July 24, 1922, the Jewish settlers received no assurance of protection. The wrathful attitude of the isolationist press in Britain only hastened the explosion in the Middle East. It served to strengthen the position of the intransigent Arab leadership against further Jewish land purchases and immigration. It was inevitable, under such circumstances, that a Jewish underground would speed refugees into Palestine when normal immigration was checked, that a Jewish army would be established and armed, and that violence would become a way of life in the Middle East for much of the remainder of the century. But over the years, it was Scott's vision of a reborn Jewish state that prevailed, and not the utter chaos of Beaverbrook. As the first president of the State of Israel, Weizmann gratefully paid tribute to his political godfather in Manchester, Scott of the *Guardian*, for his "incalculable value to the Zionist movement."

In India, seething after more than a century and a half of British rule, it was not a great newspaper but a flimsy, poorly printed little sheet in the city of Ahmedabad that precipitated a crisis after World War I. The paper was called *Young India*: the editor was Gandhi, the Mahatma, the "Great Soul" in beggar's garb. At the time of his arrest on March 10, 1922, in Sabarmati, he was fifty-three years old and described himself as a farmer and weaver. The charge against him — a disgracefully familiar one in the history of the free press — was sedition and he pleaded guilty. Nevertheless, he was held for trial — a show trial that was intended to teach India's rebels a lesson.

Born in Porbandar on October 2, 1869, into a comfortable, middle-class family, Gandhi had been educated as a lawyer in India and London and admitted to the bar in 1889. However, overcome by the injustice and harshness with which his fellow countrymen were treated in South Africa, he had abandoned the law and plunged into a lifelong struggle against persecution in 1900. Both his habitual costume of loincloth and shawl and his preaching of noncooperation and nonviolence were derived from his experience in South Africa. Upon his return to India in 1915, he had thought — quite mistakenly — that he would help the cause of Indian independence by supporting the British war effort. But when he saw that wartime censorship and suspension of civil liberties would be continued by the passage of the ill-considered Rowlatt Act of March 18, 1919, he called for his first *hartal*, a general work stoppage and suspension of business. It was the beginning of *satyagraha*, literally meaning "force of truth," but in practice nonviolent noncooperation. It was a strategy that was reinforced by his reading of Henry David Thoreau's essay on civil disobedience.

Gandhi's first campaign lasted only a month. When violence erupted in Bombay and then the Punjab, he announced that he was dropping his effort because he was deeply grieved. But it was too late. When nonresisting Indian demonstrators massed in Amritsar on April 13, 1919, British troops fired on them and killed 379 persons. In the agitation that followed, India received a new constitution on February 9, 1921, but even that did not blunt the popularity of noncooperation with British rule in India.

Gandhi placed himself at the head of the movement he had initiated. In April, 1920, he became the leader of the Home Rule League and five months later succeeded the late Bal Gangadhar Tilak as the president of the Indian Congress. Tilak's newspaper *Kesari* (Lion), which had for so long spread the arguments for Indian freedom, was replaced by Gandhi's *Young India*, which had been founded in 1919 at Ahmedabad.

In a burst of unwarranted enthusiasm, Gandhi promised India *swaraj*—independence—in 1921. The panicky British took him so seriously that they jailed his followers first by the hundreds, then the thousands, and finally by the tens of thousands.

Striking directly at the Mahatma after months of hesitation, the British government instructed the viceroy, Lord Reading, to arrest the unquestioned leader of India's millions and restore law and order at all costs. Always indifferent to his personal safety, Gandhi provided the ground for both arrest and the subsequent show trial in a series of deliberately seditious articles in *Young India*. He called it "sinful" for anyone to serve the British government in India and adopted sedition as his creed. He announced that he was in open rebellion with his followers and would accept no compromise in a "fight to the finish."

Gandhi went on trial at Ahmedabad on March 18, 1922, without a lawyer. Only his fellow prisoner, S. G. Banker, printer of the paper, accompanied him. Unlike the other famous journalistic sedition trials, this one was not based on a stalwart defense, a dramatic confrontation, or a moving appeal to a jury. There was no defense, no jury, no confrontation. Not being a professional journalist, Gandhi felt at ease with his prosecutors and saw no reason to raise the issue of freedom of the press. He was willing to go to jail; as a political leader, he was well aware of the uses of martyrdom in arousing feeling among the masses.

"The only course open to you, the Judge," he announced as the trial began, "is either to resign your post, or inflict on me the severest penalty if you believe that the system and the law you administer are good for the people." Mr. Justice C. N. Broomfield obliged him with a sentence of six years in prison; for the printer, one year sufficed. The Indians who were able to watch the strange scene knelt and wept as Gandhi was led away to jail. "Freedom," he said, "is to be wooed only inside prison walls and sometimes on gallows, never in the council chambers, courts or the schoolroom." He was released after two years in prison because he had had to undergo an emergency operation for appendicitis and was slow to recover. The British wanted to avoid blame for worsening his condition.

If Gandhi had expected that his martyrdom would stir all India, he was disappointed. In his absence, his followers had become disenchanted with nonviolent noncooperation. It didn't seem to be leading anywhere. In place of *swaraj*, which Gandhi had promised for 1921, India appeared even more firmly in Britain's grasp three years later. As the Mahatma quickly realized, a considerable credibility gap had developed between his followers and himself during his long enforced absence.

With characteristic vigor and optimism, he set about repairing the damage. On April 3, 1924, he resumed the editorship of *Young India* and proclaimed in his first issue a week later that he was still "a strong disbeliever in this government." From then on, he never slackened his attack either in the streets, in the countryside or in print. Before the first decade of the long armistice between the wars had passed, Britain's rule of the Indian subcontinent had been effectively undermined. To those who knew the strength of Gandhi and the fervor he inspired in the people, it was only a question of time before the British would have to leave their most cherished colonial domain.

2. The Conscience of Europe

Long before Czechoslovakia became a nation in the heart of an uneasy Europe after World War I, it existed as a vision for Thomas Garrigue Masaryk.

What he sought throughout his life was a parliamentary democracy for his people that would replace the tyranny of the Austro-Hungarian empire with free institutions — parliament, courts of justice, and a free press. He was well aware that free peoples had always led a precarious existence at the crossroads of Europe, surrounded as they were with powerful and ruthless enemies. He realized also that the nation he envisioned would be weakened from the outset by grave internal divisions. But for all that, he had faith that his country, once it was given life, would be proof against all danger as a symbol of liberty and the conscience of a new European comity of nations.

In the hindsight of history, all that seems tragically unrealistic. But in the atmosphere of Versailles, where the leaders of small nations thought of Wilsonian self-determination as a holy cause, Masaryk's hopes for Czechoslovakia were not considered extravagant. The warmakers of Germany had been toppled from power and their nation lay prostrate. Russia, in the throes of rebirth under Communism, had too many troubles of its own to be a serious threat to its neighbors. Austria, reduced to a giant Viennese head on a tiny body, was mainly concerned with the struggle for survival in any form. And Hungary had been ripped apart by anarchy. Thus, when the peacemakers of Versailles set about putting Czechoslovakia together, they were encouraged by men of good will in every land.

Like the great Polish pianist and patriot, Ignace Jan Paderewski, who was about to become the first premier of a new

Poland, Masaryk had worked many years for this climactic hour of his life. Had he agreed to do so, he might have become an obscure blacksmith in the Moravian border town of Hodonin, where he was born March 7, 1850, the son of a coachman on an Austrian imperial estate. For this was the trade his parents had chosen for him. But he developed into a first-rate student, if a somewhat rebellious one, and eventually was graduated from the University of Vienna. In Leipzig, where he also studied he met and married a charming American, Charlotte Garrigue, whose family name he promptly incorporated in his own. The University of Prague, which had just divided its instruction into the German and Czech languages, made him a member of its Faculty of Philosophy in its Czech division, but he was not content to limit himself to teaching.

As an ardent Czech nationalist, he turned to a combination of politics and journalism. In a monthly review, *The Athenaeum*, which he founded in 1883, he exposed the forgery of documents glorifying Bohemian culture that had been attributed to scholars in the Middle Ages. As the moral of this sorry business, he called for more realism in the movement to revive Bohemia as a Czech nation. His first step was to help found a new political weekly, *Cas* (Time) in 1887. His second was to place himself at the head of the young Czech liberals who elected him to the Austrian parliament in 1891. He found it so frustrating an experience that he resigned within two years to lead the crusade for independence from Prague.

It was a difficult and unrewarding business that often brought him into conflict with the government. With good reason, he warned against Austria's aggressiveness against the Slav peoples of the Balkans, on the one hand, and the regime's willingness to be a virtual vassal to a militant Germany, on the other. He was persuaded to stand for parliament once again as the leading representative of his people and, in 1907, was reelected. There he remained, one of the few voices of sanity in a nation that was moving step by step toward a disastrous war that would involve the world.

When the conflict came in 1914, there was no question where

Masaryk's loyalty lay. As soon as he could, toward the end of that year, he fled from Vienna and came to the United States to lead a campaign for the independence of the Czech and Slovak peoples. Everywhere, he was received as a hero. Once, at a quiet lunch with Edward L. Bernays at Delmonico's in New York, he was asked why he did not proclaim the independence of Czechoslovakia in 1914. Masaryk thought the publicity man's notion incredible. "That," he said, "would be making history for the cables."

For four years, aided by generous American support, he took his case for Czechoslovak independence to the peoples of the United States, Britain, France, Italy, Switzerland, and Russia. Wherever he could, he founded newspapers and periodicals to support his cause. In Paris, his paper was *La Nation Tcheque*. In Italy, he had the *Czeskoslovenska Samostatnost* (Czech Independence). With the help of Wickham Steed of the *Times*, he worked from London against German propaganda. In Geneva, in the summer of 1915, he issued a revolutionary manifesto. And later that year, he formed the Czechoslovak National Council, which named him as its president and chose his faithful assistant, Edouard Beneš, as secretary. This was the organization to which the United States formally pledged its sympathies for the independence of Czechoslovakia, with other Allied governments later adding their assent. In 1918, before the end of the war, Masaryk's National Council had been recognized as the de facto government of Czechoslovakia. Three days after the conclusion of the Armistice on November 11, he was elected the first president of the nation he had helped so mightily to bring into being.

Only an incorrigible optimist could have looked at the mapmaking of the peacemakers of Versailles without misgivings. For the Czechoslovakia that emerged from their deliberations was a land 600 miles long, only 100 miles wide at its maximum and less than 50 miles wide elsewhere. In addition to its 7 million Czechs and 3 million Slovaks, who had their own divisions as Slav peoples, there were 3 million hostile Germans in the Sudetenland and other minorities that were less formidable but almost as difficult to handle. Yet, with Masaryk as president and Beneš as foreign minister, Czechoslovakia boldly created all the institutions of self-government and set its press free to do as it wished. As the conscience of Europe, it showed no fear.

For five years, there was an extraordinary flowering of the press in this new, brave nation in the heart of Europe. Prague had nine newspapers, Brno had five, and others sprang up in different parts of the land. Never did free peoples support a free press with more enthusiasm, bringing up old journals from underground and reinforcing them with vigorous newcomers. All would have been well if the Czechoslovak factions had been able to handle their internal enemies. But soon enough, the dissident Slovaks and Hungarians, the Communists and rebellious Sudeten Germans and, finally, the Nazis all seized upon the free press for their own purposes. Once more, free peoples had to face up to the eternal problem of how to preserve free institutions and yet prevent their enemies from using them to destroy a free country.

Masaryk, Beneš, and their followers were determined men. Having given their lives to a cause, they did not intend to let it be crushed. Under a 1923 law for the protection of the republic, they managed to keep their enemies under control for a decade or more. Newspapers that preached hate and sedition were suppressed. Individuals guilty of such offenses were imprisoned. But with the rise once more of a powerful Germany, the moral defenses of the Czech nation were breached. Despairing and powerless at the age of eighty six, Masaryk retired from the presidency in 1935 and died two years later. He was spared the destruction of his dream at Munich.

3. The Jackal

A fine spring rain was misting over the dingy gray Palazzo Caetani in Milan on Sunday morning, March 23, 1919, when perhaps a hundred men met with an obscure editor to found a new anti-Communist organization. The editor, a reformed pacifist and ex-Socialist, was Benito Mussolini; the organization, the

Fasci di Combattimento, who styled themselves the Fascisti. The event was duly announced in the columns of Mussolini's little paper, *Il Popolo d'Italia*, but few paid much attention to it. That was a mistake, for three weeks later the black-shirted Fascisti swung into action for the first time, breaking up a Communist rally at the Arena in Milan and burning down the offices of Mussolini's old Socialist paper, *Avanti*.

Il Duce was on his way.

In his native Romagna, where he had been born July 29, 1883, Mussolini had been a passionate antimilitarist. Later, as the editor of *Avanti*, he had campaigned against Italian entry into World War I. But by the fall of 1914, an inexplicable change came over him. With a handsome sum of money (rumors credited pro-war Italian government agents and even French sources), he founded *Il Popolo d'Italia* as an interventionist paper; with Italy's entry into the war in 1915, he became a soldier. With a creditable war record, he returned to his editorial office in Milan after the armistice and resumed his career—but with a difference. Now, at thirty-six years of age, he had gone far to the right politically and was striking for power.

To the credit of the Italian press, once wartime censorship restrictions were removed, the danger of a Fascist takeover was recognized by the leading newspapers at an early stage in the movement. The fraternity of journalists well knew what kind of a jackal Mussolini was; if they did not have proof, they had well-founded suspicions of the basis of his support. Among the 150-odd Italian dailies and nearly 1,000 weeklies, few followed *Il Popolo d'Italia* at first. The greatest newspaper in Italy, the *Corriere della Sera*, with 400,000 circulation, was a resolute critic of Mussolini. Turin's *La Stampa* and Rome's *Il Messagero*, both prestigious and owned by wealthy publishers, were no less antagonistic. Many other Italian newspapers took an anti-Fascist line.

It didn't stop Mussolini. In the spring of 1921, the 79-year-old Giovanni Giolitti, five times premier of Italy, invited Mussolini and his Fascists to join a so-called national bloc in the weak government. Mussolini accepted, but with this bone-chilling warning: "Into Parliament will go a platoon of Fascists loaded with aggressiveness." With his help, the Giolitti government survived the May 15 election. He and twenty-one other Fascists were elected to Parliament; numerically, they were weaker than any other group except the Communists, who had only sixteen deputies, but they created more excitement than the 275 deputies of the leading bloc of Liberals and Democrats. Anne O'Hare McCormick wrote in the New York *Times:* "In Mussolini, Italy has heard its master's voice."

That November, Mussolini founded the Fascist Party with an initial membership of more than 300,000. He had come a long way in the two and one-half years since that rainy Sunday morning in 1919 when 100 men had answered his call for action at the Palazzo Caetani. On October 3, he published in *Il Popolo d'Italia* a series of military regulations that created in effect a Fascist army outside the discipline of the Italian armed forces. The complaisant and foolish premier, Luigi Facta, who had come to authority in February, looked on and did nothing. The end was very near. The daily and nightly rioting in the cities proved that.

Almost 100,000 Fascisti thronged to Naples on October 24 for what was billed as a party Congress. Actually, it was a one-man show. Mussolini, contemptuously rejecting a seat in the cabinet, demanded the resignation of the government. "The Fascist Party," he trumpeted, "wishes to become the state!" To his four commanders, he delegated power to march on Rome and seize the government. "Either the government will be given to us," he shouted, "or we shall take it, descending on Rome. It is now a question of days, perhaps of hours."

His black-shirted legions roared: "To Rome!"

The Facta regime collapsed. The victorious Fascists swarmed into Rome on October 28. King Victor Emmanuel III, who had waved aside a proclamation of martial law and held back the army from moving against the Fascisti, now summoned Mussolini to form a government. And on October 30 at the Quirinal, Il Duce took command of an Italy that had thrown herself on her knees before him.

The Fascist program of beatings, vandalism, rioting, and

forced administration of castor oil to political opponents took on the aura of official sanction as Mussolini consolidated his power. In both press and public, his opposition softened, partly out of fear, partly out of helplessness. On April 6, 1924, he called for an election and emerged with 65 percent of 7 million votes that had been cast. When Giacomo Matteotti, a 39-year-old Socialist deputy, demanded on May 30 in Parliament that the April elections should be voided on the ground of wholesale fraud, Mussolini bitterly attacked him. On June 10, Matteotti disappeared. When his body was found in a shallow grave north of Rome on August 16, the clamor for action against the murderers reached fighting pitch.

Mussolini, facing his first crisis, suppressed his opposition. At the beginning of 1925, he decreed that all newspapers would have to submit to a director appointed by the government and all journalists would have to register and carry a Fascist Party card in order to practice their craft. No criticism of the regime was permitted from then on. Prefects were given the authority to confiscate all papers. Thus, the first journalist of Italy treacherously stifled the very voice that had brought him into power.

Two of the greatest newspapers in Italy, *Corriere della Sera* and *La Stampa*, were closed for three months. When they reopened, their staffs were entirely Fascist. Virginio Gayda, secretary of the Fascist Party, took over the *Giornale d'Italia* in Rome and made it a party organ second only in importance to Mussolini's own *Il Popolo d'Italia*. Italo Balbo, another Fascist tough, seized the *Corriere Padona* in Ferrara as his mouthpiece. Others expropriated *Il Mattino* of Naples, *Il Messaggero* of Rome, and *Il Secolo* of Milan. To make certain that government control of all sections of the press remained effective, some 35 percent of the daily newspapers of Italy were put out of business. The government used the Stefani News Agency, once a satellite of Havas, to distribute the material it had approved for publication. To oversee the whole operation, a Ministry of Press and Propaganda was created. "I consider Fascist journalism as my orchestra!" Mussolini cried. And so it was.

Having silenced the press, it was easy enough for Il Duce to dispense with Parliament. Since the opposition had absented itself, its members were simply excluded and their seats were declared vacated. From 1925 on, Mussolini governed by decree. He had made good on his pledge to restore tranquillity and peace to Italy, but it was the tranquillity of the funeral procession and the peace of the tomb. The Italian people were to pay dearly for the security they imagined they had purchased at the expense of their free press and their civil liberties. Under Fascism, they would be dragged into the most tragic and destructive war in their history.

4. Der Fuehrer

Toward the end of November, 1918, an embittered ex-corporal in the German army drifted into Munich in search of work. His appearance was unremarkable and he possessed few skills. At thirty years of age, all that he appeared to be able to do was an indifferent kind of painting with oil and water colors and a seemingly endless amount of talking about his prejudices — the Weimar Republic, Bolshevism, Jews. However, his war record was good and the German army's District Command needed a guard, so he was hired. In the spring, he was considered reliable enough to be assigned to the army's Press and News Bureau of the Political Department. Here, his job was to investigate suspected Communist organizations and report on their leaders and membership. He was just the man for the job. His name was Adolf Hitler.

Like most rootless war veterans in Germany at the time, this one was little more than a vagabond. As a provincial Austrian, born in Braunau-am-Inn on April 20, 1889, his harsh accent was unpleasant to more sensitive German ears and his intense personality gave offense more often than not. In this strange postwar world, where money had little value and work was difficult to find, he was a bundle of neurotic frustrations. Munich, the center of discontent in a depressed and defeated land, became his spiritual home.

After Hitler had worked for the army for almost a year, he was ordered to investigate a group that called itself the German Workers' Party. As he discovered upon attending its meetings in the Sterneckerbräu Cellar, its membership was small — less than a hundred — but its principles were very close to his own. Before long, Hitler had so impressed himself and his ideas on the people he was supposed to spy upon that they dumped their chairman, Karl Harrer, a disaffected journalist. In his place, they chose Hitler and adopted his 25-point action program dominated by a demand for a union of all Germans in a greater Germany, the creation of an all-powerful central state, the abrogation of the Treaty of Versailles, the socialization of trusts and industry, and the exclusion of all Jews from the press, public office, and even citizenship. On April 1, 1920, when this platform became their code, the little group of malcontents changed their name to the National Socialist German Workers' Party. They were the first Nazis.

In the fall of 1920, with the help of a loan of 60,000 marks in cash from General Ritter von Epp of the Reichswehr, the Nazis acquired as their party organ a four-page anti-Semitic weekly, the *Voelkischer Beobachter*, which was on the verge of bankruptcy in Munich. Its publisher, Franz Eher, had died in 1918. When the paper was turned over to the Nazis, Hitler became the board chairman of the Eher Verlag, the *VB*'s parent concern, and deposed within a year that he had acquired all the Eher shares. He not only had founded a political party; in addition, he also had acquired a business that would one day own the entire German press and dictate what it should print. Through a chance meeting on a Munich street with his old wartime sergeant, Max Amann, Hitler found a general manager for the Eher Verlag. Two years later, as a result of Hitler's canny operation as a publisher, the *VB* reached 30,000 circulation and became a daily with a Baltic German anti-Semitic journalist, Alfred Rosenberg, as editor.

Through the columns of the *VB* and in his personal appearances, Hitler projected an image of such authority that opposition to his will melted away. He began attracting recruits, a noteworthy addition being a German wartime aviator, Hermann

Goering. He also adopted the black swastika as the Nazi emblem. Had it not been for his ridiculous attempt to capture the leaders of the Bavarian state government in Munich's Bürgerbraukeller on the night of November 8, 1923, he might have continued to make steady, if unspectacular, progress. But the "Beer Hall Putsch" and next day's march of 3,000 Storm Troops into the center of Munich, resulting in a fatal battle with the police, landed Hitler in Landsberg Prison, convicted of treason. The *VB* was suspended for a year. And the Nazi movement, bereft of its leader, plummeted into a decline.

When Hitler left jail after serving only nine months of a five-year term, he had the first volume of a book he had dictated to his friend, Rudolf Hess. The ever-practical Amann called it *Mein Kampf* and had high hopes for it, but it sold only 9,000 copies when it was first published in 1925. As for the *VB*, it had only 4,000 subscribers when it reappeared that same year as a weekly. Until 1927, the government refused to permit Hitler to speak in public, which gave him a chance to turn out the second and final volume of *Mein Kampf.*

What additional sources of income he developed to enable him to ride around in a $5,000 automobile and take his ease at the end of the decade in the mountains near Berchtesgaden have never been revealed; however, the renewed gifts to the party's coffers presumably helped in his rise to comparative affluence. Certainly, he didn't stay cooped up in two rooms in Munich for very long.

With the coming of the worldwide depression in 1929, the Nazis saw their opportunity and closed ranks. Of all the industrialized nations of the West, Germany was hardest hit by a shattering economic dislocation that paralyzed business, closed factories, and threw 2 million unemployed on the streets by 1930. Once again, there was widespread rioting in the cities. The Nazi Storm Troops surged to the attack, as they had in Munich, against their Communist and Socialist foes. Hitler saw that his time was approaching and singled out Heinrich Bruening, whom he called the "Hunger Chancellor," as his chief opponent.

From a total vote of 810,000 and 12 members in the Reichstag in 1928, the Nazis increased their strength more than eightfold in 1930 to 6.4 million votes and 107 Reichstag seats. They became at one bound the second largest party in the land, being exceeded only by Bruening's centrist grouping. They had passed the Communists, who also had gained substantially by boosting their Reichstag seats from 54 to 77 on 4.6 million votes. The Nationalist Party, led by the wealthy industrialist and publisher, Alfred Hugenberg, lost more than 2 million votes and the moderate, middle-class parties almost as many.

Now the industrial, financial, and military structure of Germany deliberately placed itself in Hitler's hands. On the theory that he would take power sooner or later, the old-line masters of the unhappy nation decided to "adopt" this uncouth but dangerous Austrian on the theory that they would make him their puppet. How little they knew Hitler! How poorly they had gauged the real intentions of the Nazis! While Hitler used the *VB* to persuade the army people to look more kindly upon him and his followers, some of the greatest industrialists in the nation meekly placed themselves at his disposal. Among the first to come over was Fritz Thyssen, the steelmaster; Emil Kirdorf, the Ruhr coal magnate; Baron Kurt von Schroeder, an influential Cologne banker, and others like them. Walther Funk, the editor of the *Berliner Boersenzeitung*, a financial newspaper, left his job to become a contact man and fund raiser for Hitler. And the financial wizard, Dr. Hjalmar Schacht, left the presidency of the Reichsbank to manage a fund of 3 million marks, given by industrialists, to swing new elections to the Nazis.

When Hitler became chancellor on January 30, 1933, climaxing an intricate series of election maneuvers, it was not because he had won either the electorate or the press. At the Nazis' highest point, the election of July 31, 1932, they took 230 out of 608 seats in the Reichstag on the basis of 37 percent of the total vote. But only ninety days later, in the November 6 elections, they lost 2 million votes and their Reichstag representation fell to 196 seats. When Hitler was asked by President Paul von Hindenburg to form a coalition cabinet, therefore, he didn't have a Reichstag majority and he and his Nazis were outnumbered in the cabinet 8 to 3.

Hitler soon took care of that by calling new elections for March 5 on the plea that he couldn't very well go on as a minority chancellor. The German parliamentarians fell into his trap. Goering, as Prussian minister of the interior, loaded key offices with Nazis and made 40,000 Storm Troopers members of the auxiliary police. A mild-looking former chicken farmer, Heinrich Himmler, reinforced this unit with his newer elite S.S., or Schutz Staffel. Nazi ruffians wrecked the Social Democratic newspaper offices and put the Communist papers out of business with even more devastating attacks. Then, to panic the electorate completely, the Reichstag was set afire on February 27 and a 20-year-old Dutch Communist, Marinus van der Lubbe, was seized. While the Nazi press and radio worked themselves into a frenzy over a Red revolution that was about to sweep Germany, the foreign correspondents in Berlin came to the conclusion that the Nazis had set the fire themselves as an election maneuver. Indeed, the *Frankfurter Zeitung* pointed out that so much incendiary material had been found inside the Reichstag that no one man could possibly have done the job.

But Hitler coolly proclaimed a "state emergency" next day and obtained Hindenburg's signature to a decree that suspended all civil liberties, gagged the press and the opposition leaders, prohibited freedom of assembly, and made possible unlimited seizures of property. Despite the falsehoods and the hysteria, the appeals to patriotism and the atmosphere of terror and intimidation, the Nazis could not obtain a majority. They did well enough for their purposes — 44 percent of the total vote, or 17.2 million votes — and obtained 288 seats in the Reichstag. With the addition of 52 seats carried by Hugenberg's Nationalist Party, Hitler found himself with a slim majority of 16 seats. To dispense with the Reichstag and rule by decree, he needed a two-thirds majority. In the Kroll Opera House in Berlin on March 23, 1933, with armed Storm Troopers jamming the aisles and barring as many opposition deputies as they could, the Reichstag meekly handed over all power to Hitler. The vote, taken with an exquisite parody of legality, was 441 to 84. While the opposition looked on, white-faced and silent, the Nazi deputies bellowed their victory anthem, the "Horst Wessel Song." Hitler had become Der Fuehrer in fact as well as in name.

In a little less than four months, the one-party totalitarian state came into being. One by one, Hitler knocked out the separate powers of the German states, dissolved all political parties except his own, did away with trade unions, and confiscated the entire opposition press of the Social Democratic and Communist Parties. Under an Editors' Law of October 4, 1933, drafted by Paul Joseph Goebbels as the new minister of propaganda and enlightenment of the Third Reich, all journalists had to register with the state, adopt Nazi discipline and philosophy and do exactly as they were told. The chief editor appointed to each newspaper became an official of the state, and thus independent of the proprietor, so that only material approved by Goebbels could be published. Only German Aryans were permitted to remain in journalism; the rest, being nonessential or un-persons, were excluded from the newspapers, magazines, and radio.

Amann, the genius of the Eher Verlag, now fought Goebbels for control of the business side of the German press and, to a very large extent, succeeded. Through the new Reich Press Chamber of which he became president, Hitler's old sergeant was able to dominate the Association of German Newspaper Publishers and twelve other journalistic organizations. Even more important, he was given legal power to open, close, and otherwise regulate all publishing enterprises. Nor could he be sued for damages when he expropriated any publication. If this mechanism created a conflict with Goebbels' ministry, it didn't bother Hitler. He seemed to enjoy the rivalry between Amann and Goebbels to keep the press under strict control. Whatever happened, he couldn't lose.

The first great independent publishing firm to go under was the Jewish-owned House of Ullstein, founded by Leopold Ullstein and operated by his three sons at the time the Nazis came to power. In addition to the *Vossische Zeitung*, it owned the leading German picture magazine, *Berliner Illustrierte*; the *Berliner Morgenpost,* three other major newspapers, many magazines, and the most important book publishing firm in the land. The Ullsteins were obliged to sell an enterprise worth 50 million marks for only 12 million, minus a 25 percent capital transfer tax imposed on emigrés and various other deductions. When the Nazis became the owner of the House of Ullstein, Amann boasted: "Now we have bought the largest German publishing house and it has not cost us as much as a pencil." The *Vossische Zeitung* went out of business.

That formed the deadly pattern for most of the subsequent Nazi acquisitions. Hans Lackmann-Mosse, another Jewish publisher, had to give away his precious *Berliner Tageblatt* in 1933 but it survived him by only four years. Similarly, the owners of the *Frankfurter Zeitung* and *Deutsche Allgemeine Zeitung* were forced out. Despite Hugenberg's cooperation with the Nazis, he was not spared. He had to give up his wire service, the Telegraph Union, which was combined with Wolff to form Goebbels's prized Deutsches Nachrichten Bureau (DNB). Hugenberg, in addition, had to sell his powerful Ala Advertising Agency to Amann's Eher Verlag, and was divested of his other publishing interests as well.

By 1936, the Nazi daily press could boast of more than 100 newspapers with a circulation of more than 4 million. The most profitable paper was the *VB,* which in 1932 alone contributed nearly 4 million marks to the Nazi Party treasury, and was publishing in excess of a million copies a day seven years later. In addition to wiping out the leftist press, Amann supervised the merger or sale of 500 to 600 Catholic and other special interest papers to the Eher Verlag. He took over the provincial press next. And while circulation declined several million because of the dullness, predictability, and lack of credibility of the Nazi product, there still were enough sales to show sensational profits for Eher. As for Goebbels, having banned criticism *by* newspapers, he now demanded an end to criticism *of* newspapers. The Nazi propaganda machine left nothing to chance.

With press, film, and radio under strict state control, Hitler's anxiety over criticism within Germany was laid to rest. He still had to contend with obstreperous foreign correspondents, but let Goebbels deal with them through a combination of threat, bribery, flattery, and worse. Edgar Ansel Mowrer of the Chicago *Daily News,* for example, was forced to leave Germany because he was too critical of the Nazis. But Ward Price of the London *Daily Mail,* who wasn't disposed to be mean to the Nazis, received every courtesy. The correspondents soon realized that self-censorship was being imposed on them. While a few first-rate journalists did make the accommodation without permanent damage to their reputations, a few turned themselves into little more than Nazi press agents. As for publications abroad, some of the most eminent were quite gentle with the Nazis, notably the *Times* in London, *Le Matin* and *Le Quotidien* in Paris, and smaller members of the prestige press. In the United States, William Randolph Hearst became Hitler's foremost defender.

There was a more sinister side to the Nazis' press campaign. The poison that Goebbels distributed inside Germany was also dispensed abroad through the ancient European practice of subsidizing journalists. An extreme effort was made to reach the French press and it succeeded in a number of instances. As Edouard Daladier observed sadly in 1936, about four-fifths of the French press lived on subsidy during that period. Nor were the agents of the Third Reich alone in buying up French journalists. The Italian Fascisti were even busier, contributing heavily to *Le Matin* among others. If the French public was being lulled into a false sense of security, the blame was easy enough to assign. It was not a good augury for the future.

The greatest diplomatic triumph of any German government came in 1938, the year of the Russian "blood purge" in which Stalin did away with so many of his old comrades of the Communist revolution. It was the year of the Anschluss, when Austria was overwhelmed. It was also the year when Britain and France acquiesced in the betrayal of Czechoslovakia and gave Hitler his way that dreary autumn in Munich. Prime Minister Neville Chamberlain came happily back to London and was cheered at No. 10 Downing Street. He had brought back peace with honor, or so he thought. And he said, "I believe it is peace in our time." To this, the *Times* added its journalistic accolade in the Cliveden manner: "No conqueror returning from a victory on the battlefield has come adorned with nobler laurels."

It was not the free press's most shining hour.

Only the old cabinet minister and war correspondent, Winston Churchill, growled the truth as he saw it with clear and undimmed vision. "We have sustained a total and unmitigated defeat," he said. "We are in the midst of a disaster of the first magnitude . . . and do not suppose that this is the end. It is only the beginning."

Hitler paid no attention to him, for Churchill was not in power and his words of warning were drowned out in jubilation over the false peace of Munich. The road from the denunciation of the Versailles Treaty and the reoccupation of the Rhineland had been, on the whole, an easy one for the Nazis. Why worry about a hoarse-voiced old Englishman? A few weeks, a few months at most, and all Czechoslovakia would be absorbed in the Nazi Reich. Then there would be time enough to deal with the upstart Poles, who dared to ally themselves with the Soviet Union.

Adolf Hitler, the embittered corporal of World War I, the sly undercover agent of the army's Press and News Bureau in Bavaria, had become the mightiest war lord of a dark and bloody century. Within a single generation, he and Hermann Goering, Paul Joseph Goebbels, and Heinrich Himmler had captured the land of Beethoven and Bach, of Goethe, Schiller, and Heinrich Heine. Thenceforth, these terrible genii would tell Germany what it could do, what it could read, what it could think. Out of such abject surrender of all human rights to a power-crazed paranoiac, there could be but one result — a world tragedy.

5. *The Might of Asia*

A Japanese press delegation came to Geneva in the summer of 1927 and demanded "the prevention of news reports harmful to world peace" before an international journalistic conference sponsored by the League of Nations. Even in the dreamlike atmosphere of the League, where everyone piously hoped for peace and nobody was willing to take realistic action against an aggressor, such talk was fanciful.

If the Japanese proposal had been a mere gesture of futility, it would not be worth remembering. Actually it was much more than that. Had the world conference of journalists understood what was going on in Japan at the time, it would have recognized that the resolution was a desperate cry for help, not a cover-up; a plea for understanding, not a rather transparent effort to divert attention from Japan's military preparations. The truth of the matter was that the journalists of Japan were in serious difficulties because of the rise of a dominant military clique that soon would have the power to take over the government.

From the time of Genichiro Fukuchi and Yukichi Fukuzawa, the Japanese press had waged a tenacious battle for independence. Now, the greatest newspapers in the island empire—*Asahi Shimbun*, *Yomiuri Shimbun*, and *Mainichi Shimbun*—all were being accused of publishing "dangerous thoughts." *Asahi*, the first newspaper of Japan, was under particular scrutiny, as were its chief proprietors, Ryuhei Murayama and Riichi Ueno; as always, it was the leader of the press's resistance to the military. In 1905, it had shown its power by leading in the outcry against the Russo-Japanese war settlement, a campaign that led to its suspension for thirty-five days. Again, in 1915, it outraged the government by publishing the Twenty-One Demands against China at a particularly inopportune moment. Even the suppression of the paper and its enforced publication of a denial of a story it knew to be true did not help the government very much. Then, too, in 1918, *Asahi* had printed too much information during the rice riots and suffered still another suspension. Murayama had been beaten up and the paper had been obliged to agree to follow the government line from then on.

However, as the Japanese regime discovered to its dismay, it is one thing to force a newspaper to pledge to be more discreet and quite another to police its news columns without invoking the strictest censorship. *Asahi*, like the rest of the Japanese press, had a perceptible influence on the public when it opposed the government even in a mild and seemingly innocuous manner. Consequently, the regime in 1925 adopted the most repressive censorship law in Japanese history. Under it, the press was forbidden to publish anything that might be interpreted as "undermining the existing governmental and economic system." Editors were specially warned against breaching security in the publication of anything dealing with the military; in effect, what the government was trying to do was to halt all public discussion of Japan's military buildup. As *Asahi*'s historian wrote long afterward: "Under the forces of totalitarian rule, restrictions on free speech were drawn tighter and tighter; the rattling of sabers became louder and louder. . . . The outward trappings of civilian control remained, but army arrogance was rampant."

As the decade drew to a close, such moves signified that the Japanese High Command was prepared for a military adventure in China. The time seemed opportune. Chiang Kai-shek had emerged as the strongest of the contending war lords on the Chinese mainland, but even he was so involved in his own affairs that he seemed an easy target for a foreign invader. In 1927, he had turned on his Communist collaborators and carried out a violent purge. Although he had routed Mao Tse-tung, Chu Teh, Chou En-lai, and their associates, they were still at liberty with a small Communist army force. They had even tried an uprising in Hunan, which didn't amount to anything, but it indicated that they remained as an annoyance to Chiang, if not a threat. Indeed, the only real result of the Hunan debacle was the circulation of a little military jingle written by Mao Tse-tung:

> The enemy advances, we retreat
>   The enemy camps, we harass;
> The enemy tires, we attack;
>   The enemy retreats, we pursue.

The Japanese reasoned that if Chiang could not wipe out the Communists, who were devoted to such tactics, then he could provide little opposition for a modern, industrialized army. And so, on the evening of September 18, 1931, the Japanese command reported that there had been a bomb explosion along the right of way of the South Manchurian Railroad near Mukden. This was the "Mukden Incident," the pretext under which the Japanese Kwantung Army overran Manchuria in six months to establish order and then created the puppet state of Manchukuo.

To those in Japan who questioned the wisdom of Japanese military intervention in China, the strongest kind of warning was given. On May 15, 1932, a fanatical group of young army officers invaded the official residence of the 77-year-old Ki Inukai, who had become premier the previous December, and shot and killed him. That marked the end of all serious resistance to the army's wishes. The press saw it was useless to protest. For with the inauguration of Viscount Makato Saito as premier, party government ended in Japan.

Saito lasted only two years as premier. When Admiral Keisuke Okada replaced him, Japan declared a virtual military protectorate over all China and invited the Nationalists to join in a dual crusade against Communism. But at that time, in 1934, Mao Tse-tung and his Red Army already were in retreat on their Long March to Yenan, and Chiang was not disposed to collaborate with the Japanese. The ruthless military conquest of China rolled on.

For a few brave days in 1936, there was resistance to the military in Tokyo because *Asahi Shimbun* decided to make a final stand against the China madness. In January, 1936, when the Okada government submitted itself to the electorate, *Asahi* swung into an all-out campaign against it on the issue of military interference in civilian affairs. The ultra-nationalist military faction suffered a humiliating defeat. But they took revenge at once. In a wild barracks uprising on February 26, 1936, 1,400 soldiers led by their officers attacked the homes of the chief ministers of the cabinet. Viscount Saito, then the Keeper of the Privy Seal, was killed together with the finance minister, Viscount Korekiyo Takahashi, who had warned against continued large military appropriations. Premier Okada escaped harm, but had to resign.

The *Asahi* office caught the brunt of the army's wrath, once the assassins had finished with their governmental victims. A task force of fifty officers and men wrecked both the printing plant and the editorial department. At one point during the invasion the managing editor, Taketora Ogata, coolly faced the rifles of the mutineers but was not hurt. Although the greater part of the Japanese army in Tokyo refused to support the rising, and although seventeen of the culprits were executed, the military accomplished their purpose. From that time on, no one dared even to protest the decisions of the army.

With Japan's adherence to the anti-Comintern Pact, the trend toward war gained momentum. On the night of July 7, 1937, near the Marco Polo Bridge on the outskirts of Peking, Japanese and Chinese troops clashed. Within three weeks, the second Sino-Japanese War was under way and Japanese troops were overrunning northern China. At home, the military went beyond censorship to make certain there would be no resistance. In a single day, more than 300 Japanese of liberal tendencies were arrested on the charge that they had harbored "dangerous thoughts."

Japan's war machine, confident that it now could do as it pleased in China, shrugged off disapproving noises from the United States. The warmakers resented the American decision to ship munitions to Chiang and they were angered at President Franklin Delano Roosevelt's "quarantine the aggressor" speech in Chicago on October 5, 1937, even though he did not mention Japan by name. But when nothing else happened, and the American public displayed only a colossal boredom over doing anything to any aggressor, the Japanese military saw that the American opposition could be discounted. The bombing of Shanghai, the rape of Nanking, and the bloody conquest of a dozen major Chinese cities followed. Not even the bombing and sinking of the U.S.S. *Panay* by Japanese aircraft flying over the Yangtse River on December 12, 1937, aroused American public opinion. More than 80 percent of those questioned in a national poll at the time favored a national referendum before war could be declared. A proposed constitutional amendment to the same effect failed by only 21 votes in a test in the House of Representatives soon afterward when an effort was made to discharge it from committee.

Encouraged by American indecision and even indifference, the Japanese militarists boldly proceeded to announce a "New Order" for Asia and flaunted the banner of the Rising Sun over the Greater East Asia Co-Prosperity Sphere. If they ever had been concerned about the image that Japan projected before the world, they were no longer. With the support of a militarized Germany and Italy, they intended to impose their rule wherever they pleased. They represented the might of Asia.

6. The American Ordeal

Franklin Delano Roosevelt sat alone in his bare, silent office in the White House early on Sunday morning, March 5, 1933, his first full day as president of the United States. Herbert Hoover, his thrifty predecessor, had cleaned out the place. The desk was empty. Not a pencil or pad could be found to make a note. Even the push buttons used to buzz for assistance had been removed. At a moment of deepest crisis for the panicky nation, its new president — a paralytic cripple confined to a wheel chair — seemed pathetically helpless.

Outside the White House, 13 million Americans were unemployed. Factories were shut down. With the national economy in collapse, the banks would have to be closed and an embargo placed on the export of gold. The bread lines were long and disorderly in a score of cities and the means to provide food for the supplicant citizenry was dwindling. To many, the American dream had become a nightmare. The system had torn itself apart. A bloody revolution seemed very near.

Only yesterday at his inaugural, this Roosevelt with the leonine head and the heartening smile and the courageous spirit had drawn applause from a frightened crowd before the Capitol portico with his rallying cry: "We must act, and act quickly!" During his campaign against the frozen-faced Hoover, he had assured a faltering nation: "There is nothing to fear except fear itself." And now, as he was to recall so often in later years, he was at the very center of the national paralysis and seemed himself to have contracted the well-nigh fatal infection.

He roused himself and shouted. It was the only means of communication that had occurred to him. From the White House reception room came one of his press secretaries, Marvin H. McIntyre. Leaving her own office, Marguerite (Missy) Le-Hand, the president's personal secretary, joined them. The moment of paralysis passed. The work of national restoration began. Instead of trusting less to the democratic system, Roosevelt developed it to meet the needs of the nation. Instead of resorting to half-truth, innuendo, evasion, and censorship, he held more news conferences than any other president in American history.*

At the first of his nearly 1,000 meetings with the correspondents four days later, after the banks had been closed and Congress summoned into special session, Roosevelt tackled head-on the touchy business of a largely hostile, if temporarily chastened, press. Facing two hundred members of the crack Washington press corps in the White House with that superb self-confidence of which he was master, he said: "I am told that what I am about to do will become impossible, but I am going to try it. We are not going to have any more written questions; and, of course, while I cannot answer 75 or 100 questions because I simply haven't got the time, I see no reason why I should not talk to you ladies and gentlemen off the record."

Nothing he could have done at that moment was more calculated to win him the respectful attention, and even the sympathy, of the working press; what he was offering them was in effect a partnership in the speedy restoration of full communication between the American people and their government. Most presidents had paid lip service to freedom of information, but this one really believed in it. As the first hundred days of the

---

*During FDR's first term, he held 337 news conferences; in his second, 374; in his third, 279, and his partial fourth term, 8. Total: 998.

New Deal raced by, with exciting and momentous news each day, the Washington press corps realized that Roosevelt had meant what he said. Many of the newspaper publishers thenceforth could growl at "that Man in the White House" and denounce him day by day on their editorial pages as a menace to their concept of the American way of life, but he owned nearly all the front pages and the headlines. With the vast news-making powers of the presidency, he maintained a more potent influence over public opinion than the commentators and editorialists who loathed him. And when the opposition in the press became too strident, or when in his judgment the times demanded it, he could go on the commercially owned radio networks with a full-dress speech or a fireside chat to carry his programs directly to the people.

It was clear enough that Roosevelt, in his first two terms, subscribed to the theory that continued tension between a free press and a democratic government is a healthy and desirable position. He had found through experience that he was able to get his position across to the people without trouble through the news columns of the newspapers, the radio, and the newsfilm of the time. As for the continued editorial attacks on his program, his cabinet, his family, and himself, he took that as a part of the less attractive side of the presidency and answered in kind. As he once said in another context, "I love a good fight!" He seldom pulled back from any encounter with the press; more often than not, he lashed out with blows as sharp as any he received.

"Freedom of the press," he once said, "means freedom of expression, both in news columns and editorial columns. Judging by both these columns in papers in every part of the country, this freedom is freer than it ever has been in our history."

There was reason for the average newsman (not necessarily the mighty Washington correspondents) to be grateful to the New Deal. Through the voluntary codes of the National Recovery Administration and, later, the Wagner Act, the wages of the working press rose substantially within a few years. Better still, the hours of work for many in newspaper newsrooms were reduced to forty a week or less; with the rest of the employed population, they had benefited from the Wage-Hour Act and the Social Security Act. In the process, the fledgling American Newspaper Guild had established itself as a labor union with sufficient power to conduct strikes that interfered with some newspapers and, in cooperation with the mechanical unions, forced others to suspend publication. It was an unhappy projection of things to come.

Such economic warfare, stimulated in some cases by New Deal agencies that sided with unions against employers, intensified the friction between government and a considerable segment of the press. Despite that, Roosevelt still had no real trouble in putting his case before the American people day by day. Much as he complained of unfairness and distortion, a stock posture during his first two terms, he could say just before the outbreak of World War II: "Government restrictions on the press amount to little more than laws to prevent the printing of obscene matter and articles calculated to incite rebellion. The press is as free as it cares to be or its economic condition permits it to be."

Basically, the reason for Roosevelt's triumph over the hostile newspapers of his day was the nature of the free press system in the United States and the expert professional use that he made of it. As an astute politician, he constantly reminded his journalistic enemies that they owed their prosperity to a public that was largely pro-New Deal and that they might be committing economic suicide if they failed to give the public — and the president — a reasonably fair break in their news columns. To a great extent, this is what happened; in effect, the contending interests of government and a critical press came into balance with benefit to the nation at large.

It was not Roosevelt's politics, but economic pressures, that changed the shape of the American press. From 2,200 English language dailies of general circulation in 1910, the total in the United States dropped to 1,878 in 1940 and the number of one-daily cities rose from 509 to 1,092 despite an increase of total newspaper circulation from 22 to 41 million. Between 1937 and 1939 alone, there were 165 daily newspaper mergers and suspensions. It was a time during which at least one-third of the salaried employees in the newspaper industry lost their jobs, reason enough for the remainder to be conscious of the protective measures of the New Deal. The rising competition of radio and the approach of another world conflict scarcely indicated any slackening in the process of press consolidations.

The buying, selling, and merging activities of Frank Munsey in New York City during the 1920s had only been a foretaste of things to come. In 1931, Pulitzer's New York *World* died—a victim of economic anemia—and became merely a word in the merged New York *World-Telegram*, flagship of the increasingly important Scripps-Howard chain of 19 papers. The Hearst empire, however, came apart during the depression and the lord of San Simeon had to turn his papers over to his bankers who merged and slashed in New York, Chicago, and elsewhere. Yet, it also was a time when the economics of better conducted newspaper groups favored the growth of the chains. From eight chains with 27 papers and 10 percent of daily newspaper circulation in 1900, the group publishers jumped to sixty with 300 papers and one-third of daily newspaper circulation in 1940. The Scripps-Howard, Knight, Gannett, Ridder, Cox, and Newhouse groups all based their future development on the sound management practices that enabled them to weather the depression. Moreover, it was a time when the total number of AM radio stations grew from 612 in 1930 to 814 a decade later, and the number of radio sets in use increased from 13 million to 51 million, with the new medium chipping off more than 10 percent of the advertisers' dollar.

The primacy of radio as a medium for bulletin-type news was conceded in the 1930s when the three American wire services began selling their news reports to the electronic news programs at home and abroad. Having wrested free of the restrictive arrangements of the grand cartel in 1934, the Associated Press found that it was involved in a competitive battle with its American rivals, United Press and International News Service. The UP, with the resources of the Scripps-Howard newspapers behind it, had begun selling news to radio stations as early as 1935. In the same year, the Hearst-owned INS followed suit. Toward the end of the decade, the AP no longer could hold out and offered its own radio news service. What this amounted to was that wire service news breaks were put out at the same time to all media, which gave radio an automatic lead over its slow-footed print competitor.

Thus, on the eve of World War II, an entirely nongovernmental communications network of press, radio, and film had been created in the United States under private ownership, independently operated and independently edited. Elsewhere in much of Axis-dominated Europe, the Soviet Union, Japan, and the East Asian coast, the news media either had been seized by governments or subverted to their will. Even in Britain, the first stronghold of the free press, the newspapers had remained dutifully silent during the constitutional crisis brought about by the love of King Edward VIII for Wallis Warfield Simpson until he was forced to abdicate. And in France, the national interest had been betrayed by a number of newspapers that shamefully sold out to Nazi agents. If Americans were disturbed at times by the noisy and undisciplined performance of their independent newspapers, they at least never had cause to doubt that this was in truth a press that remained free. For all its faults, it would serve them well in time of war, just as it had during the long and tragic armistice that was now drawing to a close.

On the 150th anniversary of the Congress of the United States, when people all over the world knew that the Axis powers were heading toward war, Roosevelt gave this stern response to suggestions that he should curb the free press lest it provide incitement to enter the conflict:

"I take it that no sensible man or woman believes that it [the free press] has been curtailed or threatened or that it should be. The influence of the printed word will always depend on its veracity; and the nation can safely rely on the wise discrimination of a reading public which, with the increase in general education, is well able to sort out truth from fiction. Representative democracy will never tolerate the suppression of true news at the behest of the government."

By virtue of such beliefs, Franklin Delano Roosevelt brought the United States safely through the worst economic crisis in its history without the impairment of its liberties while some of the most civilized nations on earth were yielding themselves to dictatorship. The even greater test of total war lay just ahead.

VII. Total War

1. The Fall of Europe

Hugh Baillie, president of the United Press, advised his clients confidentially on August 28, 1939 that the outlook in Europe was "extremely pessimistic ... all communications channels now thoroughly overhauled ... alternate routes arranged in event of breakdowns." With the signing of the Nazi–Soviet non-aggression pact five days before, Baillie had lost all hope that peace could be preserved. His fears that Hitler would strike against Poland were confirmed on August 31 during his last telephone call from the UP correspondent in Berlin, Frederick Oechsner. "The balloon," the correspondent said, "may go up tonight."

Never had the coming of war been so predictable. In Danzig that night, Lynn Heinzerling, an Associated Press correspondent, waited around his hotel lobby in troubled uncertainty until he heard a German officer leave a call to be aroused at 3:15 A.M. Then, he knew. As the big guns opened up in Danzig harbor at 4:47 A.M. on September 1, Heinzerling ran out of the hotel. A night watchman shouted at him: *"Es geht los!"* (It's beginning). On the waterfront, the correspondent saw the German warship *Schleswig-Holstein* hurling the first shells of World War II into the besieged Polish fortress on the Westerplatte Peninsula. Consequently, long in advance of Hitler's excited war speech before the Reichstag at 10 A.M. that day, the first war bulletins came streaming off the wires.

All that day and the next, while the British and French sought to agree on a firm position and Mussolini hesitated, the correspondents told of unbroken German successes by land and air as the weak Polish army was swept aside. For the first time, the world began to realize what Hitler meant when he threatened "total war." This was the *blitzkrieg*, awesome and frightening in its thoroughness and its impact. It was foreordained that Hitler would reject British and French demands to cease his attacks. And so, reluctantly and even fearfully, the great powers of Western Europe — with the exception of Italy — went to war.

They knew they couldn't save Poland. It was questionable, after the display of Nazi might in the East, whether the French and British could save themselves. With the proclamation of American neutrality on September 5, they had to face Hitler's panzers alone. In the temporary quiet along the Western front, there was a momentary hope that the Nazis would face trouble in the East when the Red Army suddenly moved to occupy part of Poland. But the Nazi–Soviet pact was scrupulously observed; between the two giants, little Poland was torn asunder.

Gorged with his conquest, Hitler offered peace on his own terms to the West. His press chief, Otto Dietrich, called in Louis Lochner of the Associated Press and suggested unofficial American mediation between the Third Reich, and Britain and France. Lochner picked a distinguished intermediary, James D. Mooney, president of General Motors Overseas Corporation, but Mooney's travels and conferences produced no good result. In a somewhat more meaningful signal to the Nazis, President Roosevelt persuaded Congress to repeal its arms embargo to permit American arms shipments to go to the Western Allies. But Hitler wasn't concerned. He really believed he was on the road to world dominion. With Russia as his ally in uneasy and mutual treachery, and with the United States in a posture bordering on material and moral disarmament, he turned to the West for his major attack.

In view of the traditions of Nazi journalism, which celebrated the efficacy of the monstrous lie, nobody in the West was greatly surprised when Hitler roughly thrust aside his professions of peace and shattered the false calm of the "phony war" against France. Paul Joseph Goebbels had long since served notice that total war meant the total use of the news media for belligerent purposes. As he put it: "News policy is a weapon of war. Its purpose is to wage war and not to give out information." In consequence, when the German press complained with one voice in the spring of 1940 that a new aggression was being planned by the dastardly British and French, the people of Western Europe understood that their time had come. The Nazis were about to wipe out the old scores of Versailles in blood.

Hitler gave the signal for the attack after his easy conquest of Denmark and Norway, which contrasted so sharply with Russian difficulties during the Winter war on Finland. Once again, the old Schlieffen Plan was invoked for the reconquest of France. Once again Germany struck through the neutral lowlands, this time overwhelming the Netherlands as well as Belgium. At Sedan on May 10, the heart of France's defense was pierced and the Maginot Line was outflanked. In Britain, the Chamberlain government fell. And out of the ruck of despair and defeat rose the magnificent figure of Winston Churchill, a leader to rank with the most illustrious in British history. As prime minister, he rallied a whole brave nation to combat by invoking the spirit of righteous war for the survival of free peoples and free institutions — a matchless theme against the barbarism of the Nazis.

To oppose Churchill's call to his people to endure "blood, toil, tears and sweat," the Nazis brought war correspondents to Rotterdam to show how the Luftwaffe had wiped out a great city *after* the Dutch surrender. Nothing could have been more calculated to turn world opinion against the Nazis, if they had indeed retained even a shadow of the world's respect. It was evident that neither the German High Command nor the German government had learned anything since their display of "schrecklichkeit" in 1914. If Rotterdam created an angry storm of world disapproval, the Third Reich showed no evidence that it cared. The panzers roared on.

In France, the story was different. There, an important part of the press had been subverted by the Nazis well in advance and it spread defeatism like a plague even before the Sedan breakthrough. By this means, and the added mistakes of a particularly stupid military censorship, the French people were kept in the dark while their government and their army crumbled before the aggressor. Few men fought. As the Nazis swept through the battlefields of World War I as if they had been amusement parks, the French army simply gave way. It was an affront to the heroic dead, an insult to the living.

On May 16, as Premier Paul Reynaud prepared to flee Paris, the Paris *Soir* noted: "The public is completely ignorant of the fact that the German advance has suddenly assumed such gigantic proportions." In the face of such a betrayal, the collapse of the French army could scarcely have been averted. But of the leaders who fought and lost or didn't fight at all, one still stood fast—Charles de Gaulle. In Britain, to which he fled, he raised the Cross of Lorraine, the banner of Free France, and rallied his underground Maquis to wage war without end against their conquerors. After Dunkirk, such men as Churchill and de Gaulle had to rally the human spirit against the Nazis, for they had little else with which to fight on the continent of Europe.

The effect was electric in the United States. For after the miracle of Dunkirk, the New York *Times* saluted the rescue of a British army of 400,000 men in this manner: "This shining thing in the souls of free men Hitler can not command, or attain, or conquer. He has crushed it, where he could, from German hearts. It is the great tradition of democracy. It is the future. It is victory."

Out of sheer admiration for Churchill's summons to Parliament on June 4, 1940 to "go on to the end" and "never surrender," the bonds of support for the Western Allies grew stronger and more durable in the United States. On June 10, the same day that Mussolini stabbed France in the back and put Italy into the war, President Roosevelt placed the material resources of the United States behind the opponents of force. Equally as important, the old sage of the Emporia *Gazette*, William Allen White, began organizing his Committee To Defend America By Aiding The Allies in a thousand American towns and cities. Many hundreds of speakers and advertisements, pamphlets and letters by the million besought the people of the United States to rally behind the British and oppose Nazi bestiality. Beside such an effort, the isolationist American First Committee found itself gravely handicapped by such unwelcome partners as the German-American Bund, a number of professional anti-Semites, pacifists, and William Randolph Hearst. In this manner, the struggle for America's heart and mind was joined for the second time in a quarter-century.

Britain, its faith pinned to the Royal Air Force, braced itself for the onslaught of the Luftwaffe in the closing week of the land war in France. The craven French government still clung to its censorship with the Nazi hordes pouring unchecked toward Paris. On June 10, the Reynaud regime secretly left for Tours and had the effrontery to order Jean Prouvost, the Minister of Information, to deny that it had happened. Dutifully, Prouvost repeated his official lie to the American correspondents, who didn't believe a word of it, and later told Pierre Lazareff: "*They* (the government) made me do something stupid. They told me to announce that we were staying when we knew perfectly well that we were about to leave. . . . We're running away."

Four days later, Paris fell but not a single American correspondent celebrated the Nazi triumph. The tone of the reporting to the United States was dismal. It was as if America itself had received an almost mortal blow. When Louis Lochner of the AP marched into Paris with the Nazis on June 14, he reported the swastika was flying over the Hotel Crillon, from which President Wilson had spoken to the French of a new world of peace and freedom. "It all seems so unreal," he wrote. To William Shirer of the Columbia Broadcasting System, who drove into Paris three days later, the Nazi occupation was tragic. "I had an ache in the pit of my stomach and I wished I had not come," he radioed. He met Walter F. Kerr of the New York *Herald Tribune* and Dorothy and Demaree Bess, who were among the few American correspondents remaining in the city, and from them learned of the incompetence of the fleeing French government. "I have a feeling," Shirer wrote, "that we're seeing here in Paris . . . the complete breakdown of French society."

In the Forest of Compiègne at 6:50 P.M. on June 22, the victorious Hitler forced his armistice terms on the French envoys sent by the doddering chief of state of Vichy France, Marshal Henri Philippe Petain. It was signed within view of the monument bearing this legend: "Here on November 11, 1918, was frustrated the criminal arrogance of the German Imperial Reich, defeated by the Free Peoples which it sought to enslave." And so, France fell to a ruthless conqueror who had struck from without and within. Shirer broadcast to the United States: "What a turning back of the clock, what a reversing of history." And from London, the calm voice of Edward R. Murrow assured his fellow Americans: "We wait undismayed the impending assault."

The effect of such correspondence, by radio and in print, was incalculable in the United States. For this was the impact of the news, the single most powerful force in the shaping of public opinion in a democratic society. Reinforced by Churchill's masterful oratory, to which tens of millions listened by radio, and the propaganda drive of the White Committee, Allied support reached formidable proportions in the United States by the fall of 1940.

In the presidential campaign of that year, Wendell Willkie, the Republican candidate, supported Roosevelt's pro-Allied policies and in some ways was even more of an interventionist than the leading Democrats. At this juncture, however, the country was by no means ready to go to war and the president, seeking an unprecedented third term, was well aware of it. He campaigned, therefore, on a platform of aid to the Allies that would be "short of war."

It was perhaps the strangest election in the history of the presidency of the United States. All that summer and fall, the Battle of Britain was being fought with a fury and tenacity that gripped the world's attention. Among many Americans, there was a tendency to identify themselves entirely with the British who were withstanding the Luftwaffe's bombing of London. And this was undoubtedly due, in large part, to the persuasive and dramatic reporting of radio correspondents such as Murrow and Quentin Reynolds, among others. The British came to realize that it was more important for Americans to know what was going on, in some respects, than to spread the news in England. Once, when William McGaffin of the AP pushed his way through fire lines in London's West End, shouting that he was an American reporter, a tin-hatted bobby made way for him with the cheerful advice: "Tell the States about it. Best thing you can do." And Murrow, in his deep and saddened voice, burst out on August 18, 1940, after relating the stories of London and Coventry and the Channel ports: "If the people who rule Britain are made of the same stuff as the little people I have seen today, if they understand the stuff of which the people who work with their hands are made and if they trust them, then the defense of Britain will be something of which men will speak with awe and admiration so long as the English language survives."

Roosevelt did not wait until Election Day to show the depth of his own sympathy with the Allied cause. For something more than mere sentiment was involved now. With the signature of the Tripartite Pact of 1940, the Axis powers and Japan had bound themselves to come to the aid of any one of them that became involved in an American war. It was no campaign move, therefore, that led the president to strengthen his cabinet with the addition of two Republicans, Henry L. Stimson as secretary of war and Frank Knox, the publisher of the Chicago *Daily News*, as secretary of the navy. Nor was it a mere gesture toward Britain that Roosevelt made when he approved the exchange of fifty over-age American destroyers for leases on British bases in the Atlantic. The adoption of the first peacetime conscription in American history showed the direction in which the country was moving.

In November, with the reelection of Roosevelt to his third term in the White House, the Nazis saw how solidly the public was arrayed against them on both sides of the Atlantic. Having lost the battle for Britain, they now were confronted with the certainty that American war matériel would be flowing across the Atlantic in increasing quantity—and, perhaps, American troops as well. Although, at the time, no one knew or could even guess how or when the United States would enter the conflict.

The president stated the issue before Congress in January, 1941, in the moral terms best calculated to appeal to American opinion. It was nothing less than armed support of the nations that were fighting for what he termed the Four Freedoms: freedom of speech and expression, freedom of religion, freedom from want, freedom from fear. Accordingly, he submitted the Lend-Lease Act and obtained favorable congressional action; it marked the beginning of a program of aid for the Allies in weapons and food that would amount eventually to $50 billions. That spring, with the sinking of an American freighter by a Nazi submarine, he proclaimed an "unlimited national emergency." In the following month, all Axis consulates in the United States were closed and all bank assets frozen.

With the beginning of June, reports began cropping up on wire service files and other foreign correspondence that an unusual concentration of Nazi troop strength was growing on the German–Soviet border. As early as April, Churchill privately warned Stalin that Hitler was about to attack. From American sources, Roosevelt also became convinced that Hitler's next move would be against the Soviet Union and informed the Soviet ambassador, Constantine A. Oumansky. If Stalin was suspicious of anything that came out of the West, he could have turned for confirmation to his own spy ring in Japan, headed by the pseudo correspondent, Richard Sorge; on May 20, Sorge had warned Moscow that a Nazi attack in an overwhelming strength of 170 to 190 divisions was expected on or about June 20. As a matter of fact, Stalin's own commanders outside Leningrad reported for weeks in advance that the Germans were massing in strength on the border, that the Luftwaffe was conducting daily reconnaissance flights over Soviet territory, and that enormous numbers of tanks were being brought up for undetermined purposes.

But like Hitler, Stalin was sealed off from reality. He chose to believe that the Nazis were only conducting a war of nerves against him and would not really attack in force. In consequence, he swept aside both press reports and private intelligence; in mid-June, he even authorized Tass to deny that the Nazis were about to attack the Soviet Union. It was one of the grossest miscalculations in history. For with the fall of Europe, Hitler had decided that the Soviet Union must be destroyed and he never deviated from his intention to attack.

When Hitler unleashed his invasion force on June 22, Churchill had taken the precaution to concert his views in advance with the American government and was able that night to promise aid to the Russians. In a worldwide radio address, he proclaimed: "Any man or state who fights on against Nazidom will have our aid. Any man or state who marches with Hitler is our foe.... It follows, therefore, that we shall give whatever help we can to Russia and the Russian people. We shall appeal to our friends and allies in every part of the world to take the same course and pursue it, faithfully and steadfastly, to the end."

It was the beginning of the uneasy coalition that doomed the Third Reich.

2. The Power of the Soviet Union

To the Russian people, inured though they may have been to government by secrecy, duplicity, and deceit, the Nazi attack came as a shock. It was something for which the vast Soviet propaganda apparatus and its master, Joseph Stalin, had not prepared them in the slightest. The monstrous chicanery of the Nazi–Soviet pact, through which he had hoped to involve his European rivals in a war of mutual destruction, had become instead the shield behind which the attack on his own people had been mounted. Until the last, he had refused to permit the Soviet communications network to circulate any of the well-founded reports of Nazi preparations that were current in the West.

This was Stalin's folly. Trapped by his own poor judgment, he doomed his commanders along the border with Germany by refusing to give them permission to resist even after the invasion began. No newspaper, no radio, no street corner speaker was able to sound the alarm in the Soviet Union until the people themselves came under enemy attack. Thus, when the Nazis swarmed into the Russian heartland on June 22, 1941, the Soviet propaganda machine was hopelessly thrown out of gear. The "Imperialist War" overnight had to be presented to the Russian people as the "Great Patriotic War." The partnership with Hitlerite Germany, through which Stalin had shared in the dismemberment of Poland, the rape of Finland, and the capture of the Balkan states, now had to be denounced as an infamous, inhuman betrayal.

It was no wonder that thousands of soldiers deserted the Red Army in the opening days of the war, that tens of thousands of Russian villagers in the oppressed West and South came to greet their conquerors with grateful smiles and flowers of welcome. Had it not been for Hitler's policy of wanton destruction of all who stood before him in Russia, friend and foe alike, Stalin almost certainly would have faced the prospect of major defections to the enemy. But Hitler directed his racial madness against the Russians with a virulence that was exceeded only by his bestiality against the Jews. It did not take very long for the Russian people, particularly those in the path of the Nazi advance, to learn what was in store for them if they gave themselves over to the mercies of Hitler's Germans. Between Nazi savagery and the opportunity for self-defense that their own desperate and disorganized regime offered them, there could be only one choice. The Russian lines hardened. The people of the Soviet Union massed against the invader. And soon, despite the quick advance of his armies, Hitler's opportunity to spread division and disunity among the peoples of Muscovy had vanished forever. Once more, he had underrated the potential of the human spirit.

The Stalin of those critical days, even to his own associates, was scarcely the mighty and omnipotent dictator that he pictured himself to be in the controlled literature of the time. Once Hitler had attacked, Stalin shut himself up in the Kremlin—a cringing victim of his own misjudgment. To Nikita S. Khrushchev, speaking before the Twentieth Party Congress in Moscow on February 24-25, 1956, the Soviet dictator was a well-nigh paralyzed figure for days immediately after June 22, 1941. "After the first severe disaster and defeat at the front," Khrushchev recalled, "Stalin thought that this was the end. . . . He said, 'All which Lenin created we have lost forever.' . . . Not Stalin but the party as a whole, the Soviet government, our heroic army, its talented leaders and brave soldiers, the whole Soviet nation—

these are the ones who assured the victory in the Great Patriotic War."

Khrushchev, who was in Kiev at the time, found that Stalin had neglected to provide the Red Army with sufficient tanks, artillery, and even rifles to mount resistance against the foe. He telephoned Georgi M. Malenkov, who was with Stalin in Moscow, and appealed for help. Malenkov replied coldly: "We cannot send you arms. We are sending all our rifles to Leningrad and you have to arm yourselves."

And yet, despite all the negligence and incompetence and treachery of the dictator in the Kremlin, the Russians rallied. Before Leningrad, a city of 3 million, the Nazi siege lines formed but neither bullets nor hunger nor pestilence could undermine the Russian will to resist; before the heroic 900 days of Leningrad were over, a million of the besieged were to die but Hitler would never conquer the city of Lenin, Ivan, and Peter the Great. Along the old Napoleonic invasion route, the Nazis swarmed in such overwhelming force that it seemed nothing could stop them. But outside Moscow, the hastily improvised defense lines held. In the Russian press and the radio network, the journalists, historians, and poets spread their appeals to their people to stand fast.

Less than six weeks after the invasion, Ilya Ehrenburg wrote scornfully on August 5 in the Red Army newspaper, *Red Star*, of the predictions in the captured mail of a Nazi SS officer that Nazi troops would be in Moscow within a week: "They will not enter our Moscow. They forget that brave and proud people live on the Soviet land." This was the theme that was carried in *Pravda*, *Izvestia*, and the rest of the Soviet press by the most talented and widely read of Soviet writers — among them Ehrenburg, Mikhail Sholokhov, Konstantin Simonov, and Vassily Grossman. In the age-old Russian manner, they appealed to the Russian love of their land and their pride of heritage. They sought by every means at their command to rouse their people to the defense of a system of government that had few friends in the outside world. None questioned the traditional tight censorship in the Soviet Union; with only defeats to report in the early months, the news was so bad that neither the evasions nor the distortions of the censors seemed to matter very much. In the dwindling ranks of the male civilian population, the growing shortage of food and the devastating ruin that marked the Nazis' progress, the Russian people could see quickly enough that the war was going badly and very likely would grow worse.

It didn't require much skill on the part of Paul Joseph Goebbels and his Nazi propagandists to create a worldwide impression at the outset of the invasion that Russia could not last long. The news told its own story. The well-informed Frank Knox, in the Navy's office in the Pentagon, expected the Red Army to last only about six weeks. Most American and British war correspondents wrote that it wouldn't take the Nazis even that long. The New York *Times* disliked the notion of sending American supplies to the Soviet Union because they might fall into Hitler's hands instead. Even President Roosevelt was inclined to think of the Soviet defense as a "diversion." To Admiral William D. Leahy, he wrote: "I do not think we need worry about any possibility of Russian domination."

Such beliefs worsened the Soviet position among Western nations, particularly in the United States. Where public opinion had to be taken into account in the determination of policy, the hard facts of the Nazi advance could not be disregarded. In the absence of evidence to the contrary, many Americans feared in the early weeks of the Red Army's resistance that material support for Moscow's cause might boomerang. A whole generation of anti-Soviet propaganda in the United States could not be set aside overnight.

Consequently, even though President Roosevelt had agreed privately with Churchill on the need for helping the Russians, it wasn't easy to come right out and say so in the suspicion-laden atmosphere of neutral America. The President's first step was to cancel the freezing of $40 million in Soviet funds in the United States. But when a reporter asked him at a press conference whether this meant the defense of the Soviet Union was vital to the defense of the United States, he replied with a grin: "How old is Ann?" After he noted that there wasn't too much press opposition to the release of Soviet funds, he permitted the State Department to announce that the Soviet Union would be excluded from the provisions of the Neutrality Law. Translated from the diplomatese, this meant American war materials soon would be going into such Russian ports as Archangel and Murmansk. Stalin took note of the changed atmosphere in a radio speech to the Russian people on July 3, saying: "Our war for the freedom of our country will merge with the struggle of the peoples of Europe and America for their independence, for democratic liberties."

And yet, the new champion of "democratic liberties" was hardly more enthusiastic than he had ever been to embrace the governments headed by those two erstwhile "warmongers," Winston Churchill and Franklin Delano Roosevelt. It was only when Harry Hopkins came to Moscow on July 30 as Roosevelt's special envoy that the wartime coalition against the Axis began to take substantial form. It was a mark of Stalin's desperation that he permitted relaxation of Soviet censorship to allow American correspondents to file unexpurgated accounts of an interview with Hopkins. Contrary to Khrushchev's sour view of Stalin as a wartime leader, expressed long after the war, Hopkins obligingly depicted him in an article for the *American* magazine as an "austere, rugged, determined figure" who would lead the Soviet Union to victory.

By mid-September, Stalin had gained sufficient confidence to permit foreign correspondents to take escorted tours of the front. Military briefing officers from the Red Army presented the unwarranted view that the *Blitzkrieg* already had failed. As the more realistic correspondents recognized, the estimate was overly optimistic. And yet, yielding to evidence of hardening Soviet resistance, they began revising their notion of a quick Soviet collapse. Despite Goebbels' cries that the Russians were through, world sentiment began to shift slowly as the Nazi advance slowed all along the front. It was the first damaging blow to Nazi credibility.

Through the familiar but ever-fascinating process of American self-deception, the Soviet Union's public image underwent a remarkable change. In the liberal-minded press along the Atlantic seaboard, it became fashionable to include the Soviet among the pillars of what was euphemistically known as the Free World. The Red Army, in its heroic resistance to the Nazi hordes, took its place in history somewhere between Napoleon's Old Guard and the Grand Army of the Republic. As for Stalin, his bloody crimes no longer seemed so important; in fact, his image took on such an aura of benevolence that the president of the United States publicly referred to him as "Uncle Joe." Even in wartime, such a change necessarily imposed a strain on the belief of a very large part of the American public in the good sense of its government and at least a part of the news media. The fragility of hope in the future intentions of the Soviet Union could not be disguised so readily by the tattered raiment of expediency.

3. The Misfortunes of War

Secretary of War Henry L. Stimson had just finished a leisurely Sunday dinner at his Washington home on December 7, 1941, when he was summoned to the telephone by an excited and alarmed Franklin Delano Roosevelt. "Harry, come down here at once," the president snapped. "The Japs have struck." When Stimson asked if it had happened in Southeast Asia, FDR exclaimed, "Southeast Asia, hell! Pearl Harbor!" At that moment the nation already had heard the incredible announcement over its radios: "Air raid Pearl Harbor. This is no drill." In the next few hours, the world knew that some of the American Pacific fleet had been sunk or put out of action and that the Japanese also had attacked the Philippines and other major points in Southeast Asia. The declarations of war that followed the "day of infamy" were formalities.

If the Russians had been surprised by the Nazi attack in June because Stalin chose to seal them off from all warnings, both published and private, the Americans certainly had no such excuse for their unpreparedness at Pearl Harbor in December. For weeks before the blow fell, both the government and the people of the United States had had ample notice of Japan's hostile intentions. The files of both the Domei agency and the American wire services for the fall of 1941 were full of threats of a Japanese attack, as were the columns of leading newspapers, although the precise targets necessarily were guesswork. In addition, the United States Navy had broken the Japanese code and was intercepting all messages to Japan's "peace" negotiators in Washington, which made Premier Hideki Tojo's intentions even more apparent. Finally, Joseph Grew, the United States ambassador in Tokyo, had warned Washington privately as early as November 3 that a sudden Japanese attack could be expected without a declaration of war. On November 27, the War Department's final alert message was sent to the commanders at Pearl Harbor, but they did not take sufficient precautions. And so, as *Time* sardonically reported, the Navy was "caught with its pants down."

Under the circumstances, President Roosevelt would have been justified to extend to the continental United States the curtain of censorship that was hastily lowered over the disaster at Hawaii. To the faint of heart in the American government, it seemed at the time that the island outpost would have been wide open for enemy occupation if the Japanese had realized the extend of their advantage. Whether FDR believed this or not, he proceeded two days after Pearl Harbor to frame the most liberal policy for the handling of war news in American history. The principle governing the issuance of news under the War Powers Act, he said, was that it "must be true and must not give aid and comfort to the enemy." Although he initially made the armed forces the arbiters of what would help the enemy, he became the first to realize that this was no solution.

Instead, on December 16, he announced a policy of voluntary press censorship in keeping "with the best interests of our free institutions." He rejected the fanfare and drum-beating of the Creel Committee and the other nonessential trappings of World War I by calling on the executive news editor of the Associated Press, Byron Price, to be the director of the Office of Censorship. Price was a newsman first and last and no press agent or promoter — and that was his strength.

As events were to demonstrate, no better choice could have been made to carry out the Code of Wartime Practices for the American press that was enacted on January 15, 1942. As a veteran Washington editor, Price had the respect of his colleagues and a fine reputation for impeccable news judgment. Although neither he nor his office had authority to order anybody to do anything in publishing or withholding news, it soon became evident that his office's request to defer publication of an item was usually sufficient to insure compliance. His organization, which reached a peak strength of 14,000, functioned smoothly and with remarkably little fuss or criticism throughout the war.

The Office of Censorship could not, of course, originate news or conduct the propaganda campaigns that were so necessary to the prosecution of the war. Nor was Price the man to thrust himself forward to be at the President's elbow or to fight with the secretaries of war or navy or the leaders of Congress over news policies. For these and other reasons, the Office of War Information was created by Executive Order of the White House on June 13, 1942. It was a peculiar operation in many respects, being thrown together in a merger of four other organizations of ill-defined purpose, and both the press and the military were suspicious of it from the start. It did seem like a haven for a lot of fuzzy-brained intellectuals.

What really saved the OWI from unmitigated disaster was the selection of Elmer Davis as its director; once again, Roosevelt was most fortunate in his choice of men. For as an erstwhile Rhodes scholar, New York *Times* reporter, and radio newscaster, Davis was the complete professional. It was his misfortune that he had to deal so often with amateurs in the combined government news and propaganda bureau that employed about 10,000 people at its peak and spent $132.5 million in the three years and three months of its existence.

From the outset, Davis had to contend with the familiar military resistance to any admission of defeat and the equally characteristic stance of a critical press that doubted he could change the military mind. When the first American victories occurred — the Jimmy Doolittle air raid over Tokyo and the sea battles at

Midway and the Coral Sea—the Navy had been prompt enough to announce them. But losses there and at Guadalcanal were hidden to such an extent that Ernest K. Lindley complained in *Newsweek* that the Navy might be "trying to protect itself from public examination or criticism."

There was a lot of bad news. The Japanese had taken Bataan and Corregidor, just missing the capture of the Pacific commander, General Douglas MacArthur, who had been flown to Australia. Singapore and the Dutch East Indies had fallen. Rumors flooded the continental United States of still worse to come.

Davis saw that extreme measures were needed to bolster American credibility. He went over the heads of the military directly to the president. "The only sure cure for falsehood," he said, "is the truth." Roosevelt backed him up. Bit by bit, the admissions of losses through land, sea, and air action were pried out of the armed forces. For Davis, these were hard and bitter days when every victory, however small, was to be savored and every defeat measured for the amount of war weariness and resignation it might spread among the American people.

"OWI was compelled, most of the time, to fight a war on two fronts," Davis said. "We were hired to fight Dr. Goebbels and his allies of the Japanese and Italian propaganda ministries; but for at least two or three months out of every year, while our appropriation was going through Congress, the heads of the agency had to devote more time and energy to repelling the attacks of our enemies at home than we were able to spend on Dr. Goebbels and our other enemies abroad."

Despite the enormity of the propaganda and censorship efforts in the United States, it was remarkable that there was so little interference with the correspondents either in Washington or at the various war fronts, and that the American press and radio continued to operate with minimal disruption. No matter how determined Davis was to tell the American story to the world in its best aspects, he was the first to concede that this was not really his primary job. Under the encouragement of the supreme commanders, General Dwight David Eisenhower in Europe and

General MacArthur in the Pacific, the press handled the essential task of war coverage much more thoroughly than it had ever done before.

In the face of wartime shortages and other pressures, the number of daily newspapers published in the United States decreased by only 135 during the war years. Between 1941 and 1945, paper consumption had to be cut by 20 to 37 percent, but circulation actually jumped 10 million copies a day during that time to a high of 50 million at the war's end. This gain was made in the face of competition from radio and the news magazines, a fairly general increase to five cents a copy, and the necessary omission of considerable advertising for which there was no room.

Even more important, the press went through the war with its rights under the First Amendment intact. If anything, the scope of the free press clause was actually broadened by the decision of the United States Supreme Court on December 8, 1941, the day after Pearl Harbor, which upheld the right of newspapers to publish fair comment on pending court cases. In so doing, the high court dismissed a finding that the Los Angeles *Times* had been in contempt for publishing such a commentary in a labor dispute. The test set in the judgment was whether there had been a "clear and present danger to the administration of justice" because of the newspaper's criticism. In ruling that this was not the case, the decision went on: "The likelihood, however great, that a substantive evil will result cannot alone justify restriction upon the freedom of speech or of the press."

It was a good augury for the rights of free peoples, even in time of war, and the events of World War II justified the confidence that the ruling engendered. Under the stress of necessity, the American press and radio, with few exceptions, made handsome contributions to the prosecution of the war. After Pearl Harbor, even the leader of the isolationist press, the Chicago *Tribune*, muted its attacks on the government. The pro-Germanism of the Hearst newspapers was not quite so blatantly displayed. Of the subversive sheets that the government either prosecuted or put out of business under the Espionage Act, only one, the Rev. Charles E. Coughlin's *Social Justice*, had any following of political consequence.

This is not to say that the Roosevelt administration was able to escape criticism, that the conduct of the war was not carefully scrutinized, or that the isolationist wing of the press changed character. Far from it. The unquestioned obedience that Stalin could exact from the controlled Soviet press, or even the disciplined compliance that was willingly granted to Winston Churchill by the British press, more often than not, simply could not be expected from the highly individualistic American press system.

Every now and then, something broke loose in the United States. At one point, the Chicago *Tribune* revealed that the United States had broken the Japanese code, an unnecessary demonstration of press enterprise; fortunately, the Japanese were not steady readers of the "world's greatest newspaper" and were none the wiser. As for the wartime secrecy that shrouded the president's movements, it drew protests from even liberal-minded but still competitive journalists. One of the best, Raymond Clapper, complained that Roosevelt had carried "the whole technique of the controlled press far beyond anything we have experienced in this country."

In the afterglow of history, the accusation scarcely seems justified. This war was, by all odds, the most openly reported conflict in which the United States has ever been involved, with some 2,000 correspondents in action on all fronts for American news organizations. It was also the least censored of American wars since the Revolution and the War of 1812, when censorship wasn't really a problem. Despite all the concern in the highest echelons of government that a loutish and highly irresponsible press would leak secrets, it didn't happen to a degree that mattered. There were no journalistic equivalents of the scientists who became atomic spies — Klaus Fuchs of Britain, Bruno Pontecorvo of Italy, and Allan Nunn May of Canada. The two journalists who were traitors to the United States in World War II, Robert H. Best and Douglas Chandler, received life terms in prison for making paid broadcasts from Nazi Germany while in the service of Paul Joseph Goebbels. The only damage they did was to themselves.

Unlike the ever-critical attitude of the American press toward its government, British proprietors and editors were much more generous toward their coalition war cabinet. For one reason, Winston Churchill was a symbol of national unity in a land that was in the front lines of the war from beginning to end. For another, the country was small enough to make unified action possible among the press when the government circulated a D (for Defense) notice against publishing information that might give aid and comfort to the enemy. The Defense of the Realm Act was much stiffer and a great deal tougher than the American voluntary censorship. Yet, the only paper of importance in Britain that suffered suppression during the war was the Communist *Daily Worker*.

The British press, like the British people, carried on despite all obstacles. The printing plants of the *Times*, *Daily Herald* and *Evening Standard* all suffered direct hits by Nazi bombs in London. Fires that spread from other London air raids severely damaged the offices of the *Telegraph*, *Sketch*, *Daily News*, and *News of the World*. Outside London, provincial papers also suffered, notably in Coventry, Cardiff, and Belfast.

In addition to war damage, severe shortages of paper, printing materials, and staff reduced most Birtish papers to slim sheets that could barely compete with the news services of the BBC. Yet, even with radically increased costs and much higher charges for the relatively small amounts of available advertising space, the British press yielded neither its independence nor its fidelity to the public service. It had a more difficult time with its censors, notably Brendan Bracken, the head of the British Ministry of Information, than did the Americans with their less formal machinery. However, when all else failed, an appeal to the old journalist, Churchill, usually produced the news the papers wanted. With such resources, the British newspapers came out of the war with a 33 percent increase in circulation, going from 19 million daily sales in 1938 to 25 million in 1945.

As for the Soviet Union, Stalin found it much easier to use the foreign press in his incessant campaign for a "Second Front" than to communicate with his own people. The Nazi invasion had come very close to shattering the powerful Soviet communications network. At least half the radio stations in the country were destroyed, closed down, or in enemy hands before the end of 1942. Much of the paper-producing lands were seized by the foe; as to the rest, precious transport had to be used primarily for military supplies. Close to 3,000 newspaper plants were wrecked or captured out of the 8,000 that had been operating at the beginning of the war. The rest worked only sporadically due to lack of personnel and supplies. *Pravda* and *Izvestia* still put out four pages, but the larger provincial papers had to be satisfied with two. From a high of 40 million copies daily, circulation slumped by at least 10 million and perhaps more. Soviet figures in this respect were never very convincing in wartime.

No less than the independent newspapers of the West, which for the most part freely cooperated with their governments, the controlled press of the Soviet Union played an important role in the struggle. After the initial efforts at concealment failed, notably the investment of Leningrad, it must have occurred to the Kremlin that the dullest-witted Soviet citizen could see for himself how desperate the situation of the nation really was. Consequently, Soviet propaganda often made a virtue of necessity by drumming bad news into its people. Through high-flown rhetoric and constant persuasion, the elite among Soviet writers linked forces with the Red Army's combat correspondents to call for greater resistance to the Nazis.

Describing a 600-mile journey through burned villages and looted farms where the Nazis had even machine-gunned the animals to death, the wrathful Ilya Ehrenburg wrote in the worst days of war: "My generation has lived through much. This is not the first war I have seen. But I cannot write calmly about what I see here. A Tommy gun, not a pen, is needed. We do not dare to die, we older people, without saying to ourselves before death: this will not happen again. Conscience demands vengeance, expiation, the triumph of justice."

It was a theme that was endlessly repeated in every description of the horrors that Nazi troops left behind them — piles of corpses, ruined cities, shattered homes. Hitler's bestial treatment of the Slav peoples as subhuman, something a certain class of German was always willing to believe, was turned against him. Simply by printing and broadcasting the terrible truth about the excesses of the invading armies, the Soviet propaganda organization was able to demonstrate convincingly that the only hope of the Russian people was to fight.

In addition to such appeals to the home front, the Soviet military gave careful attention to the foreign correspondents who were swarming into Moscow in the opening months of the war and who later followed the diplomatic corps to Kuibyshev. Here, the argument that was dinned into the foreign press was the Red Army's capacity for resistance, the need for help from abroad, the opening of a "Second Front," and the solidarity of the Soviet people. Even before the battle for Moscow itself had been joined, some of the Soviet briefing officers were forecasting a German defeat, which was scarcely justified by the facts at that time. It would be two years more before the German offensive could be stopped and the long and disastrous retreat from the heart of Russia would begin. Until then, the misfortunes of war in the United States, Britain and the Soviet Union would be many and there would be no way of hiding them.

4. Tragic Victory

By the summer of 1942, Hitler had 240 divisions of more than 3 million men pounding the Russians on a front that stretched from besieged Leningrad in the North to the Caucasus in the South. A threat to Moscow had been turned back, but the Nazis had pounded onward to Stalingrad. There, Hitler centered all his efforts from the middle of August, 1942, demanding a victory from his commanders that it was not in their power to achieve. In November of that year, the *Berliner Boersenzeitung* gave the German public a breath-taking view of what was going on in Stalingrad:

"Never in all the history of wars has there been such a concentration of weapons in such a small space and for such a long time. Never before has a city fought till the collapse of the last wall. Paris and Brussels capitulated; even Warsaw agreed to capitulate; but in this battle, despite our numerical superiority, we are not achieving the necessary result."

One of the principal reasons the outside world did not fully appreciate the enormity of the Stalingrad struggle at the time it was being waged was the cautious Soviet policy of keeping foreign correspondents away and, at the most critical stage, holding up the work of even the most inspired Soviet combat correspondents. Necessarily, the Soviet objective was to sustain the nation's fighting spirit, not particularly to give the news in Western fashion, until the time seemed exactly right. Different correspondents, trained in and responsible to clashing systems of government, told the story of the battle on the Volga in their own way.

On September 25, 1942, *Izvestia* reported that the front line was very near the center of Stalingrad: "There, the fighting goes on in every house and in every yard." *Pravda* wrote of the battle as "our Verdun, Stalingrad." *Red Star* appealed to the troops on October 16: "Not one step back! Every stone must become a fortress." By November 12, describing what was later recognized as the final German offensive, *Red Star* reported heavy hand-to-hand fighting.

When the Soviet counteroffensive began on November 19 with the commitment of more than a million fresh troops to battle, there was no mention of it on the Soviet side for three days. And it was not until November 27, when the Russians split the doomed German Sixth Army, that the first note of triumph crept into a special communique. No correspondent even discussed the counterattack at length until Vassily Grossman published his estimate of the battle in *Red Star*. It was the middle of December before foreign correspondents in limited numbers were permitted to see for themselves what was going on and to write about it in the stiff, stylistic cadence of the hard news format.

Lieutenant General Konstantin Rokossovsky announced the surrender of Field Marshal Friedrich von Paulus's Sixth Army, which had lost 200,000 dead, on February 2, 1943, in these terms: "As a result of the final liquidation of the enemy forces, the military operations in the city area of Stalingrad have ceased." Hitler broke the news to his people next day over the German radio with a roll of muffled drums, Beethoven's Fifth Symphony, and an order for four days of national mourning. Coming so soon after the British desert victory at El Alamein and the Anglo-American landings on North Africa, Stalingrad sounded the knell of the Third Reich.

From that time on, the military strength of the coalition was applied with ever-increasing effectiveness against Hitler's Reich. Once General Eisenhower's Anglo-American armies had secured North Africa, invaded Italy, forced Mussolini to flee, and obliged Italy to surrender in the summer of 1943, all was in readiness for the cross-Channel invasion of Normandy. When Eisenhower gave the signal, Stalin was assured of the "Second Front" for which he had campaigned for three years. With the Red Army pushing West and the Anglo-American forces rolling East, a veritable race against time began for the possession of a once-powerful Germany.

No less than the Red Army's combat correspondents, the reporters of the West did their job with a flair and heroism that gave new heart and strength to the home front. The voices of Edward R. Murrow, Eric Sevareid, William L. Shirer, and their comrades of the American radio networks and the BBC were first with the news. But the more numerous and far-ranging newspaper correspondents appealed to an even broader and more concerned public. Such young combat reporters as Homer Bigart for the Americans and Alan Moorehead for the British were everywhere along the battle lines. But the greatest of all was one of the oldest, Ernie Pyle of the Scripps-Howard Newspapers, whose inspirational reporting was often as important to the troops at the front as it was to the millions who read him at home. He was the soldiers' friend, the biographer of GI Joe, the little man who always turned up in the thick of the fighting until a sniper's bullet killed him on April 18, 1945, on Ie Shima in the Pacific.

The contrast between Soviet and Western reporting methods in the war was best illustrated by the difference between the coverage given Stalingrad and the Normandy landings. Whereas Stalin always held up the news if he thought it was likely to make a difference in the outcome of battle, no such procedures were even considered in the West. On the night of June 5, 1944, 28 of 500-odd combat correspondents were selected to go in with the Allied invasion forces massed at British bases. One of the first to move, Walter Cronkite, a 28-year-old United Press combat correspondent, was awakened and put into a B-17 bomber of the United States Army Forces for a low-altitude dawn flight over the French coast. Some went in with the vanguard of a force of 2 million troops on June 6. Others parachuted with the first airborne units. But everywhere, the correspondents went under fire with the invasion force that was borne across the Channel by the greatest armada in the history of warfare.* Roelif Loveland of the Cleveland *Plain Dealer* wrote that day: "One will never forget the sight of the ships and the landing craft heading for France any more than a knight would have forgotten the appearance of the Holy Grail."

Ernie Pyle's orders came on June 7 when he went in with the First Division—the big red 1 of the United States Army. With the rest of his fellow correspondents who survived those first days, he kept going. He was in on the capture of Cherbourg, the Normandy hedgerow fighting, and the great infantry attack on St. Lo which was prefaced by a tragic American Air Force bombing of its own troops. That day, July 25, Pyle once again had a narrow escape, but many others died, among them Lieutenant General Lesley J. McNair and an AP combat photographer, Bede Irvin. Pyle's story went through censorship quickly, for such mistakes couldn't be covered up. After describing what had happened, he went on:

"I thought an attack by our troops was impossible then, for it is an unnerving thing to be bombed by your own planes. And

---

* Total casualties of American combat correspondents in World War II were 37 killed and 112 wounded.

yet, they attacked, and within an hour they sent word back that they had advanced 800 yards through German territory and were still going. Around our farmyard men with stars on their shoulders almost wept when the word came over the portable radio. The American soldier can be majestic when he wants to be."

That was the start of the American breakout in France and the beginning of the German collapse in the West. The liberation of Paris, the breakneck dash across the French countryside led by General George S. Patton's Third Army, the capture of the Rhine bridge at Remagen, and the invasion of Germany itself followed so quickly that the Nazis had no chance to rally for an effective resistance.

In vain did Paul Joseph Goebbels try to seize on the uses of adversity, as the British, Americans, and Russians had done with such success. It had been easy enough for him to crow over Nazi victories, but he did not know what to do once the tide turned. Mainly, he appealed to the Germans by radio to follow Hitler, the glorious leader. But after Hitler narrowly escaped assassination on July 20 and took massive vengeance on all about him, including so brilliant a general as Erwin Rommel, it became evident that the German nation—if given a chance— would have followed almost anybody but Der Fuehrer. The half-mad ex-corporal now proceeded to act as the supreme commander of his forces and designated little Goebbels as the dictator over civilian life in Germany. Two worse choices could not have been made in a nation at war.

When the Allied bombers rained destruction on German cities, Goebbels tried to hearten his people with slogans. He fought the advancing Russians with a hurricane of paper decrees that were mostly brushed aside by a fearful public. He organized a Volkssturm (People's Army), proclaimed a "People's War," and tried to persuade the youth to become guerrilla "werewolves." All this amounted to was radio rhetoric.

The effect of Goebbels' program of total mobilization for war did have a noticeable affect on the press. After Stalingrad, all cities of 100,000 population or less were limited to a single newspaper. After the Normandy landings, the remaining papers in the twenty major cities of the Third Reich, including Berlin and Vienna, also were merged. What happened was that nearly all independently owned newspapers vanished. What remained was the Nazi party press in particularly dull form.

By 1944, even the Nazi party press was down to 350 papers, which accounted for 80 percent of the total daily circulation of somewhere between 10 and 15 million (it may have been much less at critical periods). Most of the rest were very small papers; indeed, by 1944, only eight papers with more than 50,000 circulation remained in private hands. The Eher Verlag, which had been such a source of profit for Hitler, Amann, and other leading Nazis, became a liability. By early 1945 nearly all German newspapers resembled mere handbills and printed nothing more than official military bulletins and obituaries. It was the end of what had been the largest press in Europe. Amann pronounced its valedictory in strange terms for a Nazi: "How could an editor publish a good paper when he sat with one foot in jail and the other in the editorial room?"

Hitler had a final shock for the world. As the coalition armies raced over Germany in the final days of the war, they came across the death factories where millions of Nazi victims had died — 6 million of them Jews. Touring the first death camp he saw near Gotha, General Eisenhower wrote in emotional terms of the "indisputable evidence of Nazi brutality and ruthless disregard for every shred of decency."

The "indisputable evidence" had been available since 1942 and had been presented to the State Department in Washington, the Foreign Office in London, and elsewhere without arousing the world against a monstrous crime. As early as July 1, 1942, the Polish Government in Exile had announced the extermination of 700,000 Polish Jews in Nazi gas chambers. In the following month, Gerhart Riegner, the World Jewish Congress' representative in Switzerland, presented evidence to the American government that Hitler had decided to exterminate at least 4 million Jews in what he called his "final solution." From then on, both official Washington and London were besieged with appeals from the World Jewish Congress and other interested groups to act to save as many of the victims as possible. Refugees who had escaped from the murder camps were produced to tell their stories. Documents from Nazi sources, obtained through private espionage efforts, left no doubt as to what was going on in a doomed and vengeful Nazi Germany. But until the war correspondents began publicizing their findings, the civilized world did not really believe that there were charnel houses like Auschwitz, Buchenwald, Belsen, Dachau, and scores of others. Here were revealed, at last, the atrocities that will never be forgotten or forgiven by humankind—the racks of ovens where cremations were carried out, the piles of corpses waiting for incineration, enormous mass graves, human skeletons, human skin stretched into parchment and even lamp shades.

The appalling reaction in the West to the disclosure of the murder camps made impossible any negotiation with the Third Reich. Even if Hitler had been disposed to yield in the concluding days of the war, which he was not, no orderly surrender could have been arranged. On April 12, 1945, when Franklin Delano Roosevelt died and a shaken but determined Harry S Truman moved into the White House, the American commitment to "unconditional surrender" remained inviolate. However, in accordance with military agreements that had been made with the Soviet Union, General Eisenhower stopped his troops at the Elbe while the onrushing Soviet armies paused not at all until they were in Berlin. It was their hour of triumph and they made the most of it.

Over a gasoline station in Milan on April 29, 1945, an angry group of Italian partisans strung up the body of Benito Mussolini by the ankles and dangled the body of his mistress, Clara Petacci, beside him. They had been shot to death while trying to escape—the end of a career of betrayal that had begun twenty-five years before in the same city. That same day, the German armies in Italy surrendered unconditionally and the Italians once again assumed sovereignty over their own land.

For Hitler the end came on the following day, April 30. With the Russians only a short distance from his command bunker in Berlin, he shot and killed himself while poison disposed of Eva

Braun, his mistress whom he had married only a few hours before. The last act of his servants was to carry their bodies to
shallow graves, pour gasoline over them and set them aflame. It
was the same fate that Goebbels chose for himself and his wife
next day. When the Hamburg radio broke the news on the evening of May 1 with the usual Nazi flourishes, a roll of muffled
drums and solemn music, Germany was in total collapse and the
war had but a week more to go.

On May 7, through an unauthorized and unnecessary bit of
journalistic derring-do, the AP's Ed Kennedy flashed the end of
the war on the basis of an Eisenhower announcement, intended
to be held for official release, that the Germans had surrendered
unconditionally. However, in the worldwide elation over the end
of the conflict in Europe, which was officially confirmed May 8,
few except the correspondents who had been professionally injured by keeping faith with Eisenhower bothered to remember
the AP's tainted beat. Thus the guns at last fell silent and a
strange and disquieting peace came to Europe in the brightness
of a new spring.

Even as Hermann Wilhelm Goering, Julius Streicher, and the
rest of the unholy Nazi crew were rounded up to face judgment
at Nuremberg as war criminals, the final phase of the war began
in the Pacific. From Guadalcanal early in 1943, General Mac-
Arthur and Admiral Chester Nimitz had directed a tremendous
campaign against the Japanese by land and sea. The Japanese
island fortresses of Tarawa, Kwajalein, Eniwetok, and Saipan
were overrun one by one. And at length, in Leyte Gulf in 1944,
the power of the Japanese Navy was destroyed. From then on,
the fanatical kamikaze suicide pilots and the desperate "banzai"
charges by Japanese troops were all that the enemy had left.
Flight after flight of B-29 bombers pulverized Japanese cities
with devastating fire raids. Tojo, his desperate gamble against
American power a complete failure, was removed from authority
in 1944.

Even in the face of certain defeat, there was such fear of the
military throughout Japan that civilian life was totally regi-
mented. The challenging and defiant bulletins still went out over

the radio. The people continued to be called on to resist. The once-independent press, cowed after two decades of subjugation, was a bare shadow of itself. Only 55 daily newspapers were left in Japan out of the 1,200 that had existed at the beginning of the war, and these frequently could publish but a single page. Except for Tokyo and Oska, there was only one paper for each prefecture and they were restricted to military notices. As for Domei, the news agency, it was a mere source of transmission for the scraps of news the military made available to the public.

Slowly but inevitably, the Japanese people learned of more reverses — the loss of Iwo Jima (where Joe Rosenthal of the AP took the famous picture of the raising of the American flag on Mount Suribachi), the occupation of the Philippines, the fanatical and losing battle to save Okinawa. It is not likely that many Japanese outside the closely knit group about Emperor Hirohito heard much about the Potsdam conference, its call for Japanese surrender, and its final warning that "the alternative for Japan is prompt and utter destruction." Even if they had, it would not have meant much to them after having endured so many bombings and fire raids. For that matter, it meant nothing to the elder statesmen around the emperor who were trying somehow to find a way to end the war without losing everything.

Bin Nakamura, a subeditor of Domei News Agency at Hiroshima, cut short the debate on August 6, 1945, when he managed to reach a radio station in Haramura with an incredible eyewitness story of how his entire city had been destroyed by a single bomb, dropped from a single American B-29 bomber. The Japanese already had picked up President Truman's announcement of the explosion of an atomic bomb over Hiroshima, the terrible weapon at which he had hinted in the ultimatum given Japan at Potsdam. If they had been disposed to disbelieve its power, Nakamura's report served to correct their impressions.

Yet, publicly, the Japanese authorities were not yet willing to reveal the truth to their own people. The most they let out over the home radio network on August 7 was that a small number of new-type bombs, delivered by parachute, had exploded over Hiroshima and "a considerable number of homes" had been destroyed. It was apparent to the American command, as it was to the White House, that the Japanese still were not ready to surrender.

On August 9, another B-29 carrying a second atomic bomb took off from its Tinian base and dropped its lethal cargo over Nagasaki. This time an eyewitness report of the mission was written by William L. Laurence of the New York *Times*, who had been borrowed from his newspaper by the government to write the history of the Manhattan Project and the first nuclear explosion. Lawrence wrote of the terrifying white light as the bomb burst over Nagasaki and the death cloud shooting up from the stricken city—"a monstrous prehistoric creature with a ruff around its neck, a fleecy ruff extending in all directions as far as the eye could see."

It was enough. The mounting death toll in Nagasaki and Hiroshima and the threat of another atomic holocaust, perhaps this time Tokyo itself, convinced Emperor Hirohito that he must sue for peace. For almost a week, the wildest confusion seized the Japanese hierarchy. The Japanese military broadcast orders to the troops to stand fast and annihilate the enemy. The emperor's intimates used the home radio network to warn the people that important developments would soon be announced. Masses of the population, fearful of new atomic attacks, deserted the cities. In prisoner-of-war camps, the half-crazed military conducted ceremonial beheadings of American pilots and similar acts of bestiality reminiscent of the death march from Bataan.

Amid such anarchy, a frightening paralysis of the governmental process and an almost complete breakdown in communications within the country, anything seemed possible in Japan. The minister of war, General Korechita Anami, vacillated between his loyalty to the emperor and his fear of his military subordinates. The army's hard-core revolutionaries were everywhere, threatening to kill anybody who dared treat with the United States. But Hirohito stood firm, once he understood that his conquerors would permit him to remain on the Japanese throne. In the end, his will prevailed.

On August 14, Domei announced an imperial message accepting the Potsdam Declaration would be forthcoming soon. The military plotters tried to block it, but the only tangible result was General Anami's suicide by hara-kiri. On the following day, in a speech recorded for radio, Hirohito announced Japan's surrender and told his people they must seek peace by "enduring the unendurable and suffering what is insufferable."

The war did not end in China, for Mao Tse-tung's Communist brigades began taking over some of the northern provinces from the lethargic Chiang. The Soviet Union, having occupied the warm water ports of Dairen and Port Arthur in the closing days of the Pacific war, did its best to set up sympathetic regimes in Manchuria and North Korea. And in Southeast Asia, an experienced Communist revolutionary, Ho Chi Minh (He Who Enlightens), proclaimed the "Provisional Republican Government of Vietnam" although the French didn't take him seriously. Yet, after the formal Japanese surrender on September 2 aboard the U.S.S. *Missouri* in Tokyo Bay, very little of this new and disturbing alignment of forces on the mainland of Asia penetrated to the joyous people of the United States and Britain and the liberated peoples of Europe. For them, the war was over and nothing else mattered. Hadn't President Truman announced that the American government was giving first priority to "bringing the boys back home"?

With remarkable celerity, the news of events in Asia shrank from the columns of the Western press. There was a momentary flareup of interest when Hideki Tojo, the fallen war lord, tried to commit suicide but was saved for later execution with his fellow war criminals in Japan. Except for that, and the always vivid interest in the personality of Douglas MacArthur, whatever foreign news circulated in the West consisted mainly of matters of mutual interest affecting the United States, Britain, and Europe. The decisions of Tehran, Yalta, and Potsdam now were to be put into effect, Stalin willing. But even such events took second place in the American mass mind to such matters as the end of meat rationing, the manufacturers' plans for new automobile models, the possibility of workable television, and the ever-present cry: "Bring the boys back home." The United States was the greatest power on earth, but acted with the irresponsibility of a country village playing host to a state fair.

In this disorderly and disheartening way, the old order passed and a new age dawned for a deeply divided and troubled world. The smoke of battle had barely been dissipated when the victorious wartime coalition was shattered. Across the immense ideological chasm that separated them, the super-powers — the United States and the Soviet Union — glowered at each other in mutual dislike and distrust. Once the war emergency was over, all pretense ended. Together, they had achieved a tragic victory. But in the postwar world, they were enemies.

5. *The Press after Five Hundred Years*

More newspapers were read on earth after World War II than at any other time in the five hundred years since Johann Gutenberg had first printed a page from movable type in Mainz. Wherever persecuted peoples were liberated in Europe, there was a pell-mell rush to publish independent newspapers and read them. It amounted to a symbolic act, a declaration of freedom. For in the long night of anguish and torment that had descended over so many great and ancient lands, and taken the lives of so many millions of people, the first freedom to perish had been the freedom of the press.

From the enthusiasm with which the liberated publics seized upon the few available papers during and immediately after the war, there was some reason to believe at the outset that a golden age was dawning for the independent newspaper. It didn't turn out that way. Freedom, once degraded and chained, is not easily restored to her rightful place in all her virtue. And the free press, once it is subverted and destroyed, cannot often be rebuilt to win its way back into public favor and public trust without enormous and time-consuming effort.

These hard and unpalatable truths were demonstrated first in liberated France. The French public, which had been starved for good newspapers, sent postwar circulation booming to 15 million daily but the phenomenon did not last. Despite rising population and restored purchasing power, newspaper sales soon slumped by 33 percent to around 10 million. It was some comfort that the newly born *Le Monde* and the prewar holdover, *Le Figaro*, retained their hold on the public as the principal quality newspapers and that *France Soir*, the largest mass circulation daily, tried to improve its news coverage. But the public's initial craze for newspapers did not make itself evident again. Once the underground press surfaced, it was no longer as exciting as it had been in wartime.

In Italy, too, the first burst of enthusiasm for a liberated press quickly died away except for the *Corriere della Sera*, a few other substantial independent papers, and the leaders of the political party press. No one shed tears over the demise of *Popolo d'Italia*, the offices of which were wrecked before the shooting stopped. The circulation level of the restored press remained below 5 million copies a day, the prewar level, for a considerable period after World War II. A disillusioned citizenry, partly because of a discouraging literacy rate but basically through lack of interest, sank to one of the lowest levels of readership in Western Europe, 11 copies for each 100 persons.

In a divided Germany, where the Western Allies and the Soviet Union struggled for influence over postwar German opinion, the situation was somewhat different. After the death of the Nazi press, the Western Allies' military governments refused to revive the famous old papers of prewar Germany for fear of being contaminated by those that had been published under Nazi auspices, and the Soviet Union preferred to start anew. In the first year after the war, under strict licensing, forty-four papers were put out in the American zone, forty-two in the British, twenty-two in the French, and seventy-one in the Russian. However, the Germans didn't take kindly to a licensed press; even Axel Springer, who was to become the great press lord of postwar West Germany, had his troubles at the outset.

After four years of licensing, when the Germans were put on their own, about 350 dailies began operating in the Western zones under a new free press guarantee, but few were successful. The eventual leaders of the prestige press—*Die Welt*, the

Frankfurter Allgemeine and the *Süddeutsche Zeitung*—based their appeal on their independence of party affiliation. But they were overshadowed by a new kind of paper, popularized by Springer, who captured the body of German readers with his lively *Hamburger Abendblatt* and his tabloid *Bild Zeitung*.

In East Germany, the Soviet Union stimulated the creation of a German Communist press headed by *Neues Deutschland*, founded in 1946, with similarly controlled publications in Leipzig, Dresden, Halle, and Weimar. They took their line from the government and published what they were told.

The free press got off to a shaky start in tiny Austria after it was wrenched from Nazi control. But in Belgium, the Netherlands, Denmark, Norway, and Finland, the traditional patterns of independent popular newspapers were reestablished with sturdy public support. As for the neutrals, Switzerland and Sweden, their newspapers rendered noteworthy services throughout the war, particularly the *Neue Zürcher Zeitung*, the *Dagens Nyheter*, and *Svenska Dagbladet*, and carried on thereafter in their accustomed manner.

In Asia, where there had never been a very broad understanding of the principles of a free press and few centers capable of and willing to support independent newspapers, General Mac-Arthur decided to make a shining example out of democratic postwar Japan. He decreed that the Japanese would "develop a free and responsible press" as one of his first acts as supreme commander of the occupation forces. Before long, the Big Three of Japanese journalism—*Asahi Shimbun, Mainichi Shimbun*, and *Yomiuri Shimbun*—were publishing first-rate if somewhat sparse newspapers and attracting an increasingly enthusiastic public. It had been more than a quarter-century since the Japanese press had made even mild pretensions to putting out independent news and comment. Unlike the discouraging experience in Europe, circulation not only held in Japan; it actually continued to go up.

There was an excellent reason for this. Having been forced into a newspaper monopoly during the war, the Japanese were not about to return to their old practices of cut-throat competition. The Japanese press therefore became the only independent press of consequence in the world that did not have to go through the painful ordeal of mergers and closings due to rising economic pressures. It was not too many years before the leaders enjoyed some of the largest circulations in the world, each selling between 4 and 5 million daily.

A few other cheerful spots existed in liberated Asia. The United States had freed the Philippines on July 4, 1946, stimulating the growth of a wild, unruly, and indubitably free press. The British decision to leave the Indian subcontinent, leading to the creation of a free India and Pakistan in 1947, was another heartening development for the comparatively few newspapers that had fought to establish and maintain their independence.

Yet, liberation from colonial rule did not guarantee that a free press would automatically arise. That was evident when the Dutch pulled out of Indonesia and other new nations began emerging in Southeast Asia and the Arab world of West Asia. Moreover, in most of Africa and a large part of Latin America, control of the press remained a way of life for the dictatorial governments of developing countries and the waning colonial empires of the West.

To this had to be added the new colonialism of the Soviet Union, which was spreading its controlled press system over its Polish, Hungarian, and Balkan satellites as well as the broad new areas that had come under its sway in the farthest reaches of Northeast Asia. With the approaching victory of Mao Tse-tung's armies in China, the influence of the Communist press would be immeasurably increased. Of course, the free press had never flourished under Chiang Kai-shek and the Kuomintang; but it was also true that Nationalist China had not been the subversive threat to its neighbors that Red China was likely to become.

In the first stronghold of the independent newspaper, the United Kingdom, there was trouble of a different nature. The war was barely over in the Pacific when the House of Commons set up a Royal Commission to inquire into the control and ownership of the British press—always a subject of keen interest to the ruling Labour Party. After two years, the Commission reported that the British press was inferior to none in the world, that there was little evidence of damage to either free expression or accurate news presentation, and that nothing even approaching a monopoly existed in the provincial press. As for the newspaper chains, the Commission argued that member papers of such groups were better able to withstand competition and often could provide improved newspapers for the public.

Despite some serious criticism dealing with a growing conformity and a tendency to tolerate both political bias and slipshod reporting, the Commission on the whole took an optimistic view of the future of the press. It seemed not too disturbed by a drop from 169 to 128 in the number of daily and Sunday papers published in England, Scotland, and Wales between 1921 and 1948. However, it expressed some concern over the decrease in the number of national newspapers from 12 to 9, warning that this was just about the rock-bottom figure to insure diversity of news presentation and opinion.

The Commission's only major recommendation, the creation of a British Press Council, aroused little enthusiasm. Probably the only reason it came into existence in 1953 was that Parliament seemed ominously close to taking some regulatory action of its own. Nor did the Council, once it came into being as an all-newspaper investigative agency without punitive powers, seek new paths for independent journalism to satisfy the critics of the press. Few newspapers have ever taken generously to the notion of investigating their own kind. In sum, the pettishness and poor grace with which the British press submitted to self-regulation did not improve its position with the public and cleared the way for further inquiries. As events proved, there was substantially more basis for fear of a further contraction in the numbers of national and provincial newspapers than the first report indicated. A wiser press, instead of fighting the inquiry, might have used the occasion to invoke public sympathy for its mounting problems.

The attack on the British press, launched with such fanfare in Parliament, had its parallel in the United States when the privately organized and financed Commission on the Freedom of the Press made its report in 1947. Congress, with its historical reluctance to engage in a feud with the press, prudently stayed out of the line of fire. The Commission, headed by Robert M. Hutchins, chancellor of the University of Chicago at the time, issued its report under the title: "A Free and Responsible Press." The source of the financing was impeccable. Henry Robinson Luce had authorized a grant of $200,000 out of the substantial profits of Time, Inc., and $15,000 additional had come from the Encyclopedia Britannica. All disbursements had been made through the University of Chicago, thus insuring that the only prejudices working on the largely academic membership of the Commission would be their own.

The Commission reported that the number of daily newspapers in the United States had fallen from 2,600 in 1909 to 1,750 in 1945 although circulation had risen to almost 50 million. There were then competing dailies in 117 cities and 10,000 weeklies still survived out of the 16,000 that had existed in 1910. Chain publishers, the report went on, controlled more than half the daily circulation and fourteen of them had 25 percent of the total paper sales.

Like the critics of the British press, the Americans attacked their newspapers for too much emphasis on sensation, entertainment and competition, political bias and distortion, and almost complete lack of internal criticism of the profession. It was, in short, the usual academic bill of complaint against the press with a studied and almost savage virulence. The Commission concluded that freedom of the press was in danger because the concentration of ownership had greatly restricted the circulation of opinions and ideas—almost exactly the opposite of the Royal Commission's finding in Britain. It made a number of recommendations, the most important of which was the creation of an agency independent of both government and press that would scrutinize and report on press performance or lack of it.

The outcry of the American press against the report, in contrast with the almost indifferent public reaction, can be understood only if it is recalled that most newspapers prided themselves on the role they had played in the prosecution of World War II. They felt, whether it was merited or not, that they deserved something better than this kind of a heavily biased view of their accomplishments and shortcomings. But nobody was pinning any medals on the press for its wartime services once the shooting had stopped.

Actually, in the postwar world, there was an insensible change in the relations of the United States government and its press that might have been explored with some profit to both by the Hutchins Commission if it had had the perception to pursue its inquiry. For with the passage of the Atomic Energy Act of 1946, the government was given the most powerful weapon in its history to maintain discipline over the press in the publication of atomic material directly related to national security. On the one hand, the press was warned that the government could impose the most extreme punishments against violators of the secrecy provisions of the Atomic Energy Act. But on the other, the act provided that "the dissemination of scientific and technical information relating to atomic energy shall be permitted and encouraged so as to provide for a free interchange of ideas and criticisms which is essential to scientific progress." Where secrecy ended and where the free dissemination of ideas began in the atomic age, no one could say, least of all the press. But it had to proceed with care in a new field.

In the wholesaling of news, the three American global services — Associated Press, United Press, and International News Service — had to meet new challenges from abroad. Reuters had become a cooperative wire service in 1941, owned in effect by the British press through the newly formed Reuter Trust; with the end of the war, it became a Commonwealth agency with the inclusion of Australian, New Zealand, and Indian newspapers as partners. Replacing the tainted old Havas Agency, the new Agence France-Presse opened for business with the support of the revived French press and a contribution of more than 50 percent of its total budget from government bureaus that bought its services. In Germany, the new Deutsche Press Agentur for the West and the Allgemeine Deutsche Nachrichten for the East replaced the former Nazi press services. In Italy, Stefani died but a new cooperative, the Agenzia Nazionale Stampa Associata, came into being. And in Japan, the revived newspapers founded the new Kyodo Agency to replace the old source of news and intelligence, Domei.

In the Communist world, Tass didn't have everything its own way, by any means, even though it concluded exchange agreements with the British, French, and American global leaders and some of the national wire services of Europe. For the Chinese Communists were preparing a challenge to Soviet primacy in the distribution of news that would test the skill and try the patience of the Russians. Within a few years, the New China News Agency would be even more carefully read in Asia than Tass.

There was one other major change in the world's news communication channels in the postwar era that was to make more difference to free peoples than anything since the production of the Gutenberg Bible. That was the birth of network television in the United States. In 1948, for the first time, the little box with the small screen brought the national political conventions to mass audiences and later reported President Truman's victory over Thomas E. Dewey in vivid pictorial detail. In the following year, the first presidential inaugural was televised for a national audience. The people were able to see for themselves what the newspapers were able to describe and circulate only hours after the event. It made a tremendous difference.

The newspaper proprietors, having survived the challenge of the news magazines, newsreels, and radio, showed comparatively little concern over the birth of network television in the early years. They had managed to do well enough in the quarter-century in which radio had been first with most of the news. In addition, as of 1949, out of a total of 2,662 stations, 711 were affiliated with newspapers in whole or in part and 41 of these were pioneering television organizations. The implication was that, in the United States at least, the newspapers would be able to make an accommodation with this new electronic giant that could command the attention of the American family in its own home and siphon off advertising dollars from the press.

It was a vain hope. In succeeding decades, some of the largest and most powerful newspapers and magazines in the United States would be obliged to fight for their lives against the inroads of television into their readership and their sources of revenue. Predictably, many would lose. Although few of the faithful in the world of print were able to recognize it immediately, a revolution without parallel had struck them and all their works after five hundred years.

The newspaper would survive, but it would never be the same.

VIII. Under the Super-Powers

1. Cold War

In the spring of 1946, while writing a speech for Bernard M. Baruch at the United Nations, Herbert Bayard Swope groped for a term that would describe the menacing postures of the United States and the Soviet Union. Shortly before, on March 5 at Fulton, Missouri, Winston Churchill had said of the difficult situation of Europe: "From Stettin in the Baltic to Trieste in the Adriatic, an iron curtain has descended across the continent." Swope decided to call this "cold war" and used the term in the first draft of a Baruch speech on atomic control. However, upon reflection, he eliminated it because he felt that it might seem too provocative to the Soviet Union. A year later, Baruch used it anyway with electric effect.

In the vivid rhetoric of journalism, such phrases often have an impact on public opinion far beyond anything intended or envisioned by their authors. To a whole generation that hoped so fervently for a peace after World War II that could be kept by the United Nations, no one had to spell out the meaning of "iron curtain" and "cold war." Everywhere, the press and the electronic media seized upon these words and magnified them into giant symbols of protracted conflict. To the independent editors of the West, they were at once an accusation against the Soviet Union and a symptom of gross betrayal. To Moscow, they became evidence of the ruthless and never-ending hostility in the West to the Socialist world. Universally, they conveyed to hundreds of millions of people the inescapable signal that the victorious coalition of World War II had collapsed. Under the new dispensation presided over by the two super-powers, the United States and the Soviet Union, the initial prospect for a settlement of the issues left over from the war were dim, indeed.

If world opinion was shocked by the abruptness of the great confrontation, there was good reason for it. Like the press at large, a majority of the American press had promoted the United Nations with such single-minded devotion from the Dumbarton Oaks meeting onward that American public opinion had been led to expect the impossible from the new world organization. With the exception of such traditionalist attitudes as those of the Chicago *Tribune* and the Hearst newspapers, many of the leading editors and commentators in the United States joined the internationalist camp with whoops of enthusiasm. Nor were they alone in their conversion. Senator Arthur Hendrick Vandenberg, the editor of the Grand Rapids *Herald* in his earlier days, abandoned the cause of Republican isolationism midway through the war and, more than any other opposition spokesman, helped Franklin Delano Roosevelt lead the United States into partnership in the United Nations.

This time, certainly, there was no cause to harp on the American press as a betrayer of Wilsonian ideals, a conspirator against the creation of a brave new world. To a degree, the same spirit was generally reflected in the independent press wherever it existed. Only in the kindly illumination of an all-knowing hindsight could it be perceived that the press after World War II erred on the side of generosity. Because the United Nations was oversold, the disillusionment that came with the cold war was all the greater.

At a crucial point in world history, when the independent press could have demonstrated its presumed role as a watchdog over the governmental process in an open society, it did little more than to report what was happening. Thus, in the United States, editors on the whole were so bedazzled by sole American proprietorship in the atomic bomb that they failed to point out the dangers of precipitous and unilateral demolition of American armed forces until it was too late. When their government choked off $45 billions in Lend-Lease to Britain, Western Europe, and the Soviet Union, there was uncritical jubilation on many an editorial page and scant consideration of the after-effects. If Stalin had had the slightest notion of carrying out his pledges at Yalta, which is unlikely, these symptoms of American disengagement would have persuaded him to stand fast. Consequently, he roughly brushed aside the notion that he would permit free elections in Poland, busied himself with building his satellite empire and encouraging Mao Tse-tung in China, and served notice on the West that the Soviet Union would permit no interference in its sphere of national interest.

The opening movements of this massive conflict were enacted at the United Nations for all the world to see. Never before had there been such a platform to test the uses of global power. Never before had the world news media been able to concentrate so heavily on a single diplomatic event, viewed almost entirely in the open. Neither at the League of Nations in Geneva nor the peace conference after World War I in Versailles had great nations so recklessly flung away all thought of reserve and staked their future on epithet, threat, and armed blackmail. Through the magic of modern communications methods, the making of news had become a very real instrument of foreign policy. The interaction of journalism and diplomacy, in consequence, served to magnify the once-passive roles of the editor and correspondent. No longer could they consider themselves to be mere bystanders; wittingly or unwittingly, they were drawn into the bubbling vortex of events as participants, often on a scale equal in influence to the combatants they sought to describe. However much they sought to avoid it and by whatever means they tried to pretend that they were mere objective viewers of events, the journalists of the middle of the twentieth century found themselves in a new role. At home and abroad, whether they liked it or not, the developing speed and power of their media caused them to become deeply and inextricably involved in the news. Through their sheer mass coverage of events, therefore, the essential meaning of the news was often strikingly changed in both character and emphasis.

Without really intending to do so, the stout and good-humored Norwegian, Trygve Lie, made the United Nations a major forum for this interaction of journalism and diplomacy. In its Geneva backwater, the League of Nations had not been able to attract consistent large-scale world attention through the press. But in New York, from the outset, the United Nations was treated quite differently. It was, as Winston Churchill had said, a "brawling cockpit." Lie, as the first Secretary General, knew that the successor world organization had to depend for its strength on world opinion—and therefore worldwide publicity—and drew about him some of the foremost journalists of the era. Among them were Byron Price, the old AP editor and wartime chief of American censorship; William H. Stoneman, the chief European correspondent of the Chicago *Daily News*; Tor Gjesdal, of the wartime Norwegian Information Service; Benjamin Cohen, a leading Latin-American editor, and others. But none of them quite anticipated the excitement and intensity of the coverage of the first United Nations meetings in New York.

Diplomats without number had retired in displeasure from uncounted international colloquia in ages past, and the world had frequently been little wiser. But when Andrei Andreyevich Gromyko buttoned his tight blue double-breasted jacket in a converted girls' gymnasium in the Bronx on March 28, 1946, and walked out of the United Nations Security Council, the excited reportage turned the event into a virtual act of war. What Gromyko had sought to avoid was a procedural decision by the Council to inquire into the presence of Soviet troops in northern Iran, upon which the United States insisted. Eventually, the troops were withdrawn and Gromyko returned to the Council in the following month with reduced fanfare.

The alarm had been sounded. The pattern had been set. The message had been flashed around the world, wherever people could hear a radio or read a newspaper, that the United Nations, conceived as a symbol of hope, had been plunged into the thick of a great power conflict. Too late, the small nations realized that the notion of a Big Five police force, as outlined in the Charter, had been nothing but a sham and the belief in the ability of the United Nations to make peace was, at best, a delusion. The truth, as it emerged from the dreary sessions of the Security Council, was that no form of world organization could succeed without the cooperation of the super powers.

Atomic control and the most elementary approach to the problems of disarmament, the first issue before the United Nations

then as now, fell into deadlock with the opening debates of the
United States representative, Baruch, and Gromyko before the
United Nations Atomic Energy Commission. In the welter of
Soviet vetoes of proposed Security Council actions on these and
other problems, and in the prolonged and often pointless debates that tied up the General Assembly, the United Nations
soon sank into near impotence in all but a few special instances.

The most dramatic and far-reaching of these was the Palestine case, in which the United States and the Soviet Union sided
together to insure the partition of Palestine and bring about the
creation of the State of Israel in 1948. This was no demonstration of admiration for a persecuted people, 6 million of whom
had died in Hitler's murder camps in World War II, but a calculated political decision brought about by Britain's inability to
maintain even the tiny part of its empire that was concentrated
in its old League mandate over the Holy Land.

The British brought the case before the United Nations on
April 2, 1947. After a seven-month struggle, during which the
more influential American newspapers threw their weight into
the campaign for partition waged by the Jewish Agency for
Palestine, the General Assembly voted 33 to 13 on November 29
in favor of dividing Palestine into separate Arab and Jewish
states with an internationalized Jerusalem. On the American
side, it was a fulfillment of many years of campaign promises,
made by both Democratic and Republican parties, in favor of a
Jewish homeland. As for the Soviet Union, with its age-old Russian suspicion of Jewish influence, the support for the Jewish
Agency's program was based primarily on the Kremlin's decision to do everything within reason to hasten Britain's departure
from the Middle East.

In the howl of protest that followed from the oil-rich Arabs,
with their many powerful American business ties, the United
States had second thoughts almost immediately. In the State
Department in particular, where there was considerably more
Arab than Jewish sentiment, a new program was proposed to try
to undo partition and place all of Palestine under a United Nations trusteeship. It didn't work. In the spring of 1948, the politi-

cal division in a special session of the General Assembly held firm. The Trusteeship plan failed. A few minutes after the final vote on the night of May 14 at Flushing Meadow, the wire services flashed the news from Washington that the United States had recognized the newly created State of Israel, which was fighting for its life against Arab armies from the moment of its birth. Without bothering to inform his State Department, President Truman had thrown American support to the struggling new nation.

On the floor of the Assembly and from the rostrum, the Arab delegates stormed about in anger. Both they and some of their allies, notably those in the Latin-American bloc, demanded to know of the American delegation how the United States had dared to act unilaterally and what was now to be done. The American delegation, without advice from Washington, could do nothing until Dr. Philip C. Jessup, on leave from Columbia University as the Hamilton Fish Professor of International Law, thought of a simple expedient. He rifled the wastebasket in the Associated Press cubbyhole at Flushing Meadow and came up with a copy of the bulletin announcing American recognition of Israel. With solemn countenance, he mounted the Assembly rostrum and read the news as it was given by the Associated Press. On that note, the Assembly ended. The Israelis were left alone in the Middle East to wage their first successful fight against the Arabs. And the Soviet Union, once the British had retreated from the Middle East, reverted to its posture of general opposition to the United States in United Nations affairs.

The Americans already had begun acting outside the United Nations to counter rising Soviet influence. Faced with Moscow-supported campaigns against the security of Greece and Turkey, President Truman declared before Congress on March 12, 1946: "I believe that it must be the policy of the United States to support free peoples who are resisting attempted subjugation by armed minorities or by outside pressures." This was the basis of the Truman Doctrine, which initially called for $400 million in aid to Greece and Turkey and the dispatch of civilian and military personnel to both countries.

A little more than a year later, on June 5, 1947, Secretary of State George C. Marshall extended the same principle to Western Europe, naming the enemies of the United States as "hunger, poverty, desperation, and chaos," and not "any country or doctrine." But the Soviet Union understood well enough what was involved, for *Pravda* soon attempted to scuttle the Marshall Plan, calling it a "disguised Truman Doctrine." But with European cooperation, a $22.4 billion, four-year recovery program was put into effect with signal success.

The process of waging a considerable part of the cold war through the press took on added impetus quite by chance in the July, 1947, issue of the prestigious quarterly, *Foreign Affairs*, when an author identified only as "X" proposed that the American government embark on a "long-term, patient but firm and vigilant containment of Russian expansive tendencies." In addition, "X" called for the application of American counterforce "at a series of constantly shifting geographical and political points, corresponding to the shifts and maneuvers of Soviet policy." It wasn't long before Arthur Krock in the New York *Times* disclosed the official nature of the "X" article, leading to the identification of the author as George F. Kennan, then the head of the State Department's Policy Planning Staff. Kennan had written the article while serving as acting ambassador to Moscow, sent it to the secretary of defense, James Forrestal, and later had assented to the publication of the essential text in *Foreign Affairs*. But the timing of the "X" article proved to be decidedly awkward although it did not interfere with the vigor of the new American approach.

The Soviet Union wasn't to be so easily "contained," however. On April 1, 1948, a blockade that had been gradually applied to West Berlin became fully effective with the announcement of Soviet-supported rail and road restrictions on all Allied traffic into the city. The United States responded to the challenge by organizing an enormous airlift, with British assistance, that soon was flying an average of 8,000 tons of food, coal, clothes, and medical supplies into the beleaguered city of 2.1 million people. Before the struggle for Berlin ended in Soviet defeat on May 12,

1949, more than 2.3 million tons of supplies had been airlifted into the Western sector.

During the 321 days of the keenly coordinated flights into Tempelhof Airport, the United States command did everything possible to mobilize world opinion against the Russians. Nearly every day, correspondents were flown into West Berlin, sitting on sacks of coal or other bulky supplies, to write and broadcast the heroic tale of resistance to Soviet harassment. As matters turned out, it was through a chance query by J. Kingsbury Smith of International News Service that Stalin gave the signal that he was ready for a settlement. Smith, a top Hearst correspondent and certainly no friend of the Soviet Union, had submitted a questionnaire to the Soviet dictator to try to get at his reasons for continuing the blockade. In responding, Stalin omitted all mention of the key Soviet demand for the use of Soviet currency in all of Berlin. That was in January, 1949. In the secret negotiations between the Soviet Union and the United States that were conducted in the weeks that followed by Jacob A. Malik, the Soviet representative, and Dr. Jessup, for the United States, Smith's role in breaking the deadlock was not forgotten. All things considered, the role of the press was greater than the role of the United Nations in achieving a temporary accommodation between the super-powers at the point of greatest danger, Berlin.

The upshot, once the blockade was called off, was the proclamation of the German Federal Republic on May 23, 1949. That fall, on October 7, the Soviet Union countered with the creation of the German Democratic Republic. The break between East and West was complete.

From then on, Soviet officials became inordinately sensitive over what was written and said about them and their country. That accounted in large part for the severity with which Western correspondents were treated in Stalin's far-reaching domain, once he had slammed down the iron curtain. Expulsions from Moscow and satellite capitals became common. Travel for correspondents was restricted and surveillance was increased. Censorship, somewhat relaxed during World War II, became tight. Visas for new correspondents became increasingly difficult to obtain. Often, when a correspondent left his post, he found that he could not return. Terror was an even more effective weapon, as was evidenced by the case of George Polk of the Columbia Broadcasting System who was shot and killed in 1948 during a venturesome mission behind Communist lines in the Greek civil war.

On the eve of the Korean War, for which Stalin without doubt gave encouragement to his North Korean allies and to which Mao Tse-tung committed the Peoples' Liberation Army, only five Western news organizations were permitted to maintain correspondents in Moscow. These men — representing the Associated Press, United Press, Reuters, Agence France-Presse and the New York *Times* — were generally restricted to copying the official Soviet line on pain of expulsion. Such difficulties accounted in the main for the relatively thin flow of news from the Soviet Union as well as from central and eastern Europe at a crucial time in postwar history. This was the way Stalin wanted it. To him, secrecy was a way of life and he enforced it on his people.

2. The Lamps Go Out in Prague

To a very large part of the Western world by the middle of 1947, all of eastern and central Europe had been written off as lost to the new Soviet imperialism. And yet, in Yugoslavia, the determined Jozip Broz — known as Tito — was standing firm against Soviet dominion and maintaining his grip on his armed forces, police, and party regulars. "Titoism" was synonymous with treason in Moscow. In Hungary and Bulgaria, Communist regimes were listening warily to talk of a Communist alliance with Yugoslavia that was intended to limit Soviet influence in the Balkans. Even in Poland, betrayed at Yalta when the West accepted Stalin's assurances of free elections there, the Soviet Union had not yet succeeded in crushing a persistent nationalist movement that troubled the pro-Kremlin faction in the government. But freest of all, and still firmly committed to its democratic faith, was the key to the heart of Europe, Czechoslovakia.

The old journalist, Edouard Beneš, and his closest collaborator, Jan Masaryk, son of the first Czech president, had come home to the ancient gray city of Prague after World War II from their long exile in London. Beneš, as president, and Masaryk, as foreign minister, maintained a democratic government in their capital under enormous difficulties, conscious that they had to placate both Moscow and the West because they were economically dependent on both. Daringly, they sought to join the sixteen European nations that associated themselves with the Marshall Plan in 1947 but Stalin refused to let them go through with it. At that juncture, both the United States and Britain appeared to have given up on Czechoslovakia. Through an ill-informed press and an even less alert intelligence service, Washington apparently concluded that the Czechs no longer were their own masters. It was a tragic miscalculation.

Masaryk labored unremittingly to reverse the course of events. He tried to persuade his British and American friends that they were wrong. "Washington and London," he told one of them, "have failed completely to understand my position and are making a serious mistake in not granting my request for funds or material assistance. This simply indicates to the Russians and to the Czech Communists that the American and British governments don't give a damn about anything the Communists might feel like doing to Czechoslovakia."

It did seem to the Western powers at the time that Communist control of Prague was inevitable. Klement Gottwald, the Communist leader, already had become premier, 114 out of 300 Assembly seats were in Communist hands, and in 1946 the Communist Party had won 38 percent of the vote. Moreover, once the Czechs had been obliged to give up hope of participating in the Marshall Plan, Gottwald had gone to Moscow and come back with a five-year Soviet trade agreement. Although he controlled but eight of the twenty-three cabinet posts, including his own, these gave him authority over such key offices as the ministry of the interior with its all-important state police.

Bravely, Masaryk talked of winning an election that had been scheduled for May, 1948. He predicted that the Communist vote total would drop to 31 percent. Then, he thought, Gottwald might try for a coup d'état. But neither he nor Beneš expected anything to happen before the election. Through their own diplomatic service and through loyal friends, they appealed to Washington and London to drop their "defeatist" attitude and predicted that democracy in Czechoslovakia would weather its most difficult period. Unfortunately, they didn't really know what was going on in their own country and for this they paid heavily. As a concession to the Communists, the wavering Beneš had restricted freedom of the press and turned over control of all newspaper staffs to a Communist-dominated Union of Journalists, which alone could give permission to a journalist to hold a job on a paper. With police and press in their hands, the Communists were well able to strike for total power at any time they chose.

When the coup came on February 21, 1948, it was swift and bloodless. Gottwald and his minister of the interior, Vaclav Nosek, moved their Communist militia into Prague and Bratislava on the ground that the democratic regime no longer could maintain order. Within four days, Gottwald was master of the unfortunate country. Journalists, university professors, and dissident army officers were the first to go in a purge. The nation's forty-four daily newspapers were cut to twenty-two and fifty of the remaining editors were expelled from the Journalists' Union. Before long, the Czech press, once the freest in Europe, was reduced to slavish devotion to its Communist overlords. A new press agency, Ceteka (CTK), was established to bring in Tass copy from Moscow and circulate the approved Communist line in Prague. The mission of the newly Sovietized press was "to assist in the constructive efforts and the struggle for peace of the Czechoslovak people and to contribute to their education toward Socialism."

Only Masaryk remained in the cabinet as an independent, non-Communist voice but his days, too, were numbered. On March 10, he was officially reported to have "committed suicide" although rumors soon circulated in Prague that he had been hurled from a window of the Czernin Palace by Soviet agents. Later that year, Beneš died at his country home, a broken man, having refused to sign the new Communist constitution and having left office. Communist control of Czechoslovakia, anticipated for two years by Washington and London, thus was accomplished without resistance, and Soviet influence advanced to the borders of Western Europe.

It was the beginning, not the end, of a harsh Stalinist rule for Czechoslovakia and the harbinger of strict Soviet control of Eastern Europe except for heretic Yugoslavia for years to come. The new Communist foreign minister in Prague, Vladimir Clementis, was ordered home from the United Nations a year after succeeding the martyred Masaryk and was himself arrested. Together with the tough secretary general of the Communist Party, Rudolph Slansky, and nine others, he was tried as a spy and a traitor. All were hanged on December 3, 1952, in Pankrac Prison in Prague.

Among their associates who escaped with prison terms was a mild-mannered intellectual, Gustav Husak, the deposed chairman of the Slovak government. But not even this widespread purge was deemed sufficient to crush the persistent underground efforts of the Czechs and Slovaks to counteract Soviet power. The outraged Anastas Mikoyan, the old Bolshevik who had served many masters in Moscow and managed to survive them all, came hurrying to Prague to charge that not enough was being done to put down "Titoism." Gottwald labored mightily to provide more sacrifices to the insatiable Russians until his death in 1953 and his successor, Antonin Novotny, went even farther.

Under the circumstances, it was evident that the foreign press eventually would feel the anger of the shaky new Czech regime. The Associated Press, with its worldwide facilities for spreading the news, was a natural target both because of its prestige and its ownership by the bulk of the American press. Two AP correspondents and several other members of the foreign press corps were expelled early in 1950, among them Nathan Polowetzky, the AP bureau chief in Prague. On April 23, 1951, his replacement, a slim, sandy-haired AP veteran from Indiana, William Nathan Oatis, was arrested and charged with activities hostile to the state. It was sheer rubbish, of course. At thirty-six years of age, Oatis was a careful and competent foreign correspondent with an excellent record. Yet, after being held incommunicado for seventy-two days and forced at one point to go without sleep for forty-two hours, he signed a statement in which he "confessed" he had gathered military information. On July 4, 1951, he was convicted and sentenced to ten years in prison. His three Czech associates in the AP were dealt with even more harshly.

The protests of the AP, in common with the remainder of the Western press, did no good. Until Stalin died in the Kremlin on March 5, 1953, ending more than a generation of paranoiac intrigue, terror, and inhuman punishment of millions of helpless people, there was no hope for the solitary prisoner of Prague. Then, there was a stirring behind the iron curtain. Faint gestures of reconciliation were discerned at intervals—the flickering of an aurora on a distant horizon. And at length on May 16, 1953, after Oatis' wife had pleaded for his freedom and President Eisenhower had sent a personal letter to the Czech government, the correspondent was pardoned. Upon his release, he uncomplainingly resumed his career at the United Nations in the service of the AP. Eighteen years later, in the brief but exhilarating freedom of a quite different Prague spring, a Czech court cleared him of spying, ruled that the prosecution had been rigged, and disclosed that the objective had been to keep the AP and other agencies from distributing news of events inside Czechoslovakia.

That result was not achieved. Yet, in so painfully divided a world, where governments strove by every means at their command to influence the shape of the news, the basic act of gathering information would never be considered normal again. To historians of the cold war, the Oatis case is perhaps a footnote at best in the tumultuous rivalry of the super-powers. But to the journalists of the West, who were charged with the responsibility of providing the raw materials of history each day, it marked an unmistakable change in their status.

No longer could correspondents assume that they would be treated as noncombatants and accorded the chivalrous protection of both sides under the Geneva Convention and less formal but common understandings among civilized nations. In a brute world where chivalry was dead and international agreements were respected only as long as was convenient, the journalist had lost his special status. Whatever romantic notion he may have entertained of his role in terms of Western civilization, he was just another agent of the state when he ventured into the great imperialist domain over which Stalin, on one side, and Mao, on the other, exercised absolute power. This was the real meaning of the Communist takeover in Czechoslovakia, the violent death of Jan Masaryk, and the imprisonment of Bill Oatis. In a time of cataclysmic change, no one — not the diplomat nor the journalist — could resort to the protective fiction that their status exempted them from harm.

3. Nehru's India

Few national leaders commanded more respect in the years immediately following World War II than Jawaharlal Nehru, prime minister of India. This calm and austere man, with the jaunty white Indian Congress cap perched on his graying head and the familiar red rose in the buttonhole of his long, high-collared coat, was looked upon by tens of millions of people as the prophet of a third world — an alternative to the dominance of the super-powers. Consequently, his country assumed a peculiar moral strength in world affairs because of its faith in a nonalignment policy between East and West.

It was an era in which political colonialism was dying, but cultural colonialism remained very much alive. Except for the decisive phases of World War II, the centers of power in the West nearly always had sent a far greater flow of information and ideas to Asia in the twentieth century than they had received. Despite the changes that were now sweeping over that vast continent, neither the Western publics nor their news media had been able to make the necessary adjustments. They simply could not appreciate the importance of Asia in this new world; with few exceptions, they clung even closer to their precious European heritage. It was this state of mind, so prevalent in the

West, that bothered Nehru and made him crochety toward the press at times.

Like so many Asian nationalist leaders, his experiences had conditioned him to demand more of the West than the West was willing to give. Born in Amritsar November 14, 1889, into a well-to-do Kashmiri family, he was educated at Harrow and Cambridge and committed to the practice of law. But when he was thirty years old, his anger over the Amritsar massacre led him into Gandhi's independence movement, to which he devoted the rest of his life. From 1930 to 1936, he passed his days in jail writing letters to his daughter, Indira, on the state of India and the world. When he emerged, one of the first things he did was to found a new newspaper, the *National Herald* of Lucknow — a "brave, true and efficient soldier in the cause of Indian freedom and world peace."

Alas for Nehru's hopes, both peace and freedom were shattered just a year after the *Herald* first appeared in 1938. The British, without consulting either the Indian people or their representatives, took the subcontinent into World War II and imposed the strictest kind of censorship on the Indian press. Gandhi announced that it would be better not to publish newspapers than to bring them out subject to British approval. In consequence, he suspended his weekly *Harijan*, the successor to *Young India*. The *National Herald, Indian Express*, and *Dinamani* were among the papers that followed Gandhi's advice.

With the adoption of the Wardha Resolution in the summer of 1942 with its demand that the British quit India, the Indian Congress explicitly supported the rebellious press although it did not go as far toward noncooperation as Gandhi had wished. Soon afterward, the British suspended ninety-six newspapers and other publications. Of these and others, security bonds were demanded as a manifest of good behavior.

Gandhi, the spiritual leader of the rebellion, went to jail, as did Nehru, who had become president of the Congress, and a number of other Indian leaders. In the United Provinces of India (later known as the Uttar Pradesh) nearly 25,000 persons were thrown into prison for offenses against the government, both real and fancied. It was against this background that the freedom movement in India read and judged Churchill for his celebrated declaration of purpose on November 10, 1942: "I have not become the King's First Minister in order to preside at the liquidation of the British Empire."

At this particular moment, Franklin Roosevelt seized the occasion to lecture the angry Churchill on his obligation to India under the "Four Freedoms." If the Indians knew about Roosevelt's representations, it made little difference to them for the irascible Churchill was unyielding. Moreover, the Indians could tell easily enough from the anti-Indian stance of many leading American newspapers that British influence over American public opinion was still powerful. It was for this reason, primarily, that a newspaper of the stature of the *Hindu* of Madras denounced what it termed the "gross ignorance of American opinion." Regardless of the economic aid that eventually came to India from the United States, the damaging impression of the United States in the Wardha era left a deep imprint on Indian consciousness. Certainly, whatever kindness the saintly Gandhi showed to Americans in his last days, Nehru never forgave them.

Until the latter days of the war, when the British felt more secure, there was no relaxation of the strictness of their rule over India. Then, with the accession of Lord Wavell as viceroy, communal rioting broke out and the government came to the Indian press to enlist its help in restoring peace. Gandhi was released from prison on May 6, 1944, primarily to try to end the murderous communal differences that had taken thousands of lives. He appealed to the leader of the Muslim League, Mohammed Ali Jinnah, for some means of insuring Hindu—Muslim cooperation. Jinnah's invariable price was partition and a Muslim nation. He called it Pakistan.

Nehru and other important members of the Congress Working Committee were not freed until after the war was over in 1945. Churchill's government made one last effort to hold India by offering dominion status to the Congress leadership. It was rejected. When Clement Attlee came in as prime minister at the

head of a Labour government, freedom for India was assured —
but it was not the kind of liberty for which Gandhi had labored
so long. The last viceroy, Lord Mountbatten, worked out a partition plan that created two independent countries, India and Pakistan, and obtained the acceptance of both sides.

With Nehru as its first prime minister, India became independent on August 15, 1947. On the same day, Pakistan came
into existence as a divided country with its eastern and western
parts separated by 1,000 miles of Indian territory. Millions of
frightened Muslims, caught in a hostile India, and as many or
more Hindus and Sikhs in Muslim areas, began a sorrowful retreat from their homes in search of a precarious future in a
strange and far-off land. While Gandhi fasted and prayed in protest in Calcutta, communal warfare reached horrifying depths.
But in the West, with the exception of pious professions of
alarm, there was almost total indifference. It was almost as if the
crimes of Hitler, now that they had become known, had hardened and paralyzed the consciences of civilized peoples to human suffering.

But there was worse yet to come. With the Pakistani army
storming into his native Kashmir on the pretext that tribesmen
were creating a threat to public order, Nehru ordered the Indian
army to the northwest border. His soldiers seized two-thirds of
Jammu and Kashmir, including the fabled Vale of Kashmir, and
proclaimed that the beleaguered Maharajah of Kashmir, an Indian ally, had "acceded" to India. Before the United Nations
could arrange a cease-fire, Indian military occupation took effect
in provinces that were heavily Muslim in population. And so the
situation remained for many years.

Gandhi meanwhile had succeeded in restoring order in Calcutta through his fast of protest against violence on the day of
independence. But the killing went on elsewhere. The Mahatma
journeyed to Delhi, causing outbreaks of violence to taper off by
the sheer force of his presence, but he was still dissatisfied. In a
supreme effort to restore harmony, he began what he called a
"fast unto death" on January 13, 1948, at Birla House in New
Delhi. In this manner, he tried to appeal to the conscience of

Hindus and Muslims alike to end the killing. As word of his fast spread and anxiety over his condition increased, thousands of his fellow countrymen filed past the porch at Birla House where he lay hunched up on a cot. Many prayed and wept over his agony.

This was something the foreign press could understand—the sacrifice of a world-famous holy man and teacher in the cause of peace for his fellow men. The correspondents came flocking in from both Europe and the United States. If anything, the heightening international attention served to increase the irresponsibility of a section of the Indian press. Some of the Marathi papers of Bombay and the surviving Urdu journals published provocative accounts of communal rioting. Others, favoring the extremist Hindu Mahasabha, maintained a steady campaign of abuse directed against the Muslims who remained in India.

Yet, despite all these provocations, the Indian leadership signed pledges guaranteeing more protection to the Muslims in India on January 18 and, to the relief of his fellow countrymen, Gandhi ended his fast. Nehru, who had himself begun a fast that day in a show of sympathy, left his duties as prime minister and came to Birla House to celebrate the Mahatma's victory. If they thought that the crisis had passed, however, they were in grievous error. For in a land maimed by violence, hatred, and sudden death, there is no easy end to the persecution and the killing of minorities. And where there is continual agitation in the streets or in the press, none can say whom the mania for assassination will strike down next.

On January 30, 1948, it was Gandhi who fell. Just before leading a congregation of five hundred in evening prayer in the quiet garden of Birla House, the Mahatma was shot and killed by a 30-year-old Hindu fanatic, Nathuran Vinyak Gadse. His last words were: "He Ram, He Ram" (Oh God, Oh God). Two members of his family who had served him faithfully, Abhu and Manu Gandhi, reverently bore his body into Birla House. There, Manu announced simply: "Bapu is dead."

The press whipped itself into a frenzy of mourning, with the *Amrita Bazar Patrika* crying: GANDHI CRUCIFIED BY FANATI-

CISM. The nation was plunged into grief. Nehru, in his broadcast to all India, said: "The light has gone out of our lives." Once again, the foreign press came to Delhi for the funeral and the final tributes to the Mahatma, who had humbled a mighty empire and led his people to freedom.

Then the attention of the West turned to other matters. India and Pakistan, still poles apart over the issue of Kashmir and their communal problems, settled into a frozen posture of confrontation and border skirmishing that lasted for many years. But scarcely a score of Western correspondents, and sometimes less than a dozen, were permanently stationed on a subcontinent of 600 million people. It is scant wonder that Nehru once exclaimed in anger:

"I have often wondered what exactly is meant by freedom of the press. What is the press? Is it the journalists, the proprietors, or editors? Whose freedom? Obviously the freedom of the press may ultimately mean the freedom not of the people who run the paper but the freedom of the proprietor who may use that freedom for other purposes than the public good."

This was Nehru's attitude toward his own press. To be sure, it was free. Under the Indian constitution of January 26, 1950, the guarantee of press freedom was set forth in ringing terms. But within a year, because of foreign exchange restrictions, there was a new government order controlling the import of newsprint. And in the Press Act of 1951 provisions were inserted to punish the publication of material that was likely to undermine the government, interfere with the maintenance of essential services, or "seduce" any member of the armed forces from his duty. All except the irresponsible papers of the extreme right and left took such measures seriously, which meant there was a certain amount of self-restraint among the responsible section of the press merely because such laws existed.

Having such powers at his command, Nehru could dominate the Indian press whenever he wished and had little to fear from any transient opposition. As he gained in world stature, he displayed the virtuoso brilliance of a Roosevelt or a Churchill in persuading both the domestic and a large part of the foreign press of India's superior moral position in world affairs. From the outset, he had managed to attract economic and military aid in increasing volume from both the United States and the Soviet Union while lecturing both on their responsibilities. In the United States, his customary arrogance frequently touched off waves of press criticism that he was "nonaligned against us." But such complaints never seemed to interfere with the golden flood of aid from Washington. Periodically, when Nehru feared Pakistan was getting more of such assistance than it deserved, or when Pakistan was more than ordinarily envious of his success, there would be a spell of ferocious talk in New Delhi and Karachi. But generally, on the restless subcontinent, there was a slow turn toward stability and economic improvement.

Toward India's neighbors, Nehru presented the image of a dedicated Asian, for India was deeply involved in the fortunes of other Asian lands and could scarcely afford to be indifferent toward any of them. Burma and Ceylon, her Asian partners in the British Commonwealth, achieved their independence in 1948 and Malaya's turn came soon afterward. The prized East Indies, over which the Netherlands had ruled for more than three hundred years, won their freedom in an uprising led by a native patriot, Sukarno, and in 1949 entered the halls of the United Nations as the Republic of Indonesia. The French, in a mistaken effort to save their colonial empire in Indochina, propped Emperor Bao Dai on a mythical throne in Vietnam in 1949 and at the same time gave Cambodia a kind of token independence within the French Union. But Ho Chi Minh and his devoted band of Moscow-trained guerrillas already had begun their long war for freedom; in Cambodia, for that matter, the less aggressive but equally determined Prince Norodom Sihanouk was making it clear to Paris that he would settle for nothing short of independence.

Nehru's India had only slight interest in far-off Japan under American rule and little more in the Philippines despite their grant of independence from the United States on July 4, 1946. As Nehru once told Carlos Romulo with ill-concealed scorn: "You Filipinos are too dependent on the United States. You must seek an Asian identity." The Indian leader had no such doubts about the China of Mao Tse-tung, which had been brought into being despite American pressure for a peaceful settlement between the Communists and Chiang Kai-shek. No sooner had Chiang and his tattered Kuomintang been expelled from the mainland than India hastened to recognize the new regime in Peking. It was Nehru's fondest hope that the two Asian giants, India and China, could stand together against the encroachments of imperialists, old and new. It was a vain dream. For this new China was a strange and powerful land that followed no one's rules. And one day, before too long, it would invade India.

4. On the Red Tide

No delusion was more carefully fostered in the United States during and immediately after World War II than the notion that Chiang Kai-shek was an authentic Asian hero and the deliverer of China's suffering millions. The faith in Chiang was so strong that the China-born Henry Robinson Luce, and his wife, the caustic and sharp-witted Clare Boothe Luce, virtually prostrated themselves before him and Mme. Chiang at their first meeting in 1942. The worshipful Luce wrote for his *Life* magazine: "We left knowing that we had made the acquaintance of two people, a man and a woman, who, out of all the millions now living, will be remembered for centuries to come."

If the Luces were unrealistic, so were a majority of their fellow countrymen. For nearly fifty years, Americans had been told by their missionaries, their public schools, and their press that they had a special responsibility for the well-being of China. This patronizing notion would have surprised those cynics of another generation, the authors of the Chinese Exclusion Act of 1882. But there was no doubt of its hold on the American imagination.

When the Japanese attacked China in 1931, American sympathy gravitated to the Chinese. As Chiang Kai-shek slowly and even reluctantly organized the main opposition to the aggression, his image lengthened in the American press until he became a giant figure. Once the United States had been plunged into World War II at Pearl Harbor, Chungking became known in American newspapers as "the farthest outpost of freedom." Such pilgrimages as those made by the Luces were marks of respect to a fighting ally. If some of the American correspondents in Chungking found new life and challenge in the fastnesses of Yenan, where Mao Tse-tung and his Communist armies were preparing a formidable bid for power, their work was dismissed by Chiang's propagandists as either the delusions of innocents or the sinister propaganda of master Communist agents. Actually, the correspondence from Yenan made more impression in Washington than it did in Chungking, for this was the period when Mao was encouraging the belief that he and his people were less traditional Communists than agrarian reformers.

Chiang's method was to pretend that the situation was better than it appeared, to demand ever more aid of the United States, to attack his critics, and to get rid of them whenever he could. He disposed in this manner of his chief of staff, General Joseph W. (Vinegar Joe) Stilwell, who was telling Washington that the war in China was being lost through graft, corruption, and sheer stupidity by the Nationalist command. Theodore H. White, the *Time–Life* correspondent in Chungking, was disciplined when he effectively supported Stilwell's findings. Among those who agreed with White and also suffered Chiang's displeasure were such eminent correspondents as Brooks Atkinson of the New York *Times*, A.T. Steele of the New York *Herald Tribune*, Harold Isaacs of *Newsweek*, and Robert P. (Pepper) Martin of United Press.

However, Washington had clearly decided by this time that the United States would have to muddle along with Chiang while concentrating its main strength in Europe against Hitler. With the collapse of Japanese resistance in 1945, the Americans had to pay the penalty for this decision. Unprepared themselves, and with an unstable and even untrustworthy Chinese ally, the forces of the United States had to face up to the awesome reality of treating with the beaten Japanese while at the same time dealing with the advancing Russians and the Communist armies of Mao Tse-tung as they poured out of Yenan.

In this extremity, the first American notion was to mediate between Chiang and Mao. The ambassador to Chungking, Patrick J. Hurley, was given this unenviable assignment and actually brought the two Chinese chieftains together at Chungking in August and September, 1945. But they could agree on nothing. It was a foregone conclusion that the same thing would happen when General George C. Marshall made a similar mediation attempt in 1945–46.

General Albert C. Wedemeyer, who had succeeded Stilwell as Chiang's chief of staff, now fell back on the old Washington formula that, when all else fails, spend more money, send more military aid, and predict victory. In the United States, leading Republicans, the Luce publications, the Scripps-Howard newspapers, and others called upon the Truman administration to stand fast behind Chiang. The president tried. By that time, there was nothing else he could do. The result was that Chiang committed his last remaining American-equipped divisions to battle against Mao's armies in the winter of 1948-49 along the Hwai River in central China, lost a half-million men, and finally had to flee to the security of Taiwan.

Appalled at the disaster, the China bloc in the American Congress and its press allies raised the question: "How did we lose China?" Secretary of State Dean Acheson replied in effect that China had never been "ours" to lose. But the so-called China Lobby, financed by the conservative businessman, Alfred Kohlberg, argued that the whole sorry business had been a Communist plot. Waiting in the wings, a young politician named Joseph R. McCarthy soon enough took up the cry. But the American public, which had never had a very clear understanding of what was going on in China, showed its disillusionment in a Gallup poll at the beginning of 1950 in which 30 percent of those questioned were for doing nothing, 18 percent were for continuing to help Chiang, 13 percent wanted American forces to protect Taiwan, and 39 percent had other opinions or no opinions at all.

But the Chiang-firsters were incorrigible. When President

Truman ordered the U.S. Navy to protect Taiwan, Henry Luce's *Life* magazine sent up editorial cheers and proclaimed Chiang's goal was a "democratic China." It would have surprised both the Kuomintang, which was sitting on top of 10 million Taiwanese, and Chiang himself.

Alas for a democratic China, that chimera of American public life, Mao Tse-tung already was fashioning a new rule for the 800 million people under his sway on the mainland which was molded on the patterns of Lenin and Stalin with some important modifications of his own. Public organization, surveillance, and thought control came with the lowering of the Bamboo Curtain over Peking and Shanghai to a greater degree than at any time in Chinese history.

Central to the whole system was a new order for the Chinese press and radio. Under Communism, Mao decreed, the role of the press would be "to organize, to stimulate or encourage, to agitate, to criticize, and to propel." It was his conviction, no less than Lenin's, that the press must be a "collective propagandist, collective agitator, and collective organizer." Hence, when he assumed power in Peking, he issued a directive to the press to devote more space to the progress of production and labor under Communism. It centralized direction of each newspaper in a single editor, approved by the regime. Throughout the country, vast correspondent networks and newspaper reading groups were created. And all published and broadcast material had to be channeled through a single high party bureau.

The ever-weak privately owned press on mainland China died suddenly. Within a matter of days, only five such papers remained. Soon, even these had to suspend publication under government duress. The Communist apparatus bodily took over the Central News Agency of China, the Central *Daily News*, and forty-three other Kuomintang papers. *Jenmin Jih-pao* (People's Daily), which had been founded in 1948 as the organ of the Central Committee of the Chinese Communist Party, became the oracle of Maoism. The once-respected independent daily, *Ta Kung-pao*, continued to come out under a Communist editor. As for the foreign language press, it simply ceased to exist. From more than 2,000 papers in 1948, mainland China dropped abruptly to 275 two years later and only the major Peking and provincial papers were dailies. They claimed a total circulation of about 8 million — a dubious figure.

That was only the beginning of Mao's new communications empire. From a single radio station in Yenan in 1945, he directed the development of a sixteen-station network at the time he came to power. To this, he added fifty Nationalist stations and thirty-three that were privately owned, the basis for his propaganda broadcasts from Radio Peking to an estimated 1.5 million radio sets.

Feeding the entire print and electronic network was the New China News Agency, Hsin Hua, which had been founded in Kiangsi in 1929 and was formally set up in 1937 as Mao's official news service. Together with *Jenmin Jih-pao* and the Peking Radio, it formed the government information pool from which the Communist propaganda service distributed all news, editorials, and policy pronouncements. Where the press and radio could not penetrate, there was still the *tatzepao*, the "paper of bold characters," which could be hand-lettered and slapped on a wall anywhere. Just about the only mode of communication that could not easily be controlled was the most ancient of all, the bamboo telegraph, through which people communicated guardedly by word of mouth.

The People's Republic of China, proclaimed in Peking on September 21, 1949, scarcely waited for such consolidations of its influence to press ahead on all fronts. Despite Stalin's lack of faith in his eventual victory, Mao made friendly gestures to paper over his messy relations with the Soviet Union. Stalin, for his part, appeared eager to show that he had made a mistake in judgment. Together, the two Red dictators approved a thirty-year treaty of "friendship, alliance, and mutual assistance" between their countries on February 15, 1950.

The first to feel the force of the new Chinese giant was the surprised and unhappy Nehru, who had been busily promoting the notion that Indians and Chinese are brothers ("Hindi Chini bhai bhai"). Early in 1950, Mao moved his troops near the border of eastern Tibet. If this maneuver had been a test, the Chinese had their answer quickly enough. Nehru went on preaching ethics and morality to the world at large, but signified to the frightened Tibetans that he would let nature take its course in their country, nature being fairly powerful in the guise of the People's Liberation Army.

The Red tide was at the flood on the Chinese mainland. With Mao in absolute control of the government, the military, and all communications, there was no way of knowing how far his venturesome spirit would carry him.

5. The "Forgotten War"

When North Korea's crack Communist army struck south across the 38th parallel on June 25, 1950, the United States began organizing the first United Nations armed intervention against aggression. For once, there was no fear of a Soviet veto. The Soviet representative, Jacob A. Malik, had been absent from all meetings since January 13, 1950, in protest against the continued exclusion of Communist China from the world organization. Instead of hurrying back to his post to defend the Soviet's client state, North Korea, Malik continued to stay away. Consequently, on the sunny Sunday afternoon of June 25 at Lake Success, an extraordinary session of the Security Council branded North Korea as an aggressor and called for an immediate cease-fire. Two days later, when the order was ignored, the Council asked all members to give the world organization assistance in repelling the aggression. And on July 7, the Council in effect handed over command of the United Nations' war to General Douglas MacArthur, the American commander in chief. By the time Malik returned to the Council on July 27, he was no longer in a position to undo the damage to his cause by diplomatic means.

Despite the high drama surrounding the origin of the Korean War and the importance of the issues that were involved, the American press and public reacted to it with curious indifference once the first shock of the conflict had worn off. It was called, almost by common consent, the "Forgotten War." It should not have been. From a scattered and well-nigh impotent fighting force at the outset of the conflict, the American armed forces expanded by 2 million men in two years and military appropriations rose from $12 billion to $41 billion. General MacArthur, as the commander of the first great force to fight under the United Nations banner, was one of the most remarkable men in American military history and by all odds one of the most colorful. He and his successors built up an army in Korea that totaled 600,000 troops, including a hard core of 200,000 Americans, 350,000 South Koreans, and contingents from sixteen other countries totaling about 50,000. Of the United Nations losses of 150,000 dead and 250,000 wounded before the signing of the agreement to end the war at Panmunjom on July 27, 1953, the Americans suffered 33,629 dead and 103,284 wounded.

It was a war of movement, of stunning surprises. At the outset, American liberal opinion was pleased because of the novelty of United Nations support while conservatives liked the idea of fighting Communism. The ever-isolationist Chicago *Tribune* grumbled: "The White House gang is today enormously popular." Once MacArthur was able to bring in his American divisions and stem the first North Korean advance in front of the southern seaport of Pusan, he struck hard behind the enemy with his amphibious landing at Inchon near the western end of the 38th parallel. It gave him an advantage that enabled him to surge back across the bordor and drive the North Koreans before him to the Yalu River by early fall.

Up to that point, the North Koreans' main support had been their chief arms supplier, the Soviet Union. But with MacArthur's forces advancing toward the Chinese border, Mao Tsetung became deeply concerned. On October 1, Foreign Minister Chou En-lai assailed the United States as "the most dangerous enemy of the People's Republic of China." Within two weeks, he warned that China would not "supinely tolerate" the invasion of its neighbor. K. M. Panikkar, the Indian ambassador to Peking, sent frantic word to Washington that the Chinese were about to enter the war.

MacArthur's response was to announce a final offensive to push to the Chinese border, end the war, and "send the boys home for Christmas." Neither President Truman, the Congress, nor the American press appeared to doubt his word, for he was the mightiest American proconsul of a martial age. By November 1, the Chinese were in action. And on November 26, a striking force of 250,000 Chinese troops attacked the American Eighth Army between Hungnam and the Chosin Reservoir, abruptly changing the entire character of the war.

As the outnumbered United Nations forces fell back, MacArthur thundered defiance. He called for an attack on mainland China in order to deny the enemy a "privileged sanctuary." That, at last, was too much. President Truman began seeking arrangements for a cease-fire. When MacArthur persisted, going to the length of issuing a statement that threatened a Chinese invasion, Truman abruptly relieved him of his command on April 11, 1951, on the ground of insubordination.

By that time, the Chinese Communist drive southward had been checked at the 38th parallel and General Matthew B. Ridgway, MacArthur's successor, had regrouped his forces. The Chinese were beginning to take heavy punishment when the Soviet ambassador, Malik, proposed a cease fire on June 23, 1951, in a United Nations broadcast. But if Moscow and Washington were ready to give up, the Chinese were not. They now had assumed a dominant role in North Korean affairs that was scarcely to Stalin's liking.

Although truce talks began on July 10, some of the hardest fighting of the war followed and American disillusionment with a far-off Asian conflict grew apace. Instead of recalling that the American presence in South Korea had come about almost by accident at the end of World War II to counter Russian armed support of North Korea, the American public blamed the United Nations for the country's involvement in the Korean conflict. Secretary of State Acheson also was criticized, quite unfairly, for a speech prior to the war in which he eliminated South Korea from the American defense perimeter in Asia, a decision that had been made by the Joint Chiefs of Staff. There was much discouraging talk, too, about the impotence of the United Nations because it had failed to force either a trusteeship or elections on the Communist North.

In this atmosphere, the promise of General Dwight David Eisenhower to end the war came to the United States as a welcome relief from an appallingly bad situation. The old hero of World War II was elected to the presidency on the Republican ticket in 1952 primarily because he had pledged himself to go to Korea, if given the power, and restore peace. He did it, but only after a wearing and frustrating process of talking and fighting with the Chinese Communists that created an even more abrasive public mood. The American people simply had had enough of an inconclusive war in Asia that did not seem to involve their national interests. No amount of argument could convince them after the signing of the truce at Panmunjom in 1953 that this had been a successful war to contain Communism because the Republic of Korea had been saved from Communist absorption.

Through no fault of the correspondents, some three hundred of whom covered the action for the American and world news media, this became a decidedly unpopular war. Because it was fought for limited objectives and with limited forces, it could not end in the kind of victory that Americans had been led to expect from their press and from their history books. The correspondents, of course, were well aware of the philosophy behind the war and some of them even criticized it as die-hard adherents of MacArthur. But in the main, this was not their business and they recognized it. Many distinguished themselves for their work under fire, among them Keyes Beech of the Chicago *Daily News*, Homer Bigart and Marguerite Higgins of the New York *Herald Tribune*, George Barrett of the New York *Times*, Stan Swinton and Relman Morin of the Associated Press, Peter Kalischer of United Press, and Jim Lucas of the Scripps-Howard newspapers. But during the concluding stages of the war, many a newspaper didn't even bother to feature the fighting on Page 1 except when there seemed to be something decisive about it. As for radio, bulletins sufficed and television was still too much of a novelty to be tried under battlefield conditions.

General Ridgway saw the disillusionment at first hand among his troops. Many a soldier asked, "Why are we here? What are we fighting for?" If it couldn't be explained to men in the field in this inhospitable Asian land, it was doubly difficult to convince the home front that this was a war worth the trouble of the United States. In vain did General Ridgway plead with the Pentagon to "wake up the people at home" and see that they were "told the truth about this war." The public wasn't interested, once the conflict had settled into a process of grinding attrition, in any stepped-up American commitment on the Asian mainland. To be sure, there was a ferocious public reaction against the Chinese Communists and a tendency on the part of conservatives to hunt for traitors in the American government who had blocked an American victory in Korea. In this respect, Chiang Kai-shek and his Chinese exiles on Taiwan were the gainers; with the additional American aid they received, they were able to establish a viable economy among the less enthusiastic Taiwanese.

Depite their losses, the Chinese Communists emerged from the Korean War with the most credit. For the first time since the Russo-Japanese War of 1904, an Asian power had been able to batter down the might of the West. The will of the greatest military power on earth, the United States, had been frustrated through Asian strength and Asian sacrifice. Both on the battlefield and at the conference table, the Chinese had shown themselves to be a match for the Americans. To the considerable discomfiture of the Soviet Union, Mao also had gained an advantage over Moscow, the fountainhead of Communist doctrine. For while the Soviets had confined themselves to a war of words at the United Nations, the Chinese had put up a fight for their Asian brethren with salutary results. In Asia, therefore, Mao had no further reason to take second place to Stalin in the highest councils of world Communism.

There was one other major development as a result of China's demonstration of its strength as a Communist power. In Indochina, where Ho Chi Minh had been fighting the French since 1946 to establish the independence of Vietnam, he gained a potent ally and the inspiration to continue his long struggle. The French, like Chiang Kai-shek, had been pretending that all was well, primarily for the sake of public opinion at home and in the United States. But with the loss of Dien Bien Phu in 1954 to the Viet Minh general, Vo Nguyen Giap, the French were through and they knew it. At the Far Eastern conference that convened at Geneva in the spring of 1954, they gave up their Asian empire.

Indochina was broken into four successor states — Cambodia, Laos, and the two Vietnams. Divided in the Korean pattern along the 17th parallel, Vietnam's twenty-two provinces with 13 million population in the north were turned over to Ho Chi Minh and his Viet Minh while thirty-nine southern provinces with 12 million population were shifted from French rule to that of a French-supported mandarin, Ngo Dinh Diem, who had come home from a refugee existence in monasteries in the United States and Belgium.

The American government, wary after the misfortunes of Korea, did not sign the Geneva agreements of July 21, 1954, on Indochina, although it could scarcely avoid a commitment to abide by them. To those who sought to involve the United States in Southeast Asia at this juncture, President Eisenhower replied: "I cannot conceive of a greater tragedy for America than to get heavily involved now in an all-out war in any of these regions, particularly with large units." The Pulitzer Prize for editorial cartooning went that year to D. R. Fitzpatrick's cartoon in the St. Louis *Post-Dispatch*, showing Uncle Sam, gun in hand, pausing before a black quagmire labeled Indochina and pondering the question: "How would another mistake help?" It was an accurate reflection of the mood of public and press in the United States.

But the Chinese and their Communist allies were scarcely in a mood to end their campaign. Following Stalin's death in 1953, Peking was the master of its own destiny and certainly no underling to Moscow. Having frustrated the United States and defeated the French, the Red alliance in Asia had little to lose in choosing to continue the struggle. With the boundless resources of Asian manpower and the patience of the East, they probed for fresh weaknesses in the ranks of their enemies. They didn't have to look farther than the first American newspaper or news magazine. For the greatest weakness in the West was the ignorance of American public opinion about the complex forces that were behind the new revolutionary movement in Asia, the terrible suspicion that led many people in the United States to fear to learn anything of their Communist enemies, and the failure of the bulk of their news media to supply the kind of public intelligence on which future policies could be based.

Out of such neglect of the very fundamentals of the democratic process, the first fissures of a tragic division in public opinion were beginning to appear in the United States — a split that would come dangerously close to undermining its position of world leadership. This was the weakness that every Communist leader would seek to exploit for his own benefit, and some would succeed beyond their wildest calculations.

IX. The Balance of Terror

1. McCarthy

The atmosphere of hate and suspicion that Joseph R. McCarthy spread through every aspect of American life can scarcely be understood — or even believed — by those who did not live through that incredible era in the United States. The junior senator from Wisconsin was able to accuse President Truman and the entire Democratic Party of "twenty years of treason." He manhandled the secretary of state, Dean Acheson, branding him "the Red Dean of Washington." General George Catlett Marshall, who had served in the Truman administration as both secretary of state and secretary of defense, was termed part of "a conspiracy so immense and an infamy so black as to dwarf any previous venture in the history of man." That same Marshall, to President Truman, had been "the greatest living American."

Such eminent citizens were able to survive McCarthy's displeasure. But hundreds of others, caught in the maelstrom of unfavorable publicity, went through agonies of suffering and had their careers torn apart. Almost the entire China service of the Department of State was wrecked, either through dismissals or resignations of officials whom McCarthy had assailed. The democratic notion that a man must be presumed innocent until he is found guilty was swept aside. The protection of civil liberties became prima facie evidence of a dangerous attraction to Communism. Anyone who invoked the Fifth Amendment before McCarthy's Senate investigating committee became a "Fifth Amendment Communist." And yet, not one person accused by McCarthy was ever convicted of a crime after a full trial or hearing.

If there was a balance of terror between the United States and the Soviet Union that kept both from venturing into atomic warfare, it scarcely prevented politicians of the McCarthy stripe from using the fear of Communism as a devastating weapon against their enemies. The terror, in such instances, was weighted entirely in favor of McCarthyism. As the angry Elmer Davis once put it in a broadcast, "McCarthy gets his effects on the front page. . . . And if yesterday's front page story blows up today, there is always today's front page story to bury the refutation."

This was the technique that McCarthy used to start his campaign. On February 9, 1950, he announced at Wheeling, W. Va., that he had a list of 205 people in the State Department who were members of the Communist Party and, at least by implication, spies. When the State Department asked for the names, McCarthy did not respond. Instead, he took advantage of the American press's tradition of objectivity, under which a speaker could rely on the publication of his most sensational charges without regard for their truth or falsity. Thus, continuing with his speaking tour, he announced at Reno that he had informed President Truman in a letter that there were 57 Communists in the State Department. More headlines. And in a Senate speech on February 20, he put the total of State Department Communists at 81.

The press now began to take notice in a big way. It didn't seem to make much difference to the Hearst newspapers, for example, if McCarthy said there were 205, 57, or 81 Communists in the State Department. Nor did it appear to matter whether the senator from Wisconsin submitted proof. Because he said it, it was so. And the Hearst newspapers were by no means alone in their support for him. The few papers that tried to oppose him were brushed off; their editors were "crypto-Communists."

McCarthy's effect on the Republican Party was even more noticeable than his impact on the press. The 1952 Republican platform seemed almost to have been written by him. It dripped with his venom—the treachery that "lost" China to the Communists, the "betrayal" of Chiang Kai-shek, the failures of the Truman administration to contain and defeat Communism. As for Adlai E. Stevenson, the lofty-minded Democratic presidential nominee, McCarthy attacked him for surrounding himself with

"Communist influences," none of them very clearly defined. Even General Eisenhower, while campaigning in Milwaukee, eliminated a passage from his speech that praised General Marshall because Wisconsin Republicans feared it might be construed as an affront to McCarthy.

With Eisenhower's victory and the return of the Republicans to power, therefore, McCarthyism became one of the facts of political life in the United States. It soon became an unwritten rule in the new administration, at least at the outset, that everybody up to and including cabinet rank had better be careful of McCarthy. Obviously, Eisenhower hoped to dissuade his black-jowled ally from continuing with the tactics that had been so instrumental in destroying the effectiveness of the Truman administration. But McCarthy was intoxicated with power. He now commanded the respectful, almost reverent, Page 1 attention of a large section of the press whenever he made a pronouncement. Certainly, he had good reason to believe that his political position was impregnable.

The Eisenhower administration had barely settled into office in 1953 when McCarthy blasted open an investigation into the Voice of America and sent Roy Cohn and David Schine, two aides who were still in their twenties, on a junket to Europe to turn up pro-Communist books in the libraries of the U.S. Information Service. Not content with that, the rampaging senator attacked Charles E. Bohlen, the eminent career diplomat whom President Eisenhower had nominated to be ambassador to the Soviet Union, as a "security risk — and that's putting it mildly." It took Senator Robert A. Taft's intervention to quiet the storm and insure Bohlen's confirmation. Finally, taking on the Eisenhower administration itself, McCarthy assailed continued American aid to Britain in the face of what he called "British blood trade" with Communist China. It was clear enough that a confrontation now was inevitable.

Early in 1954, while digging into military espionage, McCarthy made an attack on the Army that Eisenhower could neither forgive nor forget. It came about when an Army dentist, Major Irving Peress, invoked the Fifth Amendment against self-incrimination when he was called before the senator's committee to answer charges of Communist activities. McCarthy demanded a court martial of Peress from the secretary of the army, Robert T. Stevens. Instead, Peress was given an honorable discharge from the service at Camp Kilmer, N. J. In a fury, McCarthy subpoenaed the post commander, Major General Ralph Zwicker, whose reputation was above reproach, and told him he was "not fit to wear that uniform." When Secretary Stevens defended the general, McCarthy called the civilian head of the Army a "dupe." It was at this point that President Eisenhower himself entered the dispute with a defense of General Zwicker and a call to his cabinet to observe "fairness, justice, and decency" in dealing with government personnel.

The issue was joined.

At this critical point in a controversy that had embroiled the government and split the press, a new force in public communication made itself felt in a dramatic way. Just as the young radio commentators had shaken the land with their outcries against Hitler in the days before World War II when the tide was running so strongly for isolationism, television now mobilized the sentiment against McCarthy. The first blow was struck quite unexpectedly in a film documentary of McCarthy's career on "See It Now," a Columbia Broadcasting System program narrated by Edward R. Murrow and directed by Fred W. Friendly. The half-hour broadcast on March 9, 1954, concluded with these solemn words by Murrow:

"We proclaim ourselves, as indeed we are, the defenders of freedom—what's left of it—but we cannot defend freedom by deserting it at home. The actions of the junior senator from Wisconsin have caused alarm and dismay amongst our allies abroad and given considerable comfort to our enemies. And whose fault is that? Not really his; he didn't create this situation of fear, he merely exploited it and rather successfully. Cassius was right. 'The fault, dear Brutus, is not in our stars but in ourselves.'"

The reaction was fantastic. Within a brief time, more than 75,000 telephone calls, telegrams, and letters swamped CBS with the tally running as high as 10 to 1 in favor of Murrow. The press, much to its own surprise, found itself reacting to the initiative of a competing medium. Such leading papers as the New York *Times*, New York *Herald Tribune* and St. Louis *Post-Dispatch*, all of which had opposed McCarthyism, praised Murrow's crusading journalism. The Hearst papers and such conservative columnists as George Sokolsky, Walter Winchell, and Westbrook Pegler defended McCarthy. As for President Eisenhower, he left no doubt of his own sympathies when he put his arm around Murrow at a Gridiron Club dinner in Washington and remarked, "Let me see if there are any marks where the knife went in."

The broadcast, which McCarthy tried unsuccessfully to rebut on CBS, was important for two reasons. It provided the rare spectacle of a television commentator assuming national leadership in a campaign against a powerful politician. Even more significant, it was a foretaste of the climax of the struggle over McCarthy—the televised Army–McCarthy hearings that began on April 22 and lasted for two months. For 35 days of broadcasting, McCarthy was on view before the nation with his chief opponents, Secretary Stevens and the counsel to the Army, Joseph N. Welch of Boston. To some, the television exhibition became a national pastime; to others, a national disgrace. But without doubt, the constant exposure of McCarthy and his methods to public scrutiny turned public opinion against him. As an outgrowth of the hearings, the Senate voted in December to condemn the junior senator from Wisconsin for conduct unbecoming a senator. It was the end of McCarthy's power.

Elmer Davis summed up the McCarthy era in words that came to the nation first over radio:

"The first and great commandment is, Don't let them scare you. For the men who are trying to do that to us are scared themselves. They are afraid that what they think will not stand critical examination; they are afraid that the principles on which this Republic was founded and has been conducted are wrong. They will tell you that there is a hazard in the freedom of the mind, and of course there is, as in any freedom. In trying to think right you run the risk of thinking wrong. But there is no hazard at all, no uncertainty, in letting somebody else tell you what to think; that is sheer damnation."

For free people and a free press, this was worth remembering.

2. The Thaw

Ilya Ehrenburg, the first journalist of the Soviet Union, wrote a novel with a prophetic title in 1954: *The Thaw*. It became the theme of the early post-Stalin era. To be sure, under the collective leadership that succeeded the terrible dictator, freedom of thought and movement in the Western sense were almost as far off in the Soviet Union as they had ever been. The power struggle scarcely encouraged dissent. For the tough and ruthless Nikita Khrushchev, who had inherited the base of Stalin's authority as secretary of the Communist Party, already was flexing his muscles. He had brought about the execution of Lavrenti P. Beria, Stalin's chief of secret police, as an "enemy of the people." Just what the fate of the premier, Georgi M. Malenkov, would be remained uncertain, but Khrushchev was successfully fighting off his program for a shift from heavy industry to the manufacture of light consumer goods. Without doubt, either Malenkov or Khrushchev soon would be dismissed and the chances were against Malenkov.

In all truth, with this kind of intrigue increasing behind the grim facade of the Kremlin, the season didn't seem to be propitious for any kind of thaw. And yet, such was the relief at Stalin's death that a mild literary revival occurred under the patronage of Khrushchev, scarcely a figure of benevolence himself. Alexander Korniechuk wrote a play, *Wings*, based on the Beria affair and the ills of the secret police. Vladimir Dudintsev was able to write in his novel, *Not By Bread Alone*, that "once a man has started to think, he cannot be denied his freedom." And the young poet, Yevgeny Yevtuchenko, defined Communism as the "decency of a revolutionary idea," and argued it was worthy of authority only in a "state in which truth is president." Such views might have surprised Lenin.

The existence of a generation gap among Soviet writers was evident enough, but the circulation of a literature of protest was not easy to achieve. For in 1954, it was no flaming young liberal but an old poet, Boris Pasternak, who posed the issue with the completion of his huge novel, *Dr. Zhivago*. In it, Pasternak had written of history, of the beginnings of the Russian revolution and the agony through which the Russian people passed thereafter, but in effect his book was a challenge to the moral basis of the Soviet state. His friends stood by him. Even the nimble Ehrenburg, who had so lively a genius for self-preservation, went so far as to say of *Dr. Zhivago*'s treatment of the revolution: "The description of those days is excellent. Pasternak and I belong to the same generation, so I can pass judgment on this."

However, no Soviet magazine nor publishing house dared touch Pasternak's extraordinary work. It was called counterrevolutionary and worse. But outside the Soviet Union, *Dr. Zhivago* was published in seventeen languages. It became a best-seller in the United States and the subject of a world-famous motion picture. In 1958, it won the Nobel Prize for Pasternak but he had to suffer the ignominy of being forced by his government to refuse the award. For all his genius and all his prestige, neither he nor any other member of the intelligentsia could stand up against the dictatorial power of the Kremlin.

Clearly, the relaxation in the post-Stalin period had its limits. No novelist, journalist, poet, dramatist, or musician could safely overstep the bounds of Soviet propriety. What had changed was the notion of eternal *zagovor*, or conspiracy, that had dominated Stalin's quarter-century of rule. The dread of mammoth purges based on some wild figment of the dictator's imagination slowly passed. A generation of silence ended. The more courageous people in Soviet literature found their tongues; cautiously at first, then with more confidence, they began to experiment with themes they would never have dared approach under Stalin. A few were published, many were suppressed, but nobody was shot. That, essentially, was the meaning of *"The Thaw."*

Khrushchev pushed the concept of liberalization for his own purposes, very possibly because he wanted to establish before the Soviet hierarchy that he was not to be another Stalin. Whatever his aims, he showed mercy to his political opponents after the Beria purge. When Malenkov was overthrown in 1955, he was shifted to a minor job but left unharmed. The same was true of other "old Bolsheviks," such as Vyacheslav M. Molotov. At the abortive summit meeting with President Eisenhower at Geneva in 1955, Khrushchev tried to promote the notion of relaxation abroad — something he called "the spirit of Geneva."

The process known as de-Stalinization set in. On February 24, 1956, before the Twentieth Congress of the Communist Party in Moscow, Khrushchev delivered his famous "secret speech" against Stalin. Nothing that Pasternak had ever written, nothing that any Communist leader had ever said, constituted a more devastating indictment of life in a Communist world. It was Khrushchev's position that the wrongs of Stalin must be righted, so far as possible, and that the "cult of personality" must be removed from the Soviet Union. Although the speech eventually leaked out and was published in full in the Western press, the most that the Soviet people were permitted to read was a paraphrase of some of its key passages.

In central and eastern Europe, where people had had to live under the terror for so long, the repercussions were not long in coming. Although Khrushchev had taken the precaution to herd the Soviet's European client states into a Warsaw Pact organization on May 14, 1955, as an answer to NATO, that scarcely quieted the unrest behind the iron curtain. In June, 1956, Polish workers struck in Poznan for better wages and working conditions. Picket signs appeared demanding freedom, an end of the Soviet occupation, and the abandonment of Communism. The Polish Army was ordered to the seething city, precipitating a series of bloody clashes in which 38 persons were killed and 270 others wounded. While the insurrection was put down, not even a Soviet offer of more consumer goods to alleviate a chronic shortage in Poland dispelled the brooding and rebellious mood of the workers.

Heartened by the Polish outbreaks, the Hungarians began demonstrating against the repressive Moscow-supported regime of Matyas Rakosi, an unreconstructed Stalinist. When Rakosi lost control, Khrushchev removed him in July, 1956, and put in another old-line Communist, Erno Gero. But Budapest, taking the notion of a thaw seriously, turned instead to a former premier, Imre Nagy, as a true champion of liberalization. The press began to follow the brave example of the *Literary Gazette* (Irodalmi Ujsag), which had been protesting domestic censorship since 1954. It was a giddy time for the Hungarians. When the ideological indoctrination courses that had been required of all editors were dropped, they began agitating for the release of political prisoners. Among those who regained their freedom, as a result, were Dr. Endre Marton, a former editor of the daily *Kis Ujsag*, and his wife, Ilona Nylas Marton, who had served respectively as the Budapest correspondents of the Associated Press and United Press.

In the manner in which the Soviet Union settled the Polish agitation, there was further encouragement for the Hungarians. On October 9, Khrushchev permitted the return to power in Poland of Wladyslaw Gomulka, who had survived a 1949 purge by Stalin and now took up the role of a relatively liberal premier on a note of defiance. When he refused to go to Moscow, Khrushchev came bustling to Warsaw and ordered Marshal Konstantin K. Rokossovsky to alert Soviet occupation forces. Gomulka gave in, of course, but he did manage to wring a few economic concessions from the Russians. On that basis, the crisis ended on October 20 and Soviet troops withdrew.

There was more enthusiasm for the token Polish resistance in Budapest than there was in Warsaw. On October 23, thousands of demonstrators surged through the streets of the Hungarian capital to show support for the Poles. When the jittery Premier Gero ordered his security forces into action and they fired into the ranks of the protestors, a full-scale revolt began. Next day, Soviet troops came in but achieved only temporary quiet. The only solution that Anastas Mikoyan could see, when Khrushchev sent him to Budapest from Moscow, was to restore Imre Nagy to power as premier. And so, the Hungarians enjoyed their brief hour of glory.

Unlike Gomulka, who had won concessions from Moscow by negotiating within the Soviet system, Nagy rashly served notice that he was in effect leading Hungary out of the Warsaw Pact and into neutralism. He disbanded the security police, appealed to the United Nations to remove Soviet occupation forces and, in a supreme act of defiance, decreed freedom of the press. New publications sprang to life under this heady stimulus. The old Communist newspapers were burned in the streets. Like everybody else in Hungary, the journalists seemed to be acting without regard for consequences.

By an accident of history, Britain, France, and Israel selected this moment to invade Egypt. With the Communist world in disarray over Poland and Hungary and the United States in the throes of a presidential election, the time seemed favorable. If the Soviet Union had been worried at what the world might think of armed intervention in Hungary on a decisive scale, the naked Western aggression against Egypt disposed of Moscow's scruples.

As late as October 30, the day after Israel invaded Egypt, the Soviet government had promised to conduct its future relations with its satellites on "the principle of full equality, respect for territorial integrity, state independence and sovereignty, and noninterference in the domestic affairs of one another." On November 2, 200,000 Soviet troops ringed rebellious Budapest with 2,500 tanks and armored cars. Nagy was deposed. His Moscow-approved successor, Janos Kadar, appealed at once for Soviet military aid to "smash the sinister forces of reaction" and "restore order and calm." With that the Soviet invaders stormed into action. The Hungarians, under a gallant lieutenant colonel, Pal Maleter, threw a part of their army against the Russians but it was an unequal contest. In the carnage that followed, 30,000 persons were estimated to have been killed in Budapest, including nearly 3,000 "freedom fighters." More than 4,000 buildings were destroyed before the last Hungarian citadel was taken. Within a month, the brief bid for freedom was crushed.

To escape the mass arrests and deportations to the Soviet Union that followed the end of the invasion, more than 200,000

Hungarians fled to the West. Among them were Endre Marton, who had covered the fighting for the Associated Press at the risk of his life, and his wife as well as a number of other Hungarian journalists. For the first thing that vanished when Kadar took over under Russian military auspices was the freedom of the press. Nagy and Maleter, who had taken refuge in the Yugoslav embassy, were persuaded to leave their sanctuary, arrested by Soviet officials, given a meaningless trial, and promptly executed. Having witnessed the terror, Russell Jones of the United Press, the last Western reporter left in Budapest, wrote: "For the first time since I was a boy, I wept."

The Thaw had loosened an avalanche of trouble for the Soviet Union and changed the course of history.

3. The "Hundred Flowers"

With inviting opportunities for expansion on its borders, the new China of Mao Tse-tung did not take kindly to Russian talk of a thaw in the cold war or the fulsome preachment of "peaceful co-existence" as Khrushchev had defined it at the Twentieth Party Congress in Moscow. It was all very well for the Soviet Union, having achieved a role in world leadership, to seek a relaxation of tensions with the West but the Chinese hardly deemed such a policy to be in their own best interests. Under Mao, China had developed a revolutionary dynamism that was fueled by violent tactics. Peking had gained more from armed resistance to the United States in the Korean War than from the dubious Asian-African friendship meeting at Bandung in 1955. There was little doubt that Mao, having achieved the mastery of China by his own efforts, would not be afraid to oppose a regime in Moscow that was taking a course of which he did not approve.

Among the old Communists of Peking, Stalin had never been loved or even trusted. In Mao's long years at Yenan, the Soviet dictator had made little secret of his preference for Chiang Kai-shek. Nevertheless, the worldwide publicity that had accompanied Khrushchev's attack on Stalin appeared to disturb the Chinese more than anything else. It held up the Communist system to scorn. It tended to reflect on the entire range of Communist leadership, even including Mao. Consequently, in the Chinese view, Moscow no longer deserved the undeviating loyalty of all Communist parties. It was even conceivable to some Chinese theoreticians that Peking now could become a rival center of Communist authority, devoted to propagating the notion of continual pressure on the capitalist world until it collapsed.

The first sign of such an independent Chinese policy came with the Polish and Hungarian uprisings, when Chou En-lai ostentatiously visited Eastern Europe as a "mediator" between the Soviet Union and its satellites. Publicly, Chou pleaded for accession to Soviet leadership. But privately, he let such harassed leaders as Kadar and Gomulka know that China would be against further overt Soviet interference in the internal affairs of their respective countries. Chou even had a few kind words for Tito, never a hero in Peking because of his Communist heresies.

It was at this time that Mao intervened with a speech titled, "On the Correct Handling of Contradictions Among People," in which he tried to apply the lessons of Hungary and Poland to the propagation of Communist doctrine. In May, 1956, he had put forward a new policy, "Let a hundred flowers bloom together, let diverse schools of thought contend." But he did not actually campaign for this notion until his speech of February, 1957, in an apparent effort to demonstrate that China's way was superior to that of the Soviet Union.

What impression he made abroad with this poetic view was slight, but at home he suddenly found himself contending with a spontaneous uprising among intellectuals. Chinese writers and artists were the first to demand freedom to express their ideas. The journalists cried out against the lack of freedom in the press. In the universities, both students and faculties complained against the failures of Communist society and argued that no single doctrine could encompass the whole truth. There was even wild talk of another Chinese revolution. The anti-party storm, as Mao branded it in righteous anger, lasted for six weeks before he put a resolute stop to it in June, 1957.

"Certain people in our country," he said, "were delighted when the Hungarian events took place. They hoped that something similar would happen in China, that thousands of people would demonstrate in the streets against the people's government."

That brief experience with freedom of expression in China was all that Mao permitted. The lid was slammed back tight. The habitual secrecy of decision and movement resumed. Nothing more was heard of the "hundred flowers" and "diverse schools." In China, thenceforth, there was one flower, one school, and one little red book of sayings from which all wisdom flowed. Each belonged to Mao. There were small changes in the Chinese line, to be sure, but after the failure of his campaign for diversity Mao reverted to his doctrine of "permanent revolution" as opposed to the Soviet view that Communism could win its way by peaceful means.

It would be an oversimplification to contend that this was at the root of all China's moves in both domestic and foreign policy during the period of drift and indecision between Peking and Moscow. Actually, the rightist group in China still had some power although the failure of the Soviet Union to provide sufficient economic aid was making its position increasingly difficult. During the latter part of 1957, however, the rightists suffered a major defeat when Mao had many of their number sent to the countryside to perform hard physical labor. It marked the ascendancy of the Chinese left and the beginning of violent swings in foreign policy that coincided with increasing troubles at home.

Mao himself led a Chinese delegation to the conference of Communist parties in Moscow during November, 1957, to press his point of view. It was shortly after the historic night of October 4 when the Soviet Union had startled the world by pitching a 184-pound satellite, Sputnik I, into global orbit. If Mao was impressed, he did not show it. Certainly, he was not frightened by the awesome new capabilities of Soviet science that already had thrown the United States into a paroxysm of national jitters. While the world was assured at the time that all was sweet harmony between the Communist giants, it became known long afterward that Mao had taken a firm position against the Soviet doctrine of peaceful transition to Communism. He warned that the outcome could be a weakening of the revolutionary will of the proletariat. Even more important, he bluntly told the Soviets that he was not afraid of nuclear war and quoted his own words to Jawaharlal Nehru: "I said that if the worst came to the worst and half of mankind died, the other half would remain, while imperialism would be razed to the ground, and the whole world would become Socialist." It was Tito who subsequently spread the story, also attributed to Mao, that China could afford to lose 300 million people in a nuclear war and still win it.

Mao left Moscow with a Soviet commitment to help China develop an atomic capability, which never was carried out. Before the Chinese Communist Party meeting in April, 1958, he called for a policy of permanent revolution abroad. But at home he mobilized the masses of the Chinese people for a twin attack on China's grave economic ills — a multiplication of people's communes to increase farm yields and the building of backyard furnaces to produce steel in small quantities to solve a persistent industrial crisis. This was the romantic experiment called the "Great Leap Forward." Despite the fervor with which it was proclaimed in China, it didn't get very far. All it really proved was that Mao was a prisoner of his own propaganda, which made him the most menacing and the least predictable of all the world's major political leaders.

From then on, only one thing was really certain about Mao's rule in China. The time of the "hundred flowers" would never recur while he held sway over 800 million Chinese.

4. Good Neighbors — and Bad

Like its super-power adversary, the Soviet Union, the United States found itself involved in increasing difficulties after World War II in keeping order in its own hemisphere. While there was no Chinese giant that loomed in an eternally menacing posture along the borders of the greatest of the American republics, Latin America represented an almost constant source of trouble and anxiety for the "Colossus of the North." The age of dollar diplomacy and military intervention by Washington in the affairs of sister republics south of the Rio Grande supposedly had passed. And yet, despite all the admiration that had been showered on Franklin Delano Roosevelt for his widely publicized "good neighbor" policy, the hazards of dealing with the 250 million peoples of the underdeveloped lands of the Americas remained the most perplexing and least rewarding aspect of United States foreign policy.

Of all Washington's problems south of the border during and immediately after World War II, the most irksome was the challenge presented by a pudgy Argentine militarist, Juan Domingo Peron, and his noisy blonde wife, Evita. With the fall of the government of President Ramon S. Castillo in 1943, the hitherto obscure Peron, then a 49-year-old Army colonel and former Argentine military attache in Mussolini's Rome, had come to power as the head of a notorious "Colonels' Clique." Rising rapidly from secretary of labor to secretary of war and then vice-president, Peron had forced the dissolution of political parties, crushed dissent, and organized a powerful censorship section known as the Subsecretariat of Information and the Press. The only paper that held out against him was the great *La Prensa* of Buenos Aires, which had been founded in 1869, and its defiant editor and publisher, Alberto Gainza Paz.

La Prensa had led the outspoken Argentine press during the opening phases of World War II against the government's policy of favoritism for the Axis. It was Peron's conceit, when he came to power, that he could gain the leadership of the Latin American republics and embarrass the United States by maintaining his pro-Axis posture. But *La Prensa*'s continued opposition made it difficult. On April 26, 1944, therefore, Peron made his first move against the paper by ordering a five-day suspension. It was a thinly disguised warning of still worse to come unless *La Prensa* bowed to the will of the government. When the newspaper appeared again on May 1, the 45-year-old Gainza Paz's answer was to quote the Argentine patriot Esteban Echeverria: "Equality and freedom are the principles that engender democracy." It marked the beginning of a seven-year struggle.

Peron had to give ground at first. With the realization that the Axis was on the verge of defeat, Argentina belatedly adhered to the Rio declaration on January 26, 1944, by breaking relations with Berlin and Tokyo. Next, in order to qualify for admission to the United Nations, the Argentine government subscribed to the Act of Chapultepec, declared war on Germany and Japan on March 27, 1945, and thereby received grudging recognition from the United States. There was no truce, however, in the conflict with *La Prensa*. On the day war against Japan ended, and the Plaza de Mayo in Buenos Aires was jammed with happy young people waving Allied flags, *La Prensa*'s plant was invaded by Peron's hoodlums and bombed. On September 26, 1945, Gainza Paz was arrested, briefly held in prison, and released without explanation.

Encouraged by what appeared to be growing difficulties for Peron at home and abroad, the United States injudiciously intervened in the Argentine presidential election of 1946 in which Peron was the leading candidate. It was not a role in which the American ambassador, Spruille Braden, covered himself with glory. The angry Peron appealed to his followers to choose between Braden and himself and at all costs to rebuff the interference of the United States in Argentina's affairs. On February 24, Peron easily won the election, handed Washington a crushing diplomatic defeat, and assumed the legal powers of the presidency. In Argentina, he was the state. What he and Evita decreed became law for 20 million Argentine citizens.

With the abrupt retreat of the United States, Gainza Paz and *La Prensa* were left to face Peron's wrath alone. The dictator took his time about developing a campaign of harassment against his well-nigh helpless foe. First, posters appeared all over Buenos Aires asking merchants not to advertise in *La Prensa*. The government denounced its editorials in special broadcasts. Loud speakers were set up outside its editorial offices to blast away with news from rival sources. Nothing quite like this unequal contest had been seen anywhere since the early assaults of Hitler and Mussolini against their independent newspapers.

In the turbulent history of the Americas, the lot of the free press had never been easy south of the Rio Grande; yet, the spirit of independence among Latin American editors had never been completely subdued. The Argentine patriot Manuel Belgrano stated their position in his newspaper, *Correo de Comercio*, in 1810, the year of Argentine independence: "Freedom of the press is nothing but the prerogative of writing and publishing what each citizen thinks and can utter with his tongue; to oppress it is as unjust as it would be to bind the senses, the tongues, the hands and feet of all citizens." It was a tradition that had been upheld by the earliest of Latin American newspapers—*Diario de Pernambuco* and *Jornal de Comercio* in Rio de Janeiro, *El Mercurio* in Valparaiso, Chile, *El Comercio* in Lima, and by Gainza Paz's grandfather, Jose Clemente Paz, the founder of *La Prensa*.

Gainza himself now was put to a cruel test. Peron tightened his pressure on the paper with a series of assaults by hoodlums and harassing court actions. Yet, the publisher refused to give in. Because of his respected position as a leader of the world press, he became a symbol to sympathizers abroad of resistance to Peron's dictatorship and he trained the spotlight of international scrutiny on Argentina.

Peron impatiently brushed aside appeals for *La Prensa*. He worked up a scheme to collect millions of dollars in customs duties on newsprint that, the government belatedly charged, had been due from *La Prensa* for years. When Gainza refused once more to be intimidated, Peron began taking his newsprint away from him by degrees, forcing him to reduce the size of his newspaper drastically. Unsubstantiated criminal charges were preferred against him. As *La Prensa* itself said: "A nightmare of miscarriage of justice, a riot of police power, has become a tormenting reality."

On January 25, 1951, the Peron-controlled Union of News Vendors opened the climactic assault on *La Prensa* by informing

Gainza that he must make specified payments to the union treasury and submit to a union-approved audit of his books. When the newspaper refused, a work stoppage was ordered by the union but Gainza's 1,300 employees loyally remained on the job. On the night of January 26-27, a mob of Peronista thugs blockaded the plant and halted publication. Despite every appeal, *La Prensa* was doomed.

A meeting of the paper's employees on February 26 decided, nevertheless, to defy the government-supported blockade of the plant. In bright afternoon sunlight, they proceeded across the Plaza de Mayo toward their printing plant until a force of armed Peronistas opened fire on them. One workman was killed and fourteen others were wounded. The attempt to print the newspaper under its independent ownership was the last while Peron ruled Argentina. On March 20, 1951, it passed under government control and was issued shortly thereafter as an "official" newspaper. Gainza himself narrowly escaped arrest by fleeing across the Rio de la Plata in a small boat to his mother's ranch in Uruguay.

Peron, emboldened by his victory, broadened his attack on his remaining opponents. Through his control of the labor movement, he applied pressure to all elements in Argentina, including the Catholic Church and the religious schools. To the despair of those who had hoped that the United States might be able to halt his career, the growth of inter-American political organizations actually strengthened the dictator's hand. For out of the Rio Pact of 1947, which legalized the principle that an attack on one of the signatories was to be considered an attack on all, came the Organization of American States in 1951.

Thus, safely within the hemispheric structural order, Peron enjoyed enhanced prestige at home while at the same time he continued to foment opposition to the United States elsewhere in Latin America. All that Washington had to offer, in opposition, was its well-worn program of opposition to Communism. It wasn't much of an attraction south of the Rio Grande, as both the Truman and Eisenhower administrations discovered, because of the widespread economic distress among the peoples of

Central and South America. Such a position had the additional drawback of lending moral support to dictators of the Peron stripe. However, in the early 1950s, the main effort of the United States was being exerted in Western Europe; consequently, Latin America and its festering ills took a secondary position in Washington's calculations. Peron was able to do pretty much as he pleased.

In his travels in the United States and Europe, Gainza Paz became one of the few who sustained the Argentine spirit of resistance to Peron. During a campaign that was unique in the history of journalism, he managed to mobilize a considerable part of the foreign press to join the protest against the expropriation of *La Prensa*. It was no small achievement. There had never before been so united an international editorial position against the interference of any government with the press. No similar movement had been attempted to any great extent during the rise of Mussolini, Hitler, or the Japanese military clique. True, the international press could not overthrow Peron; however, it could and did give him and his country the worst kind of publicity. And, despite all the barriers he erected to insulate his people from opinions other than his own, the disapproval of the outside world eventually seeped through to unhappy Argentina. This was the purpose of Gainza Paz's campaign. During his five years in exile, he carried it out with both devotion and courage.

On September 16, 1955, Peron was overthrown by the same military forces that had put him in power, but this time they had both clerical and civilian support. The military junta that led the coup gave supreme authority to Major General Pedro Aramburu, whose first action was the restoration of freedom of the press and other civil liberties. The Peronista party and its evil offshoots were dissolved and their founder sent into exile. All expropriated property was returned, the most prominent being *La Prensa*.

Gainza Paz resumed the independent publication of his newspaper on February 3, 1956. Under Peron, its circulation of nearly 400,000 had been cut in half but it returned to normal by slow degrees. What could not be obliterated, however, were the mental and physical tortures through which the editor and his loyal staff had passed and the heavy financial losses the management had sustained in its fight against the Peron dictatorship. Such things were bound to be overlooked in Washington in the celebration of Gainza Paz's crucial role in helping bring about Peron's fall.

There was one other major development in the anti-Peron uprising. That was the election of Arturo Frondizi, *La Prensa*'s foremost defender in the Argentine Congress, as the president of the country on February 22, 1958, in the first free election in a dozen years. It was a pity that representative government could not cure the nation's persistent economic troubles and that, after eight years, another military junta was able to take over and renew the ordeal of the press.

5. *Eyeball to Eyeball*

In the fastness of Cuba's Sierra Maestra on February 17, 1957, Herbert L. Matthews of the New York *Times* found a lean and bearded 29-year-old lawyer, Fidel Castro, who for five years had been leading what seemed like an almost hopeless effort to overthrow the well-entrenched military dictator, Fulgencio Batista. From the day of his futile assault on the Moncada Barracks at Santiago de Cuba, July 26, 1953, Castro had been a marked man. Captured and imprisoned for two years, he had gone into exile for another year and in 1956 had returned to his homeland to continue the battle. At the time the 57-year-old Matthews set out to find the rebel leader, the Batista government had been spreading the rumor that he was dead. When he was found alive with eighteen of his followers, still proclaiming his ability to take over Cuba, he became an international sensation.

Both the Batista regime and its firm friends in the State Department in Washington protested the favorable publicity for the outlaw Cuban, but it did them no good. Once Batista's foes knew that Castro was alive, they began supplying him with volunteers and funds. In the Sierra Maestra, he whipped together a well-trained, disciplined fighting force that was soon able to hold its own with the dispirited government troops. On January 1, 1959, after defeating Batista's army at Santa Clara and forcing the old dictator to flee the country, Castro marched into Havana with the aura of a deliverer about him. Thereby, he opened a new era in the Americas.

Like Mao's agrarian reformers, the new hero of Cuba left some doubt initially over the extent of his devotion to the Communist cause. A considerable body of journalistic opinion, very largely influenced by Matthews' reporting, was convinced from the outset that Castro's sympathies were those of a radical democrat. There was a perfectly solid reporting job by Joseph Martin and Philip Santora of the New York *Daily News* that documented the Cuban leader's links with Communism and his devotion to the hard-line Argentine Communist, Ernesto (Che) Guevara, but it didn't have much impact. The larger part of the American press was willing to give Castro the benefit of the doubt. Even the American Society of Newspaper Editors obligingly invited Castro to its annual convention in the spring after his victory and gave him a national platform from which to lay down his terms to Washington.

By that time, the adventurer from the Sierra Maestra had tightened his hold on 8 million Cubans and their press with a reign of terror in which hundreds of his opponents were executed. Having assumed office as premier, he embarked on a program of economic and social change with little regard for practical results or outraged opinion in the United States. It became increasingly clear that the unfortunate Cubans had merely exchanged a dictator of the far Right for a dictator of the far Left.

During the ensuing 1960 presidential campaign in the United States, Senator John Fitzgerald Kennedy repeatedly branded Cuba a "Communist satellite" and accused the preceding Eisenhower administration of having followed short-sighted policies toward all of Latin America. Richard Milhous Nixon, the vice-president and choice of the old general as the Republican presidential nominee, found himself obliged to defend the administration's failures in Cuba against his vigorous young Democratic opponent in a series of national television debates, the first in American political history at so high a level. When Kennedy won by a very narrow margin, there was heightened anticipation of great events to come.

By a twist of circumstance, the first crisis of the new administration was not with the Soviet Union over Berlin or with the Chinese Communists over their continued attacks on the off-shore islands of Quemoy and Matsu, although both issues had been prominent in the Kennedy–Nixon television debates. Instead, Castro and his Cuban revolution occupied the central attention of the government of the United States, its public and press, its armed forces and its super-secret Central Intelligence Agency.

During the last days of the Eisenhower administration, preparations had been made for an anti-Castro invasion of Cuba with the support of the CIA — a supposedly top secret venture. However, on November 19, 1960, the liberal New York weekly, the *Nation*, published a circumstantial account by Ronald Hilton of Stanford University about a CIA-supported camp in Guatemala where Cuban refugees were being trained for the invasion. The supposed secret became widely known. Along the east coast of Florida, it was almost a joke. Certainly, Castro was well aware of what was going on, for he suddenly forced a cut in the United States embassy staff in Havana from 130 to only 11 officials. That indignity led President Eisenhower to order a break in diplomatic relations with Cuba less than two weeks before the new administration took office. True, Kennedy could have canceled the invasion project by withdrawing American backing for it but his military advisers were so convinced of success that he told them to go ahead.

Conscious of the need for Latin American support in his gamble against Castro, the young president called for a new program of cooperation for the hemisphere, an Alliance for Progress, on March 13, 1961. Next day, he proposed congressional approval for an appropriation of $500 million to promote social progress south of the Rio Grande. Thus fortified, he next moved directly against Castro with a White Paper early in April. In it, the revolutionary Cuban regime was denounced as a menace to peace in the Americas and warned to break off its relations with the Communist world. Cuba's answer was to accuse the United States of preparing for an invasion with an army of 4,000 exiles. President Kennedy then solemnly assured the American people and the world that there would not be, "under any conditions, an intervention in Cuba by United States armed force."

Castro, for one, didn't believe him. The American press and electronic media continued to report the buildup of anti-Castro refugees for the invasion. In one instance, Tad Szulc of the New York *Times* reported that the invasion was imminent and that the CIA was masterminding it. But the *Times,* not wanting to be blamed for a "bloody fiasco," toned down Szulc's story and used it on April 7 as a report on the anti-Castro refugee army that was training for action against Cuba. Long afterward, a sadly disillusioned John Kennedy told Turner Catledge, one of the *Times*'s editors, "If you had printed more about the operation, you would have saved us from a colossal mistake." But with the invasion only ten days off, the president refused to turn back. What he did do was to deny American air support to the rag-tag exile group, thereby denying them whatever slight chance of victory they might have had.

When 1,200 armed Cuban refugees straggled ashore at dawn on April 17 at the Bay of Pigs on Cuba's southern coast, Castro's well-armed troops were waiting for them. Within twelve hours, the invasion was repulsed. Three days later, nearly all the unfortunate members of the striking force were either dead or captured. The United States stood convicted against Cuba. As the *Guardian* of Manchester put it, "Everyone knows that sort of invasion by proxy with which the United States has now been charged is morally indistinguishable from open aggression."

Kennedy was far from contrite. In a blast at the press for disclosing his secrets, he demanded greater cooperation of the American Newspaper Publishers Association, saying, "Every newspaper now asks itself with respect to every story, 'Is it news?' All I suggest is that you add the question, 'Is it in the interest of national security?'" But no one took to the notion that the United States government had the right, legal or moral, to insist on a self-censored news media. After a good deal of grumbling, the president himself dropped the matter and faced up to the real enemy, now ensconced 90 miles off the Florida coast, the Soviet Union.

Despite its unexpected gains in the Americas, Moscow was not without its own problems. In 1959, difficulties with Peking had increased to such an extent that all Soviet technicians had been pulled out of Red China. In the following year, there had been widespread failures in Soviet farm production. Relations with the satellites had worsened because of the defiant attitude of China-supported Albania. And in Africa, the Soviet-backed premier of the newly independent Congo Republic, Patrice Lumumba, had been murdered on February 12, 1961. The principal development from which the Soviet Union could take comfort was the orbital flight of Major Yuri Gagarin, the first cosmonaut, on April 12, 1961, and the even more impressive performances of his fellow voyagers in space.

In the Soviet Union's relations with the United States, Khrushchev had been steering an erratic course. By 1959, two years after having staved off a campaign by his "old Bolshevik" opponents to overthrow him, he had felt himself strong enough to welcome Vice-President Nixon to the Soviet Union and to embark on his own spectacular coast-to-coast tour of the United States from September 15 to 28 with an entourage of nearly 400 correspondents. But his efforts to improve relations between the super-powers exploded when an American U-2 spy plane was shot down over Sverdlovsk, 1,600 miles inside the Soviet border, on May 1, 1960. When the United States denied any deliberate attempt to invade Soviet air space, he had the satisfaction of producing the downed pilot and the plane wreckage and catching the American government in a colossal lie. Subsequently, he torpedoed the Paris summit conference of May 16 with a stream of unrestrained abuse of both President Eisenhower and the United States government. That fall, at the United Nations in New York, he showed the extent of his outrage by taking off his shoe and banging it on his desk in red-faced anger.

In June, 1961, Khrushchev tried to take President Kennedy's measure at the Vienna summit conference but neither threat nor bluster over Berlin stampeded the cool young American. Two months later, on August 13, the Soviets resolved the seemingly perpetual Berlin crisis in their own fashion by authorizing the East Germans to build the wall that effectively hemmed off the West. Then, in October, came the break with China when Khrushchev used the Albanian crisis to attack Peking by implication and the incensed Chou En-lai abruptly left the Twenty-second Communist Party Congress for Peking.

From then on, it was evident enough that neither continued assaults on the old Stalinists as an "Anti-Party Group" nor the breaking of Soviet relations with Albania would suffice for Khrushchev. He badly needed a victory. In his search for one, he saw a glorious opportunity in his new relations with the "American Albania," Cuba. It was easy enough to put together a trade agreement to exchange Cuban sugar for Soviet oil, a deal that in effect caused Moscow to underwrite the sagging Cuban economy. But what followed was more complex. During the summer of 1962, a secret agreement was reached in Moscow with two Cuban emissaries—Raul Castro, Fidel's brother, and Che Guevara—to send Soviet offensive missiles to Cuba and provide Soviet technicians to build the offensive missile bases. If Khrushchev had been able to pull off this coup, it would have had a shattering effect on both American military power and world opinion.

Suddenly, the cold war began heating up. At Geneva, all negotiations for an atomic test ban treaty collapsed. On August 5, 1962, the Soviet Union resumed testing with a monstrous 30-megaton atomic explosion in the Arctic. The United States, too, set off atomic blasts in a counter-demonstration. The balance of terror still held good. And in answer to Soviet successes in putting men into orbit, Colonel John Glenn began the long and brilliant campaign of the American astronauts by circling the globe three times in five hours on February 20, 1962. The enthusiastic Kennedy proclaimed that the American goal was to place a man on the moon before the end of the decade.

Deeply troubled by its failure in Cuba and well aware that counter moves might be expected from the Soviet Union, the United States blunted the impact of its 1961 conference of the Alliance for Progress by demanding punitive economic and diplomatic sanctions against Castro. But the most the Organization of American States would consent to do was to expel Cuba from membership — a decision from which Argentina, Bolivia, Brazil, Chile, and Mexico abstained. It was clear that Washington's diplomatic offensive against Havana was a dud.

Early in the fall of 1962, both American newspapers and electronic media began circulating disturbing reports about the presence of Soviet missiles in Cuba. On October 14, a high-flying U-2 plane and its United States Air Force crew produced the first substantial photographic evidence of the very real threat to American security that the missile bases represented. While the president plunged into intensive planning for the approaching crisis, the news wires began reporting the movements of Army and Air Force units toward Florida. Even the dullest and laziest correspondent in Washington could not have failed to note the extraordinary concentration of top officials at the White House, State Department, and Pentagon.

By Saturday, October 20, it was certain that something of enormous importance was developing. Alfred Friendly, managing editor of the Washington *Post*, broke a story in his paper next day that there was a feeling of crisis in the capital. He knew more. So did James Reston of the New York *Times*. But in this instance, President Kennedy himself telephoned the publisher of the *Times*, Orvil Dryfoos, and asked him "to refrain from printing on October 21 the news ... of the presence of Russian missiles in Cuba." Dryfoos assented. A similar appeal to the New York *Herald Tribune* by Defense Secretary Robert S. McNamara also was successful.

This time it was the Soviet Union that was caught in a blatant lie. On October 18, Foreign Minister Gromyko had assured Kennedy that the missile installations in Cuba were "purely defensive." However, even as he spoke, the United States had been able to establish beyond doubt that, once the installations were completed, Soviet missiles would be able to wipe out the entire East Coast of the United States within minutes, blow up the Panama Canal, and shower nuclear explosives on great cities as widely separated as Quebec and Lima.

For once, the United States was able to make its plans for the great confrontation in secret because the press exhibited both responsibility and restraint. On the night of October 22, in a nationwide television address, President Kennedy told the American people of the menace of Soviet offensive missile sites in Cuba, exhibited the photographic evidence, and delivered a virtual ultimatum to the Soviet Union to withdraw at once.

The super-powers stood eyeball to eyeball. A rash judgment, a miscalculation on either side, would send the rockets flying between the continents and precipitate an atomic war from which neither could recover. For Kennedy left no doubt, in his speech to the nation, that "this deliberately provocative and unjustified change in the status quo" by the Soviet Union "cannot be accepted by this country."

He clamped a quarantine on Cuba, the equivalent of a tight naval and air blockade, and challenged the Russians to try to penetrate it to maintain their missile base construction schedule. At Florida bases and at sea, American bombers and fighter aircraft were at the alert. Both Army and Marine units were ready for action. Every Inter-Continental Ballistic Missile in the United States arsenal, then estimated at more than 150, was aimed at Soviet territory with atomic warheads in place. Even the atom-powered submarines with their Polaris missiles were at their action stations.

On October 23, the Organization of American States voted unanimous approval of the United States' position. In the United Nations, at the emergency meetings of the Security Council where Ambassador Adlai E. Stevenson documented the American case with dramatic flair, the NATO alliance stood firm. The Congress of the United States, closing ranks at a time of supreme danger, backed the president with a magnificent show of spirit. It was, as Secretary of State Dean Rusk told his staff, a "flaming crisis."

On October 25, the Defense Department announced that at least a dozen Soviet ships carrying offensive materials had turned back—the first sign of a break in the tension. That same day, a Walter Lippmann column was circulated with a suggestion that the United States should offer to dismantle some of its Turkish bases in return for a Soviet pledge to wipe out its Cuban missile bases. At once, the Soviet ambassador to Washington, Anatoly Dobrynin, seized on it as a trial balloon that could signify an American retreat. But the column, as it turned out, had been only Lippmann's own idea.

The Soviet Union now made its own move through the press as had been the case in the liquidation of the Berlin blockade. John Scali of the American Broadcasting Company was called to a luncheon meeting October 26 with a Soviet embassy official, Alexander S. Fomin, who asked if the United States would call off its threatened Cuban invasion if the Soviet Union dismantled its missile bases and Castro promised not to accept offensive weapons in the future. When Scali notified the State Department of this development, Secretary Rusk sent back an encouraging response but warned that time was growing short.

That night, in a long and rambling teletype message to Kennedy from Moscow, Khrushchev vaguely alluded to the same kind of proposed settlement outlined by Fomin. But it was just as well that the White House deferred any celebration, for on the next day Khrushchev came through with another teletype proposal demanding the abandonment of American bases in Turkey as the price of Soviet capitulation in Cuba.

Kennedy made a last offer. He conditionally accepted the suggestion put forward by Fomin, as elaborated on in Khrushchev's message of October 26, and offered in return to call off the naval blockade and the projected Cuban invasion. On October 28, Khrushchev caved in. "The Soviet government . . . has given a new order," he cabled Kennedy, "to dismantle the arms which you described as offensive, and to crate and return them to the Soviet Union." Within a month, in direct discussions between Moscow and Washington and also at the United Nations, the arrangements were completed. The crisis ended. Only Castro was dismayed because his Soviet allies had let him down. And from Peking, the Chinese Communists cried out first against Khrushchev's "adventurism" in Cuba and then against his capitulation to the United States.

The Chinese neglected to observe that they had grabbed huge chunks of Indian border territory in a lightning invasion at the height of the Cuban crisis. By the time the Soviet Union and the United States resumed normal relations, it was too late to do anything to help India. All Nehru could do was to express his anguish over his betrayal by his Chinese brothers and fire his violently anti-American defense minister, Krishna Menon.

Before the Supreme Soviet on December 12, 1962, Khrushchev formally ended his atomic adventure by proclaiming piously that the settlement he had achieved with Kennedy constituted a victory "for the cause of peace and security of peoples." Almost everybody except Castro, Nehru, and Mao Tse-tung would have agreed.

6. *The Great Red Schism*

Fortified by his victory over India and Khrushchev's defeat, Mao was prepared in the summer of 1963 for the open break with the Soviet Union that had been pending ever since 1957.

It came in the form of a letter from the Central Committee of the Chinese Communist Party to Moscow on June 14, which Peking took care to publicize widely in its own press and abroad. In it, the Chinese informed Khrushchev that he could not hope for disarmament and a world without war while "the system of imperialism and the exploitation of man by man still exists." The tone was scathing. The personal abuse of Khrushchev was carried on in the worst Communist polemical style.

When the Central Committee of the Soviet Union's Communist Party replied to Peking in an equally well-publicized letter of July 14, the Chinese government was accused in effect of striving to foment war and acting against the best interests of world Communism. "If both the exploiters and the exploited are buried under the ruins of the old world, who will build the 'bright future'?'' the Russians asked. That did it. When the Chinese spurned an invitation to attend the Twenty-third Congress of the Soviet Union's Communist Party, they accused Moscow of working with the United States in a "vain attempt to establish a Holy Alliance against China."

In the mounting tempest of charges and countercharges that flew back and forth between China and the Soviet Union thereafter, the solidarity of the world Communist movement was wrecked. It was not what Palmiro Togliatti, the Italian Communist leader, had bargained for when he envisioned a new "polycentrism" for the Communist system—a movement of many centers all working for the same purpose—but neither was it what the American public had been taught by its press about the monolithic solidarity of all Communists.

The world had to arrive, by degrees, at a new evaluation of the manner in which Communist governments operated. In the process, the independent press and its Kremlin and Peking specialists had to reeducate themselves. As for the Soviet Union, much against its will, it was drawn into an increasingly dangerous conflict with the Chinese along the farthest reaches of the Siberian border for the remainder of the decade.

As if the schism with China hadn't been bad enough, the faltering Khrushchev also had to face up to tell-tale signs of dissent at home. During the zigs and zags of the de-Stalinization period, the younger Soviet poets and writers had begun to display an alarming degree of independence. Yevgeni Yevtuchenko, in his poem, "Babi Yar," used the circumstances of a Nazi massacre of Ukrainian Jews to cast a rebuke as well to the traditional anti-Semitism of his own country. Another poet, Andrei Voznesensky, attacked the art of the Stalinist period as "cowsheds with cupids" and wrote to his fellow citizens of the Soviet Union: "To live is to burn."

But the dominant sensation of the time was the publication by the literary journal, *Novy Mir*, of the revolutionary novel, *One Day in the Life of Ivan Denisovich*, by Aleksandr Solzhenitsyn. Never before had so degrading an account of Soviet life—a story of forced labor in prison camps—been presented in Moscow under such auspices. Within a short time just before the open break with China, 95,000 copies of *Novy Mir* were sold out.

What did it mean? To Khrushchev, who had originally thought so highly of the notion of a "thaw," there was no doubt that the situation had gotten out of hand. Before a joint session of Communist Party leaders and a group of writers and artists in 1963, the pudgy premier angrily demanded the restoration of Soviet discipline. He spoke against "one-sided" presentations of Soviet life. He laid down the line that writers and artists should celebrate the "victory of new Communist relations in our life."

Khrushchev laid about him with blows and threats for all the new idols of Soviet life, and some of the old ones, as well. Ilya Ehrenburg and Yevtuchenko both received stern rebukes. Even the great Russian composer, Dmitri Shostakovich, was told that he was producing "music without melody," a particularly heinous crime. As for the arch-criminal, Solzhenitsyn, he went into eclipse with *Ivan Denisovich*. His novels, *The First Circle* and *The Cancer Ward*, were published outside the Soviet Union.

Viewing the plight of the author of the de-Stalinization campaign from far-off Peking, Mao had good reason to be satisfied. Defeated by the United States over Cuba, scorned by the Communist heirarchy of China, bedeviled by dissenting Soviet writers within his own domain, Khrushchev's power was gone. His downfall was now only a matter of time.

7. An American Tragedy

The United States, too, became enmeshed in Asian turmoil after maneuvering so carefully to maintain a stand-off attitude at the time of the French collapse in Indochina. After Korea, it was just about the last thing the American press and public either wanted or expected. But it happened, anyway.

Contrary to the firm position against involvement in an Asian land war taken in 1954 by President Eisenhower and Senators John Fitzgerald Kennedy and Lyndon Baines Johnson, among others, American forces were committed to the war in Vietnam during the 1960s in a curious and sometimes stealthy manner. It was as if everybody connected with the operation realized how desperately unpopular it was likely to be; and yet, the commitment was made out of the loftiest of motives.

The French had long since pulled out of Southeast Asia and, under President Charles de Gaulle's leadership, had liquidated their North African empire by acceding to Algerian independence. However, an important segment of American military opinion became convinced that the United States could win back what France had lost in Vietnam. And the military, as always, were most persuasive in winning over powerful adherents in Washington.

Hesitantly, after the disaster of the Bay of Pigs in Cuba, President Kennedy accepted the judgment of the military "hawks" that Vietnam must not be given up to Communism without a struggle. But as the initial phase of the American commitment began, the war that the Kennedy administration waged under cover against Ho Chi Minh was by no means as violent as the one that was fought against a handful of young correspondents in Vietnam.

In 1962, there were some 4,000 American military "advisers" in South Vietnam who were attached to the largely ineffective army that Premier Ngo Dinh Diem had put together. And yet, the effort at concealment was so great that the American government didn't want to award a Purple Heart to an American soldier who had been wounded in action until bad publicity forced a change in policy. Of course, Ho Chi Minh even at that early stage also had violated the Geneva accords by sending thousands of reinforcements to the Vietcong. But the net effect of the Kennedy administration's policy of restricting information on the American military buildup, modest though it appeared to be, was to keep the home front in virtual ignorance of a new war to which it was being committed. Most Americans still didn't even know what the Vietnam War was all about and many had never even heard of Vietnam itself.

The Diem government at this stage was boasting about the progress of its pacification program through the building of "strategic hamlets"—fortified villages to some, concentration camps to others — in territory controlled by the Vietcong enemy. Both Frederick E. Nolting Jr., the American ambassador, and General Paul D. Harkins, chief of the American Military Assistance Command, Vietnam, implicitly believed Diem's claims and forwarded them to Washington.

There, a state of euphoria took hold. Both Secretaries Rusk and McNamara began to predict victory in Vietnam. But the few American correspondents in Saigon who had a basic knowledge of the military situation, gained at first hand in the field, ridiculed both Diem and the American command for making preposterous assumptions. The slightest check by any impartial intelligence officer could have disclosed in good time that Diem was wrong and the correspondents were right, that the war was being lost instead of won, and that the Vietnamese army was incapable by itself of defeating the Vietcong.

Far from being complimented for their insight and their courage, the correspondents were given the same ruthless treatment that William Howard Russell had experienced more than a century before in the Crimea because he had told the truth about another small and ugly war. President Kennedy himself intervened at one point to try to oblige the New York *Times* to shift its controversial correspondent, David Halberstam, from Saigon. While he stayed put, other correspondents were expelled and some even had their loyalty to their country impugned. *Time* magazine distinguished itself at the height of these proceedings by attacking the Saigon correspondents — including its own — who were warning that the war was being lost. The *Time* correspondent, Charles Mohr, promptly shifted in protest to the New York *Times*.

When the Kennedy administration finally came to its senses and dispatched Henry Cabot Lodge Jr. to Saigon in 1963 as the new American ambassador, the United States already was deeply entangled but its military commitment still remained small. A pullout could have been arranged without too much difficulty at that stage. Instead, when Lodge reported it was impossible to deal with Diem on any rational basis, President Kennedy withdrew American support from the regime. In the military coup that followed on November 1–2, 1963, Diem was overthrown and executed but even worse confusion resulted. It was a long time before a stable government of any kind could be put together in Saigon.

Once again the press was incontinently blamed for having in effect forced a major policy defeat upon the United States. The response of the defiant correspondents was that they had only told the truth, but it didn't save them from recriminations. As James Reston concluded after the Bay of Pigs incident: "No doubt the press does have to learn greater restraint than in the days when the United States was an isolated country, but the government has to do the same. For the truth that makes men free is very often the truth they do not like to hear and also the truth that the government does not like to see published, either."

In Kennedy's memorable thousand days, not all his conflicts with the forces of world Communism brought the United States to the brink of war or forced an increase in its military commitments to its allies. The very vigor of his approach to American foreign policy caused the mercurial Khrushchev to reconsider his all-out program of atomic testing. As a result, on August 5, 1963, the United States, the Soviet Union, and Great Britain signed the limited nuclear test ban treaty—the first small step along the difficult and painful road to disarmament. "Yesterday, a shaft of light cut into darkness," the president told the American public next day. "For the first time an agreement has been reached on bringing the forces of nuclear destruction under international control."

It was the last victory. In the fullness of a brilliant career, John Fitzgerald Kennedy was cut down by an assassin's bullet in Dallas on November 22, 1963. With him perished the hope he had raised for improved relationships with the Soviet Union and Communist China, a resolution of difficulties with Cuba, and a settlement of the Vietnam War. His bumbling old opponent, Khrushchev, who had tried in his own way to relax world tensions from time to time, did not long survive him. On October 15, 1964, he was deposed by the Kremlin's conservatives and

retired to obscurity. His crimes, a *Pravda* editorial said, included "hare-brained scheming, bragging, and phrase-monger-
ing." The day after Khrushchev's removal, Red China exploded
its first nuclear device in the Sinkiang desert. A new threat had
arisen in the beclouded world of the super powers, for no pact or
promise or prayer could now forestall a whole range of Peking
atomic tests.

The balance of terror had been upset. How long would it be
before the Soviet Union or the United States would stand eyeball
to eyeball with China?

8. *The Uses of the Press*

In the aftermath of the Kennedy assassination, the American
government faced up to its most serious confrontation with the
American press since the adoption of the Espionage Act of 1917.
Although the coverage of the tragedy of Dallas itself had been
exemplary, the news media were thrown on the defense when
the accused assassin, Lee Harvey Oswald, was murdered two
days later before 50 million television witnesses. Television may
have been the prime offender as the vehicle that presented the
opportunity for the attack to the eccentric Jack Ruby, but the
press could not escape a share of the public condemnation.

The distinguished commission of investigation headed by
Chief Justice Earl Warren held that the three hundred reporters
and photographers who overran Dallas police headquarters that
day were interfering with due process and tampering with the
rights of the accused. The news media as well as the police, the
report said, "must share responsibility for the failure of law enforcement which occurred in connection with the death of Oswald." The president of the American Society of Newspaper
Editors, Herbert Brucker, agreed with the verdict saying,
"There seems little doubt that TV and the press must bear a
share of the blame."

Although the Commission received no satisfaction when it
demanded the formation of a code of ethics for the press, its
report provided the basis for an unexampled campaign by the

American bench and bar to check the broad privileges of the press in reporting both police proceedings and criminal court actions. In more than a score of states, the press with more or less grace accepted agreements worked out with lawyers and judges for voluntary guidelines in such matters. But the public's dissatisfaction with the press continued despite that. The American newspapers, directly after the Kennedy and Oswald assassinations, had not fallen so low for more than a hundred years in the esteem of the public on whose support they depended for their very existence.

The British press, which with few exceptions had been far more cooperative with its government than the unruly Americans, also found itself in deep trouble with its public as a result of the Profumo scandal. Had it not been for the probing of the sensational press, the strange conduct of John D. Profumo, secretary of state for war in the Macmillan cabinet, and his relationship with the lively Miss Christine Keeler and her protector, Dr. Stephen Ward, might never have reached public notice in 1963. As the case developed, the agitated Profumo denied the initial reports in the press but neither he nor his friends were powerful enough to persuade the newspapers to cease and desist. The scandal, together with the incidental disclosures of a Soviet agent's relationship with Miss Keeler, rocked the Macmillan government. Neither Profumo's resignation nor the conviction of Dr. Ward as a procurer and his suicide thereafter halted the press's attack on the Establishment. Several other unnamed cabinet ministers were accused of taking part in scantily attired improprieties, leading to the distinct impression that British public life had become corrupt beyond redemption.

The government's counterattack centered on what it termed "check book journalism." In Lord Shawcross' definition, this consisted of the "publicizing of pimps, prostitutes, and perverts in highly paid interviews or feature articles." It was deemed bad enough that the *News of the World* had paid £23,000 to Christine Keeler for her sordid life story. Even worse was the *Sunday Pictorial*'s publication of a series entitled, "Why I Betrayed My Country," under the name of William John Christopher Vassall, an Admiralty clerical officer who had been convicted of espionage and sentenced to eighteen years in prison.

In Lord Deming's subsequent inquiry into the Profumo case, his principal recommendation was to increase by some unspecified means the power of the voluntary Press Council "to stop the trafficking in scandal for reward." Nobody except a few impolite editors observed that it also was incumbent on government ministers to behave in a manner befitting their public trust. As for the British public, it showed an unmistakable dissatisfaction with both government and press. No one was particularly surprised, therefore, when the Labour Party and Harold Wilson came to power on October 15, 1964.

As for France during the eleven-year reign of Charles de Gaulle, freedom became a largely relative matter to the French press. During the concluding stages of the Algerian War and the uncertain peace that was achieved between 1958 and 1960, de Gaulle's government seized thirty-one editions of French newspapers and seventy-three others in Algeria for publishing material displeasing to French interests. For the high crime of printing the International Red Cross's report of French Army tortures in Algerian internment camps in 1960, the offending editions of *Le Monde*, *L'Express*, *France Conservateur*, and *L'Humanité* were confiscated. Of course, there were those who argued that such high-handed acts were justified on the ground that order had to be maintained. Yet, when de Gaulle continued to fine and jail opposition editors after the end of the Algerian crisis, it became clear that his anti-press policy was a part of his way of life.

The West German press, despite the far more serious limitations of its own past and its perpetual economic dilemma, proved to be more capable of a fight against its government over the consequences of free expression. When Defense Minister Franz Josef Strauss seized the offices of the news magazine *Der Spiegel* and arrested its publisher, Rudolf Augstein, it created a governmental crisis in 1962. What Strauss sought was the source of information for a sensational article contending that the West German Army was unprepared to defend the republic on the basis of its showing in a recent NATO exercise. Although

Der Spiegel's offices were occupied for a month and eleven persons were arrested, Strauss never did find out. But he stirred up
so much resentment among the West German public that he had
to resign as Defense Minister. In a land where the midnight
knock on the door had been heard more often than the voice of
the free press, the case of *Der Spiegel* was a favorable augury
for the future.

In Switzerland, the Low Countries, and Scandinavia, in Japan,
Canada, Australia, New Zealand, and the other nations on earth
that were hospitable to a reasonably independent press, the tensions between governments and newspapers were not always as
pronounced but they still existed. In the developing countries of
Asia, Africa, and Latin America, however, there were relatively
few governments that even understood the theory of a free press
or permitted unfettered publication or broadcast of news and
opinion. Everywhere, the fear of criticism of official acts became
almost as paranoid as in the most run-down of dictatorial regimes. Even in the traditional home of liberty in the Western
World, no government accepted the circulation of critical or dissenting material without a fight. It was a measure of the importance, if not the influence, of an independent press in the most
dangerous times through which the world had ever passed.

X. The Lonely Struggle

1. The Czech Spring — and the Fall

The lights burned late on the night of August 20, 1968 in the Prague headquarters of the Communist Party of Czechoslovakia. The eleven-member Presidium had been struggling since early afternoon to put down an attempt by the Soviet-inspired minority to force changes in the government. So far, the majority was standing fast behind the mild-mannered, 47-year-old Alexander Dubcek, who as First Secretary of the party had led the nation through a surprising and exhilarating spring—a breath of freedom such as Czechoslovakia had not known in thirty years.

The pro-Soviet group in the Presidium had been warning that it would be fatal to ignore any longer a virtual ultimatum that had been sent to Prague July 18 in the name of five Warsaw Pact powers by the Soviet Union. In it, the Kremlin had called for a purge of the political leadership in Czechoslovakia to end the swing away from Moscow-approved doctrine and—above all—to do away with the revival of free speech and a free press.

Toward midnight, Premier Oldrich Cernik left the room to telephone the Defense Department. When he returned, he interrupted the debate, blurting out: "The armies of the five countries have crossed our frontiers and are occupying us." The agitated Dubcek exclaimed tearfully, "I had no suspicion, not even the slightest hint, that such a step would be taken against us. It is a tragedy!"

In an emotion-packed hour, the Presidium buried its differences. Its members drafted a proclamation to the nation, which was broadcast over Prague Radio at 1:50 A.M. on August 21, pleading with both the Czech Army and their fellow citizens not to offer resistance to the invading troops. But they did protest bitterly against an act that was, as they put it, "contrary not only to the fundamental principles of relations between Socialist states but also as a denial of fundamental norms of international law."

Before morning, the conquest was complete. General Ivan Pavlovsky of the Red Army, the commander of the Warsaw Pact forces, had had an easy time of it. With the Czech Army of 175,000 restricted to their own posts, he sent more than 500,000 troops across the 1,600 miles of Czech frontiers. To his sixteen Army divisions, he was able to add substantial contingents of the Polish, East German, Hungarian, and Bulgarian armies. However, they weren't really needed. Even the Czech Air Force, with its 600 aircraft, had been grounded. At 4:30 A.M., the Prague Radio announced: "The defense of our state frontiers is now impossible."

This was the penalty for Czechoslovakia's all-too-brief show of independence that spring. It had begun auspiciously enough with the downfall of the old Stalinist boss, Antonin Novotny, and the election of Dubcek as his successor as First Secretary of the Communist Party. On March 22, Novotny resigned as president of Czechoslovakia. To replace him, Dubcek summoned the National Assembly to elect Ludvik Svoboda, a 72-year-old retired general, and approve a policy of liberalization—"Socialism with a human face." With the installation of Cernik as premier and Josef Smrkovsky as president of the National Assembly, Dubcek's hand was further strengthened. He then named two new deputy premiers—Ota Sik, a revolutionary economist who advocated closer economic ties to the West, and a rehabilitated Slovak leader, Gustav Husak.

Without even waiting for Dubcek to complete his new Presidium, the Czech press rushed ahead, heedless of consequences. Its emphasis was on uncovering the crimes of the Novotny era and paying tribute to his victims. The weekly paper *Student*, for example, presented evidence that Jan Masaryk had not really committed suicide. The Communist Party newspaper, *Rude Pravo*, began examining the 20-year-old theory that he had been murdered by being thrown out of a window by the Soviet secret police. One of *Rude Pravo*'s writers even demanded to know what role "Beria's gorillas" had played in the crime.

There were still other sensations when the Czech press published charges that Stalin himself had ordered the purging of Rudolf Slansky, Vladimir Clementis, and their associates in the earliest of the Czech "show trials." The sensitive subject of anti-Semitism, never far below the surface either in Eastern Europe or the Soviet Union itself, was dragged into the open with the disclosure that forced confessions had been extracted from eleven Jewish victims that they had been "spies for the imperialists." The wave of criticism of the Soviet Union in the Czech press was without precedent in any of the satellite countries.

In this atmosphere of tension and defiance, Dubcek put forward his party's "Action Program." By Western standards, it was mild; but by the Kremlin doctrine, it was treasonable. Free press, free speech, a call for criticism of the government, a check on the powers of the secret police—these were the essentials that stirred up enthusiasm throughout the land. Even the role of the Communist Party itself was circumscribed, for it was told that it could not "force its line through directives, but only by the work of its members, by the veracity of its ideals."

For the Kremlin, all this was poison. Leonid Brezhnev, the Communist Party boss in Moscow, summoned Dubcek and his associates to the Kremlin on May 4, demanded the immediate restoration of order in Prague, and an agreement to a Warsaw Pact "troop exercise" on Czech soil in June. While the Czechs bowed to Brezhnev's will, they could not control their people. On May 18, during a visit by Soviet Premier Aleksei Kosygin to Prague, thousands of Czech students marched in a violent anti-Soviet demonstration. And on June 27, in a published manifesto entitled *2,000 Words*, the Czech activists called for demonstrations, strikes, and boycotts to drive out officials who "abused their power," a thinly disguised reference to the pro-Soviet minority in the Presidium. As a crowning provocation, they pledged themselves to defend their government by force of arms, if necessary, as long as it maintained its drive toward liberalization.

The Soviet Union's reply was to move the Red Army's troops and tanks into strategic positions all over Czechoslovakia in the "exercise" of the Warsaw Pact powers to which Dubcek had been obliged to agree. Dubcek and the Czech Presidium were told to come to Moscow, but refused. For his courage, he won such support as his people had once given to Thomas Masaryk. Not even the July 18 ultimatum from the Warsaw Pact powers succeeded in breaking the national will.

Moscow stepped up its war of nerves. The reserves were called to duty. In *Pravda*, the authoritative commentator Yuri Zhukov warned that events in Czechoslovakia amounted to a "call for revolution." Under overwhelming pressure, Dubcek had to agree to a meeting of the Czech Presidium with the Presidium of the Soviet Union but he held out for a site within his own country, the border town of Cierna. Two days of meetings in Cierna and a subsequent conference with the Warsaw Pact powers at Bratislava seemed to produce a truce, for the last Soviet troops left Czech soil and the Soviet press softened its inspired attacks on Prague.

For those with long memories, the parallel with Hungary in 1956 was ominous. Then, too, Soviet troops had retreated and the Kremlin seemingly had assented to a liberalization program by a premier who did not seem to fear the consequences. Thus, while the romantics in Prague celebrated what they thought was Dubcek's triumph, the realists paid more attention to a warning that was delivered on August 12 by the hard-line Communist leader of East Germany, Walter Ulbricht, that the Czechs must meet their obligations as a member of the Soviet bloc. In all too brief a time, the realists were shown to have been right.

The short-lived Cierna truce ended in Moscow on August 14 with an all-out propaganda attack on the Czech press. Soon, the Soviet weather vane, Zhukov, displayed unmistakable storm signals with a demand for "elementary order" in the newspapers of Czechoslovakia. Once again, Dubcek rallied his forces. He did tell the editors to try to be more discreet. But it was too late. *Pravda* maintained a withering barrage of criticism, complaining on August 19 that the "enemies of the working class" in Czechoslovakia had not yet received the "necessary rebuff." On the next evening, the rebuff was delivered in overwhelming force and Czechoslovakia became an occupied country.

To the astonishment of the world in general and the Warsaw Pact occupation forces in particular, the Czechs embarked on a spontaneous campaign of passive resistance on the morning of August 21. Through an intricate system of underground publications of regular newspapers and clandestine radio and television broadcasts, the movement spread throughout the country. Youngsters outside the Prague Radio building linked arms and interposed their bodies in front of the tanks of the Red Army. Citizens in all walks of life challenged the Soviet troops to explain why they were in the capital of an allied nation.

In response to the trumped-up excuse that an invasion had been threatened from West Germany, there were angry demands by individual citizens for evidence that any country except those in the Warsaw Pact was moving against the Czech state. Posters blossomed as if by magic: "This is not Vietnam!" "Ivan, Go Home!" "Home, Dogs!" Nazi swastikas were painted on the invading tanks and half tracks. All over the country, street signs were taken down and road signs were destroyed or changed in direction with one exception, which pointed East and read: "Moscow — 1,500 KM." Farmers and storekeepers refused to give food and supplies voluntarily to the invaders and hid whatever they could.

All this was done without direction and without plan. The principal inspiration came from a fictional national hero of World War I, Jaroslav Hasek's imperishable *Good Soldier Schweik*, who confounded his country's enemies with his impudent deeds. If there was any pool of material to supply the national resistance, it came from the Czech Army and paramilitary organizations that had been trained for twenty years under Moscow's auspices to resist American aggression. Now the portable radio and printing equipment, designed for use against the "imperialists" of the United States, proved invaluable in rallying the public against the brotherly invaders.

Although the Soviet troops were under instructions to occupy all press offices and electronic media, it was not easy to pinch off clandestine newspapers or broadcasts. Even *Rude Pravo*, the Communist Party organ, came out in clandestine form and was eagerly passed from hand to hand. Through this means, the spirit of resistance was kept alive for a limited time while Soviet officials frantically sought to tighten a blanket censorship. By contrast with the foreign correspondents' reports of all this Czech activity, *Pravda*'s long historical justification for the invasion, published on August 22, had a hollow and unconvincing ring.

Inevitably, there was bloodshed despite every appeal against violence that was made by the clandestine news media. But the wonder was that the casualties were so few — less than a hundred Czech dead in the opening week of the occupation. Probably the worst of the series of street battles took place in front of Prague Radio when Soviet tank crews, taunted by the crowd, suddenly opened fire on the citizenry. Molotov cocktails began to fly as people scattered in panic. Two tanks were set on fire. From Wenceslas Square, there was more shooting and more people died. Machine guns began to chatter in the ancient streets of the city. And from thousands of transistor radios came the continual plea: "Keep calm. Don't be provoked. Try to explain their mistake to them."

Jiri Mucha, a Czech journalist, wrote long afterward: "It was pure Kafka — the whole of Prague with its narrow streets, its gargoyles and its churches. It was incomprehensible, terrifying, ridiculous. On one side, frightened soldiers firing on children, and on the other a tank crew in tears."

Now came the most astonishing part of the Czech resistance. Although Dubcek, Cernik, and Smrkovsky already were prisoners of the Red Army and awaited an uncertain fate, President Svoboda stubbornly refused, in the glowering Hradcin overlooking Prague, to install a government of pro-Soviet traitors. He was flown to Moscow — this "foolish old man," as the Russians called him behind his back — and told that he must yield. His answer was that he would commit suicide unless Dubcek and his associates were liberated to join in an acceptable settlement of the issues that had brought about the invasion.

It was the Kremlin that yielded. Although Ambassador Malik had been telling the United Nations that the government of Czechoslovakia had asked the Warsaw Pact troops to help defend their country against unspecified threats to its sovereignty, the tough Svoboda patently demonstrated the falsity of such a statement. For the Soviet Union, confronted with his defiance, could not produce a government of Quislings to do its bidding in Prague. A sadly shaken Dubcek, who had all but given himself up for lost, was flown into Moscow with his associates to join Svoboda in an effort to talk the Russians out of their all-persuasive occupation. It was in vain.

For three days and three nights the Czech leadership had to negotiate at gun point. The agreement, when it was announced on the night of August 27, was a complete capitulation. Under the circumstances, nothing else could have been expected. In return for a Soviet pledge "for the quickest normalization of the situation," the Czechs agreed in effect to give up their liberalization movement. When Dubcek returned to Prague, he had to tell his people that they would have to accept "temporary measures" to limit their democratic government with its prized freedom of opinion and put up with a continued occupation. All he had to show in return was his continued presence at the head of the Presidium. But even then, both he and his people realized that his days were numbered. In place of a treacherous replacement by a Soviet-approved Quisling government, he and his associates faced a slow and inexorable throttling of their freedom of movement until their regime collapsed.

That was the way it turned out. The "free radio" dwindled as one clandestine station after another went off the air. A new "Press Office" was established in Prague with instructions to all newspapers to refrain from publishing "negative" news and criticizing the occupation (which was henceforth not to be termed an occupation). The most rebellious of the magazines, *Politika*, *Reporter*, and *Student*, were banned. The once-militant dailies reappeared in subdued form, headed by a reformed *Rude Pravo* that hewed faithfully to the Moscow line. As the weeks passed, a preventive censorship took hold with the assent of the National Assembly. The Union of Journalists in Prague received a mounting list of "forbidden topics." Their brief time of freedom was over.

For the government itself, the shape of the future was disclosed in similar manner. The revolutionary economist, Ota Sik, was fired as deputy premier, as was the foreign minister, Jiri Hajek. Zdenek Hejzlar and Jiri Pelikan, the chiefs of the rebellious state radio and television respectively, were removed. Throughout the land, Dubcek and Cernik pleaded for friendship with the Soviet Union and thereby let the steam out of the resistance movement. The last to capitulate were the students; in imitation of their Western counterparts, they publicly burned *Pravda*, burned the Soviet flag, conducted a sit-in, clashed with police, and chanted, "Russians, Go Home." Like the Schweikism in the factories, which produced everything from sly insults to slowdowns directed against the Soviet Union, it did no good. The Kremlin continued to tighten the screws.

Premier Kosygin came to Prague from Moscow on October 16 and signed a treaty legalizing the "temporary stationing of allied troops" in Czechoslovakia. All that was achieved through this latest indignity was the removal of satellite troops, the Poles being the last to go. But the old bans were lowered on foreign travel for Czechoslovak citizens. Dubcek also indefinitely postponed the Fourteenth Congress of the Czechoslovak Communist Party. But in no case did his concessions satisfy the Russians. Applying their familiar "salami tactics," they maintained an inexhaustible stream of demands. In the end, the design was to break the will of Czechoslovakia and force the nation back into conformity with the Soviet pattern.

The future pattern for the Soviet Union's relations with its client states was laid down by Leonid Brezhnev in a speech at Warsaw on November 12. In it, the Czechs could see no hope, for the strongest voice in the Kremlin warned that whenever Socialism in a country was threatened by either internal or external forces, "it becomes not only a problem of the people of the country concerned, but a common problem that concerns all Socialist countries." He also declared that military intervention, under such circumstances, was "dictated by necessity."

The speech constituted a threat to heretic Rumania and Yugoslavia. It was also a delayed response to President Johnson's warning to the Kremlin of August 30 "not to unleash the dogs of war" by invading Rumania. Having lost a chance to persuade the president to visit Moscow for arms limitation talks, primarily because of the Czech invasion, the Soviet regime did not want to widen the breach with the United States. But it also sought to show its partners in Eastern Europe that it would not tolerate another "Czech spring," which was the real reason for what came to be known as the "Brezhnev Doctrine."

As winter set in, the gravely weakened Czech government announced the removal of Josef Smrkovsky from the presidency of the National Assembly. When the press and the unions protested, Dubcek had to announce new controls for the news media on January 8, 1969. It was the end of the nations's faith in him. "He's like a broken vase," a woman in Prague said. "You can put it together, but it will never have the same shape or shine again."

On January 16, Jan Palach, a 21-year-old student at Charles University, doused himself with gasoline and set himself aflame in the manner of the sacrificial bonzes of Vietnam. In a letter to his people, he pleaded for an end to censorship of all kinds and a ban on the distribution of the Soviet propaganda newspaper, *Zpravy*. When he died three days later, the entire nation mourned him. And on January 25, a half-million people paid their final tribute to him as his body was borne through the ancient cobbled streets of Prague in a wintry rain. Dubcek, Cernik, and Svoboda all paid their homage. And in Wenceslas Square for many nights thereafter, the mourners came to hold the Czechoslovak tricolor beside rows of flickering candles before the statue of Good King Wenceslas. In the country of Jan Hus, Jan Palach would never be forgotten.

Like all the other acts of heroism and self-sacrifice that had marked the dreary occupation era, the student's immolation had no lasting effect on the remorseless Soviet program for Czechoslovakia. Under the pressure of the Kremlin, Dubcek was removed from power by his own Central Committee on April 17 and replaced as First Secretary of the Communist Party by his fellow Slovak, Gustav Husak. After nine years in prison as a victim of the 1951 Stalinist purge of Czechoslovakia, it was inevitable that Husak would be wary of offending the Soviet Union. This time, President Svoboda no longer was defiant of the Kremlin's wishes. It was he who announced Husak's accession and Dubcek's fall. And Oldrich Cernik, the premier, publicly denounced the leader whom he had once idolized. The Russians at last had had their way.

A year passed, a terrible and tragic year for the Czech nation, and once more a call to action welled up from the dwindling ranks of the patriots who were trying to keep resistance alive. But when a few thousand agitated young people swarmed into Wenceslas Square in Prague on the night of August 20-21, 1969, to protest the "Day of Shame," Czech tanks and troops repulsed them with scant trouble. The flowers that memorialized Jan Palach's sacrifice were roughly swept from the base of the statue of Good King Wenceslas and scattered in the dust of the square. The wild excitement of 1968 was gone and with it the surge of hope that had transformed a subject people into free men and women for a brief time.

The Czech press, again bound by censorship, whispered its dissent in Aesopian syllables when it dared, but it had precious little opportunity to do so. The rebellious weeklies that dared to appear, even briefly, were suppressed. In each of the thirty dailies, there was now a pro-Russian watchdog—a new editor-in-chief for the party papers and a censor for the non-party press. Many of the 4,500 members of the Czech Writers' Union were proscribed and unable to work because they had written too much of the truth; some had menial jobs, others were being cared for by friends, still others escaped to the West.

One old journalist, sitting in a plainly furnished room in an old building near the center of Prague on a beautifully sunny summer's morning, meditated on what had happened to his country and his people since the Soviet-led invasion. It was almost a monologue, delivered in a low and unemotional voice, as he bent over a cup of thick black coffee.

"For twenty-five years," he said, "we journalists told our young people that our future lay with the Soviet Union, that they could trust the Russians, that our hope was for the development of a truly beautiful Communist society. And what happened? The Russians invaded us, occupied us, because we insisted on free discussion, a free press, on Dubcek's Socialism with a human face." He sighed and stirred his coffee with a spoon. "At one stroke, we have lost a whole generation of young people. They will never again believe anything we older people tell them."

There were, at the time, some 70,000 Soviet occupation troops left in Czechoslovakia, but no Czech took comfort in the reduced numbers. "Whether it is 7, 700 or 70,000 Russians really makes no difference," one said. "This is an occupied country and we will not rest until they are gone. The Soviet Union has lost the respect of every citizen of this country,"

For the future, there was little hope in Czechoslovakia. The bold white symbol of freedom, the name of "Dubcek!" was fading on the walls of many a building in Prague on which it had been painted. Stripped of his honors and offices, he was suspended from the Communist Party, publicly disgraced, and threatened with prosecution. His one-time colleague, Cernik, clung to the premiership until Jan. 28, 1970, when he was at last replaced by a tough hard-liner, Loubomir Strougal. The new premier was a threat to the continued power of Husak, as well, if he faltered in carrying out Moscow's will.

The people, when given an opportunity, referred wistfully to that brave time when they had been able to say and read what they wished and go where they pleased. But with the downfall of the press, the electronic media remained painfully correct within the Russian meaning of that much-abused word. The unions could mutter about slowdowns; yet, they were well aware that their leaders would face severe punishment if slowdowns persisted. The rebellious Students' Union was dissolved. A new party group took over the Writers' Union. And the foreign press went under strict surveillance with the resultant expulsion of a number of correspondents. It was not enough for the fearful Czech regime to force the New York *Times*'s Tad Szulc out of the country. His successor, Paul Hofmann, also was expelled because of what the Czechs termed "the hostile attitude taken by your paper against the CSSR." This shadow war was the only kind of conflict for which the Czechs had any stomach now. The Russians had crushed them.

The time of the Czech spring had long since passed and winter once more was at hand. In a report to the International Press Institute, a Czech journalist wrote anonymously of the experience through which his nation had passed: "The Czechoslovak people learned during that time that freedom of the press is the groundstone of all other liberties. The Soviets were so scared of that freedom that they sent soldiers with guns and tanks to suppress it. The muzzling of the free press and the reintroduction of censorship was a result of their criminal adventure. The world is not going to forget that."

It was the epitaph of a free press in Czechoslovakia.

2. *Dissent in the Soviet Union*

The Fourth National Congress of the Soviet Union of Writers received a challenge in 1967 from the nation's most distinguished living novelist, Aleksandr Solzhenitsyn. In disgrace with a regime that had banned his works inside his own country and branded him an "anti-social slanderer," he had the courage nevertheless to demand a hearing for his ideas on personal freedom. To his old associates in the Union of Writers, he addressed a letter that asked for open discussion of the "now intolerable oppression, in the form of censorship, which our literature has endured for decades and which the Union of Writers can no longer accept."

It created a sensation. Like so much of the thin stream of dissent that appeared from time to time despite all the efforts of the Kremlin to dam it up, the Solzhenitsyn letter was circulated underground. Soon enough, it got out to the West and was published in *Le Monde,* the *Times* of London, the New York *Times,* and other papers. Solzhenitsyn was called to account. In the brutal manner so often employed by repressive leadership, he was told by officials of his union that he must disavow his denunciation of Soviet censorship and condemn foreign publication of his letter as a fraud.

Three times, he refused both demands. As a result, he was almost isolated in his home at Ryazan and friends reported he was dependent on the support of his wife, a schoolteacher. The royalties from his books that had been published in the West piled up but—like other dissident Soviet authors—he could not benefit from the money. The International Copyright Convention and the practices of Western book publishers meant nothing in the Soviet Union. Eventually, both the writer and his wife became dependent on their friends for support; otherwise, no friend could help.

There were influential writers and editors in the Soviet Union who deeply sympathized with Solzhenitsyn but few had the courage to come to his defense. They remembered all too well the last days of the Khrushchev "Thaw" and the expulsion of the great Boris Pasternak from the Union of Writers even though he had obediently refused to accept the Nobel Prize for *Dr. Zhivago.* Moreover, Khrushchev's vigilant and vindictive successors had imprisoned the liberal-minded writers Yuli Daniel and Andrei Siniavsky after a 1966 "show trial" for having "slandered the Soviet Union" in works published under pseudonyms in the West.

Nobody really knew how many others had been punished thereafter, but the rumors were frightening. For dissidents there was no place to hide and few could escape. It took someone of the craft and daring of the 40-year-old Soviet novelist, Anatoly V. Kuznetsov, author of the documentary novel *Babi Yar,* to obtain permission to leave the country and then arrange for asylum in London, as he did in 1969. The only others who had a chance were eminent people like Stalin's only child, Svetlana Alliluyeva, who fled to the United States in 1967 and published two books thereafter that were critical of the Soviet regime.

There was one major figure in the Soviet literary firmament, however, who refused to remain quiet while Solzhenitsyn and his works were proscribed. He was Aleksandr T. Tvardovsky, editor of *Novy Mir*, who had survived official displeasure in the Khrushchev era. In 1959 he had told the Third Writers' Congress: "Write the way your conscience tells you ... and don't be frightened in advance of editors and critics." Early in 1968, he wrote a 6,000-word defense of Solzhenitsyn to the head of the Union of Writers, Konstantin A. Fedin, saying that the proscribed author's arguments were "irrefutable."

Tvardovsky's effort was gallant but useless, and he himself eventually lost his control of *Novy Mir*. His plea for the publication within the Soviet Union of *The Cancer Ward* and *The First Circle*, Solzhenitsyn's latest works, was answered by the expulsion of the novelist from the Ryazan local of the Soviet Writers' Union and, later, by the All-Russian parent body. Solzhenitsyn counterattacked with a furious letter on November 10, 1969, calling the Soviet Union a "sick society" and assailing his persecutors for their "hate-vigilance."

"It is time to remember," he wrote to his union, "that the first thing we belong to is humanity. And humanity is separated from the animal world by thought and speech and they should naturally be free. If they are fettered, we go back to being animals. Publicity and openness, honest and complete—that is the prime condition for the health of every society and ours, too."

The result of his defiance was a campaign to force him to leave the Soviet Union. He became a symbol of the hardening Soviet position toward its own intellectuals. Nor did he suffer alone. Anatoly T. Marchenko's small book, *My Testimony*, about his experiences in a Soviet labor camp from 1960 to 1966, caused him to be sent to prison for four years as a "slanderer of the Soviet Union." A young mathematician, Ilya Burmistrovich, was jailed for three years for circulating the works of Siniavsky and Daniel, the imprisoned writers, in typescript. Other dissidents, such as Yuri T. Galanskov, Vera Lashkova, Aleksandr Ginsburg, and Vladimir I. Bukovsky had been in prison camps in the Soviet Union for many months at a time. To those who signed petitions for support for any of these or for Solzhenitsyn, and particularly for those who appealed to the United Nations, the regime showed no mercy.

The method of expulsion from the Writers' Union had other tragic results. In 1968, Aleksei Y. Kosterin, an old Bolshevik, was expelled from both the Union of Writers and the Communist Party and died shortly thereafter. At his funeral, a former major general of the Red Army, Pyotr G. Grigorenko, blamed the "damned machine" for his friend's death and assailed the "totalitarianism that hides behind the mask of so-called Soviet democracy." Grigorenko himself had suffered for his dissident views, having lost his high rank in 1964 and been confined to a mental institution for eight months — standard treatment for the rebels against the system.

Some of the heroes of "the Thaw," too, fell from grace in the Brezhnev era. Yevgeny Yevtuchenko, whose rise had been so rapid following the publication of his poem *Babi Yar*, was dropped from the board of the publication *Yunost*, a magazine for young people. Among those who also were eliminated from *Yunost*'s board was Viktor Rozov, whose play *Class Reunion* had not shown Soviet life to be idealistic. Vasily Aksenov, the author of the novel *Ticket to the Stars*, aroused official displeasure for what was deemed a false representation of the attitudes of Soviet youth. Another writer, Viktor Nekrasov, fell into disfavor for reporting after a tour of the United States that there were some favorable, as well as unfavorable, aspects of American life. To Soviet officials, this was not really "objective" reporting.

There were a few intellectuals who resorted to desperate means to call attention to what they deemed to be injustices in the Soviet Union. At the height of the Soviet invasion of Czechoslovakia, seven Soviet citizens appeared in Red Square to lead a demonstration in sympathy with the Czechs. They included Pavel Litvinov, the son of the old ambassador, Maxim Litvinov, and the wife of the imprisoned Yuli Daniel. All were beaten up by the Moscow police and five went to prison. But all dissent could not be stifled. The irrepressible Yevtuchenko, at another time, rebuked his critics with these lines:

> They tell me: Man, you're bold!
> But that is not true. Courage was never my strong point.
> I simply considered it beneath my dignity
> To fall to the level of my colleagues' cowardice . . .
> One day posterity will remember
> This strange era, these strange times, when
> Ordinary common honesty was called courage.

The regime also was unable to stop scientists from circulating papers among themselves, and they were not always about bombs and rockets. Very often they worried about the human condition, too. One of the most eminent Soviet scientists, Pyotr Leonidovich Kapitsa, argued at the age of seventy-five that Soviet ideology was isolated and now played little part in influencing the revolutionary movements of the West. In a paper published in the journal of the Soviet Academy of Sciences in 1969, Kapitsa warned: "Our ideologists will lose the privileges they have in our country, where there are no competing views." Such was the Kremlin's respect for the dean of the Soviet scientific community that he was permitted to go abroad despite his mildly dissident views and accept an honorary degree at Columbia University in New York. Had he been a poet, he might have been treated quite differently.

Among the conformist Soviet intellectuals with contacts in the West, there were copious excuses for the reversion of the Soviet government to a tighter discipline for its people. There were also voluble assurances that a return to the excesses of the Stalin era was "impossible." Although few tried to defend the proscription of writers of the stature of Solzhenitsyn and Pasternak and the imprisonment of other dissidents, they argued that the regime had a security problem. Once, the United States had been the excuse for every unpopular step taken by Moscow. But with the rise of Peking as an external threat, the Soviet propaganda position toward the United States became curiously ambivalent toward the end of the 1960s.

It was popular among Soviet writers with close ties to the Kremlin to express the hope for a *détente* with the United States. However, the regretful observation always was made that the Vietnam War would have to be settled before any real progress could be achieved. That, in essence, was what the Kremlin meant by invoking the "Spirit of Hollybush," the name of the New Jersey house where President Johnson and Premier Kosygin had conferred briefly on June 23, 1967.

In view of the continued mistrust between Moscow and Washington, it was remarkable that any new steps could be taken to reduce the tension between them. But with the super-powers apprehensively glancing over their shoulders at an emerging nuclear force in China, a few things were achieved. The limited nuclear test ban treaty was signed, but without the adherence of China and France. An agreement was reached in the United Nations to bar atomic weapons from outer space. A Washington–Moscow "hot line" was installed for emergency communications and proved immensely useful in the six-day Mideast War of 1967, when Cairo wildly accused the United States of armed intervention. However, neither Presidents Johnson nor Nixon found it very easy to persuade the Kremlin to make a serious effort to reduce armaments or cut the size of the super-powers' missile arsenals.

During a developing era of revolutionary change, one of the best indicators of the temper of the Soviet regime was its attitude toward the foreign press in general and the American news media in particular. The break with Stalinist practice was most striking, for both the number and the volume of the work of foreign correspondents from the West who were based in Moscow showed a substantial increase. Even more important, direct censorship of outgoing foreign copy had ceased in 1963. It was now possible to send material critical of the Soviet Union out of Moscow, but too much criticism still resulted in expulsion. Anatole Shub of the Washington *Post*, for example, was ordered out of the USSR in 1969. In retaliation, the United States expelled a

Tass correspondent, Viktor Kopytin. This, and not the ceremonial exchange of visits between American and Soviet editors, was a measure of the true state of affairs between the super-powers as the 1970s began. If there were twenty-four American correspondents in Moscow and twenty-six from the Soviet Union in Washington, that scarcely meant the cold war on the journalistic front had ceased.

The so-called Soviet "Democratic Movement," a handful of dissenters, took fantastic risks to smuggle documents — some genuine, some not — to the West. An underground typewritten press called "Samizdat" (self-publication) circulated a paper bearing the name of a Soviet historian, Andrei Alexeivitch Amalrik, which predicted the collapse of the Soviet regime in the 1980s after a war with China. "The (Soviet) regime is getting old, it's as simple as that," the paper proclaimed. "Too authoritarian to permit everything, too weak to repress everything, the regime is tottering toward death." The paper was widely published in the West, after which its author was punished.

In the internal communications system of the Soviet Union, so vital to its governmental processes, the press was still the dominant force for the dissemination of political ideas at the beginning of the 1970s. However, radio for nearly a decade had been permitted to announce big news first and the people were buying television at a far more rapid rate than the newspapers were able to expand their circulations. Yet, the old hard-line journalists remained contemptuous of television for all its attractions for a bored public. Fundamentally, the journalists argued that the newspapers would continue to be the best qualified to carry out the mission of the communications media as the "front line soldiers" of the Socialist State. Seemingly, the government agreed with them. The theory was that people were more likely to remember — and to be persuaded — by what they read rather than what they heard or saw. As one editor put it, "The situation could change. We are watching television closely, but right now it is not as powerful a force as the press in our country."

However dull and conformist the Soviet press may have appeared to Western eyes, it was an unqualified financial success under the firm control of its government and the Communist

Party. And this was even more true in the time of Leonid Brezhnev and Aleksei Kosygin than it had been under Khrushchev, whose son-in-law, Aleksei Adzhubei, tried to make a newspaper out of *Izvestia* with scant success.

The publishing house of the Communist Party, dominated by *Pravda*, was the best indicator of the essential conservatism of the regime and the gauge of its success. As the leading voice of the party, *Pravda* published more than 8 million copies daily at the beginning of the 1970s. With its three companion newspapers — *Komsomolskaya Pravda*, the youth paper; *Selskaya Zhisn*, for the farm; and the feature paper, *Sovietskaya Rossiya* — the *Pravda* organization printed in excess of 25 million copies a day. There were, in addition, some thirty weekly and monthly magazines, the largest with a circulation of 10 million, and numerous book publishing enterprises. *Pravda*'s editors estimated that all the publications of the House of Pravda together earned "much more than $50 million annually." Working under government patronage, these newspapers didn't have to worry about strikes, editorial dissension, or the pinch of fluctuating advertising revenues. But they also couldn't tell the people of the Soviet Union anything the party didn't want them to know.

Izvestia, the organ of the Soviet government, was reputed to be falling slightly behind *Pravda* in circulation at the beginning of the 1970s — something its editors did not like to admit. But it also was printing close to 8 million copies daily and it probably was as profitable as *Pravda*, but it was not as influential as it had been before the fall of Khrushchev and Adzhubei. It also ceased to experiment and conformed closely to the wishes of the heads of the government.

Pravda, *Izvestia*, and six other major dailies had a combined circulation in excess of 40 million copies. Adding the lesser metropolitan newspapers and the provincial press, there were 620 daily newspapers in the Soviet Union and total circulation at the beginning of the 1970s was officially claimed to be 72 million.* Necessarily, some of these were small newspapers. The largest

* The Soviet Union, applying UNESCO standards, considered any paper published four times a week or more to be a daily paper. The only seven-days-a-week paper was *Pravda*.

editions published by *Pravda* and *Izvestia* were six pages, tabloid size, which sold for three kopeks a copy. The four-page editions were two kopeks.

For all newspaper and periodical titles in the Soviet Union,
including the smallest district ·mimeographed party sheets, the
total was said to be more than 8,000. In short, the people of the
Soviet Union were reading more newspapers than ever before and
their literacy rate was the highest in their history. Yet, by conservative estimates, the newspaper readership was still about
half of the British average of 50 copies for each 100 people. The
80 million radio receivers and 15 million television sets in the land
rounded out one of the largest and most powerful of the world's
communications systems—a massive comeback from the nearly
total destruction of World War II.

In a controlled economy, there was relatively scant opportunity
for the kind of change that would bring the Soviet news media
into a pattern closer to the Western structure of mass communications. For one thing, editorial judgments were made at the top
levels of party and government and handed down to the editors
under Soviet practice. For another, the law of supply and demand
could not apply; in the Soviet Union, the use of advertising to
move the products of the government factories and stores developed slowly through some one hundred advertising agencies lo-
cated in various major cities. If a paper did not pay its own way,
it did not automatically suspend publication; yet, it also was provided with no incentive for improvement.

The area of Soviet news communication in which competition
did make itself felt was in the news agency field. Here, Tass's
dominance was broken first by the special correspondents of
Pravda and *Izvestia* and later by a new Soviet agency, Novosti,
which worked in the feature area. Next, with the rise of Hsin Hua,
the New China News Agency, Tass found that its slow, stuffy dispatches were being shunted aside by a good many editors in Asia
who printed the Communist line in favor of the faster and livelier NCNA copy. Within the various client states, Tass also found
that it had to put up with competition from the various Communist news agencies that were supported by satellite govern-

ments. It also was not unusual, on the fringes of the Soviet orbit, for some material to be bootlegged into the Communist press from BBC or the Voice of America.

The themes of the Soviet news media at the beginning of the 1970s showed a remarkable change from those of the previous decade. Toward the United States, there was on the whole a more relaxed attitude. As Brezhnev put it in his backhanded way when he made his usual pitch for peaceful coexistence, "We make no exceptions in this for any capitalist state, including the U.S.A." In the conquest of space, once the most glamorous part of the news from the Soviet Union, both the Soviet press and Soviet television broke precedent to give comparatively generous notice to the American victory in putting astronauts on the moon in 1969. And in the field of internal reform, there was much more emphasis on the growing demands of the Soviet consumer and on the complaints that were sent to Soviet editors by mail.

It was primarily in the Soviet Union's attitude toward China that the press displayed some of the confusing twists and turns that thoroughly puzzled both its own readers and the outside world. The 1969 border warfare between Soviet and Chinese troops along the Ussuri River in Siberia touched off the most warlike recriminations in the press of both countries. Before the conference of Communist Party leaders in Moscow that year, Brezhnev sounded the theme: "We shall carry on a resolute struggle against its [China's] great-power foreign policy line." And then, following the funeral of Ho Chi Minh in Hanoi, Premier Kosygin went out of his way to meet Chou En-lai briefly in Peking to set up the machinery for a conference on border problems. Almost at once, the anti-Chinese fulminations in the Soviet press died out although the basic antagonisms between the two countries were far from resolved. Under such uneasy circumstances, the vagaries of Soviet policy were bound to be reflected in the press for some time to come, as was evident when the press war against China was renewed in 1970.

With the "Brezhnev Doctrine" in effect, and the example of a shattered Czechoslovakia to remind them of the consequences of too flagrant a dissent, the press of the Soviet's client states in

Eastern Europe remained properly respectful. It was all very well for President Ceauescu of Rumania to maintain a kind of benevolent neutrality in the Soviet–Chinese dispute. But when President Nixon unexpectedly visited Bucharest after the American conquest of the moon, the Rumanian press went out of its way to stress the country's loyalty to the Communist system. In Hungary, too, the press was careful not to arouse Moscow's ire even though the Kadar government carried on a prudent minimum of liberal policies.

The Poles made the mistake in 1968 of flocking to see a revival of Adam Mickiewicz's nineteenth-century play, *The Forefathers*, and laughing heartily at such lines as: "The only things that Russia sends us are idiots and spies." The Gomulka regime, ever concerned about the tender feelings of the Soviets, suppressed the play. Whereupon the Warsaw students, already upset by a Polish anti-Zionist campaign, broke out of control temporarily and rioted in the streets. The result was a purge of the few remaining prominent Jews in the government.

Only in Yugoslavia was there an approximation of the youthful unrest that was sweeping the West. There, the Communist flagship paper, *Borba*, could publish with impunity the demands of student sit-in demonstrators against the government. Dissent in the Western sense was still not particularly safe, but bolder spirits spoke out for more diversity and showed their courage by attending performances of the American rock musical, *Hair*.

To Milovan Djilas, Tito's one-time collaborator who broke with him and served nine years in his prisons as a dissenter, the conduct of the Soviet client nations on the whole seemed hopeful. He thought it signalized "the beginning of the end of party bureaucracy in every Communist country." There were not many who agreed with him, particularly after Anatoly Kuznetsov began disclosing in London how Soviet officials had changed his manuscripts and others to fit the party line and encouraged writers to spy on each other for the benefit of the secret police, the KGB. It was, Kuznetsov said, a "frightful story."

From the accumulated evidence, the conclusion was inescapable that the lot of the dissenter was hard within the borders of the Soviet empire and its satellite states. Theirs was still a lonely struggle and it was likely to continue without letup for an indefinite period. Neither the Kremlin nor its press gave them any cause for hope.

3. Mao's Way

At the height of Mao Tse-tung's Great Proletarian Cultural Revolution, a slender and youthful British correspondent paced back and forth for twenty-six months in a small whitewashed room near the center of Peking. His name was Anthony Grey. As the correspondent of Reuters, the British news agency, he was one of four Western newsmen in the Chinese capital, the others being from Agence France-Presse, the Deutsche Press Agentur of West Germany, and the Toronto *Globe & Mail*. Like the additional ten correspondents in Peking, including one from *Pravda* and another from Tass, the Westerners were severely restricted in their movements although none of the regulars save Grey had been penned up in solitary confinement.

Despite all entreaties from his government, his agency, his family, his friends, and his profession, the Reuters man was continually surrounded by walls of silence until his body was weakened and his nerves were at the breaking point. And yet, he had committed no crime. He had not even offended his host government with his dispatches. He was held hostage to Peking because the British had arrested, tried, and imprisoned a number of Chinese journalists, so-called, after the abortive Communist rioting of 1967 in Hong Kong.

The ordeal of Anthony Grey began on July 21, 1967 when he was twenty-nine years old and had been in Peking only four months. Until that time, Reuters' correspondents had been in Peking since 1956 for terms of service averaging two years without suffering anything worse than an incredible boredom. Grey, who had joined Reuters in 1964 after serving as a local reporter in his native Norwich, had had a three-year indoctrination in serving in Communist countries and knew what he could and could not do.

At first he was confined in a room only eight feet square on the ground floor of the three-story combination Reuters office and correspondent's residence—a brick building with a courtyard surrounded by a wall twelve feet high. On the night of August 18, about four weeks after his confinement, 200 Red Guards swarmed into his room, beat him, smeared him with black paint, hanged his pet cat, and denounced him as an "imperialist reactionary journalist." From then on, he was ignored except for two 40-minute exercise periods each day in his courtyard. He was moved to a room twelve feet square, given three books, including one on Yoga exercises, that preserved his sanity, and left to his own devices. In the entire period of his confinement, he was permitted only three visits from British diplomats, allowed to write a letter a month to his mother, and given mail at infrequent intervals.

The British meanwhile released the Chinese journalists who had been imprisoned before Grey's detention, but he was kept in solitary until thirteen other Chinese, seized and jailed in Hong Kong after the beginning of his ordeal, were freed. He was finally let go on October 4, 1969, and headed home.* Unlike the Czechs who fabricated a case against Bill Oatis of the AP, the Chinese didn't even bother to put up a defense of their position. It was symptomatic of the new and immensely difficult situation of the foreign correspondent in a world that did not believe in or even recognize his right to exist, much less to do his work.

In the unfolding of the brilliant tapestry of Chinese history, the story of Anthony Grey will account perhaps for but a few threads at best. But it was so much a part of the pattern of Chinese xenophobic behavior in Mao's last years that it had an undeniable influence on the reporting of Chinese affairs. With the line held tight against all foreign correspondents, even for a time against Edgar Snow, Mao's biographer, mainland China was a virtual journalistic No Man's Land toward the end of the 1960s. The handful of Japanese correspondents, admitted to

* Other imprisoned foreign correspondents were released soon afterward, but surveillance of all resident correspondents continued.

Peking under an exchange agreement, dwindled sharply with the two-year imprisonment of a representative of *Nihon Kezai Shimbun,* Keiji Somejima, who was released in 1970. The two remaining Russians never knew when the same thing might happen to them. As for the Americans, some two dozen had obtained permission from the State Department to visit Mao's domain but Peking would give them no visas. And so, in the main, Chinese affairs had to be reported primarily from Hong Kong and lesser listening posts on the basis of both official and bootleg intelligence. Not until Grey's release did the Chinese show any signs of a change in policy. That was the way they wanted to conduct their affairs.

The time of turmoil had begun in 1965 with Defense Minister Lin Piao's call for the spread of "People's Wars" all over the earth on the model perfected by Ho Chi Minh in Vietnam. In August, 1966, Mao himself had begun his Great Proletarian Cultural Revolution, through which he finally was able to bring down those, like the old chief of state, Liu Shao-chi, whom he called "revisionists." The terror was spread by the mobs of undisciplined students, the Red Guards, who roamed the cities and struck at anything and anybody who displeased them. This was the ultimate in dissent. Nothing was safe from these ignorant, rampaging adolescents. Theirs became a mindless, destructive crusade that spread disorder through China for more than two years.

Had not the military restored order and disbanded the Red Guards after many months of painful and intensive effort, the breakdown of government in China would have been complete. Against such anarchy, in one of the five nations with an atomic arsenal, the outside world had no defense and this was the utterly frightening thing about Mao. He didn't seem to care. During this period a dozen Japanese businessmen and as many British were under arrest, along with five Americans who had been held for years on a variety of charges. In the apartment in Peking known as the Friendship Hotel, many of the 150 or so "guests" were arrested, disappeared, or suddenly left the country if they were able to get out. Many were foreign Communists or fellow travelers who, for one reason or another, had fallen under suspicion by a Chinese regime that was raising spy scares for its own inscrutable purposes.

The turn in events came at the Ninth Congress of the Chinese Communist Party in Peking in 1969 when Lin Piao was formally designated as Mao's deputy and his eventual successor. In his report, Lin emphasized perhaps the dominant fact of life in post-Red Guard China by quoting Mao: "From the Marxist point of view, the main component of the state is the army." With the creation of a new 21-member Politburo and a 170-member Communist Party Central Committee, the rising influence of the military became apparent. For all its manifold problems, the People's Liberation Army remained the most stable force in this transitional China.

In Lin Piao's view, the United States and the Soviet Union both were China's enemies. For evidence against the Soviet Union, he pointed to the border tensions from Mongolia to Sinkiang. For evidence against the United States, he cited the Vietnam War and the existence of the Taiwan government. With the death of Ho Chi Minh in 1969, there came an opportunity for the easing of strife between the Red giants but none could say whether their border conferences would succeed. Nor was there any way of knowing how the resumed Chinese-United States talks at Warsaw would turn out. It all depended on whether Peking wanted to be a part of the world community of nations.

The one area of government that remained stable and reasonably efficient throughout the period of the Cultural Revolution and its liquidation was the communications network. Considering that China had an illiteracy problem almost equal to India's in magnitude, it was remarkable that the press remained the keystone of the propaganda system. To a far greater extent than the Soviet Union, the Chinese tried to impose a far-flung system of "thought control" on their people in the belief that 800 million souls could be taught to act as one.

Jenmin Jih Pao, with a circulation of about a million copies daily, was the prime source of instruction for the faithful of the Chinese Communist Party. It was the leader of a national and provincial press of 392 daily newspapers that circulated a total of about 12 million copies. Among the periodicals, of which there were about 1,500, the most important was *Hung Chi* (Red Flag). In addition, an assorted group of publications ranging from weeklies to the omnipresent *Tatzepao*, the wall posters, spread the messages of the central propaganda agency throughout the land.

But despite the tens of thousands of propaganda officers and the imposition of group reading practices in towns and villages, the press had to be accounted a limited instrument of communication in a nation in which only about 25 percent of the population, by the most generous estimate, could be considered literate. Daily newspapers, for example, were believed to be distributed at a ratio of 2 copies for each 100 persons.

Radio broadcasting, of necessity, became the most pervasive medium of communication in mainland China with Radio Peking spreading the same theme as the press and the New China News Agency. The system had expanded in Mao's time to more than 200 transmitters with some 11 million receivers, including 4 million wired loudspeaker outlets. Toward the end of the 1960s, television also came into use on a limited scale but receivers were few and expensive even for group viewers. The work of the propaganda agitators, the performances of traveling dramatic and dance troupes, the songs of government-inspired musicians, and the painful sessions of collective criticism in homes, factories, and the countryside rounded out the Chinese communications network.

If by some chance the correct signals could not be obtained from *Jenmin Jih Pao* or Radio Peking, the all-inclusive New China News Agency was sure to supply them. This was the journalistic trinity on which Peking depended to build its image at home and spread its message abroad. With the exception of the brief "Hundred Flowers" period, during which Mao himself complained of the dullness of the press, no liberties were permitted in the mass media and criticism of the government was synonymous with treason. It was a system that exceeded the best efforts of Paul Joseph Goebbels.

The occasional visitor who returned from mainland China in Mao's last days could not help but be impressed with China's progress toward cleanliness and the elimination of the most abject form of poverty. But the regimentation of the people, the endless demonstrations, and the mass quotations from Mao's little red book remained as a fearfully depressing factor in Chinese life among those observers who were accustomed to Western ways. From early morning on, when the loudspeakers began blaring "The East Is Red," it was difficult to escape from the propaganda activists. Even when the marching and demonstrating could not be seen, they were always in evidence. As a Canadian, Colin McCullough, wrote: "Sometimes, late at night, a roar like that of a football crowd can be heard from a stadium whose illumination lights the sky. About 50,000 people are meeting just a few blocks away, but one does not have the faintest idea of what they are doing or saying." Such were the uses of mass persuasion in the Chinese Communist state. It was Mao's way. To dissent from it was close to impossible.

4. In China's Orbit

The strength of Mao's totalitarian control of his people in the heart of Asia confronted China's neighbors with an unenviable set of options. They could either agree to the unknown dangers of a Chinese alliance, accept the protection of the United States or the Soviet Union, or go it alone in a risky neutralism, Indian style, or the kind of protracted warfare at which Ho Chi Minh excelled. There were no satisfactory alternatives, even for those areas where the vestiges of British and French sovereignty lingered. On the oldest of continents, the most ancient grievances too often arrayed neighbor against neighbor. Consequently, in an era in which one-third of the human race sought independence as its highest goal, there were relatively few lands in Pacific Asia that dared to be free. And this was as true of the client states of the United States, which looked upon itself as a citadel of freedom, as it was to the rest of Asia. Democracy, in the Western sense, was not easily exportable.

In South Vietnam, where the United States had intervened against the Vietcong and North Vietnamese, there was little to show for all the years of a frustrating war, for more than 40,000 American dead and many more Vietnamese, for the $30 billions a year that the United States had spent to try to defeat a ragged little guerrilla army and the fourth-rate military power of North Vietnam. The implications of a military stalemate and pullout were bad enough for a world power of the stature of the United States. But what hurt even worse was the damage that was done to the American moral position before the world as the self-proclaimed guardian of liberty.

Neither President Johnson's long-delayed halt of the bombing of North Vietnam nor Present Nixon's orders for American troop withdrawals could restore the unity of a fragmented America or still the protest against the war. For the South Vietnamese government, never very certain of itself or its people, and for the South Vietnamese army, never trusted to carry the main burden of their own war, the American example was scarcely inspiring. For Washington had tried since 1961, and particularly after committing a half-million troops to Vietnam in 1965, to make a losing war look like a victory, to drape the trappings of democracy about an essentially authoritarian regime. The effort had failed at considerable cost to both American prestige and credibility.

To be sure, there was little enough to begin with in Vietnam on which to develop even the theory of self-government. Few people had any sense of national identity, much less national unity. It was tribe against tribe, sect against sect, mountain people against the people of the plain, north against south. What Ho Chi Minh had given to his followers around Hanoi was a cause, a fight first against the French and later the Americans, but he was scarcely a libertarian. Nor did the French heritage of Bao Dai and Ngo Dinh Diem in the south give the suffering people a glimpse of anything better to come.

After the rise and fall of a dozen patchwork governments in Saigon in the wake of Diem's sudden end, President Nguyen Van Thieu and his fellow generals finally were propped up with American support. But almost the first thing Thieu did when he came to power in 1965 was to close down thirty-six Vietnamese language dailies around Saigon and reluctantly restore twenty-three of them to publication on sufferance. Since the papers had a combined circulation of something less than 200,000 and since South Vietnam's literacy rate was estimated at only abut 15 percent, not much except a principle was really at stake.

On behalf of the International Press Institute, Barry Bingham, its president at the time, warned Thieu: "Authoritarian suppression of newspapers defeats the claim that your government is fighting to uphold free institutions." But Thieu didn't understand that kind of language; even if he had, he wouldn't have believed in it. His National Assembly, the product of elections, had scant power. His most troublesome political opponents went to jail or fled into exile. For those in the Vietnamese press who protested too much, the same fate was in store. As late as summer, 1969, when there was much talk of a more representative government in Saigon, Nguyen Lau, a newspaper publisher, was sent to prison for five years for "actions detrimental to the national order." Censorship in its many unlovely guises was the order of the day in South Vietnam.

Although a few foreign correspondents may have been disciplined now and then, the 250 to 300 men and a few gallant women who regularly covered the war in the south were relatively free to do as they pleased. The United States could not very well have curtailed their privileges. Because they tried honestly to show the war as they saw it, the correspondents and the cameramen told more of the truth than either the American or Vietnamese governments. Not all were brave, although more than a score were killed in action and more than a hundred wounded. Few were brilliant, for this was not a war that could be written or talked about in terms that a mass public would easily understand. The horror of it was most graphically conveyed by television, which made battlefronts of millions of American homes at dinner time every night. Such combat films conveyed better than print the hopelessness of a limited war on the Asian mainland.

No evasions of government and no efforts to discredit or intimidate correspondents could cancel out the vividness of these impressions. If the Vietnam War did nothing else, it established the power of an independent news network to inflate public dissatisfaction with an unpopular war to a point at which continued fighting became intolerable. While Ho Chi Minh could not win the war in the sense of annihilating American military power, he knew at the time of his death in 1969 that he had scored a great victory in the far more important struggle for American public opinion. Through his careful balancing between Moscow and Peking, he handed over to his successors in Hanoi a policy of comparative freedom of action in wartime that enabled them to carry on in the expanded Indochina war of 1970.

In the other French successor states of Southeast Asia, there was a careful weighing of the consequences of living in an atmosphere poisoned by great power rivalry. The influence of Red China had to be balanced in both Laos and Cambodia against the consequences of offending the United States, for China was a neighbor and the United States was a new and erratic force in Asia. Consequently, in Laos, the government of Souvanna Phouma gave permission for the use of its bases during the Vietnam War in return for a fabulous flow of American aid but desperately tried to avoid publicizing either activity for fear of offending China. With almost no information complex in the small, land-locked country, it didn't prove difficult to keep Laos' share in the Vietnam War to a minimum of public attention until a new crisis arose in 1970.

For Cambodia, the problem was even more difficult; having broken relations with the United States in 1965, Prince Sihanouk soon found that China's close attentions were even less welcome. In addition, with his small military force, he was comparatively helpless to halt the use of Cambodian borderlands as sanctuaries by the North Vietnamese and the Vietcong. His solution to all these embarrassments was to try to keep them as secret as possible by denying his country to all Western correspondents for months at a time, with the exception of his court favorite, a representative of Agence France-Presse. When his less than a dozen papers gave him trouble, he simply closed down the lot. It was all very well for others to concede the exis-tence of the manifold Ho Chi Minh trails through northern Laos, which were far out of Souvanna Phouma's control. But it didn't do to have stories published, as frequently happened, that Cam-bodia was sheltering Ho's soldiers. This was why Sihanouk would wrathfully deny what every journalist, diplomat, and sol-dier in Southeast Asia knew to be the truth. But at last, in 1970, his venturesome diplomacy failed and he was overthrown when the Cambodian military and students tried to force Vietcong and North Vietnamese troops out of their country. With the subse-quent invasion of Cambodia by United States and South Viet-namese troops, protests against the spreading of the war sent demonstrators swarming across American cities — the end result of the loss of credibility in Washington's intentions.

There was greater secretiveness in Thailand during the early part of the American buildup in that proud and ancient land, when American bombers first began flying from six Thai bases against North Vietnam. But by the time 50,000 American troops were scattered from Bangkok to outermost Sakon Nakhon, visit-ing correspondents had pretty well shattered the myth that the bombers were based on some distant Shangri-la. Even though the Thai press had been dutiful about keeping the secret that wasn't a secret, it scarcely prevented the Thai people from knowing what was happening around them.

From 1958 on, when their National Assembly was dissolved by a coup d'état led by Field Marshal Sarit Thanarat, they had lived for years under a military dictatorship. Their government-con-trolled radio and television, with some 350,000 sets serviced by two-score transmitters, were their chief reliance for news and opinion. Their independent newspapers — the leaders being *Thai Rath*, *Siam Rath*, and *Phim Thai* — accounted for only about 300,000 circulation, less than 1 percent of the population of a country with about 70 percent literacy. The threat of Communist insurgency in the north, stimulated by the ever-dangerous Chinese, was enough to keep the newspapers in line until Than-arat, the old dictator, died in 1963. Then, under the encour-agement of the new premier, Thanom Kittikachorn, the press disclosed the scandals through which Thanarat had amassed a fortune of $140 million. From this unwonted experience with freedom, the newspapers took on a livelier hue, led by the witty and courageous Kukrit Pramote, editor of *Thai Rath*. The outburst was temporary, however. With the slow liquidation of the Vietnam War, there was no telling what the Americans would do, but the prudent Thais knew that their old enemies, the Chinese and North Vietnamese, would always be with them. Inevitably, the Thais chose security from Communist incursions over the luxury of democratic freedoms. They did not want to become an Asian domino state.

For another American client state, Taiwan, the protection and patronage of the United States had also brought a high level of economic stability. But in the measured transition of its rule from the octogenarian Chiang Kai-shek to his son and deputy, the 60-year-old Chiang Ching-kuo, Taiwan remained a garrison state and the press was held to strict account under self-censorship regulations. There was no fear of the little band of Taiwanese exiles who agitated for independence. But to the dissidents on Taiwan, particularly the Chinese journalists and returning students, there was no mercy. In a typical case, a Taipei newspaper editor known as Po Yang was imprisoned on charges of having been a Communist agent in 1949 although his friends said his real offense was to publish a Popeye cartoon satirizing the ever-sensitive Chiang Kai-shek. It is no wonder that the thirty-one daily papers of Taiwan, with their total circulation of 700,000, submitted to the leadership of the two Kuomintang organs, the *Central Daily News* and the *China Daily News*. If the *United Daily News* was independent in ownership and the most popular paper on the island, it did not let its success delude it into criticism that the government would resent.

In prospering South Korea, which was just as dependent on the United States, the government of President Chung Hee Park of necessity maintained equally strict security. The threat of incursions from the north was always very real in Seoul. Yet, despite the regime's repressive powers, the fiercely independent Koreans could not be held down. The historic stance of most of their daily press had always been in opposition to the government; with 2 million circulation daily, of which four papers in Seoul accounted for half, this was a considerable force in a land with some 90 percent literacy. No matter how tightly the rules of self-censorship were observed, editors generally found a way around them if the issues were big enough to justify the risk. To the students, a notable political force south of the 38th parallel, freedom of the press was something more than a tiresome figure of speech. When they rioted against a constitutional amendment to permit President Park to run for a third term, their chief protests against his regime were its press policies and its secret police. This was not a country that would easily sink into servitude once again.

Of all the American client states within the sphere of Chinese influence, the Philippines was the most unrestrained and allowed its independent press and electronic media the greatest privileges. But for all that, the one-time "little brown brother" of the United States was far from a democratic model for the non-Communist Asians who sought an alternative to domination either by Red China or the Soviet Union. The gap between rich and poor in the Philippines was widening. The contrast between the few privileged and enormously wealthy families in such glittering suburbs as Makati and Forbes Park and the impoverished barrios of the countryside was both depressing and appalling. Corruption, always a problem for developing countries, was so widespread in the Philippines that President Ferdinand Edralin Marcos had to take repeated public notice of it, and student rioters accused him of doing too little to stop it.

Among the newspapers, the dominant publication was Joaquin P. Roces' Manila *Times*, which commanded about one-third the total circulation of the twenty-two daily papers in the island republic. Like Pramote of Bangkok, Roces tried to run an open forum in the *Times* by permitting a wide range of comment among his columnists. When he cooperated with his government, it was usually on his own terms. But as for cooperation with the United States, that was something else again. Roces was no uncritical admirer of Washington; in consequence, he was often cited among his fellow journalists in Asia as an example of a publisher who could be both morally and financially independent. The trouble was that there was exceedingly few like him in the Philippines.

Throughout the sphere of dying British influence in Pacific Asia, the signs of independence among peoples and their press were lamentably few. Even in the seeming freedom of Hong Kong, the government of the tiny British Crown Colony worried continually over what Red China might think or do. For the few English language newspapers of the colony, and the two dozen or so Chinese journals of all shades of political faith, the Government Information Office maintained the right of licensing and strictly rationed its official news.

The outside world assumed that the Chinese Communists were glad to permit Hong Kong to stay in business pending the expiration of the British lease in 1997, primarily because it provided Peking with more than a half billion dollars annually in much-needed trade. But the government of the colony, after the fierce 1967 Communist rioting, had no such illusions. While it maintained a stiffly correct attitude toward recognized foreign correspondents with business in Hong Kong, it could be sticky and even critical of its own journalistic nationals. The security of an island of 4 million people, 99 percent of them Chinese and more than one-third refugees, was a far more important consideration with the last of the British colonial administrations in the Far East than the ritual observance of freedom of the press. No less than Ceylon or Afghanistan, Nepal or Sikkim, Hong Kong did not intend to let its press give offense to Red China without good cause.

In other former British colonies where there were overseas Chinese in large numbers, developing nations faced grave problems of civil strife and worse. Under such circumstances, there was more shadow than substance to the manner in which a self-proclaimed democracy was able to operate in Asia. There were innumerable dangers. To guard against them, despite the noblest of intentions, compromises had to be made.

Malaysia was a case in point. Having survived the bullying

and the armed attacks of Sukarno's Indonesia during his small "confrontasi" war of the early 1960s, Malaysia could have used a breathing spell. But the brutal 1969 rioting between Malays and Chinese in that prosperous but unhappy land emphasized the shaky foundations of its experiment in multiracial democracy. Within two years of its foundation in 1963, Malaysia had expelled its largest city and chief source of world trade, Singapore, precisely because it was a city with a Chinese majority.

But that bill of divorcement settled nothing. The antagonism between the races persisted. And because it did, so independent and prosperous a newspaper as the *Straits Times* had to be very careful what it printed about its government. With nearly 250,000 circulation, it had almost half the combined circulation of the twenty-six daily papers in the country that were published in English, Chinese, Malay, and Punjabi. But in time of crisis, the *Straits Times* had to be circumspect in its reporting if it wanted to continue in business. It was not an easy situation for a supposedly free press. And the regulations imposed by the equally vigorous government of Lee Kuan Yew in the city-state of Singapore did not make the problem any simpler.

It was much worse in Burma, where General Ne Win permitted no dissent among his people and no criticism of his government. He had destroyed the independence of the Burmese press, which had once numbered no less than thirty-two dailies, and had held one of the most distinguished of Burmese journalists, Edward Law Yone, under house arrest for five years. The isolation of the Burmese from the world was almost as great as that of their Chinese neighbor, whom they had good reason to fear.

In the two great Muslim nations, Indonesia and Pakistan, dictatorships far more powerful than Ne Win's toppled in the latter part of the 1960s but the freedom that the revolutionaries demanded came with aggravating slowness to the people and their press. In both countries, military regimes assumed power with vague assurances of the eventual restoration of democratic forms. But the military, as always, had an inborn mistrust of the processes of uninhibited public criticism. For whatever relaxation there was, excuses were found soon enough to warn the press not to interfere with national security. Among these, the always difficult relations with Red China played a part.

When Sukarno decided to take Indonesia into a close relationship with Communist China in 1965, his first move was to wipe out the anti-Communist press. After purging nearly fifty newspapers, he ordered the expulsion of several score journalists from the government-controlled Journalists' Association, thereby depriving them of their jobs. For those who entertained the notion of defying him, the nine-year imprisonment of Mochtar Lubis, the editor of the independent-minded *Indonesia Raya*, proved to be a sufficient deterrent.

It was scarcely a triumph for freedom, however, when Sukarno's "guided democracy" was overthrown and replaced by the "new order" of Suharto, his cautious military successor. The hundreds of thousands of Indonesians and Chinese who were slain in the anti-Communist purges, following the failure of the Peking-supported takeover of 1965, left a heritage of hate and suspicion across the land. Even toward the end of the decade, Indonesia's economic plight was grave; aid from the United States had been slow in coming because of the more urgent demands of the Vietnam War.

Suharto tried to institute reforms, nevertheless. In what he called a "refreshing" process, he permitted the functioning of a limited kind of party system, enlarged the Parliament, cut down the number of military people in government and did what he could to stamp out corruption. A lively and thoroughly functioning press could have helped him, but he had only a semblance of a communications system left from the shambles of the Sukarno regime. Mochtar Lubis, upon his release, began publishing his *Indonesia Raya* once more and won back readers with his *Prison Diary*. But few other independent editors were as successful. The government and party press outnumbered them, and the military papers were the most important of all. But throughout the whole of Indonesia, the press circulated scarcely a million copies a day. In a nation of 110 million with a literacy rate of 15 to 20 percent, that meant the main dependence of the people for information had to be the government radio with its sixty transmitters and 800,000 receivers. The outlook for a free press, under such circumstances, was dubious; yet, it was given more privileges than it had had in a decade.

In Pakistan, the change in military dictatorships did little to liberate the press. General Mohammed Ayub Khan was overthrown in 1969 because his people no longer could tolerate his manipulated courts and subservient police, his controlled press and his total effort to suppress dissent. In a nation of 100 million people, he had permitted only about a hundred closely supervised papers to circulate a total of a half-million copies daily. When editors did something of which he disapproved, they went to jail. In a typical instance, Shorish Kashmiri, the editor of *Chatan* of Lahore, published a mild article on the Ahmadi sect in April, 1968, was sent to prison for eight months for violating defense rules, and lost his printing plant.

Pakistan's undoubted prosperity saved Ayub for a time. In foreign affairs, he played a bold game by bidding for Red China's trade and friendship while maintaining the facade of an alliance with the United States and putting up a brief battle against India in 1965 for Kashmir. But his luck ran out finally because he had done too little to help East Pakistan and too much for the handful of wealthy families that were most influential in West Pakistan. Once the rioting began in the cities, it was not halted until Ayub stepped down on March 25, 1969, and handed power over to the military commander, General Aga Mohammed Yahya Khan. As a farewell gift to his persecuted press, he restored a measure of freedom to the editors. It didn't last long. Before Yahya had been in power a month, censorship was clamped down tighter than ever before and the press of Pakistan might just as well have been issued in a mortuary.

Thus, if there was any functioning containment policy in Red China's orbit at the beginning of the 1970s, it was a containment of the press. There were few places in which an independent paper could be published, even fewer in which an editor could speak his mind without punishment. Given a choice between freedom and security, the governors for the most part chose security without hesitation; the governed were either too weak or too uninterested to care.

5. *The Fate of India*

In India, the largest and most vulnerable of the world's democracies, there was a stubborn — sometimes an almost despairing — adherence to the practices as well as the forms of open societies despite seemingly insuperable difficulties. As the decade of the 1970s opened, the decisive test of India's survival as a nation was at hand. A less dedicated land would long since have collapsed under continual threats of famine, fragmentation, secession, strife in the national government, near-anarchy among the states, of hesitant leadership and partial to noncommunication among more than 500 million people.

But somehow, India kept going. The government of the slender but durable Indira Gandhi was able to plan for the 1972 elections with an outward show of confidence despite the undeniable pull away from New Delhi's influence, the rout of the once-dominant Congress Party in 1967, and the suspension of leftist administrations in six of the sixteen states in favor of nationally imposed governments. Had it not been for $8 billion in aid from the United States, including some 47 million tons of wheat to make up for drought failures, there would have been widespread starvation and economic disaster in India. Had it not been for a show of military support from both the Soviet Union and the United States after the Himalayan rout of 1962, the Indians would have been at the mercy of the Chinese along their borders. Had it not been for United Nations intervention and Soviet mediation after the brief war with Pakistan over Kashmir in 1965, the strain of that long-simmering dispute might have torn all South Asia apart.

After twenty years of independence, here was a nation with a per capita income of only a little more than $50 a year, a literacy rate of about 15 percent, and an exploding birth rate that doomed all hope of rapid improvement in appalling social conditions. With 80 percent of the people living in 500,000 villages and hundreds of thousands leading a wretched existence on the

streets of Calcutta and Bombay, there were enormous gaps between the relatively few wealthy families and the helpless armies of the poor. There was always danger of strife between the
fiercely nationalistic Hindu rightists and the 60 million Muslims
who still lived in India, the third largest Muslim community in
the world. Even in differences of language, the Tamil, Marathi,
and Bengali peoples could riot against what they feared was an
attempt to impose the Hindu tongue on them. Finally, violence
was the weapon of the extreme left, particularly the Maoist faction that split off from the pro-Moscow Indian Communist Party.

In a nation so beset with troubles, an effective mass communications system to link the government with its people was a
desperate necessity if even a semblance of democracy was to be
preserved. Indira Gandhi recognized the problem quickly enough.
She used the All-India Radio so much that it began to be called
the All-Indira Radio. She also initiated an American–Indian
agreement to make possible television broadcasts from an orbit-
ing space satellite by 1972 to bring both news and education to
the villages by means of inexpensive receiving sets.

A large, aggressive, and independent press would have filled
an important void in India's national life if it had been able to
develop to the fullest extent. But unhappily, newspaper expansion was sharply limited. Although the Indian constitution guaranteed freedom of the press, shortages of newsprint and of foreign exchange combined to keep the nation's dailies on a short
leash. Even if the government had been willing and able to find
means of being more generous, the lack of literacy and general
impoverishment of the people would have kept circulation down.

Of the approximately 6 million copies of daily newspapers that
were sold, nearly 80 percent were published in the various Indian languages, but the numerically inferior English language
press was by all odds the most influential. For regardless of the
agitation for the use of Hindi as India's sole official language,
English remained the nation's lingua franca — the language of
the government in large part, of the intellectuals, teachers, and
scientists. How long it would last was problematical; in Pakistan, a tentative deadline of 1975 had been set for phasing out

English in favor of Urdu in the West and Bengali in the East. Only India's multiplicity of languages — All-India Radio used fourteen — kept English going there as an alternative to Hindi.

It was clear enough to the great newspaper chains that their only safety for the future lay in diversified publication of both English and Indian language newspapers and magazines. And since the chains accounted for nearly two-thirds of the total circulation of the daily press and probably nine-tenths of its influence, this was the shape of the future.

With the exception of the *Hindu* of Madras, which alone among the leaders was dominated by a family of journalists, each of the other major newspapers had some close connection with industry. Such links were bound to arouse suspicion and even hostility in government and harsh criticism from the liberal-to-radical left. Yet, it would have been difficult in Asia to find newspapers that were more professional and more animated by a genuine feeling for their independent status than the *Indian Express*, the *Times* of India, the *Hindustan Times, Amrita Bazar Patrika*, and the *Hindustan Standard* with their Indian language counterparts.

In certain areas of the news, the press generally agreed with a policy of self-restraint rather than risk the wrath of the government. The most important of these was in the reporting and publication of civil disturbances. Here, at the suggestion of the government, all except the most irresponsible Indian language papers were careful about publishing casualties, identifying religious organizations or using extravagant and perhaps offensive language. In the continuing crisis with Pakistan over Kashmir, the Indian press also was generally responsive to the government line.

In foreign affairs, despite the enormous assistance that had come from the United States, it was almost an article of faith for most Indian newspapers and journalists to be anti-American in varying degrees. For the Soviet Union, however, the press treatment was more considerate; as for Red China, the tone was more likely to be respectful than intemperate. The difference, of course, was the hard reality of geography that dictated prudence toward a powerful neighbor and a great show of independence toward a distant friend. These, too, were part of the uses of freedom, irritating though they might be to Washington.

Indian foreign correspondents generally could write just about what they pleased from abroad but the handful of foreign correspondents of Western news organizations within India found new difficulties put in their way. The biggest complaint was the inability or the unwillingness of the Indian government to permit very many correspondents to visit sensitive border areas. This, plus an informal and often clumsy system of surveillance of some Western correspondents, was just about as far as any Indian government went toward limiting the news into or out of India. To be sure, Indira Gandhi complained often that the foreign press seemed to search out the worst of India's troubles and exiled a BBC man in 1970 to show his resentment. But in all truth, so few good things happened in India that the foreign press — like the domestic newspapers — had little choice.

6. Japan: Forge of Asia

Many of the considerations that motivated governments from Hong Kong to India in their relations with the press also applied in some respects to Japan. Here, as the beneficiary of MacArthurean postwar policies, the greatest and most pervasive information system in Asia had been developed in cooperation with, but independent of, its government. It was exceeded in size only by the American and British networks of mass communications outside the Communist world.

To a greater extent than their Western counterparts, the major Japanese newspapers appeared to have a deep-rooted conviction that they were more the protectors rather than the critics or watchdogs of their country's welfare. Without doubt, this feeling on the part of the proprietors and editors was an outgrowth of the closely knit pattern of Japanese society. But it was also based on the phenomenal recovery of Japan from the ruin of World War II. In less than twenty-five years, the Japanese people had transformed their shattered and defeated land into the third greatest industrial power in the world, directly behind the United States and the Soviet Union. The Japanese press, which had survived in the loneliest and most desperate struggle of all in Asia, could scarcely be blamed for its well-nigh universal belief that it had something very precious to defend.

At the outset of the 1970s, the Japanese economy was within reach of a gross national product of $200 billion annually, second largest in the non-Communist world after the nearly $900 billion of the United States. It is true that Japanese per capita annual income was still $1,100 — far below the American standard. But, at that period, it is equally true that the exchange rate of the yen to the dollar was unrealistic. By every outward indicator, the Japanese living standard was going up rapidly. With a growth rate that could exceed 13 percent annually, the increase in foreign trade was a particular matter of national pride and celebration in the press. For the Japanese were the largest shipbuilders in the world, the second largest producers of automobiles after the United States, and ranked near the top in steel, chemical, and photographic equipment. Its $15 billion foreign trade was closely linked to the American economy, for no less than $6 billion annually was with the United States and 15 percent came as a result of the Vietnam War. In 1969 alone, it was estimated that Japan had achieved a $1.3 billion balance of trade over the United States.

To a greater degree than in the United States and Britain, the daily press in Japan looked upon itself as a part of the Japanese Establishment. It gloried in Dai Nippon's prosperity. Under the Liberal Democratic Party, the government's attitude toward the newspapers was paternalistic even toward its critics. Each government minister of consequence, and some leading industrialists, had their coterie of loyal journalists — a reporters' club — with which each worked in close harmony. From time to time, ministers and proprietors could consult directly and informally, since they moved in the elevated echelons of Japanese society. Such things could be done on a very polite, very proper basis and nobody resented it, least of all the people. For public opinion in Japan was not really a dominant factor in most decision-making. The independent press was more important.

Truly, the Japanese information system was formidable. Even with the rapid expansion of television by both government and private ownership, the press remained of enormous importance to the Japanese communications complex. Calculated by American standards, the total daily circulation of 118 newspaper companies approached 50 million* in the early 1970s in a nation of 100 million people with a 98 percent literacy rate. Nearly one-third of these sales were accounted for by the "Big Three" — *Asahi*, *Mainichi*, and *Yomiuri Shimbun*. In excess of 90 percent were by annual subscription. What this amounted to was a total subscription rate of nearly two newspapers a day on the average among 22 million households.

The income from this enterprise amounted to nearly a half-billion dollars a year, almost evenly divided between income from advertising and circulation. The favorable aspect of the press's operations was due in part to the development of more advertising revenue, but the comparative docility of Japanese labor was an even more important factor during the boom years. Television was the major danger to newspaper stability. For despite the financing of the government-controlled NHK network through license fees, the expansion of independent television and its attraction for advertising cut into the press's revenue.

Few newspapers outside the fat and monopolistic provincials could get by on their own earnings. While the law theoretically protected the press from domination by commercial interests, many a proprietor found he had to go to the banks to draw loans at tight periods. The banks were not displeased. Nor were industry and government greatly concerned. It made for a satisfactory situation all around and the public, with the exception of the discontented students and intellectuals, seemed utterly disinterested. Many a newspaper had to turn to more diversified sources of income — books, magazines, radio, and TV.

Pleasant as the government-press relationship seemed to be,

---

* This is on the basis of the American system of counting morning and evening sales separately. The Japanese put them together as "sets."

no one could doubt that the press had muscle. In 1960, during the Japan–United States mutual security treaty riots, the Japanese press had helped touch off an unexampled outburst of anti-Americanism. It brought down the Kishi government and forced the cancellation of President Eisenhower's visit to Tokyo. Only when the opposition faltered did *Asahi Shimbun*, the leader, give the signal for a change of front that helped save the treaty. A decade later, when the treaty once again was at issue, the position of the press was no less critical at a time when the Sato government was insisting on the reversion of Okinawa to Japanese sovereignty. On such issues, it took a tough line.

The Japanese newspapers could be quite severe toward the United States, their conqueror, ally, protector, and No. 1 trading partner. During the Vietnam War, an American ambassador to Tokyo, Edwin O. Reischauer, took the unusual step of protesting the combat reporting of the Japanese correspondents as "unbalanced." Toward Communist China, however, there was a solicitude in a largely conservative press that very closely paralleled the government's attitude. For all their misadventures on the Chinese mainland, the Japanese had never forgotten that China remained potentially their largest remaining area for trade expansion and the provision of raw materials.

In the peaceful creation of the Greater East Asia Co-Prosperity Sphere, the wartime dream that had turned into a nightmare, a firm Japan–China friendship was essential. If Peking was rude, threatening, and hostile by turn, that did not seem to disturb Japan. As Premier Eisaku Sato put it in response to his critics in the Diet, the maintenance of Japan's pipeline to China outweighed considerations of national prestige. The press's favorable attitude toward the conclusion of a 1969 trade agreement with China showed that the premier had public opinion solidly behind him. Only one newspaper of consequence, Tokyo *Shimbun*, grumbled that it had not been a "negotiation between equals, but a master-servant relationship." But the rest of the papers, like the leadership of the Liberal Democratic Party, were content. They could not forget that China would always be their neighbor and that the United States, while important to them today, might very well withdraw across the Pacific tomorrow. And this was the key to much of Japan's policy-making in its critical years for, whatever happened, the island colossus meant to remain the forge of Asia, the industrial heart of a system that encompassed one-third of the world's peoples.

Unlike the complaisant press under the military dictatorship before World War II, the postwar newspapers regarded very little as sacred outside the Emperor and his immediate family. A weekly, *Shukan Asahi*, disclosed in an interview with the 61-year-old Mrs. Hiroku Sato in 1968 that her husband, the premier, had been a somewhat less than devoted bridegroom. It became the talk of Tokyo. The tale was not a glorious moment in the history of the independent press in Japan. But it did testify eloquently to the changed relationship between the people and their newspapers.

As for the government, it seldom seemed outwardly disturbed by the excesses of the Japanese press. More often than not, when Japanese journalists were in trouble, the regime would go out of its way to give them support. Toward the foreign correspondents who were concentrated in Tokyo in greater number than in any other place in Asia except Saigon, the Japanese were even more indulgent. The "low posture" of the government was not particularly calculated to make news. Nor were the reporters' clubs in the government any more friendly to foreigners, although one or two such organizations did let down the bars slightly. But in the main, for ease of living, efficiency of communications, and freedom of movement, Tokyo deserved its status as the prime news center of Asia. In time, that in itself would make an enormous difference to the people of the Asian mainland.

For Japan was not permanently committed to a "low posture" in world affairs. There would come a period, in the not too distant future, when Dai Nippon would assert itself again as a world power. What happened then to the press would provide the test of whether Japan's hard-won liberties could be preserved.

XI. Into a Revolutionary Age

1. The Third World

After enduring four years of military-supported government in Brazil, a 32-year-old journalist celebrated his country's Independence Day in 1968 with a gesture of contempt for the Army. He asked people to stay away from the military parade in Rio de Janeiro that September 7.

To most Brazilians, it was just another of the journalistic darts that Marcio Moreira Alves had been throwing regularly at the military in his speeches as an opposition deputy in the National Assembly and his widely read column in Rio's *Correio de Manha*. But to the indignant military supporters of the government of President Arthur da Costa e Silva, a former Army marshal, it was the last straw. They wanted the rebellious journalist's parliamentary immunity removed so that he could be tried for violation of national security.

When the National Assembly refused to do so, Costa e Silva proclaimed an effective military dictatorship on December 13. The National Assembly was suspended indefinitely. Censorship was imposed on the press. And a widespread purge of all dissenters began, in which editors and proprietors of newspapers were the leading victims. Moreira Alves' little dart of criticism had been seized upon by the Army to do away with the troublesome forms of self-government. As the president himself put it: "The entire nation understands that the military does not accept criticism and abuse covered by cowardly immunity."

In the developing nations of Latin America, which had been searching for so long for a new way of life, the Brazilian experience was painfully familiar and disheartening. Left to themselves, there is little doubt that many of the 250 million Latin Americans would have associated themselves with that Third World of new lands in Asia and Africa that were seeking a middle ground between the super-powers, the Soviet Union and the United States. But few had such freedom of choice.

There had been nearly forty military coups south of the Rio Grande since 1930, at least a dozen of them following President Kennedy's proclamation of the Alliance for Progress in 1961. Out of every four people in Latin America, three were living under some form of military rule. The press, whether formally censored or not, was nearly always on the defensive. It made little difference whether the dictatorships were of the Left or Right, for the result was usually the same as far as the independent newspapers were concerned. In Castro's Cuba, where the newspapers had become government chattels, some forty journalists had been in prison for years as opponents of the Communist regime. In French-speaking Haiti, the rightist dictatorship of Francois Duvalier was no less thorough in its persecution of the press. When military governments seized power in Peru and Panama in the fall of 1968, the extreme Right promptly cracked down on the press. Nor was the situation much better in Argentina, which had been under military rule since 1966, although both *La Prensa* and *La Nacion* served notice that they would continue to maintain the right of dissent as long as possible.

Despite worldwide protests led by the Inter-American Press Association, the Brazilian suppression of 1968-69 followed a predictable pattern. From the outset, the military dictatorship spread its censorship over all foreign correspondents as well as the domestic press in an effort to conduct its persecution in utter secrecy. But Moreira Alves' paper published a list of those who had been arrested and the government had to make a formal disclosure to the nation. The leading newspapers — *Jornal do Brasil*, *O Globo*, *Correio da Manha*, and *O Estado* of Sao Paulo — attacked the spreading censorship without regard for consequences. For their temerity, Mrs. Niomar Moniz Sodra Bittencourt, publisher of *Correio da Manha*, and her managing editor, Osvaldo Peralva, served prison terms. Thereafter, Mrs. Bittencourt was deprived for ten years of the right to publish her paper. Alberto Dines, editor of *Jornal do Brasil*, and Helio Fernandez, publisher of *Tribuna da Imprensa,* were jailed. Less prominent journalists received similar — and sometimes even more brutal — treatment.

After a visit to Brazil, Agustin E. Edwards, publisher of *El Mercurio* of Chile and president of the Inter-American Press Association, reflected sadly: "It seems clear that for a long time to come, freedom of expression will be restricted in Brazil." When Costa e Silva died after a heart attack in 1969 and was replaced by a military junta, there was a brief breathing spell. But as the regime of President Emilio Garrastazu Medici gained strength, reports of police torture spread through the land, and censors bore down hard on the press. A news magazine, *Veja,* was forced to delete news of military repression; other publications warily practiced self-censorship. Edwards' worst fears were quickly realized.

Much the same thing was going on elsewhere in Latin America. The Peruvian military dictator, General Juan Velasco Alvarado, decreed fines and jail terms in 1970 for any journalists who were deemed to have insulted his government. He also forced through a law barring absentee press owners, a direct blow to former Finance Minister Manuel Ulloa, owner of the influential Lima papers, *Expreso* and *Extra,* who had been hounded into exile after the coup of October 3, 1968. Another exile, Enrique Zileri, was threatened with the loss of his new magazine, *Caritas.*

With the crushing of press freedom in Peru, even the usually liberal nations of Chile and Uruguay adopted menacing postures toward their press. The Chilean regime of President Eduardo Frei Montalvo enforced a law prohibiting the publication of "alarmist" news following the appearance of press criticism of the government and reports of dissatisfaction within the armed forces. In Uruguay, a 1969 law obliged the press to withhold reports about planned strikes and demonstrations. And in Panama, the government simplified matters by installing its own editors to make certain that neither it nor its military supporters were criticized.

The military regime of President Juan Ongania in Argentina

suspended most civil liberties and effectively gagged most of its press, the exceptions being *La Prensa* and *La Nacion*, without even bothering to invoke a formal censorship. The leading weekly, *Primera Plana*, was closed. As for Communist Cuba, if any editor thought of criticizing Fidel Castro's rule, he could reflect on the fate of Alfredo Izagurri, editor of *El Crisol*, who had been in prison for eight years.

If there was any hope of relief in the widespread anti-press campaign, it lay in the activities of the Inter-American Press Association in rallying world opinion against the weaker dictators. Beginning with its defense of Gainza Paz in *La Prensa*'s struggle against Peron, IAPA (Yapa south of the Rio Grande) grew in two decades into an organization that represented more than 1,000 publications and editors in the Americas. It was able to save Demetrio Canelas, a Bolivian publisher, from execution and it helped obtain the release of Pedro Beltran, publisher of *La Prensa* of Lima, from prison. But even IAPA was appalled at the enormity of the task before it. At the opening of the 1970s, it reported the decline in press freedom in Latin America had become alarming.

In Africa, where the developing nations for the most part had little experience or patience with the forms of self-government, the press was in an even less favorable position. Including the newspapers of the Union of South Africa and the United Arab Republic, there were less than 200 dailies in the entire continent at the start of the 1970s. Twelve new countries had no papers of any kind and seven others used only bulletin sheets. With 80 percent of the population concentrated in rural areas, most of them not easily accessible, it followed that newspapers had to be produced mainly in the cities. And since most newsprint had to be imported at a steep rate above the market price and literacy in Africa was the lowest of all the continents, even the existing press was in deep trouble in the few places where it had a foothold. Such was the state of public communication in the Third World as it existed in Africa.

Most of the sub-Sahara nations had one-party governments

and insisted on owning or controlling their press. Ghana, Nigeria, and Kenya permitted minimal independent ownership of newspapers, but watched the editors and publishers with deep suspicion. Others imitated them. The going became so hard for Lord Thomson, largest owner of newspapers in the world, that he cut his losses and made television his main interest in sub-Sahara Africa. The International Publishing Corporation, which had gone into West Africa in 1947, also reduced its commitments sharply. The East African Standard group remained active with newspapers in eight countries, but both the government-owned press and the Aga Khan's Nation group of papers provided challenges at the beginning of the 1970s.

Even native journalists were punished if they became intractable. President Milton Obote warned the Uganda press that it would not be allowed to interfere with the government. "We cannot have a government and a press enjoying the same responsibility," he warned. Acting under this philosophy, he caused the editor of the magazine *Transition*, Rajat Neogy, to be detained for five months without trial and bore down hard on other nonconformist editors. Seeing native journalists treated so harshly, the foreigners in the new African nations realized their influence was gone.

It was scarcely a surprise, therefore, that both foreign investment and foreign personnel dropped off in the African press. It was unfortunate, primarily because there were so few journalists in sub-Sahara Africa who had either the training or the experience to build a system of independent newspapers. Only one African newspaper proprietor, Dr. Nnamdi Azikiwe—the dynamic "Zik"—had been able to command respect among his European colleagues. As the founder of Zik's Press Ltd., and of the *West African Pilot* of Lagos, he became so important a figure in his native Nigeria that he served as its first president from 1960 to 1966. But during the thirty-month civil war with Biafra, his fortunes went into a decline because he supported his rebellious Ibo people almost until the end came in 1970.

Few in sub-Sahara Africa emulated "Zik's" independence either in journalism or politics. For one reason, the privately owned African press was small and pitifully weak. But more important, as the governments in the new countries took over the proprietorship of the existing newspapers, the consequences of independence became calamitous. Latif Jakande, the managing editor of Allied Newspapers in Lagos, was imprisoned for four years by the Nigerian government. In Uganda, journalists who criticized the government were often arrested and imprisoned on charges of sedition. When the *East African Standard* and other newspapers of Kenya reported that the government was trying to break the grip of Indians on the country's trade, the regime threatened reprisals. "The local press," it warned, "is expected to identify itself with the aspirations of this country."

As for the white governments of Rhodesia and South Africa, they were in no mood to make any concessions either to the blacks or their liberal supporters. By expelling foreign correspondents who gave offense and disciplining the domestic press through a variety of repressive steps, the South African government substantially undermined the principle of dissent in a democratic society. Much the same thing was done in Rhodesia.

In the face of outraged world opinion, the South African regime enforced the policy of *apartheid* at the expense of the first truly independent press to flourish on the African continent. In its most notorious prosecution, the government undertook a four-year campaign against the *Rand Daily Mail* for exposing prison brutality and tied up its editor, Laurence Gandar, and its chief reporter, Benjamin Pogrund, in the courts. In 1969, Gandar was fined $280 after being found guilty of publishing his prison exposé without "reasonable" verification, and Pogrund received a suspended sentence. The case cost South African Associated Newspapers Ltd., owners of the paper, about $280,000 — a powerful deterrent against future efforts in South Africa to improve the lot of the downtrodden — and Gandar soon afterward left for London. It was no wonder that the tough dictators of the new lands in sub-Sahara Africa were encouraged in their harsh treatment of their own press.

If the peoples of the Third World in Africa had any curiosity about what was going on in their own countries or the world at large, they had an unenviable choice—the government radio or the local press. What little information either was able to provide did not spread over a very large area. Nor was it credible in some instances. Censorship thus was not as much of a problem in Africa as the sheer complexity of maintaining contact with the news media. For example, in one of the most advanced nations in West Africa, the Ivory Coast, only the urban elite bothered to try to keep themselves informed. With a literacy rate of 10 percent and a per capita annual income of $186, every 100 citizens had access on the average to 1.7 radio stations and only 0.4 of a daily paper. In Nigeria, Kenya and Ghana, which were more advanced, the press had a better chance. But it was still a negligible force in the governing process in Africa.

When Dr. Kofi A. Busia became the first premier of Ghana's Second Republic in 1969, dramatically resuming parliamentary rule after the Nkrumah dictatorship, there were only eight newspapers with 300,000 circulation in a country of nearly 7 million people with a 25 percent literacy rate. In Kenya, with about the same literacy rate for the same number of people, there were just four dailies with 150,000 circulation. And in strife-torn Nigeria and Biafra, some eighteen dailies were functioning during the Biafran war with about 350,000 circulation for 35 million people. It was clear enough that the oral tradition of communication south of the Sahara still carried far greater weight than the printed word. A press that was so weak and so much at the mercy of government, even where independent ownership was tolerated, could have few opportunities to assert itself.

There were several major differences between the situation of the press of Africa, however, as compared with that of Latin America. The most important was that the journalist in Latin America tended to be well-educated, generally representative of the middle or upper classes, and steeped in a centuries-old tradition of free publication. In Africa, the number of journalists who had been exposed to higher education was minute and they had almost no background for an appreciation of the right to publish an independent newspapers. It followed that when repression came in Latin America, there was always a chance of resistance. But in Africa, especially in the new nations below the Sahara, the dictator had little trouble in exacting obedience from his tiny press.

"Many countries where the press is relatively new live in the twilight zone of freedom of information," the International Press Institute reported. "There, newspapers are at best tolerated, generally face harassment or suppression, and at worst are supplanted by propaganda organs aimed at telling the people what the governments wish them to know."

This condition, so typical of Black Africa, was aggravated in the broad band of Arab nations that spread from North Africa across the face of West Asia. While their governments did more talking about the need for a liberalizing Third World force than almost any other group of national leaders, their people with few exceptions did not know the meaning of civil liberties or the uses of dissent. At the beginning of the 1970s, censorship was almost general in Arab lands. The United Arab Republic limited the movement of foreign correspondents, censored their copy, and kept tight control of its own press. Libya and the Sudan had total censorship. Syria, Iraq, and Jordan varied their censorship practices with the state of their continual war against Israel. Even in once liberal Lebanon, news censorship was imposed and three papers were suspended during the country's conflict with Arab guerrillas.

Such practices were directly responsible for the confused state of public opinion in Arab countries from North Africa through the Middle East, and for much of the disillusionment that came with the six-day June war with Israel in 1967. Just before the conflict broke out, Jordan suspended all press licenses and reinstated the practice of running the newspapers by fiat. In Iraq, the same thing happened, with five government newspapers replacing a dozen that were suppressed. Such measures long since had been the rule in both Syria and the UAR. In consequence, it was relatively easy to promote the belief among eager and unsophisticated peoples that Gamal Abdel Nasser and his allies were about to wipe out 2 million Israelis and destroy their country.

When Arab forces were so quickly and utterly humiliated, the errors of total censorship became all too tragically evident. In a melancholy post-mortem, President Abdel Hamid Hassan of the Egyptian Students' Federation pleaded for a free press to avoid such disasters in the future. He was, of course, ignored. The war went on. And instead of being relaxed, Arab censorship spread.

Not unnaturally, it was in Israel that free institutions and a free press flourished to a greater extent than anywhere else in the adjacent lands of Africa and West Asia. As a Socialist nation with a high degree of industrialization, it should have been a model for many an underdeveloped country of the Third World, but it was not. Under the constant threat of war and extermination as an object of Arab hatred, Soviet displeasure, and European indifference, 2 million Israelis managed somehow to maintain an effective military posture and at the same time preserve much of their democratic way of life. True, military censorship had been a part of Israel from the very beginning, but it was unavoidable.

Because the Israelis were a nation of newspaper readers, they were usually aware of what was at stake inside and outside their own land. In this respect, they were much like the Americans on whose support they so mightily depended. With a literacy rate of about 95 percent, they managed to maintain some thirty daily newspapers at a level of about a half-million circulation. Their readership of 21 copies for each 100 people compared favorably with that of France (27 per 100) and was double that of Italy. Although radio was important, with some 400,000 receivers and eleven transmitters, it could not take the place of the press, with the highest rate of circulation in the Middle East. Whether they published in Hebrew, the dominant language, or a dozen other tongues, the newspapers invariably were lively and competed for the public's interest.

In a war-oriented economy, it was a foregone conclusion that few except the largest and most influential dailies could support themselves. Some, therefore, represented political parties; others, religious organizations. The state gave subsidies to maintain a few among the 300-odd publications of general interest as well as the daily press. As for the Israeli Broadcasting Service, that was, of course, government-owned.

No less than the British, on whom the Israelis also patterned themselves on occasion, there was a strong sense of cooperation between government and press in times of great national crisis. If there was a government ban on discussion of some major topic, such as the celebrated Lavon spy case in the 1950s, the Israeli journalists usually went along. The penalties for disobedience could be quite stiff and public sentiment, in such cases, was almost certain to be with the government. It was well understood, too, that the Israeli press was not to disclose military information that could give aid and comfort to the enemy. Such restrictions applied also to the large number of foreign correspondents who moved in and out of Israel, seldom with trouble. The Israeli government and its communications system were so thoroughly disciplined and in tune with each other that both the attacks of 1956 and 1967 against Egypt achieved total surprise. It was a mark of the respect accorded to the journalist in Israel that Gershon Agron, the founder of the English-language Jerusalem *Post*, became the mayor of Jerusalem.

Almost alone among the new nations of West Asia and neighboring Africa, Israel sought a new way of life by building on the oldest and most cherished of democratic forms — parliamentary democracy and a free press. Its society was in striking contrast with much of the surrounding Third World, where human freedom was often discussed but seldom practiced.

2. The Divided House of Europe

"When a whole people are being oppressed, the fate of individuals is of little consequence," wrote Christos Lambrakis from a Greek prison in 1967. In common with other Greek journalists, he had been the victim of a military coup that had crushed freedom in the first of the world's democracies on April 21. Some, like him, had been hauled off to prison for inflicting imaginary dangers on state security. Others, like Helen Vlachos, had closed their papers and fled from the country. But all without exception had been reduced overnight to the ignoble posture of a mindless creature of a police state. In Greece, the home of the spirit of free inquiry, all inquiry was forbidden; in a land once dedicated to the pursuit of truth, the living lie was supreme.

As the publisher of two Athens newspapers, *To Vima* and *Ta Nea*, Lambrakis might have made his peace with the military junta merely by renouncing all thought of political activity. Instead, soon after his arrest, he smuggled out a warning to the International Press Institute that no press worthy of the name existed in Greece. "In Greece today," he wrote, "the press is not being simply censored or dictated. It is being violated." An International Commission of Jurists, meeting in Geneva, soon agreed: "Experience shows that when freedom of the press vanishes, the press vanishes with it. The responsibility lies with those who deprive the press of its freedom."

King Constantine, in an eloquent bid for power, appealed to the Greek people on December 13, 1967, to help him restore democratic government but the military rulers remained unmoved. The king and his family had to go into exile. Andreas Papandreou, the son of an ex-premier, joined him within a month upon release from prison; like his king, he besought the democratic nations, mainly the United States, to withdraw its support from the junta. But as in its relations with Turkey, where the press also was in difficulty, the United States was in no mood to further weaken a NATO alliance that already sprawled in disarray.

During the dwindling years of the decade of the 1960s, the military tightened their hold on a tortured land. They made many promises of liberalization, none of which amounted to much. Under a new Greek constitution of 1968, for example, freedom of the press was "guaranteed" with a flourish in one section and as quickly taken away in others. The press was prohibited, on pain of severe punishment, from promoting the views of Communist or other outlawed political parties, insulting the royal family, reflecting on any recognized religion, or interfering with the security of the state. For two offenses against the government in five years, a newspaper could be confiscated. In spite of gestures of liberality and fulsome promises of relief from government pressures, this remained the stultified position of the journalists of Greece under military rule. Like the once-free people they had served, they were the prisoners of circumstance.

In the divided House of Europe, the fate of Greece was a forbidding omen of worse to come. Over more than half the continent, with its traditions of respect for self-government and the rights of man, few words could be uttered in criticism of authoritarian governments at the opening of the 1970s and none could safely be published. All channels of information remained under government control in a dozen once-great and famous lands, with the consequent growth of widespread surveillance, intimidation, restriction, or outright censorship. It was as if the governors were trying to seal off their peoples from the revolutionary winds of change that were sweeping the earth.

As was the case in many of the developing countries of Africa, Asia, and Latin America, it made no difference whether the authoritarian regimes of Europe adhered to the Right or Left; toward the press, their attitude was the same. In most of Central and Eastern Europe and the Balkans, and in Portugal and Spain, the journalist could not exercise his basic function of seeking out and publishing the truth. Now and then, as in Francisco Franco's Spain in 1966, censorship was officially ended but the prosecution of journalists continued with cruel regularity under various sections of the penal code. A single paper in Barcelona, for example, was prosecuted eight times in two years. Another in Madrid was suspended for four months. In one year, supposedly liberalized Spain brought governmental proceedings against eighty-two publications in more than 300 instances and imposed punishment in 180 cases. Franco's decision to name Prince Juan Carlos as his successor did not make any material change in the press at the outset of the 1970s.

Watching what was happening in Spain, the Portuguese press

moved with understandable caution when Marcello Caetano came to power as premier after forty years of authoritarian government under Antonio de Oliveira Salazar. Censorship, instituted in 1928, continued although it became a bit more permissive and journalists showed sufficient pluck to ask for its removal. But a press accustomed to doing its government's bidding could not easily throw off its bonds.

Elsewhere in Western Europe, from the Bay of Biscay to the Baltic Sea and from North Cape to the Tyrrhenian Sea, the press remained free but it had to stand up against the stress of changing times. Almost everywhere, under the pressure of competition from television and the new mass circulation dailies, the old European political press was contracting. To save their faltering papers, publishers proposed all manner of schemes from outright subsidies to remissions of taxes and government contributions to reductions in the price of newsprint and printing equipment. Some demanded that governments seize a part of television's profits and give them to the political press. Others wanted the circulations of the new mass appeal dailies to be limited by law. Yet, even though some of these desperation measures were enacted, they could not preserve a press that had either lost the interest or the confidence of the public, and sometimes both.

In Finland, where the damage was not as great as in other European countries with an independent press, no less than thirty-three papers suspended publication in the twenty years after World War II. By 1965, television had made such inroads in the advertising revenue of the party press that its publishers asked for and obtained a government subsidy of $3.3 million. Under a 1967 law, the fund was handed out to political parties in proportion to their representation in Parliament, each being permitted to decide how much to give to its particular newspapers. It did not by any means affect the continued dominance of the greatest newspaper in Finland, the *Helsingen Sanomat,* with a circulation of 257,000 daily. It continued to sell more than 15 percent of the 1.6 million copies published by the sixty-odd Finnish papers.

The inability of the party press to compete with such great national newspapers as the *Aftenposten* of Oslo and the *Dagens Nyheter* and *Svenska Dagbladet* of Stockholm led to proposals by both the Norwegian and Swedish government press commissions to emulate the Finnish experiment. But even the sponsors of the scheme to keep the political press going realized that government subsidies couldn't really maintain newspapers in which the public wasn't interested. In Sweden, papers owned by the unions had been subsidized for years by a press tax on their members without noticeably contributing to their longevity. Nor did the political press subsidy scheme insure the existence of its beneficiaries. There were just too many papers.

In Norway also the laws of journalistic economics were being defied daily by a press of some four-score newspapers that circulated 1.7 million copies in a nation of 3.7 million. Much as the Scandinavian peoples disliked and feared a monopolistic press, this was the trend of the times and there was very little that government subsidies could do to change it.

In the Netherlands, the concentration of the press was well advanced at the beginning of the 1970s and a broad system of government-supervised benefits had been worked out to help the survivors. Whether this would serve eventually to curb their independence remained a grave question; in the initial period, it seemed to make little difference to such independent papers as *De Telegraaf* and the merged *Nieuwe Rotterdamse Courant*. The Dutch press had been declining steadily in numbers since the end of World War II. From a total of 115 newspapers issued by sixty concerns in 1950, the industry had dropped in less than twenty years to about forty firms publishing less than 100 papers. Some journalists feared that eventually only two national dailies would remain out of the ten that had survived a series of mergers.

The pattern of government support for newspapers was perhaps the broadest and most comprehensive in Italy. There, the press in large part was treated with the respect accorded some of the great foundations in the United States, being granted generous remissions of taxes, subsidies, and favoritism in freight and communications rates. In a way, many newspapers resembled charities or even the church as far as special priveleges were concerned. For example, any paper that qualified under the broad Italian rules as one with special cultural, labor, or political interests was exempt from income taxes. Those without printing plants of their own received tax reductions. To help meet the high cost of newsprint, papers were granted a subsidy of one-third their market price up to 20,000 copies. In addition, the state railway gave them lower freight rates for carting newsprint and they also enjoyed a break in rates for telegraph, telephones, and leased wires. Government advertising was an extra source of revenue for the favored press.

Aside from the understandable interest of political parties in the press, a pattern of industrial and business support for a broad range of newspapers also was evident in Italy. Some of the most distinguished dailies in the country had close links to industry, among them the *Corriere della Sera* of Milan (textiles), *La Stampa* of Turin (Fiat), *Il Messagero* of Rome (vintners), and *Il Tempo* of Rome (shipping). In a land with relatively skimpy advertising and the lowest daily newspaper readership ratio in Western Europe outside the Iberian peninsula, the press had to get its financial support wherever it could. Against the competition of television and the new mass circulation dailies and weeklies, the traditional press had a difficult time. Despite the prosperity of much of Italy at the end of the 1960s, perhaps half the eighty-odd dailies did not share in it. They circulated about 5 million copies daily in a country of 50 million, but they choked each other by their competition. In Rome alone there were thirteen dailies.

As the process of consolidation took effect and the smaller political papers began dying off, the stronger survivors became more important. None achieved the prestige of *Corriere della Sera*, with a half-million daily circulation, and *La Stampa*, with 325,000. In a country that had gone through thirty governments in twenty-five years, such papers had more stability than the successive regimes they alternately supported and criticized. Such newer papers as *Il Gazzettino* of Venice and *Il Giorno* of Rome, which catered to popular taste more than the politicals, helped to change the course of Italian journalism. The pro-Communist *Paesa Sera* of Rome and the Christian Democrats' *Il Popolo* both took on more modern trappings and profited thereby. But the fatal weakness of the politicals for giving a party slant to the news persisted in Italy.

Even in wealthy and conservative Switzerland, the stronghold of the old European journalism of the political specialist, the critic, and the essayist, new times were having an effect at the beginning of the 1970s. A jazzy illustrated paper less than ten years old, *Blick*, achieved a circulation of 200,000 — 10 percent of the 2 million copies that were sold by the nation's 120-odd dailies. It soon had imitators, although not all of them succeeded. But the wave of popularity that swept the new press along brought doubt and anguish to many an old-time journalist. Peter Duerrenmatt, the editor of the *Basler Nachrichten*, warned, "Decisive influence on news and comment is passing to a few big concerns."

No one, however, could say that either the prestige or the quality of the greatest of Swiss newspapers, the *Neue Zürcher Zeitung*, had diminished in the slightest. After nearly two centuries of publication, the seemingly ageless *NZZ* was still one of the few most influential and highly regarded newspapers in the world. With a total circulation of only 80,000, it was sold and read in every world capital of consequence except Peking. It was no small matter for a country of 6 million people to be represented before the world by such a formidable and independent journal. In some of the other small nations of Europe — notably Denmark, Belgium, and Austria — prestige newspapers had survived the attack of the new populars and television as well. But the *NZZ* had become something more than a newspaper. It was the proudest exhibit of Swiss democracy.

The power of popular journalism in Europe reached its apogee in the Federal Republic of Germany, miraculously risen from wartime ruin and dictatorship in less than twenty-five years. Through brilliant exploitation of the mass appeal of the newspaper, as practiced in the United States, Britain and Japan, the publishing house of Axel Springer managed to capture nearly 40 percent of West Germany's daily circulation of 17 million copies. His *Bild Zeitung* alone sold more than 4 million copies daily in a nation of 55 million — a figure exceeded only by the largest British and Japanese dailies. At fifty-five years of age, he ruled a press empire without parallel in German history. Even more remarkable, he had created his journalistic monument in less than a generation against the difficulties of press licensing in the earliest years of postwar Germany and the appeal of television in the 1960s.

Springer was no political spellbinder. Nor was his personal magnetism overwhelming. He was a rather diffident and aloof figure from his earliest days in his native Hamburg, when he learned whatever he could of journalism during the worst period of Nazi repression. Spared from wartime military service because of a physical disability, he managed to survive both Nazi purges and Allied bombings in Hamburg. But when he applied to the British occupation regime for a license to publish a newspaper after the end of the war, he was refused. However, once the licensing privilege was turned over to German authorities, Springer was empowered by his friend, Max Brauer, Lord Mayor of Hamburg, to begin publishing an independent newspaper, the *Hamburger Abendblatt*.

This was the modest beginning of the most spectacular success story in modern European publishing. With his popular touch, Springer soon towered over the tiresome old German political papers. Within a few years, his *Hamburger Abendblatt* was the largest of West Germany's 160-odd dailies. With the founding and phenomenal success of *Bild Zeitung*, his future was assured. Next, he acquired the prestige daily, *Die Welt*, through the British authorities in Berlin. He also took over the properties of the House of Ullstein, which had tried to come back to its old position of prestige after World War II with indifferent success.

These and subsequent ventures enabled the aggressive German press lord to scale the peak of personal power. In 1966, he opened as his publishing headquarters a $20 million, twenty-story building in West Berlin just a short distance from the Berlin Wall. Outraged by Springer's influence and his conservatism, the militant Student Socialist League stirred up a series of riots against him, hurled Molotov cocktails at his Berlin building, and set fire to his delivery trucks. It didn't deter him.

At length, in 1968, the West German government took a hand in the affair. Its press commission reported that press freedom was "endangered" when a publisher corralled 20 percent of the market and "impaired" when he had 40 percent. Springer took the hint. That year, he sold one newspaper and four magazines for $25 million. Two years later, he transferred his Ullstein book publishing subsidiary to his rival, Bertelsmann A. G., effective in 1972. But the two deals, which accounted for more than one-third of the Springer interests which then had an annual turnover of $245 million a year, did not appease his critics. As the *Frankfurter Allgemeine Zeitung* put it, he was not renouncing power.

Not content with dominating the press, Springer soon began trying to set up a private TV network — a field in which the eleven West German states had retained a monopoly. Then, when Willy Brandt's Social Democratic government came to power, Springer fought the regime's policy of seeking a better accommodation with East Germany. The chief spokesman of the regime, Conrad Ahlers, struck back. He charged the Springer papers with "falsifying the news" and verging on violation of the Federal constitution. Chancellor Brandt himself was reputed to have warned Springer: "If he wants it rough, he will get it rough."

The feud enlivened the languishing fortunes of a substantial part of the German press, which inevitably was drawn into the conflict. While many of the old-line papers were suffering, and the party press was in a decline, the quality papers for the most part were able to maintain their position. Moreover, the booming German economy bolstered at least a part of the weaker papers. In the first nine months of 1969, for example, advertising in all the news media jumped to $650 million, a 19 percent gain over the previous year. Of this total, news and picture magazines

held 40 percent, the newspapers, 27 percent; television, 20 percent, and radio, about 6 percent, with the rest going to scattered
sources. The secret was that television was limited by law to 20
minutes of advertising a day before 8 P.M. If the press had had
to contend with unrestricted television advertising as well as
Springer, the result would have been a near disaster.

In the lively German magazine field, there continued to be
ferment, excitement, and controversy. Knowing of the power of
Le Monde's staff in formulating policy and selecting an editor,
the staff of *Stern*, the West German picture magazine, touched
off a virtual press revolution when it was faced with the threat of
sale to a rival publisher. Its 165-member editorial staff won the
right to elect a seven-member council with power to help set policy and choose an editor. The idea spread to *Der Spiegel*, but
Springer remained inflexible.

Even without major television competition, the contraction of
the daily press in terms of numbers, circulation, and financial
strength was more marked in France than it was in West Germany. The total readership of approximately ninety daily newspapers of general circulation in France, nine of them in Paris,
was only about 12 million. This was just a slight gain over the
total circulation of more than a hundred dailies that had been
published in France before World War II. In view of the 33 percent increase in France's population during that period, it meant
that the per capita readership of newspapers had dropped
sharply. Put another way, as a French researcher dolefully reported, France's dailies over a test period in the 1960s suffered a
decline in circulation that was almost exactly equal to the death
rate.

The decline of the daily press was most marked in Paris.
From eighty daily papers in 1904, the French capital was reduced to forty-four at the beginning of World War I, thirty-two at
the outset of World War II, seventeen in 1948, and nine in 1970.
Moreover, the total Parisian daily newspaper circulation of 6
million in 1939 had fallen to 4 million three decades later when
the population of the metropolitan region had doubled. Thus, the
provincial press, which in 1939 accounted for only 37 percent of

the daily circulation, jumped in thirty years to 66 percent of that total. However, there had been a high mortality rate among the press in the provinces, too, with more than a hundred newspapers suspending publication in the decade after World War II. In sixty-three towns and cities outside Paris at the outset of the 1970s, there were only about eighty newspapers and the chances were that some of these would merge or die.

The reason for the parlous state of the French press was not hard to find. Unlike their counterparts in other advanced nations, France's independent newspapers had never been able to develop advertising as a major source of revenue, a failing they shared with the Italian press. In the mid-1960s, for example, French advertising revenue was only 2.8 percent of the world total compared with 60.5 percent in the United States, 9.1 percent in West Germany, and 6.8 percent in Britain. In terms of national income, France's .97 percent expenditure on advertising ranked twenty-sixth (on a par with Mexico and Jamaica) after the 2.71 percent of the United States, 2.70 percent in West Germany, 2.09 percent in Britain, and 1.43 percent in Japan.

Of France's total annual advertising expenditure of 3,200 million francs (about $600 million), it was estimated that the press as a whole received less than 50 percent, and this at a time when television advertising was restricted on the government's network, the only one in the nation, to just a few minutes each evening. One authority, Robert Salmon, publisher of *France-Soir*, estimated that if the government permitted full development of television advertising on the nation's 9 million TV sets, the newspapers could lose as much as half their advertising income. "It is clear," he wrote, "that if newspapers lose half their advertising income to television, the press will be in exceptional danger. Most newspapers will simply disappear and others will be bought up. This diminution of diversity of expression will put the freedom of the press itself in question, for there is no liberty without diversity."

Aside from such doleful views, which were quite generally held by experienced journalists both inside and outside France, the brightest spot in French journalism was the flowering of *Le*

Monde as a great international newspaper. In 1944 upon the liberation of Paris, General Charles de Gaulle inspired the creation of *Le Monde* by demanding of one of his ministers: "Make me a great newspaper." Under the editorial direction of Hubert Beuve-Méry, a prewar foreign correspondent of *Le Temps*, *Le Monde* qualified but not in a manner that pleased Le Grand Charles. It was a stubbornly independent publication from the time it was founded in 1944 and never hesitated to strike out at de Gaulle himself. Certainly, in the rejection of the 1969 referendum that virtually forced de Gaulle's resignation, *Le Monde* played an important part. In so doing, it helped to overthrow its creator.

Le Monde was designed to be the successor to the tarnished old *Le Temps*, the assets of which were leased by the government to the new publication after the liberation of Paris. Under a reorganization plan adopted in 1951, the original shareholders gave 28 percent of the paper's stock to its editorial staff and then decreed that all policy decisions must be taken by a three-quarters majority. Since *Le Monde*'s staff held 80 of the 280 votes, it became the real power in the newspaper. As a nonprofit organization, it was difficult to influence financially. The fact that its circulation more than doubled, from 200,000 to in excess of 400,000 at a time when most French metropolitan dailies were losing, demonstrated its strength.

Le Monde's independence and its honesty gave it a tone that broadly appealed to the professional and intellectual classes. This was enhanced by the disinterested *grand reportage* of a distinguished staff of a dozen or so Paris-based regional experts in foreign affairs and ten foreign correspondents. The most influential people rallied to such a journalistic standard. They could be confident, no matter what the pressures, that Beuve-Méry would not yield either to his own government, Whitehall, or Washington. And until his retirement in 1970 at the age of sixty-eight, he did not compromise. It was typical of *Le Monde* that Jacques Fauvet, its editor-in-chief who became Beuve-Méry's successor, commented after Georges Pompidou's election as president of France in 1969 and the sudden devaluation of the franc: "Things were getting better and better but not enough to prevent them from going from bad to worse." Fauvet's replacement as editor, André Fontaine, was just as keen and as tough.

The independence of *Le Monde*, its most precious asset, was fortified by a further grant of power to its editorial staff on the eve of Beuve-Méry's retirement. Through his insistence, the journalists won the right to own 40 percent of the stock of the newspaper and to hold veto power over editorial policies and top editorial appointments. It was, indeed, as Parisians jested, "A newspaper of the left that is read by the right."

Le Monde's only serious rival as a prestige daily, the conservative *Le Figaro*, was torn by a bitter struggle between its owners and its editorial staff over the issue of editorial independence toward the end of the 1960s. Always inclined to support whatever government was in power, *Le Figaro* nevertheless had created an imposing audience of more than 500,000 daily readers. During the de Gaulle era, it was one of the general's strongest advocates, which scarcely hurt it with its advertisers. Yet, despite the stability of its circulation and its undeniable prosperity as a top-ranking advertising medium, *Le Figaro* fell on evil days.

As was the case with so many French newspapers, the roots of *Le Figaro*'s difficulties went back to World War II and the German occupation. It was then owned by the perfume maker, François Coty. Pierre Brisson, its wartime editor, moved the paper to Lyons and, in 1942, closed it when the Nazis seized the so-called "free zone" of France. That was what saved the paper. Once the war ended, Brisson was able to reestablish *Le Figaro* in its old building at Rond Point with the support of the government. Even more important, he forced the owners to enter into a contractual agreement to let a group of editors run the paper.

The octogenarian wool manufacturer, Jean Prouvost, principal postwar owner of *Le Figaro* and of the glossy picture magazine, *Paris Match*, was dissatisfied with these arrangements, even though they gave him the right to collect 95 percent of the profits of the paper. After Brisson's death in 1964, he began a battle to resume editorial control. Five years later, upon the expiration of the post-World War II contract, Prouvost offered the paper's editorial association one-third of the profits and representation on the board of directors provided that management received the right to exercise full editorial control. The staff rejected the proposal, resulting in a strike that closed the paper for fifteen days. It was a peculiarly French strike, with the staff insisting that a great moral principle was at stake and the owners holding out financial rewards for a settlement. Following the example of *Le Monde*, the journalists of *Le Figaro* sought no less than complete editorial control including the right to exercise veto power over the designation of top executives.

A lesser newspaper might have been destroyed by the dispute, which resulted in the temporary appointment of a judicial administrator while the affair was before the French courts. To the credit of *Le Figaro*, when it reopened, both its readership and its advertisers continued to give it their support even though the dispute continued to create difficulties. Complicating the newspaper's situation still further was the necessity for finding a more practical location for the plant than the old quarters at Rond Point. It meant that the owners would have to make a further large investment in a property which they could not control, a predicament unique even for French journalism.

The largest newspaper in France, the powerful Hachette group's *France-Soir*, had an entirely different problem but one that appeared to be even more critical than that of *Le Figaro*. During the 1960s, it had achieved a circulation of 1.35 million but toward the latter part of the decade its readership began dropping. Within a few years, it lost more than 300,000 circulation. As a mass medium, *France-Soir* did not lack either aggressiveness or imagination under its veteran director, Pierre Lazareff. Like *Le Monde*, it came to terms with its editorial staff association by granting it 15 percent of the paper's stock and a seat on the board of directors. It covered the news in sensational style for its working-class audience. When the first three American astronauts reached the moon, *France-Soir* was the victorious bidder for their stories. Yet, its circulation continued in the doldrums.

Soon, the largest newspaper in France found that operational economies were necessary. In consequence, it became the first daily in the nation to experiment with facsimile publication in a novel attempt to share the plants of other newspapers outside Paris. The objective was to send provincial editions of the paper by electronic means to centers, such as Marseilles, where the idle presses of noncompeting provincial papers could be used. It was a daring scheme, but whether it would work was something else again.

Among the rest of the Parisian press, the process of consolidation inevitably took its toll. The old *Paris-Presse* became a mere edition of *France-Soir*. The Socialist *Le Populaire* died. *Le Parisien Libéré*, the second largest newspaper in France, dropped its political staff to try to sharpen its popular appeal. The rightist *L'Aurore* depended on the support of its principal owner, Marcel Boussac, a textile magnate. The tiny *Combat*, too, was kept alive by a wealthy owner, Henry Smadja, merely as a matter of principle. *Paris-Jour*, the Communist *L'Humanité*, and the Catholic paper, *La Croix*, all had to have substantial help from one source or another. It was a time of vast change in France, as the 1968 rioting and the subsequent changes in government so graphically demonstrated, and the press could not help but be affected. Had not the government severely restricted television advertising for the time being, the toll among the newspapers would have been far greater.

Aside from *Le Monde* and *Le Figaro* in Paris, about twenty to twenty-five medium to large provincial newspapers came to represent the real backbone of the French press. Among them were such leaders as *Ouest-France* of Rennes, with 650,000 circulation; *Le Progrès* of Lyons, with 550,000; *La Voix du Nord* of Lille, with 425,000; *Le Sud-Ouest et La France* of Bordeaux, with 450,000, and *Le Provençal*, of Marseilles, with 350,000. These were scarcely the stodgy, provincial papers of yore; on the contrary, they were among the leaders in the experimentation with new methods of producing and presenting news.

As for France's global wire service, Agence France-Presse, its dependence on the patronage of government bureaus and foreign subscribers was even more marked than ever before. With so small and precarious a base of domestic support, AFP had no alternative other than to accept patronage wherever it could be found. Toward the end of the 1960s, it was estimated that sub-scriptions from 130 to 135 French government bureaus provided it with more than half its revenue. Much of the rest of its income had to come from the newspapers and electronic media outside France, notably in the former French colonies in Africa and Asia and some of the newspapers of Latin America.

Perhaps the most important new phase of French journalism was the development of the high quality weeklies headed by *L'Express*, a news magazine edited by Jean Jacques Servan-Schreiber and modeled on *Time*. It ran up a circulation of 500,000 in a short period. The older *Le Canard Enchainé*, with 330,000, and the leftist publication, *Le Nouvel Observateur*, with 200,000, both maintained strong positions in the weekly field. But *Paris Match*, the giant of the Prouvost publishing chain, had its troubles despite its continued circulation of more than 1 million. The challenge of the newcomers and of television had to be met.

Altogether, the whole enterprise of French publishing was in a difficult and unsettled state. Without doubt, since it constituted 1 percent of the gross national product, it was affected by the declining French economy that forced the 1969 devaluation of the franc. For the 90,000 workers on some 9,000 publications of all kinds, including some 10,000 journalists, it was a serious mat-ter for which there were no simple solutions.

Under such circumstances, questions were bound to be raised about the prospects for the continued independence of the French press. For the most part, French editors worked on a leash — and the leash was not in the hands of government. What did the editors and their proprietors fear? During de Gaulle's reign, he did not have the power of life or death over them, as he did with French television, and he could not banish some of the leading journalists in the manner in which he had treated televi-sion people. However, his journalistic enemies were always wor-ried over what he *might* do. The government, after all, did con-trol the import of paper, taxation, and the degree of advertising that could appear on television. Journalists in addition had certain privileges, such as the deduction of a substantial percentage from their gross earnings for income tax purposes and travel conveniences on French railroads and Air France. These could have been stopped.

Even after de Gaulle relinquished power and Pompidou succeeded him, however, there was no particular show of independence among French newspapers. Nor did Pompidou himself do more at the beginning than talk about trying to improve relations between his government and the press. He did attempt to institute reforms in television to try to convince people that it did attempt, despite government control, to tell the news honestly. But the nation on the whole showed little enthusiasm for its network of news communication.

With only a few exceptions, the French press displayed little confidence either in itself or in its role as a leader of public opinion. After its many vicissitudes, it appeared to be less highly regarded in the land than at any time since 1939. The public was well aware that it was a much better press — certainly a more honest press — after the bitter experiences of thirty years. But it did not command the kind of popular support that it merited, and for the most part let itself be carried along by the unfavorable economic tide that was sweeping France. One newspaper of courage and independence, *Le Monde*, became more sensitive to the process of democratic government than nearly all the rest of the French press combined. It was not sensible. It was not even logical. But it accurately reflected the state of the French press. In the divided House of Europe, it was one of the weakest inhabitants. It should have been the strongest.

3. The Decline of Fleet Street

There was nothing quite like Fleet Street anywhere in the world during the latter part of the twentieth century. It was at once a short and grubby thoroughfare in the heart of London, an area dominated by the British press, and a rather outdated symbol of British journalism. It also represented a state of mind — an almost fatal affinity for the glories of the past and, to a surprising extent, a gloomy and almost unreasoning fear of the future. Dour and forbidding in appearance, grimy, unplanned, and choked with traffic at the most inconvenient hours of the day, Fleet Street was at best a handicap to the modern process of communication. At worst, it had become an anachronism in the electronic age. Yet, the driving genius of its people in the mid-1960s gave Britain the highest per capita sale of newspapers in the world — 50.6 copies for every 100 people.

It is difficult to say just when the decline of Fleet Street set in, but it antedated television. The public's first real alternative to the press, radio news, was provided by the government in the years between the two world wars. But although the British Broadcasting Company's service soon established an enviable reputation for honesty and reliability, it seemed only to whet the British appetite for newspapers. Yet, a tendency toward concentration of ownership took shape to such an extent that several national dailies perished before World War II, mergers began among the Sunday papers, and only three London evening papers survived of the eight that had been published in 1900.

Circulation boomed throughout World War II and advertising increased thereafter. In 1957, the sale of newspapers reached a peak of 26 million daily. However, two more London papers folded in the 1950s. With the coming of the 1960s, the dismal contraction of the press began in earnest and a howl of outrage echoed through Fleet Street. From the prime minister down, angry questions were raised about the concentration of press ownership and its likely effect on the future of the democratic press. The British took their papers seriously.

Their indignation, however, could not blunt the economic forces that were buffeting both the nation and its press. For if the national outlook was glum at that particular time, the future of an important segment of the newspaper industry appeared much worse. Primarily, the press had been severely damaged by a combination of rising costs, archaic management practices, union resistance to change, and the growth of competing media. The addition of commercial television, which took its place beside the BBC in 1956, served to intensify the adverse trend among the most important national newspapers with only three exceptions. Circulation and advertising revenue dropped. In 1960, the *News Chronicle*, with a readership in excess of 1 million, was obliged to merge with the *Daily Mail*. The *News Chronicle*'s associated evening paper, the *Star*, with 735,000 circulation, vanished. It was a shock even to hardened Fleet Street.

What could be done? Very little, as an immediate remedy. After all, two Royal Commissions and an industry-sponsored economic inquiry had closely examined the straitened circumstances of British journalism over a quarter-century without being able to reverse the trend. In its 1966 report, the Economist Intelligence Unit had warned of the particular weakness of the national dailies. Four of the eight, it said, were operating at a loss and a fifth was losing money as a newspaper but making it up on fringe activities. Moreover, of the three profitable nationals, the EIU found that one was in what it called a "declining trend." By 1970, it forecast that four national papers would be out of business and the London evenings would be under heavy pressure as well. While the prediction proved to be premature, there was little doubt that it could be realized in the future.

Among the quality national newspapers, the *Daily Telegraph*, with nearly 1.5 million circulation, alone was in an impregnable financial position. Of the popular nationals, the leader was the tabloid *Daily Mirror*, with more than 5 million circulation, while the *Daily Express*, with nearly 4 million, was a distant challenger. These were the reasonably healthy ones. Only time and circumstance could determine the fate of their rivals. Nor was the situation much better in the once-thriving Sunday field. What had happened, in effect, was that the crisis-ridden British economy had channeled advertising mainly to the leaders in the national quality and popular press, as well as television, with insufficient quantities left over for the No. 2 and No. 3 papers. Consequently, in order to survive, the laggards either had to effect major economies in their operation, raise their circulation prices, or in some cases do both. The penalty for failure was merger or extinction.

The one newspaper to which this prognosis did not fully apply was the old "Thunderer," the *Times*. Although it was passing through still another era of uncertain fortune, and was vastly changed in both content and appearance, it remained the leader of the British press and the most important independent influence on the governmental process outside the major political parties themselves. Its septuagenarian owner, Lord Thomson of Fleet, had lavished a fortune on its limp pages to keep it alive — a performance that astonished his competitors and exceeded even Northcliffe's historic rescue operation at Printing House Square.

To the ambitious Thomson, who had accumulated many millions of pounds in his seventy-seven years, nothing seemed impossible in the world of Fleet Street. Two years after buying the *Times* in 1966, he told an interviewer at Thomson House that he stood to lose £10 million ($24 million) in the five years he had given himself and his organization to pull the faltering old giant out of a financial morass and back on secure ground. By the end of the third year of his ownership of the *Times*, it seemed likely to take all of that — in addition to the thumping purchase price he had paid the Gavin Astor interests.

Thomson was grim, but determined. His circumstances had been far more difficult in his earlier years when he had sold cheap radio sets in the Canadian town of North Bay and started a little radio station at Timmins, Ontario, to stimulate business. After his fiftieth year, he had accumulated the bulk of his chain of 160 newspapers, nearly 50 in the United States, plus additional holdings in magazines and the electronic media. In 1959, as a result of an intricate financial deal, he took over the entire Kemsley chain, headed by the prestigious *Sunday Times*, and including 4 other Sundays, 13 provincial dailies and some weeklies. But he still wasn't satisfied. The acquisitive instinct was highly developed in this hearty, round-faced salesman with flint in his blue eyes and iron grey in his hair. Not even his peerage in 1963 diverted him from his strenuous life.

Why the *Times*? "It is a symbol of Britain," he was accustomed to say in a booming voice, "and more characteristic of Britain than any paper in the country. To make this paper pay presents me with the greatest challenge of my life and I want to be successful at it."

There were those in Fleet Street and elsewhere who criticized Thomson's management, saying that he pauperized the editorial operations of many of his newspapers and really cared for nothing except the eventual return of a good profit. Whatever the truth of the matter, the philosophy of cheap operation did not apply to the *Times*. As his most successful competitor put it, "Thomson is spending money like a drunken sailor."

When the *Times* became a part of the Thomson organization, it was only a shadow of its old self—an anemic paper with less than 275,000 daily circulation and a loss of more than $2,000,000 a year. Between 1967-69, the first three years under Thomson's management, he lost $13.2 million on the *Times*, boosted its circulation to 430,000, jacked up the price per copy from 3 to 4 pence (6 to 8 cents), took on 25 percent more employees to put his total staff at 2,500, and approved a growth in the size of the paper from an average of 22 to 32 pages. But these heroic methods weren't enough to bring in the needed advertising.

Clearly, more drastic moves were necessary. Thomson's optimistic schedule was revised. The British devaluation of the pound made things even more difficult for him. Eventually, he and his chief executive for the *Times* and *Sunday Times*, Denis Hamilton, had to consider more daring plans, for the outlook for 1970 was an additional loss of $2.4 million. "The *Times*," Hamilton announced in a letter to his staff, "is fighting for its life." He appealed for their cooperation and soon was assured of it.

Hamilton, born on the Tyne in 1918, was a veteran of Dunkirk with an outstanding World War II combat record—a soft-voiced but hardheaded newspaperman who had worked his way to the top from unpromising beginnings as a reporter in Middlesbrough. He had been editorial director of the Kemsley newspapers when Thomson had acquired them, and in 1961 had been made editor of the *Sunday Times* with excellent results. It was now the first newspaper in its field with a circulation of nearly 1.5 million and an annual profit of about $5 million.

Once Thomson acquired the daily *Times*, Hamilton made

rapid changes. He put William Rees-Mogg of the *Sunday Times* in charge of the old "Thunderer's" editorial page. Next, he expanded the foreign service and began sending reporting teams out to cover the news. "Very expensive," Thomson grumbled, but he did not interfere. Following Sir William Haley's precedent-shattering decision to put news on Page 1 of the *Times*, Hamilton increased the size and boldness of both the type and the kinds of articles that were displayed. With Sir William's retirement as editor, there were some on Fleet Street who said the *Times* would never be the same.

Thomson and Hamilton made the *Times* more of a mass circulation paper than it had ever been before. But they did not hurt the *Daily Telegraph*. They also gave the *Times* a complete business section to try to rival the *Financial Times*, but did not improve their position as much as they had hoped. With such stunts as the first publication of color pictures of the American astronauts on the moon in 1969, they scored brilliantly. But these, too, failed to reverse the trend.

Soon Hamilton was writing: "A major bonus of any merger (of the *Times* and *Sunday Times*) should be the sharing of common services. But the *Times* is still situated in Printing House Square and the *Sunday Times* in Gray's Inn Road. If you have two newspapers in two buildings that are 20 minutes' drive apart through heavy traffic, the possibilities of sharing are limited."

The answer was a plan to merge the two properties physically. It meant the abandonment of Printing House Square after nearly two hundred years of publication there, latterly in a fine new building. What Thomson and Hamilton contemplated was a new $15 million building in Gray's Inn Road where printing presses, communications centers, picture departments, libraries, and other editorial and production services could be shared by the losing daily and the prosperous Sunday paper. Even so, it seemed probable that Thomson might have to economize still more, perhaps raise the sales price of the *Times* again, and gamble on a loss in his hard-won circulation. In the early 1970s, the fate of the "Thunderer" could go either way. And all Fleet Street knew it.

If the weakness of the Thomson organization was its preoccupation with the nationals in the prestige field, its strength lay as always in the prosperous provincial newspapers, the new suburbans and the weeklies, the latter being what Thomson so often called his "little cash boxes." In Reading, Luton, and Watford, all in suburban London, he bucked a trend by starting new dailies using the most advanced composing and printing methods at a cost of about $5 million. In the United States, at about the same time, he acquired the Brush-Moore chain of 12 small-city dailies and weeklies for a reputed $75 million. In addition to his newspapers, he now owned 153 miscellaneous publications, nineteen printing companies, seven book companies and widespread electronic interests. It was no wonder that the second Royal Commission had warned, "Concentration of ownership carries with it the potential danger that variety of opinion may be stifled."

Thomson argued that he permitted his editors to conduct policy as they saw fit and concentrated his own efforts on business and advertising. But it would have been naive to suppose that, in a critical matter affecting himself or his holdings, his own views would not prevail. Under his ownership, the *Times*'s positions were discreet rather than daring and it did little thundering in its old manner. But then, as one of its editors conceded, it has been many years since the *Times* had bowled over cabinets. If that reflected a decline in the influence of the *Times*, it was also a measure of the very real loss of power among the British press as a whole.

Slowly, the main strength of the press in the United Kingdom was shifting from London to the countryside. Sheer numbers and points of publication told their own story. Toward the end of the 1960s, in addition to the 10 national morning newspapers, there were a total of 117 daily and Sunday newspapers and 6 specialized daily publications in England, Wales, Scotland, and Northern Ireland. Of these, the provincial press in England and Wales alone accounted for 14 mornings, 69 evenings, and 3 Sundays, with the rest scattered. London itself was down to 2 evenings.

The International Publishing Corporation was the first to perceive that the future of the daily press would depend, in large
part, on more efficient and decentralized operations. The *Daily
Mirror* soon followed the lead of the Japanese in pioneering with
facsimile transmission of its Northern Ireland edition to Belfast.
At the same time, an effort was made to include somewhat more
serious content in the generally light and frothy fare that was
served by Britain's largest daily. For all its efforts, however, the
Mirror dropped close to 200,000 readers toward the end of the
1960s and both its profit margin, and that of its parent IPC, were
reduced.

As an entirely practical matter, the *Mirror* occupied the political ground to the left of center that most of the British national
press either had abandoned or never sought to capture. It was
that strange combination of journalistic virtues and vices peculiar to Britain—a tabloid built on sex and sensation that espoused liberal causes. But despite the *Mirror*'s seeming
strength, and the widespread interests of the parent IPC, the
whole organization ran into stormy weather beginning in 1968. In
that year, despite the IPC's pre-tax profit of around $6 million, it
abruptly dismissed its autocratic old chairman, Cecil Harmsworth King. To most of Fleet Street, he had seemed to be the
dominant force in IPC. It was a shock to find out that he was a
hired publisher, subject to instant dismissal.

Hugh Cudlipp, who took over from him, deliberately went
about unloading the IPC's worst loser, the *Sun*, on a bustling,
37-year-old Australian press lord, Rupert Murdoch, in 1969.
Murdoch had only lately invaded Fleet Street as the ruler of an
Australian journalistic empire that included fourteen newspapers and seven broadcasting outlets. His first move had been to
beat the millionaire Socialist owner of the Pergamon Press,
Robert Maxwell, in a battle for control of the trashy Sunday tabloid, *News of the World*, which had a circulation of 6 million and a
profit of nearly $5 million annually. Although Maxwell bid $82
million for the paper, Murdoch won out and soon began looking
around for a daily in Britain, as well.

The *Sun*, his choice, had been the successor to the ill-fated

Herald, darling of the Labour Party and the Trade Union Congress. In taking over the publishing house of Odhams, IPC in the 1950s had inherited the *Herald.* After seven years, all efforts to salvage the paper failed, so it was allowed to die. But next day, in its place, the *Sun* was born in a bid for both the old readership and new people. Neither responded very well; as a result, the *Sun* was an even bigger loser than the *Herald.* According to Fleet Street reports, IPC let Murdoch have the *Sun* for a down payment of only $100,000. He proceeded to turn it into a tabloid, went into a hot competition with the *Mirror,* and in a few months put the racy new *Sun* up to 1.3 million circulation, a gain of 400,000.

Another executive shakeup then hit IPC. Early in 1970, S. T. Ryder, chairman of the Reed Paper Group, bid for the IPC and projected a combined organization with assets of close to $100 million. Under the proposed reorganization, which the Labour government favored, Cudlipp was offered one of three deputy chairmanships. Prime Minister Wilson, during his government's vain attempt in 1970 to achieve re-election, wanted the pro-Labour *Mirror* in sure hands. The whole business, however, caused Fleet Street to wonder, for IPC had owned 27 percent of Reed's ordinary shares; in effect, the child was swallowing up the father and no one was very sure what the outcome would be.

An even greater Fleet Street puzzle was the continued failure of the Establishment to embrace the *Telegraph,* which for decades had held aloft the banner of conservatism and won numerical leadership among middle-class readers. Its detractors said that its losing Sunday paper showed it was vulnerable, but the *Telegraph* was a power for all that. Its news report was the broadest among all the nationals and its staff of foreign correspondents the largest in its field. Its features, sports, and women's pages were attractive, its financial pages authoritative. Yet, among the molders of British opinion, the *Times* and *Sunday Times,* the *Financial Times,* and sometimes even the wobbly *Guardian* were ranked ahead of the *Daily Telegraph* in their impact on the processes of government.

Somewhat the same critical attitude affected the flagship of the Beaverbrook newspapers, the less successful but still profitable *Daily Express*, under the leadership of Sir Max Aitken, son of the fabulous Lord Beaverbrook. Although its policies were conservative, the *Daily Express* and its prospering Sunday newspaper broadly appealed to all classes of people except the elite. It was perhaps the best of the populars, so-called, in the competition for domestic news and frequently scored with its consistently good foreign report.

But, hobbled as the *Express* was with an enormous investment in conventional newspaper production and distribution methods, there seemed to be little it could do either to decentralize or otherwise cut its costs. This was the factor that led the more knowledgeable leaders of Fleet Street to speculate that the *Express* eventually would work out a merger with its old popular competitor, the *Daily Mail*, flagship of the Associated newspapers. It was not something that either the Beaverbrook or Rothermere (Associated) interests liked to contemplate, for scarcely a generation had passed since they had been at the top of the heap. But public taste had changed, and the old-fashioned populars had not really changed with it.

While Lord Rothermere's *Daily Mail* had barely 2 million circulation and merged with his *Daily Sketch*, under 1 million, the old Harmsworth publications in the Associated group were far from helpless. Their *Evening News* was the dominant paper of the two surviving London evenings with a circulation of 1.2 million, almost double that of the Beaverbrook *Evening Standard*. With its provincial evenings and other profitable interests, the Associated group appeared able to carry its losers for a limited time. But eventually, its losses would have to be cut in one way or another. Although Fleet Street was not what it once had been, it still was not a philanthropic thoroughfare.

The paper that attracted the most interest — and the most sympathy — was the *Guardian* of glorious history. It was being supported in the Scott Trust by the highly profitable but mundane Manchester *Evening News*, its associated publication. At the outset of the 1970s, despite a certain improvement in the *Guardian*'s position, its fate was dubious. Its reputation was still imposing, and its voice was still respected among the liberal-minded, but it had been outdistanced by the *Times*, among others. All in all, the *Guardian* was eking out a precarious existence on a circulation of less than 300,000 and a skimpy diet of advertising. Just how long the Manchester *Evening News* could carry its distinguished associate remained a problem for the Scott Trust.

To a certain extent, the Thomson organization was a factor in the future of both the *Guardian* and the *Sunday Observer*, with 900,000 circulation. For some years, the *Guardian* had been printed at Thomson House and the *Observer* had used the old *Times* presses at Printing House Square. There was a fair possibility, if the *Times* consolidated with the *Sunday Times*, that the *Guardian* and *Observer* would inherit Printing House Square. But there was no disguising the decline of the liberal wing of the British press. As for the radicals, the *Morning Star*, official Communist Party successor of the *Daily Worker*, had only 50,000 circulation in all Britain.

Where the British press appeared to make its greatest progress was among the largely nonpolitical evening newspapers in England outside London. In most of the fifty towns and cities in which they were published, these unassuming provincial journals had a virtual monopoly of circulation and local advertising. Their total sales reached 7 million daily, as compared with 1 million daily for the provincial morning papers in a dozen cities. Such competition against the dominance of the nationals and television showed the vitality of the British press.

But Prime Minister Wilson was far from satisfied. His Labour Party, ever suspicious of a largely conservatively owned press, did what it could to stimulate a greater diversity of opinion. As Wilson himself put it: "I start from the doctrine that in a free and democratic society such as ours the British people need, and are entitled to demand, a free press representing every point of view. ... If this is to be achieved, this country needs, and is entitled to have, something like the present number of papers, local and national."

This, in turn, raised the question of whether the government could or should guarantee the survival of failing newspapers by a subsidy along Scandinavian, Dutch or Italian lines. Such measures had been discussed for a long time, but Prime Minister Wilson saw no hope in them. "In a free and democratic society," he pointed out, "there would be appalling risks in government intervention. . . . It might threaten the whole philosophy of a free press."

As a result of such governmental concern over the future of the independent newspaper in Britain, there was one beneficial development. That was the reconstitution of the British Press Council as a more effective impartial arbiter between press and public and press and government. Its early failure had been due to lack of support from the press; however, in important quarters, that view changed and newspapers came to the rescue. Lay members joined the Press Council, along with journalists. But the crucial change was the addition of Lord Devlin, a distinguished jurist, as impartial chairman. With his encouragement and under his careful guidance, the Council became a respected and effective organization beginning in 1964.

Although the Council had no punitive powers, its appeal to conscience and fair play proved to be extraordinarily strong and its resort to publicity for its decisions became an unexpectedly powerful weapon. Abjuring force, it relied on persuasion. Laying aside the role of inquisitor, it became in the main a source of education for press and public alike in ways of maintaining communication over the proper approach to troublesome areas in the news.

The process of lodging a complaint, instituting an impartial inquiry, holding private hearings, and issuing public findings became familiar over the years in the proceedings of British journalism. By the time Lord Devlin finished his five-year term and stepped aside for his successor, Lord Pearce, another jurist of repute, the Press Council had become an accepted institution. While the complainants from the public who appealed for justice were not always satisfied by its conclusions, its impartiality and integrity could not be challenged successfully. Among the newspaper defendants, at the same time, there was a growing awareness that the Council, far from being an infringement on the freedom of the press, actually served to defend the newspaper's right of publication in a number of cases. The proprietors also saw that the Council, by requiring an appellant to give up the right to sue for libel, helped keep some troublesome cases out of the courts.

The fiercely independent and well-nigh anarchistic spirit of Fleet Street thus became a thing of the past.

In foreign affairs, the essential character of British journalism also underwent an irreversible change in the quarter-century after World War II. For with the dissolution of empire, the ancient fear of British influence on the shape of world news was laid to rest. Few except Irish extremists and others with historic grudges worried any longer about London as a central transmission point for foreign dispatches. The old penny-a-word Empire rate, which had stimulated so much British-oriented news, had to be abandoned under the pressures of inflationary times. If foreign correspondents still clustered in London in greater numbers than elsewhere, it was more a matter of superior accommodations and convenience than a fatal attraction to the majesty and glory of Britain.

Nor did the British outdo the rest of the world press to any considerable extent in lavishing banner headlines on news of Rhodesia, South Africa, India, or Pakistan; with the end of empire, local and national concerns had become far more important to the average citizen. It took something closer to home, like the anti-Catholic rioting in Northern Ireland, to upset him.

There also were monumental changes in Reuters, which once had ranked with the Crown and the Union Jack as a symbol of empire. With a budget of $12 million a year for the gathering and dissemination of foreign news on a worldwide basis, the giant news agency could hardly afford to remain oriented to the needs of Fleet Street alone. In the keen competition with the Americans and the French, and with the Russians and Chinese in many developing countries, it was a positive disadvantage to Reuters to be accused of putting Britain's interests first, of being anti-American, anti-French, or anti-German.

Under the Reuter Trust, created in 1941, the agency had become a nonprofit cooperative jointly owned by the British press through the Newspaper Proprietors Association of London and the Press Association, which circulated domestic news and was dominated by the provincial newspapers. In 1946, Australian and New Zealand newspapers joined the ownership. Two years later, Indian newspapers also took a proprietary interest. Exchange agreements were completed with national agencies in Canada, South Africa, and various countries outside the Commonwealth.

Since all domestic news coverage was the business of its ally, Press Association, Reuters boldly strengthened its bureaus in Pacific Asia, the Middle East, and Africa after World War II. Under a vigorous general manager, Gerald Long, who had come up through the ranks as correspondent and executive, the agency also expanded its most valuable asset, Reuters Economic Service. It went into television through its association with the commonwealth agency, Viznews. In association with electronics manufacturers, it kept pace with the Americans in using computers and complicated data circuits for high-speed transmission.

Finally, climaxing an intensive rivalry that developed with the Associated Press and the Dow Jones service over the distribution of financial news, Reuters staged an American invasion in the late 1960s by breaking out of New York and Washington to open bureaus in other major cities. The agency business had come a long way from the old days of news-gathering cartels. Independent journalism was stronger because of it.

With the severance of so many ties to Britain, the newspapers of the Commonwealth developed in a far different manner. Riding the crest of booming economies, the press systems of Canada and Australia showed a strength and prosperity unmatched by anything outside the United States. Far from dismaying them, the rivalry of television actually increased their competitive urge.

Under such conditions, their independence was unchallenged.

While the newspapers of New Zealand also had no cause to worry about inroads on their freedom, a stagnant economy slowed their development and weakened all but a few of the leaders. The Indians, while far from well off, made the best of what they had and found sufficient support in their hard-pressed economy to maintain the independence of their press. But in South Africa, despite its mounting prosperity, the government's insistence on support for its *apartheid* policy made a mockery of its claim that its press was unfettered. Under the circumstances, the South African press could be no more independent than that of Pakistan, where freedom to publish the truth was unknown.

Canada provided a brilliant example of press participation in the governmental process through the diversity of opinion made possible by an independent, two-language press. Like the Swiss, the Canadian government was ever sensitive to the wishes of its multi-language constituency, so frequently expressed through editorial pages. But unlike the Swiss, the Canadians had undergone a consolidation that had insured the prosperity and ultimate survival of most of their papers.

In a nation of 20 million, there were a few more than a hundred daily Canadian papers with a total circulation of close to 5 million, of which eleven were published in French. Despite the government-owned Canadian Broadcasting Corporation and a privately owned network replete with advertising, the Canadian press was in robust health. Profits of 10 percent after taxes were not uncommon and one large daily reported earnings in excess of $2 million a year net. Over a twenty-year period, failures among Canadian newspapers had been held to only 2 percent.

The leading characteristic of the Canadian press was its group ownership, which extended to more than half the daily papers. The Thomsom organization owned twenty-eight, all of them small; the Southam Press, ten; F P Publications, eight, and smaller groups had four or fewer. It is doubtful, however, if the chains exerted influence comparable to the great Canadian metropolitan dailies, both English and French, for Southam and F P each controlled less than 1 million daily circulation spread over a large area of the country, and Thomson had less than 400,000.

The largest newspapers in the land had more punch and more prestige. The outstanding dailies were the Toronto *Star*, with

400,000; the Toronto *Globe & Mail*, and the Vancouver *Sun*, each with 260,000; the Toronto *Telegram*, with 235,000, and the Montreal *Star*, with 200,000. Such smaller but prestigious newspapers as the Winnipeg *Free Press*, the Ottawa *Citizen*, Ottawa *Journal*, *Le Devoir*, and *Le Droit* also packed a punch as far as the government was concerned.

Undeniably, there was a strong American influence in the Canadian press, no less than in Canada itself. The pull of the American economy and American trade, which made itself evident in the volume of American-originated advertising, probably accounted for a considerable part of the prosperity of the Canadian press. It was understandable, too, that American columnists and other news features were bound to be widely published. But if American news was used in large volume in the Canadian press, the reverse was far from true and this was one of the points of contention with the United States.

Nothing, of course, could be done about American journalism's characteristic refusal to take more than passing note of its good neighbors. But it served to solidify the growing nationalism of the Canadian press. Ever determined to be independent of its own government, it took a certain amount of pleasure in tossing darts at its powerful southern neighbor — something that could not help win the Canadian public's approval. The Canadian press kept pace with every journalistic advance in the United States. In the expanding suburban and provincial press, a premium was placed on efficient management and labor-saving devices. Consequently, future growth was assured. The outlook was for a rise in evening papers and a standstill or decline in morning papers. But neither the dependence of the Canadian economy on the United States nor the strains of the English-French relationship within Canada itself were likely to upset the self-reliant pattern of the Canadian press.

In Australia, too, a buoyant economy in an open society during the 1960s provided optimum conditions for the growth of a vigorous and independent press. Here, the main strength of the sixty-odd dailies was concentrated in the cities. In a land of 10 million people, the newspapers sold about 4 million copies a day regardless of television and all other forms of competition. Advertising was plentiful. Despite the continuance of a "white Australia" policy, the government did not make the error of trying to use it as an excuse to regulate the press. One firm, the *Herald and Weekly Times,* owners of two newspapers in Melbourne, was able to pay an annual dividend of 30 percent in the latter 1960s. Profits of 15 to 20 percent were fairly common.

Sydney, a city of 500,000 population, supported four morning papers, two evenings and three Sundays headed by the Sydney *Morning Herald* which, with the *Age* of Melbourne, set the standards for the press. Neither paper was particularly large, the *Herald* having about 300,000 circulation and the *Age* about 200,000, but they were the leaders, respectively, of the conservative and liberal press of Australia. Curiously enough, the firm of John Fairfax & Sons, owners of the *Herald,* was closely allied with the owners of the *Age,* David Syme and Company. It was a reflection of one of the less appealing aspects of group ownership.

As in Canada, Britain, and the United States, the chains were a dominant force in Australian journalism in the latter third of the twentieth century. Fairfax, in addition to the *Herald,* owned the *Sun, Sun-Herald,* and *Financial Review* in Sydney, together with the Syme interests. Queensland Newspapers, West Australian Newspapers, and Australian Consolidated Press also were powers in the land. But the chain with the most spectacular growth was Rupert Murdoch's company, News, Ltd. When he acquired London's *News of the World* and the daily *Sun* in addition to his Australian holdings, he became a world figure before his fortieth year—the embodiment of the Northcliffes and Beaverbrooks of other and more free-swinging eras in British journalism.

What made Murdoch so impressive a figure was the venturesome spirit that led him to start a new paper, the *Australian,* in Sydney in 1964. He used facsimile equipment to transmit an electronic edition to Melbourne, put in computers to set type, smashed all conventions in layout and typography, and rivaled the Sydney *Morning Herald* and the *Age* by setting up his own staff of foreign correspondents. To make the *Australian* a nationwide paper, he loaded his various editions on aircraft for distribution to every major city in the nation. Toward the end of the 1960s, despite his rivals' predictions of failure, his experiment in the new journalism had passed 100,000 copies a day.

While computers were setting type and web offset presses were printing papers in Britain, there was nothing as new as the *Australian* in Fleet Street. Nor was there much left of the refreshing spirit of papers like the Toronto *Globe & Mail* or the Sydney *Morning Herald* in the heartland of British journalism. True, there were vast differences in economic conditions. But little remained in the mother country of the adventurous spirit that had once led the young Delanes, Russells, Harmsworths, and Aitkens into Fleet Street. That, in a very real sense, was the difference between the old and the new.

4. The American Giant

At the pinnacle of world leadership a quarter-century after World War II, the people of the United States were bombarded with more news, pictures, opinions, and advice than the inhabitants of any nation in history. It was the age of the 96-page daily newspaper, the five-pound Sunday newspaper, the round-the-clock radio newscast, the all-day (and sometimes three- or four-day) television news program for great events, the full-color slick magazine compounded of pictures, exposés, and irrelevancies, the participatory and often nude theater, and the instant paper newsbook describing yesterday's events and foretelling tomorrow's. What this did to the American image at home and abroad was predictable. It was sometimes like living in a vast hall of mirrors of uneven quality that magnified some things, distorted others, and made reality a fleeting quality that often defied comprehension. Yet, as an admiring Indian editor once observed during one of the numerous crises in American life, "Whatever happens in the United States, good or bad, the whole world will know about it at once." It was a comforting, if scarcely complimentary, assurance that the freedoms guaranteed under the First Amendment to the Constitution were being observed.

No nation ever before had developed an independent system of mass communication of such power and scope. As might have been expected in a land of more than 200 million people that had become the richest and strongest on earth, it published more newspapers and periodicals than any other country, offered the largest television and radio audiences, spent more money on advertising than anybody else, and provided the broadest distribution of news through its global wire services and syndicates. The result was a veritable landslide of information, transmitted by the most advanced — and expensive — methods.

High-speed transmission and reproduction of news was the order of the day, whether it came by print or electronic means. Banks of computers, communications satellites, multichannel undersea cables, microwave overland systems, intercontinental facsimile, and even the use of light beams gave promise of still more spectacular developments yet to come. In the declining years of the twentieth century, more information was available in the United States than any democratic society could possibly use or even comprehend. What was needed, in the words of Wes Gallagher, general manager of the Associated Press, was "a clear cold light to illuminate the problems of the day." This ever complex problem of illumination became the principal function of the journalist in the United States. Standing on the threshold of the twenty-first century, he bore the greatest responsibilities he had ever assumed.

As the most independent and aggressive of the American news media, newspapers retained their traditional position as a rallying point for public opinion and principal critic of the governmental process. They had, of course, suffered heavy losses during the period of consolidation that had begun with the turn of the century and was now approaching its end. But with relatively few exceptions, primarily in metropolitan areas, the survivors were enjoying a larger measure of prosperity than they had ever known before. True, television was taking away advertising revenue and holding the bulk of its vast audience in prime evening time. But it was at the expense of the once-thriving magazine field, in the main, although the press continued to feel the electronic competitive pressures. However, the remaining quality newspapers in the biggest cities, the efficiently operated groups, the dominant regionals and suburbans, and the small city dailies and weeklies that enjoyed a monopoly of local advertising, all proved themselves capable of resisting the best—and worst—of television's attractions. The world of print was not about to disappear at the waving of a television press agent's wand.

At the beginning of the 1970s, some 1,750 newspapers were selling a record total of 62.5 million copies daily in more than 1,500 American cities and towns, a circulation increase of about 22 percent since 1946. It coincided roughly with the growth in the nation's adult population during that period. However, advertising revenue had shot up by 352 percent in that time, substantially ahead of the 308 percent gain in the value of the gross national product. For the first time, newspaper advertising exceeded $5 billion a year, as compared with $3 billion for television, $1 billion for radio, and $1.3 billion for magazines. Newspaper employment, too, showed a substantial increase in exceeding 360,000,* a gain of 46 percent over 1946, as compared with a 31 percent gain during that period in total national employment. By every measurement, the U. S. Department of Commerce noted, there had been "unprecedented growth" in the newspaper industry during the decade of the 1960s. With 60 million Americans in school, nearly 8 million of them enrolled in higher education, it was to be expected that there would be broadened interest in the printed word.

American newspapers cost more, jumping in 1969 to a total of $2.4 billion in circulation revenue. But they also were substantially larger in total size and editorial content. The average daily in 1969, for example, ran 56 pages, divided into 21.3 pages for editorial and 34.7 pages for advertising. This was more than

---

* In early 1971, a recession created a job scarcity but it did not seem to affect many of the 40,000 on newspapers' editorial staffs. For the 20,000 in other media, however, times were more difficult.

double the size of the average daily in 1946, which ran 27 pages, divided into 12.3 pages for editorial and 14.7 pages for advertising. The gain of 20 pages in advertising to only 9 pages for editorial reflected the reality of inflationary times. Even American newspapers in small cities were larger than the best of the foreign press, but quality was another consideration.

As an industry that grossed nearly $8.2 billions in 1969 in total advertising and circulation revenue, the American newspaper became a more important factor in the nation's economy. Profits of 10 percent were common and some returned margins of 20 and 25 percent. A small daily in the Thomson group was reputed to have earned $1 million in a year. Another daily, this one of independent ownership, was said to have shown a 19 percent profit of $2.5 million on a gross of $13 million. Newspapers such as the New York *Times*, Los Angeles *Times*, Washington *Post*, and *Wall Street Journal* reported record and near-record earnings, as did such expanding newspaper groups as Gannett and Knight. But the weekly field of more than 8,000 newspapers was overcrowded and, in 1970, signs of recession and a drop in advertising created a job squeeze and a cut in profits even among some giants of the press.

There were additional debits to be considered as well as credits. Only forty-five cities, most of them small, retained competing dailies. It didn't help very much, as enthusiastic spokesmen for the proprietors pointed out, that there were nearly 5,000 competing electronic or printed media in some 1,300 cities. It was the voice of the independent newspaper that counted most with a discerning public. The disappearance of significant competition in the presentation of news and opinion could not be glossed over. It was popular, but misleading, for otherwise responsible newspapers to hire columnists of diverse views or permit editors in group organizations a loose leash on matters of political policy. The public didn't believe for one moment that, in a showdown, the proprietors' views would not prevail. The most respected newspapers frankly conceded that they were operating in a monopoly situation and conducted themselves as a responsible public trust.

There was need for such an attitude. In the quarter-century after World War II, the whole substance, direction, and thrust of metropolitan newspaper journalism changed in a drastic manner. The aggressive drive of big city minorities for greater power, the flight of the middle class to the suburbs, the rise of the outer shopping centers, and the breakneck spread of inflation combined to touch off an upheaval in most major metropolitan centers. Particularly in the Northeast and Far West, the metropolis became a megalopolis as cities spread until their suburbs ran into each other. Such a basic change in the organization of urban society, combined with the rise of national television, the weekly news and picture magazines, and the suburban dailies, had a crushing effect on the old metropolitan press, centered as it was in the inner city.

Through sales, mergers, and a combination of slipshod management and irresponsible strikes, the already hard-hit big city newspapers suffered still more losses. In twenty-one metropolitan centers of 1 million or more population, the inner city newspapers dropped from 79 to 57 from 1950 to 1968 while the well-entrenched suburban and outer community press rose from 305 to 310. For the same period, the mets lost 2.5 million circulation, most of it in New York, while the suburbans gained 3.3 million for an overall increase in newspaper reading. Naturally, the papers that survived in the inner cities were even greater beneficiaries and showed substantial increases over eighteen years in fifteen of the twenty-four major areas of population. So it turned out that, for metropolitan papers of general circulation, New York City was reduced to two mornings and one evening; Chicago, two mornings and two evenings; Philadelphia, one morning and two evenings; Boston, three mornings and one evening; Washington, one morning and two evenings; Baltimore, one morning and two evenings; Fort Worth, one morning and two evenings; and a single morning and evening paper each remained in Los Angeles, San Francisco, Detroit, Cleveland, Pittsburgh, Kansas City, Cincinnati, St. Louis, Dallas, Minneapolis, St. Paul, Milwaukee, Seattle, Houston, Buffalo, Atlanta, and San Diego. In some of these cities, there was a common ownership of some or all dailies; in others, plant-sharing arrangements in whole or in part. Still others were supported by group managements. The independent, individually owned big city daily was becoming very close to being a museum piece.*

The group-owned dailies were making by far the most rapid gains in the newspaper field, and in most cases the largest profits. They were also well in advance in using every major new scientific development. By the outset of the 1970s, more than 150 such groups owned in excess of 800 papers that accounted for 58 percent of total daily circulation and 63 percent of Sunday circulation. Of these, the seven largest — Chicago *Tribune* group, Newhouse, Knight, Scripps-Howard, Gannett, Cowles, and Ridder — controlled more than one-quarter of the daily and Sunday newspapers that were sold in the land.

It would have been difficult to pick out press barons in this field who ruled their publications, magazines, and electronic media in the manner of a Hearst and sought to sway national opinion for personal ends. Most modern group managers were executives whose functions were sharply separated from influence on editorial policy in the better-run news organizations. Perhaps the least centralized of all the big groups were the nine Cowles newspapers, which were split into three autonomous units. Among the eleven Knight newspapers, which became the third largest group in total circulation after the acquisition of the Philadelphia *Inquirer* and *Daily News* for $55 million in 1969, editorial independence was the gospel preached by their guiding spirit, John S. Knight, who insisted on keeping business influence out of his newsrooms. This tradition, so respected by Edward Wyllis Scripps, was handed down to his journalistic heirs, Charles E. Scripps and Jack Howard, but the sixteen surviving Scripps-Howard papers appeared to be more centralized. In the surviving eight papers of the Hearst chain, the nominal editor-in-chief, William Randolph Hearst Jr., exercised less authority over individual editors than top management. For the Gannett group,

---

* *Newsday*, largest suburban newspaper in the country, became part of the Los Angeles *Times* family in 1970 when Captain Harry Guggenheim sold his 51 percent interest to the *Times-Mirror* Corporation.

with a number of medium-sized and small papers, corporate management was centered in Paul Miller, a former Associated Press executive, who carefully walled off the business side from purely editorial concerns. In the largest group of all in weekly circulation, the Chicago *Tribune* chain, corporate managers little known to the public had replaced the pugnacious Colonel Robert R. McCormick and set aside some of his arbitrary ways.

The group that came closest in the public mind to the old image of mass ownership of the press was the Newhouse chain, second in circulation after the Chicago *Tribune* papers. The twenty-two Newhouse papers, including sixteen dailies, were part of a giant combine that also included twenty magazines, seven TV and seven radio stations, twenty cable TV systems, a gravure printing plant, and part ownership in a newsprint firm. While the whole enterprise was profitable, it also made a national impression for public-spirited achievement with Pulitzer Prizes for the St. Louis *Globe-Democrat* and the Portland *Oregonian*, and other awards for the *Long Island Press* and other papers. The result was continued growth.

This was the achievement of Samuel I. Newhouse, who, like Lord Thomson, made most of his large purchases after his fiftieth year. He had build his chain in the pit of the depression in the 1930s by bidding for readers for relatively small, shaky newspapers on the fringes of New York's metropolitan area against the indifference of most advertisers and the hostility of most unions. He survived a series of the worst strikes ever conducted against any newspaper proprietor and turned most of his suburban properties into money-makers. It was only late in life that he ventured into the inner cities, where so many newspapers had died, by buying such papers as the Cleveland *Plain Dealer* for a reported $50 million. Throughout, he often aroused more antagonism than good will, although much of the criticism of his methods was undeserved.

Yet, he built so well that he achieved his greatest gains during the painful contraction of the metropolitan press after World War II. In the period of strikes and consolidation in the New York area beginning in 1950, his *Long Island Press, Staten Is-*

land Advance, Jersey Journal, and Newark *Star-Ledger* were among the principal beneficiaries of the million-copy circulation increase that came to the suburban dailies as a whole and gave them 40 percent of the total area readership. He had only one loser there, the *Long Island Star-Journal.* With the Gannett chain in Westchester, and such successful suburban dailies as *Newsday,* with 425,000 circulation, and the *Record* in northern New Jersey, with 150,000, Newhouse probably had as much effect as the electronic media in undercutting the faltering metropolitan dailies.

The New York newspaper world had been contracting steadily. Of fifteen newspapers in 1900 and a dozen in 1930, only seven survived in 1950. With the middle class already in flight to the suburbs and inflation boosting costs to record highs, the remaining newspapers and the ten unions with which they had contracts began fighting a paralyzing economic battle. There was a 10-day strike in 1953, a 19-day strike in 1958, and a 114-day strike in 1962-63 that seriously damaged both sides. An immediate victim was the second largest paper in the country, Hearst's *Daily Mirror,* which suspended publication while it had a million circulation.

The strikes continued with a 25-day tieup in 1965. Thereafter, Hearst's *Journal-American* and Scripps-Howard's *World-Telegram & Sun* combined in a single evening paper and joined John Hay Whitney's New York *Herald Tribune,* a morning paper, in what they hoped would be a 24-hour-a-day operation in a single plant. However, the unions never gave the merger a chance. On the opening day of publication, April 25, 1966, they struck before any papers of the new combine appeared. When the struggle dragged on through the summer, Whitney folded his *Herald Tribune* and agreed with his partners, Hearst and Scripps-Howard, to put out a single evening paper, the *World-Journal-Tribune,* if the unions would permit it.

After 140 days of wrangling, the worst and costliest strike in New York's annals ended. On September 12, the *World-Journal-Tribune* appeared but it wasn't much of a paper. When the owners' losses passed $10 million, they suspended publication on

May 5, 1967. Thus, Hearst and Scripps-Howard both were forced out of New York City and one of the greatest papers in the nation, the *Herald Tribune*, died in the process. As for the unions, which waged so senseless a fight to save jobs, they lost a sizable proportion of their newspaper members.

Two of the three surviving papers, the *Times* and the *News*, always had been profitable as the leaders respectively in the quality and popular morning fields. But the third, the *Post*, the surprising remnant of the once-numerous evening papers, had lost at least $6 million for its owner, Dorothy Schiff, before becoming profitable.

All three now enjoyed a virtual monopoly in their respective fields. The *Times*, at the end of the 1960s, soared to more than 900,000 daily and 1.5 million Sundays, set new advertising records, and showed a consolidated net income of almost $7.5 million for the first six months of 1969 on an operating revenue of nearly $120 million. As the largest newspaper in the country, the *News* improved its traditionally strong position by exceeding 2 million circulation on a five-day-a-week basis and passing 3 million on Sundays. The *Post*, with more than 700,000 circulation, claimed to be the largest evening paper in the nation.

In less than a year, however, the situation changed after still another ordeal of union bargaining. Soaring inflation and rising payrolls obliged the *Times* and the *Post* to raise their daily sales price to 15 cents a copy with losses of advertising and circulation.

The lessons of New York did not prevent reckless union leaders from striking elsewhere in an attempt to win gains for their members. Their own inner politics, in many places, proved to be a complicating factor in achieving settlements. As in New York, the practice of multi-union bargaining at staggered intervals, with each contract negotiation separate, had the result of causing one group to charge that it had been given less than another. In the inter-union rivalry that resulted, labor people jockeyed for advantage among themselves as savagely as guerrilla warriors. This is not to say that some less far-sighted newspaper managers did not attempt to take advantage of such divisions by maintaining an inflexible bargaining posture. But as the economic conflicts dragged on, the heaviest damage was sustained by the independent press and its people. Few dictators could have done worse.

Wherever there were cities without newspapers, television and radio tried without success to replace the printed word by extending their news coverage. In the very real vacuum that was created through the loss of the inner city press, it was an observable phenomenon that economic activity slackened, local government went into a decline, and social and cultural life on the community level almost ceased. Nor was it easy to repair the damage once strikes ended. As the New York *Times'* A. H. Raskin observed, "The surest way to become convinced that you can do without newspapers is to have to do it over and over again for weeks or months on end."

The bitterest, longest, and most senseless strike of all occurred in Detroit against the independently owned *News*, an evening paper with a pre-strike circulation of 700,000, when the circulation drivers of the Teamsters Union walked off the job on November 16, 1967. On the following day, the other major daily, the Knight-owned morning *Free Press*, with a pre-strike circulation of 590,000, suspended publication on the ground that union members were violating joint contracts.

Thereafter, the other thirteen newspaper unions entered the struggle, with each bargaining separately, some long after the Teamsters had settled their differences with the *News*. Both papers had been out of business for 134 days in 1964 as a result of a strike, but the new paralysis was even more serious. It was not until August 9, 1968, a lapse of 267 days, that both newspapers reappeared after the last union had accepted a package increase in benefits that amounted to $33 a week. When it was all over, and the papers had raised their circulation prices to meet increased costs, the *Free Press* commented: "Actually, there were two strikes involved, separate and distinct. Ironically, neither one of them now seems to have been necessary."

Lesser tieups occurred elsewhere in the country during this strange and costly period in American journalism. In Toledo, the public-spirited *Blade*, published by Paul Block, was shut down by its unions for 148 days in 1966-67. As was the case in Detroit, the Toledo paper was among the few that appeared to have suffered no lasting damage. But in Boston and smaller communities throughout the land, such economic warfare served only to weaken both the press and the unions.

It is remarkable, despite the proliferation of strikes and the length and intensity of the bargaining between managements and unions, that the underlying cause—the need for modernizing archaic production and distribution methods—was so seldom mentioned. For in all truth, what the unions really feared was the introduction of job-saving machinery and what the publishers really insisted upon was the right to modernize their plants to cut costs. Such things could not be indefinitely delayed, however.

By the beginning of the 1970s, nearly 500 dailies already were being printed on offset presses or were due to make the change.* More than 350 were using computers for typesetting. Widespread experiments were being conducted with photocomposition to replace hot metal typesetting. Quicker methods of platemaking to serve the presses also were being developed. Standard daily data compilations, such as stock market reports, could be transmitted at thousands of words per minute. Nearly 1,500 dailies, about 90 percent of the total, were offering color printing to their readers and advertisers, although the full-color daily was still just a dream. All in all, the annual expenditures for plant expansion and modernization were approaching $200 million in the United States.

While the home printing of mini-newspapers had become possible, it was scarcely practical in terms of either cost or results. Yet, such great newspapers as the Los Angeles *Times* took a serious look at the possibilities of electronic delivery systems. Few housewives could be enthusiastic at the prospect. There was no outpouring of joy in the nation's living rooms because electronics manufacturers had promised soon to produce an attachment

---

* Offset, an adaptation of the lithographic printing process, was first used for daily newspaper publication in the U.S. in 1939.

that would enable television sets to spew out their own printed news. It was one thing to have a 96-page New York *Times* dumped on one's doorsetp, to be retrieved at breakfast time. It was quite another to have such a monster jump out of a black box in one's living room. There was scant danger of it, for the immediate future. The best the electronic press attachments could produce was a little printed matter on small-sized sheets.

The electronic media had far more pressing problems in the United States than such risky ventures in print. Radio, with six thousand stations and 165 million home receivers, had reached saturation. Television's 700 stations were changing over from black and white to color transmission with more than 60 million black-and-white sets and nearly 15 million for color in existence. Profits were slumping and the industry's troubles were rising. As if it had not been bad enough to be accused of fomenting violence by covering the race riots of the 1960s, TV also had to fight off wholesale charges of news management from the highest sources in government as well as angry minority groups. Even worse, the first Alfred I. duPont-Columbia survey of broadcast journalism called television "a hideous waste of one of the nation's most important resources" and indicted its news handling as shallow and uneven.

The once-docile Federal Communications Commission meanwhile came to life with a denial of the renewal of a major station's license for TV in Boston and an order for hearings in other cases. A drive was on, backed by the Congress, that forced the removal of cigarette advertising from TV on the ground of harm to public health. Despite a decade of TV protest, the Supreme Court strongly upheld the so-called "Fairness Doctrine" of the FCC which guaranteed the right of reply to injured individuals and groups. Sharply separating the electronic media from the Constitutional protection given the freedom of the press, the majority decision held: "There is no sanctuary in the First Amendment for unlimited private censorship operating in a medium not open to all."

The masters of the networks, facing a determined drive by foundations and dedicated individuals to create an educational television system that would be popular, cast about for ways to maintain themselves in the style to which they had become accustomed — and hit upon the notion of domestic satellite transmission. The use of satellites for overseas communication already had been successful. What Frank Stanton of CBS now proposed was to send four satellites into orbit for domestic use alone. But the changeover, to nullify the rising costs of the American Telephone and Telegraph Company's lines, would take time.

Just about the only satisfaction for the television proprietor was his profit, but even that was dwindling at the outset of the 1970s amid signs of a recession. For 1967, television's pre-tax profits were $414 million, a thumping 18 percent. The fifteen network stations realized 39 percent, but some of the locals earned up to 54 percent. For 1968, television's profits went up by an additional 11 percent. And in 1969, CBS alone boosted earnings by 24 percent on a 17 percent gain in revenues, which exceeded $1 billion. Net income for the year was nearly $72 million, equal to $2.65 a share. It was no wonder that a station such as KFMB, the CBS-TV affiliate in San Diego, which was sold for $1 million in 1950, was worth twenty times more in 1970. But in 1971, television was hit for the first time by the financial jitters despite its past profits.

Since the press was deeply involved in the ownership of the electronic media, it could not very well look the other way when television, on top of its increasing troubles, became subject to widespread criticism for failing adequately to represent the public interest. In 1968, no less than 183 of 671 television stations, or 27.2 percent, were owned by newspapers. For FM radio, the percentage was much lower, 191 of 1,917 stations, or 9.9 percent; for AM radio, it was lowest of all, 381 of 4,235 stations, or 8.9 percent. Something more than mere numbers was involved, however, as both regulators and legislators were quick to point out. Commissioner Nicholas Johnson of the FCC said that newspapers owned at least one television station in each of thirty of the top fifty marketing areas in the nation. It was the basis for the FCC's attempt to force some newspapers to divest themselves of their electronic affiliates. The finding that some broadcast affiliates actually supported some failing newspapers did nothing to lessen the official pressure for diversification.

At about the same time, the press was put on the defensive to an even greater extent when the Supreme Court ruled in 1969 that it was illegal, under antitrust statutes, for competing papers to share advertising and circulation departments. The decision affected forty-four newspapers in twenty-two cities. To find new and legal ways of entering into such economical combinations, the press had to turn to Congress, which in 1970 passed a law permitting failing papers to share some costs. However, for all the laws that a helpful Congress might consider, none could require people to read a nonessential newspaper.

By contrast with the generally healthy state of the bulk of the nation's daily press and its electronic media, the magazines were developing glaring weak points at the beginning of the 1970s. Of the 4,000-odd American periodicals, there were perhaps 250 after World War II that had a particular influence by reason of size, prestige, specialty, or particular appeal. Of this total, nearly 35 of the largest and best known vanished in a little more than a decade as costs went up and income failed to keep pace with expenses.

Some of the greatest names in American magazine journalism dropped out. *Collier's* and *Coronet*, each with 4 million circulation, suspended publication. An even bigger shock came with the death of the *Saturday Evening Post* in 1969. It had lost more than $50 million in a decade, primarily because both *Life* and *Look*, the big picture magazines, became more vital to younger audiences. At the end, the *Post* still had 3.5 million circulation but couldn't find the resources to stay in business.

The seriousness of the magazine industry's downturn became even more apparent at the end of the decade with a change in the fortunes of its leader, Time, Inc. At the death of the group's founder, Henry Robinson Luce, on February 28, 1967, it had been calculated that the total operation was worth $690 million. Having begun in 1923 with $86,000 in borrowed capital, Luce's own share at his death was put at $109 million. Record revenues

of $503 million and net earnings of $37.7 million had been reported for 1966. Three years later, Time, Inc., reported a net
operating loss of $300,000 for the first quarter of 1969; its stock,
which had sold as high as 100 earlier that year, dropped more
than 60 points.

One of the troubles appeared to be with *Life* which, despite 8
million circulation, was losing advertising. It had also been
obliged to abandon its Spanish edition. *Time* itself, with 4 million
circulation, was changing its old-fashioned style in answer to the
growing challenge of *Newsweek*, owned by the Washington *Post*,
a lively news magazine that was approaching 3 million circulation. The Luce publications also suffered from ill-judged ventures into both the motion picture and book fields, but now were
trying to expand into the even more competitive newspaper industry. True, there were reasonable answers to the troubles of
Time, Inc., as its reduced but still substantial earnings indicated
at the end of the decade. However, if the leader had troubles, it
was self-evident that relatively few magazines could be considered safe.

Pressures were building up, as well, against the other great
American pictorial giant, *Look*, the pride of the Cowles empire.
In a fabulous publishing industry, the magazine had paid rich
dividends for years. But with the founding of the Suffolk *Sun* in
1966, Cowles Communications soon realized it had an expensive
loser on its hands. The Long Island daily was reputed to have
lost $4 million in 1967 and nearly $3 million in 1968. In 1969, after Cowles had to reduce its dividend, the Suffolk *Sun* suspended
publication. The lesson was clear enough. In the television age,
there was a limit to the advantage that could be gained from
expansion and diversification. Too much was dangerous, as both
the Luce and Cowles publications had discovered to their cost.

Such magazines as the *Reader's Digest*, the citadel of conservatism with 15 million circulation, and the *TV Guide*, Walter
Annenberg's program directory with 10 million, were impervious
to the effect of television. The McGraw-Hill publications, controlled circulation magazines with heavy readership in business

and industry, also maintained a steady and profitable pace, as did the leaders in such specialized fields as fashions, home-making, and sports.

But among the once influential intellectual magazines, the struggle for survival intensified. *Harper's* and the *Atlantic* both clung to modest audiences, as did the *Saturday Review*, al-though the *Reporter* had to quit. What was left of the old radical periodicals, the *Nation* and *New Republic*, got along on consider-ably less than the prestige monthlies. It was a sign of the times that even the *New Yorker*, the dowager of class magazines, dropped sufficient advertising to show a tremor of nervousness at the competition of a new publication, *New York*.

There was one other part of the American mass communica-tions system, the most basic of all, that displayed signs of strain. It was the news agency field, in which the Associated Press and United Press International* each served more than 4,000 newspaper, magazine, and broadcast clients in the United States and at least 2,500 others abroad. The increasing demands on these wholesalers of news had boosted their annual budgets in the 1960s, the AP's to $57 million and the UPI's to $50 mil-lion, with resultant rate increases for their respective members and clients. With the introduction of computers and high-speed transmission methods, the outlook for further cost increases served to intensify the competitive pressures. Still worse, the growth of such syndicate services as those of the New York *Times* and the Los Angeles *Times*–Washington *Post* combine, plus the expansion of Reuters in the United States, created new problems for the wire services that would have to be faced in the foreseeable future.

The 2,000-odd employees of each agency constituted, in ef-fect, the foundation of a journalistic system of checks and bal-ances in the United States that insured a very high level of swift, accurate, and truthful reporting and was generally impervious to extraneous influence. To have reduced the system to a single

---

* The United Press became the United Press International in 1958 when it absorbed Hearst's International News Service.

super-agency, as the economically minded suggested, would
have swept away at one stroke the protection of 90 percent of
the American press that depended on agency-supplied foreign
news and of 60 percent that used only agency-supplied national
news. It could be argued that responsible newspaper monopolies
at the local level had been beneficial on the whole in producing a
better news report. But at the national level, the concept of a
single wire news service for a large part of the American communications system was an open invitation to disaster.

In a country as large and as varied in regional and local interests as the United States, there could be no dominant national
leader for the news media, nor even a single like-minded group
that exerted overwhelming influence on all the other disparate
elements. There was not even a national daily newspaper on the
model of the *Times* in Britain, *Le Monde* in France, *Asahi* in
Japan, and *Pravda* and *Izvestia* in the Soviet Union. Whatever
influence the news media exerted at the national level was usually
spread among a dozen or so quality newspapers in various parts
of the country, the news magazines, a few intellectual periodicals,
and a handful of major columnists and television commentators.
This could scarcely be regarded as a select group, for it varied
in accordance with the peoples, places, and issues that were
involved.

In the various regions of the country, the leaders became still
more numerous and diffuse in their outlook, but there was no
question of their impact on specific issues. Among the newspapers, there were as many as 200 to 250 that made a particular
point of public service through investigative reporting and campaigns for regional and civic improvement. Here and there, a
few local broadcast media and some of the new locally oriented
magazines made an effort to emulate them. But in the main, at
the base of the pyramid, the press was often the only common
medium of social or political interchange that exerted an independent influence of its own on the public.

Radio, it is true, had been the fastest medium for reporting
the news for more than a half century. Nor could anything sur-
pass the effectiveness of television in presenting the pictorial

record of a moon landing, a war, an earthquake or hurricane, the uproar of a political convention or the election of a president, or the coronation of a king or the selection of a pope. But however useful the small screen may have become to a democratic society, it could not by its very nature make the commitments and assume the risks of a responsible newspaper. Nor did it, with rare individual exceptions, display the moral courage that such commitments involved.

The single news organization that came closest to exerting leadership among the news media and a dominant national influence was the New York *Times*. This was no longer the good gray *Times* that Adolph Ochs had created nor even the larger but still sober and sedate *Times* of Arthur Hays Sulzberger's day. The new *Times* was a giant that displayed many of the virtues of its distinguished predecessor together with some of the unpleasant aspects of a mass circulation journal. But despite the injection of a large amount of women's page trivia, social chatter, and sheer press agentry in the pages that went under the generic heading of "cultural affairs," the news report was still prepared in the old tradition. And this continued to be the saving grace of the economy-size *Times*. That was why the paper was still read carefully and with respect in government offices in Washington from the White House down and why leaders of public opinion at all levels sought its favor.

There were growing pains, of course. Having doubled in size since the era before World War II, the *Times* had problems of direction and leadership. The proprietorship rested now in the young Arthur Ochs Sulzberger, Arthur Hays's son and the grandson of Adolph Ochs, who was even less inclined than his father had been to intervene in editorial affairs. With the old guard passing from the newsroom and younger men pressing for advantage, the consequences of the *Times*'s policy of editorial laissez-faire were predictable. The editorial paladins soon began contending among themselves with such colorful results that a modest body of literature, including a best-selling book, was based on their doings.

Against his wishes and perhaps his own best interests, James

Reston, the first reporter of his time, was impressed into service as executive editor to resolve the conflicts. In due course, responsibility for the news report, the life blood of the *Times*, was given to a former foreign correspondent and Pulitzer Prize winner, A. M. Rosenthal. He had risen through the ranks from campus correspondent at the City College of New York. When he became managing editor in 1969 at the age of forty-seven, he fulfilled the judgment of a former executive editor of the *Times*, Turner Catledge, who had persuaded him to abandon a brilliant career in the foreign field to assume executive responsibilities.

There was nothing static about either the *Times* or its principal competitors. The *Wall Street Journal*, for example, had developed from a small, parochial paper in the financial community into the second largest newspaper in the land with a circulation of more than a million daily at a sales price of 15 cents a copy. The Washington *Post* and the *Evening Star*, the capital's distinguished rivals, both expanded their services and usefulness as well as their size. The Los Angeles *Times* transformed itself from a stodgy, provincial journal into a great newspaper of national and international repute. The St. Louis *Post-Dispatch*, maintaining the Pulitzer tradition, was recognized as the foremost champion of liberalism in the Midwest and a power in the nation. Starting as a tabloid that had to fight for its life, the Chicago *Sun-Times* climbed to first place in the second city in the land and continued its expansion. The Miami *Herald*, dominant in the Southeast, was able to overturn two separate murder convictions in a single year and set free two persons who had been wrongfully imprisoned. The *Christian Science Monitor* turned itself from a religious tract into a unique newspaper of news and commentary that was read throughout the country. In Boston, Providence, and Philadelphia, Baltimore, Detroit, Cleveland, Milwaukee, Des Moines, Louisville, Atlanta, Denver, and San Francisco, other major newspapers flourished with undiminished vigor.

Among the regional and small-city press there were, in addition, many medium- and small-size newspapers that had an impact on life in their respective areas. The Hutchinson *News*, for example, successfully conducted a four-year campaign to force legislative reapportionment in Kansas and do away with many of the state's "rotten boroughs." The Riverside *Press-Enterprise* in California upset the misrule of the courts in the affairs of an otherwise helpless tribe of Indians. In North Carolina, two small weeklies successfully fought a resurgence of the Ku Klux Klan. And in Pecos, Texas, another tiny newspaper uncovered the misdeeds of Billy Sol Estes, a national scandal that reached into the White House. From top to bottom, this was a virile press that took itself and its news reports with the utmost seriousness. On occasion, the periodical press made significant contributions in the examination of government, such as *Life*'s exposé that forced the resignation of Justice Abe Fortas from the Supreme Court. But since the days of Edward R. Murrow, the broadcast media with few exceptions had not lived up to the high standard of public service that he had displayed.

The American legal system, with its broad insistence on civil rights, encouraged the process of surveillance of government by a press of such demonstrated independence. In the 1960s, the interpretation of these basic rights expanded the protection of the press to a degree unknown since the adoption of the Constitution. The landmark decision of 1964, known as the New York *Times* Rule, held that a journalist could not be made responsible for libel even if he committed errors of fact in his criticism of public officials, as long as he did not act with "actual malice" and a "reckless disregard" of the truth.

In a companion decision in 1967, in a suit brought against *Life* magazine, the high court made almost exactly the same distinction in knocking down the protection of public figures under the laws protecting privacy. It ruled that a "newsworthy person's" right to privacy did not entitle him to collect damages for reports containing false information unless there was proof that errors were knowingly and recklessly made.

Besides these two favorable legal decisions, the Congress adopted a Federal "Freedom of Information" law that obliged government departments, with certain national security exceptions, to provide news of their work to the press. And in more than half the states, similar and even broader "open records" laws were provided. In more than a dozen states, the right of a journalist to withhold identification of his sources was also protected by law.

Under the circumstances, it might have been expected that the public in the United States would be properly grateful to its press. But unfortunately, much of the evidence pointed in exactly the opposite direction. Late in the 1960s, Dr. George H. Gallup said, "Never in my time have the media of communications been held in such low esteem." James Reston, in a lecture before the Council on Foreign Relations, observed, "The credit of the American newspapers with the American people for accuracy and good judgment is not high." The International Press Institute, in its annual report issued in 1969, found that there was growing mistrust of the news media in the United States, together with a feeling that the press and broadcast media "incite the violence they report."

To all this the manager of the information service of the American Newspaper Publishers Association, Stewart Macdonald, retorted, "The evidence today is that many people do not understand the press, do not see why the press has to cover bad and unpleasant news, do not see why the press must report the violence of our troubled times, do not want to look at the record of misdoing and corruption that dots the pages of the daily newspaper."

This was something more than a case of the people blaming the herald for proclaiming bad news in the market place instead of keeping it to himself. The malaise went to the very roots of American life. For if the American people were not pleased with their press, they also were not particularly inspired by the acts of their government, the burning of their cities, the riotous conduct of their militant minorities and sometimes their police as well, the rise of crime in their streets, the rebellion in their universities, and the soaring inflation of their daily living costs.

It would have been a mistake to attribute this very real and widespread public dissatisfaction to any one cause, whether it was the uselessness and frustration of the Vietnam War or the outrages in the cities, the constant drain of inflation or the well-publicized excesses of the young. But, quite properly, the people held their government responsible for the end product and, regardless of the critical stance of a substantial proportion of the press toward the government, they considered the press as a part of the nation's Establishment. The dismissal of the Democrats from national power and the advent of Richard Milhous Nixon at the White House, with a new Republican policy of de-emphasizing conflict, did little to change the sour public mood at the end of the 1960s. Neither peace nor national serenity, unhappily, turned out to be just around the corner. And lowering one's voice, as Nixon counseled, did not reduce America's troubles.

In this extremity, the press did very little to help itself return to the public's good graces. At first, there was a tendency for the press and broadcast media to blame each other for being mainly responsible for this melancholy turn of events. Once that phase passed, a certain amount of sulking and even resentment set in, together with a sense of bewilderment over the public's lack of appreciation of a lot of first-rate news reporting and public service. Some journalists argued angrily that the public was unappreciative of the blessings of American life, including the works of the news media. Others muttered that they were dealing with an ignorant people that had lost both the will and the inclination to read, much less to govern themselves. That was just as irresponsible an exaggeration as the most critical public attitude toward the press.

The truth of the matter was that the press, to a frightening degree, had lost touch with a large area of public opinion, including most of the people under twenty-five who constituted almost half the nation, the blacks and other underprivileged urban minorities, and other disadvantaged groups that had been virtually abandoned in the nation's rural areas. The crusade of bench and bar against the excesses of the press in the reporting of the administration of justice, while a serious matter, by no means accounted for the sum total of public displeasure. Nor could the damage be repaired overnight, as the more optimistic journalists believed possible. Consultations between press and bar and the drafting of voluntary codes of conduct were all very well. And the small but respectable initial experiments with community press councils on the British model were admirable in concept. But something much more sweeping in nature was required.

The ills of the American press were not material but spiritual. Instead of reaching out for the poor and the disadvantaged of another era as Pulitzer and Scripps and Greeley and Medill would have done, in an altogether sincere effort to improve their lot, a very large part of the press of the United States was satisfied to be the comfortable and prosperous representative of a middle-aged, middle-class society. It wouldn't do. The nice people had too many advocates, the not-so-nice but far more desperate people too few. Out of the uproar of the 1960s, and without doubt the 1970s as well, a new kind of American society was emerging and it had a right to seek a new—or at least a different—kind of press to give it the representation it deserved. The American newspaper, in effect, had to find a new philosophy or forfeit the trust of the people to whom it appealed and on whom it depended for support.

XII. Free Press/Free People

1. The Press Today

Few journalists live in Happy Valley. Nor do very many view
the world from the clear and heady atmosphere of a mountain
top. Those who contemplate life through the closed and clouded
windows of a smoky newsroom are not likely to be overcome by
hope. They are, more often than not, suspicious of the past, dissatisfied with the present, and highly dubious of prospects for
the future. It is completely in character, therefore, for the news
agencies and journalistic societies responsible for such things to
report, as they have on many a recent new year, that the free
press no longer exists over two-thirds to three-quarters of the
earth's surface. The assumption based on a logical projection of
this news, of course, is that the days of the free press are numbered and it soon will be the unmourned companion of the stylus
and papyrus, the quill pen and foolscap.

Aside from demonstrating that news and truth are not necessarily identical, this melancholy statistic is wrong in two respects. It is questionable, to say the least, whether space in the
sense of *lebensraum* is the best measurement of the state of the
press. There are about forty places in the world, from Swaziland
to New Guinea, where the daily paper doesn't exist, and
wouldn't be of much use to a largely illiterate populace if it did.
But even more to the point, the independent newspaper has
always been handicapped, and, in many countries, unknown
over much of Asia, Africa, Latin America, and most of Eastern
Europe. To observe, consequently, that there is no free press in
two-thirds or three-quarters of the world today is just about as
valid as it is to report that Julius Caesar is dead today. This is,
on the whole, a peculiar way to present the news, much less the
truth. The scorekeepers had better give up. This is no mere
game, in which each year is an inning to be scored for or against
the free press, but a worldwide struggle for the control of public

opinion. The press is in enough trouble without further confusing the public about its own situation.

There are other demonstrable fallacies in the use of the world's surface as an operating table for the examination of the health—or indisposition—of the independent newspaper. The control of the press over the vast area of the Soviet Union, for example, is scarcely a new development; the czars, certainly, were just as mistrustful and censorious of their editors as the masters of the Kremlin who followed them. Moreover, the success of Mao Tse-tung's revolution did not change the basic practices of Chinese press control, for Chiang Kai-shek had never permitted his press to be a model of freedom. It is a palpable error, therefore, to measure the change in the Soviet and Chinese press either in area or in methods of control. What really matters is that both these powerful entities are being used today by their respective governments as weapons in their deadly rivalry. Under these circumstances, for all their growth, the two Communist press systems can do less damage to the independent press than to each other. With the destruction of the myth of the Communist monolith, it is no accident that some of the Soviet Union's dissident associates in Eastern Europe have struggled to loosen their ties to Moscow.

If the Western press has thus overreacted in general to its supposed losses, it has been almost as mistaken in surveying its gains. For the lingering death of colonialism and the emergence of so many new nations have stimulated a hopeful tendency to equate fealty to the West with an impression of tolerance for independent journalism. It isn't in the nature of humankind to create virtue by association, sad to say. A Latin American dictator may be the darling of Washington and yet toss all his editors into solitary confinement. And the same is true of the African oligarch who swears by Socialist brotherhood as expounded by Moscow and/or Peking, or subdivisions thereof.

There is, in addition, a grievous lack of reality in crying out, as editorialists do so often, that the dominance of an anti-Western or pro-Communist native dictator over a few small and hapless papers or a small radio station is a "blow" to the free press.

Some blow! Some papers! In all truth, in most such developing nations, there has been only an exchange in control between a colonial governor and a new native government. As in the new China, the loyalty but not the status of the news media has changed. The situation of the press is not often visibly improved, as it was when India's people and press became independent together, or clearly downgraded, as it was in Greece with a military junta's dismissal of king and government. There are even fewer uprisings of a popular nature, such as the Czechoslovak revolt of 1968, in which freedom of the press was such a major factor. Changes in the status of the press, on the whole, tend to come rather slowly.

Instead of keeping score or measuring the areas of press freedom and control, the West may be well advised to disentangle itself from its own propaganda about the nobility of its cause. After fighting beside the czar in World War I to make the world safe for democracy and enlisting under the banner of the four freedoms with Generalissimo Joseph V. Stalin and Generalissimo Chiang Kai-shek in World War II, the West should have wearied by this time of such meretricious intellectual baggage. Opposition to Communism is not really a very satisfactory test of a government's willingness to tolerate and support an independent press. The "Czech spring," with its savage outburst of criticism of the Soviet Union in a wholly Commmunist press, was no isolated phenomenon. Nor was "Papa" Duvalier, Haiti's dedicated anti-Communist dictator, to be regarded as anything other than one of the bitterest enemies of the free press in the Western hemisphere, along with Fidel Castro.

There are, on the whole, more reasons for hope than for mourning over the future of the independent newspaper despite its difficulties in a rapidly changing world. After all, the most important development in the situation of the press during the last twenty or thirty years was not Mao's victory in Red China, but the liberation of Europe, most of Pacific Asia, and key parts of Africa from the domination of Hitler, Mussolini, and Tojo. It was not the Communization of the relatively small and almost thoroughly controlled Chinese press that mattered. Rather, it was the rebirth of the free press in Europe, its reestablishment in Japan and, with Britain's withdrawal, its emergence in India.

Thus, far from the decline and fall that is implied in the statistical measurement of the free press over the earth's surface, there has been a very real and demonstrable improvement in the situation of the newspaper as an independent force in organized societies. Mere numbers are as misleading as space in making such a determination, but they do say something about the concentration of the press. Of the 8,000 daily publications in the world today, ranging in size and importance from national dailies to mere bulletin sheets in poor lands, 60 percent are published in the continents most hospitable to the free press, Europe and North America. This breaks down into 35 percent in Europe, including the Soviet Union; 25 percent in North America; 23 percent in Asia; 10 percent in South America; and about 2.5 percent each in Africa and Oceania. The United States, with 22 percent of the total, possesses by far the largest number of dailies although it still lags behind the British, Scandinavians, Japanese, and others in the ratio of newspaper readership to total population. Despite a gratifying increase in its statistics for literacy, the Soviet Union's controlled press and its news agencies are still outdistanced by their independent competitors in everything from size and quality to credibility.

True, there continue to be grave public questions over the total performance of the free press, or lack of it, the purposes of the proprietors, their other private interests, and their motivation. No thoughtful person can help but be disturbed at the rising encroachments of conglomerate corporations into an area of journalism that should be free of all suspicion of outside financial pressures. Nor is the inner weakness of the press, and its susceptibility to union and other employee pressures, something that can merely be shrugged off.

The truly astonishing prosperity of the American press, as the world leader, is not as reassuring a guarantee of independence as it once was; at home, there are too many weak spots. Abroad, with the exception of Canada, Australia, Switzerland, and a few other places, the situation is even less satisfying. There is no disguising the strength of television as a rival medium, wherever it exists. The serious economic position of a number of national and metropolitan newspapers of independent ownership in the Western world is not to be denied.

Yet, for all their probing and questioning, free peoples are not about to dispense with a free press. By every standard and requirement of the open societies in the world, the independent newspaper remains indispensable to the functioning of any system of self-government. Both have their shortcomings, but they are easier to bear than the out-and-out control and the lying of opposing systems. Nor can television, by any stretch of the imagination, meet the public's daily need of information on the complexities of a free and not very orderly society. In short, it is not in the democratic system, but in the world's closed societies, that pressures are rising for a change in the nature and concept of the press. Such pressures, in the long run, may prove to be greater than the dictatorships against which they are directed.

2. *New Roles for the Press*

This is the paradox of the free press in the declining years of the twentieth century:

It is, and by its very nature must continue to be, an independent critic of the manifold processes of government. Yet, in a world of five atomic powers and a dozen others with atomic capabilities, there are well-defined limits to what the most efficient and dedicated watchdog of government can attempt. No editor, regardless of his devotion to the public interest, can turn aside official pleas against the publication of critical information when national survival may be at stake.

In so crucial a situation, the self-restraint of the independent press usually approaches in effectiveness the government-enforced censorship of the controlled press. As the 1962 missile crisis between the United States and the Soviet Union so clearly demonstrated, the time-consuming practices of democratic societies can scarcely be invoked when life-or-death decisions have to be made at the top level of government within a matter of hours—or even minutes. Could *Pravda* or *Izvestia* have responded to the wishes of their government any better than the two great American dailies that voluntarily withheld disclosure of President Kennedy's naval blockade until he had announced it to the nation and the world? In matters involving the highest national security, the individual proprietors of newspapers, like their editors and fellow citizens in all walks of life, have learned that they must trust their government to act in the best interests of the nation and make their value judgments later. There is precious little room for maneuver in crises where tens of millions of lives can be wiped out and whole cities destroyed, where a silent earth bereft of humankind is ultimately possible.

All over the world, in consequence, the new destructive power of atomic nations has increased the tendency among peoples in open societies to trade a measure of freedom for what they imagine to be greater security. Sometimes it pays off, as in the case of the Cuban missile crisis or de Gaulle's decision to pull out of Algeria. But on other occasions, notably in the case of President Johnson's decision to escalate the Vietnam War in 1965, it can lead a great nation into a quagmire.

In any event, the leaders of an opposition press in a democratic nation (in the Western sense) frequently find it is no longer as popular as it once was for an individual newspaper to attack its own government, even when there is justification. No Indian editor was ever very anxious to assail Nehru during his lifetime. Few French editors were willing to take on de Gaulle. And a considerable section of the British national press was hurt in campaigning against its government. There is more to this than the risk of defeat, embarrassing though that in itself may be. Governments can—and often do—retaliate. Violent nationalists, always noisy in every land outside the Iron Curtain, regardless of numbers, frequently attack the independent press as a grievous handicap to a nation that has to compete with the controlled press. Dissent may be highly popular with the gilded Western and Japanese youth of the hapless universities, but it is looked upon with askance in nations that are dominated by their middle classes.

There are other factors that intensify the tendency of weaker and more cautious independent newspapers to tone down their critical views of government. The compression of most provincial dailies into monopolies in the West and Japan has inhibited risk-taking to a certain extent. Only the strongest and most public-spirited proprietors now dare to maintain an independent position against government pressure. Here, too, the growth of television has made a difference. For very often, because of television's inherently weak position as a licensee or creature of government, it may be used by public officials in an effective competition against an unruly, unreasonable, or undisciplined press. De Gaulle used to love French television for that reason, even though most of his French newspaper opposition was usually meek. And in the United States, President Johnson on occasion used to denounce his press critics on television, a practice that Vice-President Agnew followed in the succeeding administration. It is particularly galling to a journalist or a newspaper, locked in a dispute with the government, to be forced to respond to such television attacks. As if it isn't bad enough for the broadcast media to be first with much of the news!

There is one favorable aspect to this new and scarcely pleasant role of the independent newspaper. Few people in the great industrial nations, considering the current situation of the press in Western society, take stock any longer in Upton Sinclair's turn-of-the-century notion of a conspiratorial press, in league with cruel trusts against an impoverished and helpless people. It isn't that kind of world now, either in the United States, much of the British Commonwealth and Western Europe, or Japan. As Walter Lippmann once put it: "If the press is not so universally wicked, nor so deeply conspiring, as Mr. Sinclair would have us believe, it is very much more frail than the democratic theory has yet admitted. It is too frail to carry the whole burden of popular sovereignty, to supply spontaneously the truth which democrats hoped was inborn." These words, written in 1922, bear repeating almost a half-century later when the frailty of the independent press is so well understood by both its friends and its enemies.

Newspapers that have prided themselves on their durability and their independence are now being used in ways that would have brought roars of protest from the great editors of other days. In such situations as the Korean and Vietnam wars, the ever-strained Middle East and Kashmir, and the tensions between Washington and Moscow, the press has been employed as a convenient medium for the exchange of signals between the contending sides. If a trial balloon in *Pravda* is more closely examined in Washington than is a chance remark by the Washington *Post* in Moscow, that is a reflection of a difference in journalistic method. But it does not in any sense deter the grim business of signaling. Of course, it can happen that the State and Defense departments in Washington get their signals crossed and tell the press just the opposite things, as occurred in the long effort to reduce the level of combat in Vietnam. And it is also decidedly inconvenient for everybody when the Soviet government accepts a dim-witted suggestion by a columnist as a plant by the American government, as occurred during the Cuban misile crisis. *Pravda* may warn, as it did after a 1969 border clash with Red China, that a Soviet–Chinese war would inevitably involve the use of atomic bombs and "would not spare a single continent." But was this psychological warfare against Peking—or Washington? Or both?

These are the hazards of the new role of the press in the atomic age. The Americans and British may try to guard their news columns more zealously than their contemporaries in Paris, Bonn, Rome, New Delhi, and Tokyo, but they can scarcely fail to give prominent notice to awesome shifts in nuclear power. Such developments, like rival accomplishments reported from Moscow, constitute the very heart of the theory of deterrence through which the world hopes so prayerfully to avert atomic warfare. In a very real sense, it would be impossible to maintain what many call a "balance of terror" without the press on both sides of the Iron Curtain.

Neither the United States nor the Soviet Union has ever left the slightest doubt of the size of their respective atomic arsenals. Their respective news media have dutifully circulated authorized estimates regarding both the smaller "tactical" atomic weapons as well as the "strategic" hydrogen bombs that could destroy a city. Still, among both super-powers and their principal allies, a nagging fear has remained with regard to the lesser but still dangerous atomic capabilities of the Chinese under Mao Tse-tung. The United States in particular went to great lengths to try to downgrade the Chinese atomic achievement through advance disclosures of Peking's early testing. It was not a mistake that was duplicated in Moscow. Such publicity gimmicks could scarcely discount the atomic clouds that rolled up from the Sinkiang desert. The gathering of Soviet troops on the Sinkiang border was surer evidence of the importance of China's new strength, which touched off near-hysterical editorials in the Soviet press. The Chinese, in return, publicized their military preparations for defense.

The inescapable conclusion that is derived from these public convulsions is that journalism has replaced diplomacy to a large extent as a substitute for warfare on the battlefield. The ambassador whose silken manipulations once were deemed so essential to a Metternich or a Talleyrand now is seldom more than a glorified postman, delivering messages when directed to the foreign office to which he is accredited. His life too often is an exercise in frustration, his reports for the most part are filed and forgotten. His opposite number in journalism, the foreign correspondent, has superior means of communication and far more efficient media for displaying his intelligence. On occasion, the correspondent's information is also better than an ambassador's and his assessment of its importance frequently makes a good deal more sense.

It is no idle jest, but a bitter and perhaps unpalatable truth, that an American ambassador attracted the attention of the White House to his views by leaking them to the New York *Times* instead of entrusting them to the coded top secret State Department cables. It is equally true that another American ambassador was accustomed to show his top secret reports to the State Department to trusted journalists in the hope that they would make use of his information. More often than not, they did.

Scant wonder, then, that governments wage their bloodless battles for primacy in the headlines and on the small screen in an effort to avoid the ultimate disaster. Of course, a communications system that is not under government control always has the option of refusing to circulate threats and alarmist views, even if governments choose on their own responsibility to put them out. But the option is seldom, if ever, exercised.

The cynic will observe, with sour and curdled logic, that shock, fear, and bad news are the journalists' stock in trade, and reason enough for his prominent role in the war of nerves. It isn't quite as awful as that, for newsrooms aren't exactly hospitable to paranoiac monsters. The principal consideration in dealing with psychological warfare is quite different. No journalist can foretell, in a darkening time in the history of humankind, whether the warning that has been handed to him is merely news or a terrible and bloody truth. To withhold publication of the formal views of a government that soon may go to war is scarcely in the public interest.

This undoubtedly has something to do with the sharp reaction against war-making in a very large part of the independent press in the Western world and Japan. To be sure, national considerations of circumstance and policy play a major role in determining such editorial attitudes, as do dominant public feelings. But a swing in the press to an underlying theme of peace — sometimes peace at almost any price — is a decided change of front. It is less than a century, after all, since Hearst proudly told his staff that the Spanish-American War was "our war" because he had helped foment it. The Boer War, for that matter, was "our war" to an important segment of the British press, which treated the dissenting *Guardian* as a virtual traitor. Much the same thing happened in 1918 to the New York *Times* because it mildly suggested in an editorial that a chance for peace was near in World War I. Even as late as the 1930s, the wildly war-bent Hitler had his admiring supporters in the British, French, and American press and Mussolini, the hero of the war against Ethiopia, was saluted editorially in many parts of the world.

The development of the weapons of mass destruction, together with the demonstration through televised space shots that they can be dropped anywhere, has wrought a powerful change in public consciousness of the risks of war. And this, in turn, has had its effect on the press. The editorial Napoleon, at last, has been interred unmourned in an unmarked grave. For in the face of a public so obdurately set against bearing the human suffering as well as the costs of war, only maniacs today would counsel a newspaper to support preparations for new conflicts. In most industrialized countries, notably the United States, most editorialists face in exactly the opposite direction and campaign for reduced military expenditures.

This has had a strong influence on the moral outlook of the press. In Japan, where millions of citizens each year make an atomic pilgrimmage to Hiroshima, the newspapers have an almost fanatical compulsion to oppose the rise of a new military class. In West Germany, the target of so much Soviet suspicion, the press is almost the only effective force that has tried to restrain military expansion. In Britain and France, particularly after the disastrous Suez War of 1956, the press led the outcry against military adventuring and, in general, supported the troop withdrawals that came with the collapse of empire. And in the United States, the long campaign against the Vietnam War by an important section of the press almost certainly helped put Richard Milhous Nixon in the White House, only to turn against him. Even among such old and bitter foes as India and Pakistan or Israel and the Arabs, the newspapers almost universally profess to seek peace although they know that peace is nowhere in sight.

The image of the jingo press has vanished, a casualty of the atomic age. But tragically enough, the exertions of a large part of the independent press for the creation of a peaceful world have done little to dissipate the ever-present war clouds. It was so easy — and so irresponsible — to lead the outcry for war. It takes so long — and requires so much patience and effort — to achieve even a small step toward peace. In consequence, the press has pitifully little to show for all its good intentions. The new dispensation may have created far better and more responsible newspapers, but it has not helped them much with the impatient young who demand immediate and nonnegotiable solutions (usually their own) for the world's most intricate problems.

3. The Explosion of Techniques

It is not too many years since Vermont Royster, the editor of the *Wall Street Journal*, was both surprised and delighted in San Francisco when he was handed a printed proof there of an article within an hour after he had written it. "In that space of time," he said, "it had gone by teletype 3,000 miles across the country (to New York), been edited for my awkward spelling, had a headline written for it, and returned by wire 3,000 miles across the country to be set in type automatically at our San Francisco plant."

The technological revolution that Royster celebrated with such enthusiasm has shaken the press to its foundations. Once again, after a static and stagnant century, change has become the first law of journalism. True, there are still many newspapers on which John Delane or Horace Greeley could work without a great deal of instruction. But among dailies as different in political philosophy and journalistic practice as the *Wall Street Journal*, the London *Daily Mirror*, *Asahi Shimbun*, and *Pravda*, there is a common interest in facsimile editions published long distances from the home office by electronic means. Visitors to such modern plants as that of the Miami *Herald*, which is highly automated, come away wondering where the mechanical staff keeps itself and what it actually does. Through the marvel of high speed transmission, the Associated Press is able to edit its entire report from its New York headquarters with the exception of major news bulletins. United Press International is experimenting with still more marvels. And in London, over a closed circuit television set, Gerald Long can scan whatever he wishes of the intelligence carried by Reuters, of which he is general manager.

Such techniques give newspapers and wire services advantages such as they have never had before. For the independent daily press, in particular, it opens up the prospect of swift circulation of interesting material that can't be used by television either because it is impractical, inaccessible, or unknown. The newest methods also are easily adaptable either to a single national edition, as put out by the *Wall Street Journal*, or numerous suburban or regional editions, as developed by the Los Angeles *Times*. Despite the large costs that are involved in modernization, the chains and individual dailies that can afford the investment often find that enormous labor savings are possible in places where unions either are weak or nonexistent. Some pull back for fear of crippling labor disputes. Still others perceive the distant threat of government intervention if the press, by some unhappy turn of events, should ever become a rival of the broadcast media in the use of overcrowded wire circuits or radio channels. But the movement goes on.

One of the most successful ventures in the relatively brief span of the technological revolution is the London *Daily Mirror*'s electronic transmission of its Northern Ireland edition from Manchester to Belfast. It is an efficient and carefully planned operation that was put into effect in the late 1960s. The *Mirror*'s parent concern, the International Publishing Corporation, provided new Muirhead (British) facsimile equipment, web offset presses and plate-making machinery, and invested heavily in transmission by a combination of radio and coaxial cable under the Irish Sea. At the rate of three minutes to a page, the entire edition was sent to Belfast, where local news was added as needed. The plate-making and printing followed without incident.

The *Mirror*'s venture into modern production methods was expensive, for electronic transmission and photo-offset printing presses require heavy initial investment. But some savings were achieved in manpower. Where 450 mechanical people had been employed in Belfast under conventional printing arrangements, only 70 were required to keep the electronic photo-offset system functioning. By 1970, about 200,000 papers were being printed and sold by IPC in Belfast on a Saturday night under the new dispensation.

Despite its internal troubles and changes in management, the

IPC was encouraged by its Belfast experiment to do more planning in the facsimile-offset field. One of its more ambitious projects was a proposed new offset plant for Glasgow to publish its *Daily Record* and *Sunday Mail*, with a capacity for 500,000 papers daily and 800,000 on Sunday. Considering the state of the British economy, it was a venturesome business to think of expansion for the press in a period of generally reduced growth and profit plus an overall slump in circulation for the British press. But as the position was expressed by Edward Pickering, one of the IPC's top managers, "We grow or we die."

The Japanese, as pioneers in newspaper automation devices including facsimile, might have been expected to develop a major trend in labor-saving but it didn't turn out that way. For although Japanese newspaper union leaders were relatively docile and the membership on the whole created little fuss, the Japanese tradition of virtual lifetime employment by a single company stood in the way of major reductions in force. It could have been done very easily. But the Japanese press lords were well aware of what the consequences of such a social overturn could have been. They were content to continue in their traditional way. With wages slowly rising, the number of press strikes sharply decreased. Of the 65,000 total newspaper employees, printing maintained its share at 27.5 percent between 1965 and 1970, editorial slightly decreased from 26.2 to 25.7 percent, and publishing employment fell off from only 2.4 to 1.6 percent.

This indicated a remarkable stability for the industry at a time when *Asahi*, which introduced facsimile and offset printing to Japan in 1959, was publishing a regular edition in Sapporo and a multi-color edition in Hino; *Yomiuri*, a regular edition in Takaoka; and three major provincial dailies were turning to offset publication, one with a multi-color plant in Nagoya.

The explosion of techniques, which had such a varied worldwide effect, achieved its most impressive results in the United States with the expansion of the *Wall Street Journal* over a twenty-year period. From a modest and highly regarded economic daily with a circulation of less than 200,000 in 1950, its readership increased sixfold by 1970 under the stimulus of brilliant editorial direction and the imaginative use of every major innovation in printing and production. Its daily takeouts, or long team reporting enterprise stories on Page 1, its digested general news, its fresh writing style, and its policy of developing its own news put it in a class by itself. Much as it tried to hold down its size, the number of pages slowly increased in response to both editorial and advertising pressures.

What happened to the *Journal*'s New York edition was typical of the enterprise as a whole. From its main editorial office at 30 Broad Street in downtown Manhattan, all copy was sent by high-speed tape to its plant in Chicopee Falls, Mass., to be set in type. It was planned that the pages, when made up, would then be photographed and transmitted by facsimile to a new plant at New Brunswick, N.J., where the edition would be run off and trucked to New York.

A network of 100,000 miles of leased wires at the same time directed the flow of copy from New York and Chicopee Falls to eight other plants throughout the United States where editions of the *Journal* were published. For the Midwest edition, new presses were installed at Highland, Ill. And at Riverside, Calif., pages were printed from facsimile sheets that had been made up and sent from the *Journal*'s plant near San Francisco. At another plant in Silver Spring, Md., which served the area including Washington, D.C., the thrifty parent firm, Dow Jones Co., founded a new weekly newspaper, the *National Observer*, to cut down unused press time. After only a few years of publication here and at other *Journal* plants, the new paper built a respectable following and had hopes of becoming a profitable enterprise.

Such has been the manner in which some of the leading independent newspapers of the world have tried to meet the twin problems of rising costs and the explosion of techniques. As expenses continue to increase in the 1970s, there is little doubt that more proprietors will be forced into new labor-saving operations and more efficient use of their facilities. And this is even more true of Europe, the British Commonwealth, and Japan than it is of the United States. Everywhere, the remaining weaker units of the press have little choice between plant-sharing, merger, absorption by chains, or suspension of publication. In fact, this will apply just as much to the broadcast media, if they continue to proliferate, as it does to the press.

By every economic indicator for both the short and long term, however, automation is more likely to strengthen than to weaken the position of the independent newspaper of substance and quality. Group operations are bound to increase, as well. The staggering growth of the computer industry, in itself, will eventually transform printing from a narrow and inefficient craft to a broadly efficient technology. Satellite plants, so effectively used by the *Wall Street Journal*, will be a necessity for large papers as traffic clogs the decaying inner cities. New plates, new inks, and better color processes all will improve the product. And for the future, the concentrated light beam of the laser and the developing electrostatic printing process (which does away with ink in favor of pigmented particles that cling to paper by electricity) can produce changes of an even more startling nature. As for the complete electronic paper, presumably delivered by cable television on microfilm at the rate of 100 pages with the flick of a button, that is still less of a dream than a nightmare.

What these innovations will do to the human condition can, as yet, be only dimly perceived. One of the probable consequences over the next decade or so is an intensification of the trend toward union consolidation in the newspaper field. The formation of one big union out of a dozen or more smaller ones has been regularly predicted in Britain. But as one editor commented bitterly, "The unions are taking their bloody time about it." Why not? Even the condemned, as a rule, take the time to eat a hearty breakfast.

Yet, it is probably true, both in the United States and Britain, that the old union tactics of stalling, diversion, and delay through multiple bargaining negotiations are approaching the point of no return. But there is nothing resembling a statesmanlike posture among most employers' associations, either. Much as some hope for it, this perpetual confrontation will not end by decree. On that basis, *Pravda* may be going ahead smoothly with a new Moscow plant and facsimile transmission to its automated units in client cities, but the Soviet Union's method of handling labor disputes has no admirers of consequence in the West. The use of the new techniques as a weapon to beat down organized labor can only produce more strife, not less.

As for the individual journalist, the introduction of more centralized control already has made a difference in his professional work. To be sure, it has not turned him into a mere cog in a machine, as some feared it would. The efficiency experts' notion that a reporter could come running from a two-alarm fire to impart his singed prose to a computer proved to be just as impractical as most of their schemes to oblige journalists to act like accountants. What has happened, instead, is a rise in the demand for sub-administrators, or deskmen, to use the generic journalistic term. When columns of prose or type are spewed out quickly by machines untended by human hands, somebody has to read the lot, evaluate it, and make decisions about its use. No cathode ray tube has yet been devised to replace human judgments, good or bad.

To the business mind, the delivery of ready-made copy by the pound, neatly ground to fit particular editorial percolators, makes a lot of sense and the necessity for processing can be understood. It is far more appealing than the hit-or-miss assignment of a reporter to search for news that he may or may not bring in for an hour, a day or—inefficient dub that he is—a week. Standardized autos, food, and clothing are snapped up by an eager public. Why not news?

It is perfectly obvious, under the new technological dispensation, that the responsible editor is bound to be under pressure very often to take the pre-packaged, mass-circulated material and dispense with much of his staff-originated news. Except, of course, for the stuff that comes in such volume from the police, courts, City Hall, and press agents of all degree. To their credit, the better editors put up a fight for the right to gather and prepare their own news and wise proprietors give in, as long as they have the means to support such an expensive news staff. This, by all odds, is the most effective answer to centralization and standardization on any newspaper. No computer, high-speed teletype, or light beam is ever going to question a president or a king, demand an accounting of a mayor, sound the alarm for international crisis or local riot, uncover a crime, or find a missing child. It takes people to do the job and usually, of necessity, most of them must be young, energetic, and imaginative people. And this, finally, is the most vexing of the problems that confront all forms of journalism, but particularly the press.

The shortage of talented youth among the news media is not a new phenomenon, nor is it confined to a particular country or class. Among the youthful elite, from Oxford and Cambridge to Tokyo University, and from the Sorbonne to Harvard, there has never been a concerted rush into the underdeveloped profession of journalism. And it is almost as true today as it ever was. For better or worse, there is often a feeling of mutual mistrust between the editor, college-trained or not, and the distinguished academic who holds a First or Phi Beta Kappa key or a similar distinction. All too frequently, neither has much confidence in the judgment of the other—a peculiarity that is unhappily characteristic of the relations between the scholar and the journalist. The former publishes too little, the latter too much.

It is primarily in the Americas and Western Europe that the holders of single or multiple degrees will be found in journalism to any extent. Partly this is due to stuffy recruitment policies and lack of attractive opportunities, partly to a greater preference among the better-educated youth for more appealing professions or even the drab monotony of government security. But it is popular to blame the lag—some call it a "brain drain"—on the low pay and rag-tag existence that were the mark of journalists from the time of Jonathan Swift. That is not as true as it once was.*

The difficulties vary from one country to another and, very

---

* It is, of course, impossible to compare prevailing wage rates in different countries, and even cities in those countries, without figures on living costs. But, merely for illustrative purposes, British Information Services reported in July, 1968, that a journalist of age twenty-three in London earns an average of £30 a week ($72) working for a national newspaper and a salary of £5,000 a year ($12,000) is "not exceptional" in the top grades. In Japan in 1969, the *Nihon Shinbun Kyokai* reported an average beginner on a large newspaper, with a university degree, earned about $2,500 a year, but the system of supplemental wages and bonuses was rising sharply for experienced people. In the United States, the American Newspaper Guild editorial top minimum was $300 a week.

often, between different types of publications and broadcast media. In Japan, where a staff affiliation with the press or broadcast media generally amounts to a life job with assured benefits, the "Big Three" papers set the pattern with exhaustive tests that often discourage rather than attract the most talented applicants. In India, where so many university people contend for the security of government jobs or try to travel and work abroad, most newspaper publishers feel themselves helpless to attract the better qualified youth. As one executive put it: "Why fool ourselves? We can't compete in pay or security." In most of Western Europe, there is too much uncertainty in a still overcrowded field, except for the prestige or quality publications and the big chains, which still find more available talent than they can use. As for Britain, the chief problem for many a journalist in his developing years is a lack of sufficient opportunity for higher education. That may be remedied at least in part by the flowering of the new universities. The training programs that publishers have self-consciously operated in Britain and France are little more than low-grade vocational schools intended to deliver bodies into routine jobs.

Whatever the prospects for young journalists may be elsewhere, they have all but vanished in Czechoslovakia. There, when the standard of the free press was briefly raised for a few inspired months in the spring of 1968, the youth of the nation rallied to it with enthusiasm. It was an act of faith and a deed of bravery in a society that already had suffered greatly under both Nazism and Communism. But the Soviet-led troops that crushed the uprising in August did more than silence the gallantry of the broadcasters and the defiance of the press. It turned the young people away from the kind of society they had been taught was the sole hope of mankind. In the newsrooms, the old and compliant journalists bowed their heads and resumed the hard task of apologizing for the misdeeds of their masters. But for the youth, in Czechoslovakia as in other parts of Eastern Europe and the Balkans, such work was beneath their contempt. And so it remains, as freedom lies interred in Czechoslovakia.

In the United States, with its annual need for at least 3,000 recruits for all forms of journalism, the nature of the problem of attracting the youth is quite different. Every proprietor and editor concedes it is serious. Yet, relatively little is done to assist or even bring long-deferred recognition to many of the journalism schools that have provided so large a proportion of the young people for the news media during the last quarter-century or more. It is an incredible and indefensible neglect of one of the strongest resources of American journalism—the only practical and thoroughly developed system of education for independent journalism in the world

Partly as a result of such professional callousness, which affected all but a few top schools, less than half the 17,037 holders of journalism degrees from 1964 through 1968 went into the news media. A survey by the Newspaper Fund, which reached a maximum of 126 journalism schools, showed that news organizations took 7,830, or 46 percent. The rest went elsewhere as follows: graduate schools, 2,077, or 12.1 percent; military, 1,921, or 11.3 percent; teaching, 838, or 4.9 percent; other fields, 1,223, or 7.2 percent; and the remainder unreported, married, or traveling.* The daily newspapers, with proportionately larger news staffs and a greater need for new people than their competitors, attracted only 17 percent; the weeklies, 2.5 percent; the wire services, 1.3 percent. The rest were distributed as follows: public relations, 9 percent; advertising, 7.7 percent; magazines, 3.4 percent; television, 2.5 percent; and radio, 2.2 percent. While the newspapers continued to lead the media in recruitment of journalism graduates, public relations, advertising, and television made impressive gains over the five years while magazines and radio dropped.† Because of the insistence on prior

---

* Attendance at graduate schools and some forms of teaching were grounds for military service deferment during the five-year period, which coincided with the escalation of the Vietnam War, but this scarcely accounts for the growth of the adverse trend. It had set in some years before the 1965 escalation of the war and the call for larger draft quotas.

† The Newspaper Fund's 1969 report shows that the average American journalism graduate with a BA degree earned $128 a week and the average MA earned $168 (most MA's have some outside professional experience). TV paid $124 for BA's and $162 for MA's as compared with the dailies' $122 and $146 respectively. The best pay was in advertising (BA's, $131; MA's, $178) and public relations (BA's, $140; MA's, $190). True, one or two hit the television networks for $18,000 a year, but the lucky ones did almost as well in newspapers and news magazines. These were the exceptions.

journalistic experience among most television employers, there also were fewer opportunities in television for beginners. The daily newspapers' hiring of women at double the pace of male employment for the five-year period also was a new development for American journalism, the total additions to the newsrooms from journalism schools being 1,091 women, or 37 percent, and 1,865 men, or 63 percent. For the rest of their young recruits, the news media had to turn to the other parts of the educational system, from high school to the graduate faculties of the universities, and resort to the hard-nosed old on-the-job training practices.

The point of the American experience is inescapable. Keeping up with the latest techniques, important though it may be, isn't the main task of journalism for the future. For if the largest and most affluent of the world's independent news media systems has such personnel problems, it spells trouble for others as well. Surely, the daily newspaper in particular will have to find a way to improve its appeal to the young journalist if it is to have any hope of attracting the young readers who are so important to its survival. For the youth, and not computers or light rays or even cameras, are the hope of the future.

4. Television vs. the Press

Prime Minister Indira Gandhi, no admirer of the independent press, has dreamed for years of a state-owned television network that would serve the 500 million people of India. Having absorbed some of her distinguished father's mistrust and even disdain for privately owned newspapers, Mrs. Gandhi's faith in the government's own broadcasting media is understandable. It reinforces her image as a devoted Socialist, first of all; in addition, it has a rather dampening effect on her less respectful critics in independent journalism. All-India Radio may not be precisely the wave of the future as a communications medium, even in Mrs. Gandhi's eyes. But her commitment to satellite-diffused television, under government auspices and with American help, will bring the small screen to many of India's 500,000 villages during the 1970s if it can be done without diverting too much money from more urgent needs such as food, housing, and a broader industrial base.

The pattern of long-term investment in a state-owned television system, with interim reliance on radio and doubt about the nature and purposes of an independent press, is fairly typical of a number of developing non-Communist nations. Relatively few have Mrs. Gandhi's tolerance for the practices, as well as the forms, of a self-governing society. Some of the leaders of the new nations defend their restrictions on the news media by proclaiming once more the outworn values of old-fashioned European Socialism, which held a self-supporting press to be an unmitigated evil. But for most dictators, the assumption of power needs little justification; they simply impose controls on their newspapers and take over the broadcast media. This was what happened in Cuba when Fidel Castro seized power. And in Czechoslovakia, when the invading Russian tanks appeared on the small screen, the people knew it was the end of "Socialism with a human face."

Where newspapers lead a vigorous and independent existence, however, the uses of television and radio in government hands are not as likely to be arbitrary. And this is as true in a number of developing countries as it is in the highly industrialized nations.

All modern experience shows that, despite their economic and sometimes partisan rivalry, there is a strong element of moral dependence among the news media. This amounts to considerably more than acting as mere alternative or supplementary sources of news and opinion. It can become a matter of survival.

For while it is true that broadcast media in government hands are in no position to defend the press, it has been demonstrated time and again that the independent newspaper is among the first to protest manipulation of radio and television for governmental purposes. The British press rose up unanimously against hot-tempered criticism of BBC news coverage by a cabinet minister, Richard Crossman, and called it an effort to manipulate television for the government's ill-defined ends. The French press, similarly, attacked President de Gaulle's wholesale removal of French television people who had displeased him and promoted the cause of television news services that would not be so subservient to the government's aims. On the issue of news management in the Vietnam War, the press and broadcast media in the United States invariably stood together. The expulsion of a television correspondent from Saigon was just as serious an issue as the disciplining of the respresentatives of the press.

In the 1970 controversy over the American government's efforts to amass evidence against the Black Panthers and other radical groups by subpoenaing unused newsfilm, tape recordings, reporters' notes, and unedited files of various news organizations, the opposition of both the print and electronic media was firm and furious. What was at stake here was the ability of a free press to protect its news sources, historically the first point of attack by any hostile regime. Thus, the growth of television, far from reducing the role of the press, has actually strengthened its moral position as the leader of the news media.

For those who have never had much confidence in the press and consider it both a nuisance and a blight on society, this is difficult to understand. To such people, there seems to be limitless power in television—a medium that can transport viewers anywhere on earth and even to the moon. And yet, the proprietors who are committed to both media believe with few exceptions that the press has a more vital function as an articulate and independent leader of public opinion. The septuagenarian Japanese press lord, Matsutaro Shoriki, used to boast that he made far more money from his independent television network than from his great newspaper, *Yomiuri Shimbun*, and did it with a fraction of the people needed by the paper. But when he was asked shortly before his death in 1969 whether he would have given up his newspaper if he had had to do it all over again, his reply was: "I would never give up my newspaper. A newspaper means power." It was an assessment with which another multi-media proprietor, Lord Thomson, fully agreed.

Curiously enough, the same conclusion was reached in the heart of the Communist world, but for entirely different reasons. In the mid-1960s, the Communist Party's theoretical journal complained of an "inertia of attitudes ... that interferes with giving television the role it ought to occupy." A few years later, after some improvements in Soviet television news programs, a panel of Soviet journalists still complained of the "narrow-mindedness of information and poverty of content" in such newscasts. The continual protest, strangely enough, was that Soviet television news was not sufficiently timely. What this amounted to was the hard-nosed old newspaperman's mistrust of the electronic media rather than any ideological split.

The distribution of *Pravda* and *Izvestia* at the rate of about 8 million copies each daily seemed to the leaders of the Soviet government and the Communist Party to be more effective, politically, than any television program that could be devised. Partly, it was suspected that the policy of continually emphasizing print journalism might be due to the reluctance of the leaders of the Soviet hierarchy to exhibit themselves regularly to their people on television. None seemed to have any particular talent in that regard. But mainly, it was a commentary on the cautious state of mind of both the powerful secretary of the Communist Party, Leonid Brezhnev, and the nation's premier, Aleksei Kosygin. They were comfortable with print, uncertain of what television might do to them and their policies. It was big news when Brezhnev risked appearing on television for a series of speeches, in which he revealed himself to be something less than a spellbinder.

This may help explain why, in the Soviet Union, alone among the world's major powers, there has been an increase in the numbers as well as the circulation of the daily and periodical press. Nor is this phenomenon confined to Moscow, Leningrad, Kiev, and a few other large cities. At the University of Moscow Journalism School, where several thousand Soviet journalists are trained each year, graduates are shipped off as far away as Kamchatka to begin their newspaper careers. In fact, the press in the outlying parts of the USSR seems to be receiving greater attention than formerly in the declining years of the twentieth century.

In the United States, the argument over the relative merits of television and the press has gone on interminably for two decades. Each has appealed to the public through intensive advertising. Each has engaged rival poll-takers who, like rival psychiatrists examining the same defendant, usually have produced evidence to support their respective clients. Predictably, the public in the mass has not shifted its preferences violently. As a result, both print and electronic media have tended to become unduly defensive.

The statistical battle, instead of settling anything, has led to a number of exaggerated and even conflicting claims. An Elmo Roper survey for TV in 1965, for example, showed that 58 percent of those polled received most of their news from television and 41 percent believed television news to be more reliable, as compared with 23 percent for newspapers. But in 1969, a Louis Harris survey for *Time* magazine showed that 44 percent of those polled would be "very upset" if they couldn't read their newspaper for a month, but only 33 percent would react similarly to the loss of their favorite television program for a month. Walter Cronkite, the managing editor of CBS News, commented on the report of television's 58 percent superiority as a news medium: "If that's the case, 58 percent of our public is inadequately informed."

Another Harris report, this one in 1967, showed that television viewing was dropping off among college-educated people in middle income brackets. But the standard-bearer for television ratings, the A. C. Nielson Company, replied that the hours of weekly television usage among middle income families had shown a gain. This was typical of the kind of thing a long-suffering public had to endure. It was no wonder that all news media had to contend with a lowering of public credibility.

With or without benefit of polls, there can be no argument that both television and radio are able to present major news well ahead of any newspaper. And there is no doubt, aside from exclusives in the daily and periodical press, that they do so. But in the average 30-minute national news summary, no more material can be presented than is covered on a single newspaper page, and that only in bulletin form — a sentence or two to each item. As David Brinkley of NBC has explained so candidly: "It is impossible — physically and otherwise — to cover news in complete and voluminous detail on television. It just cannot be done. ... Television is a pictorial medium essentially, and if there is no picture, if there is no movement, if there is nothing happening, nobody is going to listen."

In the matter of trust and responsibility, many a newspaper editor is just as bluntly critical of his product as are the stars of television about their limitations of content and full interpretation. In a 1969 poll of twenty-eight editors and twenty-five public officials and civic leaders, a committee of the Associated Press Managing Editors concluded that there was widespread public mistrust of the American newspaper. The major cause, as pinpointed by 75 percent of the public representatives, was given as "over-attention to sensational news of violence and insufficient attention to serious news of community-wide consequence." Only 9 percent of the editors agreed with this finding. However, 64 percent of the editors and 65 percent of the public representatives concluded that newspapers are mistrusted for "half-told or misleading stories resulting from lax standards for reportorial research and backgrounding of news stories." Imprecise or inaccurate headlines and articles, inexpert specialized reporting, and a reluctance to censure professional misconduct by other journalists also were singled out for blame by the public representatives. As for the belief that the public more readily trusted television news rather than the press, 52 percent of the public's representatives believed this to be a substantial cause of the press's troubles but only 19 percent regarded it as a major cause.

Thus, the American journalist goes forth to face his fellow countrymen and the world in the 1970s in the strange and unaccustomed garb of sackcloth and ashes. He beats his breast and cries, "Mea culpa!" And he admits to faults of large and small degree. To those who are accustomed only to the bumptiousness of the journalist, this is a decided change of front. Normally, he has invariably resented criticism from all quarters and displayed a cheerful willingness to mind everybody's business but his own. Can it be that he has become an humble soul? Probably not. The current condition is temporary, a manifestation, very likely, of the familiar American disposition toward public self-examination and self-depreciation. The patient will recover.

But will he ever be the same? That, too, is problematical. The frenzy of revolution that is sweeping the world is no respecter of either nations or their most cherished institutions. It is churning through the great cities and the whole of urban society, the universities, all the professions, and even that rock of human faith, the Catholic Church. As the recorder of change, the journalist cannot escape the storm in the United States or elsewhere.

Under the circumstances, it is a rather empty exercise to try to calculate to what extent the fate of the press in general can be separated from that of the broadcast media. There are perfectly valid reasons why television, being part carnival and part news medium, should not be lumped with the press. But when a life or death issue arises, these differences vanish. All the news media — the newspapers and the magazines, television, and radio — made a concerted bid for greater freedom in Czechoslovakia in 1968, with the support of government and people, and all went down together before the Russians. Nor was it any different in Nazi Germany, Fascist Italy, or militarist Japan.

Amid the dangerous and divisive pressures that beset modern society, there are also times when it becomes an academic matter to try to measure separately the influence of the news media for good or ill, as if they existed independently of each other and served entirely different publics. What, for example, is the difference between a race riot that begins in Newark, N.J., after a false report is heard over a taxicab radio and another such disturbance that is attributed to a racial slur published in a newspaper in Hartford, Conn.? How can anyone be sure in these calamitous situations that a needlessly provocative picture flashed over television does more harm than an exaggerated headline in a newspaper? One can only shudder at the theoretical prospect, raised by Hugh Cudlipp of the London *Daily Mirror*: "Suppose my newspaper with its 5 million circulation went racist tomorrow? What would that do to England?" Fortunately, it won't happen. The news media in the West, after a period of trial and error, have learned from hard experience that there is good reason to be circumspect in the telling of news when racial or religious passions boil over. There is no question here of tampering with the course of events. What is involved, basically, is the exercise of good judgment in a difficult situation.

It is self-evident, therefore, that the press and television will have to reach a better working accommodation wherever they have joint responsibilities for informing the public. The expert election coverage in the United States is sufficient evidence that such teamwork may yield superior results. For the hard truth is that the press and the broadcast media are stuck with each other. Until something better comes along, which is likely to be quite a while, the public will be obliged to depend on both.

5. *The Free Press on Trial*

There is widespread public dissatisfaction today with representative government and the imperfections of the system of free discussion and free press upon which its value ultimately depends.

In the third decade of the atomic age, when man has grasped the means of his own destruction, the governors have become too far removed from the governed in almost every land where self-government exists. The governed suspect, too, with good reason, that they often are being told too little and taxed too much.

When they feel there is a lack of sufficient information or understanding of their problems in the higher reaches of government, they not unnaturally attach a share of the blame for their plight to the press. And they are not always so terribly wrong. Before a war breaks out, or before people take to the streets to seek redress of their grievances, the press does have a positive duty to blast off with a warning trumpet and make it loud and clear. That doesn't often happen.

After an existence of nearly three centuries, therefore, the relationship between free peoples and a free press has been placed under an increasing strain. It is scarcely an exaggeration to say that the free press is on trial in every open society, and its partnership with free peoples is being called into question by some of those who were once its strongest supporters. This may be tragic, but only the blindest of editors (and quite a few are still around) would deny it.

If the record of this uneasy partnership had been bad, the decline in the amount of mutual trust that exists between free peoples and their press might be more easily understood. But on the whole, the accomplishments have outweighed both the errors and the lapses in watchfulness since the beginning of World War II and the area within which the free press operates has substantially increased.

Consider, if you will, the progress that free nations have made in so brief a time span. Much of Western Europe, devastated in World War II as never before since the Hundred Years' War, has been rebuilt. The British Commonwealth, despite the severe economic trials of the United Kingdom and the defiance of racist regimes in Rhodesia and South Africa, remains a power in the world. France has survived the collapse of her empire, as have Belgium and the Netherlands. West Germany, through an economic miracle, once again is a dominant force in the assembly of free nations. Japan, restored to representative government, has become the third greatest economic power on earth.

As for the United States, keystone in this mighty arch, it has outstripped all others in wealth, productivity, and military power and has demonstrated its scientific genius by placing its astronauts on the moon. Most important of all, despite every threat of a catastrophic atomic conflict inherent in every war since 1945, that ultimate disaster for mankind has been averted until now.

If so much has been accomplished under an admittedly imperfect system of representative government and public communication, what has gone wrong? No one can be quite sure. In

Western Europe, the British Commonwealth, Japan, and the United States, it is one of the commonplaces of public discourse to ascribe every difficulty to a "crisis of confidence" in the forms and institutions of democratic societies on the Western model. This is a round, mouth-filling phrase that may cover any number of grievances, depending on the person or group involved. It may mean anything from dissatisfaction with the failure of the government of India to solve its food problems to the agitation over racial conflicts in the United States, the economic problems of Britain and France, or the concern almost everywhere over the disorder in the universities and the outrageous conduct of youth.

The common quality in all these problems is that they are not easily solved. It is therefore difficult for either the governors or the governed to find anybody outside each other to blame for their troubles. Under the circumstances, a certain amount of critical fallout is bound to descend on the press. For one reason, it is a convenient and visible symbol of national torment; for another, the press has become over the years a ready target for the release by all sides of accumulated frustrations and abuse. Nobody has asked it to pay reparations for past indignities, but perhaps nobody has yet thought of it. Give them time. Almost anybody in or out of government these days, no matter how weak his leadership, can create a temporary impression that he is a veritable St. George by denouncing the press for crimes that are either fancied or real.

As the position was put somewhat despairingly by Roger Tatarian, the widely respected editor of United Press International, "We are clearly in a period when 'news media' to many Americans is a dirty word, and when any conflict of views between press and government automatically elicits an endorsement of the official view."

This is not to suggest that the press is in the process of being turned into a national scapegoat and the inheritor of original sin. In his unprincipled political attack on the news media for criticizing President Nixon, Vice-President Spiro Agnew tried to rally public opinion against the press because it was too independent to suit him. He may have been able to scare some editors, but on balance their numbers were few. For his was a pernicious attempt at intimidation which, being so rare in the United States, resulted in an almost immediate closing of ranks between the press and the rival media.

True, as Tatarian observed, the Spironic attack drew cheers from the unthinking who rejoiced because someone in government had lashed out against a stiff-necked, independent press. But even among these zealots for autocratic conduct of the government's business, a certain amount of doubt must have been raised by two related moves—the use of government subpoenas that could have uncovered sources of press information about radical causes and the infiltration of the Saigon press corps by American military agents posing as newsmen. Of course, official Washington at once disavowed harmful intentions against the press. But doubts in such cases, once raised, are hard to put down.

Eventually, of course, the press will have to deal with the central issue that Agnew and others in government have raised, no matter how ignoble their motives may have been in so doing. For if it is the independent newspaper's contention that it is the principal common medium for discourse between the American government and the American people, then it cannot complain if it is blamed for clogged channels or an actual breakdown in communications between the governors and the governed. Certainly, television can't do the job in 30 minutes of newscasting, or even an hour a day. And radio for more than forty years has been little more than a vehicle for bulletin news, with a few notable exceptions. It is a hard and observable truth that no network, radio, or television, is going to do a great deal with budgets, social security, new tax schedules, public welfare, foreign aid, or other intricate issues that take up whole pages and sections of good newspapers. There may not be much sex in such stuff, as the saying goes, but it makes an enormous difference in peoples' lives.

News may be too important to be left to newspapers, but they remain the only available medium that can publish necessary information and background in sufficient volume and detail to make it understandable to the public day by day. If the public doubts or doesn't choose to read such voluminous presentations, that is something else again.

What it all comes down to, in reality, is whether the daily newspaper, as presently constituted, is capable of publishing all this news and at the same time getting at the truth. This is the nature of the communications gap that will have to be bridged, in one way or another, in the United States and elsewhere. For people are weary in every self-governing land of the nonparliamentary aspects of parliamentary democracy, through which so much of the business of elected representatives is done behind closed doors. There is rising impatience, too, with the evasions, half-truths, self-righteous justifications, and outright lies that are so much a part of accepted government procedures.

It is a narrow question whether people have lost more faith in the credibility of the government or of the press; quite possibly, both have slumped together in an era when few can claim victories for anything and peace seems a distant, far-off dream. There is no doubt that the public, on the whole, is not much interested any longer in the calculated and stage-managed government events that masquerade under the headlines and on the tube as news. Nor is there any real belief in the gyrations of nongovernmental public relations circuses. And this, in essence, is what rebellious youth on American campuses talk about when they ask their elders to "tell it like it is."

Necessarily, truth is hard to come by in the complicated modern world. But neither the elite of democratic governments nor the paladins of the press can shrug off public dissatisfaction by pleading that the job is difficult and perhaps even impossible to do to everybody's satisfaction. Two thousand years ago, nobody was satisfied, either, with Pontius Pilate's crafty evasion, "What is truth?"

Socrates had a better answer. When he was condemned to death on false charges in 399 B.C., he phrased the never-ending quest for truth to his fellow-Athenians in these immortal words: "In me you have a stimulating critic, persistently urging you with persuasion and reproaches, persistently testing your opinion and trying to show you that you are really ignorant of what you suppose you know. Daily discussions of the matters about which you hear me conversing is the highest good for man. Life that is not tested by such discussion is not worth living."

When Socrates was obliged to drain the cup of hemlock, his fate sharply discouraged the practice of the art of the "stimulating critic" among the politicians in the agora of ancient Athens. Nor are such people, regardless of their wisdom or lack of it, any more popular in the modern world. In the closed society of the Soviet Union, they are generally packed off in the night to work camps or prisons. In the open societies of the West, every excuse from the needs of national security to the precipitous flight of officeholders to the country over the week-end may be invoked to escape the Socratic persuasion and reproaches, the persistent testing of opinion.

As for the news media, television will invite a few well-chosen and controversial nonconformists to perform now and then if they are capable of a good show and rapid talk. The press, of course, continues to publish a handful of letters to the editor daily, and usually more on Sundays. But for all practical purposes, public access to the news media is even more limited than public access to officeholders. People do have a chance to see a congressman or an alderman, a mayor or a judge, at election time, but how many — outside small towns — have ever seen the editor of their local newspaper? Let alone talk with him!

If communication between the governors and governed is to be restored and enlarged in democratic societies, if the testing of ideas is to be resumed as a matter of national policy and public necessity, the independent newspaper is the only available force that can set a proper example. Such newspapers of quality and conscience as the St. Louis *Post-Dispatch* have recognized the problem, but only to the extent of denying the government's right to force them to open their columns to dissenting opinion. The *Post-Dispatch* wrote editorially:

"The newspaper (which is in no way licensed by the government as a broadcasting station) has an obligation to the community in which it is published to present fairly unpopular as well as popular sides of a question. Enforcing such a dictum by law is constitutionally impossible, and should be. As a practical matter, a newspaper which consistently refuses to give expression to viewpoints with which it differs is not likely to succeed, and doesn't deserve to."

This begs the question, in a way. The point is not to force newspapers by law or by codes of conduct, voluntary or not, into performing their proper duty. That is just as much a violation of the rights of the free press as the scattered attempts that have been made, here and there, to license reporters or revive taxes on news and other levies on knowledge. Nor can reasonable people differ with the *Post-Dispatch*'s conclusion that a newspaper should not suppress unpopular opinions. The fact is that, with a number of brilliant exceptions, too many newspapers in every open society still pay insufficient attention to minority causes and unpopular opinions generally. Righteousness is rationed in too large a section of the press and the unpopular critics and the minorities are the first to say so.

It is no answer to contend that the press hasn't space enough to recognize the protests of every crack-brained agitator, the first response of many an outraged editor. The description could have been applied, among others, to Thomas Masaryk and Mahatma Gandhi, who had to found their own papers to put their views before the public. So did Lenin, for that matter.

The modern newspaper in the more prosperous democratic countries has space for everything from pants for women (pages of pictures, even in the New York *Times*) to the most voluminous and detailed reports on sports and the financial markets. Why cannot the human condition and the quality of life on this unhappy planet be treated just as frankly, honestly, and persistently? Why is it so difficult to stimulate the testing of ideas so that the practice will be pursued at every level of society and in every matter of importance to public opinion? The Socratic method, which can't be squeezed into the format of a humpty-dumpty news story, may try the patience of those who are satisfied with life as it is, but it is still the last resort of those who are determined on change before they take to the streets and fight.

The British Press Council, which gives the public a better break in matters that require redress in the newspapers, has recovered from a poor beginning and earned such wide support at home that its example has been followed in a half-dozen other lands. The mere excuse that the United States is "too big" can scarcely be considered sufficient for postponing a fair trial of the system. It could be set up with little difficulty in New York City, Chicago, Los Angeles, and a half-dozen other metropolitan areas. The first experiments in smaller places like Seattle and the town of Bend, Oregon, did not come off too badly. Nor are the extensions of the Press Council idea, Norman E. Isaacs' notion of a Grievance Committee, or the Scandinavian "Courts of Honor," without merit as a place in which the public has at least a slight chance of communicating with its print peerage. At the very least, such things have more basis than the customary philosophical anarchy so beloved by most journalists.

There are other proposals worth considering. The Louisville *Times* and *Courier-Journal* have not exactly been forced to their knees, or otherwise lost their standing as independent publications, because they picked up the notion of employing an Ombudsman, or public defender, to represent people in the Swedish manner. And the Milwaukee *Journal*, owned by its employees, demonstrates anew the feasibility of diversifying membership of the boards of directors of newspapers, particularly when their stocks are offered to the public. *Le Monde, France Soir, Stern* and *Der Spiegel*, all publications of standing, have welcomed employee representation on their boards and made additional grants of power to them. Why not public representatives — and in particular *young* public representatives — on American newspaper and broadcasting boards?

Aside from changes in management practices, the newspapers could also look into the matter of a greater allotment of space — and time — in the shaping of public policy through broadened public participation. What is needed here is a more imaginative approach than the syndicated public opinion poll and a more universal instrument than the occasional letter to the editor. It could be someone called, for want of a better name, a public correspondent. Philip Meyer, in his widely admired inquiries into the opinions of black communities in Detroit and Miami for the Detroit *Free Press* and the Miami *Herald*, established the validity of this amalgam of sociology and journalism. Of course it is expensive; it also takes journalists who are trained in the social sciences, and it can't be done in a ten-minute curbstone interview. The development of such new forms of public communication could do much to help restore public confidence in the role of the press as a fair, honest, and disinterested representative of all forms of public opinion.

A public confrontation with the press on a regular basis, too, is not as impossible as it seems. True, it is impractical except in small towns for an editor to maintain open house for any citizen who decides to call on him. But, as a few brave editors have learned in various parts of the United States and Western Europe, the citizenry is perfectly willing to accommodate any proprietor or editor of a newspaper who wants to take the trouble to engage a large enough hall for a meeting. Such confrontations have been lively, even bruising to the ego of the journalist, but they have not been without value. If the great corporations of the West feel inclined to report publicly to their stockholders once a year, the editor of a newspaper is scarcely justified in neglecting a regular — and personal — accounting to his readers.

There is a certain advantage to this. The American Assembly, which regularly brings together public representatives of business, industry, labor, the professions, and government for debates on public questions, has learned that the records of such meetings in book form sell 50,000 or more copies and spawn still other conferences. It is something for newspapers to consider along with guessing games, beauty contests, and soapbox derbies, if they are to become more responsive to the public's needs. Their judgment, as well as their news, will have to be more deserving of the public's trust.

Whatever the method and however difficult it may prove to

be, the revitalizing of the press is a matter of the first priority for the cause of representative government and the health of democratic societies in these declining years of the twentieth century. It cannot be put off much longer. And it cannot be left merely to committees of editors who pass high-flown resolutions. Like any other key element in public life, the press will have to make out a more convincing case for its continued existence—a better one, certainly, than it is now able to present.

To that end, the familiar words of Judge Learned Hand deserve to be framed over every editor's desk: "The First Amendment presupposes that right conclusions are more likely to be gathered out of a multitude of tongues than through any kind of authoritative selection. To many this is, and will always be, folly; but we have staked upon it our all."

This is the shield of free peoples. To strengthen it is, and must always be, the mission of a free press.

Epilogue

The free press, like the free peoples who support it, is going through difficult times. In the two years since the completion of this study of their relationship, independent newspapers all over the world—with the exception of prosperous American papers and some others—have suffered from tightened economic conditions. Nor has independent television been able to maintain its role of seemingly perpetual prosperity; here, too, the pinch has been felt and the result has been an unmistakable decline in the volume and quality of broadcast news and public affairs. Just what will happen if cable television shatters the monopoly of the American networks by opening many new channels cannot now be predicted, but it is evident that the days of the automatic electronic money-making machine are numbered.

Equally as dangerous as the new economic problems of the free press is the growing contentiousness of many governments that seek, in so many different ways, to control the shape of the news and often the actual content of news reports as well. What totalitarian regimes do in this area is not really pertinent here, for their ways and their enforcement measures are foreordained by their very nature. It is the libertarian government, which proclaims its fealty to the principles of the free press while deliberately undermining its foundations, that raises a far greater threat to the democratic process.

Because too many journalistic properties are, on the whole, not very well managed, and the profession itself is subject to intense technological change, a threatening climate can create complications in and of itself. And this is particularly true in times of intense social change when the independent news media (I use the term as synonymous with free press) are almost always most vulnerable. For it is then that economic pressures rise, governments grow progressively more defensive, and the forces of revolutionary reform make menacing gestures on both the right and left. Under such circumstances, a hostile government—even though it passes no new laws and issues no openly repressive edicts—can have a considerable impact on what the free press does or does not print or broadcast. Today, more than ever before, the gathering and dissemination of most important news is a political act, and the struggle to control it can become virulent.

Thus, however optimistic the long view may be for a continuation of the troubled but ever-essential partnership between free peoples and their free press, the short view is clouded, obscured. For in the United States, citadel of the free press, new restraints have been applied to the news media through governmental action in the courts. The economy, too, has taken its journalistic toll. One of the greatest magazines in the land, *Look,* with a circulation that once exceeded eight million, was forced to give up, as were three newspapers in major cities: the *Boston Herald-Traveler,* the *Washington Daily News,* and the *Newark Evening News.* As for broadcast journalism, staffs were reduced and budgets were cut except for the biggest and most spectacular news—the Presidential campaign, moon shots, and the like. And all this occurred at a time when the American economy on other fronts was expanding and forging ahead at more than a trillion-dollar-a-year pace.

When such things happen in the United States, it is not surprising that the journalistic landscape takes on an even grimmer hue in most other parts of the world. Britain's industrial crisis is increasingly reflected in its press, with the loss of still another mass publication, the *Sketch,* and rough going for the national papers and numerous others (with the exception of Rupert Murdoch's sensational *Sun*). France has only 81 daily newspapers left, out of the more than 200 that started up in 1945, and the government has handed out a subsidy of 15 million francs (a little more than $3 million) to the survivors. With the exception of the giant Springer chain, most West German newspapers are in even deeper trouble. And, elsewhere in Western Europe, except for such authoritative publications as the *Neue Zürcher Zeitung,* the clamor for government subsidies and tax breaks for the press has become so widespread that editorial independence and even survival are clearly threatened for the weaker and less essential newspapers.

If the trouble in Britain and Western Europe is economic for the most part, the woes of the Latin American press are due primarily to the pressures of authoritarian regimes. For 1972, the annual free press report of the Inter American Press Association said:

At this moment there is hardly a country where the press is not subjected either to a frontal onslaught of its many enemies or to severe tension and threats....Even if practically every one of our Constitutions guarantees freedom of speech—written as well as oral—secrecy and news management and sometimes even prior restraints as well as open censorship are the order of the day.

Much the same thing is true of the tiny, struggling handful of independent newspapers in Africa and of the newspapers of the Republic of South Africa. What freedom they have is likely to be withdrawn on any given day.

In Asia, outside increasingly prosperous Japan and its thriving news media, the free press has always had a hard time making both ends meet and at the same time satisfying the governments that consider serious criticism as verging on treason. While China's emergence from self-imposed isolation has dispelled fears of aggression by Peking, and renewed Sino-American and Sino-Japanese relationships give promise of stronger journalistic contacts, the fundamental press patterns in the area have not changed. Indeed, in some respects there is more repression rather than less, greater risks for the press rather than greater security. For in Singapore, where Lee Kuan Yew's government does so much talking about its multiracial democracy, the *Singapore Herald* was ruthlessly put out of business because it criticized the regime, and several Chinese editors of other papers were thrown into jail on unproven charges. In the Philippines, where a kind of shotgun democracy prevails, two Chinese editors were suddenly deported to Taiwan, where they were cast into prison for years despite all outside protests. Very little, of course, could be expected from South Vietnam, but President Nguyen Van Thieu confounded even his firmest supporters in the American government by censoring or stamping out every vestige of opposition in Saigon's fledgling press at a time when peace negotiations seemed promising. As for the subcontinent, India's 16-day victory over Pakistan in the 1971 war effectively subdued the surviving press critics of Indira Gandhi's policies and placed an overwhelming burden on the shackled press of truncated Pakistan. Nor was there very much to cheer about in resurgent Indonesia, where the Suhar regime kept the country's tiny press "in its place."

The Australian and Canadian news media, like those of Japan, have had their problems, but they are well able to cope with them. They remain among the principal lands where the free press is able to fulfill its role as a watchdog and critic of government, sometimes more effectively than in the United States, Britain, and Western Europe. Elsewhere, the islands of freedom are weak and small or, as in India, forced into a species of self-discipline which some day may compromise their independence in one way or another.

Regardless of what has happened elsewhere, however, it is in the United States that the decisive battles for press freedom will be fought in the years to come. This is not only because of the pre-eminence of the United States as a world power, but also because of the essential strength and resilience of its massive engine of public communication and the broad guarantees of a free press in the First Amendment of the Constitution. Certainly, if the independence of the news media cannot be perpetuated in the United States without serious damage, then it follows that the entire theory and practice of a free press are in mortal danger everywhere.

Although the Nixon administration of 1968-72 bears much of the blame for governmental attacks on the press, and clearly neither President Nixon nor Vice President Agnew can plead innocent to an antipress bias, the problem did not originate with them and their associates. Five presidents since World War II, together with their Secretaries of State and Defense and their Attorneys General, have contributed to the tightened governmental attitude toward the press. Once the first atomic bomb was dropped over Hiroshima, it was inevitable that this would be so. For, under the Atomic Energy Act of 1946, for the first time in the history of the nation the news media were made subject to a legal system that involves both prior restraint of publication and advance censorship on sensitive news of atomic developments. The mania for secrecy was furthered by the National Security Act of 1947, which set up the Central Intelligence Agency.

Scant wonder, then, that successive occupants of the White House for more than a quarter of a century have sought, openly or deviously, to regulate what the news media can print or broadcast in areas that are sensitive to national security! It was, moreover, not exclusively a policy of either Democratic or Republican administrations, having been common to both. For example, it was no mudheeled conservative, but the liberal-minded Harry S Truman, who issued executive orders that led to the overclassification of many supposedly sensitive documents to keep them from public knowledge. The Eisenhower administration went far beyond that with its order to the Pentagon to issue information only on work that would make a "constructive contribution" to the mission of the armed forces. Both these measures proved impractical and had to be modified.

However, an atmosphere already had been created in which it became possible for the highest officials in the United States to issue deliberate misinformation to the public on grounds of national security. It happened during the Eisenhower administration in the U-2 case and in the Kennedy administration over the Bay of Pigs fiasco. But even the most libertarian government, once imbued with a mania for security, does not change its policy because of such setbacks, as the conduct of successive administrations in the Vietnam War has demonstrated. Yet, no President, no adviser to the Chief Executive, and none of their apologists could have hoped to keep secret for very long the record of falsehood and double-dealing that marked the course of the United States in Vietnam. Once Secretary of Defense Robert Strange McNamara ordered the compilation of that fateful record by a team of two-score people in the

Pentagon, it was only a matter of time before the news would leak.

When the *New York Times* obtained the Pentagon Papers and began publishing them on June 13, 1971, it fell to President Nixon to decide whether the government should oppose further disclosures or let the whole story come out. An earlier President, Theodore Roosevelt, angry at the *New York World* because of a row over the Panama Canal, had chosen to prosecute the paper on the ridiculous ground that it had violated an obscure law to protect harbor and other defenses from "malicious injury." Like TR, Nixon elected to fight, but his administration chose the broader issue of damage to the national security and thereby sought to avert the failure of the government in the case against the *World*. The result was an historic confrontation between government and press that went directly to the United States Supreme Court. It was a case that drew global attention to the basic issue: the people's right to know versus the government's right to withhold information in the national interest.

Strangely enough, the American press itself did very little about the Pentagon Papers during the first three days of publication, and relatively few news organizations published either the syndicated accounts or press association summaries. It was only after the Justice Department obtained a temporary restraining order against further publication from the Federal Court in the Southern District of New York that the story assumed top priority in the day's news. That was late on June 15, after the *New York Times* had run three installments. For 15 days thereafter, the *Times* was unable to publish additional material from the Pentagon Papers—the first time in American history that such a restraint had been successfully applied through the courts on grounds of national security. When the *Washington Post* subsequently obtained a copy of the Pentagon Papers and began publishing, it also was forced temporarily to abide by the restraining order. Other papers, although not a party to the issue before the courts, similarly were silenced.

During the 15 days of effective censorship through the courts, it became evident that a new and somewhat more abrasive relationship was taking form between the American government and the press. The use of the courts to bludgeon the press had something, but not everything, to do with this. Almost equally important was the climate created by the Nixon administration, which in its first three years had forcefully promoted a running battle with the press. Vice President Agnew's scathing attacks on the media, as well as President Nixon's more-or-less benign neglect (he held only nine news conferences in all of 1971) were among the factors that further poisoned the political atmosphere. The attitudes of the Nixon cabinet, notably that of Attorney General John N. Mitchell, contributed to the uneasiness (and even the alarm) of the press.

When the United States Supreme Court voted by 6 to 3 on June 30, 1971, to permit the *New York Times* and the *Washington Post* to resume publication of the Pentagon Papers, therefore, the first reaction of the press was one of jubilation. But, on closer examination, it was not a victory worth cheering about. For the court's majority ruled only that the government in this instance had not been able to justify its demand for a prior restraint on publication, and all nine justices submitted separate opinions. Only three stood squarely on the First Amendment and condemned the application of prior restraint of publication. Of these, Justice Hugo L. Black was the most outspoken:

Only a free and unrestrained press can effectively expose deception in government. And paramount among the responsibilities of a free press is the duty to prevent any part of the Government from deceiving the people and sending them off to distant lands to die of foreign fevers and foreign shot and shell. In my view, far from deserving condemnation for their courageous reporting, The New York Times, The Washington Post and other newspapers should be commended for serving the purpose that the Founding Fathers saw so clearly. In revealing the workings of government that led to the Vietnam War, the newspapers nobly did precisely that which the founders hoped and trusted they would do.

It was significant, however, that Chief Justice Warren E. Burger and three other members of the court—just one short of a majority

—took the view that other cases involving national security could in the future involve prior restraint if the government was able to prove its case. The dominant opinion here was that of Associate Justice Potter Stewart, who held that the President must protect state secrets and that prior restraint might well be the outcome of a case in which the government shows that "direct, immediate and irreparable damage to our nation or its people" would result from the publication of secret papers. In the Pentagon Papers case, however, Justice Stewart voted with the majority because he did not believe the situation was that critical.

Associate Justice Byron R. White gave a more direct warning. He said that the newspapers were "now on full notice" that the Justice Department may bring future prosecutions. He himself went on record as saying that he would have no difficulty in sustaining convictions in cases of security violations even if prior restraint was not involved.

It is apparent, therefore, that the press has won what amounts to a Pyrrhic victory in the Pentagon Papers case. The government has been encouraged to bring further actions in the event of what it considers to be serious violations of national security by the news media. And it is on this basis, presumably, that investigations and prosecutions in the Pentagon Papers matter continued long after the highest court granted the press the right to continue to publish them. The Solicitor General of the United States, Erwin N. Griswold, gave the government's reaction when he commented directly after the decision was made public: "Maybe the newspapers will show a little restraint in the future."

Maybe so. Maybe not. For the Advisory Board on the Pulitzer Prizes, which includes some of the most powerful editors and publishers in the land, unanimously voted the 1972 Pulitzer Prize for Public Service to the *New York Times* for the publication of the Pentagon Papers. And, at the same time, the Board voted the National Reporting Prize to nationally syndicated columnist Jack Anderson, for his reporting of American policy decision-making during the Indo-Pakistan War of 1971. The Trustees of Columbia University, while they did not favor the granting of these prizes, nevertheless declined to veto them, on grounds that the Pulitzer Board has a greater responsibility in such matters.

Just why the government chose to prosecute the *New York Times* and the *Washington Post* for publishing the Pentagon Papers, and failed to act against Anderson's publication of the far more immediate and damaging secret records of government decision-making, is something that has never been publicly explained. In all probability, it was a matter of tactics. Anderson did everything he could to invite prosecution, and at one point seemed almost to be challenging the government to take him to court. But nothing was done about it at the time of publication. Eventually, after a series of brilliant coups, he came a cropper when, during the brief period in 1972 when Senator Thomas Eagleton of Missouri was a Democratic Vice Presidential nominee, he lent credence to the accusation that Eagleton had—at least once—been arrested for drunken driving.

It is certain that neither the government nor the press is satisfied with the position in which each has been placed. Nor is the United States Supreme Court finished with the delicate business of interpreting the law in an area in which the Constitution forbids any law to be made. The Burger court, in reviewing decisions of the liberal-minded Warren court, has swung over to the government's philosophy in several cases not involving the press. And, further appointments of conservative members could alter the balance by which the press was enabled to publish the Pentagon Papers.

If there had been any doubt about that, it was dispelled by the Supreme Court's 5 to 4 decision on June 30, 1972, in which journalists were denied the protection of the First Amendment and ordered to tell grand juries the names of confidential sources of information given to them in confidence in criminal cases. The case was that of Earl Caldwell, a *New York Times* reporter who had won a decision in a lower Federal court that rejected his contempt citation and upheld his refusal to testify before a Federal grand jury about information he had been given by the Black Panther Party. The high court not only overturned that decision in the Caldwell case, but also applied its order to two other newsmen in related cases. They were Paul M. Branzburg, then a reporter for the *Louisville Courier-Journal*, and Paul Pappas, a television reporter for a station in New Bedford, Massachusetts.

Justice Byron R. White, supported by the four Nixon-appointed members of the court, handed down the majority decision which rejected the legal theory that the First Amendment is a shield behind which journalists may protect their confidences. Justice White held:

We cannot accept the argument that the public interest in possible future news about crime from undisclosed, unverified sources must take precedence over the public interest in pursuing and prosecuting those crimes reported to the press.... There is no First Amendment privilege to refuse to answer the relevant and material questions asked during a good-faith grand jury investigation.

The result has been to draw the Congress increasingly into the field of government-press relations. As far as the press is concerned, the way to offset the Supreme Court's decision against the current State "shield" laws protecting newsmen's confidences is for Congress to pass a national "shield" law. Just how constitutional that will be depends on many things, including the political climate in which any future court test occurs. Because the House of Representatives in 1971 rejected an attempt by a subcommittee to cite the Columbia Broadcasting System for contempt in retaliation against its documentary "The Selling of the Pentagon," it does not necessarily follow that the Congress of the United States will always be a sympathetic forum for the press. For the Congress, even more than the Supreme Court, follows the election returns. Thus, the unofficial truce between press and government during the 1972 Presidential campaign can scarcely be expected to herald a subsequent era of good feelings.

It is a nice question whether the government's antipress offensive has changed the tone, if not the actual content, of the news media. There are no calipers by which measurements of so sensitive a nature can be taken, and most news executives do not issue orders on how to handle every controversy in the news. But there is an impression, and it can only be an impression, that the television networks have, with few exceptions, become more circumspect about the handling of sensitive news impinging on national security. As for the press, while it is impossible to know at one moment the position of 1,750 daily newspapers, there is reason to believe that even the most determined opponents of government are going to give more careful consideration in the future to any new major confrontations on the issues that have gone before the Supreme Court. For one thing, such actions can tie up a newspaper in interminable and unpredictable details; for another, they are, as a rule, too expensive for all save the wealthiest and most important papers.

There also appears to be more interest in moderation on both sides in the press-government conflict. The growth of the numerous committees to resolve press-bar differences in the States is one symptom of the strength of the moderate view. Another is the national interest that was aroused by the formation of the Minnesota Press Council, the first voluntary State organization of its kind in which the news media have participated. True, most of the great newspapers of the land still oppose press councils and similar devices to increase public participation in their affairs. Yet, recognizing that the public deserves greater access to both publication and broadcast, every responsible newspaper is doing a good deal more than it ever has before to make available more space for minority news and opinions. The time has passed when a newspaper can be merely the personal instrument of its publisher; in fact, the relatively few that still exist in one way or another are on their way into limbo. In this sense, the revitalizing of the press has begun; if it is proceeding far too slowly to please the champions of wholesale reform, that is because large and complicated enterprises cannot be made over quickly or easily. Uncertainty is the foe, not the stimulus, of institutional change.

The continued development of the American communications system, one of the principal factors in the success of the American political system, now depends in large part on the eventual resolution of the simmering crisis over the nature and powers of the free press. While the adversary relationship of press and government is necessary to self-government, it simply will not do to have the two constantly at war. The daily business of government cannot be conducted in so poisonous an atmosphere. And a press that is under continual government surveillance cannot command the kind of public confidence and public support that are the very under-pinning of its existence. If Presidential trips to Moscow and Peking are in the public interest in order to seek an accommodation with the two greatest Communist powers on earth, perhaps an attempt at some future time to work out a better relationship with the news media at home will seem worthy of the attention of some future occupant of the White House.

Before there can be a revival of confidence, there will have to be a revival of trust on one basis or another. And this is as true of free peoples and their free press outside the United States as it is within the American system. There is no set manner in which this can be achieved; certainly it is not going to come about overnight or merely through wishing. Nor is the restoration of the economic well-being of the press as a whole, much as it is needed, going to be enough to sustain its usefulness.

For those few who may be attracted to totalitarian solutions, there is no comfort in the manner in which dictatorial regimes handle the basic issues affecting human rights. For, as Soviet Academician Andrei D. Sakharov has written of conditions in his country (in "The Sakharov Memorandum," *New York Times*, August 18, 1972, page 31):

Our society is infected with apathy, hypocrisy, narrow-minded egotism, hidden cruelty. The majority of the representatives of its highest stratum —the party and government apparatus, the most successful strata of the intelligentsia—hang on tenaciously to their open and secret privileges and are deeply indifferent to violations of human rights, to the interests of progress, to the security of future mankind. Others, in the depths of their souls, are concerned, but cannot allow themselves the slightest free thinking and are doomed to tortuous conflict within themselves....With hurt and alarm I am forced to note, in the wake of illusory liberalism, the growth of restrictions on ideological freedom, of striving to suppress information not controlled by the government, of persecution for political and ideological reasons, of an intentional exacerbation of national problems.

To this was added an eloquent warning for all nations in Aleksandr I. Solzhenitsyn's Nobel Prize lecture in 1972:

Woe to that nation whose literature is disturbed by the intervention of power. Because that is not just a violation against "freedom of print." It is the closing down of the heart of the nation, a slashing to pieces of its memory.

It may prove to be exceedingly difficult over the short run to sustain a satisfactory working relationship between free peoples and a free press. But if the effort can be made in the United States, the outcome could set a worthy example for a world in which there has always been far more repression than freedom. After all, no alternative has yet been devised that offers greater protection for self-government under a viable system that guarantees the preservation of human rights. The free press, being guided by human beings, has decidedly human weaknesses. But to shackle it is to shackle mankind. For almost 300 years it has dedicated itself to the preservation of human liberties. If there were no other reason for its existence, that would be sufficient. Its cause is a cause for all peoples. It is still the best cause.

Index

Abolitionist press, 115–18
Adams, John, 49, 51, 53–54, 61, 63, 66, 67, 68
Adams, Samuel, 51, 56, 57
Addison, Joseph, 46
Adzhubei, Aleksei, 369
Africa, press in, 275, 350, 400–4, 465
Agence Frances Presse, 279, 289, 373, 381, 420–21
Agencia Nazionale Stampa Associata, 279
Agnew, Spiro 468, 491–92
Agron (Agronsky), Gershon, 203, 406
Aitken, Sir Max, 431, 439
Akron (O.) *Beacon Journal*, 201
Aksenov, Vasily, 365
Albania, 337
Albany (N.Y.) *Register*, 69; *Evening Journal*, 121
Alexander, James, 40
Allgemeine Deutsche Nachrichten, 278
Alliluyeva, Svetlana, 364
All-India Radio, 482
Amalrik, Andrei A., 368
Amann, Max, 221, 222, 225, 226, 266
American, 253
American colonies, press in, 27, 28–45, 47, 48–59; number of newspapers, 59; *see also* United States, press in
American Newspaper Publishers Association, 335–36, 459
American Society of Newspaper Editors, 333, 347
Annenberg, Walter, 453
Archer, Thomas, 21, 22
Argentina, newspapers and press in: *La Prensa* (Buenos Aires), 327–32, 398, 400; *Correo do Comercio*, 329; *La Nacion* (Buenos Aires), 398–400
Asia, newspapers in, 465
Associated Press, 98, 123, 159, 160, 199, 237–38, 241, 245, 264, 268, 269, 278, 286, 289, 292–93, 302, 309, 323, 435, 440, 454, 473, 487
Assyria, 8
Astor, Maj. John Jacob, 208
Athenaeum, The (Czech), 214
Atkinson, Brooks, 302
Atlanta (Ga.), newspapers in, 443
Atlantic, 454
Augstein, Rudolf, 349
Automation of newspapers, 473–76
Australia: press in, 97, 200, 278, 435, 437–38; *Age* (Melbourne), 200, 438; *Morning Herald* (Sydney), 200, 438, 439; *Financial Review, Sun,* and *Sun-Herald* (Sydney), 438; *Herald and Weekly Times* (Melbourne), 438; *Australian*, 439
Australian Consolidated Press, 438
Austria: *Wiener Zeitung*, 92; *Die Presse* (Vienna), 105, 107; *Neues Weiner Tageblatt*, 181; press in, 274
Austro-Hungarian Empire, 192; press in, 19, 91, 92, 104–6, 181; *Beobachter*, 92; *Arbeiter Zeitung,* and *Neue Freie Presse*, 181
Azikiwe, Dr. Nnamdi, 401

Babylonia, 1–2, 8–9
Bache, Benjamin Franklin, 65
Bacon, Sir Francis, 21
Bailey, Dr. Gamaliel, 116
Bailey, William, 116
Baillie, Hugh, 240
Bainham, James, 19
Baltimore, Md.: press in, 63, 443; *Federal Republican*, 70; *Sun*, 97; *News*, 202
Banker, S. G., 212
Barnes, Thomas, 108
Barrett, George, 309
Bayfield, Richard, 19

Bayonne (N.J.) *Times*, 201
Bay Psalm Book, 29
Beaumarchais, Pierre, quoted, 71–72
Beaverbrook, Lord, 208–9
Beaverbrook papers, 430–31, 438
Beech, Keyes, 309
Belgium, press in, 92–93; 274; *Courrier des Pays Bas*, 92
Belloc, Hilaire, 145
Beltran, Pedro, 400
Bennett, James Gordon, 97, 115, 118
Berger, Victor, 183
Berkeley, Sir William, 27
Berling, Ernst Heinrich, 94
Bernays, Edward L., 182, 215
Bernhard, Georg, 176
Bess, Demaree and Dorothy, 244
Best, Robert H., 258
Beuve-Méry, Hubert, 417
Bigart, Homer, 263, 309
Bingham, Barry, 380
Birney, James Gillespie, 116
Bismarck, Prince Otto von, 141–43
Black, J. R., 138
Blanc, Louis, 101–2
Blick (Swiss), 412
Block, Paul, 448
Boer war, 143–46, 471
Bohemia, *Cas*, 214
Bolivia, press in, 400
Bolts, William, 131
Borthwick, Algernon, 113
Boston, Mass., newspapers in, *Publick Occurrences*, 30-32; *News–Letter*, 32–33; *Gazette*, 33, 49, 50, 52, 53, 55; *New England Courant*, 33–35, 38; *Evening Post*, 50, 52, 55; *Massachusetts Spy*, 51–52, 54, 58; *Columbian Centinel*, 66, 70; *Liberator*, 114–16; press in: 63, 443, 449
Bourne, Nicholas, 21–22
Boussac, Marcel, 420
Bowles, Samuel III, 118
Bracken, Brendan, 259
Bradford, Andrew, 36
Bradford, William, 49
Brady, Mathew B., 124–25, 126
Braham, D. D., 153

Brazil, newspapers and press in, 28; *Diario de Pernabuco*, and *Jornal de Comercio* (Rio), 329; *Correio de Manha* (Rio), 397, 398; *O Estado* (Sao Paulo), *O Globo*, and *Jornal do Brasil*, 398; *Tribuna da Imprensa*, 399
Bremundan, Francisco Fabro, 94
Brewster, William, 29
Brinkley, David, 487
Brisson, Pierre, 418
Brissot de Warville, Jacques, 73
British Broadcasting Company (BBC), 371, 423, 483
British Press Council, 433–34, 496
Broadsides, 13, 17
Brooker, William, 33
Broun, Heywood, 184
Brown, David, 67
Browne, Rev. Edmund, quoted, 29
Brucker, Herbert, 347
Buckingham, James Silk, 132
Buckley, Samuel, 26–27
Buffalo (N.Y.), newspapers in, 443
Buist, Dr. George, 130
Bukovsky, Vladimir I., 365
Burma, press in, 386
Burmistrovich, Ilya, 364
Butter, Nathaniel, 21–22
Byoir, Carl, 182

Caesar, Julius, 6
Callender, James Thomson, 67
Cambodia, press in, 381–82
Campbell, John, 32–33
Canada: press in, 97, 200, 435, 436–37; *Mail*, and *Globe* (Toronto), 200; *Star* (Toronto), 200, 203, 436; *Star* (Montreal), 200, 437; *Globe and Mail* (Toronto), 373, 437, 439; *Citizen*, and *Journal* (Ottawa), *Telegram* (Toronto), *Sun* (Vancouver), *Free Press* (Winnepeg), *Le Devoir*, and *Le Droit*, 437
Canadian Broadcasting Corporation, 436
Canard Enchainé, Le (French), 421
Canelas, Demetrio, 400
Canton (O.) *News*, 201–2
Caritas (Peruvian), 399

Carlile, Richard, 86–87
Carter, William, 19–20
Castro, Fidel, 332–36, 400, 464, 483
Catledge, Turner, 335, 457
"Cato" papers, 38, 39, 45
Cave's Gentlemen's Magazine (British), 47
Cavour, Count Camillo Bensi di, 91
Caxton, William, 20
Censorship and control of news: Great Britain, 19–26, 47, 83, 175–76, 185, 196, 259; American colonies, 30, 31, 34, 39–43; United States, 64–65, 66–69, 121–22, 179, 182–84, 254–55, 257, 258–59, 278, 345, 467; France, 71–72, 73–77, 78–79, 100, 102, 103, 177, 179, 180, 349; Switzerland, 90; Austro-Hungarian Empire, 91, 92, 105–6, 181; Germany, 91–92, 106, 141–42, 176, 181, 224, 225, 226, 266; Belgium, 92; Spain, 94, 95, 408; Russia, 96, 150–51, 152, 155–56, 186, 189; India, 129–32, 133–34, 212, 295, 299; Japan, 136, 137, 138, 139, 140, 229–30, 231–32, 269–70; China, 157, 463, 464; Soviet Union, 191–92, 319, 343, 362–65, 463; Czechoslovakia, 216, 291, 292–93, 357–58, 360, 362, 464; Italy, 219; Soviet satellites, 275; Hungary, 321; Argentina, 327–32, 398, 299–400; Vietnam, 380; Cambodia, 381–82; Taiwan, 383, 463; Thailand, 383; Pakistan, 388, 436; Panama, 398, 399; Peru, 398, 399, 400; Cuba, 398, 400, 464; Haiti, 398, 464; Chile, 399; Uruguay, 399; Brazil, 399–400; Bolivia, 400; Ghana, 401; Kenya, 401, 402; Uganda, 401, 402; Nigeria, 401–2; Rhodesia, 402; South Africa, 402, 436; Iraq, 404; Jordan, 404; Lebanon, 404; Libya, 404; Sudan, 404; United Arab Republic, 404; Syria, 405; Israel, 405, 406; Greece, 406–7, 408, 464; Portugal, 409; *see also* Libel; "Seditious" publications
Central News Agency (China), 304
Ceteka (CTK), 291
Chamberlain, John, quoted, 20–21
Chandler, Douglas, 258

Charles I, king of England, 22–23, 24
Charleston, S.C., 63; *American General Gazette*, and *South Carolina*, 57
Chesterton, G. K., 145
Chiang Kai-shek, 230, 232, 271, 275, 301–4, 310, 314, 323, 383
Chicago, newspapers in, 443; *Tribune*, 118, 121, 123, 198, 203, 204, 257, 258, 282, 307; *Times*, 121–22; *Daily News*, 227, 246, 309; *Sun-Times*, 457
Chicago *Tribune* group newspapers, 444, 445
Chieh, Wang, 10
Chile, *El Mercurio*, 329, 399
China, 10–11, 230, 271; newspapers in: *Gazette* (Peking), and *Miscellanies*, 11; *Wai Kung-pao, Shih Wu Pao*, and *Shih Pao* (Shanghai), 156, 157; *Hsinmin Ts'ung Pao* (Tungshan), 158; *Central News,* and *Ta Kung-pao*, 304; number of newspapers, 304; press in: 156–59; Central News Agency, 304
China, Nationalist, 301–6; press in, 275, 302, 382; *China Daily News*, and *United Daily News*, 383
China, People's Republic of, 305–6, 307–9, 310–11, 323–26, 341–42, 373–78; *Central Daily News*, and *Ta Kung-pao*, 304; *Jenmin-Jih-pao*, 304, 305, 377; press in, 304–5, 376–77, 463, 464, 470; number of newspapers, 305, 376; *see also* New China News Agency
China Weekly Review, 203
Christian Science Monitor, 457
Churchill, Winston, 145, 228, 242, 245, 248, 251–52, 258, 259, 284, 296
Cincinnati (O.), newspapers in, 97, 443
Civil War, press during, 118–25
Clapper, Raymond, 258
Clay, Cassius M., 116
Clemenceau, Georges, 176–77, 179–80, 193, 195
Clemente Paz, Jose, 329
Cleveland (O.), newspapers in, 443; *Plain-Dealer*, 264, 445
Cobbett, William, 65–66, 86, 87, 88
Coke, Edward, quoted, 21
Colden, Cadwallader, 49

Cold war, 281–89, 337–41, 469
Collier's (periodical), 202, 452
Colored America (Abolitionist), 118
Columbia Broadcasting System, 224, 289, 316–17, 451
Columbus, Christopher, 16, 45
Committee on Public Information (U.S.), 181–82
Constant, Benjamin, 77
Control of news, *see* Censorship and control of news
Cooper, Thomas, 67
Cornish, Rev. Samuel, 117–18
Coronet, 452
Correspondents, 470; German, 107; Crimean War, 110–12; British, 110–12, 113–14, 130, 145, 153, 175–76, 185; Civil War, 113–14; Boer War, 145; Japanese, 149, 228, 374–75, 395; World War I, 174, 175–76, 184; American, 174, 175, 184, 194–97, 218, 235; in Russia, 189–90; at Versailles Peace Conference, 194–97; in Nazi Germany, 224, 227; World War II, 240, 241, 243, 244, 245–46, 258–59, 264; in German Democratic Republic, 288; in Soviet Union, 289, 367–68; in Czechoslovakia, 292–93, 362; in India, 298, 392; in Nationalist China, 302; Korean War, 309; in Hungary, 321, 323; in Cuba, 332–33; in Vietnam, 345, 380–81; in Chinese People's Republic, 373–75; Indian, 392; in Rhodesia, 402; in South Africa, 402; in United Arab Republic, 404; in London, 434
Cotta, Baron Johann, 92
Coty, François, 418
Coughlin, Rev. Charles E., 258
Cowles newspapers, 444, 453
Cox newspapers, 237
Creel, George, 181–82, 194–95
Crimean War, 110–12
Crisis, The, 204
Cromwell, Oliver, 24–25
Cronkite, Walter, 264
Croswell, Harry, 68–69
Cuba, 332–36, 337–41, 467, 469; press in, 398, 400, 464; *El Crisol*, 400

Cudlipp, Hugh, 429, 430, 489
Czechoslovakia, ix, 213–16, 289–94, 351–62, 464, 480, 483; newspapers in: *Czeskoslovenska Samostatnost*, and *La Nation Tcheque*, 215; number of newspapers, 216, 291; *Rude Pravo*, 352, 256, 358; *Zpravy*, 359; press in: 215, 291, 292–93, 352, 357–58, 360–61, 371, 464, 480; Ceteka press agency, 291; Union of Journalists, 291; Czech Writers' Union, 360, 362

Dallas (Tex.), newspapers in, 443
Dana, Charles A., 119
Daniel, Yuli, 363, 364, 365
Daniels, Josephus, 179
Davis, Elmer, 255–56, 314, 317–18
Davis, Richard Harding, 145
Dawson, Geoffrey, 205, 208
Day, Benjamin, 97
Daye, Stephen and Matthew, 29–30
Defoe, Daniel, 44, 46
De la Harpe, Jean François, 95–96
Delancey, Justice James, 40–43
Delane, John Thadeus, 107–14, 439
Democracy, Greek ideal of, 2, 4; *see also* Freedom, ideal of
Denmark, press in, 93–94, 274; *Berlingske Tidende*, 94
Denver (Colo.) *Rocky Mountain News*, 181
Dernburg, Dr. Bernhard, 171, 174
Desmoulins, Camille, 70–71, 74, 75
Detroit (Mich.), newspapers in, 443, 448; *News*, 448; *Free Press*, 448, 497
Deutsche Nachrichten Bureau (DNB), 226
Deutsche Press Agentur, 278, 373
Devlin, Lord, 433
Dickens, Charles, 113
Dietrich, Otto, 241
Dih Ch'u-ching, 157
Dines, Alberto, 398
Diurnall Occurrences, 22
Domei News Agency (Japan), 254, 269, 270–71
Douglass, Frederick, 118
Dow Jones, 476; service, 435

Dryfoos, Orvil, 338
Duane, William, 65, 67, 131–32
Dubcek, Alexander, 351, 352–62
Du Bois, William E. B., 204
Dudintsev, Vladimir, 318
Duerrenmatt, Peter, 412
Dumas, Alexandre, 78, 79, 80, 82
Durrell, William, 67
Dutacq, Armand, 81

Eastman, Max, 183, 190
Ecuador, press in, 28
Edes, Benjamin, 49, 50, 52, 54, 55
Eher Verlag, 221, 225, 226, 266
Ehrenburg, Ilya, 250, 260, 318, 319, 343
Eisenhower, Dwight D., 263, 267, 268, 309, 311, 334, 336, 343, 395
Elevator (Abolitionist), 118
Elizabeth I, queen of England, 19–20
Emporia (Kan.) *Gazette*, 197, 243
England, *see* Great Britain
Euripides, 4, 5
Europe, newspapers in, 465
Express, L' (French), 421

Fairfax, John & Sons, 438
Fascism, 216–20
Fatherland, 171
Fauvet, Jacques, 417–18
Fedin, Konstantin A., 364
Fenno, John, 64, 65
Fereos, Rigas, 93
Fernandez, Helio, 398
Fielding, Henry, 47
Finland, press in, 94, 274, 409; *Helsingen Sanomat*, 409
Fitzpatrick, D. R., 311
Fontaine, André, 418
Ford, Guy Stanton, 182
Foreign Affairs, 287
Foreign correspondents, *see* Correspondents
Fortune, 203
Fort Worth (Tex.), newspapers in, 443
Fourdrinier, Henry and Sealy, 98
Fox, Charles James, 84
FP Publications, 436
France: press in: 16th century, 16–19;

French Revolution, 70–77; 19th century, 100–4, 152–53; World War I, 172, 175, 176–77, 179–80, 200, 215, 227; World War II, 243; 20th century, 272–73, 278, 349; decline, 415–16; contemporary, 415–22, 455, 472; revenues, 416; newspapers in: *Gazette de France*, 17–19, 20, 71, 72, 76, 81; *Journal Officiel*, 18; *Les Nouvelles Ecclesiastiques*, 72; *Les États Généraux*, and *Le Patriote Français*, 73; *L'Ami du Peuple, Le Père Duchesne, Mercure de France*, and *Revolutions de France et de Brabant*, 74; number of newspapers, 74, 272–73, 415, 421; *Journal de L'Empire*, 76; *Phare de la Loire*, 81; *La Presse*, 81, 103; *La Justice*, 152; *L'Homme Libre*, 176–77; *L'Homme Enchaîné*, 177, 179, 180; *Bonnet Rouge*, and *Le Journal*, 180; *France Conservateur*, 349; newspaper readership, 415; *La France*, and *Le Sud-Ouest* (Bordeaux), *Ouest-France* (Rennes), *Le Progres* (Lyons), *Le Provençal* (Marseilles), and *Voix du Nord* (Lille), 420; *see also* Paris, newspapers in
Franklin, Benjamin, 35–38, 40, 44, 48, 52, 53, 55–56
Franklin, James, 33–36
Frederic, Harold, 149–50
Freedom, ideal of, 272; Sumerian, 1–2; Greek, 4–6, 7; Israel, 8–10; Massachusetts Bay Colony, 28–29; France, 73, 77; post-Napoleonic Europe, 96; John Stuart Mill, 127–28; Roosevelt's Four Freedoms, 247, 296
"Freedom of Information" law, United States, 458–59
Free press, 272; characteristics of, xi, 126–28; Greece, ancient, 2–4; Rome, 6–7; China, ancient, 11; 15th century, 15; "Areopagitica" (Milton), 23–24; American colonies, 38–45, 53–54, 58–59; Zenger case, 39–42, 44–45; United States, 59-60, 63–70, 96, 97–99, 235–36, First Amendment in Constitution, 59–63, 440, 498, Commission on

Free press (*Continued*)
Freedom of the Press, 276–78, recent decisions and laws, 458–59; France, 71–74, 77–78, 272–73; Great Britain, 83, 96, 146, 275–76; Belgium, 92–93, 97; Netherlands, 93, 97, 274; Denmark, 93–94, 274; Sweden, 94, 274; Spain, 94–95; Russia, 95–96; Australia, 97, 350; Canada, 97, 350; Scandinavia, 97, 274, 350; Switzerland, 97, 274, 350; India, 133, 274, 436, 464, 465; Japan, 136–37, 140, 274–75, 350, 396, 465; post-World War II, 272–80, 350; Italy, 273; Nationalist China, 275; New Zealand, 278, 350; Argentina, 331, 398; Greece, 407–8; contemporary status, 462–66; Czechoslovakia, 464, 480; future of, 464–66; as critic of government, 466–68; future responsibilities of, 466–73; and nuclear power, 469–70; as platform for opposing national points of view, 469–72; and psychological warfare, 470; and antiwar opinion, 471–72; relation to free people, 489–97; and dissenting opinion, 494–96; *see also* Censorship and control of news
French Revolution, 70–71, 74–75
Freneau, Philip, 64–65
Friendly, Alfred, 338
Friendly, Fred W., 316
Fukuchi, Genichiro, 138, 229
Fukuzawa, Yuchichi, 229
Funk, Walther, 223
Füssli, Johann Heinrich, 89–90
Fust, Johann, 13

Gainza Paz, Alberto, 327–32, 400
Galanskov, Yuri T., 365
Gallagher, Wes, 440
Gandar, Laurence, 402
Gandhi, Indira, 389, 390, 482
Gandhi, Mahatma, 210–12, 295–96, 297–98, 495
Gannett, Frank E., 202
Gannett newspapers, 237, 442, 444–45, 446
Garrison, William Lloyd, 114–15, 127

Garvey, Marcus, 204
Gazeta Nueva (Spanish), 94
German Information Office, New York City, 171–72
Germany, 11–15, 220–28; newspapers in: *Avisa Relation oder Zeitung, Frankfurther Journal,* and *Frankfurter Postamtzeitung,* 17; *Allgemeine Zeitung* (Augsburg), 19, 78, 89, 92; *Argus,* and *Rheinische Merkur,* 76; *Hamburgische Correspondent,* and *Kölnische Zeitung,* 92; *Vossische Zeitung,* 92, 106, 164, 176, 225, 226; *Rheinische Zeitung,* 100; *Neue Rheinische Zeitung,* 106; *Frankfurter Zeitung,* 142, 164, 180, 224, 226; *Berliner Tageblatt,* 162–71, 176, 181, 226; *Norddeutsche Allgemeine Zeitung,* 163, 165; *Kreuz Zeitung,* 164; *Vorwärts,* 165; *Breslauer Volkswacht,* and *Zukunst,* 176; *Berliner Boersenzeitung,* 223, 261–62; *Berliner Illustrierte, Berliner Morgenpost,* and *Deutsche Allgemeine Zeitung,* 226; number of newspapers in, 226, 266; press in: 17, 76, 91–92, 97, 106, 141–43, 162–72, 200; under Hitler, 221–28 *passim,* 241, 265–66; Association of German Newspaper Publishers, 225; Editor's Law of *1933,* 225; Deutsche Nachrichten Bureau (DNB), 226
Germany, Democratic Republic of, 288; press in, 274, 288; *Neues Deutschland,* 274; *Hamburger Abendblatt,* 274, 413
Germany, Federal Republic of, 288; newspapers in: number of newspapers, 273, 413; *Die Welt* (Berlin), 273–74, 413; *Süddeutsche Zeitung,* 274; *Bild Zeitung,* 274, 413; *Frankfurter Allgemeine Zeitung,* 274, 414; revenues, 415, 416; press in: 273–74, 349–50, 412–15, 416, 472; *Allgemeine Deutsche Nachrichten,* and *Deutsche Press Agentur,* 278
Ghana, press in, 401, 403
Gill, John, 49, 50, 54, 55
Ginsburg, Aleksandr, 365
Girardin, Emile de, 81, 103

Glover, Rev. Jose, 29
Godkin, Edwin Lawrence, 146, 147
Goebbels, Paul Joseph, 225, 226, 227, 228, 241–42, 252, 259, 265–66
Goerres, Joseph, 76
Gordon, William, 38
Gorki, Maxim, 190
Government control of news, *see* Censorship and control of news
Grand Rapids (Mich.) *Herald*, 282
Great Britain: press in: 16th century, 19–27; printing regulation act of *1662*, 25, 26; 18th century, 44–45, 46–48, 82–85, 96; newspaper stamp tax, 85, 86, 99, 112–13; 19th century, 85–88, 98, 107–14; Boer War, 143–46, 471; World War I, 172–73, 176, 185; 20th century, 205–10, 238, 416, 472, 480; World War II, 259, 263; Royal Commission inquiry, 275–76; British Press Council, 276, 349; Profumo scandal, 348–49; revenues, 416; contemporary, 422–35, 455; British Press Council, 433–34, 496; Newspaper Proprietors Association, 435; Press Association, 435; salaries of journalists, 479n; *see also* American colonies; newspapers in: *Gazette* (Oxford), 25; *North Briton*, 47; *L'Ambigu*, 76; *Guardian* (Manchester), 145–46, 166, 209, 210, 335, 430, 431–32, 471; number of newspapers in, 259, 276, 423, 428, 432; newspaper readership in, 423, 432, 465; *Evening News* (Manchester), 431–32; *see also* London, newspapers in
Greece, ancient, 2–6
Greece: press in, 93, 406–8; *Ellenika Chronika, Ephemeris,* and *Greek Telegraph,* 93; *Ta Nea* (Athens), 407; *To Vima* (Athens), 407
Greeley, Horace, 97, 98, 99, 118, 119, 125, 127
Green, Bartholomew, 32, 33
Green, Samuel, 30
Grey, Anthony, 373–74
Griffith, Arthur, 207
Grossman, Vassily, 250
Guiana, press in, 28

Gutenberg, Johann, ix, 12–13, 14–15
Gutenberg Bible, 13

Hadden, Briton, 202
Haiti, press in, 398, 464
Halberstam, David, 345
Hale, William Bayard, 175
Haley, Sir William, 427
Hamilton, Alexander, 59–60, 61, 62, 64, 68, 69–70
Hamilton, Andrew, 40–43
Hamilton, Denis, 426–27
Hammurabi, 1–2
Hand, Learned, quoted, 498
Hansard, Luke, 86
Harden, Maximilian, 176
Harley, Robert, 44
Harmsworth-King, Cecil, 429
Harper's, 454
Harrer, Karl, 221
Harris, Benjamin, 30–31
Harvard Press, 29–30
Havas, Charles, 80–82, 103–4
Havas Agency (Agence Havas), 18, 81–82, 103–4, 142, 199, 200, 278
Hearst, William Randolph, 146–48, 175, 227, 237, 244, 444, 471
Hearst, William Randolph, Jr., 444
Hearst newspapers, 146–48, 257, 282, 288, 314, 317, 446, 447; *see also* International News Service
Hébert, Jacques Rene, 74, 75
Heine, Heinrich, 78
Heinzerling, Lynn, 240
Hemingway, Ernest, 203–4
Henry, Patrick, 50, 62
Herzen, Alexander, 151
Hickey, James Augustus, 131
Higgins, Marguerite, 309
Hills, Lawrence, 193
Hilton, Ronald, 334
Hitler, Adolf, 220–28, 240–48, 261–68 *passim,* 471
Hittin, Thomas, 19
Hoe, R. & Co., 98
Hofmann, Paul, 362
Holt, Charles, 67
Holt, John, 49

Hong Kong, press in, 385
Hopkins, Harry, 252
Hopkinson, Francis, 54
Houston (Tex.), newspapers in, 443
Howard, Jack, 444
Howard, Roy, 184, 204
Hsin Hua, *see* New China News Agency
Hudson (N.Y.) *Wasp*, 68
Hugenberg, Alfred, German editor, 226
Hugo, Victor, 102, 103
Hui, Ch'ian Hsio, 156
Hungary, 320–23; newspapers in: *Diet Bulletin*, 104; *Pesti Hirlap*, 105; *Kis Ujsag*, 321; *Literary Gazette* (*Irodalmi Ujsag*), 321; press in: 275, 321, 372
Hung Chi (Chinese Republic), 377
Hunt, Leigh, 86
Hutchins, Robert M., 277–78
Hutchinson (Kans.) *News*, 457

Illinois, newspapers in, 97
India, 129–35, 210–13, 275, 294–301, 341, 389–92; newspapers in: *Indian World* (Calcutta), 67; *Som Prakash* (Bengal), 130; *Times of India* (Bombay), 130, 134, 391; *Amrita Bazar Patrika* (Calcutta), 130, 298, 391; *Gazette*, and *Journal* (Bengal), *India World*, 131; *Journal* (Calcutta), 132; *Sambad Kaumidi*, 132; *Civil and Military Gazette* (Lahore), *Pioneer* (Allahabad), *Statesman* (Calcutta), 134; *Kesari*, 134, 211; *Hindu* (Madras), 134, 296, 391; *Young India*, 210, 211–12, 295; *National Herald* (Lucknow), *Dinamani*, and *Harijan*, 295; *Indian Express*, 295, 391; *Chatan* (Lahore), 388; number of newspapers in, 390; *Hindustan Standard*, and *Hindustan Times*, 391; press in: 129–35, 210–12, 275, 278, 295, 298–99, 390–92, 436, 472, 480
Indonesia, 275, 300, 386–88; press in, 387–88; *Indonesia Raya*, 387
Inter-American Press Association, 398, 399, 400
International Monthly, 171
International News Service (INS), 238, 278, 288, 454n

International Press Exchange, 171
International Press Institute, 380, 404, 407, 459
International Publishing Corporation, 401, 429, 430, 474–75
Iraq, press in, 404
Ireland, 206–8; Dublin *Daily Express*, 160
Irvin, Bede, 264–65
Isaac, Norman E., 496
Isaacs, Harold, 302
Israel, ancient, 8–10
Israel, 208–10, 286; newspapers in: *Ha'aretz*, 203; *Palestine* (later Jerusalem) *Post*, 203; newspaper readership, 405; number of newspapers, 405; *Jerusalem Post*, 406; press in: 404–6, 472
Israeli Broadcasting Service, 406
Italy, 14, 216–20; newspapers in: *Acta Diurna*, 6–7; *Il Risorgimento*, and *Giovine Italia*, 91, 92; *Il Popolo d'Italia*, 217, 218, 219, 273, 412; *Corriere della Sera* (Milan), 217, 219, 273, 411; *La Stampa* (Turin), 217, 219, 411; number of newspapers, 217, 273, 411; *Il Messagero* (Rome), 217, 411; *Corriere Padona* (Ferrara), *Il Mattino* (Naples), *Il Secolo* (Milan), and *Giornale d'Italia*, 219; *Il Gazzettino* (Venice), and *Il Tempo* (Rome), 411; *Il Giorno* (Rome), 411–12; *Paesa Sera* (Rome), 412; press in: 90–91, 97, 200, 215, 217, 219, 273, 410–12; Stefani News Agency, 219, 279; Agencia Nazionale Stampa Associata, 279
Ives, Frederic Eugene, 125
Ivory Coast, press in, 403

Jakande, Latif, 402
James I, king of England, 20–22
Japan, 135–41, 149, 227–33, 268–70, 392–96; press in: 137–41, 227–32, 238, 268–71, 274–75, 393–95, 396, 416, 455, 472, 475, 480; Domei News Agency, 254, 269, 270–71; salaries of journalists, 479n; newspapers in: *Nichi Nichi* (Tokyo), and *Jiji Shimpo,* 138;

Mainichi Shimbun (Tokyo), 138, 139, 229, 274, 394, 395; *Mainichi Shimbun* (Yokohama), 139; *Yomiuri Shimbun* (Tokyo), 139, 229, 274, 394, 475, 484; *Asahi Shimbun* (Tokyo), 139, 229–30, 231–32, 274, 394, 395, 455, 473, 475; *Kokumin*, 140; number of newspapers, 275, 394; *Nihon Kezai Shimbun*, 375; newspaper readership in, 465
Jefferson, Thomas, 57, 60, 62, 64–65, 67, 68, 69
Jersey Journal, 446
Jewish Correspondence Bureau, 203
Johnson, Lyndon B., 343, 359, 379, 467, 468
Johnson, Nicholas, 451
Johnson, Samuel, 47
Jones, George, 119
Jones, Russell, 323
Jordan, press in, 404
Journalists, 479–82; labor relations, 446–49, 477; salaries, 479n; shortage of, 479, 480–81; training of, 479–80, 481

Kalischer, Peter, 309
Kansas City (Mo.), *Star*, 203; newspapers in, 443
Kapitsa, Pyotr L., 366
Kashmiri, Shorish, 388
Kennedy, Ed, 268
Kennedy, John F., 333, 335, 337, 338–40, 343, 344–46; assassination of, 346–48
Kent, James, 68
Kenya: press in, 401, 402, 403; *East African Standard*, 402
Kerr, Walter F., 244
Kipling, Rudyard, 134
Knight, John S., 201, 444
Knight newspapers, xii, 237, 442, 444
Knox, Frank, 246, 251
Knox, Tom, 124
Kopytin, Viktor, 368
Korea, South, 383–84
Korean War, 306–10, 469
Korniechuk, Alexander, 318
Kossuth, Louis, 104–5
Kosterin, Aleksei Y., 365

Krock, Arthur, 287
Kuznetsov, Anatoly V., 363, 372

Lackmann-Mosse, Hans, 226
La Harpe, Frederic, 151
Lambrachis, Christos, 406–7
Laos, 381
Lashkova, Vera, 365
Latin America, 327, 330–31, 334–35, 339, 397–98; press in, 27–28, 275, 327–32, 350, 397–400, 403–4, 463; Inter-American Press Association, 398, 399, 400; number of newspapers in, 465
Laurence, William L., 270
Lazareff, Pierre, 419
Lebanon, press in, 404
Lenin, N., 153, 154, 155, 187–88, 189, 190, 192
L'Estrange, Roger, 25
Levy, J. M., 113
Lexington (Ky.), *True American*, 116
Liang Chi-chao, 156–59
Libel: in American colonies, 27; in Great Britain, 38–39, 83, 84–85, 86, 434; in United States, 148, 458–59; in India, 131, 133; in Japan, 137, 138, 139; *see also* Sedition; "Seditious" publications
Libya, press in, 404
Life, 202, 301, 302, 304, 452, 453, 458
Lilburne, John, 44–45
Lindley, Ernest K., 256
Lippmann, Walter, 190, 199, 340, 468
Literary Digest, 202
Litvinov, Pavel, 365
Living newspapers, *see* Newspapers, living
Lochner, Louis, 241
London, newspapers in: *Corante*, 21; *Weekly Newes*, 21–22; *Mercurius Britannicus*, and *Swedish Intelligencer*, 22; *Mercurius Aulicus*, 23; *Mercurius Politicus*, 24; *Intelligencer*, *Newes*, *Publick Intelligencer*, and *Gazette*, 25–26; *Daily Courant*, 26–27; *Post*, 31, 108; *Review*, 46; *Champion*, and *Critical Review*, 47; *Times*, 82–83, 85, 87, 88, 98, 107–14, 144, 149, 153, 155,

London, newspapers in: (*Continued*)
166, 176, 202, 205–8, 227, 228, 259, 363, 424–27, 430, 432, 455; *Daily Universal Register*, and *Oracle*, 83; *Chronicle*, 83, 108; *Morning Post*, 83, 113, 196; *Sun*, 83, 429–30; *Public Advertiser*, 84; *Morning Chronicle*, 85; *Examiner*, and *Political Register*, 86; *Republican*, 86–87; *Daily News*, 103, 113, 114, 145, 166, 259; *Morning Advertiser*, and *Morning Herald*, 108; number of newspapers, 108; *Daily Telegraph*, 113, 259, 424, 427, 430; *Morning Leader, Star*, 145, 424; *Westminster Gazette*, 145; *Kolokol*, 151; *Daily Mail*, 176, 206, 227, 424, 431; *Evening Standard*, 208, 259, 431; *Daily Express*, 208, 424, 431; *Daily Herald*, 259, 430; *Daily Sketch*, 259, 431; *News of the World*, 259, 348, 429, 438; *Sunday Pictorial*, 348–49; *News-Chronicle*, and *Daily Mirror*, 424, 429, 430, 473, 474, 489; *Sunday Times*, 425, 426, 427, 430, 432; *Financial Times*, 427, 430; *Evening News*, 431; *Morning Star*, 432; *Sunday Observer*, 432; *see also* Great Britain, newspapers in

Long, Gerald, 435, 473
Long Island, N.Y., *Long Island Press*, 445; *Long Island Star-Journal*, and *Newsday*, 446; *Suffolk Sun*, 453
Look, 452, 453
Los Angeles, newspapers in, 443; *Times*, 257, 442, 449, 457, 474
Los Angeles *Times*–Washington *Post* press service, 454
Louisville (Ky.), *Courier-Journal*, and *Times*, 496
Lovejoy, Elijah Parish, 117, 127
Loveland, Roelif, 264
Lubis, Mochtar, 387
Lucas, James, 309
Luce, Henry R., 202–3, 277, 301, 303, 452

Macdonald, Stewart, 459
Madison, James, 60–61, 62, 63, 67, 70
Magazine of Russian Letters, 95, 151
Malaysia, 385–86; *Straits Times*, 386

Mallett, Elizabeth, 26
Mao Tse-tung, 150–59, 203, 230, 275, 283, 289, 301, 302, 304, 307, 310–11, 323–26, 375–76, 377–78, 470
Marat, Jean Paul, 74, 75
Marchenko, Anatoly T., 364
Markov, Eugene, 156
Martin, Joseph, 333
Martin, Robert P., 302
Marton, Dr. Endre, 321, 323
Marx, Karl, 100, 106–7
Masaryk, Thomas G., 213–16, 495
Massachusetts Bay Colony, 28–31, 50, 51–53; *Freeman's Oath*, 29; *Essex Gazette*, 55
Masses, The, 183, 190
Matthews, Herbert L., 332, 333
Maxwell, Robert, 429
Mazzini, Giuseppe, 90–91
McCarthy, Joseph R., 303, 313–18
McCormick, Anne O'Hare, 218
McCormick, Col. Robert R., 204, 445
McGaffin, William, 245–46
McGraw-Hill publications, 453–54
McIntyre, Marvin H., 234
Medill, Joseph, 118
Mellett, Don R., 201–2
Memphis (Tenn.) *Appeal*, 123
Meredith, Hugh, 36
Mexico, press in, 27–28, 416
Meyer, Philip, 497
Miami (Fla.) *Herald*, 457, 473, 497
Middle East, 208–10, 469; press in, 404–6
Mill, John Stuart, quoted, 127–28
Millaud, Moise, 103
Miller, Paul, 445
Milton, John, x, 23–25
Milwaukee (Wis.), newspapers in, 443; *Leader*, 183; *Journal*, 496
Mirabeau, Comte de, 73
Minneapolis (Minn.), newspapers in, 443
Mohr, Charles, 345
Moniz Sodra Bittencourt, Mrs. Niomar, 398
Moore, Arthur, 176
Moorehead, Alan, 263
Moreira, Alves, Marcio, 397, 398

Morin, Relman, 309
Mount Pleasant (N.Y.) *Register,* 67
Mowrer, Edgar Ansel, 227
Mucha, Jiri, 356
Muddiman, Henry, 25
Munsey, Frank, 198, 237
Murayama, Ryuhei, 229
Murdoch, Rupert, 429–30
Murdoch newspapers, 429–30, 438–39
Murrow, Edward R., 245, 246, 263, 316–17, 458
Musgrave, Philip, 33
Mussolini, Benito, 165, 216–20, 240, 267, 471

Nakamura, Bin, 269
Napier, David, 98
Napoleon Bonaparte, 75–77
Narushima, Ryuhoku, 138
Nation, 198, 334, 454
National Observer, 476
Nazism, 220–28
Negro press, 204; Abolitionist press, 117–18
Negro World, 204
Nehru, Jawaharlal, 294–301, 305–6, 341
Nekrasov, Viktor, 365
Neogy, Rajat, 401
Netherlands, 72, 242; press in, 21, 76, 92–93, 274, 410; *Gazette de Leyde,* 76; *Nieuwe Rotterdamse Courant,* 93, 410; *De Telegraaf,* 410
Nevinson, Henry W., 145
Newark (N.J.) *Star-Ledger,* 446
Newburyport (Mass.) *Herald,* 115
New China News Agency (Hsin Hua), 279, 305, 370, 377
Newhouse, Samuel I., 201, 445–46
Newhouse newspapers, 237, 444, 445–46
New Jersey Gazette, 59
New London (Conn.) *Bee,* 67
New Orleans (La.), newspapers in, 97
Newport (Ky.), *Free South,* 116
New Republic, 190, 454
News, control of, *see* Censorship and control of news
Newspapermen, *see* Journalists
Newspapers, world statistics, 465
Newspapers, "living": Greece, ancient, 2–3; China, 10, 11; France, 16, 19; Japan, 136–37; Chinese People's Republic, 305
News services, *see* Press services
Newsweek, 256, 302, 453
New York, 454
New York City, newspapers in, 63, 97, 443, 447; *Weekly Gazette,* 39; *Weekly Journal,* 39–43, 45, 52; *Gazette,* 49; *Gazetteer,* 53, 55; *Evening Post,* 59, 68, 146, 156; *Gazette of the United States,* 64; *America Minerva,* 66; *Tribune,* 97, 98, 107, 118–19, 123, 124, 136, 184, 196; *Herald,* 97, 98, 115, 118, 124, 160, 184; *Times,* 97, 119–21, 123–24, 147, 184, 199, 204, 218, 243, 251, 270, 287, 289, 302, 309, 317, 332, 335, 338, 345, 362, 363, 442, 447, 450, 456–57, 470; *Sun,* 97, 193, 196, 198; *National Intelligencer,* 98; *Morning News,* 99; *Freedom's Journal,* 117–18; *World,* 121, 146–48, 193, 196, 197, 199, 237; *Journal of Commerce,* 121, 202; *Journal,* 146–48; *Evening Mail, American,* 175; *Call,* 183, 190; *Daily News,* 198, 333, 447; *Staats-Zeitung,* 202; *World-Telegram and Sun,* 237, 446; *Herald Tribune,* 244, 302, 309, 317, 446, 447; *Journal-American,* 446; strikes in, 446–47; *World-Journal-Tribune,* 446–47; *Post,* 447
New Yorker, 454
New York *Times* syndicate service, 454
New Zealand, press in, 200, 278, 350, 435–36
Nigeria, newspapers and press in: *West African Pilot* (Lagos), 401; Allied newspapers, 402; number of newspapers, 403
Nipho y Cagigal, Francisco, 94
Niva, (Russian), 152
Nixon, Richard M., 333, 336, 367, 372, 460, 472, 491
Nobel Prize for Literature, 203, 319, 363
North America, newspapers in, 465
Northcliffe, Lord, 176, 178–79, 205–8, 438
Norway, press in, 94, 274, 410; *Aftenposten* (Oslo), 410

Nouvel Observateur, Le (French), 421
Novosti (Soviet News Agency), 370

Oatis, William Nathan, 292–93, 374
Ochs, Adolph S., 147, 199, 456
Oeglin, Erhard, 13
Ogata, Taketora, 232
O'Higgins, Harvey, 182
Oliphant, Lawrence, 108
O'Sullivan, John L., 99

Paine, Thomas, 56, 57–58, 84–85
Pakistan, 275, 297–98, 299, 300, 389, 391; press in, 388, 436, 472
Palestine, 285–86
Palm, Johann, 76
Palmer, Frederick, 184
Panama, press in, 398, 399
Paoli, Giovanni, 18
Paris, newspapers in, 415–21; *Mercure Galant,* 19; *Le Journal de Paris,* 72–73; *Les Revolutions de Paris,* 74; *Le Vieux Cordelier,* 75; *Le Moniteur,* 76, 77; *Le Quotidien,* 76, 227; *Le National,* 78, 100; *Le Temps,* 78–79, 417; *Le Constitutionnel,* and *Le Siècle,* 81; *La Revue Parisienne,* 83; *Reform,* 101; *Chatiment,* and *La Petit Presse,* 103; *Le Figaro,* 103, 273, 418–19; *Le Matin,* 227; *Le Soir,* 243; *Le Monde,* 273, 349, 362, 415, 416–18; 422, 455, 496; *France Soir,* 273, 416, 419–20, 496; *L'Express,* 349; *L'Humanité* 349, 420; *L'Aurore, Combat, La Croix, Parisien Libèré, Paris-Jour, Paris- Presse,* and *Le Populaire,* 420; *see also* France, newspapers in
Paris Match (French), 418, 421
Parker, Gilbert, 172
Parliamentary Debates (Hansard), 86
Pasternak, Boris, 319, 320, 363
Pearce, Lord, 433
Pecke, Samuel, 22–23
Pecos, Tex., 458
Pegler, Westbrook, 317
Peralva, Osvaldo, 398
Pericles, 4, 5, 6
Periodicals in the United States, 452–54; *see also individual titles*

Peron, Juan Domingo, 327–31
Perry, James, 85
Peru, newspapers and press in, 398; *El Comercio,* 329; *Expresso,* 399; *Extra,* 399; *La Prensa,* 400
Peter the Great, 19, 95, 150
Philadelphia, newspapers in, 63, 443; *Pennsylvania Gazette,* 36–38, 44, 49–50, 57; *Pennsylvania Journal,* 49, 52, 57; *Pennsylvania Evening Post,* 57, 63; *Pennsylvania Packet and Daily Advertiser,* 63, 65; *National Gazette,* 64–65; *General Advertiser,* 65; *Aurora,* 65, 67; *Porcupine Gazette,* 65–66; *Public Ledger,* 97; *Pennsylvania Freeman,* 116; *Press,* 121; *Inquirer,* 121, 124, 444; *Evening Journal,* 122; *Daily News,* 444
Philanthropist (Abolitionist), 116
Philippines, 384; press in, 275; 384–85; *Times* (Manila), 384
Pickering, Edward, 475
Pittsburgh (Pa.), newspapers in, 443
Pogrund, Benjamin, 402
Poland, 320, 321–22; press in, 275, 372
Politika (Czech), 357
Polk, George, 289
Polowetsky, Nathan, 292
Poor Richard's Almanac (Franklin), 37
Portugal, press in, 408–9
Potter, Louis de, 92
Powell, J. B., 203
Pramote, Kukrit, 383
Presses, invention of, 98, 124; *see also* Printing
Press services, 278–79, 289, 454–55; network of correspondents in American colonies, 51; *see also under individual name, e.g.,* Agence France-Presse
Price, Byron, 254, 284
Price, Ward, 227
Printing: cuneiform, 1; movable type, 10–13; lithographic, 449; offset, 449, 474, 475; facsimile reproductions, 473–75, 476; electronic, 473–76; *see also* Presses
Prouvost, Jean, 244, 418–19
Prussia: newspapers in, 19; *Intelligenz Blätter,* 91

Pulitzer, Joseph, 146–48
Pulitzer Prizes, 172, 311
Punch (British), 166
Pyle, Ernie, 263, 264

Quebec, press in, 28
Queensland Newspapers, 438

Radio: as news source, 160–61, 317–18, 455–56, 492; in China, 305, 377; in Great Britain, 371, 423, 483; in Indonesia, 388; in Israel, 406; in Canada, 436; in India, 482; *see also* United States, radio in
Radio Peking, 377
Raleigh (N.C.) *News and Observer*, 178
Raskin, A. H., 448
Raymond, Henry J., 97, 118, 119–21, 122, 125, 127
Reader's Digest, 453
Reading (Pa.) *Weekly Advertiser*, 67
Record (New Jersey), 44
Red Star (Red Army newspaper), 250, 262
Reed, John, 190–92
Reed Paper Group (Great Britain), 430
Rees-Mogg, William, 427
Reformation, 14, 19
Reischauer, Edwin O., 395
Renaissance, 14
Renaudot, Theophraste, 17–18, 20, 72
Reporter (American), 454
Reporter (Czech), 357
Reston, James, 338, 457, 459
Reuter, Julius, 81–82
Reuters Economic Service, 435
Reuters News Agency, 82, 104, 142, 159, 199, 200, 278, 289, 373, 434–35, 454, 473
Revere, Paul, 53, 54
Revolutionary War, press during, 55–59
Reynolds, Quentin, 245
Rhode Island Mercury, 35
Rhodesia, press in, 402
Ricardo, Antonio, 28
Ridder brothers, 202
Ridder newspapers, 237, 444
Riverside (Calif.) *Press-Enterprise*, 45
Rivington, Jemmy, 53, 55, 58

Robert, Nicolas Louis, 98
Roces, Joaquin P., 384
Rochester (N.Y.) *North Star*, 118
Rome, 6–7
Roosevelt, Franklin D., 233–39; 246–47, 251–52, 253–54, 266, 296, 327
Rosenberg, Alfred, 221
Rosenthal, A. M., 457
Rosenthal, Joe, 269
Rothermore newspapers, 431
Roy, Raja Ram Mohan, 132
Royster, Vermont, 473
Rozov, Viktor, 365
Rumania, press in, 372
Russell, Maj. Benjamin, 66, 70
Russell, William Howard, 110–12, 130, 439
Russia, 149–56, 184–93; press in, 19, 94, 95–96, 149–56, 186–87, 189; newspapers in: *Vedomosti*, 95, 150, 152; *Golos*, *Russkoe Slovo*, and *Savremennik*, 151; *Novoye Vremya*, 151, 152; *Journal* (St. Petersburg), 152; number of newspapers, 152, 154; *Iskra*, 153; *Novaia Zhizn*, 190; *Glavlit*, 191; *see also* Soviet Union
Russian Information Bureau, New York City, 185
Russian Speech, 156
Russian Telegraph Agency (Rosta), 191
Russwurm, John B., 118
Ryder, S. T., 430

St. Louis (Mo.), newspapers in, 97, 443; *Observer*, 117; *Post-Dispatch*, 146, 311, 317, 457, 494–95
St. Paul (Minn.), newspapers in, 443; *Pioneer Press*, 202
Salmon, Robert, 416
San Diego (Calif.), newspapers in, 443
San Francisco (Calif.), newspapers in, 97, 443; *Examiner*, 147
Santora, Philip, 333
Sarnoff, David, 160–61
Saturday Evening Post, 202, 203, 452
Saturday Review, 454
Scali, John, 340
Scandinavia: press in, 93, 97, 200, 274, 410; newspaper readership in, 465

Schiff, Dorothy, 447

Schoeffer, Peter, 13

Scotland: *Courant,* and *Scots Postman* (Edinburgh), 44; *Daily Record,* and *Sunday Mail* (Glasgow), 475

Scott, Charles Prestwich, 145–46; 209, 210

Scripps, Charles E., 444

Scripps, Edward W., 204, 444

Scripps-Howard newspapers, 237, 238, 263, 303, 309, 444, 446, 447

Sears, Isaac, 49

Seattle (Wash.), newspapers in, 443

Sedition: Alien and Sedition Acts (U.S.), 65, 66–68, 183; Alien and Sedition Laws (Switzerland), 90

"Seditious" publications: in Great Britain, 21, 31, 38, 84–85, 86–87, 145–46; in American colonies, 31, 34, 40–43, 49, 53–54, 55; in U.S., 64–65, 115, 183, 257–58; in Germany, 142; in India, 133, 135; in Russia, 151, 155–56; in Czechoslovakia, 216

Serle, Ambrose, 58

Sevareid, Eric, 263

Shaw, Flora, 144

Shengi, Pi, 10

Shirer, William, 224, 245, 263

Sholokhov, Mikhail, 250

Shoriki, Matsutaro, 484

Shub, Anatole, 367

Shukan Asahi (Japanese), 396

Simonds, Frank H., 196

Simonov, Konstantin, 250

Siniavsky, Andrei, 363, 364

Sission, Edgar, 182

Smadja, Henry, 420

Smith, J. Kingsbury, 288

Smollett, Tobias, 47

Snow, Edgar P., 203, 374

Social Justice, 258

Socrates, 4, 6, 493–94

Sokolsky, George, 317

Solzhenitsyn, Aleksandr, 342–43, 362–63, 364

Somejima, Keiji, 375

Sons of Liberty, 48–50, 52

Sorge, Richard, 247

South Africa: press in, 200, 400, 402, 436; *Star* (Johannesburg), and *Daily Mail* (Rand), 200

Southam Press, 436

Soviet Union, x, 248–53, 261–62, 318–23, 336–43, 362–73; newspapers in: *Pravda,* 187, 191, 250, 260, 262, 287, 347, 354, 356, 358, 369, 370, 373, 455, 473, 477, 485; *Izvestia,* 187, 191, 250, 260, 262, 369, 370, 455, 485; *Novy Mir,* 185, 342–43, 364; *Red Star,* 250, 262; number of newspapers, 260, 369–70; *Komsomolskaya Pravda, Selskaya Zhisn,* and *Sovietskaya Rossiya,* 369; press in: 191, 215, 238, 250, 259–61, 262, 264, 342–43, 347, 354, 368–71, 455, 463; Tass News Agency, 191, 200, 247, 279, 291, 368, 370–71, 373; Union of Writers, 362, 363, 364, 365; attack on authors and intellectuals, 362–67; Novosti news agency, 370

Spain, press in, 94–95, 408

Spanish-American War, 146–49, 471

Spencer, Ambrose, 68

Spiegel, Der (German Republic), 349–50, 415, 496

Springer, Axel, 273, 413–14

Springfield (Mass.) *Republican,* 118, 121

Stamp Act, 48–50

Stanton, Frank, 451

Staten Island Advance, 445

Stationers Company, 19, 23

Steed, Wickham, 178, 206, 208, 215

Steele, A. T., 302

Steele, Richard, 46

Stefani News Agency (Italy), 219, 279

Steffens, Lincoln, 204

Sterling, Edward, 85

Stern (German Republic), 415, 496

Storey, Wilbur F., 121–22

Strikes: U.S. newspapers, 446–49; Japan, 475

Strünsee, Johann Frederick, 93–94

Student (Czech), 352, 357

"Subversive" publications, *see* "Seditious" publications

Sudan, press in, 404

Sulzberger, Arthur Hays, 456

Sulzberger, Arthur Ochs, 456

Sumeria, 1
Sweden: press in, 94, 274, 410; *Dagens Nyheter*, and *Svenska Dagbladet* (Stockholm), 274, 410
Swift, Jonathan, 44, 47
Swinton, Stanley, 309
Switzerland, 17; newspapers in: *Zürcher Zeitung*, 88–89; *Neue Zürcher Zeitung*, 89–90, 274, 412; *Basler Nachrichten*, 412; press in: 88–90, 200, 215, 274, 412; Alien and Sedition Laws, 90
Swope, Herbert Bayard, 193, 196, 199, 204
Syme, David, and Company, 438
Syria, press in, 404
Szulc, Tad, 335, 362

Taiwan, *see* China, Nationalist
Tao, Feng, 10
Tass news agency, 191, 200, 247, 279, 291, 368, 370–71, 373
Tatarian, Roger, 491
Tatzepao (Chinese wall posters), 377
Taylor, Bayard, 136
Television: as news source, 279–80, 409, 468, 484–88; in Soviet Union, 368, 371, 485–86; in Chinese Republic, 377; in Thailand, 382; in Japan, 394, 484; in Great Britain, 423, 435, 483; in Finland, 409; in German Republic, 414, 415; as press rival, 466, 482–89; in India, 482–83; in Cuba, 483; in Czechoslovakia, 483; in France, 483–84; polls on vs. newspapers, 486
Teukesbury, John, 19
Thailand: *Phim Thai, Siam Rath,* and *Thai Rath*, 382; press in, 382–83
Thiers, Adolphe, 78, 100
Thomas, Isaiah, 51–52, 54–55, 58
Thomas, John, 22
Thomson, Lord (Roy), 202, 401, 425, 445
Thomson newspapers, 425–28, 436
Thorbecke, Jan, 93
Tilak, Bal Gangadhur, 134–35, 211
Time, 202, 254, 302, 345, 453, 486
Time, Inc., 452–53
Toledo (O.) *Blade*, 448–49
Townshend Acts, 50–51
Toynbee, Arnold J., 172

Transition (Uganda), 401
Trenchard, John, 38
Trotsky, Leon, 153, 154, 155, 185, 189, 190–91, 192
Truman, Harry S., 267, 269, 271, 279, 286–87
Tumulty, Joseph, 195
Tvardovsky, Aleksandr T., 364
TV Guide, 453
Tyndale, William, 19
Type, *see* Printing

Ueno, Riichi, 229
Uganda, press in, 401, 402
Ullstein, Leopold, 225–26
United Arab Republic, press in, 400, 404, 405
United Nations: and Cold War, 283–84, 286–88; and Palestine question, 285–86; and Korean War, 306–10; appeal of Soviet writers to, 365
United Press, 184, 200, 238, 240, 264, 278, 289, 309, 323
United Press International, 454, 473
United States (*see also* American colonies)
—— newspapers in: number, 63, 97, 98, 236–37, 257, 277, 279, 441–42, 443, 465; newspaper readership, 441; average daily newspaper issue, statistics, 441–42; *see also individual cities*
—— press in: Revolutionary War, 55–59; 18th century, 59–60, 63–70; Alien and Sedition Acts, 65, 66–68; 19th century, 97–99; Civil War, 114–26; Spanish-American War, 146–49; World War I, 175, 181–84, 193–204; Espionage Act of *1917*, 183–84; 20th century, 215; World War II, 227, 241, 243–44, 254–59, 263–64; Office of Censorship (World War II), 254–55; Office of War Information (OWI), 255–56; Commission on Freedom of the Press, 276–78; Korean War, 309; McCarthy episode, 314, 317; Cuba crisis, 332–33, 335, 338, 339; Vietnam War, 345, 380–81, 467, 469, 472; 20th century, 348, 416; revenues, 416, 441, 442; contemporary, 439–61; strikes,

United States (*Continued*)
446–49; antitrust actions, 452; periodicals, 452–54; recent decisions and laws on freedom and reporting, 458–59; negative public opinion of and dissatisfaction with, 459–60, 487; contemporary weaknesses, 460–61; salaries of journalists, 479, 481*n*; employees, 480–82

—— radio in, 161, 171, 237–38, 244–45, 263, 264, 289, 315, 316–17, 371, 439, 441, 450–52, 486

—— television in, 279–80, 439, 440–41, 450–52, 484, 486–88; McCarthy episode on, 316–17; and Kennedy assassination, 347

United States Constitution, x, 58; First Amendment, 59–63, 448, 498

United States Federal Communications Commission, 450, 451

Uruguay, press in, 399

Urukagina, king of Lagash, 1

Usteri, Dr. Paulus, 89–90, 96

Utica (N.Y.) *Standard and Democrat*, 116

Vega (Brazilian), 399

Viereck, George Sylvester, 171

Vietnam, 310–11; press in, 380

Vietnam War, x, 343–46, 367, 376, 379–83, 387, 393, 467, 469, 472, 484

Villard, Oswald Garrison, 198

Villemessent, Hippolyte, 103

Virginia colony, 27, 50

Vlachos, Helen, 407

Voice of America, 315, 371

Völkischer Beobachter (German), 221–22, 223, 226

Voss, Christian, 92

Voznesensky, Andrei, 342

Vperyod (Russian), 153

Vsiakaia-Vsiachina (Russian), 150

Walley, Henry, 23

Wall Street Journal, 442, 457, 473, 474, 475–76, 477

Walpole, Robert, 44

Walter, John, 83, 86; II, 85; IV, 208

Washington, George, 56, 57–58, 60, 63, 64, 65

Washington D.C., newspapers in, 443; *National Era*, 116; *Chronicle*, 121; *Post*, 338, 367, 442, 453, 454, 457; *Evening Star*, 457

Webster, Noah, 66

Wesley, Edward B., 119

West Australian Newspapers, 438

White, Theodore H., 302

White, William Allen, 193, 197, 243

Whitney, John Hay, 446

Whittier, John Greenleaf, 116

Wilkes, John, 47

Williams, Roger, 28–29

Williams, Wythe, 184

Wilson, Robert, 185

Winchell, Walter, 317

Wire services, *see* Press services

Wolff, Bernhard, 81–82

Wolff, Theodor, 162–71, 176

Wolff Agency, 82, 104, 142, 159, 226

Woodfall, Henry S., 85

World War I, 162–98

World War II, 240–72

Yanagawa, Shunsan, 138

Yang, Po, 383

Yevtuchenko, Yevgeni, 318, 342, 343, 365, 366

Yone, Edward Law, 386

Yugoslavia, press in, 372; *Borba*, 372

Yunost (Soviet), 365

Zang, August, 105

Zenger, John Peter, xii, 39–43, 44–45

Zik's Press Ltd., 401

Zileri, Enrique, 399